D0849657

15.00

Exposition of

ISAIAH

Volume I

Chapters 1–39

Volume II

Chapters 40–66

Exposition of

ISAIAH

Volume I

Chapters 1–39

By H. C. LEUPOLD

BAKER BOOK HOUSE
Grand Rapids, Michigan

Formerly published in two volumes:

Exposition of Isaiah, Volume I (Chaps. 1-39) and
Exposition of Isaiah, Volume II (Chaps. 40-66).

Copyright 1968, 1971 by
Baker Book House Company

ISBN: 0-8010-5577-6

Library of Congress Catalog Card Numbers:
Volume I: 68-29786
Volume II: 68-29787

PHOTOLITHOPRINTED BY CUSHING - MALLOY, INC.
ANN ARBOR, MICHIGAN, UNITED STATES OF AMERICA
1977

Foreword

The theory that some "Great Unknown" wrote chapters 40-55 of Isaiah is quite generally accepted in the field of biblical scholarship. This "Great Unknown" goes under the name of Deutero-Isaiah. A corollary to this theory is this: A number of "Great Unknowns" contributed chapters 56-66 of the book. Much painstaking scholarship has been poured into the establishment of these theories. We do not deny that many a piece of valuable insight has been gained in the process of arriving at these conclusions. But still this approach cannot lay claim to being more than a theory.

We shall not at this point argue the issues involved.

But together with many earnest Christians we still accept the theory, held so long in the realm of biblical scholarship, that Isaiah the son of Amoz wrote the entire book.

This *Exposition* has not as its ultimate purpose to maintain and defend the unit authorship of the book. Strangely, the message of the book remains virtually the same whether multiple authorship or unit authorship be upheld.

We believe that there is need for a practical commentary that stresses the abiding values of this rich prophetic work.

H. C. Leupold

October 1968

INTRODUCTION

Introduction

In this Introduction we purpose to follow the simple outline that was used by *Procksch* (only for the major parts):

I. Historical Situation Prevailing in Isaiah's Day
II. The Prophet
III. The Book

    A. Brief Outline and Authorship
    B. Theology of Isaiah
    C. Forms of Prophetic Utterance
    D. Dead Sea Scrolls
    E. Detailed Outline
    F. Selected Bibliography

I. THE HISTORICAL SITUATION

In the days of the Golden Age of Israel's history, when David and Solomon reigned, Israel occupied a position in the world of that time commensurate with her destiny as it had been divinely outlined. The nation in whose midst the salvation of mankind was to develop ranked with the world kingdoms of that day. David's territory extended from the River of Egypt to the great river Euphrates. Everyone felt that that was as it ought to be. The position of Israel after the death of these two monarchs rapidly declined, to the sorrow of all. About the middle of the eighth century a new aspect of international politics began to develop. Assyria appeared on the scene and not only grew to large proportions but also began to try to dominate all nations within her reach, including Israel in the course of time. To see Israel reduced to the level of a tributary to one of the ungodly world-powers seemed to do violence to the very promises that God had bestowed upon his ancient people. It was into a situation like this that Isaiah, among others, was sent to guide and direct Israel's course

11

We need a bit of background in order to be able to evaluate the historical circumstances as they prevailed in those days.

It was around 750 B.C. when Assyria began to emerge as the first of the great world empires in the international politics of the Near East. A notable ruler began to head the destiny of this nation, a man by the name of Tiglath-pileser, who reigned, and reigned very capably as far as empire building was concerned, from 744-727. When he first appeared on the scene, Israel and Judah had experienced a resurgence of her one-time greatness, not so much because of true strength as because of the weakness of the neighboring nations. Jeroboam II (785-745) had reigned over Israel and had extended her territory once again as far as the Euphrates; and Uzziah (790-738) had extended the dominion of Judah far to the south. That this expansion of dominion was not built on very stable foundations did not become apparent at the time, but it was only a pseudo-strength, because the moral fibre of the Israelites had degenerated. But the successors of these two great kings of Israel and Judah soon became tributary to Tiglath-pileser, as did also Phoenicia. At first, however, Judah and Philistia refused to make common cause against Tiglath-pileser with Israel to the north and with Syria and Damascus, as Isa. 7 abundantly indicates. In other words, Judah was at first strongly pro-Assyrian under King Ahaz. So Tiglath-pileser came along with his invading armies, conquered Hamath and the Phoenician coast to the north, and sadly devastated the northern half of Israel down as far as Hazor and Naphtali. In fact a major deportation of Israelites took place at that time (see II Kings 15:29). In proof of the devastation of the land see Isa. 9:1. The Assyrian forces penetrated farther down to the south, conquering in the land of Philistia, Ashkelon and Gaza. Damascus and Ephraim were subdued easily after this. Pekah, king of Israel was dethroned and murdered by Hosea during the upheavals that occurred in this connection, and Tiglath-pileser officially sanctioned Hosea's seizure of the power.

After the Assyrian monarch died, Hosea attempted a revolt, but only brought down upon the land of Israel the avenging Assyrian hosts, which besieged Samaria three years and finally took it (722 B.C.), although by this time Tiglath-pileser had died and Sargon II (721-705) had to complete the task of taking Samaria. Isa. 28:1-4 bears on this subject. Twenty-seven thousand two hundred ninety deportees were dragged away from Samaria at this time, and settled in the region of the upper Euphrates.

Somewhat earlier than this, in the days of Ahaz, king of Judah (735-715 B.C.) a last clash had taken place between Israel to the north under Pekah together with Damascus under King Rezin lined up against Judah under Ahaz. The two allies to the north were trying to compel Judah to join in their anti-Assyrian coalition, an enterprise for which Ahaz could not be won, being too strongly pro-Assyrian. Although the Biblical account gives no details as to the resultant clash, it is usually assumed that a Syro-Ephraimite attack against Judah took place about 734. Judah at this time controlled Philistine cities like Gath, Ashdod, and Ekron. Ahaz, however, not only refused to enter into the proposed alliance but persisted in his attitude of friendliness toward Assyria, even going so far as to invite the Assyrian king to come to his aid.

The fortunes of the Assyrians during the ensuing years ran briefly as follows. Sargon, the successor of Tiglath-pileser, was not a man of the stature of his predecessor, but he did manage to hold the Assyrian empire together, though he too had to wage many a campaign to achieve his objective. He fought in Armenia and in Asia Minor, and won the battle of Carchemish, an ancient Hittite stronghold and sacked the city (cf. Isa. 10:9). He met his death in a battle against the Cimmerians. During his reign he had to tolerate the opposition of Merodach-baladan, who sought control of the southeastern corner of the Assyrian empire around Babylon. Sargon overthrew him in battle and so Merodach-baladan vanished from the scene. Note the reference to him in Isa. 39:1.

In the southwest corner of his empire as well as in the northwest he also encountered opposition. In Gaza his opponent was Hanno. In Hamath it was Jaubidi. Hanno

was finally brought fettered to Assyria and there disposed of.

Hezekiah (715-687 B.C.) then became king of Judah
(II Kings 18:2). As to his attitude to the God of Israel,
he was radically different from his father Ahaz, but politi-
cally he was as inept as he. He gets high praise from the
Book of Kings as having walked faithfully in the ways of
the Lord and as having taken summary steps against the
idolatry then rampant in Judah. But in the nature of the
case he inherited a sort of vassalhood under Assyria. In
his relation to Isaiah, his counsellor and father-confessor,
he may not have been as clumsy as some claim ("lacking
in gifts and marked by indesion" — *Volz*) but he certainly
left much to be desired, and gave Isaiah plenty of trouble.
Time after time he attempted to establish his independence
and to shake off the yoke of the Assyrians. With each new
development he made a fresh attempt. Within the kingdom,
groups were continually agitating and keeping policies in
flux. Outside the nation, Philistines, Edomites, Moabites,
and Arabians kept stirring up the troubled waters. In a
sense the greatest of the agitators was Egypt, who promised
much help to the smaller nations but gave precious little.
She, whose fame had made her the mistress of the Nile,
seemed about to stage a come-back and unfortunately was
prized as a promising ally. So the whole picture is one
of continual turmoil practically all the days of Isaiah.

When Hezekiah came to the throne in 715 B.C. Isaiah
had to warn him not to be drawn into the alliance that
the Philistines sponsored. Hezekiah heeded the warning and
withdrew. Since his victory at Carchemish, Sargon had a
free hand to deal with those who caused trouble. He qui-
eted Samaria and made the remnant comparatively harmless
by settling people of various nationalities in their territory.
Feeling his strong hand, a number of the conspirators submitted to Sargon. Yet he overran Moab and the Arabians,
perhaps as an object lesson to the other conspirators. But
Egypt, with an Ethiopian ruler on the throne, always
kept posing as the deliverer of the oppressed. Of the Philistine cities, Ashdod kept seeking the help of Egypt, and so
brought down the wrath of Assyria upon herself, and was

conquered in 711. The usurper on the throne of Ashdod fled to Egypt, who gave proof of her lack of reliability by allowing him to be extradited to Assyria, where he perished. Judah had avoided involvement, backing away in the last moment.

Sargon died and Sennacherib (704-681 B.C.) succeeded to the throne of Assyria. What came into his hands was a well-knit empire. There were trouble spots on the eastern and western fringes. After Hezekiah had been approached by Merodach-baladan (Isa. 39) he became a strong agitator against Sennacherib, going along with that group of Philistine cities that were anti-Assyrian. All of this adds up to a very confusing situation, where it is almost impossible to see clearly.

Confronted by these several opponents Sennacherib proved his mettle in a good display of military skill. He started down the coast from the north, where Sidon had to be put into her proper place (701 B.C.). He did not destroy the cities that were conquered. He vanquished some of the Philistines. Then he encountered the rest of the Philistines at Elteke, led by Tirhaka, an Ethiopian incumbent of the throne of the Pharaohs, and beat them back. He likewise subdued the strong city of Ekron. Then he set up his headquarters at Lachish, so as to be able to reach out either to the Philistines or to Judah. Jerusalem was not immediately attacked but Judah was overrun, and Sennacherib boasted in his famous inscription that he had taken forty-six towns and cities of Judah and had shut up Hezekiah like a bird in a cage. Of the people of Judah he claims to have made 200,150 captive. The territory taken from Judah was distributed to the Philistine cities, Ekron, Ashdod, and Gaza. Hezekiah virtually declared himself defeated and paid a heavy tribute to Sennacherib, as the price of sparing the capital city — thirty talents of gold and eight hundred talents of silver (II Kings 18:14 says 300). All of which was sent back to Nineveh.

Here the records present difficulties. Sennacherib seems to have dictated the terms in question and to have guaranteed immunity to the city. Then, beginning II Kings 18:17, it would appear that the king regretted the bargain he had made and in spite of all demanded the total capitulation of the holy city, ignoring the terms to which he had agreed.

From here on many writers, following the trail blazed by *Alt*, declare that the Biblical account does not follow the true course of events, but rather idealizes history, describing what would have happened if Hezekiah had faithfully followed Isaiah's advice. In other words the close of Isa. 37 is declared to be a colorful legendary account, and not at all a factual record. We hope to show in connection with our exposition of Chap. 37 that the Biblical text may be accepted at face value without resorting to rash claims about a legendary approach. *Herntrich*, an otherwise very sober expositor, goes afield so far as to claim that where Isaiah had had a dream that the Assyrian world-power would crack up before the gates of Jerusalem, this dream was not fulfilled. At the same time Judah's confidence that the deliverance, promised by the prophet with such enthusiasm, was beyond the power of God to bring it to pass.

One rather significant fact should yet be noted, which has tremendous bearing upon the case, namely that Sennacherib, though after his return from Judah he continued to wage war for another twenty years, never again ventured to go back to the land of Israel, or Judah.

II. THE PROPHET

The name of this prophet is Isaiah, which means, according to the Hebrew, "Yahweh is salvation" — a name which to an extent epitomizes the message of Isaiah.

It has been aptly remarked that "it is impossible to construct a biography of the prophet Isaiah." The material available is too scant. Besides, the book makes only casual mention of what the prophet did, touching only on those things that are essential to the understanding of certain of the words of the prophet. Yet for all that, as has also been remarked, the prophet strides through the events involved with calm composure and a certain majesty, sure of himself and impressing his ministry on them.

The few details that are available are the following: he was the son of Amoz (not Amos, the prophet); he was married — his wife is called "the prophetess" (8:3), which name may signify that she also had the gift of prophecy, but more likely she is so designated merely because she was the wife of the great prophet; he had two sons, Shearjashub and Maher-shalal-hashbaz, the first name meaning, "A remnant shall return," the second, "The spoil speeds, the prey hastes," (see 7:3 and 8:3). We also have an account of the commissioning of the prophet (chap. 6); and he was told to seal up his teaching (8:16). Then we, too, know a few details of his encounter with King Ahaz on one occasion (7:1-17). Lastly we are informed that in a particular instance Isaiah went about for the space of three years "naked and barefoot" (20:2-3). It is possible that 8:17 may indicate that Isaiah withdrew from the scene for a length of time, perhaps almost twenty years. But the statement involved in this passage seems to furnish too meager support for this conclusion.

The ministry of Isaiah falls within the range of the reign of four kings of Judah: Uzziah (783-742 B.C.), Jotham (750-742 as regent and 742-735 as king), Ahaz (735-715) and Hezekiah (715-687). There is always the possibility that Isaiah may have lived even into the days of the reign of Manasseh, of whom an account is given in II Kings 21:1-18, in which account v. 16 indicates that good men lost their lives. It is often assumed that in Heb. 11:37 the reference "sawn in two" has been traditionally construed to refer to the death of Isaiah. But for this view nothing more than a vague tradition may be cited. If Isaiah lived until the time of Manasseh (an interpretation not warranted by Isa. 1:1) his ministry could have been one of fifty years.

Since the days of Isaiah were marked by a continual clash with Assyria, it will be of interest to list the Assyrian kings involved during this period. They are: Tiglath-pileser (744-727 B.C.), Shalmanezer (726-722), Sargon II (721-705), and Sennacherib (704-681).

The ministry of the prophet could be outlined very simply as involving three periods — early, middle, and late. *Hast-*

ings, Dictionary of the Bible, (2nd. edition, 1963) divides the ministry into the following periods:

— his call in 738 (chap. 6)
— the Syro-Ephraimitic war in 734-733 (7:1–8:18; 17:1-6)
— the siege of Samaria in 724-722 (9:8–10:4; 5:24-30)
— the siege of Ashdod in 711 (chap. 20)
— the invasion of Sennacherib in 701 (chaps. 36-39).

This approach makes the ministry center about major historic dates, although the chapters cited cannot always be easily fitted into the history involved.

C. R. North (*International Dictionary of the Bible*) utilizes the first pattern mentioned above but inserts between the early and the middle a period of "withdrawal from public life" running from 734-715 B.C., although, as already indicated, this is but poorly substantiated.

So we could go on at great length presenting divergent patterns. The sampling given suggests a few reasonable possibilities.

In Isaiah we see for the first time a prophet appearing in the Southern Kingdom. In that respect Isaiah's ministry is a landmark. True, men like Nathan had appeared as early as the reign of David, but on a rather personal mission, not with a mandate for the kingdom.

It would appear that our prophet is at home in court-circles. He seems to have had unquestioned access to the royal court whenever he was minded to appear before the king. This has led some to assume (the Jewish tradition) that Isaiah belonged to the royal family. At least he may have been "of noble descent." His life centered about the royal city of Jerusalem.

Hardly any one would question the claim that Isaiah is a prince among prophets. His eloquence is very evident. His major theme is Yahweh's sovereignty. He has at his command a vocabulary richer than that of any prophet, even more comprehensive than that of the Book of Psalms.

Since the problem of dating successive chapters keeps arising continually, we shall deal with it on a chapter to chapter basis, not attempting any elaborate combinations on the basis of these dates but merely fixing them as a convenient point of departure in the exposition.

III. THE BOOK

A. BRIEF OUTLINE — AUTHORSHIP

We submit first of all a few outlines of the material of Chaps. 1–39 of Isaiah.

This first outline is patterned largely after *von Orelli*.

Introduction (chap. 1): A typical message of Isaiah

Chaps. 2–6. Through judgment to the fulfilment of God's gracious promises

Chaps. 7–12. The Immanuel book

Chaps. 13–27. Oracles of judgment, mostly on foreign nations (Babylon, immediate neighbors, distant neighbors, Jerusalem, and Tyre)

Chaps. 28–35. The Book of Zion

Chaps. 36–39. A historical interlude

In this outline the time sequence, which is very difficult to determine in many a case, has not been the determining factor. But large, overall themes that ring through larger areas of the book have largely controlled the outline, which we freely admit is an oversimplified outline.

By way of comparison we shall submit a few other types of approach to the outlining of the subject matter of Isa. 1–39.

Procksch uses the following rather workable pattern:

A. Chaps. 1–12. Words concerning Judah and Jerusalem (mostly from the early ministry of the prophet)

B. Chaps. 13–27. Oracles concerning the nations (mostly from the middle period of the prophet's ministry)

C. Chaps. 28–35. Oracles of Woe (dating from the closing period of the prophet's ministry)

D. Chaps. 36–39. Narratives about Isaiah (later ministry)

Another simple, and not so adequate outline divides the material into three parts, somewhat after the pattern of Jeremiah:

A. Threats against the prophet's own people (chaps. 1–12)
B. Threats against foreign peoples (chaps. 13–23)
C. Promises to the prophet's own people (chaps. 28–35)
Chaps. 24–27 are partly in B and partly in C.

When we come to the question of the authorship of these thirty-nine chapters, a very difficult problem, we must take particular note of headings that are given at several points throughout the book. 1:1 attributes the "vision" to "Isaiah the son of Amoz," although nothing specific is said as to how much area is covered by the term "vision." It could well be the whole book, a position which grows out of the observation that this type of heading corresponds to the purpose served by the title page of a printed book in our day. The fact that this vision is said to concern itself "with Judah and Jerusalem," fits in well with this approach, because no matter what is treated in these thirty-nine chapters, it all is viewed in its relationship to Judah and Jerusalem and is practically touched upon only in so far as the interest of this capital city and this country are concerned.

The heading of 2:1 is similar and may have first stood as a heading of a collection made by the prophet of a number of chapters, but was allowed to remain when these chapters were placed in a larger collection. At least this is as reasonable an assumption as any. It is not unnatural to assume that this early collection ran to the end of Chap. 12.

The next heading is to be found in 13:1, and introduces what may originally have been a separate collection, the oracles of judgment on foreign nations. But the material set off by this heading is again clearly ascribed to "Isaiah, the son of Amoz." Inserted in this corpus of chapters is the statement of 14:28, which merely indicates the time when the following oracle "came." Nothing is said of authorship by Isaiah. Yet this silence does not mark the passage as not coming from Isaiah's pen. Several times from Chap.

13 to Chap. 23 the word "oracle" appears in the chapter-heading, without any ascription of authorship. The only other related passage is 8:16, which may or may not have involved the writing of some part of the prophet's message, but is not specific enough for use in this connection.

The conclusion that we draw from all this runs as follows: Since the material of these thirty-nine chapters is well integrated, the evidences of the references just given gives warrant for the conclusion that Isaiah is the author of the whole. We are well aware that this conclusion is not popular nor commonly accepted by the world of Old Testament scholars, but we are ready to defend it as being as reasonable as any conclusion offered. From chapter to chapter we shall attempt to demonstrate the coherence manifest throughout the book, and suggest the following consideration: If there is evidence of logical, editorial work done by some competent writer, this writer could well have been the prophet himself. Subjective opinion frequently rules out this possibility; but it takes more than subjective impressions to effect the cancellation of this evidence.

A factor that is more important than is usually conceded is the testimony of the New Testament. We refer to the passages Matt. 13:14; 15:7; Mark 7:6; John 12:38, 39, 41; Acts 28:25; Rom. 9:27, 29. In two of these passages (John 12:39 and Acts 28:25) the reference is specifically to Isaiah "the prophet." We are not minded lightly to brush this specific reference aside with the remark: By metonomy the name of the person is used for the book. For there is always the possibility that these statements are meant literally.

The view generally prevailing on this subject as a whole will show how complicated Old Testament scholarship, whose motives we do not impugn, has found this problem to be. We intend to offer, largely on the basis of the presentation of *Eissfeldt*, how a good bit of the world of scholarship stands on one related question, viz., how much of the material of this half of Isaiah's book is genuine and how much is questionable. No two authors agree completely as to the questions of genuineness.

The following describes the general position held by a large part of modern scholarship.

Material dating back to Isaiah (*Eissfeldt*): Chap. 1

2:6-21. To be traced back to the youthful activity of the prophet and patterned after Amos.

3:1-9. Also from the early ministry of Isaiah.

The "woes" found in the early part of the book, which should be rearranged as follows: (1:19-21; 5:8-10, 17, 11-13, 22, 14, 18-21; 10:1; 5:23; 10:2-4a; 5:24).

6:1ff. An "I-report" (*Ichbericht*), to be dated 746 B.C.; originally it stood immediately after superscription 1:1.

7:1ff. After the days of Ahaz. The chapter speaks about Isaiah in the third person (*Fremdbericht* — i.e., written by a person other than the prophet).

8:1ff. An "I-report" of the time of the Syro-Ephraimite war.

9:7-20 plus 5:25-30. From Isaiah's early ministry, showing dependence upon Amos.

10:16-23. From Isaiah's early ministry, and is to be removed and is to be taken out of 10:5-34.

10:5-15, 24-34. Here the oracles against foreign nations begin. Late in the prophet's ministry.

14:24-27. Also late.

14:28-32. (dated) after the year of the death of Ahaz (726). Dated like 6:1; 7:1; 20:1.

17:1-11. Before 732, the year of Rezin's defeat and death.

17:12-14. Refer to the confusion of nations serving in the Assyrian army.

18:1ff. Not before 715, about 711; begins with Ethiopia and adds the fall of Assyria (v. 4-6).

20:1ff. About 711.

22:15-25

28:1-22. Difficult to date. Contains thoughts that Isaiah always maintained. 713 or 705

28:23-29. Like v. 7-22 to be dated 713 or 705.

29:1-8

29:9-12, 13-14, 15

30:8-14, 15-17, 18-26

31:1ff. Mostly genuine.

32:9-14

Material of which the authorship by Isaiah is often classified as dubious. (in chaps. 1–35)

This material attempts to relieve and modify the words that have an undertone of threat, by adding promises of good for Israel, and threats of punishment for the nations that are hostile.

11:10-16
14:1-2
29:16-24 } It is claimed that these are commonly acknowl-
30:18-26 } edged to be of a much later date than the min-
32:1-8   } istry of Isaiah
4:2-6
12:1ff.

2:2-5   }
9:1-6   } Opinions differ widely as to genuineness. 9:1-6
11:1-9 } is probably genuine.

In fairness to those whose position as to genuineness is rather critical it may be quoted that at about this point *Eissfeldt* remarks that "words like 2:2-4 carry their worth within themselves, quite apart from the question from whom they stem and from what time."

13:2-22. Cannot come from Isaiah, for v. 17 refers to the Medes, who first come into prominence about 540 B.C.

14:4b-21. Might be traced back to Isaiah, if it referred to an Assyrian king, but it happens to refer to a king of Babylon.

Chaps. 15, 16. Authorship by Isaiah is but poorly evidenced. Here *Eissfeldt* remarks that the oracles against foreign nations (chaps. 13–23) are *herrenloses Gut* (anonymous material) which might be attributed soon to this author, soon to that.

Chap. 19. Impossible to determine the time.

Chap. 21. From around 538.

Chap. 23. This would fit in well with the rest of Isaiah's message, except for the reference to Tyre which was taken 332.

Chaps. 24–27. Make up a separate unit and are hardly a
composition that is constructed according to a unified
plan. Yet on the other hand this piece dare not be
thought of as an incoherent hodge-podge (*sinnloses
Durcheinander*). Rather the insertions that are found
appear to have been made deliberately and well.

We disgress at this point to give a typical example of
how little agreement is to be found among the various
writers who have only this in common, that they do not
attribute Chaps. 24–27 to Isaiah. Four possible patterns
for these chapters are suggested:

(1) *Duhm*. To a collection of predictions and an assort-
ent of hymns have been added a number of prophecies.
(2) *Sellin* and *Procksch*. The foundation is 24:1-23, which
passage was expanded in successive stages.
(3) *Rudolph*. Here we have ten prophecies, analogous as
to content, and stemming for the most part from the
same author.
(4) *Lindblom*. This section is made up of five eschatological poems and four hymns of thanks and jubulation.

Eissfeldt takes his position with *Duhm*. Then he goes
on to report that writers differ even much more widely
when they attempt to arrange the material of these four
chapters in chronological sequence. He concludes his remarks on this section with the warning that in interpreting
the chapters involved a man dare not take an unswerving
position on any one of the approaches indicated.

We continue with the listing of the passages usually
classified as dubious of authorship.

Chap. 33. Labelled as doubtless of exilic or post-exilic
authorship.
Chaps. 34–35. The poet has patterned after chaps. 40–66.
There cannot be any thought of genuineness. Date:
end of sixth century.
Chaps. 36–39. A repetition of II Kings 18:13–20:9, in an

effort to gather all material available concerning Isaiah under one cover. The psalm of Hezekiah has nothing to do with Hezekiah. Three legends have been appended.

Yet for all that, *Eissfeldt* insists that most assuredly as far as the religious kernel of his message is concerned, Isaiah always presented the same truth. The following items are clearly in evidence: Isaiah champions with unabating zeal the sole majesty of Yahweh, and attacks vehemently everything and every individual who rises up against his divine majesty or seeks in any way to cloud it. This is the mark of his preaching from beginning to end.

We have already clearly indicated that we do not accept the somewhat negative position advanced especially on the subject of portions that are not accepted as genuinely Isaianic. But for the sake of rounding out the picture we would also submit at least one example of how able writers envision the process of the composition of the book, Chaps. 1–39. We shall condense the story that *R. B. Y. Scott* offers in the *Interpreter's Bible*.

He advances the claim that first of all a collection of early prophecies of Isaiah was made after Ahaz, king of Judah, had in 734 B.C. refused to heed the prophet's message. This collection was made up of three types of material: (a) oracles concerning Judah and Jerusalem (selected material from chaps. 1–5); (b) "two earlier oracle complexes" inserted in the preceding material — like 2:6-22 and 9:8–10:4, supplementing Chaps. 5 and 8; (c) "memoirs," mostly Chap. 6.

Then a second collection of prophecies was written, also by Isaiah, after the conferences with Egypt had been denounced (*ca.* 704) but the prophet's denunciation had gone unheeded: e.g., 28:1-4, 7-13 plus parts of Chaps. 29, 30, and 31.

Then these two collections were supplemented by oracles that had reference to the Assyrian thrust (701 B.C.). To the first collection there were added portions like 10:5-16, 24-27c; 14:24-27. To the second were added: 29:1-8; 30:27-33; 31:4-9.

Then these first two collections were expanded soon after Isaiah's death by "authentic material concerning him or his message." To the first collection there were added "dynastic oracles" (9:2-7; 11:1-9); also some "biographical narratives" (like 7:1-7 and 18-25). Also there were added "minor oracles and fragments" (like 10:17-19, 10-13; 17:12-14; 17:1-6). Lastly there were added oracles concerning foreign nations (like 10:27d-32; 14:28-32; 17:1-6, etc.). Some of these were "doom oracles."

To the second collection there were added oracles from Isaiah "of uncertain date" (like 28:23-29; 29:9-12, etc.).

Now each collection was further expanded by material that did not originate with Isaiah. (a) To the first collection there were added oracles concerning foreign peoples (like 13:1-22; 14:1-23); then material from Chaps. 15, 16, 21 and 23, mostly again "doom oracles." Also there were added brief "oracles and fragments" (like 1:27-31; 5:24b; 9:1; 17:7-11). To the second collection there were added a wisdom poem (32:1-9) and a prophetic liturgy (33:1-24).

Finally these two collections were joined and further materials were inserted in the form of "eschatological prophecies" dating from the latter part of the Exile or even from the post-exilic period, passages like 2:2-5; 4:2-6; 11:10-16; 12:1-6, etc., down to 32:15-20.

By this time chaps. 1–33 were complete. There remained the last step — the addition of "material from outside sources," like chaps. 34 and 35 and chaps. 36–39, the last four chapters being largely a modification of II Kings 18:13 20:19, plus sizable additions like 37:4d-21 and 38:1-8 and 39:1-8.

There can be no question about it that the above story of the composition of Isaiah chaps. 1–39 is based on much and intensive research. Many possibilities are explored and have arrived at some helpful results. But very strong doubts begin to assail the reader as he begins to observe the intricacy and infinite detail with which the whole process is depicted. To be able to analyze and dissect a book like this as to how it came to be as it is and to detect the exact procedure followed, borders on the humanly impossible. Thousands of subjective impressions enter into a process which is indeed intended to be a purely objective evaluation of facts. Some measure of superhuman ingenuity is required to do such a piece of work with such detailed reconstruction. The degree to which writers differ from one another in trying to tell the story of the composition of the book is in itself a refutation of their so often positive claims.

Besides it must be conceded that certain foregone conclusions enter very strongly into the critical appraisal of chapter after chapter. Anything that savors of prediction is allowed to reach into the future only to a very limited extent. Certain concepts like "Babylon" are not taken in their full Biblical connotation. Headings ascribing portions of the book to Isaiah himself are allowed to extend only over a minimum of the material following. Much latitude in the area of textual criticism is granted to the commentator. Textual emendations are made with the utmost of freedom. The proof advanced for certain positions often has done no more than to demonstrate a certain approach as *possible*, without even attaining to the level of the *probable*, let alone the level of the *necessary* and the conclusive.

Then altogether too little is made of the possibility that the writer may have resorted to the use of the purely objective, referring to himself by the use of the third person, as writers often did in days of old. Still another possibility has been too little explored — namely that the prophet himself may have engaged in constructive editorial activity in preparing his own book. We would certainly not entirely eliminate the possibility that there may have been minor editorial changes (or copyist's errors) and additions made at a later date by a person other than the original author. But clear evidence for the *extensive* character of such activity is not available.

B. THEOLOGY OF ISAIAH AS REFLECTED IN CHAPS. 1–39

The Gospel in Isaiah

It would be very proper to begin by dwelling on the gospel in Isaiah, for he is the most evangelical of all the

prophets. In that connection we do well to emphasize that
he has a very clear conception of free grace. Having scored
the children of Israel very sharply for their ingratitude
and ungodly conduct, he, rather abruptly, introduces the
note of grace, totally undeserved, when he represents the
Lord as promising: "Though your sins be as scarlet they
shall be white as snow" (1:18). On a basis such as this
he can well issue the call to repentance in the words:
"Turn to him from whom you have deeply revolted." All
this does not cancel out the fear of the Lord, but underscores its necessity: "Let him [the Lord of hosts] be your
fear" (8:11-13). That faith then becomes the means of
the acceptance of the grace so freely offered is set forth
in words like: "Thou wilt keep him in perfect peace, whose
mind is stayed on thee" (26:3-4). Approached from the
other point of view the subject can also be stated thus by
the prophet: "If you will not believe, surely you will not be
established" (7:9b). Cf. also 26:20.

Some make a strong point of the fact that the truth that
Isaiah preaches is deeply rooted in the standing tradition
of the chosen people, particularly the tradition of the holy
war, as is clearly the case in 30:30, where the Lord is
depicted as himself going forth to do battle for his own.
This faith then also is the very opposite of self-help (see
7:4), as is clearly shown in the word: "In quietness and
in trust shall be your strength" (30:15).

The Messianic Future

Very closely related with the preceding is the subject of
God's Anointed One and the future which he will in his
own good time inaugurate. Sometimes this aspect of the
case is set forth without mention of the Messiah himself
who brings in this new age, as is clearly the case in 2:2-5,
where the change of attitude on the part of the foreign
nations toward God's ancient people is described, and also
in 4:26, where indeed the "branch" appears, without its
being made apparent that of necessity a person is being
thus designated, but where the Zion of the future is pictured in all its purity and holiness.

Whatever relation the next two passages may have had first of all to the then-time incumbents of the royal office, may here be left out of consideration, but that 9:2-7 and 11:1-10 had a very definite Messianic content is beyond the shadow of a doubt. Both passages describe, almost like full-length portraits, the character and work of God's Anointed One. The two hymns 12:1-6 and 35:1-10 depict the jubilant praise that men will offer when they experience the dawning of the new day as well as the transformation of the physical world and the spiritual situation that the One who is to come will bring to pass.

The Day of the Lord

All of what was said concerning the Messianic future ties up very naturally with the thoughts that bear on the new era, or the Lord's day. This day is thought of first of all as one in which all human greatness and arrogance must be brought low, in order that the Lord alone may be exalted, as 2:12-17 repeatedly sets forth. In addition many other facets of the Lord's day are introduced from time to time. The prophet sets forth how the physical aspects of God's creation will shine forth at their best and every human infirmity will be overcome. No more shall the people of God be marked by misunderstanding of God (29:17-24). Or again, all of God's work upon his people will blossom forth in the glory and beauty that are native to it (4:2ff.). All the cruel and destructive aspects of God's created work will be cancelled out and perfect harmony shall pervade this world (11:10). All of which shall fill the hearts of God's people with such superlative joy that they will break forth into singing (12:1ff.). Spiritual insight will be on so high a level that the Lord himself will be the object of all their aspirations (28:5f.). All deficiencies of the lower level of living will then be a thing of the past (32:1-8).

The Holy God

The sole sovereignty of God is one of the major emphases of the prophet. This, as partly already indicated, is to be made evident by the overthrow of all human greatness that exalts itself against the Lord, so that "the Lord alone will be exalted in that day" (2:11, 17). This insight may indeed be said to stem from the experience that the prophet had in his inaugural vision (chap. 6). Never, perhaps, did the eye of man behold a sight more exalted, as is in part manifested by the title that the prophet uses by preference for the Lord ever thereafter — "the Holy One of Israel." This holiness, which is so strongly stressed, has first of all the positive connotation of being separated from all things inferior and sin-stained — some might prefer to call this a negative aspect. But without a doubt both negative and positive aspects of God's holiness are in evidence in the fact, also clearly set forth, that the Lord is an avenging God (9:8ff.; 10:4). This by no means implies that God's justice and vengeance are inferior qualities in the divine character. For sin is a grievous evil and the removal of it is a work of divine perfection. How the Lord's justice and his mercy blend with one another is an issue that defies adequate human definition. It is in this connection that we may draw attention to the fact that Isaiah is the prophet who originated the expression concerning the "strange work" of God (28:21). For God is a God who works in a manner that is often quite incomprehensible to the children of men.

The Inadequacy of Formalistic Worship

If then God is so great and majestic a Lord, he surely dare not be offered a type of worship that is pure formalism, or even, for that matter, vitiated by the taint of formalism. Few prophets come near to the sharpness of denunciation of such worship that is reached by Isaiah. First of all this is revealed in 1:10-15, where God is said to hate and abhor the unspiritual worship of his people. But 29:13f. also treats of this subject with deep insight, aside from the occasional references to the subject that appear in his book.

Related to this is that of the futility of idol worship. The passage 2:18-24 depicts in a rather colorful way how, in a time of crisis, idols utterly fail mankind and will have to be spurned and summarily cast off by Israel. Idolatry

more and more became a major issue in Judah coming more
and more prominently to the forefront as Judah ripened out
for judgment. Isaiah did his part to utter stern warnings
against this most prevalent vice. Cf. also 31:7.

God and the Nations

This subject had to be driven home to Judah by the
prophet with more than usual emphasis. It had become
an issue in a very definite sense. For the first time a world-
power was threatening to engulf the people of God and to
make impossible the high purposes that God had revealed
concerning them and their great hope. But things were
not at all what they appeared to be on the international
horizon. No one had ever set this forth quite as clearly as
Isaiah. It may safely be claimed that after him no one
surpassed him in the effective treatment of this subject.

One might designate as the point of departure of his
treatment the basic concept, which appears often in later
writings, namely that of two cities that are set in sharp
antithesis to one another. There is a city, but an ungodly
one, which is destined to destruction. Of this 25:1-11 speaks
quite clearly. Over against it stands a "strong city," whose
destiny and impregnable character are set forth in 26:1-6.
Practically all history may be said to be the story of the
conflict of these two through the ages.

This is declared more specifically by the prophet as
pointing to Assyria in his day as the most prominent exponent of the "city" that is doomed to be ultimately overthrown. But before Assyria's overthrow comes she will have
some success, as 7:1-17 indicates: she will overthrow, among
others, also Syria and Samaria, who will for a time constitute a threat to Judah, before the time of their own
overthrow comes. These complicated historical developments are shown to be under the total control of the Lord.
See 7:1-17.

More light is thrown on this whole issue when the
prophet sets forth the view that all these nations, no matter
how prominently they may loom up on the horizon for a
time, are nothing more than tools in the Lord's hands,

governed and used by him, not as the tool pleases, but according to his own sovereign plans (10:33f.).

One factor seems a bit puzzling in this connection. It would appear that heathen rulers had some sense of being directed by the Lord even when they proceeded against Israel, as 36:10 clearly shows. But we grope in vain for an answer to the question how this commission was conveyed to the heathen powers.

But quite a bit is made of the fact that *all* nations are wholly under the Lord's control, as Chaps 13–23 abundantly indicate. The fact that God foreknows the ultimate outcome, namely how these nations will finally be cast down and punished for their pride, vindictiveness, and other sins, is merely a part of the whole subject of divine control of history. It is interesting to note in this connection that the overthrow of Babylon is also clearly foretold, at a time when Babylon had not yet become a leading world-power, or a formidable empire. But in the Scriptures Babylon happens to be the epitome of all those powers that attempt, Titan-like, to storm heaven and to dethrone the Almighty, a tendency, the earliest manifestation of which is set forth in the tale of the Tower of Babel, Gen. 11. Isa. 13 and 14 stand out particularly in the treatment of this subject.

Analogous is the subject of Egypt, "the mistress of the Nile." She had enjoyed some measure of prominence from very ancient times. She early manifested hostility against Israel in the days of the Egyptian bondage, a spirit which found strongest expression in the answer of Pharaoh to the Lord's demand to let his people go, when Pharaoh said: "Who is the Lord that I should heed his voice?" (Exod. 5:2). Through the early part of the second millennium B.C. Egypt frequently dominated the destinies of the peoples resident in Canaan and adjacent countries, without destroying their identity as Assyria did when she appeared on the scene. Egypt was still making pretences of superiority in Isaiah's days when a resurgence of Egypt seemed to have taken place. But Egypt's claims were hollow, not backed by the great power that she had once had. No statesman had insight into this aspect of the case as did

Isaiah, though we by no means imply that his insight was the result of his astute political discernment and evaluation. God enlightened him on this score. The following passages are particularly instructive: 30:1-14 and chap. 31. The most famous words under this head are 31:3: "The Egyptians are man and not God," and v. 1: "Woe to those who go down to Egypt for help."

That all nations come under the purview of this approach and must ultimately be judged by God and experience his vengeance is by way of summary set forth in chap. 34: All the enemies of God's people must ultimately appear before the judgment seat of the Lord. So, as a kind of climax, when the Lord is done with his work of judgment upon Zion and Jerusalem, he will punish the arrogant boasting of foes of his like Assyria (10:12). One of the grandest passages in all prophetic literature is to be found in 30:27-33, which describes in summary all judgments of God including the last and greatest of all.

Zion

Zion, as the ideal embodiment of the nation, occupies a prominent place in the thinking of Isaiah, so much so that writers of times past (like *von Orelli*) even ventured to caption Chaps. 28–35 as "The Zion Book," though in these chapters the word "Zion" seems to appear only about seven times. Yet the holy city, beloved of God and by his people is the subject under continual consideration. Perhaps all this is brought to a head in the passage 28:16, where Zion is designated as a "precious cornerstone." Again a choice name is given to the city in 29:1f. — "Ariel" — God's hearth, where his altar-fires burn and his home among his people is to be found. Lowly though she now often is, and even though her future seems imperiled and very uncertain, the prophet sees it as glorious and sketches it in sublime colors in chap. 27, as a restored vineyard (cf. also 5:1-3). Or he dwells on the security that God's city will in the end enjoy, when all conflicts are past. Though chap. 35 gives the impression of being a description of the whole land in its rejuvenated blessedness, this is merely a sketch of the domain over which the beneficent rule of Zion extends. It just cannot be denied that the Zion tradition in all its glory is perpetuated by no one more eloquently than by Isaiah.

God's Spirit

Though the subject does not come in for lengthy treatment by the prophet, it still comes under consideration in two very significant instances. The Spirit of the Lord is the major equipment of the "shoot from the stem of Jesse." It enables the Messianic Servant to do his work as effectively as he does. But it is for that matter even the power that is poured out upon the nation (30:15) making such a thorough-going change in the people of God that the very land is transformed together with the nation and all things belonging to the national existence.

The Remnant

Isaiah very significantly names one of his sons Shear-jashub — "a remnant shall return." This concept, however, is not developed at length by Isaiah, though at times, when the term as such is not used, the concept proper is nevertheless under consideration, like in 6:13. Sometimes the term is used in reference to any nation that has lived through the vicissitudes of war and has been sadly reduced in numbers. What is still left is then called "the remnant." In reference to Israel the remnant is made up of those who, after the nation has been visited by the judgment of God, are the believing ones left after this experience, with whom God makes a fresh start, having preserved them for this very purpose. Pertinent passages are 4:3; 10:20, 22; 11:11, 16; 37:4, 31. The emphasis lies partly on the extent to which God will have to let his judgment strike the guilty, and partly on the low estate to which his people will be reduced. The statement, "a remnant shall return," is both a threat and a promise. But the chief emphasis is on the fact that God can revitalize his people after they have been most severely punished.

C. FORMS OF PROPHETIC UTTERANCE

Kraeling (*Commentary on the Prophets*, p. 24) has well said in approaching this subject: "Recent study of the prophetic books has been much concerned with the literary forms, their origin and development." It would, however, appear that concern for the form has often outweighed the net profit derived from such study. Not that these studies have been misdirected or fruitless. But sometimes they have been overvalued.

Gunkel began the work in this direction, followed by *Hoelscher*. For both the starting point was the "ecstatic experience" of the prophet. It was naively assumed that prophets regularly went into a state of "ecstasy" before making a prophetic pronouncement. Later writers, recognizing the untenability of this claim, noted that the starting point for prophetic utterances was: receiving an assignment to bear a divine message. Everyday experiences furnished the pattern that the prophets followed. Or, it might be said with equal propriety, that prophets spoke in the common idiom of their day. So, for example, when Jacob wishes to send a message to his brother Esau (Gen. 32:1-4) he instructs the messenger to begin the message with the words: "Thus says your servant Jacob." This pattern of approach is certainly being used by Elijah, when he delivers the Lord's message to Ahab after the slaying of Naboth (I Kings 21:17-19): "Thus says the Lord." Numberless instances of this type of introduction of the prophetic message could, of course, be cited.

In this connection the effort was made to determine which was the basic element or prophecy. *Gunkel* advanced the theory that it was the threat. *Westermann* has shown the inadequacy of this term and has substituted the expression "announcement of judgment." But it still remained a question which came first, the weal-message or the woe-message. The attempt seems to be made to force the issue, as though one of these two possibilities *had*, in the nature of the case, to come first. Fact of the matter is that logically and historically neither can be called the original form. This is especially the case when the approach is used that where primacy of the woe-message is asserted, the claim is made that, where weal-messages then follow, they are always later additions. That is a verdict that has not been established and cannot be. At least it may be admitted that the woe-messages were "most typical of the early prophets."

By way of sampling the approach here developed it may be pointed out that *Westermann* has suggested the following pattern for woe-passages: (a) introductory invitation to hear; (b) the accusation; (c) the elaboration of the accusation; (d) the messenger formula, often reduced to a simple "therefore"; (e) the announcement of divine action; (f) the elaboration of this announcement. Of course, many variations of this pattern may be observed as well as clear departures from it.

But as may readily be imagined, the "terminology" involved is still under dispute. So many attempts have been made to reduce these approaches to categories, that uniformity can hardly be achieved. No man can rise up and say: My findings are final. All this becomes still more apparent when we begin to recognize what these studies are doing is to employ "western rationalization" (*Kraeling*). The prophets and the people they addressed were not in the habit of thinking in terms here used. So that when all the work of form criticism is done, and passages have been successfully categorized, all that has been achieved is that the passages in question have been inserted in their proper pigeon-holes. Their content has only been glanced at. Their rich meaning still needs to be determined. None of those who work in this area are, of course, content merely to determine the form involved. But they frequently devote far more effort to the form than to the content.

It is rather instructive to note how many different forms of utterance are employed by the prophets. It may be quite instructive to compare all examples of pattern that come under one heading. A listing of patterns or classifications may be briefly submitted here. We follow *Wester-mann* (*Grundformen der propetischen Rede*) who has done more than any recent writer to clarify the issues. He has observed that the prophetic word may appear:

(a) as word of a messenger (somewhat after the analogy of some Mari letters that have been found)

(b) as a word of judgment on an individual

(c) as a word of judgment on Israel. The following forms are possible under this head: Briefer forms, expanded forms, words of woe (or curse), court-trial patterns, disputations, parables, laments, prophetic tora, liturgies.

(d) words of judgment against Israel's enemies

(e) words which are a departure from the proper pattern (*Aufloesung*)

As our exposition progresses we frequently shall indicate what form is, by almost common consent, being used by the prophet. This may in most cases help to make the passage stand out more clearly over against other related passages. Men need to be on their guard against becoming obsessed by form-criticism studies.

D. THE DEAD SEA SCROLLS

The remarkable find of the great Isaiah scroll in 1947 has to be referred to briefly in connection with the text of the Book of Isaiah. Since this scroll may date back to 150 B.C., it is well nigh ten centuries earlier in the text that it offers than the familiar Masoretic text.

For critical use this scroll text in its major variants is to be found in the *Biblia Hebraica*, ed. Rud. Kittel, for the American Bible Society, published by privel. Wuertt. Bibelanstalt, Stuttgart, 7. edition, 1951. It appears under the familiar critical apparatus. *Eissfeldt-Kahle* remarks: "Only a selection, however, could be made of the large number of variant readings of (this) manuscript."

Not many references needed to be made in our Exposition to these variant readings from the Isaiah Scroll. In very few instances did these readings materially alter the sense. They serve to convince the careful student that the Masoretic text is, by and large, a reliable text, carefully transmitted.

E. DETAILED OUTLINE

I. PROPHECIES CONCERNING JUDAH AND JERU-
SALEM (chaps. 1–12)

Introduction: A Typical Message of Isaiah (chap. 1)
1. Heading (v. 1)
2. The Divine Indictment (vv. 2-4)
3. The Desolate External State of the Nation (vv. 5-9)
4. The Current Type of Worship Ineffective as a
   Remedy (vv. 10-15)
5. Call to Repentance (vv. 16-20)
6. Indication of the Corruptions in Jerusalem (vv. 21-
   23)
7. Israel to Be Redeemed by Judgment (vv. 24-31)

A. Through Judgment to Fulfillment of God's Gracious
   Promises (chaps. 2–6)

Heading (v. 1)
1. Zion's Glorious Future in the Messianic Age (2:2-5)
2. Zion's Inglorious Present (2:6–4:1)
   a. Description of the Spurious Values That Are Cur-
      rent (vv. 6-9)
   b. Indication of a Terrible Judgment about to Come
      (vv. 10-11)
   c. What the Lord's Day Will Do to All Spurious
      Values (vv. 12-17)
   d. The Fate of the Idols (vv. 18-21)
   e. The Lord's Indictment of Irresponsible Leaders
      (vv. 2:22–3:15)
      (1) The Resultant State of Anarchy When the
          Lord Takes Away All Supports (3:1-12)
      (2) The Guilt of the Leaders That Brought
          on This Calamity (3:13-15)
   f. The Lord's Indictment of the Vain and Frivolous
      Women of Jerusalem (3:16–4:1)
   g. Zion Purified (4:2-6)
   h. God's Judgment on His Guilty People (chap. 5)
      (1) The Parable of the Vineyard (vv. 1-7)

a. The Summoning of Warriors for an Assault (vv. 2-3)
b. The Description of the Assembled Host (vv. 4-5)
c. The Terrors of the Day of the Lord (vv. 6-8)
d. The Destruction Wrought by the Day of the Lord (vv. 9-16)
e. The Medes — God's Agent for the Overthrow of Babylon (vv. 17-19)
f. The Total Desolation of Babylon (vv. 20-22)
g. The Overthrow of Babylon in Relation to God's Gracious Purposes for Israel (14:1-2)
h. Israel's Taunt Directed against Babylon's King (vv. 3-21)
   (1) Introduction (vv. 3-4a)
   (2) The Fall of the Oppressor Signifies the End of All of Babylon's Cruelty and Oppression (vv. 4b-6)
   (3) The Song of Exultation That Greets This Overthrow (vv. 7-8)
   (4) Sheol's Reception of the Shade of Babylon's King (vv. 9-15)
   (5) The Estimate of Babylon's King Made by Those Who Behold His Corpse Lying Unburied on the Field of Battle (vv. 16-21)
i. God's Verdict with Regard to the Whole Empire of the King of Babylon (vv. 22-23)
2. Against Israel's Immediate Neighbors (14:24–17:1ff.)
a. Assyria (14:24-27): The Lord's Unalterable Purpose in Regard to Assyria
b. Philistia (14:28-32)
c. Oracle Concerning Moab (15:1–16:14)
   (1) Cruel Invasion and Drought for Moab (15:1-9)
   (2) The Appeal for Asylum Addressed by Refugees to Judah (16:1-5)
   (3) Indication of Further Affliction, Especially of Moab's Grape Culture (16:6-12)
   (4) An Epilogue Fixing the Time of Disaster (16:13, 14)
d. Damascus-Ephraim (chap. 17)

a. Praise of God for the Overthrow of the Ungodly City That Had Oppressed His People (vv. 1-5)
b. The Good Things That God Has Prepared for His People (vv. 6-8)
c. The Overthrow of Moab, a Typical Enemy of God's People (vv. 9-12)

3. A Hymn Glorifying the Works of God Done for His People (chap. 26)
   a. Praise for the Strong City (vv. 1-6)
   b. Prayerful Reflection on God's Judgments (vv. 7-15)
   c. The Prayer of Hope (vv. 16-19)
   d. Exhortation: the Nation Must Wait Quietly for God's Constructive Judgments (vv. 20-21)

4. The Overthrow of the Kingdoms of This World vs. the Prosperity of Zion (chap. 27)
   a. Overthrow of the Mighty World-powers (v. 1)
   b. Another Song of the Vineyard: God's Kindly Protection (vv. 2-5)
   c. The Fruitful State of the Vine in the Last Days (v. 6)
   d. God's Purposes in Dealing Gently with Israel (vv. 7-9)
   e. God's Stern Dealings with the "fortified city" (vv. 10-11)
   f. The Gathering of the Scattered Children of Israel (vv. 12-13)

III. THE BOOK OF ZION (chaps. 28–35)

A. Zion's Precious Cornerstone (chap. 28)
   1. The False Crown of Glory vs. the Right Crown (vv. 1-6)
   2. The Doom of Judah's Dubious Security vs. the Solid Endurance of the Lord's Project (vv. 7-16)
   3. A Further Announcement of Doom: the Lord Will Do a "strange" Work (vv. 17-22)
   4. A Parable Illustrating How Judiciously the Lord Does His Work upon His People (vv. 23-29)

F. SELECTED BIBLIOGRAPHY

Bewer, J. A., *The Book of Isaiah* (Harper's Annotated Bible) New York, Harper & Brothers, 1950

Delitzsch, Franz, *Biblischer Commentator ueber den Propheten Jesaia,* (Biblischer Commentar, Keil und Delitzsch), Leipzig; Doerffing u. Franke, 1866

Fischer, Johann, *Das Buch Isaias I. Teil* (Die Heilige Schrist des A. T.) Bonn, Peter Hanstein, 1937

Fitch, W., *Isaiah* (The New Bible Commentary, Davidson, Stibbs, Kevan), Grand Rapids: Wm. B. Eerdmans Publishing Co., 1958

Gray, George Buchanan, *The Book of Isaiah* (International Critical Commentary) New York: Charles Scribner's Sons, 1912

Haller, Max, *Das Judentum* (Geschichtsschreibung, Prophetie, etc. 2. Auflage) Goettingen, Vandenhoeck & Rupprecht, 1925

Kissane, Edward, *The Book of Isaiah, Vol. I.,* Dublin, Brown & Nolan, Ltd., The Richview Press, 1941

Koenig, Eduard, *Das Buch Jesaja,* Guetersloh, Bertelsmann, 1926

Leslie, Elmer, *Isaiah,* New York and Nashville, Abingdon Press, 1963

Luther, Martin, *Auslegung ueber die grossen Propheten,* (Walch, vol. 6, pp. 1-470) 1543, Reprint, Concordia Publishing House, 1897

von Orelli, C., *Der Prophet Jesaja,* (Strack u. Zoecklers Kommentar, 3. Auflage) Munich, C. H. Beck, 1904

Procksch, Otto, *Jesaia I* ("Kommentar zum A. T.", Sellin) Leipzig, Deichert (Scholl), 1930

Rogers, Robert W., *Isaiah* ("The Abingdon Bible Commentary") New York & Nashville, Abingdon-Cokesbury Press, 1929

Scott, R. B. Y., *The Book of Isaiah* ("The Interpreter's Bible"), New York & Nashville, Abingdon Press, 1956

Skinner, J. *Isaiah* Chapters I-XXXIX, (Cambridge Bible) Cambridge University Press, 1951

Smith, George Adam, *The Book of Isaiah*, Vol. 1, ("The Expositor's Bible"), New York, George H. Doran (n.d.)

Wright, G. Ernest, *The Book of Isaiah* (Vol. 11, The Layman's Bible Commentary), Richmond Va., John Knox Press, 1964

PROPHECIES CONCERNING
JUDAH AND JERUSALEM

Chapter I

I. PROPHECIES CONCERNING JUDAH AND JERUSALEM (Chaps. 1–12)

Many hold that this section is best covered by an overall historical approach which divides it as follows: Chaps. 1–6 could well date from the more prosperous days of Uzziah (767-739 B.C.) and Jotham (739-735); then Chaps. 7–12 are to be assigned to the days of distress which prevailed under Ahaz (735-715) when the Syro-Ephraimite threat hung over the land, and Judah was defeated in battle (II Chron. 28:5f.) rather disastrously.

Even so Chap. 1 is in the nature of a prologue, or a "typical message," and Chap. 6 (the inaugural vision) is in the nature of an epilogue. But Chap. 1 may still date from the days of the great Assyrian invasion (*ca*. 701).

INTRODUCTION: A TYPICAL MESSAGE OF ISAIAH (Chap. 1)

As far as this chapter is concerned, it is not difficult to determine why it should have been set first in the book. It gives the impression of being both a typical instance of the message of Isaiah and serves at the same time as a convenient summary of much of what he preached.

Since there is no indication of the time when this message was delivered, we are thrown back upon conjectures. The well-nigh total devastation of the land would seem to point to the days when the Assyrians were threatening to take Jerusalem, and had done their worst to the whole country round about (cf. II Kings 18:13ff. and 19:25, 26), tearing Judah away from the City of David. So the message would date from the latter part of the prophet's activity, that is to say, about 701.

1. The Heading (v. 1)

1:1 1. The message of Isaiah, the son of Amoz, which is received concerning Judah and Jerusalem in the days of Uzziah Jotham, Ahaz, and Hezekiah, kings of Judah.

Verse 1. The word we have rendered "message" (*chazon*) perhaps should have been rendered "vision" as is rather commonly done. However the English connotation of "vision" is quite different from what is meant here. The word really implies all that the prophet *perceived* without the actual beholding of visions by day or by night. That which he perceived he transmits to his people. We call that, "message." But it should always be remembered that the word strongly implies divine revelation and communication. The message did not grow out of reflection, nor was it the result of intense wrestling with a problem. It was not of human discovery or manufacture. It was divinely given.

The verse is broad enough to cover not only the first twelve chapters of the book, as many concede, or even the greater part of Chaps. 1–39, or even, for that matter, all of these chapters, as some will be ready to grant. We maintain that it may rightly be regarded (unpopular as this approach is in our day) as covering the entire book, Chaps. 1–66.

The only identification of the prophet that is offered is contained in the words, "the son of Amoz." This name, being spelled differently than the name of the other prophet, Amos, indicates a different personage.

The ministry of Isaiah touched the period of the reign of four kings: Uzziah, Jotham, Ahaz, and Hezekiah. Though very likely only the last years of Uzziah were involved, we yet have a prophetic ministry that may have run from 739-690 B.C.

It is true that this superscription indicates that the message following concerns "Judah and Jerusalem." It is equally true that Chaps. 13–27 concern themselves with the heathen nations round about. From this evidence it could be deduced that the heading 1:1 applies at most only to Chaps. 1–12. However on further reflection it will appear that even though Chaps. 13–27 deal with heathen nations, these nations are under consideration mainly in their relation to Judah and Jerusalem, and so the heading of 1:1 is still very much to the point.

In any case it will be impossible to determine whether 1:1 was written by Isaiah himself or is perhaps a later editorial addition — and a very valuable one at that.

2. The Divine Indictment (vv. 2-4)

1:2-4 2. Hear, O heavens, and give ear, O earth;
    for the Lord has spoken:
  Children have I reared and exalted,
But they have rebelled against me.
3. The ox knows his owner and the ass his master's crib;
  but Israel does not know, my people do not consider.
4. Ah, sinful nation, guilt-burdened people,
  a brood of evil-doers, children that deal corruptly!
They have forsaken the Lord; they have despised the Holy One
  of Israel;
  they have turned their back on him.

This first piece bears some resemblance to a court trial (*ribh*). There is a great Judge (who He is goes without saying); there is a defendant — the nation Israel. There are witnesses. For this reason this chapter has been given the heading "The Great Assize." However, regular court-procedure is not followed consistently. Therefore we have chosen another caption, which is from the same general area. The three verses involved do present an "indictment" that God charges against his people.

Verse 2. What purpose does it serve to call upon heaven and earth to note what is happening? It makes the whole scene more solemn and impressive. We often use a somewhat similar approach, when we say that the heavens look down upon what happens here below. In this instance, however, by calling upon witnesses so mighty, one is made to feel the grave importance of the things about to be uttered. Similar is the approach of passages like Deut. 32:1; 4:26; 30:19; 31:28. By regarding the issue from this point of view we are relieved of the necessity of determining whether heaven and earth are merely to listen, whether they are

formally to serve as witnesses, or whether they are to participate in the judgment about to take place. But this much is
quite obvious; when the Lord speaks it behooves all things
animate and inanimate to pay respectful attention.

Now comes the indictment proper: "Children have I
reared and exalted, but they have rebelled against me."
That is a flagrant instance of the basest ingratitude. The
pain such behavior has caused the Father is clearly indicated. It takes two words to cover all that God has done for
Israel: He reared them first; that is: He brought them up,
manifesting much patience with them in the process. He
made of them a great nation among the nations of the earth.
So he exalted them, giving them position and reputation in
the eyes of their neighbors. For the many things that he
bestowed upon them in the process, they might have given
many evidences of gratitude. Instead: "They have rebelled
against me." That means both fall away from, and rise in
opposition against God. Though it may be true that the
terms used are quite appropriate for the entire history of
mankind as well, they are singularly applicable to the history
of God's chosen people.

Verse 3. Such behavior, however, stamps them that have
become guilty of it as having sunk down to a brutish level.
The ox and the ass know better and behave better. But
Israel is completely defective in understanding and insight.
By expressing no object for the verb "know" in this case
the writer makes the expression all the stronger. One might
supply "me" as object. But leaving the expression as it
stands, the indictment becomes all the more scathing. At
that they were "my people," procured by God at the price
of many a kindly and undeserved favor. One stands ap-
palled at such base ingratitude. The words spoken were
calculated to sting a nation into a sense of shame.

Verse 4. At this point God begins to address himself
directly to the people, though as the verse progresses the
discourse turns back into the third person. Aside from the
basic ingratitude referred to in v. 3 there is a depth of moral
depravity that beggars description. "Sinful nation" presents
the issue in summary. The exclamation introducing the remarks indicates how shocking is the degree of sinfulness.

By a rhetorical device (*hoi goi*) the outcry is made the more startling. The harmless expletive ("Ah") could be rendered more appropriately in this connection as "Shame!" Besides the word for "nation" (*goi*) is one that is usually used for the heathen nations round about Israel, the implication being that Israel has dropped to this level. The various new titles now following show how many-sided Israel's guilt is. So they are described as a "guilt-burdened people," for sin always involves guilt. They are a "brood of evildoers," a figure taken perhaps from a nest of serpents, a sight anything but attractive. They are "children that deal corruptly." Everything they touch is defiled.

The rest of the verse seems to reach back into the causes for this sorry state. First, "they have forsaken the Lord." The personal relationship with their covenant God was lost. But that would never have happened but for a deeper-seated fault — "they have despised the Holy One of Israel." The verb used is strong, seemingly too strong. Who would despise the Lord? Actions prove that Israel did nothing less than that. A name of singular dignity appears here for the first time in the book, "the Holy One of Israel," a title that is a special favorite of Isaiah (cf. 5:19, 24; 10:17, 20; 12:6; 17:7; 29:19; 30:11, 12, 15; 31:1; 37:23; 41:14; etc.). He who is so far above human defects has reached forth nevertheless to his people; but they have repelled his advances. Lastly "they have turned their back (on him)"; from having been indifferent they have advanced to the point of insulting behavior.

If all these charges are true, Israel's moral plight must have been extreme and desperate.

3. The Desolate External State of the Nation (vv. 5-9)

1:5-9 5. Why will you still be smitten? You continue in your apostasy.
The whole head is sick, the whole heart is faint.
6. From the sole of the foot to the head there is no soundness in it,
but bruises and stripes and fresh wounds,
which have not been pressed out, or bound up, or softened with oil.

7. Your land is a desolation.
As for your cities, they are burned with fire.
As for your fields — before your eyes strangers devour them.
It is desolate as though overthrown by strangers.
8. And the daughter of Zion is left like a booth in a vineyard,
like a hut in a cucumber field, like a besieged city.
9. If the Lord of hosts had not left us a few survivors,
we should have been almost like Sodom,
we should have resembled Gomorrah.

Verse 5. Again the Lord addresses himself directly to his people as he unfolds before their eyes a picture of the extremity to which the desolation of the land has advanced. For what is here offered is not a description of the moral state of the nation given in figurative terms, but a description of the external appearance of a land ravaged by war. The opening statement involves that the Lord has tried every possible expedient that could have turned their minds to repentance, having done at least all that could have been done by way of chastisement. But the net result of each new attempt on his part was that they would "continue in [their] apostasy." So the futility of this course of action on his part has been amply demonstrated.

Now follows the frightful description of the state of the land. By way of summary description the Lord says: "The whole head is sick; the whole heart is faint." It would appear that "head" refers to those who are in positions of rule. There is nothing sound in the government of the nation. "Heart" in this connection could refer to courageous outlook, of which there is none left in the land.

Verse 6. The description continues in terms of a person badly wounded perhaps in war, bruised from head to foot. There is not a part of the body that is left sound. It is a mass of "bruises and stripes [left by the lash of the whip] and fresh wounds [so recently has the cruelty been inflicted]." None of the ordinary methods of treatment as yet have been applied: they "have not been pressed out [as older wounds should be] or bound up [as those that bleed ought to be] or softened with oil [for purposes of promoting healing]."

Verse 7. At this point the figurative description is abandoned and a literal description takes its place. The land as a whole "is desolate." One city after the other is "burned with fire." The fields that provided the much-needed food of the nation have been stripped of whatever produce they had grown by the ravaging enemy in the very sight of the ones who had cultivated them, making the experience all the more disheartening. The description adds the term "overthrown," a word usually reserved for the total destruction that befell Sodom in days of old (cf. Deut. 29:22; Amos 4:11; Isa. 13:19; Jer. 50:40).

Verse 8. At this point a few striking comparisons are again resorted to. "The daughter of Zion" (appositional genitive) is referred to here; that is to say, either the city itself — Jerusalem — or perhaps even the nation as a whole. She is, in the face of this otherwise total destruction, to be likened to a booth for a watchman in a vineyard, a fragile structure to begin with and almost total ruin after the vintage is past and the windswept poles stand half-collapsed in the field. "A besieged city" is a figure that carries the same import. So does "a hut in a cucumber field."

Verse 9. Now by way of summing up this desolate description — that total extinction has not resulted is due to the fact that the "Lord of hosts" (a title indicative of "majesic authority" — *Scott*) had graciously intervened and had left "a few survivors" (literally a "remnant"). Else there would be no description more apt than that which is used to describe the fate of Sodom and Gomorrah of old. The point being made is: like guilt; therefore like fate. Sodom had been the epitome of deep-dyed guilt in days of old. Jerusalem was equally guilty in these latter days.

4. The Current Type of Worship Ineffective as a Remedy (vv.10-15)

From this point to the end of v. 20 possible solutions of the difficulty involved are considered — solutions or remedies — first one that is inadequate, then one that will meet the needs of the case.

1:10-15 10. Hear the word of the Lord, you chiefs of Sodom;
give ear to the instruction of our God, you people of
Gomorrah:
11. "Of what value to me is the multitude of your sacrifices, says
the Lord:
I am surfeited with your burnt offerings of rams and the fat of
fed beasts;
in the blood of bulls and lambs and he-goats I take no delight.
12. When you come to appear before me,
who demands this at your hands — to trample my courts?
13. Don't keep on bringing vain offering;
incense is an abominable smudge for me.
New moon and Sabbath and solemn assembly — I cannot endure
them — wickedness and worship!
14. Your new moons and appointed assemblies my soul hates;
they have become a burden to me, I am weary of bearing them.
15. And when you spread forth your hands I will hide my eyes
from you.
Also if you make many prayers I will not hear you.
Your hands are full of blood!

Verse 10. Leaders and people are now addressed by the
prophet. Leaders set the pace; people follow. In line with
the last allusion made in v. 9 both groups are identified
again with the iniquity of these two notoriously wicked
cities: the chiefs are like those of Sodom; the people like
those of Gomorrah. Nevertheless a "word of the Lord" is
about to be offered to them. This word begins at v. 11 and
runs to the end of v. 20. The word was the special means
by which the Lord brought his influence to bear upon
history, especially the history of his people. The parallel
expression for "word" is "instruction" (the basic meaning
of what is frequently designated as "law"). When men sin,
there is always an element of ignorance involved. God's instruction removes such ignorance, if men will accept what
he says.

Verse 11. Now follows perhaps the most scathing indictment of formalistic worship to be found anywhere in Sacred
Writ. It runs parallel to the other classic passages on this
subject, such as: Hos. 6:6; Amos 4:4; 5:21-25; Micah 6:6-8;
Jer. 7:4, 21 ff.; Ps. 50:8-15. It is not true that the prophet is
hostile to sacrifices as such. This is indicated by what he
says in 19:21. It could not be hostility; for sacrifices as such

were sanctioned by the very law of Moses that the Lord
himself gave. What Isaiah opposses is sacrifices that are offered in an unwholesome spirit — for merit's sake or in an
impenitent spirit or with trust in the mere outward performance of them as such.

In addition, from what now follows it becomes very apparent that the people of Israel at this time were fulfilling
every external religious obligation meticulously. Here is the
proof. Their sacrifices were being offered by "multitude."
"Burnt offerings" were much in evidence. "Fat" and "blood"
— the chief ingredients of offerings — were in evidence
every day. Even choice victims were being presented continually. Technically every requirement of the law was
being met. But since they were soulless sacrifices, done without a spirit of humility and dire need, the Lord's reaction is
to be described thus: they are "of no value" to him; he is
"surfeited" with them; he "takes no delight in them." Such
an accusation must have been painful, especially since the
persons involved thought themselves in this respect entirely
above reproach.

Verse 12. Besides they thought they had divine sanction
for what they did. Had not the ordinances of the Lord prescribed such procedures? Not in an unwholesome attitude
of meritoriousness! Therefore he challenges them to produce
proof to legitimize such doings of theirs: "Who demands
this at your hands?" Then comes the damning disclosure:
all that they do amounts to nothing more than "to trample
(his) courts" as long as the present reprehensible attitude
continues.

Verse 13. Now comes the itemized condemnation. In fact,
what the law seemed to demand, is now forbidden by God:
their approach to the matter has made the good unacceptable. The long procession with sacrificial victims coming to
the high altar is rejected: "Don't keep on bringing" these.
For the smoke that rises from the altar is polluted by their
cheap attitude and so is only "an abominable smudge."
The various types of sacred assembly, which could well have
gladdened the heart of God and man — "new moon and
Sabbath and solemn assembly" — God asserts that he cannot

even "endure." This is all capped by the climax-assertion summing it all up: they are "wickedness and worship." The two factors stand unreconciled in the lives of these men and therefore in their worship.

It is true that there is a break in the construction at this point. In his indignation, feeling wells up strong and the regular sentence structure is broken. But the condemnation goes on. Three verbs serve to express to the full how repulsive these seemingly holy acts become to God when the heart is not right: his "soul hates" them; "they have become a burden" to him; he "is weary of bearing them." All this (vv. 11-14) is specific repudiation of sacrifice, which was really the epitome of all worship in days of old.

Verse 15. To this is added a repudiation of prayer, at least of the prayer offered by this ungodly generation. One would suppose that nothing could delight the heart of the Creator more than to see his children come before his throne as suppliants. All Scriptures assure us that such is the case. But when behind the prayer is an unsanctified life with no intention of changing it, then prayer becomes repulsive to a holy God. When men therefore spread forth their hands in the typical gesture of days of old, hands open to receive what the grace of God is ready to give, God turns his face away. Also if prayer persists, he refuses to hear. By way of one sweeping indictment the reason for this refusal is found in this that their "hands are full of blood." It is immaterial whether we take this expression literally or figuratively. There will have been cases where men were guilty of bloodshed in secret and yet faithfully resorted to the temple to perform their religious obligations according to the letter. If this was not literally true of others, their impenitence had made whatever evil deed they had done equally heinous in the sight of the Lord. Spoken with force, this concluding statement was in the nature of a sharp exclamation.

Further denunciation after these stinging words would obviously have lacked purpose. Therefore there follows a strong call to repentance, one of the most moving in all the messages of the prophets.

5. Call to Repentance (vv. 16-20)

1:16-20 16. Wash yourselves, make yourselves clean.
Remove the evil of your doings from before my eyes;
cease to do evil, 17. learn to do good.
Seek justice, rebuke the oppressor.
Uphold the rights of the fatherless, plead the case of the widow.
18. Come now, let us reach an adjustment, says the Lord:
though your sins be as scarlet, they shall become as white as snow;
though they are red as crimson, they shall become like wool.
19. If you are willing and obedient,
you shall eat the good of the land.
20. But if you refuse and rebel,
you shall be devoured by the sword.
For the mouth of the Lord has spoken it."

Now for three verses various deeds that are to be done and various acts that are to be performed are indicated in curt imperatives. Yet the thought involved is not that the people are to set things right between themselves and their God, as though such a result could be achieved by human endeavor. Where the final adjustment lies will come to light in v. 18. But a man, aware that he has displeased his God, can do at least this much as an indication that he means it sincerely: he can lay aside those things that have caused God's displeasure. He can begin to do those things that God has pointed out as having been omitted. That does not clear all issues between himself and his God but it will at least remove obstacles that he himself would otherwise have allowed to stand in the way of a reconciliation. To say that "repentance and conversion can win Yahweh's favor" overlooks that repentance and conversion are his gracious work.

Verses 16, 17. Assuming now that the preceding indictment has struck home and that a man is sincerely intent on getting right with God, there are certain negatives that he can take in hand. He can remove obvious wrongs and mend his ways. So to speak he can "wash" himself and "make himself clean." He can "remove the evil of (his) doings from before (God's) eyes." He can "cease from evil and learn to do good." All these are broad areas of action which are, in the last analysis, the test of sincerity. To continue in flagrant wrongs and still expect favorable consideration from God is the approach that the prophet and his God utterly abhor. Since so many cases of obvious injustice had been chargeable against this people, it is also quite in order to indicate the course of conduct to be followed as "Seek justice, rebuke the oppressor, uphold the rights of the fatherless, plead the case of the widow." Contrasted with what had gone before the spirit of this admonition is in short: "To obey is better than sacrifice" (I Sam. 15:22; cf. Amos 5:21 ff.; Hos. 6:6; Micah 6:6-8). But all this is merely preparatory to the great issue involved, which is now set forth in v. 18.

Verse 18. "Come now" seems to carry a bit more emphasis than it usually does, when it introduces a hortatory word. It would appear that under the impact of the prophet's stern rebuke his hearers, so to speak had stepped back from him, unable to face him directly. The tone of his words now becomes friendly and winning. He invited them to draw near for a kindly mutual conference. The essence of his suggestion is "Let us reach an adjustment," or as it also could be translated: "Let us settle our difference," or even: "Let us adjust our misunderstanding." Things are not right between the nation and its God. This calls for adjustment: Israel must get into the clear with Yahweh. But the initiative cannot lie with the nation. Her strength is paralyzed by her many sins. Therefore all that is left is an offer of pure grace; and that is exactly what follows. It must be admitted (and the prophet does not close his eyes to obvious realities) that Israel's sins are of a deep hue that almost defies erasure. But not so in the face of a God who is gracious and long-suffering beyond man's ken and certainly beyond any possible desert of his. If Israel is but ready to accept with the *salto mortale* of faith, these sins "shall become white as snow" and "like wool," which was normally a clear and pure white also. Complete and absolute pardon is thus indicated, a pardon that reason could not have anticipated and that human insight could not have foreseen. After the denunciation that had preceded, only complete and total rejection and damnation would seem to have been the logical next step. But such is the nature of grace, that it exceeds our boldest thoughts. If ever the gospel was expressed in the Old Testament, here is the classical formulation of it. To heighten the total effect, "scarlet" and "crimson" are used as the native color of the nation's guilt, terms reminiscent of bloody deeds that are not to be regarded as light transgression.

Unfortunately the force of this truly evangelical approach can be much weakened and the total comfort of the passage be undermined by certain translations, which have come to enjoy quite a bit of favor in our day. The positive and hopeful assertion, "they shall become as white as snow," is removed out of the category of promise and assertion and is rendered interrogatively: "Will they?" or "Can they become white?" Or even a half-sarcastic turn is indicated by making it to be an exclamation involving the impossible. It is even claimed that such an approach alone meets the implications of the entire connection in which the statement is found. Three major arguments may be presented to support our position. First, in cases of this sort the long-standing tradition of the church cannot calmly be brushed aside. The faith of men in passages of strong comfort should not be tampered without good reason. Then there is the strictly grammatical argument: To have a passage of this sort to be taken interrogatively without the least indications of such a character by the use of some interrogative particle, is, as one of the most thorough grammarian's has said "utterly without analogy." Thirdly, there is the context, which the opposition strongly claims for its approach. Verse 19 becomes meaningless when it continues, "If you are willing and obedient. . . ." A bit more consideration might be given to the translation which renders these words, "Let them become white as snow. . . ." But in that event the emphasis lies more on what man can do in his utter extremity; and besides, his case may be rendered quite hopeless if he finds his strength quite unequal to the task of breaking with sin-habits strongly entrenched.

We must yet deal with the fact that we have translated the word of the initial summons not: "Let us reason together" but: "Let us reach an adjustment" or: "Let us settle our difference." As *George Adam Smith* has already pointed out, the familiar translation ("Let us reason . . .") fails to make good sense. For after you have been reasoning with a man for quite a while, you do not suddenly invite him to start reasoning. This led *Smith* to the translation "Let us bring our reasoning to a close." *Koenig* comes even more to the point with a translation much like the one we have used above, *"Wir wollen uns miteinander ausgleichen."*

Verses 19, 20. Pleadings are added to the offer of grace, making assurance doubly sure. A people faced by starvation in a land blasted by marauding armies are promised that they shall yet eat "the good of the land" if they will let the Lord forgive them. The tremendous reach of God's grace could hardly be set forth more attractively. But there is another side to the question (v. 20) to which the Lord will not let them close their eyes: refusal will result in being "devoured by the sword." This is not an unworthy emphasis on material blessings but factual prediction of what the actual outcome will be. Cannot a father bestow tokens of his pleasure on obedient children to make their obedience still more delightful? A play on words is involved in the verse — "eat" or "be eaten." A solemn affirmation that this message stems from the mouth of the Lord gives a strong close to the passage.

6. Indication of the Corruption of Jerusalem (vv. 21-23)

1:21-23 21. How has the once faithful city become a harlot,
She that was full of justice!
Righteousness once used to lodge in her, but now murderers!
22. Your silver has become slag;
Your wine mixed with water.
23. Your rulers are rebellious and associates of thieves;
Every one loves a bribe and runs after gifts.
They do not uphold the rights of the fatherless,
And the case of the widow does not come before them.

The preceding verses had opened up two possibilities: men would either accept or reject God's grace. In view of the inveterate habits of the nation, the latter of the two was the more likely outcome. The prophet apparently felt this. He, therefore, dwells again on the corruption that prevails in the city to make the tone of warning included in the

preceding section the more incisive. In a sense these verses
(21-23) take on the form of a lament, a type of literature
that customarily began with "how." See Lam. 1:1; 2:1; 3:1.
Isaiah contrasts a rather glorious past with a most deplorable
present.

Verse 21. There was a time when Jerusalem had been "a
faithful city." Now she had dropped to the level of "a
harlot." That Israel was the wife of Yahweh, figuratively
speaking, traces back to Exod. 34:15 f. The thought was
developed more at length in Hos 1:2 ff.; Isa. 50:1; 54:1; etc.
A more glaring contrast in station could hardly be imagined.
There was a time in the days of David and Solomon when
one might with full justification have claimed for the city
that she "was full of justice." It could be maintained with
equal propriety that "righteousness once lodged there."
God's own righteousness displayed itself there, as well as
the righteous conduct of good men. They were both quite
at home there and had taken up a permanent residence.
"But now murderers." Murders, and most of them un-
avenged, seem to have been so commonplace as no longer
to stir men's indignation. This form of crime is always
particularly heinous.

Verses 22, 23. Then there was corruption of high officials,
which is first described figuratively as follows: "Your silver
has become slag, your wine mixed with water." The direction in which this figure points could be manifold, but the
key is the explanation that follows at once in literal speech
indicating that the two figures described the deterioration
of high officialdom. Instead of being examples of good conduct they were themselves (v. 23) rebellious, and therefore
unwilling to obey the plain behests of the law of the land:
they were "rebellious" and "associates of thieves." Corruption of justice through bribery was much in evidence. They
not only loved bribes, they even ran after a gift. The rest
of the verse is reminiscent of v. 16. For when men are so
corrupt and have so little sense of high obligation to office,
the weak and the defenseless will be the ones that must
suffer most, widows and orphans.

All this leads up to the next part which indicates that the
Lord must follow a stern course with people and rulers such

as these, but the stern course will be one productive of good results.

7. Israel to Be Redeemed by Judgment (vv. 24-31)

1:24-31 24. Therefore thus says the Lord, the Lord of hosts, the Mighty One of Israel:
"Ah, I will ease myself of my enemies,
And avenge myself on my foes!
25. I will turn my hand against you and throughly purge your slag,
And remove all your alloy.
26. And I will restore your judges as at the first,
And your counsellors as at the beginning.
Afterward you shall be called the city of righteousness, the faithful city.
27. Zion must be redeemed by judgment,
And her converts by righteousness.
28. And the destruction of rebels and sinners shall take place together;
And they that forsake the Lord shall utterly perish.
29. For they shall be ashamed of the terebinths in which you delight;
And you shall blush over the gardens which you chose.
30. For you shall be like a terebinth whose leaf has faded,
And like a garden that has no water.
31. And the strong man shall become tow,
And his product a spark.
And they shall both burn together,
And no one shall quench them."

We have in this section one of the themes that comes to the surface repeatedly in Isaiah. It is formulated especially in v. 27. It might be rephrased: Through judgment to Salvation. The former leads up to the latter; the latter is not possible without the former. Stern measures, in the nature of the case, will have to be resorted to.

Verse 24. The pronouncement about to be made is specially reinforced by the emphatic statement that it comes from the Lord himself. Nowhere in Isaiah are the divine names used cumulatively in quite such a measure. The last title employed especially points to the need of emphasis on God's mighty rule, a rule which under the circumstances might well have become dubious in the minds of many. Cf.

another use of this name in Gen. 49:24. When the assertion
is made that God will proceed against His enemies and foes,
these are not to be thought of as strangers outside of Israel.
They are those members of the chosen people who have so
stubbornly refused to walk in the Lord's ways. On them he
must vent his wrath — for that is the basic meaning of the
expression, "to ease (oneself) of."

Verse 25. Since (v. 22) the deterioration of the silver or
of the wine was interpreted to refer to rulers who had gone
to seed, the second member of this verse in the use of the
same figure has the same class of persons in mind. Therefore
the first member of the verse ("I will turn my hand against
you") appears to refer to the nation at large. The people as
a whole and the rulers in particular become the object of his
dealings. The third member of the verse continues the
reference to the ruling classes. "To turn one's hand" against
another means as much as to assail or to attack, as Amos
1:8 and Zech. 13:7 would indicate.

Verse 26. Apparently the rulers were very sadly in need
of stern correction, for God's dealings with them continue
to be the subject matter of this verse. But already here the
emphasis is on the beneficial results that will develop as he
takes these officials in hand. Their judges will be restored
as they once were and their counsellors as at the beginning.
There is quite an array of passages indicating how affairs
stood at the beginning. Passages like Gen. 14:18 (Melchise-
dek); Josh. 10:1 (Adonizedek, whose name meant righteous
lord, even though he was a Canaanite); I Kings 3:9, 28;
II Chron. 19:5 ff. show what a notable record Jerusalem
had in the area of righteousness all through the past
centuries. So God's corrective dealings will result in the re-
establishment of her most honorable name, "the city of righteousness." The second title, "the faithful city," could be
a good parallel to the first; but as *Scott* has pointed out,
this adjective ("faithful") is used in reference to the dynasty
of David in II Sam. 7:16 and Ps. 89:37 in the sense of
"enduring." This would indicate that the city will have a
promising future, not only as city, but as what it represents
in essence, the eternal city.

The fact that in this picture of the restored city the king

has no place might be purely accidental. It might also be a subtle allusion to the fact that the ultimate future involves a strict theocracy without an earthly king (cf. Isa. 24:23).

Verse 27. Finally, the point at issue is formulated as a principle that holds good now and for the rest of the history of this great city. We have sought to capture the force of a principle by using "must" instead of "will" and so have followed *Luther's* lead. The two nouns used must be most carefully evaluated in indicating the policy that is to be followed in God's dealing with the holy city. The first is "judgment." This implies first of all the harsh work of the "execution of judgment" (*BDB*) which includes "judicial removal" (*Koenig: richterliche Ausscheidung*) of all undesirable elements. But the other, positive and constructive, aspect of his dealings is covered by the term "righteousness." This, in this connection, refers to either "justification" or "salvation" (*BDB*), for it is the type of dealing that is in evidence in reference to the "converts." In this latter term there is an undertone of the Messianic work (cf. 9:7). So the negative and the positive achieve a marvelous blend in this passage, which reaches down through the ages as a description of the manner in which the Lord deals in his kingdom. Neither of these two aspects of his work appears without the other. "Redeem" in this verse carries the general sense of "save" or "deliver."

Verse 28. For the moment, the emphasis lies the stronger on the negative aspect of this great work, when it is indicated that the Lord will not let rebels and sinners stand in his way. "Destruction" shall be their lot — the noun standing first with unique emphasis. Equally effective will be the removal of all those who "forsake the Lord"; they shall utterly perish.

Verses 29, 30. From this point on to the end of the chapter attention is given to the idolaters within the nation. No doubt they were a considerable group. They had long been admonished. They had stubbornly clung to one of the besetting sins of the nation. Only if that be borne in mind will the propriety of having an issue made of this matter become clear. In other words, the close of the chapter is not some extraneous material that by some strange chance became attached to the foregoing part of the chapter and must be regarded as a later addition by a hand other than Isaiah's, as many writers insist.

Two types of current idolatry are specially mentioned: the tree-cult and the garden-cult. We do not know too much of either of them. Usually it is the trees that are mentioned as having been the scene of the one type, if not perhaps in some way included in this abomination as special cult objects. Cf. II Kings 16:4; Hos. 4:13; Jer. 2:20; 3:6-13; 17:2; Ezek. 6:13; Isa. 57:5. Reference is made to gardens in Isa. 65:3 and 66:17. The number of these references is indicative of the prevalence of this abomination. It is difficult to identify positively the type of trees referred to: translators waver mostly between "oaks" and "terebinths" (i.e., the terpentine tree). Where the verse begins with an objective reference to those who participate in this type of worship it unexpectedly turns into the second person ("you delight") — a flexibility of language which we are not in the habit of sanctioning. But the people themselves were involved; so they are directly addressed. For continuing the last part of the thought of v. 28 ("utterly perish") it is shown how these sinners will find their idolatry quite unavailing; they shall in fact become ashamed that they ever engaged in these foolish practices, being ashamed of the terebinths and blushing over the gardens which they once so ardently chose for themselves. For, continuing in the use of the figure introduced (v. 30), they shall themselves be like a wilted tree and a garden gone to ruin due to lack of water. The more attractive use of a similar figure for the truly godly man is found in Ps. 1:3; 52:8; and Jer. 11:16. How completely Israel abandoned her idolatry after the Babylonian Captivity and as a result of it, is well known. Then this word of the prophet achieved its fulfillment.

Verse 31. The utter destruction of this infamous cult is lastly described in a figure that has its difficulties, but cannot be unclear as to its ultimate import. It is asserted that the "strong man" (that seems to imply: the ruler, who led in movements such as introducing idolatrous worship) shall be the kindling "spark." Instead of saving the imperiled one in the hour of danger, the idol shall be as harmful to the tow as a spark. Both shall burn together in a fire that cannot be quenched. Where thus the passage seems to close on a strong negative, yet it cannot be denied that the destruction, the utter destruction, of idolatry involves a major achievement. Not so negative a note after all!

Notes

Verse 2. It will be noted that *weromamti* does not resort to the waw consecutive construction. This is due to the fact that the two verbs employed are synonyms. See *KS* 370 f.

Verse 3. *Be'alaw* is plural because with suffixes only the plural of the noun is found. See *KS* 263 v.

Verse 4. "Guilt-burdened" in the original runs thus: "a people heavy of guilt" — *'awon* in the construct relationship is an accusative of specification. (*KS* 336 h.)

Verse 5. *'al meh* can be translated either "why" or "where." The latter translation, though much favored, seems to imply that he who is administering the punishment is looking for an unbruised area on which to let the blow fall. They that administer punishment are hardly so over-refined. Again, although in *kol ro'sh* and *kol levav* the *kol* can be translated either "every" (see *KS* footnote p. 286) or "whole," neither can be maintained positively.

Verse 7. The last word *zarim* happens to have appeared earlier in the verse. They who feel that Isaiah would not have used the same noun twice resort to conjectural emendation, substituting *zedhim* ("proud"). We feel that personal taste in such a matter is not sufficient ground for emendation.

Verse 9. We agree with those who would move the *athnach* back one word and place it under *saridh*.

Verse 10. In "chiefs of Sodom," Sodom is a genetive of quality (*KS* 335 c).

Verse 12. *Panay* must be regarded as an adverbial accusative (*KS* 330 k).

Verse 15. The Isaiah Scroll (Dead Sea Scrolls) adds to this verse: "and your fingers with iniquity."

In view of the many types of sacrifice with which the people seemed familiar in Isaiah's day ("sacrifices" — *zebhach*; "burnt offerings" — *'olah*; "offerings" — *minchah*; "fat" — *chelebh*), it seems most likely that Israel had an extensive sacrificial system, formulated and detailed. In other words this passage conflicts with the theory of a late formulation (fifth century) of the Priestly Code of Israel.

Verse 25. *Kabbor*, "as with potash," may be translated "thoroughly." *BDB* remarks that *bor* is "alkali used in smelting metals."

Chapter II

A. THROUGH JUDGMENT TO FULFILLMENT OF GOD'S GRACIOUS PROMISES (Chaps. 2–4)

The approach to the next three chapters (following *von Orelli*) indicated by the above caption still seems to have most merit. A glorious future is in prospect, but the attainment of it is by way of severe judgments that must first be visited upon God's people. The glorious future appears at the beginning of the section, 2:1-4, and again, with obvious modifications at the close, 4:1-6. Between the two stands many a sharp word of judgment. The glorious future is Messianic. Not that there is any reference to the Messiah in 2:1-4, or even for that matter in Chap. 4. But the kinship of both passages with 9:1-7, where the Messiah appears quite obviously, stamps these two passages as among those that have the *age* of the Messiah in mind. The case might be stated thus: It was so utterly clear to the people of God that only in the Messianic days would the glorious future be realized that descriptions of the *age* may well take for granted that only Messiah himself can achieve these things. The fact that he alone produces such results goes without saying.

Chapter 2, as the heading also indicates, has no direct relation to Chap. 1, which is strictly in the nature of a general introduction.

Whether the first section, 2:2-4, can be dated within the ministry of Isaiah, may well be left as an open question. Since the messages of the prophets were often closely related to the growth and inner development of the prophet, the most suitable time in Isaiah's life might have been after the glorious deliverance of Jerusalem from the Assyrians in 701 B.C. That experience may have conditioned the prophet for the understanding of the glorious future that

73

God's city had in prospect. The distinctive role that Jerusalem is to play in the future with reference to all the nations on the face of the earth is so clearly the focal point of this short passage that headings like *Bewer's,* "Vision of universal peace through the arbitration of the Lord," lack an essential factor. Very suggestive is *G. A. Smith's* approach who designates the first five verses as coming from Isaiah, "the Idealist," and the rest of the chapter as from Isaiah "the Realist."

The Heading (2:1)

2:1   1. The word which Isaiah the son of Amoz saw concerning Judah and [especially] Jerusalem.

Verse 1. In the original "the word" carries so general a significance (thing, matter) that Luther does not even translate it, saying: "This is what Isaiah saw." This approach removes the next difficulty: How can a prophet "see" a "word"? "Saw" here means perceived, or received. The manner of communicaion of the message to the prophet is not in any wise described. This heading as such looks like a caption that was set over a smaller message like Chaps. 2–4, which may have been published by the prophet separately. The caption was retained when the unit was inserted into the book that was in process of compilation. Still it need not be thought of as covering more than the three following chapters. When the word "Jerusalem" is added, its purpose is to specify more precisely where the center of interest lies.

1. Zion's Glorious Future in the Messianic Age (2:2-5)

2:2-5   2. And it shall come to pass in the latter days:
the mountain of the Lord's house shall be established at
the head of the mountains,
and shall be exalted above the hills,
and all nations shall flow to it.
    3. And many peoples shall come and say:
"Come, let us go to the mountain of the Lord,
to the house of the God of Jacob;

that he may teach us somewhat concerning His ways
and we may walk in his paths."
For out of Zion shall go forth instruction
And the word of the Lord from Jerusalem.
4. Then he shall judge between the nations
and arbitrate for many peoples.
and they shall beat their swords into plowshares
and their spears into pruning hooks;
Nation shall not lift up sword against nation,
neither shall they learn war any more.
5. O house of Jacob, come and let us walk in the light of the
Lord!

At once we are confronted by the fact that this passage
occurs also in Micah 4:1-3 (4), which raises the question:
Which prophet spoke it first? Though the question could
be examined at great length, it is now quite commonly
conceded that the more likely explanation is that both
Isaiah and Micah were quoting from an anonymous earlier
prophet. For Micah seems to be at the point of already
amplifying the original when he adds v. 4. This would
seem to make Isaiah the author. But Isaiah begins as Micah
does: "And it shall come to pass. . . ." Beginning with an
"and" seems to point to a passage taken from another context. This brief consideration of the problem may suffice.

Verse 2. This vision that the prophet sees, comes to pass
"in the latter days." This phrase, which occurs already
in Gen. 49:1; Num. 24:14; Deut. 4:30; 31:29 may in these
earlier passages carry a reference to the Messianic age.
It certainly does at this point in Isaiah. As an expression
it is more than a neutral "in days to come." It marks the
last part of the future into which the prophetic glance
penetrates. Since not all have the same depth of glimpse
into the future bestowed upon them, the "latter days" may
not reach equally far into the future for the different
prophets. Isaiah's glimpse in this case would seem to penetrate down to the time where "old things have passed
away, all things have been made new." In other words,
the scene depicted would lie beyond the point of the return of Christ.

What he sees is this: In some way, not clearly described
here, he detects that an unusual pre-eminence attaches to

"the mountain of the Lord's house" i.e., to Zion. Whether it had physical exaltation that raised it higher than all other mountains, or whether it was surrounded by a glorious light, we are unable to determine. Perhaps the physical and the spiritual values so blended into one another as to be inseparable. But it was obviously marked by some distinction. The Hebrew expression used (*bero'sh*) does not necessarily mean "on the top of" (lit. "on the head"), but "at the head," as the use of the phrase in Deut. 20:9; I Sam. 9:22; I Kings 21:9 clearly shows. The *Septuagint* practically says it shall be outstanding. But that which occurs in reference to Zion is the significant thing, namely "all nations shall flow to it." A vast scene is depicted. All nations on the face of the earth are "streaming" to Zion. That which this house stands for is what attracts them. Here the mountain of the Lord's house is the symbol of God's revealed truth, or, as some might say, of Israel's religion. One striking thing, observed already by *Calvin*, should yet be noted. Zion was a small mountain, being little more than a handful of earth in comparison with huge mountains. Still it shall stand out as pre-eminent.

Verse 3. The parallel expression for "all nations" now becomes "many peoples," not in the sense of denying the universality of approach, but merely adding in a colorful way that many nationalities are going to be represented in this mass-movement. This verse takes us down into the many crowds that are approaching. It allows us to overhear what they are saying and so to understand their purpose. They are mutually encouraging one another to press on in their pilgrimage. After saying that their goal is the "mountain of the Lord's house," they continue, that more precisely it is "the house of the God of Jacob." This points to the deeper spiritual values that Israel has been granted by her God. These nations would have a share in these values. They know that these values are destined to be the common property of all in the end. This is a thought spoken by all the prophets; cf. Jer. 3:17; Zech. 8:20-22; Hag. 2:6f; Isa. 60; 66:22ff. If God be called "the God of Jacob" that seems to be an attempt to get a more choice phrase for the commonplace "God of Israel."

Further attention to what these persons are saying discloses that they want to be instructed by Yahweh concerning "his ways." They imply that there is so much to be learned that they can only hope to learn something concerning them, but even that will be precious knowledge. When they speak of "his ways" they are thinking in terms of ways that God has marked out for bewildered man, so that he may not miss the proper road. But on the whole these persons display such a fine spirit in their search that they indicate that, as soon as they have learned what his ways are, they, on their part, want to "walk" in them, that is, do what his commandments prescribe. Moral conduct will keep pace with spiritual insight. With this significant remark their words come to an end. What a remarkable attitude in contrast to the attitude proverbially displayed by the hostile nations in previous days. Then there was unvarying hostility; now there is hopeful friendliness. Then there were wars; now there is a peaceful quest. Once there was arrogant pride; now humble inquiry.

The prophet himself speaks in the words: "For out of Zion shall go forth instruction." Note, that it had just been said: ". . . that he may instruct." Now the assertion is made that such instruction emanates from Zion. The statement is laid down as a kind of axiom. It is analogous to "Salvation is of the Jews" (John 4:22). The word used for "instruction" is *torah*, usually translated as "law," to indicate that it is a word spoken with firm authority. But at the same time it is "word of the Lord," that great creative force that made the world and governs it and imparts all needed guidance to men. Historically this word has proved itself true. At the city of Jerusalem, after Pentecost, the church was established as the great agency for spreading saving gospel. Ever since, both aspects of the case have been in evidence: messengers have gone out; prospective converts have come in. This great movement is here foretold and vividly depicted in a highly idealized scene rich in color.

Verse 4. After this new attitude on the part of the nations, just described in v. 3, shall be in evidence, "then" an entirely different attitude on the part of all nations shall be observed on that important issue that has always been the greatest curse of the human race — war. Since God's word has become normative, it will be obeyed and so the Lord himself shall be the arbiter, should misunderstandings arise. This approach does not necessarily imply that misunderstanding will come up, but this is actually an attempt to describe the perfect situation in terms of the customary imperfections with which we are only too familiar. That he can "judge between the nations" is well understood; cf. Isa. 31:8; 37:36. The "nations" are mentioned as the ones who had an inveterate hatred for Israel — a common connotation of the word. The type of arbitration covered by the next line ("arbitrate for many peoples") involves that the one perfect norm — the Word — is always the court of last appeals. Whatever verdict the Almighty renders, it is unquestionably accepted. As a result, wars do not come about. In due time it becomes apparent that the weapons of war are no longer of any use. So they are taken in hand and converted into utensils and tools of peace. Swords become plowshares (or the small colters on Oriental plows). Some find warrant for translating the word "sickles" or even "hoes"; and spears become pruning-shears. Weapons of destruction become implements of constructive effort. The opposite course had only too often to be followed in days of old already, as Joel 4:9f. describes. But now the very use of weapons falls away: one nation does not lift up the sword against another. Neither is there any occasion for learning the techniques of war. Micah in his version of the passage adds the delightful picture (Micah 4:4): "But they shall sit every man under his vine and under his fig tree, and none shall make them afraid." This entirely new attitude with reference to war is found in other prophetic words. See Isa. 9:5; 11:6-9; Hos. 2:18; Zech. 9:10. But note well that there is a strict sequence of events. The abolition of war cannot come about before the nations have learned to submit to the Word of Lord.

Verse 5. By an unexpected turn of the thought Israel is addressed and the truth just set forth is effectively applied to the prophet's own people. If all nations will in due course of time come to the point where they will come to

the Lord and his Word and submit to it, how much the
more ought Israel walk in the light of the truth which is
her ancient heritage. In a friendly tone the prophet invites
Israel to do this and includes himself as among those that
need to give heed to this invitation ("let *us*"). God's revealed truth is conceived of as a "light" which makes going
in the right path easy and plain. "Come" is an obvious
parallel to the "come" of v. 3.

2. Zion's Inglorious Present (2:6–4:1)

a. *Description of the Spurious Values That Are Current (vv. 6-9)*

2:6-9 6. For you have abandoned your own people, O house of Jacob;
for they are filled up with things from the East,
and with soothsayers like the Philistines;
and they conclude bargains with foreigners.
7. Their land is filled with silver and gold,
and there is no end to their treasures.
Their land is filled with horses,
and there is no end to their chariots.
8. And their land is filled with idols.
They bow down each one to the work of his hands,
to that which his own fingers have made.
9. And the plain fellow bows down,
and the big fellow humbles himself.
And Thou couldst not forgive them!

This section dates possibly from the prosperous days of
Uzziah and Jotham.

Verse 6. It fits better into the context to translate, as we
have above, letting these words be addressed to Israel and
not to God, and taking "abandoned" in the sense of the
nation's having given up the best part of its heritage. They
have abandoned their own people by giving up the best
things that the nation stood for. This statement is immediately followed by a listing of the substitutes that have
taken the place of the solid values of a better day. Chiefly,
Israel has let things that are ranked high in the East fill
the land, in the East where Assyria was the fast-rising
power; and nothing lends glamor to values, like the success

which the Assyrians were having. For "things from the East," *Koenig* says rather well, *Orientalismen*. From here on the verb "filled" stands out, indicating with emphasis that each of the spurious values was in evidence in great amounts. But there were also importations from the West, "soothsayers like the Philistines." There had been a clash with the Philistines in Uzziah's day (II Chron. 26:6). But as so often in history, the ones conquered vanquished their conquerors. That soothsaying was something distinctively Philistine is indicated by I Sam. 6:2 and II Kings 1:2. That such devices for ascertaining the future were of only too dubious a value was obvious to more observing persons. But Israel dropped to this lower level. In fact they were only too inclined to take an unwholesomely friendly attitude toward foreigners. That is the attitude criticized by the statement, "they concluded bargains with foreigners." Whether this refers to the area of commercial contacts as well as to political connections, need not be argued. Both tendencies seem to have been in evidence.

Verse 7. Isaiah comes to another area where unwholesome values had been substituted by Israel, and here in clear defiance of a word of warning dating back to the days of Moses (see Deut. 17:16f.). Silver and gold and many other kinds of treasures were at hand in great profusion; and as is always the case, men had put their trust in them as solid values that make for the wealth of a nation. In like manner horses had been collected as a strong factor in setting up military strength and defenses. Solomon had inaugurated the trend (I Kings 10:14-29). Uzziah had carried such preparations much farther (II Chron. 26:6-15, although horses are not in this instance specifically mentioned). Isa. 30:1ff. and 31:1ff. may also be compared.

Verses 8, 9. Isaiah is building up to a climax. The worst of the spurious values are the idols. They, too, are in evidence in great abundance. By a unique turn given to a grammatical form the prophet makes it appear that each man had an idol of his own. So utterly widespread idolatry had become, in the face of the urgent warnings of Moses and the prophets. With a mild touch of irony these idols are described as "that which his own fingers [small

and weak things that they are] have made." These idols
are not only available; they are in regular use: in Israel
men "bow down" to them. In fact (v. 9) idolatry has
invaded all classes of society: "the plain fellow bows down;
and the big fellow humbles himself." For a chosen nation, the recipient of so many and so rich mercies from
Yahweh, to drop to such levels of ingratitude and blindness makes the prophet question whether even the great
mercy of Yahweh could pardon what has been done: "Thou
couldst not forgive them!" Doubt and hope wrestle in this
word. "Forgive them not" (*RSV*) is too blunt and too
little warranted by the facts of the case (see the *Notes*).
It is true that the forms used could yield the translation,
"Forgive them not." It is also true that prophets were at
times forbidden to intercede for their people; cf. Jer. 7:16;
11:14; 14:11; 15:1. But that is not yet remotely like praying
that the Lord may not forgive.

b. Indication of a Terrible Judgment about to Come (vv. 10-11)

2:10-11 10. Crawl into the rock and hide in the dust
from before the terror of the Lord and before the
glory of his majesty.
11. The haughty looks of man shall be brought low
and the pride of man shall be bowed down
and the Lord himself shall be exalted in that day.

Verse 10. In a land that abounded in caves of every
description, it had become traditional among other things
in days of disaster, especially when the enemy overran the
land, to seek a hiding place in such caves (cf. Judg. 6:2;
I Sam. 12:6; 14:11). In the present instance the Lord
himself, or the terror that his coming induces, is the danger
from which the prophet bids men to flee (cf. Luke 23:30).
Any kind of hollow will do, whether it be in rock or earth.
The Lord's coming will impress some as being sheer "terror."
Others will see a manifestation of the "glory of his majesty."
In any case they will look upon the Lord from the angle
of their sinfulness, and that will be so keenly felt that all
benign aspects of his being will be suppressed. That the

terror-aspect of God's being is a very real thing in Biblical revelation from most ancient times, appears from passages such as Gen. 31:42, 53; 35:5.

Verse 11. Summing up the total effect to be achieved by this appearance of the Lord unto judgment, the prophet indicates that all "haughty looks," which result from an attitude of pride will be "brought low," that is, will be turned into the very opposite of what they now are; and the very "pride of man" itself shall be cancelled out. For there is but One who may be high and exalted without having his exaltation degenerate into pride, and that is the Lord. This world reappears for emphasis at the conclusion of v. 17 as a skillful refrain.

c. What the Lord's Day Will Do to All Spurious Values (vv. 12-17)

2:12-17 12. For the Lord of hosts has a day
against all that is magnificent and impressive
and against all that is exalted;
and it shall be brought low;
    13. against all the cedars of Lebanon, tall and lofty,
and against all the oaks of Bashan;
    14. against all high mountains,
and against all lofty hills;
    15. against every high tower,
and against every fortified city;
    16. against all the ships of Tarshish,
and against all prized objects.
    17. And the haughtiness of man shall be humbled,
and the pride of man shall be brought low,
and the Lord alone shall be exalted in that day.

Verses 12-17. The concept of the Lord's day appears here for the first time in Isaiah's message (cf. Amos 5:18-20). The implications of what that day will bring are not pleasant in this instance. For men of faith, in days when men walked in God's ways, there may be occasion for stressing the brighter aspects of what that day may offer. Here the one who acts is described as "the Lord of hosts," in view of the great resources of power for punishment that he has in reserve. In line with what had just been said about the reprehensible pride of man, the things against which the

Lord on his day must lash out are now listed in pairs. The picture of a storm sweeping the land is involved: it begins at the north and sweeps out toward the sea. First all things destined for destruction are summed up under the adjectives: magnificent, impressive, and exalted, which here apparently are used with a mild ironic touch. They appear high and mighty; they shall soon be brought low.

In the list of objects that follows it may be questioned whether the separate items are to be taken literally. The objection called for against such an interpretation might seem to be: What have these inanimate objects done to deserve God's punishment? But here it must first be noted that for the Old Testament point of view the physical and the spiritual are not set over against one another in sharp contrast. They are both parts of one world. When one suffers, the other is drawn into such suffering. When one is exalted, the other shares in the glory. When a nation sins, she and the land she inhabits may share in the one judgment that comes. So the literal interpretation is not far-fetched. On the other hand objects like high mountains may be thought of as symbols of the pride and self-exaltation of man. Or for that matter, if strong fortresses are built on high mountains, by metonomy the mountain may be referred to with the thought of that which stands out upon it. We may well have here a kind of half-figurative description in which the literal and the figurative blend inextricably.

Verses 13, 14. To this consideration may be added the observation that as far as the cedars of Lebanon were concerned, they often suffered ravages when invading armies hewed them down for military purposes. In any case, such cedars together with the oaks of Bashan will be ravaged to bring about a thorough and all-inclusive desolation. The mountains upon which these trees stood are thought of next (v. 14). These had been the scene of fortifications by Amaziah (II Chron. 26:10) and of heathen abominations by Ahaz (II Chron. 27:4).

Verse 15. Many a fortress and watchtower seem to have dotted the landscape as fine defensive measures, in which, however, the nation had put its trust rather than in the living God. Consequently "fortified walls" would soon be found far from impregnable.

Verse 16. And then there were the ships of Tarshish (presumably in Spain), big ocean-going vessels that first appear on the scene in the days of Solomon, as having their harbor in Elath, which Amaziah held for a time (II Kings 14:22) and Ahaz lost again (II Kings 16:6). The last item mentioned as involved in the general crash of all things high and desirable we have ventured to translate as "prized objects," a very uncertain term, for which any number of translations have been offered from "beautiful craft" to plain "treasures." In any case, it is abundantly clear that when men abandon faith in the living God they grow proud of their own achievements and treasured objects more than of God, making it necessary to disabuse them of their mistaken and misplaced confidence. God has a time when that shall be done. That time is "the day of the Lord."

Verse 17. Refrain-like, this verse tells what it is that actually is being brought low when all prized possessions crumble and fall, namely, the haughtiness and the pride of man. But when it is said that "the Lord alone shall be exalted in that day" the thought is also this, that through his overthrow of the spurious values that man has amassed, God's honor will be increased; for his greater power and sole excellence will stand forth all the more clearly when he has wrought such a necessary overthrow of the spurious.

d. The Fate of the Idols (vv. 18-21)

2:18-21 18. And as for the idols — every last one of them shall pass away.

19. And men shall go into the caves of the rocks and the holes of the ground,

from before the terror of the Lord and before the glory of His majesty,

when he arises to terrify the earth.

20. In that day a man shall cast his idols of silver and his idols of gold,

which he made for himself to worship,

to the moles and to the bats;

21. that he may himself enter into the rock caverns and rock clefts
from before the terror of the Lord and before the glory of his majesty,
when He arises to terrify the earth.

Verse 18. Now the prophet comes to the subject of the chief object of the Lord's displeasure, the idols, that had already been referred to briefly in v. 8. First of all, the total abandonment of them by those who made them is indicated. In fact, they shall not even be an issue any more. The time will come when the nation shall recover from its folly. They shall be in reality what their name in the original implies: "nothings."

Verses 19, 20. Exactly what will be done on that great and terrible day of the Lord is described quite graphically. With a reference to what had already been suggested as the only feasible course of action on that day in v. 10, it is first pointed out that men actually shall flee from the terror of the Lord into the rocks and caves of the earth. The close of the verse should not be overlooked — "when he arises to terrify the earth." This actually will be the Lord's purpose (the Hebrew reinforces the idea by a strong alliteration). At first when a man starts to flee on that day he may take his idols, as precious objects to which he is attached, along with him, especially since they are made of precious materials, silver and gold. But presently (v. 20) he shall find them only to be encumbrances in his flight. So, the objects that had been made for what could be regarded the highest purpose, worship, he shall cast away. But their uselessness at that time will be so keenly felt that he shall not hesitate to cast them "to the moles and the bats" — creatures that inhabit dark and repulsive places. But in their disgust over the delusion under which they have been, such places will appear most proper for the once-revered objects. If, as some claim, "moles" are not found in Palestine, some such creature is involved in any case.

Verse 21. The object of the casting away of the idols was to make entrance into "the rock caverns and rock clefts" possible. Any dark and difficult place will be preferable to encountering the Lord. The thoughts of vv. 10 and 19 are freely reworked in this verse to build up an impressive refrain. Some measure of repetition is inevitable and intentional and should not be regarded as casting suspicion upon the integrity of the text in this verse.

Verse 22 is best regarded as belonging to the next section.

Notes

Verse 3. The *min* of *midderakhaw* seems best regarded as a *min* partitive, the idea being that there is so much to be learned that the nations despair of mastering more than a part of it. Cf. *KS* 81.

Verse 4. "Many peoples" is construed with a dative rather than as direct object. A dative of advantage can easily become the equivalent of a direct object. Cf. *KS* 2.272, note 1.

Verse 6. The suffix on *'ammekha* may be regarded as covering the reflexive pronoun idea. Cf. *KS* 30.

Verse 8. By using a plural verb (*they* bow down) and a singular suffix (*his* hands) an effect is secured which we believe is covered by our translation "each one to the work of his hands." Cf. *KS* 348 n.

Verse 9. We regard the imperfect *tissa'* as potential: "*couldst* not forgive" rather than assertive for the future. Cf. *KS* 186 c. This verb also appears without the object *'awon* (guilt). Cf. *KS* 209 b.

Verse 10. The initial *bo'* is absolute infinitive used for an imperative. Cf. *KS* 359 k.

Verse 18. By using the singular after the plural subject ("idols") an effect is produced which seems to be covered by rendering *kalil* as "every last one." See *KS* 348 y.

Verse 20. A similar use of singular and plural appears here. See *KS* 346 d. The singular is used first (a man) the plural follows (which *they* made).

Chapter III

e. The Lord's Indictment of Irresponsible Leaders (2:22–3:15)

The prophet is still on the subject of Zion's Inglorious Present. A sharp indictment from the mouth of the Lord against the current leadership in Zion is about to be uttered. How helpless the idols will be in the face of the impending calamity has just been indicated. The section dealing with the poor leadership is about to begin. It is prepared for by a general statement on the virtual helplessness of man in the face of disaster and an admonition not to stake one's hope on man as the redeemer of the nation. In that sense this verse (2:22) is meant.

2:22 22. Abandon your trust in man who has breath in his nostrils. For of what account is he?

The inclination of man to depend on man as his adequate deliverer is only too common. It takes the grace of God to eradicate this baleful tendency from his mind. Here God (or perhaps the prophet) shows man's weakness, inasmuch as man is merely a creature "who has breath in his nostrils." Should that breath cease to flow from his nostrils, man would perish on the spot. Breath as the index of man's frailty is elsewhere referred to in Scriptures (Job 34:14f.; Ps. 104:29). At the same time the general sentiment of the verse is expressed in Ps. 118:8f.; 146:3; Jer. 17:5).

There is no warrant for a hidden reference to the Messiah in this passage, as some writers thought in days of old.

We now proceed to Chapter 3.

(1) The Resultant State of Anarchy When the Lord Takes Away All Support (3:1-12)

3:1-12 1. For behold, the Lord, Yahweh of hosts, will take away from Jerusalem and Judah every staff and stay, the whole staff of bread and the whole staff of water;
2. the mighty man and the soldier;

the judge and the prophet;
the diviner and the elder;
3. the captain of fifty and the eminent citizen;
the counsellor and the skilled craftsman and the skilled enchanter.
4. And [says the Lord]: "I will give boys to be their princes,
and irresponsible young men shall rule over them.
5. And my people shall mutually tyrannize one another,
and the young fellow will treat the old man disrespectfully,
and also the base fellow, the honorable man."
6. When a man will take hold of his brother in the house of
his father,
saying: "You've got clothes, you shall be our leader,
you shall be in charge of this catastrophe."
7. Then he shall protest loudly in that day:
"I'll not be the doctor; furthermore in my house is neither bread
nor clothes;
you shall not make me leader of the people!"
8. For Jerusalem shall totter and Judah shall fall;
for their tongue and their deeds are directed against Yahweh
to provoke his glorious eyes.
9. The very expression of their faces testifies against them;
they declare their sin like Sodom, they do not hide it.
Woe to them! for they have inflicted evil on themselves.
10. Say to the righteous that it is well with him,
for they shall enjoy the fruit of their doings.
11. Woe to the wicked! it shall be ill with him,
for what his hands have done shall be done to him.
12. As for my people, wilful children are their oppressors
and women rule over them.
As for my people, your leaders lead you astray
and obliterate the path you should go.

Verse 1. God is referred to by a very solemn, full-sounding title, "the Lord, Yahweh of hosts," as in 1:24; 10:16, 33; 19:4, where also judgment is about to be pronounced. The center where the impending devastation shall chiefly be displayed is the holy city itself; but the whole land of Judah shall experience the same judgment. This judgment shall consist in the removal of all agencies that might support the state and the city — all visible supports, material, and personal. These are here referred to as "every staff and stay." By using the same word in a masculine and in a feminine form a unique device is being resorted to which would equal our use of "every" in such a case, which we have ventured to insert in the translation. The original involves a play on

words something like that found in the expression "bag and
baggage." Though every imaginable prop is to be taken
away, in the enumeration which follows, the prophet limits
himself to a few areas without trying to be exhaustive.
There is, therefore no good ground for questioning the
correctness of the text when it goes on first to enumerate
under the general heading: "the whole staff of bread and
the whole staff of water." These two are important mainstays of the state. One is reminded of a state of siege of a
city where all food and drink are shut off from those shut
up within.

Verse 2. From this point on a detailed enumeration of
personages that can be of great help to a nation's or a city's
welfare is listed, always, however, in pairs, except the very
last item. Historically one is reminded of the course followed
by Nebuchadnezzar, when, as II Kings 24:14; 25:12 report,
all qualifiied leadership was taken away from the city in the
first major deportation. Deprive a city of all those that are
here listed and you have all activity hamstrung. First of all
"the mighty man and the soldier are listed." The first term
also is translated as "hero" at times. He excels in action by
virtue of physical strength. The "soldier" mentioned
apparently is the professional. Together these two make up
the defensive and offensive strength of the nation. Next
follow "the judge and the prophet." The "judge" is usually
a personage who can effectively serve as ruler rather than in
a merely judicial capacity. The "prophet" might seem to be
a professional prophet, without reflecting on his divine
mission. Then come "the diviner and the elder." The former of these is one of whom the law of Moses disapproved;
but he still was found only too commonly as a man in whom
men reposed confidence for leadership. The "elder" is the
man who, because of maturity, occupies a position of leadership in many of the affairs of the community.

Verse 3. That the listing used by the prophet is more or
less promiscuous appears at several points, also here, in that
a man of military standing is listed with an "eminent citizen." For the latter the Hebrew really says: "lifted-up of
face." We believe our translation comes close to the original
concept. The next two have nothing in common except that

they are persons of some distinction. The function of the "counsellor" was to give solid advice in matters great and small, especially in matters of policy of state. "The skilled craftsman" was the solid citizen well versed in his particular line of activity and would always be regarded as one of the mainstays of the community. Though quite a case can be made for the translation which renders this second personage, "skillful magician" (*RSV*), the last term "skillful enchanter" would become redundant, aside from other considerations. But the mention of the "enchanter" after the "diviner" of v. 2 indicates that occultism played an unduly heavy role in the life of the nations, all divine counsel to the contrary (Deut. 18:10ff.). What has a nation left when all representatives of these many classes are taken away? Note that the king is not even referred to. This could have been due to his total ineffectiveness.

Verse 4. Not only will the best stock be removed, but by the very implementation of the Almighty, inferior persons shall take over the direction of affairs. For he is represented as speaking and indicating that he is raising the irresponsible and the inexperienced to positions of authority: "boys will be their princes," i.e., the ruling class, and "irresponsible young men" shall have rule. This last class is designated by an abstract noun in the original, which connotes willfulness, utter irresponsibility. Some suggest the translation "outrage" (in German, *Ausgelassenheit*). Is there perhaps a subtle allusion to Ahaz in these words, hidden under the generalizing plural? Cf. II Kings 16:2. In any case, one is reminded of the other youthful ruler of whom Isa. 9:5ff. knows and who shall be the embodiment of all that is desirable.

Verse 5. But because the reins are in weak hands, anarchy is the result, and everybody takes advantage of everybody else. The due respect that the old man might expect is noticeably absent. The Old Testament inculcated respect for one's elders (Lev. 19:32) but these "young fellows" — again with the connotation of following the merest whim of the moment — throw such sound traditions to the winds. In fact, every "base fellow" behaves similarly to the honorable man, whose very character carries well-deserved weight in the community. This verse most effectively reflects the utter confusion that prevails.

Verses 6, 7. The next two verses indicate how hard it will be to find a good man to direct the affairs of the community or of the nation. The little incident portrayed takes place in the "house of (the) father," presumably because when the brothers of a family congregate, each having his own house, the father's home is still the logical place for meeting. As long as a one of their number might seem to have at least a decent coat to wear that would give him more qualification for office than others have, so utterly destitute shall they all be. But when these men single out a brother of theirs as having at least this one qualification and shall endeavor to put the whole sorry mess ("this catastrophe") "under his hand," that is to say, "put him in charge," then this brother shall loudly protest, indicating how desperate and even beyond recovery the whole situation is. His remonstrance covers, first of all, the idea that he is not competent to heal what is wrong. In Hebrew he says: "I will not be the binder-up," sometimes translated "healer" *RSV*, or "physician" (*Luther*). We have a more modern idiom when we say, "I'll not be the doctor." The patient to be healed is the state. It appears that his brothers were mistaken in their assumption that this one of their number had clothes or bread. He is as badly off as the rest. He refuses therefore to take any official responsibility.

Verse 8. This telling episode being ended, the prophet now tells in unmistakable terms what is going to take place. It could not be stated more bluntly: "Jerusalem shall totter and Judah shall fall." An especially strong form of statement is used to indicate that Judah and Jerusalem are as good as down on the ground, the so-called prophetic perfect. The obvious cause for this disastrous overthrow is nothing other than their advanced state of sinfulness. By not submitting to the word of reproof or to the instruction of that divine law which Israel alone possessed, they virtually directed both their tongue and their deeds against Yahweh himself. The disobedient and unresponsive ones, according to this word, fight God by word and deed. Or to use an unusually challenging form of statement, they "provoke his glorious eyes." This compact statement goes on the assumption that God's people are able to see his divine majesty shining forth upon them from His holy countenance. But though his eye is upon them and warns them that they are dealing with the Holy One of Israel, they sin flagrantly before his very eyes and so "provoke" him. The unholy defiance of their attitude is stressed.

Verse 9. In fact, sin has become so ingrained in their very character that the "expression of their faces" testifies against them. Their ungodliness and irreverence is written all over their faces. They are beyond the point of sinning in secret, trying to preserve a semblance of godliness. In fact, they have achieved the brazenness of the people of Sodom of days of old, who purposed to sin publicly and proclaimed their intention without a trace of shame. The woe that the prophet pronounces (or is it the Lord?) is abundantly called for: "they have inflicted evil on themselves." They have none other to blame than themselves for the evil that is coming. God may let it come but, more directly, they themselves have self-inflicted it.

Verse 10. Now the prophet, reiterating what he has already said in 1:19, reduces the outcome of the present situation to basic principles. The nation could have repented, for it had many prophetic messengers, and could so have been counted "righteous" in the Lord's sight and so it might have been well with them; they would have "enjoyed the fruit of their doings." For the Lord loves to reward those who walk in his ways and give obvious tokens of his good pleasure. Though there may be exceptions to this rule, as we well know, it is nevertheless of so general a nature and so commonly observed by the Lord in his dealings with men that it may be here set forth as a general maxim.

Verse 11. The obverse of this statement is equally true: It goes ill with the wicked. But this is not arbitrariness, for in the providence of God nothing other is done to the wicked than what he has done to others. He sets the pattern of what shall be done to him. By casting these statements in the forms of proverbs like the sayings of wisdom literature, the prophet indicates that old truths long known, are involved. This constitutes no new or hidden wisdom! The ancients knew these things and formulated them correctly.

Verse 12. If again we encounter a word that could have been spoken by the prophet or by the Lord himself, this dual character of the prophetic utterance may be due to the fact that prophets often identified themselves with their message so completely that for them God's word and their message flowed together into one. They spoke what their own consciousness led them to speak. At the same time it was a message that God gave them. Assuming that the prophet largely speaks for himself, the opening statement, "as for my people," indicates how thoroughly he identifies himself with his own nation. He reverts to the subject of the immature rulers, who are not only guilty of grave irregularities and actions that smack of inexperience; they are actually "oppressors" of those for whose good they should rule. In fact, in the absence of good masculine leadership, tyrannical women have taken over. Apparently such cases as Jezebel and Athaliah (I Kings 18:4; 21:5; II Kings 11:1) would be good examples of what the prophet had in mind. Two further formulations of the situation as it prevails are appended.

The very ones whose business it is to guide the nation are the ones that mislead them. Instead of clearly marking and pointing out the road to be followed they have themselves "obliterated" (literally: "swallowed the way of your paths") the course that should be followed. One shudders to think how thoroughly disorganized the situation must ultimately have become in the land of Judah.

(2) The Guilt of the Leaders That Brought on This Calamity (3:13-15)

But the prophets are not merely oracles of doom that vie with one another in bold attempts at effective rhetorical descriptions of woes to come: they make a special effort to lay bare the roots of conduct that bring about a given situation, so that they may sharpen the sense of moral responsibility. This calamity is laid squarely at the door of the nation's leaders.

3:13-15 13. Yahweh has taken his place to conduct a trial,
And he stands ready to judge nations.
14. Yahweh enters into judgment with the elders and princes of
his people:
"As for you, you have devastated the vineyard;
the plunder taken from the poor is in your houses.
15. What do you mean by crushing my people and grinding
the faces of the afflicted?"
says the Lord, Yahweh of hosts.

Verses 13, 14. Psalmists and prophets frequently sketched scenes of judgment in an effort to make it clear to their hearers that there is a Judge and a judgment. So here Yahweh is represented as just having entered the courtroom to conduct a trial, to use modern terminology. This single act of judging his own people is set against the background of God's universal prerogative to judge "nations." From days of old his right to exercise such judgment was well known (see Gen. 18:25; Judg. 11:27). One part of that broad obligation is to take Judah in hand when the circumstances make it imperative. In this case (v. 14) it is particularly "the elders and princes of his people" that must give account of their doings. Several charges in the area of social wrongs are raised by him who is both Judge and Prosecutor. First is the general charge, "You have devastated the vineyard." To liken the people of God to a vineyard that is the object of special attention of its owner, is a point of view especially developed by Isaiah (cf. chap. 5). But for those who should guard it against devastation to be the very devastators themselves is the height of criminal action. It is the leaders who have left the nation in a state of desolation; so furiously have they followed their own wicked course. More specifically, they are charged with having the very plunder which they have stripped from the poor now laid up in their own houses, ready to convert it into cash when opportunity presents itself. That leaders should treat the poor thus, when they are supposed to be the protectors of the helpless, has something peculiarly base about it.

Verse 15. With strong indignation the Lord addresses the question to the leaders who are on trial before him: "What do you mean by crushing my people?" Wherever a sense of justice is left even in a small measure, conduct such as this provokes a strong feeling of indignation on the part of any man. How much more Yahweh himself must be outraged. His charge reaches a climax in the indictment, couched in strong terms: You "grind the faces of the afflicted." Apparently the figure is that of a man fallen prostrate, face in the dust, having his face pushed cruelly into the earth again and again. See Micah 3:1-3. Apparently the enormity of the transgression corresponds to the enormity of the judgment just pictured as descending on the guilty nation and especially the guilty leaders.

f. The Lord's Indictment of the Vain and Frivolous Women of Jerusalem (3:16–4:1)

3:16–4:1 16. Furthermore Yahweh said:
Because the daughters of Zion have become proud
and walk with outstretched necks, casting coquettish glances,
walking along with mincing steps and jangling their anklets,
17. the Lord will smite with a scab the head of the daughters
of Zion,
and Yahweh will lay bare their shame.
18. On that day the Lord will take away the beauty consisting
in their anklets, neck ornaments, crescents,
19. ear pendants, bracelets, veils,
20. turbans, step-chains, sashes, perfume-boxes, amulets.
21. signet rings, nose rings,
22. robes of state, overtunics, cloaks, hand bags,
23. mirrors, linen wrappers, head bands, and large veils.
24. And in place of perfume there shall be rottenness,
and instead of a girdle, a rope;
and instead of a coiffure, baldness;
and instead of a rich robe, a girding of sack-cloth;
branding instead of beauty.
25. Your men shall fall by the sword,
and your strong warriors in battle.
26. And her gates shall groan and grieve,
and she, quite depopulated, shall sit upon the ground.
4:1. And seven women shall lay hold of one man in that day,
saying, "We will eat our own bread and provide our own garments;
only let us be called by your name;
take away our reproach!"

Verse 16. If irresponsible leaders have inflicted damage upon the nation, for which it shall dearly pay, similar damage was done by the type of women who set the standards of conduct in those days, in Jerusalem in particular. They are called by a special title to remind them of their noble destiny — "daughters of Zion." Women can exercise a tremendous influence for good or bad on the nation. Here it was all bad. The opening description traces their misconduct to its source: they are "proud." Instead of walking naturally they go along with outstretched necks, trying to attract attention. Instead of looking at things naturally they are seen to be "casting coquettish glances," trying to attract men. To make their femininity doubly apparent they go with fine mincing steps, which are pure affectation, and they go along "jangling their anklets," making everything about them seem artificial, and calculated to center unnecessary attention on themselves.

Verse 17. Since everything they do is calculated to promote their charm as though they were mere objects of beauty and not useful creatures with any wholesome purpose and destiny, the Lord himself will bring upon these voluptuous ones the very opposite of what they aspire to display. A repulsive "scab" shall cover their head instead of the beauty they sought. Where they seek to advertise their charm and attractiveness, the Lord will make the most repulsive to be seen, when, perhaps half naked, they are led away captives and are unable to cover their shame. Similar sharp words were spoken by other prophets in their day (see Amos 4:1-3; Jer. 44:15-30; also Isa. 32:9-13); but none quite so colorful and scathing as this passage. Isaiah may have known the Amos passage.

Verses 18-23. Then follows a long list of things which, perhaps in war and captivity, will be removed from them, all articles of vanity — all superfluous, all indicative of the rigor with which the women will be treated in place of the soft indulgence which was characteristic of them. It would hardly be proper to assume that every one of the daughters of Zion had all these articles of vanity here mentioned in her possession. But beauty-culture in its cheaper aspects was certainly overdeveloped already in the prophet's day.

Besides, it may be that some of the articles mentioned were in the nature of amulets and lucky pieces. It has even been noted that the Canaanite goddess Ishtar had many of these in her makeup, which fact might point to aids in idolatry. But this is largely conjecture.

In any case the articles of beauty-culture mentioned cannot always be identified with total certainty. We shall not attempt to give a full discussion of all possibilities with complete justification of our translation. We have followed a large measure of consensus of opinion that prevails among lexicographers and commentators. By a rare construction of the genetive, the Hebrew word "beauty" (v. 18) has twenty-one words dependent upon it, a construction which is in itself perfectly clear but quite unusual especially in the original. These are, of course, appositional genetives, which fact has led us to translate the relation by the words "consisting in." Lastly it may help to recall that, no doubt, no woman ever wore all these ornaments at one time.

After 2:12ff. this long enumeration of articles will not seem strange to us. It is one of Isaiah's favorite devices. Basic garments, lighter and larger tunics and cloaks, sashes, shawls and veils, great and small, articles of jewelry and perfumes, rings and hand bags and mirrors, all follow one another largely in a sequence that groups them euphonically. Any basic pattern of arrangement of items need not be sought and cannot be found. The bewildering mass of things is what should impress us. Indeed, in the pursuit of idle vanity and surface beauty an unbelievable amount of money must have been spent and the creatures that spent it must have been pretty vain and frivolous. When such emphasis is placed upon looking pretty and attracting men, solid virtues cannot be achieved at the same time. This frivolity is bound to be shallow and wicked and the source of many sins that engulfed the nation. Frivolous women breed a sensual and frivolous nation.

Verse 24. Instead of being able to live softly and luxuriously, they shall fall into the very opposite in the judgment of God. A number of striking contrasts is listed by the prophet. For perfumes they shall have a rotten stench. In place of a well-embroidered girdle shall be the rope that

binds the captives hands and feet. The place of an elaborate hair-do will be taken by baldness which results from
not being in a position to give the hair even the most
necessary attention. Baldness may also be a mark of grief
(cf. 15:2). For all the rich robes they shall have sackcloth,
either as the only kind of meager covering they can find
or as a token of mourning or even as "a mark of abject submission" (cf. I Kings 20:31; 21:27). In a strikingly compact
and untranslatable phrase all is summed up in the words
"branding instead of beauty." The branding referred to is
the branding put on the forehead of prisoners to mark
them as prisoners forever, a mark which often must have
seriously disfigured the person branded. On that sad picture the description closes.

Verses 25, 26. Behind the entire chapter, lurks the specter
of captivity with all its horrors, a captivity coming as the
result of cruel war. To this aspect of the case, reflecting
not only upon the frivolous women and their lot, the prophet
now goes on to describe the effects of war on the nation
as a whole, and on her manpower in particular (v. 25f.).
When men are said to fall by the sword, that signifies their
death as well as the defeat of the nation. Even the "strong
warriors" will not be able to save themselves in the day of
disastrous battle.

At this point a new female figure appears in the place of
the daughters of Zion, which have stood in the forefront
of attention since v. 16. It is personified Zion, or Jerusalem,
itself. Her gates shall "groan and grieve." By metonomy
"gates" stand for the city itself. For all of the city's activity centered in her gates. We used the translation "groan
and grieve" in an attempt to capture a similar turn of the
alliteration in the original. In a word, disaster shall be
heavy on that day of judgment. Next the city itself is
depicted as sitting upon the ground in total dejection and
grief, having lost practically all her men and people, either
by death or by deportation into the land of captivity, as it
actually came to pass in the fall of Jerusalem in 586 B.C.
at the hands of Nebuchadnezzar.

4:1 closes the scene with the poor women of the previous

chapter now reduced to the extremity of pursuing men, no longer being the objects of pursuit. In fact they are said to go so far that seven (this number signifies a maximum) of them will cling to one man, one of the few still left, and beg him to take them over at least in some kind of token marriage. They will not expect him to fend for them and provide them with their due support of food and clothing (cf. Exod. 21:10). They will be glad to supply all that for themselves. If only the shame of not being able to get a man may be taken from them, and, possibly the reproach of being childless, which the Oriental women dreaded so much. They will be content to be allowed to bear the man's name. This is a far cry from their bold attitude in the days of their luxury and vanity!

Notes

Verse 1. On the subject of coupling together a masculine and a feminine noun of the same root to express full compass of the concept involved, one may compare *KS* 91.

Verse 3. In the expression "eminent in regard to face" the noun face is to be regarded as an accusative of specification (*KS* 336 h).

Verse 6. The phrase "in the house of his father" involves a noun used adverbially without a preposition (*KS* 330 k). The *lekhah* after *simlah* is the dative of the second person singular in the fuller style of writing and is, of course, a dative of possession (*KS* 376 k).

Verse 8. It fits the context better to take the verb *kashelah* as a prophetic perfect, indicating what will befall Jerusalem in the future. *Naphal* do.do. KS 133.

Verse 7. After the verb *yissa'* the customary object is taken for granted: "lift up (the voice — *qol*)." KS 209 b.

Verse 8. On the form *lamroth* with the *he* of the hiphil infinitive elided see *GK* 53 q.

Verse 11. Since the adjective *ra'* represents a whole clause, according to the connection, with an obvious omission, the necessary verb can readily be supplied — "it shall be . . ." (*KS* 354 b).

Verse 14. The condensed expression found in "the spoil of the poor" is readily seen to imply some such thought as "the plunder taken from the poor" and is therefore an objective genitive (*KS* 336 e).

Verse 15. The opening word *mallakhem* consists of the interrogative *mah* plus *lakhem*, dative plural masculine. See *GK* 37c.

Verse 16. The two absolute infinitives expressing both the continuous nature of the action and the manner of it are explained in *GK* 113 s and u.

Verse 24. The word *ki* translated "branding" is unusual, but fits the context and is defensible grammatically. See *KW* and *BDB* 465 a.

Chapter IV

g. Zion Purified (4:2-6)

We come to the conclusion of this portion which began with 2:1. There Jerusalem was under consideration; here she again is the center of interest. There the emphasis was chiefly on the impression that the converted (or about-to-be-converted) Gentiles have of the city of God; how highly they think of her. Here the emphasis focuses on her spiritual glory, chief factor of which is God's continual presence. These two descriptions very effectively supplement one another.

It is true that the transition from 4:1, which concludes the previous portion, to 4:2, which opens the one under consideration, is abrupt, unmotivated. Nothing indicates what should have brought about a change of attitude on the part of the Almighty so as to induce him again to show favor to his covenant people. But it has rightly been pointed out (*Herntrich*) that what man does is not the factor that motivates God's action. The source of all constructive action in the realm of God's kingdom lies exclusively in God and God's unmerited grace. Grace is beyond human logic and not connected with man's strivings. Therefore, whatever is done, is, especially in vv. 3 and 4, attributed solely to God's activity. Let it be noted also that the fact that this passage is eschatological in tone does not fix a late date upon it after the age of Isaiah. Such verdicts as to the measure of truth that can be attained in a given age are largely subjective speculation. Nor is there any need of changes in the text. Here, as usual, the available Hebrew text is easily to be supported on the basis of careful textual criticism, and also makes good sense from the point of view of good coherence and reasonable logic.

4:2-6   2. In that day the *tsemach* [sprout] of Yahweh shall
              be beautiful and glorious.
and the fruit of the land shall be the pride and glory of the
      ones of Israel who have escaped.
   3. And it shall come to pass that he who is left in Zion
      and survives in Jerusalem — holy shall he be called,
every one who has been noted down for life in Jerusalem.
   4. When the Lord shall have washed away the filth of the
      daughters of Zion
and shall have cleansed away the bloodguilt from her midst
by a spirit of judgment and a spirit of burning,
   5. then Yahweh will create over the whole extent of Zion
      and over her assemblies
a cloud by day, and smoke and glow of flaming fire by night;
for over it all shall be glory as a kind of canopy.
   6. There shall also be there a sheltering pavilion
as a protection by day against the heat,
and as a refuge and shelter against storm and rain.

Verse 2. The time for this situation is fixed as being "in
that day." In prophetic language this refers to the "day
of the Lord." This day is not only one of judgment, though
that aspect of it may be stressed at times. When, after
judgment, God continues to act in constructive endeavors,
that is merely the continuation of his day in which great
things are achieved. In general the expression means:
when the time has come for God to act. The item on
which attention now centers is a concept that in our language is almost untranslatable. So we have let the original
stand — *tsémach.* "Sprout," "shoot," or "branch" are all
inadequate, as equivalents. It is not only a part of a tree
(branch). It is more than a little beginning of growth
(shoot or sprout). It is the "growing thing," with the
connotation of abundant vitality and fresh life. If it be
Yahweh's *tsémach*, then it is best understood in this connection as being the great work of salvation which Yahweh
has undertaken for the good of mankind. Oftentimes this
great work lay hidden and forgotten. It was totally lost
sight of at times. It became submerged in the movements
and processes of history. Whether it was still alive, might
often have become doubtful even in Israel. This statement
claims that it shall most obviously appear and be so "beauti-

ful and glorious" that none will fail to see both that God
has achieved something and that which he has achieved
is a thing of rare beauty. The remaining verses of the
chapter unfold the full glory of this work of the Lord's,
chiefly from one outstanding point of view. For that matter
every description of the Lord's work can do little more
than unfold at some length a major aspect or two of this
magnificent project. So here the emphasis lies on how
"beautiful and glorious" it is. The term always implies
something living and growing. The Messiah is included
indirectly.

Another thing will stand out to make the hearts of men
glad. "The fruit of the land" shall be an object of "pride
and glory." The reference is to vegetation, which oftentimes is described in the Messianic age as being particularly
rich and exuberant (cf. Amos 9:13ff., etc.). Those who
are first mentioned as appreciating the marvelous growth
of vegetation are "the ones of Israel who have escaped."
The prophet has in mind the returnees from Babylonian
Captivity, that is to say, the ones who will be left over
when the judgments described in Chaps. 2–4 shall have
befallen Israel. Many others, that is to say, all the saved,
however will take like joy in the fertility of the new heavens
and earth that the Lord shall bring to pass.

Summing up the glorious project — man's salvation —
on which God has long worked, will become obvious and
will be seen in all its glory. A part of that glory will be
the abundant fertility of a rehabilitated world. This is the
substance of v. 1.

However our interpretation of *tsémach* requires further
explanation and justification. The favorite interpretation
of the term in our day seems to be that it signified "vegetation." Then the two terms, *tsémach* and "fruit of the earth"
are synonymous. In support of this interpretation one can
cite the fact that the same root used as verb is often used
in the Scriptures to describe the springing forth of vegetation. However, it should be specially observed that Isaiah
likes to use this verb to describe the growing up of projects
that the Lord is sponsoring (42:9; 43:19; 55:10; 61:11).
Furthermore, if the factor of extreme glory that shall be in

evidence in the Messianic age is only exuberant vegetation, that fails to agree with the importance of the issues at stake.

This leads us to the consideration of the second interpretation, which is much more to the point. This is the interpretation which says that *tsémach* is none other than the Messiah himself, an interpretation found already in the Jewish *Targum* on the passage. What lends special weight to this interpretation is the fact in later passages *tsémach* clearly becomes a sort of title for the Messiah (Jer. 23:5; 33:15; Zech. 3:8; 6:12). However, the difficulty that this interpretation creates in this instance is that the next statement, "the fruit of the earth," constitutes a strange parallel to the Messiah. Some attempt then to make this second expression to be a description of the human origin or nature of the Christ. But to make "fruit of the earth" bear such a meaning is far-fetched in any case. So the truth of the matter appears to be that, where in the earlier instance of the use of the term *tsémach*, it covers the whole work of God, later on in prophecy it specifically and appropriately describes the Christ himself, who is the greatest branch, or sprout, or shoot, that God's providence ever brought forth. Therefore we conclude that in this instance the whole of the saving work of God is meant by the term.

It should yet be noted that where, for two chapters, God's work of judgment on Israel had been under consideration, the use of the term "the ones who have escaped" indicates that Israel shall not be exterminated. It allows for the final escape of a goodly number of them.

Verse 3. Now the attention concentrates on these survivors. When two terms are now used ("he who is left" and "survives") this seems to imply that only after a severe trial shall there be any escapees. But the chief emphasis in the verse lies on the fact that this remnant shall be "holy." The sentence structure pushes this term into the forefront. The word used has a connotation somewhat different from the one we associate with the idea. As *Skinner* aptly puts it, the term indicates "consecration to God and inviolability." Each person is set apart to God and by virtue of this consecration stands under God's providential care in an unusual degree. Therefore being "holy" is not something that man achieves, but something that is divinely given. This aspect of the case is covered also by the second descriptive expression used: they are persons who are "noted down [or, written down] for life in Jerusalem." The notion of a book enters the picture, as in Exod. 32:32; Ps. 69:28; 139:16; Dan. 12:1. Behind the expression lies the fact that cities, even in days of old, kept citizenship lists containing the names of all who could claim to be accepted citizens of a given town. So, to make the distinctive honor involved clear to our human way of thinking, all of God's true children may be thought of as clearly inscribed in the records of heaven. The high honor associated with being in the community of the people of God is thus strongly highlighted.

Verse 4. There is, however, a negative aspect of the case which must be thought of as having been brought about before this holy community can come into existence. There first had to be a cleansing of those who were at length described in the second half of Chap. 3 as having a spurious glory and adornment, the daughters of Zion. Their proud and wanton attitude is here described as "filth." That filth had to be washed away, not by these sinful women but by the Lord himself. Then there were the men of 2:6ff. who in their self-sufficiency and cruelty had heaped up "bloodguilt," who had to be cleansed — not cleanse themselves. So in chiastic order Chap. 4 describes the cleansing of the sinners who had provoked the anger of the Almighty. The same one whom they offend, by his spirit cleanses them, bringing first "judgment" as just retribution and to awaken a sense of guilt, and bringing secondly "burning to purge away the accumulated guilt. His "Spirit" appears to be the strong reaction of the Lord against the things that call for adjustment.

Verse 5. When such cleansing will have been accomplished, then a new beauty and glory will become apparent (v. 5). This verse is the apodosis of v. 4. The descriptive terms are borrowed from the days of the wanderings in the wilderness. Exod. 13:21f., concerning the pillar of cloud, and Exod. 40:34-38, concerning the cloud that covered the tent, are the passages on which the description here given is based. More than the area of Zion is under consideration. These new glories are not confined to the hill in Jerusalem. They express a reality which transcends such narrow bounds. But the opening word ("Yahweh will create") indicates that a special work of divine grace is under consideration. Only Yahweh can achieve results like these. When the cleansed people of God come together ("her assemblies") to worship the Lord there shall be a spiritual truth in evidence like the visible presence of the days of old. The cloud, the symbol of his presence, will be there, not as a visible entity but as a spiritual reality. The terms "smoke, and glow of flaming fire by night" describe a second reality — God's presence in its protective aspect. As "cloud" it stressed its guiding and enlightening aspect. Still speaking the language of the wilderness days to describe the great truths of New Testament living, the prophet envisions the cloud and the smoke as covered by a canopy of sheer glory, enhancing the whole scene and raising it above the realities that were encountered in the days of Moses. For then there was no comprehensive overshadowing glory.

Verse 6. Thus far the glory aspect of the scene that the prophet has painted is the feature that has been most in evidence. This again was based on the concept of a people pardoned and cleansed. It is amazing how the truth concerning the forgiveness of sins gets proper evaluation in the Old Testament. But there is one more feature that the holy seer would weave into the picture, and that is the feature of protection against hostile elements that might be encountered. These hostile elements, according to this thumb-nail sketch of the church of God, are conceived of in terms of the extremes of weather: heat, and fierce and uncomfortable storm. That which provides such protection is the "sheltering pavilion," in Hebrew a *sukkah*, a term usually meaning "a hut." Where this "pavilion" — for "hut" carries a connotation out of keeping with the whole of a dignified and glorious scene — is to be thought of as located on Mount Zion does not seem to concern the prophet. It is enough to know that it is there and serves its purpose, and is not a feature out of harmony with the scene as a whole.

More than this was not granted to this holy man to see at this time. Men have pointed out that the whole now really presents a picture of a city which had been hit by a violent storm and has been washed clean by the waters that swept down upon it when the thunders of divine judgment were heard. Now that purified city lies on Mount Zion bathed in pure sunshine, a picture of supreme attractiveness and beauty.

But it has been objected that the last feature touched upon in v. 6 concerns itself with the "lesser inconveniences" that man may be exposed to and so "reads like an anticlimax," and so Isaiah is charged with having offered a "weak conclusion," and this conclusion in turn is used to question the verse as having come from the pen of Isaiah. This is a purely subjective criticism. Because a writer feels that he himself would have made a far stronger conclusion, is that valid criticism of what a prophet has to offer? Rather, note the construction of the oracle in vv. 2-6; the passage mounts to a climax in vv. 4 and 5, then it subsides in v. 6. It apparently was not the writer's intention to list all the mighty forces of evil that had been overcome. According to v. 4 he was not ignorant of what these forces were. Verse 6, for that matter, may even be construed to say that *not even* the "lesser inconveniences" will disturb the peace of God's people.

Notes

Verse 4. The initial "when" is not so much conditional as temporal, as is also the case in 6:11 and 28:25. Thus v. 4 is cast in the form of the protasis to which v. 5 is the apodosis. The word for "blood," being in the plural, means "masses of blood," or "blood-guilt." Cf. *Ks* 259 c. *Ba'er* ("burning") is the absolute infinitive used with a noun in the construct. Cf. *KS* 224.

Verse 6. In *mechorebh* the *min* of separation expresses the idea of counteracting the heat (*KS* 406 n).

Chapter V

b. God's Judgment of His Guilty People (Chap. 5)

(1) The Parable of the Vineyard (vv. 1-7)

The prophet is about to indict his people for their extreme sinfulness. Rather than use another reproach of the form previously used, he varies his tactics to stir their jaded interest. He assumes the role of a sort of minstrel, or "ballad-singer." He may have rendered this ballad for the first time at some public gathering, even, for that matter at some major festival. It is well calculated to attract and hold attention. As to literary form it has been described as one "of the most perfect" of the parables of the Scriptures. The basic idea of the vineyard appears prominently elsewhere in the Scriptures: see Jer. 2:21; 12:10f.; Ps. 80:8ff.; Matt. 20:1ff.; 21:33ff.

It will be difficult to discover a point in history when this parable was first set forth. The majority of opinion inclines to the latter part of the reign of Jotham, or to the time of the transition from Jotham to Ahaz. At least it appears that the prophet's ministry has gone on for some time, at least long enough for some opposition to develop; therefore Isaiah's attempt at a fresh approach to gain a hearing.

The title that has become popular for this parable, "a love song," is of dubious value. On the basis of other usage this title could be defended. But here the title as such is inappropriate.

Lastly, it should be noted that there is no specific connection between this chapter and the one that precedes. Still the general theme of Chaps. 2–4 may be kept in mind, "Through Judgment to Fulfilment of God's Gracious Promises," only that in Chap. 5 the judgment note prevails; there is practically nothing of the thought of grace in evidence in the chapter.

5:1-7 1. Let me now sing about my Beloved, a song of my Beloved concerning his vineyard.
My Beloved had a vineyard on a very fruitful hill.
2. He hoed it and cleared it of stones and planted it with choice vines;
he built a watchtower in the midst of it,
and hewed out a wine-vat in it;
and he waited that it should produce grapes,
and it produced sour grapes.
3. And now, O inhabitants of Jerusalem and men of Judah,
you be the judges between me and my vineyard.
4. What more was there to be done by my vineyard that I did not do for it?
Why, when I waited for it to produce grapes, did it produce sour grapes?
5. And now, let me tell you what I will do to my vineyard.
I will remove its hedge and it shall be devastated;
I will break down its wall and it shall be trampled on.
6. And I will make it a gully; it shall not be pruned or hoed;
and briars and thorns shall spring up;
And I will command the clouds that they rain no rain upon it.
7. For the vineyard of the Lord of hosts is the house of Israel,
and the men of Judah are his pleasant plants;
and he looked for justice, but, lo, bloodshed;
for righteousness, but, lo, a cry!

Verses 1, 2. The opening statement seems to have a certain verbosity which is hard to understand. The second term, translated "Beloved," seems unnecessary. The two terms translated by this one word are of the same root in Hebrew but differ a bit as to form (*yedhidhi* and *dodhi*). Both can, and seem here to mean "Friend," or "Beloved." The prepositions cause further trouble. We prefer the perfectly defensible translation: "Let me sing *about* my Beloved." For though on the surface the theme of the ballad is the vineyard, on further reflection it becomes apparent, that the Lord and what he did is more obviously under consideration. Admitting that this does not fully solve the difficulties involved, the problem remaining does not materially affect the interpretation. To translate the first "beloved" as "uncle" or "cousin," as some do, merely complicates a complicated situation. The identity of the "Beloved" is not revealed until the parable has progressed a bit farther. At v. 4 it begins to appear that

it may be the Lord. In v. 6 this becomes fully apparent.
Verse 7 may be an explanation offered by the prophet
himself. It should lastly be remarked that the title given
the Lord, "Beloved," is an unusual one for Isaiah, bordering a bit on the familiar, for Isaiah is the prophet who
above all others is impressed with the fact that the Lord
is "the Holy One of Israel."

The ballad proper begins with a claim to the effect that
the prophet's Beloved had a vineyard on a very fertile hill.
The choice of ground for the vineyard was carefully made.
The hill is very fertile (Hebrew: "a son of oil," or fatness).
Being a hill, it is on all sides open to the sunlight, a
feature that vines particularly love, as the poet Virgil in
his day already pointed out. Now follow the various steps
taken in creating a situation where grapes could be effectively raised: the ground is hoed, stones are removed —
always a problem in stony Palestine; choice vines are
planted. A watchtower is centrally located to enable the
watchman to guard against theft at the time when the
grapes ripen — a piece of standard equipment for a good
vineyard. Even the wine-vat is hewed out in advance in
anticipation of the harvest, this vat being, strictly speaking,
the lower container cut in solid rock into which the juice,
after it had been trodden out in the upper and larger
container flowed through a small opening. All this having
been meticulously attended to, the owner waits for the
good grapes to ripen. Result: "it produced *sour* grapes."
The term used is a bit stronger: "stinking grapes." Some
feel that "wild grapes" covers the term, except for the fact
that wild grapes, as we know them, may be very sweet
and produce a very good wine.

Verses 3, 4. At this point the hearers, mostly people of
Jerusalem and also the men of Judah, are asked to leave
their strictly objective approach to the whole matter and
pass judgment upon the merits of the case. The issue
appears to be: What should the owner of a vineyard do
under such circumstances? The case is stated a bit more
fully (v. 4) so that there be no mistake as to what the
hearers were to pass judgment on. Was anything omitted
of that which owners were in the habit of doing? Could

he have done more? For that matter, did any one do more
than what was described above? Bringing the whole issue
into sharpest focus, why, instead of the good grapes to be
expected, were sour grapes produced? No answer is given
by the hearers of the prophet. It is assumed that they
strongly arrived at one conclusion as the only reasonable
one that men of that time would all have arrived at. Since
that might tacitly and correctly have been assumed, the
writer does not stop to give the hearers' verdict. He
formulates the proper decision for himself and for them
in v. 5.

Verse 5. His decision begins with a somewhat ominous
ring: "Let me tell you what I will do." The "hedge" often
made of material like prickly pears would be removed so
that all manner of beasts have easy access to the vines.
The "wall," usually made of stone, and the second line
of defense, would be broken down to given vent to the
owner's exasperation. The result would be that the vines
could and would be trampled by creatures, wild and domestic. The Hebrew construction at this point employs a
device calculated to make the reader feel the owner's disappointment.

Verse 6. The description of the destruction that will be
resorted to is carried several steps further, making the
reader feel that there were certain very important issues
at stake that called for the ultimate of abandonment and
destruction. The owner will see to it that the once fruitful
hill becomes the equivalent of a "gully" — a precipitous
place where nothing can grow or would be planted — a
perfectly worthless plot of ground, an area that no man
would think of hoeing or doing any pruning of what grows
there. The only things that will flourish there will be briars
and thorns. And now, of a sudden, it becomes apparent
that the highest issues are at stake and that the Almighty is
the speaker, when he announces that he will issue orders
to the clouds not to drop their rain upon it.

Verse 7. An authoritative interpretation is appended at
this point so that no one may misread the message. The
vineyard involved is "the house of Israel." At this point
this expression does not reflect on the northern kingdom

except in a secondary sense. The point seems to be that the entire nation, was the recipient of God's abundant mercy and loving care; both kingdoms were equally dear to him, as far as salvation of men was concerned. Both had sinned with little difference of the degree of iniquity involved. A bit more care could be bestowed upon the "house of Judah," where the line of David held the throne and where there was more response to the pleas of the prophets. So they are called "his pleasant plants." By a very effective paronomasia in the original Hebrew the case is now summed up. In the Hebrew it is said: He looked for *mishpat* and behold *mishpach*, for "justice" came "bloodshed"; He looked for *tsedhaqah* and there came *tse'aqah*, for "righteousness" came a "cry." An attempt has been made to reproduce the play on words in English: Looking for *measures* he found *massacres*, and for *right* he found *riot*. The Lord was justified in expecting the finest of godly fruits among his people and found instead the most horrible of crimes. This last indictment must have stung them to the quick. One cannot help but feel that the strategy employed was like that which Nathan used against the guilty David. Cf. II Sam. 12:1-4; also 14:6f.; I Kings 20:39f.; and also Isa. 24:24-28; Ezek. 24:3-5.

The two points of strict analogy set forth by v. 7 are these: The vineyard is Israel, or Judah; God looked for good fruits and was disappointed. Beyond that we dare not resort to specific interpretation trying to determine exactly what the vines were, what the watchtower or the wine-vat. These latter items are inserted into the parable to give the needed color and make clear the point that the Lord had done all that reasonably could be expected to be done. Though one may think of the items involved that *Luther* specifies, as being no more than good illustrations, it still would exceed the limits of strict interpretation to say the choice vines are the judges; the towers are divine services and the Word; the winepress is the mortifying of the old Adam.

So by an ingenious device the prophet has no doubt reached the heart and conscience of at least a few more of the chosen people, who by now had become well-nigh impervious to the strictures of the prophetic utterances. We may well believe that Isaiah spent much time and ingenuity on the planning of this device to reach his hearers. This inspired word gives evidence of having been most carefully worked out in detail and with sharp precision, not one word too many, not one too few.

Echoes of this parable appear in the New Testament; see Matt. 21:33-46; Mark 12:1-12; Luke 20:9-19.

(2) The Sour Grapes Produced by Israel (vv. 8-23)

Unfortunately the term "sour grapes" in our idiom carries the connotation of the unattainable and therefore the thing that the speaker claims he cares nothing about. We are using the term in the sense of bad fruit. It appears on the surface that six classes of men producing bad fruit are listed. However, since the writers of Scripture are, as a rule, careful to respect the symbolical use of numbers, it seems at least quite permissible to supply a "woe" before v. 23 (which the sentence structure in the original well allows for) and so increase the number of Woes to seven. Nothing would seem to indicate that these Woes were "uttered at various times," and later conveniently grouped under one head. The slight changes of semi-poetic rhythm may well be a device for achieving some variety. Rather a dismal picture develops as one Woe follows the other. The state of morals in the land of Judah must have been at a low ebb, to say the least.

5:8-10 8. Woe to those who array one house next to the other, and add field to field, till there is no more room; and you are made to dwell alone in the land.
9. The Lord of hosts has sworn in my hearing:
"Surely many houses shall be desolate, houses large and splendid, without an inhabitant.
10. For a vineyard of ten acres shall produce only a few gallons; and ten bushels of seed shall produce only one bushel."

Verse 8. The ones upon whom the Woe is being pronounced are the greedy landowners. The word "woe" is stronger than "shame on." It involves more than an "alas." *BDB* says well that the term is "preparatory to a declaration of judgment." In blunt terms, land-grabbing is under consideration. They who already own some property desire more. They crowd out poorer and weaker home-owners till they have control of entire blocks of the city, "one house next to the other." Out in the country they follow the same tactics till they have added "field to field," and "there is no more room" for others. Mere possession, no matter how many are dispossessed or crowded to the wall! The landowner then ultimately "dwells alone in the midst of the land." He does not need all this land and these houses. He cannot successfully work it all. He glories in the mere possession. In Israel the ideal set forth in the law of Moses was that as many persons as possible should each have their own holdings of lands and houses — many small property owners. These sinners set out to nullify such a purpose.

Verse 9. The doom that the prophet foretells is reinforced by the claim that it is a word directly revealed by none less than the Lord of hosts to his own servants. The Hebrew puts it more abruptly: "in my ears Yahweh of hosts." That means, it has been conveyed to me with unmistakable clarity, as good as "sworn," as the *Septuagint* supplies. The doom is this: land and houses shall lie there desolate, not as indications of the prosperity of the owners. Apparently the ravages of war are being thought of by the prophet. A further result of such ravages will be that little can be sown and little will be reaped. An area of "ten acres" (strictly as much as a yoke of oxen might plow in ten days) will produce "only a few gallons." The Hebrew says at this point, "a bath," which is a measure somewhat in excess of eight gallons. As to the grain raised on the extensive fields of those who acquired so much land, "a homer of seed shall yield but an ephah" (*RSV*). The point is that the homer contained about ten ephahs. In other words men will reap only one-tenth of what they sowed. Their cruel oppressions and foreclosures apparently are not going to lead to a very successful life financially.

Next comes a Woe on hard-drinking worldlings. Strangely, as other writers have also remarked, the acquiring of wealth and the spending of it on hard liquor so commonly go hand in hand when a nation rushes on to its own down-fall. This Woe gets the most extensive treatment of all, perhaps because the sin involved was the most flagrant. It runs from vv. 11-17. Some commentators disapprove of this approach and decree that either vv. 14-16 or vv. 15-17 are out of place. However what *we* may describe as disproportionate treatment is no index of what a writer may set forth. It must also be considered that the shameful disregard of the Lord and his work may indeed have stirred the prophet's strongest indignation and led him to dwell on the subject more at length.

5:11-17 11. Woe to those who rise up early in the morning
only to pursue strong drink,
who sit up late in the evening until wine inflames them.
12. And they have zither and harp, tambourine and flute and
wine at their feasts;
but they do not regard the work of Yahweh,
and the deeds of his hands they do not see.
13. Therefore my people will go into exile for want of knowledge,
and their honored men will die of hunger,
and the common crowd will be parched for thirst.
14. Therefore the realm of the dead [Sheol] will enlarge its
appetite,
and will open its mouth without limit;
and the elite of the city and her mobs shall go down,
the noisy throng and the "happy souls" in her.
15. And the plain fellow bows down and the big fellow humbles
himself,
and the eyes of the haughty are humbled.
16. And Yahweh of hosts shall be exalted in judgment,
and the Holy God shall display his holiness by righteousness.
17. And lambs shall graze there in their pasture,
and strangers shall feed on the waste places where the rich had
been.

Verses 11, 12. First a brief sketch is given of these hard-drinking worldlings with a Woe written across the head of the page. Where men ordinarily have a worthy objective in mind when they rise up early, here the goal is merely "to pursue strong drink." One is reminded of Eccles. 10:16f. where a similar charge is raised against princes. "Pursue" implies putting forth efforts worthy of a better cause. And as the day begins so it ends: they stay up till the evening breeze (here "evening") comes up, aiming to achieve a degree of inebriation where they are really inflamed with wine. There always will be such and they will take some pride in their cheap attainment. In this instance an embellishment is added to the bouts of revelry to give them an aura of refinement: musical instruments are present and music is being made to testify to the cultured habits of the wine-drinkers. There is quite an array of instruments — zither, harp, tambourine and flute. As an appendage to the list comes "wine." Amos 6:5f. is much of the same sort. But true culture, insight, and refinement is completely wanting at these bouts. Spiritual discernment has become a rare commodity in these groups. They never turn their thoughts to "the work of Yahweh," that is, to his achievements as he guides the destiny of his people. Yahweh is carrying on a mighty work in his *Heilsgeschichte*; they have never noticed it. Besides, "the deeds of his hands they do not see," referring to the individual instances of achievement as he carries forward his purposes. In Israel they are blind to the purposes of the covenant God of Israel as they unfold generation after generation. The spirit of wine has dulled their senses to discern the presence of the Spirit of God.

Verse 13. This is not merely an unfortunate situation; it is a very blameworthy one. It calls aloud for judgment. This judgment is now announced as impending. It will take the form of an exile. The reason for the judgment is again briefly stated summing up what v. 12 pointed out — "want of knowledge." Ignorance can be damnably culpable. Cf. also Hosea 4:1, 6, 12. A most gloomy picture is drawn of the results and the process of going into exile: "their honored men will die of hunger," no matter how highly they may have been esteemed in the nation in their day. Their lot will be no better than that of the "common crowd" who will "be parched for thirst," and will, of course, die in the process. In picturing scenes of judgment the prophets often lavish color on their canvas, though they may depict only isolated scenes by way of illustration. Yet the prophet is not devoid of sympathy for his people as the

possessive adjective indicates when he says all this will befall "my people."

Verse 14. By another bold description the prophet indicates that the number of lives to be lost in the judgment
will be exceedingly great. There seems to be an echo of the
fate of Korah in the description (Num. 16:30, 33). The
underworld, or "realm of the dead" (called *she'ol* in
Hebrew), is here, as elsewhere, represented as an insatiable
monster (cf. Hab. 2:5; Prov. 1:12; 27:20; 30:16). She
"will enlarge her appetite," or desire. She is so voracious
that in the process of feeding she grows hungrier. She
opens her mouth unbelievably wide; and down, as out of
mighty bowl from which she is drinking, go all classes of
those now to be found in the seemingly happy city: the
elite, the mobs, also the noisy throng and the "happy souls."
This is not an indiscriminate judgment befalling unsus-
pecting and innocent people because of the drunken excesses of some few. The presupposition is that where such
excessive drinking prevails other equally destructive crimes
prevail on other levels of society, and therefore there has
to be mass-punishment.

Verses 15, 16. This stern judgment of God will have its
effect. This is stated with a free repetition of a sentiment
expressed earlier by Isaiah (2:9, 11, 17): the pride that
made men self-satisfied and dumb to all reproaches and
rebukes will have gone clean out of them. The "plain fellow"
will bow down and "the big fellow" will humble himself,
chiefly because there will be neither high nor low left;
they all will have been pressed down to the lowest level.
A third statement indicates how effectively God's judgment
will have worked: "and the eyes of the haughty are humbled." Only after man's cheap pride will have been cleared
out of the way can there be room for what is destined to be
high and exalted, namely Yahweh of hosts himself. But
his glory shall be revealed "in judgment." This indicates
that the end result of the judgments that he is forced to
bring upon his people will be tokens of glory to them
that look on with deeper discernment. The constructive
objectives of his judgments shall be manifest and actually
shall be achieved — the effective correction of his people.

Then a new understanding of the holiness of the "Holy God" shall come about: "He shall display his holiness by righteousness."

Verse 17. Some have taken this verse to mean that those left in the land after the deportation of the great majority shall live peacefully upon the word of God. It is better to regard this passage as a strictly literal description of the appearance of the land after the judgment has descended. The whole of the land shall be used for the grazing of flocks. It was not really pasture, but that is the only use to which it can be put. That is why sheep shall graze there "as in their pasture." And since the land shall be completely desolate of its inhabitants and be a sort of "no man's land" it is not surprising that "strangers shall feed on the waste places where the rich had been."

A logical sequence in which the Woes of this chapter could be listed is out of the question. They appear in a loose assortment. The next Woe has to do with men who may be described as the willing slaves of sin who at the same time have cultivated a certain defiant attitude toward the Almighty.

5:18-19 18. Woe unto them who draw iniquity with cords of falsehood,
and sin with wagon-ropes;
19. who say: "Let his work come quickly and speed on, that we may see it;
let the plan of the Holy One of Israel draw near and come that we may know it."

Verse 18. This verse has its difficulties of interpretation. We shall not examine every approach. One attempt to make the meaning more readily apparent is to take the word "iniquity" in the sense of "punishment for iniquity," which is a legitimate meaning of the word. Then the passage means that these men bring down their own evil on their heads, having been duly warned. But the figure rather seems to be this: these men have not been enticed unawares into sin; they have rather willingly laid its fetters upon themselves and have made themselves its slaves. Their bonds of enslavement are upon them by their own free choice. Sin has not sought them out; they have sought sin out. Such an attitude seems impossible, but at times such abandonment to sin may actually take place. "Cords of falsehood" is an expression that in this connection almost defies definition. We take it to mean that the force that binds them to their sin is one of total self-deception.

Verse 19. The brazen attitude of these sinners makes them quite defiant of the Lord. Their sentiments here are boldly expressed. They have heard it said that God is at work in the history of his covenant people and is continually achieving his purposes. They have been admonished to reckon with this fact and with God's control of their and the nation's destiny. They have been unable to discover a single trace of God's activity in their day. They hurl their challenge at high heaven: If God is at work let him make it apparent; they want to see that displayed which only the eyes of faith can discern. They want it to be written across the heavens, even as Christ's contemporaries, similarly challenged him to show them a sign. They behave as though the Holy One of Israel had to be at their beck and call. A similar spirit is described in Isa. 28:14ff. Such high-handed dealing with the Exalted Lord of heaven and earth condemns itself for what it is. There is no need of further comment.

5:20-23 20. Woe unto them that call evil good and good evil, who, put darkness for light and light for darkness, who put bitter for sweet and sweet for bitter.
21. Woe unto them that are wise in their own eyes, and prudent in their own sight.
22. Woe unto them who are heroes at drinking wine, and valiant men at mixing drinks.
23. [Woe to them] who acquit the wicked for a bribe, and deny the righteous man his righteous claims.

Verse 20. The authors of moral confusion are taken in hand here. Moral values no longer exist for these men. Clear cut terms such as light and darkness can even be perverted to mean their opposites. As men sink deeper and deeper into sin, moral values become completely clouded, or else they are purposely confused till no absolute moral distinction any longer prevails. *Vilmar* cites a few telling instances how murder has been described as a "sacred duty," or adultery as a "moral necessity," or theft and the seizing of territory as "a divine mission."

Verse 21. Long-drawn-out descriptions of the classes of sinners involved could weary the reader and the hearer. The trenchant incisiveness of this proverb-like Woe is very effective. Conceited men are condemned, who are so sure that they are right and wise and prudent, that they look down upon others. The point at issue is that these men have the quality they claim only "in their own eyes," and "in their own sight." Others are not impressed. They themselves are. The Scriptures frequently take occasion to condemn such a self-satisfied attitude; see 28:9-13; 29:14; 31:1, 2; Jer. 9:23; Prov. 1:7; I Cor. 1:18-25.

Verse 22. The key word appears to be "heroes," a term used to describe men mighty in war. The only distinction however that these army-men have is that they have on occasion out-drunk others and have made a name for themselves by the drinks that they could mix, new formulas, new combinations! If with this second group of drinkers the subject of drunkenness comes to the fore a second time (cf. v. 11) the reason would appear to be that drinking to excess had become one of the most prevalent and damaging sins of the day. The prophets could not treat excesses like these lightly.

On the insertion of a "woe" at this point in the text see the remarks just before v. 8.

Verse 23. Corrupt judges are under consideration. They allow themselves to be bribed, a sin most strongly condemned by the Mosaic law and by many examples of Sacred Writ. Cf. Exod. 23:6-8; Deut. 16:19. It is also a sin that outrages all finer sensibilities: The upholders of righteousness themselves pervert righteousness. In a special sense judges are thought of in the Scriptures as the very men who represent the righteous God on earth and speak and judge in his name. When morals decay courts of justice become perverted. One can almost feel how the prophet's indignation became hotter and hotter as one

Woe after the other was pronounced. One summary condemnation closes the case at this point (v. 24).

(3) The Impending Judgment Brought on by the Assyrians (vv. 24-30)

5:24 24. Therefore as the tongue of fire devours the chaff, and dry hay caught by the flame sinks down,
their root shall be rottenness and their blossom shall go up as dust;
because they have despised the law of Yahweh of hosts,
and have spurned the word of the Holy One of Israel.

Verse 24. Now all the sinners, of whom a rather complete sampling has been taken in the seven Woes just pronounced, are regarded as combustible material ready for the fire of judgment. Being all ripe for the judgment they shall burn quickly and completely like chaff or like dry hay. To make the thought clear that this destruction will be complete, the Hebrew resorts to a device characteristic of the language: Both ends or extremes of an object are mentioned to indicate the entire object. Here the extremes are "root" and "blossom." They shall become rottenness, that is, be utterly dissolved, and vanish completely. But once again in a very effective summary which goes to the very root of the matter, all sins are described as being in essence only one: It has been a wrong attitude toward the Word of the Lord, here first designated as "the Law of Yahweh." When men have the Word of God and refuse to give heed to its precepts then they are rightly said to have "despised" and "spurned" that Word. This is a sin that could not be done by nations outside of Israel. In those days Israel was the only one that had the Word of the Lord for guidance. Therefore having much, much was expected of them by way of better lives and holier conduct. They failed to produce what they should. Therefore their evil fruits would be consumed by fire. This judgment is unfolded a bit more fully in the following verse.

5:25 25. Therefore the anger of the Lord was kindled against His people,
and He stretched forth His hand against them and smote them;

and the mountains quaked and their corpses became like refuse
   in the midst of the streets.
For all that his anger is not turned aside
and his hand is stretched out still.

Verse 25. Already one instance of the flaming forth of
God's anger has occurred: there was a recent earthquake.
Perhaps the one of the days of Uzziah is meant (cf. Amos
1:1; Zech. 14:5). Such letting loose of the forces of nature
was not regarded as nature working autonomously. God's
anger was manifesting itself: He was stretching forth his
hand against his people. He smote them by touching the
mountains and making them quake. The earthquake must
have been unusually disastrous, for dead bodies lay about
like refuse in the streets of the city for some time thereafter.
For Israel of old, the anger of God was a very real thing
and to be viewed with extreme seriousness. But this earthquake was merely the forerunner of other judgments to
come. Therefore, after having fetched one mighty blow
with his all-powerful hand, the Lord is represented as still
standing with hand outstretched to fetch the next blow.
A number of blows followed in this series, for v. 25b becomes a refrain that reappears in 9:12, 21; 11:14.

From this point on the description begins to concern
itself with the instrument that God intends to emply to
further strike his people, vv. 26-30. This is a description
of the armies of the Assyrians. It is true that they are not
mentioned by name in this passage. But in the light of 7:18
and especially 10:5ff. it seems likely that no other enemy
could be meant.

5:26-30 26. And He will raise a signal to a nation afar off,
           and whistle for it from the end of the earth;
and, lo, it will come swiftly, speedily.
27. None is weary among them or stumbles,
none slumbers or sleeps;
the girdle of his loins does not become loose,
nor the thong of his sandal torn.
28. Their arrows are sharp and all their bows bent;
the hoofs of their horses are reckoned as flint,
and their wheels like the whirlwind.

29. He has a roar like that of a lion,
yea, a roar like that of a young lion;
He growls and seizes his prey and carries it off,
and none can rescue.
30. And there will be a roaring over them on that day like
　　the roaring of the sea;
and they will look to the earth but, lo, there will be
　　distressing darkness;
even the light will be darkened by its clouds.

Verse 26. In this brilliant description of the effective Assyrian war-machine strict accuracy can hardly be expected, but at least an abundance of color. The description begins by representing the Lord as himself gathering these forces together. He does it by raising a signal, or ensign, a banner on a high pole raised on the mountain top as a preconcerted signal for the assembling of all forces who see it. Cf. 13:2; 11:10. On the whole Deut. 28:49ff. may be in the background of the writer's thought. The figure of whistling, or hissing, may be the common one that we know for attracting attention, or summoning someone. It appears that bee-keepers did the same thing when they sought to attract a swarm. In either case the meaning is clear. The response of those summoned is very prompt; note the two adverbs "swiftly," "speedily." Further details of assembling the hostile forces are passed by.

Verses 27, 28. Already the army is on the march. Every soldier is at the peak of physical perfection, well fed and in excellent condition: "none is weary among them or stumbles." Always total alertness is the order of the day: "none slumbers or sleeps." We regard the next two lines as most effective if understood to mean that the military equipment of this army is so perfect that not a girdle becomes untied, so as to hamper a man's advance or action, and not a single sandal-thong tears. Such a situation could hardly be literally true. But the description is somewhat idealized. The next statement takes us to the place where they have arrived and join the battle: the bows are already drawn; at the given signal the arrows will fly. During the pause that ensues the writer casts his eye back to the chariot contingent. The horses are such excellent beasts that every hoof is to be counted as hard as flint, and the chariot-wheels themselves seem imbued with the power and speed of the whirlwind.

Verse 29. The battle gets under way. With a fierce shout the warriors throw themselves at the enemy. Their shout is said to have all the terror of the roar of the lion in it, or that of the lusty young lion. Carrying this figure further this king of the beasts, growling, seizes his prey and carries it off — total victory over the foe, Israel — "and none can rescue." Israel has nothing to match this devastating Assyrian strength.

Verse 30. A number of factors make this verse difficult. We shall not attempt to list them but merely to offer an interpretation of the verse that seems to do justice to the original and fit into the total picture. The verb "roar" used in the previous verse is used again, but apparently its subject is the sea, as is expressly stated, though in both cases the verb is rather "growl." In other words, we have the figure of a ship at the mercy of the waves of the sea, a second terrifying experience. The second line of the verse could be paraphrased: No matter where one looks everything is gloom; no hopeful prospect can be discovered anywhere. Look down and you have distressing darkness; look up and the prospect is darkened by the clouds that make up this distress. On this gloomy note the description comes to a close.

Notes

First the question of the arrangement of the material of this chapter. Many are quite sure that vv. 15-17 are out of place. We believe and trust we have indicated that the sequence of material here offered by the prophet is quite coherent as it stands. In like manner it must be regarded as reckless treatment of the text to move vv. 25-30 up after 9:8-21 or else after 10:4. Such conjectural criticism is merely a test of ingenuity that rearrangement can devise.

It should be noted that in v. 14 we have a unique example of the use of the abstract for the concrete, where in every one of the four instances involved we have offered the concrete in the translation: for "its pride" we have: "the elite of the city"; for "its multitude" we have "hermobs"; for "its confusion" we have "the noisy throng"; and for "one happy in her" we suggest "the happy souls in her."

Verse 1. In the Hebraism "a son of oil," "son" is a relation word, and the whole expression means "very fertile." Cf. *KS* 306 h.

Verse 4. Here the verb "was" has to be supplied. *GK* 114 k.

Verse 5. For "I will remove" and "I will break down" the Hebrew uses the absolute infinitive, the most concise form available, thus giving an unusual abruptness to the sentence structure. (cf. *KS* 217 a and 413 d).

Verse 11. The construct state relationship appears at the beginning of the verse followed not by a noun but a phrase. See *GK* 130 a.

Verse 13. The perfect *galah* here is quite obviously a prophetic perfect. *KS* 133.

Verse 17. For "strangers" the Septuagint suggests "kids"; in other words, *gedayim* for *garim*. But "strangers" makes very good sense in this connection. The strangers are the shepherds of the flocks.

Verse 26. It improves the meaning if the singular *goy* is read for *goyim*, assuming that dittography of the *m* has taken place.

In connection with v. 19 it may be noted that *Johannes Fichtner* has a helpful article on "God's Plan in the Message of Isaiah," in *ZATW*, 1951 [Heft ½], p. 16 ff.

Chapter VI

i. The Judgment of Israel as Involved in the Prophet's Original Call (Chap. 6)

In the face of the customary approach to this chapter — that it is the record of Isaiah's commission to his prophetic office — one might hardly dare venture to suggest that the chapter has a primarily different purpose. No one could justly question the fact that the chapter does recount how the prophet was called. But we do question whether this was the chief objective of the entire chapter — merely to tell how this call took place. We at least suggest that this different approach be given some consideration. The chief reason for suggesting a new evaluation is that, to begin with, practically the latter half of the chapter tells of the message he is to deliver and that is only secondarily related to his call as such. Besides if the present arrangement of the book means anything — and we honestly believe it to be the most carefully done — then this chapter ties up well with what preceded, for Chaps. 2-5 dealt with the general theme: Through judgment to salvation, as many writers in the past have suggested. Chapter 6 belongs into this same general approach. It dwells heavily on the judgment that shall fall to the lot of Israel, indicating in fact that this judgment was prominent already in the initial call of Isaiah. That appears to be what *Luther* in his day had in mind when he said: "This chapter contains a vision of the future extinction of the synagogue."

By using this approach we have also in part answered the question that all raise at this point: Why does the chapter, telling of the prophet's call, stand here and not at the beginning of the book, where other prophets are wont to tell how they were commissioned? Yet we are well aware of the fact that many problems about the composition of the early part of the book, especially Chaps. 1–12, remain unsolved. We do well to hold our opinions in reserve as to whether certain earlier groups of utterances once constituted an earlier form of the prophet's written message. Speculation usually nets very few positive results on such questions.

In so far as an account is also given here of how the prophet was called, it must be admitted that this is a most striking record of the event, most dramatic, most instructive, and most impressive. No end of comfort and instruction has flowed forth from the chapter, especially from the first part.

Historically it should be noted that this chapter seems to stand at the turn of a major change in the affairs of the children of Israel. Hitherto, in spite of the division of the kingdom, the people had, by and large, been a relatively prosperous nation, but from the days of King Uzziah on, a tremendous slump in her affairs occurred. Israel fell into a terrific decline. From here on everything tends toward collapse and ruin, which comes slowly but relentlessly. Uzziah's death, so to speak, marked the significant turn. Some have compared the significant juncture marked by the mentioning of Caesar Augustus in the Gospel of Luke (2:1), or of Pontius Pilate in the Creed.

The question whether the chapter be prose or poetry is perhaps best disposed of by taking the position disclosed by the printing of the *RSV*. All found there is prose except v. 3b and vv. 9b-13.

We suggest the following simple outline for the contents of the chapter: vv. 1-3, the prophet's vision; vv. 4-5, his reaction to the vision; vv. 6-7, his absolution; vv. 8-9, his commissioning; vv. 9b-13, his message.

Therefore it will appear that we are leaving certain questions unanswered, questions that are suggestive, but the answers of which are quite problematic and can contribute little to the fruitful interpretation of the chapter. We refer to questions such as these: Did Isa. 6 once stand first in the book? Or, Was it later added at this point because as Isaiah was preaching judgment strongly he wanted to show that he had warrant for treating this unpopular subject as he did? Or, Did Isaiah's call first come sometime after he had been preaching to the nation? Or, Should we rearrange the material of the book in such a way as to give Chap. 6 first place?

(1) The Prophet's Vision (vv. 1-3)

6:1-3 1. In the year that king Uzziah died, I saw the Lord sitting on a high and exalted throne, and the sweeping length of his robe was filling the palace [or, temple].

2. Seraphim stood above him. Each had six wings. With two he kept covering his face; with two he kept covering his feet; and with two he kept flying.

3. And they kept calling to one another and they said:
"Holy, holy, holy is the Lord of hosts;
That which fills the earth constitutes His glory."

Verse 1. Uzziah, the king involved, also goes under the name of Azariah (II Kings 15:1ff., cf. with v. 32). There is scarcely any doubt that this is the one to whom Tiglath-pileser refers by the name of *Azrijau Jaudaa*. He died around 742 B.C. This is the year to which the prophet refers. The prophet is not saying that he had his vision after the king's death. In fact, *Gray* seems to offer fairly strong arguments in support of the other interpretation that the expression means, while this king was still living. So this adverbial phrase of time marks nothing more than a date. It does not contrast the earthly mortal monarch with the immortal One.

When Isaiah says that he "saw" the Lord, he does not describe the manner of his seeing. Whether it was a pure vision, or a dream experience, or some type of seeing with the physical eye, is not revealed. In fact, direct looking upon God with the naked eye seems totally excluded according to Exod. 19:21; 20:19; 33:20; Deut. 18:16; Judg. 13:22; John 1:18. The manner of seeing is not reported for it is of little moment. Enough for us to hear what he did see. And here it should be remarked at once that no description of the appearance of him who sat upon the throne is offered. Perhaps sinful man can so little comprehend what he sees, or perhaps the prophet never ventured to gaze upon the Almighty, being so keenly aware of his own smallness. Still, though nothing in the text directly

points in this direction, according to John 12:41, it was
none other than the Christ who appeared to him. No man
on the Old Testament level ever became aware of this aspect of the Christ. Among the things that the prophet did
recall as seen was the divine throne as one that was "high
and exalted," perhaps like Solomon's with steps (I Kings
10:18ff.; cf. also I Kings 22:19). He also recalled most
distinctly that "the sweeping length of his robe was filling
the temple." We have used a new expression, "sweeping
length of his robe" for what is usually designated as "train."
For train involves the part of the vestment that trailed
after a monarch when he walked. "Skirts" is equally inadequate, being a piece of feminine apparel. In any case,
so imposing was the majesty of him that occupied the throne
that if you regarded so secondary a matter as the sweeping robe, it already filled the available area of the sanctuary
where all this took place.

In identifying the scene involved, interpreters differ
sharply as to whether the earthly temple at Jerusalem is
meant or the heavenly sanctuary. Some major points must
be noted concerning this discussion. Without venturing to
speak with finality, we suggest first of all that in the sanctuary at Jerusalem the type of heavenly, or angelic, being
that was in evidence was the cherubim. See I Sam. 4:4.
Here are only seraphim. Besides there is a *heavenly* sanctuary as the following show: Micah 1:2f.; cf. Ps. 29:9;
18:6, 9; 11:4; I Kings 22:19. That the earthly sanctuary
bore some analogy to the heavenly could be inferred from
Exod. 25:40. Nor can it be argued that since the prophet
saw the foundations of the thresholds shake it must have
been the temple at Jerusalem. He could with equal propriety have observed the same phenomenon in the heavenly sanctuary. But the cherubim vs. seraphim argument
carries the greater weight. Therefore it is precarious to
assert that the entire vision took place as Isaiah was worshipping at the temple in Jerusalem, or even that he, as
prophet, was performing certain cultic functions.

Verse 2. The picture is further filled in. There are seraphim (a Hebrew plural because of the ending *im; KJ*
makes a double plural by adding *s*) present, most likely a

great number of them, if the analogy of other heavenly visions may be thought of. Their name is suggestive of flame-like beings. The rest of their description gives them wings, faces, and feet. Therefore they must have been largely after the human pattern. Their essence, as far as it could be discerned then, may have appeared flame-like. In the context in which they appear it may be most pertinent with *von Orelli* to assert that they are beings that reflect the holiness of God, whereas the cherubim reflect his power and glory. They "stand," or as Num. 14:14 suggests, they "hover above" the Lord. In the original the "above" with the verb "stand" merely implies a readiness to be of service, as Gen. 18:8 indicates. Face and feet are kept covered by these angelic beings. For being only relatively holy they dare not presume to gaze upon the Holy One. Besides, feet are the member of the body that had contact, especially in days of old, with the dust of the earth, and so they became the marks of the less clean. They were, therefore, appropriately covered. If with two of their wings they finally fly, that would seem to indicate that they are equipped to go on divinely assigned missions.

Verse 3. But more than silent adoration marks the behavior of these heavenly ones: they chant a hymn of praise. Apparently it is done antiphonally "to one another," but the song as a whole goes on uninterruptedly. The divine attribute that they especially rejoice in extolling is God's holiness. Perhaps *Skinner* has the clearest and simplest definition of this attribute. He says: "As a predicate of deity it expresses first of all the awful contrast between the divine and the human, and then those positive attributes of God which constitute true divinity. . . ." It is at this point that the overpowering holiness of God becomes apparent to Isaiah. No man before Isaiah had caught the impact of God's holiness quite as clearly as he did. His message frequently reflects this. Isaiah is the one that loves especially to speak of the Holy One of Israel. In that respect he had advanced beyond others of his class.

If the threefold "holy" is here employed, we must take care not to overestimate as well as not to underestimate what this implies. To see here a *revelation* of the Holy

Trinity is more than the words can bear. To regard this merely as a grammatical device to assert the superlative, represents the opposite extreme. Jer. 7:4 and Ezek. 21:27 indicate that there is something in the nature of a superlative achieved by threefold repetition. But it must not be overlooked that enlightened heavenly beings of high angelic rank are using this repetition. For them it may have reflected their insight into the Trinity. In the light of the New Testament we may see this aspect of the truth thus reflected without calling this a proof passage for the Holy Trinity.

God is designated here as the "Lord of hosts," a term which is best defined as describing him as the Lord of the whole host of created things that his own omnipotence has made. He made and still controlled them all in spite of his being holy, that is to say, free of every earthly limitation. Hosea comes nearest to Isaiah in catching the emphasis of divine holiness. See Hos. 11:9.

The second half of the verse is not so readily interpreted. Two major approaches claim attention, the traditional — "The whole earth is full of his glory" — and the one we have rendered above — "That which fills the whole earth constitutes his glory." We are following the latter. It says that the sum total of all created things that man encounters throughout the entire earth, if added together into one word, spells "glory." That these things are so many, are so skillfully adapted to one another, are so well adapted to the needs of God's chief creature, man, and are so remarkable and beautiful in themselves, all adds up to glory. So the seraphic hymn asserts the Lord's holiness but defines his glory, at least indicates what it is that makes this glory evident. The one attribute (holiness) is and must largely remain hidden, being of the very essence of God; the other (glory) is manifest and is designed to be so. Therefore the hymn stresses both the mysterious and the displayed nature of the being of the Lord. We might add a word, traced back to *Oetinger* and *Bengel*: "God's glory is His uncovered holiness, even as His holiness is His inner glory." Apparently it was a matter of deep joy and intense devotion on the part of the seraphim thus to chant the

Lord's praises, a procedure which has become the object of cheap jokes and supercilious frivolity. Yet it may justly be asserted that it belongs to the very essence of blessedness to be enabled and allowed to sing the praises of the Lord of hosts continually.

The expression "that which fills" is a single noun in Hebrew, "the fulness." Num. 14:21 may be compared; also Isa. 11:9 and Hab. 2:14.

No vision quite like this was granted to any prophet to prepare him for the high and holy work of his calling. Equipped with a more adequate knowledge of the Lord, Isaiah could stand his ground and do his work more effectively.

(2) His Reaction to the Vision (vv. 4-5)

6:4-5 4. And the foundations of the thresholds shook at the voice of their calling, and the house was filled with smoke.
5. Then I said: "Woe is me, for I am ruined; for I am a man of unclean lips and dwell in the midst of a people of unclean lips. For my eyes have seen the King, the Lord of hosts."

Verse 4. Now it is, of course, entirely possible that though the vision represented a heavenly scene that the Prophet was allowed to see — whether in the body or out of the body is hard to determine — yet he may have stood on or near the "foundations of the thresholds," and so could observe that the powerful reverberations caused by the mighty song of the seraphim produced vibrations, even as the deep bass of an organ may cause a cathedral to carry noticeable vibrations of the whole structure. The observer is merely trying to show how majestic and powerful this great hymn was, and how impressive. (See *Notes* for further discussion.)

At the same time "the house was filled with smoke." We encounter a fresh difficulty here. The cause and the purpose of the smoke are hard to determine. To equate the Exod. 40:34 and Ezek. 10:4, goes on the unwarranted assumption that since there are instances where a house was filled with a cloud, everything that fills a house must be a cloud, even though it is designated as not being a cloud.

Since neither the origin nor the purpose of the smoke is described, we may cautiously draw inferences. According to v. 6 there is an altar in the heavenly palace. Being in the sanctuary, it would, after the analogy of the Tabernacle, be the altar of incense, having live coals upon it. Incense placed on these coals would cause waves of smoke to arise, a scene commonly witnessed in Israel's sanctuary. So this feature would merely serve to recall that it was for all its novelty still a sanctuary-scene.

Another possibility must at least be entertained. Often smoke, appearing in a theophany, is an index of the wrath of the Almighty (cf. Ps. 18:8; etc.; etc.). So here, since the words of explanation that follow give indication of the wrath of God, this same wrath might proleptically be indicated at this point in the vision; the features therefore noted in this verse added to the awesomeness of the scene that the prophet beheld.

Verse 5. It is not to be wondered at that a cry of alarm at this point breaks from the prophet's lips. He feels that heavy things must befall him. Though we have translated what he feels must happen, or virtually has happened, as "I am ruined," the expression is very hard to render. *RSV* says simply: "I am lost," a strong translation but it lacks the color of the original. *KJ* still seems to have caught the force of it all best with its "I am undone." Being an archaic expression, it appeals less to our day and age. *Luther* did very well with his *Ich vergehe* ("I am dissolved"). According to the root meaning of the word, "cease, cause to cease, destroy" the passive implies being put out of existence, being made utterly to perish. Most likely, had Isaiah here beheld the Lord with the naked eye in the fulness of his dazzling revelation it would have meant the total undoing of the man (cf. Gen. 32:30; Exod. 33:20; Judg. 13:22). He felt that keenly. He even says so when he gives the second of his reasons for this strong feeling of ruin that has come upon him. The first reason, however, indicates that a sense of sinfulness, strong as never before, had flashed upon the prophet's consciousness. He felt a desperate sense of iniquity. In this case it

happened to be concentrated in one area of his consciousness — his lips: they were unclean. What he had till now
acknowledged perhaps in somewhat routine fashion, of a
sudden became an overpowering conviction that burned
to the core of his being. He felt sin as we would feel it if
our insight were not so blurred and dulled. That which
made him conscious of sins of the lips no doubt is correctly
explained as being due to the fact that he had just heard
holy lips sing perfect praise. It flashed upon him in this
connection how deeply stained with sins of the tongue were
his own lips. If at the same time the consciousness finds
expression that he also dwells "in the midst of a people of
unclean lips" that does not even for a moment contain an
element of self-excuse. It rather reflects how tremendous
the amount of sin is that the prophet feels surrounds him —
his own and that of his people. He feels well nigh buried
under the total mass of it all. Incidentally the title given
the Almighty in the last part of the verse sums up the total
aspect of the being of the Lord that filled his thoughts at
the moment. He said that his eyes had seen the "King."
Somehow that should be written into the title of the scene,
if full justice is to be done to it, as *Ewald* in his day had
already pointed out. Summing up, the prophet's reaction
to what he beholds is one of *despair.* At this point he may
have lain on the ground crushed in contrition. The particular designation of the Lord that he uses ("Lord of
hosts") may have been borrowed from the hymn that he
has just heard.

(3) His Absolution (vv. 6-7)

6:6-7 6. Then flew one of the seraphim to me having a live
coal in his hand which he had taken with tongs from
off the altar.
7. And with it he touched my mouth and said: "Lo, this has
touched your lips, and your iniquity will depart and your sin will
be covered."

Verse 6. A kind of sacrament of absolution is involved
in what follows. There is more than the spoken word.
A manual act accompanies the word in order to make the

word, which in a sense is enacted, apply to the total man, body and soul. The angel will hardly have acted on his own initiative. The account suggests strongly that the act performed had divine sanction. To an extent, the seraph acts as a priest functioning at the altar might act. He uses tongs. One of the hot coals, used for strewing incense on it, is removed with tongs. It is carried to the prophet and with it his lips are touched. It is futile to inquire whether there was a searing of human flesh by the contact. We know too little about heavenly visions to know the physics of what there transpires. In any case the symbolism of the act of the seraph is detectable. Burning, cauterizing, signifies purifying. The word spoken, so interprets the act. It may help but little, if at all, to see an analogy between certain Akkadian and Egyptian ritual "mouth purifications" and this act. This act speaks for itself.

Verse 7. The word spoken carefully indicates what will come to pass: iniquity will depart and sin be covered. That the future is used perhaps indicates that the outward act of touching the lips does not convey the benefit involved, it merely symbolizes it. In some manner, known only to God, the act of cleansing will take place. "Iniquity" implies guilt and could be so translated. So both the misdeed and the resultant guilt are taken care of. Though the parallelism used in the statement is poetic as to form, the repetition involved is still apparently of design. Man needs strong reassurance. God's mercy gives him a reinforced statement for his comfort.

We should take issue with the fact that though there is a sort of ritual procedure involved in the absolution, there is no indication of a sacrifice offered. This does not minimize physical sacrifice in the least. But it does point to the truth that the time will come when the need for such outward acts of reassurance with their symbolic import will be left behind. The sacrifices of the Old Testament find their abrogation in the full and perfect sacrifice of Christ. Some things in the Old Testament point in that direction. Some of God's prophets were not ignorant of the *relative* necessity and importance of the cultus.

(4) His Commissioning (vv. 8-9a)

6:8-9a 8. And I heard the voice of the Lord saying: "Whom shall I send and who will go for us?" Then said I: "Here am I; send me."
9a. And He said: "Go and say to this people. . . ."

Verse 8. After the vision, Isaiah is no longer the man that he was. He has undergone a radical change of insight and of attitude. Being absolved and having the burden of guilt taken from off his conscience, he possesses a new freedom and new compelling insights that make him an instrument far more fit for service than he could have been otherwise. He feels this keenly. So much so that when the Lord's question is addressed to no one in particular, but largely in the sense of a call for volunteers who will go in perfect freedom and without a trace of unwholesome compulsion, Isaiah responds with alacrity and with joy, offering himself without reservations of any kind. Then he gets his commission: "Go and say. . . ."

What is involved in the use of the plural pronoun, ". . . go for *us?*" Again a direct and open reference to the Trinity is ruled out, as was already the case in v. 3. Though the triune God is speaking, nothing in the text clearly bears a reference to the three persons of that Trinity. But it is known that on other occasions, God is represented for human understanding after the manner of a monarch of this earth who sits upon a throne and has a royal court in attendance; so here there is the court of heaven, to the existence of which, at least in descriptions offered in Sacred Writ, belong certain attendants, who would obviously be the heavenly angels. See especially I Kings 22:19; Job 1:6ff.; 2:1ff. Without implying that these court attendants have a share in issuing the commission here involved, at least it is a sign of divine condescension that he lets his heavenly attendants be thought of as vitally sharing interest in, and concern for, that which here transpires. So there is more involved than the use of a majestic plural.

It should yet be noted that under the circumstances the brevity of the reply of Isaiah indicates that he clearly felt how small he was in the sight of such a Lord and in the

face of such an office. Modesty impels him to say as little
as possible. Two words in Hebrew cover the answer he
gives.

Verse 9a. Then he gets his commission and his message.
Both are spelled out quite fully and precisely (vv. 9b-13).

(5) His Message (vv. 9b-13)

6:9b-13 9b. "Keep on hearing but do not understand;
Keep on seeing but do not perceive."
10. Make the heart of this people fat; make their ears dull and
besmear their eyes; lest they see with their eyes and hear with
their ears and understand with their hearts and turn and be
healed."
11. And I said, "How long, O Lord?"
And He said:
"Until cities lie in ruins without an inhabitant, and houses without people and the land is left utterly desolate.
12. And the Lord have moved men far away,
and the forsaken places be many in the land.
13. And yet there will be a tenth in it,
but it shall again be burned, like a terebinth or an oak,
whose stump is left when it is cut down.
A holy seed is its stump."

Verse 9b. The first two verses are given in some form or
another by each of the Four Evangelists as having been
used by Jesus to describe the effect of his message on his
contemporaries at a given point in his ministry (cf. Matt.
13:13ff.; Mark 4:12; Luke 8:10; John 12:39ff.). It should
be noted that the first part of this verse contains a reference
to "*this* people." When the demonstrative is thus used, as
has been remarked, this involves a note of "disdain." The
word puts a distance between the people and God. Cf.
Isa. 7:4; 22:15; 23:7. Besides the word is a word of judgment as well as a description of the nation's sin. The
judgment described will come, but only because the people
by their strangely antagonistic attitude have fully deserved
it. The nation's sin came first, not the decision of God to
let this result come to pass. But there are several noteworthy things involved. One is that the word coming from
God to man calls for decision: it must either be accepted
or rejected. When rejected it produces certain effects on

man. He who has said "No" to God is no longer the same person that he was. His refusal has done something to him. To be more precise, God has done something to him. God's judgment already has overtaken the man. There is never anything of a predestination-character involved in what befalls a man. But he that hardens himself stubbornly and repeatedly, as Pharaoh of old did, finds a special kind of judgment reserved for him and this judgment is that, in addition to his hardening of himself, he experiences a further hardening from the hands of God. To understand this a bit more adequately it might be well to give an extended quotation from *Skinner*: "The difficulties created in our minds by this startling and even harsh statement of a great law of the spiritual world, are partly due to the tendency of Scripture writers to refer all things immediately to the will of God. To the Hebrew mind that what we call secondary causes scarcely exist, at least in the sphere of religion." Add to this a very helpful remark of *Fisher's*: "The boundary of God's mercy is marked by his righteousness."

It should be noted well that the reference to this significant word made by Jesus in the New Testament describing what was happening to his hearers in terms of what happened to the hearers of Isaiah, indicates that we have here a momentous and ever-valid truth.

The burden imposed by this principle upon Isaiah was in no sense a light one. It may almost have dismayed the prophet. It opens up a dreary prospect to a man. But so all-decisive is the nature of the hearing of God's truth. We may too often have glamorized the preaching of the message from God. He who faces the truth squarely must reckon with this outcome as a possible and sometimes a relatively frequent one.

Now for the message. As such it is made up of two statements. Though given on the face of it as something that is to be preached to the people, obviously these were not the very words to be spoken. The process that takes place rather than what is to be said, is offered. The effect is stressed. Repeated hearing will not lead to understanding. Repeated seeing will not increase godly perception.

That which will be heard will be messages that God gave Isaiah and he on his part gave to the people. That which will be seen is works of God done prominently in the sight of his people as evidence of his divine providence. In the case of the dull and impenitent hearers neither of the two will make an impact.

Verse 10. After this is offered, as the substance of the message, or rather, as the effect of the message, the commission itself of what the prophet is to accomplish is clearly stated. By way of a strange paradox designed to create an unusual effect, the prophet is commanded what no man would ever set about to do. It is made to sound cruel and heartless and even almost vindictive. But it is totally clear that this cannot be the purpose of this paradoxical assignment. It rather means: This is what will happen but it will happen as a result of your preaching; and you yourself are to be conscious of what is happening. You will make the "heart of this people fat." Since, in Hebrew the heart is the seat of understanding, the activity here described will be that understanding will be lessened. At the same time hearing will be dulled, not made more acute ("make their ears dull"); and insight will be lessened ("besmear their eyes"). What could have produced such favorable results will, due to the hardness of the hearer's heart, produce the very opposite effect.

The second half of the verse is another part of the striking and startling way of stating the issue. "Lest they see with their eyes . . ." really means that God would have this result come about in the case of the impenitent hearer. Man cannot play with God's word. He dare not trifle with it. If he does, it produces a most unwelcome effect, a judgment fully deserved. And so the ultimate result during this state of hardening will be: they cannot and will not "turn and be healed." That is actually God's purpose as long as a man does not submit to the word of the Lord.

Verses 11, 12. But the prophet senses that what has just been stated can never be God's ultimate design with man. It expresses a passing phase of what is calculated to bring man to time, if he is still capable of being brought to time. So Isaiah asks, "How long, O Lord." God's answer amounts to this: Things must get worse before they can get better. God does not retract what he has threatened. Since a nation and not individuals only are involved, nation-wide afflictions must occur: cities must lie in ruins without an inhabitant, houses must stand without people; the land must be left utterly desolate. To round out the picture (v. 12) there comes the strange expression of another result: "and the Lord have moved men far away." That can hardly be intended to mean anything other than a captivity and a deportation. In other words, Israel and Judah must go into captivity. Of course, that would also have as a result that "the forsaken places be many in the land." God's judgment on the impenitent hearers will not be a light one; not one from which the nation quickly recovers.

Verse 13. In fact this difficult verse seems to foresee a nation brought down to the level where only a tenth part of the inhabitants are left in the land. Even that will not be the end of what shall befall. That tenth "shall again be burned." A nation could hardly be brought lower and still be called a nation. The picture used to illustrate this more fully is that of any big tree (terebinth or oak are mentioned as examples) that is left standing on a field otherwise desolate. Then that tree is caught in a fire that sweeps over the field. Then the seemingly dead tree is cut down. The stump that is left is, however, not yet dead. It has a "seed" in it, that is, some trace of life that can yet spring forth in a new shoot. Desolation of the impenitent could hardly be described in terms more strongly indicative of all but total and final desolation. On this note of slight hope, the commission of Isaiah ends. Not a very cheering prospect! Not an inspiring commission!

We shall not try to gloss over the fact that there are grave difficulties involved, especially in the close of this verse. The word rendered "stump" carries that meaning only here. It usually means "pillar" — this being the only passage where the meaning "stump" seems to be required. This alone makes it slightly questionable. But *BDB* does not hesitate to give the second meaning as valid. The radical treatment of the problem, which removes the verse as a later interpolation is not warranted. It further would conclude that when the prophet said: "O Lord, how long?" he was wrong in assuming that there would be some point at which God's judgment would terminate before the end. Besides, interpreting as we have above, we stay in harmony with the doctrine of the "remnant" which prophets have in general (see I Kings 19:18; Amos 3:12) and Isaiah has in particular (cf. Isa. 7:3 — the name of his son — etc.). Nowhere is Isaiah the exponent of utter hopelessness, as he would be if these last three words be removed.

Notes

Verse 1. Additional light may be thrown on the problem of where the vision took place by considering the word for what is commonly translated as "temple" (*heykhal*). This word originally means "palace." Only where the large structure known as the palace of the Lord is definitely meant should it be translated as "temple." It is for this reason that we set the word "palace" in the translation and gave "temple" parenthetically.

Verse 2. The fact that the root *saraph*, is used for serpent (cf. Num. 21:6 ff.) in no wise necessitates that this meaning of the root must apply in this instance in v. 2. Oftentimes one and the same root is known to bear two or more basic meanings. It would be derogatory to these angelic beings to suppose serpent-like qualities as manifested by them. Since the same root means "to burn" something more like "fiery ones" would be far more appropriate.

Verse 3. Since *weqara'* is a converted perfect, following the imperfects of the previous verse, the iterative idea of the imperfect dominates the whole picture: they kept covering themselves with their wings; they kept flying; they kept calling. Each of these activities was continually to be observed by the onlooker.

Verse 4. The translation, "the foundations of the threshold," is perhaps the most satisfactory. The Greek translators thought in terms of the lintel above the door. The word here translated "foundations" is used here in an unusual sense. Perhaps: "sill."

Verse 5. The construct relationship is found in the expression literally, "unclean of lips." Cf. *KS* 336 h.

Verse 6. *Ritzpah* is rightly translated by *RSV* as "hot coal," in spite of the insistence of many that it should be a "red-hot stone." The latter [rétseph] is first of all a different form and at the same time something that appeared on the hearth for baking purposes, whereas an altar is not used for baking purposes.

Verse 10. For "lest they see. . . ." The Hebrew has the singular form of the verb, being the verb form that often indicates the indefinite subject ("one") and may thus very appropriately be translated as a plural. Cf. *KS* 324 d.

Verse 11. "Desolate" is really a noun which is used as an accusative of effect, the noun *shemamah* (*KS* 113).

Verse 13. In the expression "shall again be burned," the "again" is covered by the unique idiomatic use of the verb *shubb* ("return and be burned" which equals: "again burned"). See *GK* 120 d.

Excursus

The reader may feel that the above treatment of the hardening of Israel has left certain aspects of the case too much out of consideration. We grant that. Some instances of the more recent treatment of this subject should at least be presented for their suggestiveness. We refer, by way of example, to *Hesse's* treatment of the subject in the *Beiheft* of *ZATW*, 1955, "*Das Verstock-ungsproblem im Alten Testament*" as well as to *von Rad's* analogous treatment of Isaiah's call in his *Theologie des Alten Testaments*, Vol. 2, p. 162 ff.

Our treatment above has made the problem appear less acute. It inserted two things that clearly do not appear in the text. First of all the possibility that Israel's judgment of hardening came about as a logical result of her having been disobedient and inattentive to the divine word that the Lord sent by his prophets; and secondly that the hardening is something that God causes, not man. At least the divine causality is the only side of the issue that the prophet brings to the fore in this chapter. Other prophets did avail themselves of the approach that we use. Isaiah doubtlessly does stress the divine causality of what happens to man or to the nation to the exclusion of the measure of guilt that man may have previously accumulated.

So these writers emphasize that we are here dealing with a "theological dilemma." Israel dashes to its ruin in its collision with God, the very God who chose Israel and made the nation his own people. The God who elected Israel is the God who hardens Israel. How can this be? The prophet poses a riddle which he does not solve for his hearers. Besides, the hardening referred to comes not *at* the conclusion of, nor *as* the conclusion of, this prophet's ministry, but at its very beginning, at the time when the prophet receives his initial commission.

Another way out of the dilemma in which the prophet's account puts us theologically is by taking recourse to the doctrine also developed by Isaiah, the doctrine of the "remnant." (Our treatment above works this element into the picture.) For though the prophet seems to present the hardening as final, he still gives some indications of hope, as in the concluding words of this chapter. The hardening will be followed by the inevitable judgment. This judgment will cause a small remnant to turn from their evil ways and so be saved in spite of everything.

But a certain measure of the mysterious factor of divine causality remains, no matter how you approach the subject of the hardening of Israel, which the prophet presents as an inevitable doom.

So the God of Israel and his work cannot easily be put into categories that man has developed for purposes of theological classification.

Chapter VII

B. THE IMMANUEL BOOK (Chaps. 7–12)

1. The Immanuel Sign (Chap. 7)

A brief historical sketch of the situation that prevailed in the days of Ahaz, king of Judah, must be presented first of all. The entire situation was extremely complicated. In the days of Jotham, father of Ahaz, the Northern Kingdom, Israel, had become subject to Assyria. But both Israel and Syria attempted to revolt from Assyria in 735 B.C. At that time Egypt seems to have been making a bid for power, as words of Hosea might seem to indicate (7:11; 8:13; 9:3, 6; 11:5, 11; 12:1). Judah managed to keep from getting involved, for Uzziah, the father of Jotham, had been rather strong (II Chron. 26:5ff.). Jotham then continued his father's policy of independence, but nevertheless became involved when Israel and Syria attacked him (II Kings 15:37). But this attack apparently was motivated by trying to compel Jotham to join an alliance against the Assyrians. Somehow this attack is not fully reported. In the meantime Jotham dies and Ahaz comes to the throne (735-715).

It may be that the major defeat, which Chronicles alone reports (II Chron. 28), was the outcome of the attack which got under way in Jotham's day. Judah is said to have suffered the loss of 120,000 men — no doubt an exaggerated figure. Women and children in still greater numbers (again an exaggerated figure! exaggerated by copyists, no doubt) having first been taken captive to Samaria, were released at the behest of the prophet Oded. So the defeat did not become as disastrous as it might have. But Syria, according to II Kings 16:6, went farther south and captured Elath, but turned the captured port over to the Edomites, who about that time staged a separate minor assault upon

Judah (II Chron. 28:17). Even the Philistines ventured
to attack Judah (v. 18).

In the midst of these complicated developments the Assyrian threat seems suddenly to have loomed large on the
horizon again, prompting Rezin, king of Syria, and Pekah,
king of Israel to make strenuous efforts at a major anti-
Assyrian coalition, drawing in Judah, if possible. Since
Ahaz refused to join, the two kings to the north prepared
to compel Judah's cooperation. When Isa. 7 opens, Syria
had already come down to Israel and its armies were encamped on Israel's soil, some three days' march from the
territory of Judah. Perhaps certain misdeeds that Ahaz
became guilty of had not yet occurred: for example, his
worship of Moloch (II Kings 16:3) may not have become
a reality as yet, for Isaiah still calls the Lord, Ahaz' God
(Isa. 7:11). Perhaps, also, the attempt to enlist the aid of
Syrian gods had not yet happened (II Chron. 28:23). But
somewhere in this juncture Ahaz officially summoned Tiglath-pileser to come to his aid, presumably after the events
of Isa. 7 (cf. II Kings 16:7). But somewhere shortly after
this the incident occurred where Ahaz had a copy made
of an Assyrian field-altar that Tiglath-pileser had erected
at Damascus, and set up in the temple area at Jerusalem.

By and large, Ahaz was weak and unduly impressed
with the might of Assyria. He had little, if any, faith in
Yahweh. As king of Judah he falls far short of the ideal.

To show how rapidly things developed after this — Tiglath-pileser, summoned by Ahaz, appeared on the scene in
734, destroyed the coalition Rezin-Pekah, went farther south
and punished Philistia, especially Gaza, and penetrated
even to the borders of Egypt. Then he struck again in 733,
thoroughly devastating Galilee and Transjordan. In the
meantime Pekah was murdered by Hoshea, who succeeded
him (II Kings 15:30) and shortly after that (732) Damascus was ravaged — all of which goes to show how utterly
the picture changed within a short space of time, just as
Isaiah said it would in this chapter.

So this section (chaps. 7–12) may be thought of as
playing in the days of Ahaz, king of Judah.

The chapter may be outlined as follows:
a. The Incident at the Upper Pool (vv. 1-9)
b. The Sequel to That Incident, the Word Concerning Immanuel (vv. 10-17)
c. The Further Sequel, the Predicted Devastation of the Land (vv. 18-25)

a. The Incident at the Upper Pool (vv. 1-9)

7:1-9 1. And it came to pass in the days of Ahaz, the son of Jotham, the son of Uzziah, king of Judah, there came up to Jerusalem, Rezin, the king of Syria, and Pekah, the son of Remaliah, king of Israel, to make war against it; but they could not effectively make war against it.

2. When it was told to the house of David, "Syria has encamped on Ephraimite territory," his heart and the heart of his people shook, as the trees of the forest shake before the wind.

3. Then Yahweh said to Isaiah: "Go forth now to meet Ahaz, you and your son Shear Jashub, to the end of the aqueduct of the Upper Pool, to the highway of the Fuller's Field, 4. and you shall say to him: 'Watch yourself and keep calm! Do not be afraid, neither let your heart be faint at two such smoking stumps of firebrands, at the fierce anger of Rezin and Syria and the son of Remaliah. 5. Just because Syria also Ephraim and the son of Remaliah have devised evil against you, saying, 6. "Let us go up against Judah and fill it with fear and split it wide open for ourselves and set up as king in the midst of it the son of Tabeal"; 7. thus says the Lord Yahweh:

"It shall not stand;
and it shall not come to pass.
8. But the head of Syria is Damascus,
and the head of Damascus is Rezin,
and within sixty-five years Ephraim shall be broken
so as to be a people no more.
9. And the head of Ephraim is Samaria,
and the head of Samaria is the son of Remaliah.
If you will not believe,
you will not endure." ' "

Verse 1. If the Chaps. 2–5 may be dated as belonging into the reign of Jotham, it becomes clear at v. 1 of this chapter that we find ourselves in the days of Ahaz. The conspiracy or coalition between Syria and Ephraim and its purpose is briefly described. Two nations were pitted against one, against little Judah, which had recently suf-

fered extensive territorial losses. (See the opening words
under this chapter for a fuller presentation of the historical
situation.) This opening verse appears almost word for
word in II Kings 16:5. Perhaps it will never be clearly
determined whether Isaiah is quoting from the book of
Kings, or vice versa, or whether both are drawing on a
third source (cf. II Chron. 32:32). This initial statement
is essential for getting the historical situation involved in
the clear. We have translated the last statement of the
verse: "but they could not effectively make war against it,"
even though the verb simply says "make war." Apparently
however it is meant in the sense of our translation. However, in typical Hebrew narrative, the situation and the
outcome are given, headline-fashion, and the reader already
knows before he reads on, what to expect. Now follow the
details.

Verse 2. We are taken to that point of time where the
bad news came to Judah that the Syrians together with
Israel, were already close at hand for the invasion of the
territory of Judah. When it is stated that this news came
to "the house of David," a term which would seem to apply
to the entire royal court, this may be construed to mean
that the court just happened to be convened when the
messenger arrived. As a result the king did not learn of this
threat first, but the entire royal court heard the tidings
together. It seems better to construe the verb that carried
the burden of the message as meaning: Syria "has encamped," literally "rests upon," Ephraim. This could mean:
"is confederate with Ephraim" (*KJ*), or as modern English
has it: "is in league with Ephraim" (*RSV*). But the verb
involved more likely is taken in the purely physical sense
of: "is encamped on Ephraimite territory." In effect this
meant: the combined forces of the enemy are only about
three days' journey away.

Judah's reaction to this ominous news is graphically described as being: "his heart and the heart of his people
shook, as the trees of the forest shake before the wind."
The singular pronoun ("his") in this case singles out the
king in contrast to the people, though he had not previously
been mentioned. The figure used, dramatically described

a panic. And well might Judah be thoroughly afraid. Each one of the two combined enemies alone was no doubt stronger than Judah at the time.

Verse 3. Into this situation the word of Yahweh came to Isaiah. It should not be thought unnatural that the prophet should here refer to himself in the third person. Writers of old frequently used the same pattern — Xenophon, Caesar, even Josephus. It seems to be implied that Isaiah already knew what sort of message had been received at Ahaz' court. The king was out, perhaps at the city walls, examining in anticipation of an attack a crucial point in the water supply of what was about to become a besieged city (cf. 22:9). The same spot is mentioned in another connection in 36:2. We seem to be unable to determine exactly where this aqueduct lay, whether to the north or to the south, or whether it may in any way be identified with the Siloam aqueduct. In any case, Isaiah's orders ran to the effect that he was to go forth and personally encounter the king, taking with him his son Shearjashub, a lad of some three years at the time. The Fuller's Field, also unidentified, may have gotten its name from the field where men engaged in bleaching clothes spread out for drying.

If the name of the child is given because the father was to take the lad along at divine command, the significance of the name must be meaningful in this connection. In Hebrew it signifies "a remnant shall return." Two thoughts are contained in that brief statement. The name is either a threat to the effect that *only* a remnant shall return, or survive; or it can imply that a remnant *shall* return, and so it involves a promise. Ahaz must have known the child's name, otherwise this procedure would have to be stamped as meaningless. But by the side of Shearjashub stood Isaiah, with a name equally meaningful: the salvation of the Lord, or the Lord is salvation. The entire cue to the course to be taken plus an indication of the outcome was mapped out in this significant name. This encounter was suggesting to Ahaz to let the Lord be his salvation and then at least a remnant would survive.

Verse 4. Now comes the message to the king, as given verbatim to the prophet. It runs to the end of v. 9. It deals first of all with the problem of the general attitude to take in this emergency. "Watch yourself" implied that careful and cautious procedure was imperative. Nothing was to be done rashly on impulse or out of panic. "Keep calm" suggested that the emergency was not so extreme as to cause anyone to lose his head. The third imperative practically demanded that fear was to be banished — "'Do not be afraid, neither let your heart be faint." We seem to hear echoes of Josh. 1:6. Half contemptuously a description of the two leading adversaries is given — "two such smoking stumps of firebrands." The point is that two *flaming* firebrands could indeed kindle a dangerous conflagration. These two brands are already *extinguished*. Some volume of smoke may still emanate from them, but they can do no damage.

The precise meaning of the use of the figure of firebrands appears from the apposition employed in this word. This apposition is "fierce anger of Rezin," for anger is in all languages likened to a fire that burns hot. But even then this anger is described as having practically burned itself out. There is no confusion involved, as some claim in that first *two* firebrands are mentioned, and then *three* individual names — Rezin, Syria and the son of Remaliah (i.e. Pekah, the regicide, whom this word does not deign to mention by name). On the contrary, on closer inspection the meaningfulness of this careful enumeration of three makes very good sense. Rezin and his nation, Syria, may well have felt a common anger at Judah's refusal to join their alliance against the Assyrians. Pekah may have felt equally angry. But Pekah's people are not included, as were Rezin's. This is due to the fact that very likely at the time the northern nation did not feel angry at the southern, Judah. Israel and Judah often felt themselves to be brothers, in spite of occasional clashes.

Verse 5. If then in v. 5, Ephraim *is* mentioned, it should be noted that another verb is employed. Verse 4 indicated that Ephraim had no anger against Judah on this occasion. Verse 5 shows that Ephraim did, however, plan evil against the brother nation. This careful analysis of the situation should be evaluated, not just rejected because of a seeming disparity of numbers. Grammatically it should be noted that v. 5 is the protasis of a longer statement whose apodosis appears in v. 7.

Verse 6. Now is presented the battle plan as these two confederate northern nations had formulated it. The first objective of the campaign was to fill Judah with fear and apprehension. Something in the nature of a war of nerves could be said to be involved. This phase of the struggle apparently was already working, as v. 3 showed: Judah was terribly afraid. The second objective was "to split it wide open." The verb is strong. It involves the idea of cleaving an object apart, and then that which remains is to be partitioned between the two assailants. The third step of the plan is to set up a puppet king, whom they already have in readiness for the occasion. His name is not given, only that of his father, because only the latter lends itself to an effective play on words. For though it is acknowledged that Tabeel could be a good Syrian name, Tabeal means about as much as "Good-for-nothing." That is all the puppet king amounted to in the eyes of the Prophet. This pun, however, was possible only by using the slightly altered form of the name.

Verses 7, 8. Now comes the Lord's verdict and the true conclusion of the matter. And since the word offered is of such great importance it is cast in a poetic form easily remembered by virtue of the clever balance of statements. First comes the double statement to the effect that the plan as such will fail (not stand, not come to pass). This passes sentence on the entire project. Something quite other and something quite obvious is the true situation as here depicted (v. 8). The adversative "but" indicates this. This statement of the obvious geographical and governmental relationship seems to require a slight adverbial modification to give its exact weight. For "the head of Syria is Damascus" is meant in the sense of "the head of Syria *only*, is Damascus." She may aspire to be the head of Judah also. That is destined not to be the case. In exactly the same fashion the next statement has the force of "the head of Damascus *only*, is Rezin." He may aspire to be more. It shall not come to pass.

At this point, with a perfectly logical sequence at least, the writer might have continued with the same pattern and offered the first half of v. 9. But just because that could logically have been done, and some present-day writers would have been inclined to present the matter thus, does not yet prove the present sequence of clauses wrong or out of order, or v. 8c to be a later addition to the text. With equal propriety it may be claimed that the statement, v. 8c: "and within sixty-five years . . ." makes very good sense where it now stands. For already here the total collapse of the second partner to the dreaded coalition is indicated. Ephraim, is shown to have a very limited future, and in fact shall be completely out of the picture. Sixty-five years are the utmost limit of existence that Ephraim dare hope for.

At first glance the figure seems altogether too large. If the date of the incident (v. 1) be about 735 B.C. and Samaria fell is 721, should not the period of fourteen years be here mentioned? Sixty-five years would bring us down to 670, when Esarhaddon was the Assyrian king. Of him, however, it is said that he brought colonists to Samaria to replace the last group that had been removed; and this step was really the one that spelled the total end of the national existence of Ephraim (cf. II Kings 17:24ff.; Ezra 4:2, 10). So the statement — v. 8c — is both correct in itself and very much in place at this point. All it does is that it interrupts the sequence that *we* might have expected. But then the next verse (9) falls back into the pattern that had marked v. 8. It is only that the doom-passage about Ephraim comes before the statement of the obvious limitations that are laid upon Samaria and Pekah.

Verse 9. In line with what was indicated in reference to v. 8, we must now read v. 9 in the sense of: "the head of Ephraim *only*, is Samaria"; also: "the head of Samaria *only*, is the son of Remaliah." The nation and its capital may have ambitions to annex Judah and be its head and also dominate Jerusalem. In the book of destiny of God this is not provided for and cannot be.

At this point there is the possibility that a sort of inference might have been intended. Some would add as such an inference: "the head of Jerusalem is Yahweh." However this is so significant a thought, towering so much above the level of the argumentation of v. 8, that it would have to be expressed and could not merely be implied. The prophet could have made an effective argument along the line suggested. Apparently he did not. We should hold back from such a bold inference.

The actual climax of this particular word of the Lord is plainly offered in the text: "If you will not believe, you will not endure." The emphasis for the present does not lie on the predetermined counsel and will of God in reference to the place nations and capitals of nations shall occupy. Emphasis lies on the personal attitude of faith that men shall take. Man has his free position to take, be the divine destiny of nations what it will. If he fails to take the proper attitude, he has no share in the good things that may develop. This attitude is one of clear, unwavering trust in Yahweh, who in this case is addressing this very challenge to Ahaz. He and his people will endure if they continue in faith. They shall go under if they fail to do so.

Men rightly make much of the basic importance of faith that is here so clearly set forth. *Procksch* goes so far as to claim that this insight at this point illuminated the inner consciousness of the prophet like a flash of lightning and he broke forth into a challenging utterance. Other words prepare the way for this key-word. They have the same interpretation of faith, that it is a basic trust that leans wholly on the Lord; that in essence it is trust and confidence. These earlier words are, for example: Gen. 15:6; Isa. 28:16; 30:15; Hab. 2:4; II Chron. 20:20. But this utterance of Isaiah surpasses them all for clarity and effective statement. To call this the "birth hour of faith" (*Bewer*) overlooks that Gen. 15:6 already expresses a similar purpose of faith as involved in the life of Abraham. —But summing up, the nation's destiny is tied up with her readiness to believe. If she and her king believe, they have a future. If not, their doom is sealed. For effective statement this word resorts to a play on one and the same word used in two different stems. No one came closer to reproducing the paronomasia involved than *Luther*, with his famous: *Glaubt ihr nicht, so bleibt ihr nicht.* Other efforts have produced the following: "If you will not be sure, you cannot be secure" or: "If you will not affirm you will not be confirmed"; or, "If ye have not faith ye cannot have staith." It must be admitted that the issue had been made clear for Ahaz and had been formulated in such a way that he could not evade it.

b. The Sequel to That Incident, the Word Concerning Immanuel (vv. 10-17)

7:10-17 10. Once more Yahweh spoke to Ahaz, saying: 11. "Ask a sign for yourself from Yahweh your God; go as low as you please; go as high as you please." 12. And Ahaz said: "I will not ask, so as not to put Yahweh to the test." 13. So he said: "Hear now, O house of David. Isn't it enough for you to weary men? Must you weary my God also? 14. Therefore the Lord Himself will give you a sign: Behold, a virgin shall conceive and bear a son, and shall call his name Immanuel [God is with us]. 15. Curds and honey shall be his food when he knows enough to reject the bad and to choose the good. 16. For before the lad knows enough to reject the bad and to choose the good, that area before whose two kings you tremble, will be forsaken. 17. Yahweh will bring upon you and upon your nation and upon your father's house such days as have not come since the time Ephraim seceded from Judah — the king of Syria."

Verses 10, 11. At this point it may well be asked whether this section (vv. 10-17) followed immediately upon the one that precedes. The connection between this section and the one that precedes is very close. At least a brief pause must have occurred after v. 9. But to demand that from v. 10 on, the incident involved must have taken place in the king's palace and no longer by the conduit of the upper pool, seems to fail to see that v. 9 in particular had made such an issue of faith, that the words that give that faith something to build on, are a necessity almost at once. When it is said that "Yahweh spoke," it is rather obvious that it is implied that this speaking took place through the prophet. It is equally obvious that v. 9 had asked something of the king that called for a much stronger faith than Ahaz had.

The demand on Ahaz was virtually exorbitant. Considering the weakness of Ahaz' faith, none recognized that more clearly than Yahweh himself. Therefore, not to ask more than Ahaz could bear, the Lord very graciously allows the king to ask for a sign to provide for himself some ground on which to build. This sign should be asked from Yahweh himself. By calling him "your God" it is admitted that the king still stands in some sort of special relation to God. Ahaz had not as yet openly or virtually denied the God of his father David. The sign to be asked for could appear in one of two areas: either down on earth or up in the skies. The king is even granted the liberty of penetrating as deeply as he wished in either of these two areas. Down on earth he may, if he so desires, penetrate into the area of Sheol, the underworld, or the hereafter. Under this head one might think of the sign granted to King Saul when Samuel reappeared from the realm of the dead (I Sam. 28:11ff.). On the other hand a striking sign way up in the skies would be allowed. In that area there might be signs in the sun, moon, or stars, eclipses, and the like. We have sought especially to catch the wide latitude given by the divine permission by translating: "Go as low as you please; go as high as you please."

Verses 12, 13. The answer of Ahaz is most disappointing from every point of view. He claims he is afraid to put the Lord to the test in an unseemly way. He seems to have a word like Deut. 6:16 in mind, where putting God to the test is forbidden. But, as has long been pointed out, when *God* proposes a sign, man is not putting God to the test. For it is quite obvious that certain religious scruples are not what restrains Ahaz. The point at issue is that Ahaz would be under necessity of believing if the sign asked came to pass, and Ahaz does not want to be under necessity of believing, strange as that may sound. He has a course of his own plotted. If the sign happens, this course must be abandoned. The pious sound of his answer masks a very stubborn unbelief.

So the prophet's answer comes promptly and with emphasis (v. 13), cutting through all sham and pretense. The king's vacillation and inability to take a wholesome attitude already weary all right-thinking men in Judah. The prophet indicates that they are a severe trial of God himself. At this point Isaiah's protest indicates that this refusal of Ahaz has severed the last bond that still tied him to the God of his fathers, by telling him that God is no longer the God of Ahaz. In v. 10 Isaiah had still called Yahweh Ahaz' God; now he says: "You weary *my* God also," not *your* God. The word appears to have been spoken with some vehemence and with a justifiable measure of impatience.

Verse 14. Now Isaiah asserts that the sign that God would have given will take a particular form and will be given in spite of the refusal of Ahaz. There is a note of threat for Ahaz involved under the circumstances, though the overall import of the sign is beneficent. Apparently Ahaz's punishment consisted chiefly in that he never saw any light as to the meaning of the sign Yahweh threatened to give. However, it should be noted at once that the term "sign" does not necessarily involve some striking miracle. The sight of a babe "wrapped in swaddling clothes" was a "sign" for the shepherds by way of identification. Aside from that, nothing miraculous appeared to them nor was it expected. So also in I Sam. 10 Saul is promised a "sign." But only three commonplace things happen; but that they come to pass as predicted by Samuel does constitute a sign. The sign is that "a virgin shall conceive and bear a son and shall call his name Immanuel." Almost every term in this pronouncement calls for investigation. Are we justified in still using the term "virgin" here, where *RSV* uses "young woman," in line with the claim of many commentators in our day?

It should be noted at once that the *RSV*, by putting the translation "virgin" in the margin, at least conceded that it is a possible translation, deserving to be noted. In the Hebrew the word used is *'almah*. The root meaning of this word points in the direction of "young woman," i.e., such a young woman as is of marriageable age. However *usage* must also be carefully considered in determining the meaning of words. In Biblical usage, the word, clearly referring to young persons, appears six times. We pass by those instances where the plural is used in a technical term in the heading of psalms. We do not know exactly what the term signifies in that connection. But in a passage like Gen. 24:43, in reference to Rebekah, the whole context implies that the girl in question is a virgin. The same is true of Exod. 2:8 in the case of Miriam, Moses' young sister. Ps. 68:25 obviously has reference to women of honorable repute who are worthy to appear in solemn religious processions at the sanctuary. The use of the term in the Song of Solomon, in 1:3, certainly does not imply questionable reputation; the young lady is worthy to be desired by Solomon. In the same book in the passage 6:8, the word is used in reference to such as stand over against both queens and concubines. So virginity is implied. Finally, though all kinds of constructions have been put on the expression "the way of a man with a maiden" (Prov. 30:19f.), it should not be overlooked that immediately the contrasting conduct of the adulteress is noted in v. 30. This contrast puts the "maiden" in the category of the unblemished. Adding up the results of this investigation we conclude that *'almah* in Hebrew signifies a marriageable young lady of unblemished reputation. It cannot be denied that such a one is to be classified as a virgin.

One should not however close one's eyes to the fact that the specific term that connotes strict virginity in Hebrew is, as has often been pointed out, *bethulah*. Since this term is not here employed it follows that the passage in question does not lay the major emphasis on virginity, but upon the fact that the person in question is physically capable of producing children. The secondary emphasis lies on the concept of virginity nevertheless. Noteworthy also is the fact that the earliest translation of the Old Testament that we possess, the Septuagint done in Greek, uses the regular Greek word for a virgin, *parthenos*. If the evangelist Matthew builds on this fact and adduces this passage in partial support of the virgin birth, it must be said that he has caught a valid emphasis that lies in this passage. The translation "virgin," therefore, deserves to be moved out of the margin and into the text; and the translation "young woman" merits no more than marginal status.

This leaves us faced with the question of the identity of the virgin spoken of. Possibilities without number crowd upon us if we consult commentators: a queen of King Ahaz, the wife of Isaiah, some princess at court, a generic use of the term implying that many mothers will designate their children by the name Immanuel in this period, even an ideal child, not a real one, etc. The major difficulty happens to be that a contemporary person is almost demanded by the very situation involved. Yet no such a one can be pointed to with any measure of assurance. At the same time a contemporary *child* seems to be inexorably demanded by the passage. Where shall we turn in this bewildering array of conflicting possibilities?

We suggest two approaches as contributing to the understanding of the passage. First of all, in this passage the major purpose of the appearance of the child involved is to serve as a measure of time, a sort of chronometer. In fact, it should be continually borne in mind that v. 15ff. is part of the pronouncement that the prophet is making. So the child is essential from this point of view. Before the child has achieved years of discretion, the total picture confronting the king and the nation will have changed. The child, however, is so real to the prophet that he actually measures the lapse of the next few years by the child's time of birth. That is then the part of the prophecy on which we have comparatively little difficulty. And that was the immediate relevance of the passage. The facts predicted actually came to pass, and in very short order.

The next important factor to be borne in mind is that in prophetic words of prediction there are known to have been delays. Where a certain development was definitely expected, the situation changed and either the good promised or the evil threatened was for the time being deferred. Such deferring may have come about as a result of a change of attitude of the persons involved. In Jonah's day

Nineveh was given a period of forty days' grace. Still the punishment so definitely threatened was put off for years. It is true that we do not have definite knowledge what it was that could have caused a postponement of a part of this word (the birth of the child) in this instance. We may even use the approach that it might at that time have been possible in the wisdom of God to let the promised Savior appear in the days of Ahaz. Again we say we are now quite unable to determine what happened to change this possible plan. But changed it was. The rest of the word was accurately fulfilled. In some way, which is perhaps providential, the fact is stressed that the one who gives the child its name is the mother, a procedure which was occasionally followed, but appears to have been the exception.

The fact that the child shall deserve to be called *Immanuel* does not necessarily imply that the child is divine, though Immanuel means "God with us." Even as the names of the other children of Isaiah (Shearjashub and Maher-shalal-hashhaz) reflect facts then important, so this name could merely stress that in the prevailing emergency God would not forsake his people. Yet the other possibility must be cheerfully conceded, namely this, that in his own person this child could embody this truth. He himself would be, God among his people. It is impossible to say with any certainty in which direction the word points.

No explanation of v. 14 will ever be *entirely* satisfactory. The best a commentator can hope to achieve at this point is to relieve some of the difficulties that the reader encounters. But that the child plays an important role in the thinking of the prophet nevertheless is apparent from the fact that the child Immanuel appears again, twice, in the next chapter (8:8, 10 — though in v. 10 the name is *translated* — "God is with us"). Again a mysterious and important child has to be reckoned with in 9:6 as well as in 11:1. In the latter two instances by almost common consent, the implication is indubitably Messianic. By inference the same must be the case here in the first mention of the child. Therefore the child repeatedly referred to is always this same child, which is here called Immanuel. It is for this reason that the title "Immanuel Book" is apt for Chaps. 7–12.

Verses 15, 16. In approaching this verse we should note that the major issue is whether "curds and honey" represent an abundance of food or a scarcity of it. They that advocate the idea of abundance try to show that the expression is to be interpreted in line with the famous description of the Land of Promise, "a land flowing with milk and honey." But necessity compels us to admit that the expression is a different one. So also is its use. In fact these verses dare not be separated from the passage 20ff. toward the close of the chapter. The same situation prevails there and here. In fact in our verse, "curds and honey" are mentioned specifically as all that a man will have to eat. The expression is meant in the sense of *"nothing but* curds and honey." That means no cereal food, no bread, no meat, no vegetables that are raised in fields and gardens. A bare minimum of two articles of diet on which he can keep alive, but hardly more than that. And this diet shall be that of this child at the time "when he knows enough to reject the bad and to choose the good."

Here again two issues lie open before us. Either this means the child has come to years of *ethical* discernment, or to years of *physical* discrimination between the good and the bad. In other words, either the words point to about fifteen years, or to about three years. Apparently the latter of the two choices has to be made. For a comparatively short space of time is under consideration. The point being made is that in a surprisingly short time, first of all, the physical situation in the land of Judah itself will have changed so completely that population will be sparse and food will be scarce. That the terms "evil and good" may refer to physical discrimination between what is good and bad for the child will be demonstrated later. In fact (v. 16) the point that is being made is, *before* the child can distinguish between what is good and what is bad for it, the land of the two confederate kings of v. 1, Rezin and Pekah, shall be forsaken, that is, largely depopulated. The big threat that Syria and Israel posed against Judah will have collapsed completely. Instead of being objects of fear, these lands will be objects of pity.

Verse 17. This situation is now more accurately described as being, first of all, one that does not come about by some concatenation of natural causes, but as brought on by Yahweh himself. It is next told the king that he himself shall have to share in this hard lot; so shall his people; so shall the entire royal house, whose princes and princesses might often be expected to be exempt from hardships that afflict the common run of the inhabitants. The affliction that is anticipated is described as "such days as have not come since the time Ephraim seceded from Judah." As to dates, that involves all the time from the famous division of the nation in the days of Rehoboam — 933 B.C. — until the present — 735 — a space of about two centuries. The situation must have been much more grievous than we are usually led to expect at the time of the division. It shall be equally bad in short order (cf. II Kings 15:29; 16:9). Now comes the dangling apposition — "the king of Assyria." This is supposed to be an obvious addition to the text by a later hand, because it somewhat mars the smooth flow of the thought. But, for that matter, appositions often do just that. Is lack of smoothness of style a criterion of later and spurious additions? Are we sure that explanatory appositions lie outside of the scope of the prophetic style of Isaiah? All such norms of judgment are so purely subjective as to lie outside of the sphere of what can be demonstrated. We see good reason for considering the expression to stem from Isaiah's pen, and to hold that it strikes in with "penetrating force" (*mit durchbohrender Gewalt* — *Delitzsch*). What makes the expression so particularly emphatic is that it was the very king of Assyria on whom Ahaz had pinned his hopes for *deliverance*, and to whom he was shortly going to send an urgent appeal for help, or had already done so.

c. The Further Sequel, the Predicted Devastation of the Land (vv. 18-25)

7:18-25 18. Namely, it shall come to pass at that time that Yahweh will whistle for the fly which is at the mouth of the rivers of Egypt and for the bee which is in the land of Assyria. 19. And they shall come and settle all of them in the steep ravines and in the clefts of the rocks and on all underbrush and on all watering-places. 20. At that time the Lord will shave with a razor hired from beyond the river (namely with the king of Assyria) the head and the hair of the feet, and he will also remove the beard. 21. Also it shall come to pass at that time that a man will keep a young cow and a couple of sheep. 22. And it shall come to pass that because of the amount of milk that he gets, he will eat curds; for curds and honey shall be the food for everyone left within the land. 23. In that day it shall come to pass that in every place where there used to be a thousand vines worth a thousand shekels, this shall indeed be for briers and thorns. 24. With bow and arrow men will come there, for everything shall be covered with briers and thorns. 25. And as far as all the mountains are concerned that used to be hoed with the hoe, people will not come there for fear of briers and thorns; but they shall be used to drive oxen there and let sheep tread there.

Verse 18. From this point on to the end of the chapter it is usually assumed that we have here a few disconnected, or loosely related words of the prophet, which have been put together by some disciple of Isaiah. The fact that we have not the same close coherence which is in evidence in a historical piece where item follows item in close sequence may be due to the fact that this is supplementary and explanatory material, spoken, as it would seem, at this time by Isaiah, but appearing to be less strictly coherent, because figure crowds close on the heels of figure, and illustration on the heels of illustration. What was in the previous paragraph given in a summary fashion is now broken down into detailed pictures. In fact, what had been previously stated in the chapter would lack in effectiveness, being merely indicated, not spelled out. For that reason the initial "and" may well be translated "namely."

Verse 19. It had previously been indicated that Assyria would sweep down on the Promised Land. Now the picture is rounded out in that it is indicated that Egypt shall also crowd into the picture. But more important is the fact that the coming of both is to be traced to Yahweh's activity. He will whistle for both of them, that is, summon them;

though on their part they may be utterly unaware that his sovereign control brings them on the scene and uses them. Pestiferous flies were found in those days, too, in the land of Egypt, and bees in Assyria. The hosts of these two nations are likened to these numerous creatures. The two creatures are pictured as coming in huge swarms, so as to cover the countryside: ravines, clefts of the rocks, underbrush, and watering places, as well. Whether this swarming over the land is thought of as involving either Israel or Judah, or both, is not clearly indicated. It would appear that the entire ancient land will suffer. Whether these two will clash on the soil of Palestine again is not indicated. It is enough to know that the land will suffer.

Verse 20. Then an entirely different figure is used to describe the plundering of the land and the removal of its inhabitants. Assyria's activity alone is now described as being, no doubt, the more disastrous for Israel. The nation is likened to a "razor," a "hired" razor at that. Ironically, it would seem, reference is made to the fact that Ahaz sent Tiglath-pileser a substantial sum of money to induce him to come. He came, but went much farther than Ahaz thought at the time. For in the light of Ezek. 5:1ff. it would seem that shaving indicates removal by forceful means of the inhabitants of the land. There seems to be no reference to different classes of people in the terms used, but only to the removal of *all*, or practically all. Ultimately two deportations came to pass, which practically achieved this result ("hair of the feet" is a euphemism for pubic hair).

Verses 21, 22. Now for two verses we have another brief illustration of how grievous the times will be. The issue is how tragic the food problem will be in the devastated land. A typical inhabitant of the land is looked at for the moment. What will his possessions amount to? He shall own nothing more than "a young cow and a couple of sheep." That is a far cry from what men formerly held. Having at least one article of diet in fair amount — milk — that shall constitute the chief article of diet, fresh milk or curds. In addition, he shall manage to find a bit of wild honey occasionally. It will be enough to keep him alive, but no more. As remarked above (v. 15) the curds and honey here referred to are to be taken in the sense of "nothing more than curds and honey." Nor will anybody in the land have access to anything other than this monotonous and the meager diet. As *Delitzsch* again appropiately remarks, this will be what men will eat to the point of utter disgust (*bis zum Ekel*).

Verse 23. Here follows another thumb-nail sketch indicative of the sad state of land and people. Take a walk out into a place where pleasant vineyards used to thrive, where the choicest of vines were the only ones planted, rated at a shekel per vine — top price for those days. What do you find there? Everything shall be so utterly neglected that all that meets the eye is "briers and thorns." Already wild beasts will have taken over, so much so that a man would not think of going out into such an area without taking along bow and arrow. It will be noted that with a certain dreary monotony, verse for verse, we encounter the expression "briers and thorns," just as the land is overrun with them, the choicest land at that. There just are not enough people left to till the land, nor do the circumstances permit it. All has been war-swept.

Verse 25. When the mountains are now referred to, it must be remembered that the whole land is mountainous. So "mountains" means the whole land and would, of course, include pleasant hillsides that, as a rule, had been cultivated, being land that "they used to hoe with the hoe." Now they will not even venture there because of the tangled weeds and thorns. These formerly good fields will be used to drive their oxen there, what few oxen there are, of course; and they will "let sheep tread there," what few sheep they have. On this sad note the chapter comes to a close; a dismal note of sadness. The king — and to an extent the people, for they were likeminded — did not want a helpful sign. This is the state of affairs that he shall see with his own eyes.

Notes

Verse 1. The verb *yakhol,* being singular, makes the sentence regard Rezin as the dominating figure of the coalition against Judah, and says of him that he was unable to war effectively against Judah. The parallel passage, II Kings 16:5, uses the plural and so puts both kings of the coalition on an equal footing.

Verse 4. The demonstrative pronoun almost has the flavor of the derogatory, i.e., "such." Cf. *KS* 48.

Verse 6. Whether the form *Tabeal* dated from the prophet originally or from copyists who added in the vowel points at a later date will be impossible to determine.

Verse 8. *KS* regards the initial *ki* as adversative, "but." With this approach the following words (v. 8 ff.) stand in contrast to the apprehensive understanding of the situation that Ahaz was inclined to adopt. See *KS* 372 e. So also the *ki* of v. 9 is merely the index of the apodosis and, therefore, hardly to be translated (the "surely" *RSV* is superfluous). See *KS* 415 l.

Verse 11. *KS* maintains that *ha'meq* and *hagbe(a)h* are to be construed as absolute infinitives, used gerundively, "going as low," etc. See *K* 402 d. It is just as simple to view them as imperatives. *She'alah* may be no more than a pointing of *she'olah* that has been chosen because of similarity to the final *lema'elah.* By itself *sha'alah* could be a cognate accusative object of *she'al.*

Verse 12. Though the second clause is coordinated "and I will not put Yahweh to the test," yet it makes better English to subordinate it in a consecutive sense, "so as not to" (*KS* 364 e).

Verse 13. The imperfect *tal'u* involves the potential (*KS* 188).

Verse 14. To remove a misconstruction that has been put on the verse, note that *hinneh* cannot bear a conditional meaning [*KS* 390 o.] Since *yolédheth* the fem. part. is used with *himneh,* the usual rule holds good that such a construction refers to the future (*KS* 367 v). This construction then carries with it the adjective *harah* (*KS* 237 h). This at once eliminates any reference to a pregnancy which already is in evidence or has begun.

Verse 15. The warrant for translating "*when* he knows . . ." is found in the fact that the *le* before *da'to* is a *le* temporal. (*KS* 331 f).

Verse 18. That Egypt was trying to get into the picture is indicated by a number of passages from Hosea, like 9:3.

Verse 20. If in II Sam. 10:4 and I Chron. 19:4 the shaving away of the beard was a major insult this does not seem to bear upon the case in hand.

Verse 24. The *yabho'* represents the impersonal use of the verb or the indefinite subject (cf. *GK* 144 h, and *KS* 324 d). The verb *tabho'* of v. 25 amounts to the same thing, the ideal use of the second person (cf. *GK* 118 l). The *heharim* at the beginning of the verse represents a nominative absolute (*KS* 341 f).

P. *Boehmer* [*ZATW*, 1923, p. 84ff.] has an interesting article in which he attempts to establish that the last part of 7:9 ("If you will not believe/you will not endure"), does not stem from the prophet Isaiah. He arrives at the same conclusion in regard to the similar word found in 28:16. In both cases a hypercritical approach to the Hebrew text coupled with heavy reliance on subjective impressions control the conclusions arrived at and so make them very questionable.

H. *Junker* (Supplements to *Vetus Testamentum*, IV, 1956, p. 181 ff. *Ursprung und Grundzuege des Messiasbildes bei Isajas*) stresses a few points to which reference should be made, points not touched upon in our above treatment. He indicates that there are passages in Ugaritic texts that seem to refer to an *'almah* bearing sons. *Junker* shows how the attempt to establish a parallel between these King Keret passage and our passage as referring to the wife of Ahaz is rather far-fetched. Besides, *Junker* maintains, and we believe rightly, that this passage (7:14) is fundamental to the development of the Messianic concept in Old Testament prophecy.

Chapter VIII

2. The Stirring Times (734-732 B.C.) and How to Meet Them (Chap. 8)

We are still within the confines of the Book of Immanuel, whose name appears twice in the chapter (vv. 8 and 10). Where the previous chapter saw the prophet confront the king, we see him now confront the people (*Procksch*). These were to be stirring times; they would test men to the utmost; men would need clear guidance to know how to live through these days without mortal harm to themselves. The prophet provides such directives for Judah and Jerusalem. For first of all this was the time of the Syro-Ephraimite war, of which Chap. 7 had given some intimations. Furthermore the big Assyrian invasion of Tiglath-pileser was impending. A serious threat hung over Samaria, as we read in 7:3ff. Isaiah is about to tell what will happen in both these areas and aims to show what guidance God offers his people for the impending emergencies.

a. The Plundering of Damascus and Samaria (vv. 1-4)

8:1-4 1. Then Yahweh said to me: "Take a large tablet and write on it in plain script in reference to the speeding of the spoil, the hastening of the prey." 2. And I got as witnesses for myself certain faithful men, Uriah the priest and Zechariah, the son of Jeberechiah. 3. Thereupon I went in unto the prophetess and she conceived and bore a son. Then Yahweh said to me: "Call his name Maher-shalal-hash-baz; 4. for before the child knows how to cry 'My father' or 'My mother,' the wealth of Damascus and the spoil of Samaria shall be carried away before the king of Assyria."

We have no indication how much time may have elapsed between what took place in Chap. 7 and the present chapter. *Kissane* surmises about one year. The last part of Chap. 7

could have been the prophet's interpretation of the will of the Lord, as it was given to him to see (vv. 18-25). Now comes a direct word of Yahweh. Isaiah is to take a large tablet, perhaps of wood or metal, perhaps even of some animal-skin. In any case it is to be material capable of bearing an inscription, which the prophet is to write out in its striking brevity, but in easily legible script (Heb. "the pen of man"; cf. Deut. 3:11, "cubit of a man" — "common cubit") as we might copy out an inscription in capital letters. The substance of what is written bears upon the "speeding of the spoil and the hastening of the prey." In Hebrew transliteration it read as follows: *Maher-shalal-hash-baz.* Though by itself such an inscription would be utterly obscure, it is quite possible that for the contemporaries of the prophet — who were aware of the things previously stated by him, especially in 7:3-9, that an early collapse of the threat against Judah would occur and that both Damascus and Samaria were headed for trouble — for these contemporaries, this inscription would readily be tied up with the earlier pronouncement. This was all the more likely because Isaiah himself was at hand to help clarify the otherwise most mysterious word. There is the further likelihood that if "plain script" was to be employed, the tablet itself was designed to be publicly displayed. His brevity and its enigmatic content would challenge attention and inquiry. The explanation offered vv. 3-4 would give all needed comment. The striking name would make the message all the more easy to remember. For further certification that the meaning of it all was not an afterthought but a prophetic prediction two witnesses are brought into the picture. They are Uriah the priest, of whom we read, II Kings 16:10-16, that he co-operated with Ahaz to make a model of a heathen altar to be set up in the temple area at Jerusalem, apparently an Assyrian altar indicating that Ahaz would offer sacrifices for the success of the Assyrian king. Zechariah on the other hand was the father-in-law of Ahaz. Both are called "faithful men," or witnesses, because they would not have sided with the prophet against the king. They could be depended upon to offer unimpeachable testimony on the subject in hand. The issue appears to be that Isaiah unquestionably had predicted the early plundering of Samaria and Damascus.

Now another thing occurs (v. 3). The prophet begets a son. The "prophetess" mentioned is naturally his wife. The name involved is a mere title, not an indication that she exercised any prophetic functions. The manner of statement used seems to imply that the son was begotten after the tablet incident had taken place. Upon divine orders a name is given to the child, a rather cumbersome one. What was the substance of a message in v. 1 now becomes a proper name of a child. By this second incident, the message of the prophet on this subject is underscored somewhat heavily. In fact, the prominence given this child seems to counterbalance the greater prominence attached by the prophet to the other child, Immanuel. But a fuller interpretation is added (v. 4) to the name of the child, that men may not struggle vainly after dubious possibilities. The meaning is unmistakably clear. Before the prophet's son will be old enough to say the words: "My father," or "My mother," both Damascus and Samaria will have been plundered and the spoil carried away by the king of Assyria.

The king of Assyria referred to is Tiglath-pileser, who overran northern Israel already in 734 B.C. and before whom Damascus fell in 732 (for the former event see II Kings 15:29).

It should be noted that the passage 7:3-9 was rather mysterious. If it was to be meaningful for Judah at all it demanded some such word as Chap. 8 now offers. So the material of these two chapters is closely integrated.

b. The Assyrian Invasion of Judah (vv. 5-8)

The just-mentioned incident implied hard things for Israel. Judah might seem immune from invasion, for Ahaz had courted the favor of the Assyrian monarch. But no, calamities were in store for Judah also, more specifically, an invasion. Of this the following verses tell, though Israel, of course, will be involved.

8:5-8 5. And Yahweh went on to speak to me yet again, saying: 6. "Since the people despise the waters of Shiloah, that flow gently, and because of their rejoicing with Rezin and the son of Remaliah, 7. therefore, behold, the Lord is bringing upon them the strong and abundant waters of the River [Euphrates], the king of Assyria, and all his glorious host; and it shall rise over all channels and go over all banks. 8. And it shall flow into Judah, and sweep along and swell, and reach even to the neck; and the spread of its wings will fill the breadth of thy land, O Immanuel."

So far there has been only an indication that Assyria shall be Israel's nemesis. Such a claim, however, almost demands further clarification. This word from Yahweh gives that fuller treatment. It is again a specific word from Yahweh. It attributes the invasion to two basically wrong attitudes, involving a negative that was wrong and a positive that was wrong. The first wrong then was the despising of the gently flowing rivulet of Shiloah. This was a very meager runlet that flowed along the east of the city of Jerusalem. In its insignificance it typified rather well the esteem in which God's work and his holy city were held by men of that time. Contrasted with the mighty and famous Euphrates it was a ridiculously small body of water, not deserving to be mentioned in the same breath. Judging by mere outward appearance, even the people of God despised God's mighty work in the midst of his holy people as utterly inconsequential, small, weak, and unimpressive. That was the first aspect of their sin. Then by contrast at least some of them (the Northern Kingdom) took great pride in the fact that they had become aligned with Rezin, king of Syria, as though such alliances made for success and were all-important. One attitude was as shortsighted as the other. Each was indicative of a large measure of spiritual blindness. Sins like these were the total antithesis to faith and understanding.

Verse 7. By way of just retribution, since another aspect of the case was involved, and since Ahaz in particular had sought the help of Assyria, whose outward strength could very aptly be likened to the mighty sweep of the River, the common designation of the Euphrates, therefore the

Lord would bring upon them that for which they longed — at least in Judah — and so greatly admired, namely the Assyrian nation itself. They are the ones signified by "the strong and abundant waters," the king himself and all his glorious host. But due to the irony of events, where this oncoming host had been envisioned in terms of deliverance and much-needed help, in reality it was the very opposite. The king would bring his mighty war-machine. He would overrun Israel to the north. He would find plunder so easy and conquest so successful that he would not stop short at the boundary of Judah, which was supposedly his ally, but would, though mostly at a later date, take Judah in hand for prospective plundering.

This plundering of Judah is described in v. 8 in terms of a stream at flood-stage. For since due to the nature of the terrain, the Euphrates could never flood the land of Judah, it was still a very effective figure to picture these Euphrates floodwaters as actually flowing "into Judah" where they would then "sweep along and swell, and reach even to the neck." Ironically that was the type of help Ahaz had brought into the land by inviting the Assyrians to come to his rescue. At this point two figures blend into one another. The first is that of the River at flood stage. The second is that of a mighty bird with tremendous wing-spread, flying over the land and darkening with its "spread of its wings." The second figure thus adds the thought of total coverage of the land. But it should be noted that at this point the prophet addresses his discourse to Immanuel, whose coming had been predicted in 7:14. Now the added fact appears that this mysterious Immanuel is lord of the whole land of Israel. Though it has not yet been said that being "God with us" he is divine and the Lord of the whole land, thoughts like these are implied, as well as the possibility that he is the only one who in this extremity can deliver the land and the people.

The turn of the thought at this point is like that which so often follows after a grievous threat. The prophet now indicates where safety lies.

c. The Safety That Immanuel Can Give (vv. 9-10)

8:9-10 9. Rage, you peoples, and be broken. Give ear, all you distant countries. Gird yourselves and be broken; gird yourselves and be broken. 10. Take counsel together, but it shall come to nought. Formulate a plan, but it shall not prevail; for God is with us [Heb. Immanuel].

In a series of imperatives, that constitute a sort of challenge, the prophet effectively shows how futile all attempts like the Assyrian invasion must prove in the end, because they are directed at the overthrow of the people of God. Various aspects of such assaults are suggested. On the one hand they involve something of "rage." For the enemies of the people of God frequently become filled with rage against the Lord and against his work (cf. Ps. 2). But whenever this aspect of their attitude appears, the outcome always has been and always is bound to be: "be broken." The Almighty utterly overthrows them. Again, the enemies of the Lord make vast preparations, i.e., they "gird themselves." Vast lands, far off in the distance, even may be involved. But their preparations, too, can have only one result: "be broken." Or, still another aspect of the situation (v. 10) is this, that they who seek the overthrow of the kingdom of God "take counsel," but there always is only one possible outcome: "it shall come to nought" — "it shall not prevail." The simple answer by way of explanation of these drastic defeats is one word, "Immanuel." Here, naturally, this word is not used as title but in its native meaning: "God is with us." That bulwark can be pitted against any danger. Thus the threat of the opposition is met with a ringing, triumphant position of faith. In fact, the whole paragraph breathes an atmosphere of resolute and unimpeachable faith. Parallel passages where taunting verbs are used by the author are 23:1-7; 29:9.

d. Whom and What to Fear (vv. 11-15)

From reassurance given to the faithful, the tone now shifts to warning for the prophet and for all the faithful followers and for the entire nation.

8:11-15 11. For thus has Yahweh spoken to me, his hand upon me being strong, and he warned me not to walk in the way of this people, saying: 12. "Not shall you [you, Isaiah, and your followers] call all this 'conspiracy' which this people calls 'conspiracy'; and do not fear what they fear, nor shall you be in dread. 13. Yahweh of hosts, him shall you regard as holy, he shall be the one whom you fear and whom you shall dread. 14. And he shall become a sanctuary, but also a stone of offense and a snare to the inhabitants of Jerusalem. 15. Many shall stumble thereon, and they shall fall and be broken; they shall be snared and taken."

Another one of the words follows, that instructs the prophet but does not necessarily give him the actual form of words to be used in conveying this information to the people. Isaiah may have been under necessity of recasting the message in order to transmit it to his hearers. But the substance of the truth came from Yahweh himself. It was conveyed to his prophet by some strong form of compulsion, indicated by the expression "his hand upon me being strong," the Hebrew being: "by strength of the hand." Before the actual words themselves are given, a summary of their import is offered in the words, "He warned me not to walk in the way of this people." At the time there was a trend developing among the people which was dangerous and bore watching. It was in effect an attitude which had become quite common.

Verse 12. This unwholesome attitude first of all involved a certain popular form of expression which was getting to be the habit-pattern in referring to the attitude which Isaiah and his followers advocated. The mode of speech that was becoming habitual was this, that the policy of the Isaiah-group was regularly being described by the term "conspiracy." Here the word almost seems to bear a connotation like the word "treason" in our day. Not to follow the party line of the political leaders who chiefly advocated alliance with Assyria was accounted treasonable and so the stinging designation of "treason" was attached to it. Not to agree with the ones who dominated the policies of state at the time was spoken of as undermining the very existence of the state. On this score Isaiah and his followers were not to yield ground, no matter how loud the clamor to the contrary might be. Though every one insisted that this course was treasonable, it was the policy which was dictated by the Lord and at the same time was true to the best interests of the national state. Parallel with this first unwholesome attitude was the one which is described in the terms: "Do not fear what they fear, nor shall you be in dread." This applied chiefly to the political trends which saw in one or the other of the surrounding nations a specially dangerous threat. Some said Assyria was dangerous; others, Syria. The real threat lay within the nation, but reverential respect was to be developed in another direction, as v. 13 indicates.

Verse 13. The statement does not begin, as might have been anticipated, with a demand that the nation should truly fear Yahweh. Rather, that statement is prepared for by the other one: "Yahweh of hosts, him shall you regard as holy." This may be stated first for the reason that Yahweh is not to be too readily associated with the political trends of policies of the time. He has his place in the scheme of things, in fact his is the dominant place. But the fact of his superiority over the weaknesses, foibles and sins of man should be primarily kept in mind — that is to say: his holiness. Yet at the same time he who is to be regarded as so very high and holy, him and his punitive justice should the evil-doer fear and dread. For in this case fear is the reaction of the lower type, according to the context, and not so much the holy reverence that characterizes a true godly man. All the sights of the nation, in other words, were to be reset and correctly aligned. The Lord practically calls for a reversal of all current trends in the nations.

Verse 14. But the more positive side of the matter is now added. Not only shall the Lord and his anger be the matter for which they have a wholesome respect but they should also flee to him for refuge, for he is always a very present help in trouble. Therefore they should resort to him as to a safe sanctuary from the evils that threaten. But a sinful nation should also be aware of the fact that if he be not sought as refuge, he will become for the sinners "a stone of offense and a rock of stumbling," and that shall be an issue with which "both houses of Israel" shall have to reckon; but as far as "the inhabitants of Jerusalem" themselves are concerned, he shall be "a trap and a snare." The Old Testament already clearly reveals that aspect of the truth which shows the Lord to be the One who is set "for the fall and rising of many in Israel." Such a time of decision seemed to be upon Jerusalem and Israel in a special sense at this particular season. The appeal made here rings out on a strong note of warning (v. 15): "Many shall stumble thereon; they shall fall and be broken; they shall be snared and be taken." It will be observed that the note of a possibly disastrous outcome is the stronger in this instance. Apparently there was much more likelihood of the unwholesome reaction at the time when the prophet spoke. All this prepares for the next portion of the chapter, where the offers of grace are to be, at least temporarily, withdrawn.

e. *The Patient Waiting of Faith (vv. 16-18)*

8:16-17 16. [God]: Bind up the testimony, seal up the law for my disciples! 17. [the prophet]: But I will wait for Yahweh that is hiding his face from the house of Jacob, and in him will I hope. 18. Lo, here am I and the children whom Yahweh has given me for guarantees and portents in Israel from Yahweh of hosts who dwells in Mount Zion.

Did some time elapse between the speaking of this word and the one that preceded? *Kissane* suggests about a year. However we are completely at a loss in reaching any conclusion. It could have been spoken almost in the same breath, because of the unreceptive attitude that the people obviously displayed. In any case, he who has testified in the name of the Lord, and has spoken law, or instruction, to the people, is to desist from both activities. He is, as it were, to tie up the sheets that have his messages written on them and put a seal on the package. We said, "as it were," because the words constitute a figurative description of the temporary cessation of his activity. Strictly speaking, it is not he that ties up the messages. The nation and their attitude have done that and made it ineffective. This command from God, "Bind up" in brief demands that the

prophet discontinue, at least for the time being, his prophetic activity, at least as far as its public aspect is concerned. For the command contains the added phrase, "for
my disciples." They will continue to hear, read and take
to heart. Strictly speaking, the prophet's activity is to
limit itself to the very small circle of the receptive ones.
The nation at large has forfeited the right to hear messages
from the Lord.

Verse 17. Now the prophet indicates what attitude he
personally must take in the meantime. His must be the
attitude of waiting patiently until the Lord again allows
him to resume his activity. The Lord's attitude for the
present may be described as one of "hiding his face from
the house of Jacob." He refuses to look upon them with
favor. But no matter how many others there are who
reject God's message, his faithful follower can do nothing
less than "hope" in him. Hope is the banner of the faithful.

Verse 18. Once again in brief, the prophet sets down
for the nation what the issue continues to be. When he
says, "Lo, here am I," he says in effect: Look at me and
my children; we are the epitome of what I have taught up
till the present. We are first of all "guarantees," promises
of good that Yahweh has in store for the obedient. This
aspect of the case lies embodied in the names "Isaiah" and
"Shearjashub" (cf. 7:3). For *Isaiah* means "the salvation
of Yahweh," and *Shearjashub* means "a remnant shall return." For them that believe, the Lord is always their
salvation. For them that return there is always the prospect of restoration — for Israel, restoration to the land, for
every penitent soul, restoration to God's favor. These two
supplementary truths Isaiah had been preaching unremit-
tingly. They still stand, if any man will but recall and
believe them. But there was also an ominous note to all
that the prophet said. This note applied to the impenitent
and unbelieving. It lay embodied in the name of the son,
Maher-shalal-hash-baz, which meant (v. 1), "the spoil speeds,
the prey hastes." Though that meant primarily the early
plundering of Damascus and Samaria, it meant, in more general terms, the swift punishment of every stubborn sinner.

That was the "portent," or warning, enclosed in the name of the second son.

So there was for Isaiah a time for preaching as well as a time to refrain from preaching. The latter was now upon him. How long it lasted, he did not say. In fact what he next offers is a second interpretation of how to meet this time of keeping silence. He offers, so to speak, the right slogan for the day.

By a rather bold use of the passage, the author of the letter to the Hebrews uses the words of v. 18b in reference to the Messiah (Heb. 2:13). In their native context these words do not appear to have such a connotation. They are used however by way of adaptation.

f. *The Right Slogan for the Day (vv. 19-22)*

8:19-22 19. And when men shall say to you: "Consult the mediums and the fortune tellers, who chirp and mutter," should not a people consult their God? Should men consult the dead in behalf of the living? 20. To the law and to the testimony! If they for whom there is no dawn will not speak according to this word, 21. they will pass through the land greatly distressed and hungry. And it shall come to pass that when they are hungry, they shall grow angry and curse their king and their God. And they shall look upward; 22. and down again to the earth, and, lo, nought but distress and darkness, the gloom of anguish, and in thick darkness will they be banished.

From the tone of this entire passage it appears that the prophet has moved forward to a situation where the judgment of God is beginning to descend upon the impenitent and stubborn majority in Israel. What they are here represented as saying, is spoken in a spirit of panic. Since they will not have a safe word of guidance, clear and adequate as from God himself, they resort instead to the questionable and dubious. They will want to take refuge in words of diviners and soothsayers. As the German can so aptly put it: From *Glauben* they turn to *Aberglauben* (from *faith* to *superstition*) (cf. Jer. 2:13). It may not be strictly the fortune tellers and mediums that they have recourse to, but to the spirits of the departed that speak through them. For those consulted are in the last part of the verse described as "the dead." Such procedure was, of course, typically heathen in character, as Deut. 18:14 also shows. The use of the descriptive verbs "chirp and mutter" seem to indicate that trivial, unclear, and unwholesome sounds emanate from the characters consulted. It all amounts to trivial and unsatisfactory stuff. No more unhappy slogan for the unhappy times impending could be found than the word of these speakers in v. 19. Very properly the prophet challenges to resort to God, as the only one who can afford safe directives in critical times. Especially, should a nation like Israel be challenged to fall back upon the living God, seeing he has never failed his people in times past, but has always provided adequate words of guidance through his prophets. The folly of Israel's procedure is well epitomized in the challenge: "Should men consult the dead in behalf of the living?" Equally sensible would be the procedure of having a man who sees, seek as guide the man who is blind, or he that has keen hearing, him whose hearing is impaired. Such folly has never been practiced.

Verse 20. Slogans abound in this portion of the prophet's message. Verse 16 is a slogan which describes the course necessary for the present; "bind up the testimony. . . ." Verse 19 describes a slogan against the following of which men are to be warned: "Consult the mediums. . . ." Verse 20 again gives the best slogan of all, in the very concise form: "To the law and to the testimony." It is true that "law" means "instruction." It is also true that from an early date the Mosaic law was regarded as a primary instance of such instruction. "Testimony" again was another synonym for the "law." Apparently then the two terms together imply that men should turn back to all instruction, oral or written, that may have been brought to their attention at any time. Such instruction may have been largely ignored. It was important then. It is important now. In fact, the giving heed to it is the most important issue of the day. It could therefore be aptly paraphrased: Let the nation turn back to that basic instruction which has come to it from God in the past; to do so is their only hope.

It is this latter note that the rest of the chapter dwells upon, the hoplessness if the nation fails to heed this summons. Already, since they have failed to give heed they are the ones "for whom there is no dawn." But unless they go according to the directive of this divine imperative, "they will pass through the land greatly distressed and hungry." It would seem that the figure in the prophet's mind is that of a group passing through a dry desert, burned by the heat, lacking food and drink. Their sorry plight will make them impatient of all leadership. For they will not blame themselves for their sorry lot. They will rather charge the heads of the nation, particularly their king, with being the cause of their misfortune. Being impenitent people they will be inclined to blame even the Almighty himself. Both courses were, from days of old, rightly regarded as most reprehensible (Exod. 22:28; I Kings 21:10). But to see miserable men staggering along breathing curses, does not present a pretty picture.

Verse 22. The description goes on (taking the last part of v. 21 together with v. 22) abandoning the desert scene and concentrating on another scene where everything is dark and gloomy, or even murky. Perhaps the figure is that of men struggling along in the dark, lost and miserable. No matter where they turn and whither they look, their eye lights on things that spell misery: "And they shall look upward and down again to the earth, and lo, nought but distress and darkness, the gloom of anguish." There is a certain vagueness about the description. It could apply to a number of calamities — war, national disasters, deportation, and the like. Perhaps the prophet himself could not at this point detect what the future might bring, except to indicate that it would be extremely gloomy. The emphasis seems to rest on the captivity idea, for he concludes: "and in thick darkness will they be banished."

To treat all this from the angle of slogans has its shortcomings. The point at issue still is to return to the Lord and the guidance which he has in the past amply provided for his people through lawgivers and prophets.

Notes

Verse 1. In the expression that later becomes a proper name, *maher* and *hash* are participles, not imperatives. Cf. *KS* 399 y.

Verse 2. In spite of the contrary evidence of the Septuagint, the Targum and the Syriac, we still feel that the first person should be retained in the expression "and I got as witnesses."

Verse 3. It is unnatural to make *wa'eqrabh* to read as a pluperfect, so that the prophet had already gone in to his wife before the order was received to write the long name on a tablet.

Verse 4. The passive "shall be carried away" is merely the impersonal use of the verb in this instance. Cf. *KS* 324 d.

Verse 6. The initial "since" or "because of" as it also can be translated carries through to the word *mesos*, and if the statement be interpreted as we have it above, there is no need of corrections of the text. *Mesos* is an infinitive used as object of the initial "because of."

Verse 9. Though "rage," as to form, is imperative, its force is in actuality concessive. See *KS* 363 c. The verb *ro'u* could be translated "raise the war-cry" (see *ZATW*, 1964 (2) an article by *Saebo*, pp. 132ff.).

Verse 16. The verbs *tsor* and *chathom* are both absolute infinitives. So they could be translated, "Binding up the testimony, sealing the law." Then some words such as: "This is what needs to be done," would fill out the ellipsis.

Verse 20. After the opening slogan the clauses may be so arranged as we have them. In fact, only thus does the thought become clear. For the initial slogan again a verb has to be supplied, although the slogan is clear as ellipsis. "Through the land" is expressed so consisely that it reads *bah*, i.e., "in it." But still that obviously means in this context "through the land."

Verse 22. Another possibility must be noted here. The last part of the verse can be translated: "And thick darkness will be scattered." This could be taken in two senses. Perhaps it is intentionally ambiguous. In line with our above interpretation it could mean: Darkness will be scattered around. It could also mean: Darkness will be dissipated, i.e., removed. It is this latter interpretation that provides a good transition to the next chapter (or to v. 23 of this chapter).

Chapter IX

4. The Child with the Four Names (9:1-7; Hebrews 8:23 — 9:6)

We are still in the Immanuel Book (chaps. 7–12). In Chap. 7 the Child first put in its appearance; a very mysterious person. In Chap. 8 we were moving through stirring times and finding directions how to cope with them. Though very difficult days were in the offing, the conclusion of the chapter indicated that the gloom might break; see the alternate translation of v. 22 in the Notes on Chap. 8.

Now that hopeful possibility is explored more fully. In particular, the one through whom this significant change is to come to pass is identified and described. But again as a Child! This leads to the conclusion that the Immanuel of 7:14 and the Child of 9:6 are identical. Only by thus relating them do both passages take on meaning. There will be found a further tie-up in Chap. 11 — the mystery-Child will again receive attention. But already in Chap. 8 it had appeared twice — in each case as a person of rare authority (cf. v. 8 and v. 10).

Though we can engage merely in suppositions, yet as far as the time-factor is concerned, it may well be that the date for the passage in question is still shortly after Tiglath-pileser's invasion of Syria and Ephraim in 734-32 B.C. That would account for the desolate state of upper Galilee with which we meet at the beginning of the chapter. But the issues involved are, of course, far more than the purely political.

9:1-7 1. For there will be no more gloom for her that was in anguish. As in bygone days he [Yahweh] brought into contempt the land of Zebulon and the land of Naphtali, so in days to come he will bring glory upon the area by the Sea Road, the land beyond the Jordan, Galilee of the nations.

2. The people that walked in darkness will see a great light,

Those that dwell in a land of deep darkness — light will shine on
them.
3. Thou wilt multiply the nation; for it thou wilt increase joy.
They will rejoice before thee as men rejoice over a harvest, as
men exult when they divide spoil.
4. For its burdensome yoke, the rod laid on its shoulder, the
staff of the oppressor —
all these thou wilt break as in the day of Midian.
5. For every boot of the warrior tramping in battle tumult and
the blood-stained warcloak —
this is destined to be burned — fuel for the fire.
6. For unto us a child will be born, unto us a son will be given;
and the government will be upon his shoulder.
And men will call his name: Wonderful-Counselor, Mighty-God,
Father-forever, Prince of peace.
7. Of the increase of his government and of peace there will be
no end upon the throne of David and upon his kingdom,
to establish and to uphold it with justice and righteousness from
henceforth even forever.
The zeal of the Lord of hosts will achieve this.

It may well be, as is often claimed, that in their original
form the prophetic pronouncements, especially of earlier
literary prophets like Isaiah, were small units. These were
later grouped together, though not always necessarily in
a sequence such as that in which they first appeared. Nevertheless their present sequence may indeed date from the
prophet himself. They therefore deserve to be examined
in their present connection rather than as unrelated units.

a. A Summary (v. 1)

Verse 1. This is both a transition verse as well as a
summary of what follows in the next six verses. The picture
of total gloom which closed the preceding chapter gives
way to a picture of brilliant light. Since this word in some
way looks to the future, we ventured to insert at the opening the words "no more" before "gloom." The extreme
devastation that the Assyrians visited upon north Galilee
is to give way in the course of time — the prophet himself
does not seem to know how soon or how late — to a bright
glory. The areas involved are the tribal territory of "Zebulon" (which lay directly west of the Sea of Galilee, except

that Naphtali, which extended farther north pushed down between the sea and Zebulon) and "Naphtali," also "the area by the Sea Road" (which, coming from the northeast passed along the west side of the Sea of Galilee) "the land beyond the Jordan" (which here means: east of the Sea of Galilee) and "Galilee of the nations" (which refers chiefly to north Galilee). All this region had suffered from the "scorched earth" policy of the invading Assyrians.

b.　The Great Happiness (vv. 2-3)

Verse 2. In this connection the opening statement ("the people that walked in darkness") seems to us to refer specifically to the region just described. So Matthew construes it (Matt. 4:14-16) thinking in terms of the beginning of the Galilean ministry of Jesus. The "great light" referred to is Jesus Christ in person, as we can now clearly see in the light of the fulfilment that the New Testament brings. The parallel statement concerning those "that dwell in a land of deep darkness" still refers to the same area where Jesus had grown up and began his public ministry (cf. Matt. 4:14-16). The word used for "people" (Heb. *goy*) though usually signifying the hostile Gentile nations, is sometimes referred to Israel (as in Gen. 12:2; 18:18; Exod. 19:6; Isa. 1:4). "Light" in a connection such as this refers primarily to joy, but surely can include every possible blessing that the age of the Messiah can bring.

For sheer beauty and wealth and weight of insight this chapter, as commentators remark, deserves to be classed with other great passages of the Bible like Genesis 1 and John 1, which also speak of the coming of light.

Though the familiar versions render the verbs involved as being in the past tense (or present, in German) they are all what the Hebrew describes as prophetic perfects, and point clearly to the *future*, which, in the Hebrew idiom, is as sure to come as though it had already transpired.

Though the "child" seems to be thought of as appearing in Isaiah's day, this is neither said nor implied — an example of prophetic perspective.

Verse 3. At this point the passage turns to address the

Lord in a spirit of devotion and praise. *He* does the things
that are to be recounted as part of the great light that is
to come. First there is attributed to him the fact that he
will "multiply the nation." From being sparsely settled
and depopulated, as it was after the Assyrians were done
with their ravaging, it will again be populous and thriving
in the days under consideration, the Messianic days. The
Scriptures often associate a people strong in numbers with
this age; see Isa. 26:15; 66:8; Zech. 10:14f.; also: I Kings
4:20. In Jesus' time, as also Josephus reports, Galilee was
dotted with numerous prosperous villages. The added
statement, "for it thou wilt increase joy," by the "for it"
indicates that this sorry-looking land would be the very
one that shall undergo so tremendous a change of circumstances, impossible as it might have seemed to the one
who beheld it in its desolation at Isaiah's time. By the
use of various verbs and nouns descriptive of joy the author
indicates how vast this joy will be. Two notable comparisons are also used. On the one hand the joy involved will
be like that when "men rejoice over a harvest," a type of
joy indicative of unusual satisfaction. On the other it will
be like that when "men exult when they divide spoil."
What makes such joy deep is that it sets in after the
pains and griefs of war have been resolved into victory and
peace. Both figures used, bespeak rare joy. When above
it was said, "They will rejoice *before thee*" this emphasis
indicated that a pure and wholesome type of joy is under
consideration, such as must not hide its face before the
Almighty (cf. Ps. 42:2).

c. *What Is Taken Away (vv. 4-5)*

Verse 4. While the prophet exultingly describes some
still undefined great joy, or light, he turns from the idea
of good things that are to be received to the idea of evils
that are to be removed. The happiness under consideration
involves a great deliverance, which, in turn, is described
by a variety of figures. It is as though a "burdensome
yoke" had been removed from the one that toiled under
it. We believe this translation (involving a descriptive gen-

itive) to be simpler than the traditional "yoke of his burden." It is as though "the rod laid on its shoulder" had been done away with. Thoughts like those of the Egyptian bondage of Israel seem to lend color to the figure (Exod. 5:6). The idea of "the staff of the oppressor," which had time and again been laid heavily on the poor slave in cruel blows runs parallel. All three — yoke, rod, staff — will be broken in the deliverance involved, and broken at that in a deliverance as triumphant and complete as was the deliverance of Gideon when the Midianites afflicted Israel (Judg. 6–8). Since that also was a blessing that the *northern* tribes especially enjoyed, the allusion is all the more appropriate.

Verse 5. Since war had brought these Galilean areas so very low, the deliverance in question can also be described in terms of ending wars, as is now done. A few items to be consigned to burning are mentioned, colorful items taken by way of a few significant samples — warriors' boots and blood-stained soldiers' robes — samples of things to be consigned to the fires when men clean up after wars are outlawed. Weapons are just not mentioned because it is quite obvious that they all will be given a similar treatment. Perhaps the thought of passages like Deut. 13:16f. enter in here. War booty may be unholy stuff to be consumed by flames, not to be gloated over.

d. The Author of the Great Happiness (vv. 6-7)

Verse 6. Now the author of all the blessings enumerated thus far is prominently brought into the picture. According to the statement involved it will not be a famous man, a renowned hero, but — "a child" and "a son." The choice of the terms is without a doubt partly motivated by the thought introduced in 7:14, the Immanuel. It is not claimed, of course, that as child this individual shall achieve all these things. But he will in some significant way appear on the scene as a child. He will "be born," as human beings are; he will "be given," for in a special way he will be divinely sent to the children of men. That he will in his own way occupy a position of great dignity is indicated by the fact that it is said: "the government shall be upon his shoulder." "Shoulder" may here involve a reference to the golden chain that hangs around the neck of, and lies upon the shoulder of, the great ruler as a symbol of authority.

And now come the four famous names. The parallelism requires that they be four compounds, as it were, compound names because the unique dignity of this deliverer cannot be covered by single names; and four of them because no one name can comprehend the multitude of blessings that he brings or the manifold works that he successfully achieves. Besides, all four of the compound nouns used are objects, not some subjects and some objects. The only objection to this simple regular construction of the names comes from the desire to remove some of the high claims that are made for the child by his names. It should also be noted that the expression, "his name shall be called," in line with the meaning of the Hebrew "name," means: This is the type of *character* that will be his. Besides, it is implied that he is called by these names because he actually is the kind of person that the names say he is.

Comprehensive synonymns for these four titles would be, assigning them to various areas of activity: statesman, hero of war, guardian, and ruler (*Herntrich*). However this is but a modest unfolding of the more obvious. "Wonderful-Counselor" emphasizes primarily that he will be most effective in planning, in formulating a plan for action. A great work is to be done by him, even the greatest ever attempted. But he had an adequate plan, the only one ever devised that measured up to the things to be attempted. In fact the very plan as such is a marvel; therefore: "a marvel of a counselor," as the term may also be translated. From the rest of revelation we know that these divine plans for action are not of a recent date but reach back into the eternities. The same thought in a different context appears also Isa. 28:29.

The immediate connection of the second, "Mighty-God," with the first is that the individual in question possesses the capacity for carrying out to the full all that his brilliant

plans call for: He has nothing less than the full omnipotence
of God at his command. What he devised, he is also well
able to achieve. He is himself God. That the divine
character of the "child" is here asserted appears also from
the fact that Isaiah uses the same title unequivocally for
God in 10:21. Again, therefore, in the compound name
the emphasis lies on the second member. The Hebrew
says literally, "God-hero," using a title for God (*'el*) that
signifies: "the Strong-one"). *Luther* used the translation
Kraft-held, showing how difficult of translation the name is.
We have translated the next name "Father-forever" rather
than "Everlasting-Father," because the emphasis obviously
lies not on the fact of the individual's eternal existence
but on the thought of his being everlastingly a father. "Father" in his connection refers to the loving, paternal concern he has for those who have been committed to his
charge. There is not even a remote reference here to an
intertrinitarian relationship — the Son being called the
Father. The thought to be associated with the father-con-
cept in the Old Testament is that of Ps. 103:13, "Like as
a father pitieth his children, so the Lord pitieth those
that fear him." If previously, effective plans and capacity
for carrying out such plans were the thoughts set forth,
this third title leads us to probe deep into the spirit and
attitude that motivates this "child" in what he undertakes;
deep, loving concern for his creatures.

The translation "father of booty" — once quite popular —
has fallen by the wayside as quite out of keeping with the
dignity of the great names involved.

The conclusion of this character-sketch is made by the
title "Prince of Peace." After all his work is done and he
has gathered to himself a redeemed people, he rules over
them as "Prince." The methods by which he achieved his
success were peaceful. The people whom he rules are men
of peace. The principles according to which he still carries on his work are all peace. In fact, through him the
word peace has taken on a much richer spiritual as well
as physical connotation. The very antithesis to what he
does would be to attempt to build a successful empire by
the methods of brutal war. Cf. Zech. 9:9f.; Micah 5:4f.

When this era of peace will set in is in no way indicated by this word of the prophet.

Verse 7. What this child inaugurates in a seemingly small beginning will have within it potentialities of growth well-nigh unbelievable. His rule and the peace he achieves will develop endlessly. At this point he is definitely identified with the famous throne of David. Even if this reference to the basic statement of II Sam. 7:12ff. had not been inserted, the assumption that a connection with this famous pronouncement exists, would have been made almost inevitably. For by the time Isaiah appeared on the scene the great promise to David about the continuance of his line was very well known and accepted in Israel. To be sure, it is not specifically asserted that the Child will be of David's lineage, but is he to be thought of as an usurper who has taken to himself without warrant possession of the throne of David? In his righteous position he does the work of his kingdom with "justice and righteousness" and he is also said to "establish and uphold it," all of which implies solid and successful building. "Justice" would refer more to the official pronouncements that he makes in connection with his work. "Righteousness" is the quality that governs all that he personally does. All this is indicative of the sound ethical basis on which all his work rests. No thought here of nationalistic preference for a certain nation apart from moral qualifications!

Though the "light" appears in Galilee, it somehow is related to the land of Judah through David.

The description closes with two emphatic declarations: first, his work reaches into the vast vistas of eternity; and secondly, the Lord with burning zeal for this whole undertaking stands continually behind his chosen one. It goes without saying that this is one of the clearest and most meaningful Messianic prophecies in the whole Old Testament.

4. "His Hand is Stretched Out Still" (9:8–10:4)

This section now presents a sharp dissonance over against the serene peace that pervaded the first part of the chapter.

Some commentators would object to having this section at this point, assuming that they must rearrange the material. However, as *Herntrich* very aptly points out, this is all by obvious design. The prophet is saying that the glorious age of the Messiah just described is not to be ushered in at once: the people are not ready. As long as they continue in their present state they have nothing to look forward to but judgments. So this is a doom passage.

It is quite difficult, however, to fit it into the picture of the days of Isaiah, as we know them. We can hardly tell whether things past, present, or future are being described. Nor, for that matter, does it make too much difference. Some of the situations described seem already to have taken place, some are in the making. We have, therefore, not a historical record of what took place, but a sort of indictment describing how things are going and will yet go for some time. The coming of the "child" cannot take place soon.

How the thought-units progress is not difficult to determine. The recurrence of a refrain (vv. 12, 17, and 21) marks the end of the three sections of this chapter. (10:4 belongs here too.)

a. Because of Unholy Pride There Will Be Defeat by the Enemies (vv. 8-12)

9:8-12   8. A word was sent by the Lord into Jacob,
And it has fallen into Israel.
9. And the people — all of them — will know,
Ephraim and the inhabitants of Samaria:
(who say in the pride and arrogance of mind:
10. "Bricks have fallen, but we will rebuild with hewn stones;
sycamores have been cut down but with cedars we will replace
   them").
11. [They will know:] that the Lord exalted the adversaries of
   Resin,
and spurred on his enemies;
12. [also] the Syrians on the east and Philistines on the west;
and they devoured Israel with open mouth.
For all this his anger is not turned back,
his hand is stretched out still.

The sequence of thought of vv. 8-11 must be determined briefly at the outset. The content of the "word" referred to in v. 8 is not given at once. Verse 9 means that the people will know what that word is as a result of the course that things take after the word has been pronounced. The word is the outgrowth of the haughty attitude that the people of the Northern Kingdom have taken, as described in v. 10. They as a nation will see a connection between this attitude and that which befalls the nation. As a result they will know that the Lord had a hand in the success of the powerful enemy, Rezin, king of Syria, which enemy will be exalted in the wars that follow. Of course this enemy is Assyria first of all. Yet before Assyria has this success, the Syrians and the Philistines will have done much damage to Israel (v. 12). Apparently the attack by the Philistines must be regarded in this instance as having been directed first against Judah, against whom the Philistines were perennially waging war. But from the connection it appears that the Philistines will not stop with attacks on Judah but will reach farther north and afflict Israel. Verse 12 then must be thought of as introduced by some connective as "also." The enemies of v. 11 and those of v. 12 are obviously not the same. It cannot be denied that whatever construction is put on these verses, particularly on v. 11, there will always be some rough spots for the explanation.

Now for the details on these verses.

Verse 8. A unique conception of the "word" of God is in evidence here. It is almost personalized as though it were a messenger. Again it falls with an ominous thud on a certain area. We incline to resort to a figure that was certainly foreign to the prophet's way of thinking, when we say that the word is like a sort of delayed time-bomb, which lies in Israel for a time and finally explodes. This is merely in line with the typical thought set forth by the prophets that the word of the Lord is an unusally effective thing.

Verse 9. In due time the people of the Northern Kingdom will become aware of the fact that a word of doom has been sent forth against them. Before the prophet goes on

to say what doom is impending he delays for a moment
to indicate that there is reason for the doom involved.
We have included this reason in the parenthesis that includes the last line of v. 9 and all of v. 10. A pronouncement that the Israelites have made indicts them; it reveals
their pride and haughtiness. This pronouncement (v. 10)
seems to be more in the nature of a proverbial saying. It
could be taken literally, though there seems to be no occasion for such an interpretation. It could be spoken after
an earthquake. It would be equally appropriate after the
ravages of war after homes and city-walls had been destroyed. We prefer to take it in a more general sense.
Something of the existing order has been overthrown by
the judgments of the Lord. The people are not humbled
or rendered contrite. Immediately they have grandiose
plans ready for building bigger and better and more ex-
pensively. There is not even an inkling of the fact that the
calamity that has befallen is a judgment from God and
seeks to brings them to their knees. Their intention on the
other hand is to replace bricks — cheaper building material
— with hewn stones — more elaborate and costly material.
The sycamore-cedars pattern involves the same arrogant
plans. On the value of sycamores compare I Kings 10:27.

Verse 11. At the beginning of this verse the sense seems
to demand that we repeat the verb "will know" from v. 9.
This means they will, by the turn that events take, be
compelled to admit that when the Assyrians were successful (i.e., "the adversaries of Rezin," king of Syria) it was
that the Lord had a hand in it, having in his own way
"exalted" them, i.e., given success to the arms of Assyria,
and "spurred" them on. God's direction of the affairs of
world-history can often be detected by those who observe
carefully. Sometimes it thrusts itself upon those who are
more obtuse.

Verse 12. In any case, in the wild irregularities of the
times that will develop, attacks will strike Israel behind
and before and Israel will be cruelly devoured. The picture
is lurid with scenes of battles and a nation brought very
low in suffering. Though that might evoke pity on the
part of the beholder and though the nation might well

pity itself, the Lord will show no pity, for apparently the nation has not actually taken its lesson to heart. For that reason comes that ominous refrain, "for all that his anger is not turned away, his hand is stretched out still." Of this word G. A. *Smith* says rather aptly: "Over the storm and battle comes booming like the storm bell the awful refrain, 'For all this. . . .'"

b. Because of Continued Impenitence There Will Be Overthrow of Leadership (vv. 13-17)

9:13-17 13. But the people have not turned back to him that smote them,
and they have not sought the Lord of hosts.
14. Therefore the Lord cut off from Israel head and tail,
palm branch and reed in one day.
15. (The elder and the man of rank, they are the head,
and the prophet and the teacher of lies are the tail).
16. And the leaders of this people mislead them,
and those who are led by them are swallowed up.
17. Therefore the Lord did not rejoice even over their young men,
nor did he have pity over their widows and orphans.
For all of them are profane and doers of evil,
and every mouth speaks folly.
For all this his anger is not turned away,
his hand is stretched out still.

With more force than we can catch in the translation the emphasis lies on the fact that the people did not *turn back*. The last line of v. 12 had asserted that Yahweh's anger had not *turned*. The first line of v. 13 indicates that there was no turning back on the part of the people. The word order (subject first) indicates in Hebrew that "the *people*," who had been the object of special attention on the Lord's part were the ones who had failed in this encounter. Bluntly speaking: They had failed to repent, when everything pointed to the extreme need of repentence. Right-minded people recognize who smote them and are wont to turn to him that did it. Not these. Nor "have they sought the Lord of hosts," a form of expression that signifies a special effort or even a pilgrimage to a sacred place to get a word of guidance from the Lord (cf. Gen.

25:22; Exod. 18:15; I Sam. 9:9; II Kings 22:18). But this nation has been dull and unresponsive.

Verses 14-15. Without elaborating any more fully this subject of the impenitence of the nation, the prophet launches at once into a description of the punishment that shall fall upon Israel as a result — overthrow of leadership. It is true that there is no particular connection between the form of sin and the form of the punishment, except that which is not here expressed: because they as a nation would not listen to their leaders that called them to repentance, therefore these warning voices together with all effective leadership would be taken from them. It may be that the time of this pronouncement falls into the days when the last kings of Israel were succeeding one another in quick succession, perhaps even the very time of Hoshea is meant. In any case, "head and tail, palm branch and reed" shall be cut off from Israel "in one day." These appear to be two expressions of the kind that mention the two extremes and by so doing include everything that lies in between. But since this all refers to leadership it would mean: all sorts of leadership, high and low.

At this point (v. 15) the prophet allows himself a sarcastic aside, or parenthesis. He puts a somewhat arbitrary interpretation on two of the extremes mentioned, interpreting the head to mean, "the elder and the man of rank," and elucidating the tail as an apt reference to "the prophet and teachers of lies." This is the element of interpretation that involves the sting. About as unstable as a dog's tail were some of those prophets who professed to offer leadership. And into that same class Isaiah puts the "teacher of lies." So it must have been a case where bad leadership undermined the effects of the good and the people were only too ready to give ear to those undeserving of confidence. The prophet does not attempt any special explanation of "palm branch and reed."

Verse 16. Now vv. 14 and 15 are explained a bit more fully. Many, if not almost all, of the leaders were leading this people astray. Yet it is well known that the first quality of any leader should be his utter reliability. But in Israel's last evil days there was a total collapse in this area. So men who let themselves be led by such irresponsible persons "were swallowed up," a figure expressive of some form of complete destruction.

Verse 17. This all explains how it came about that the Lord himself no longer seemed to care what befell his people. Where, for example, the young men would seem to be the objects of the special delight of the Lord, that was no longer the case. Where in another sense "orphans and widows" were the objects of his special protection that, too, no longer would be the case. For these two classes also, like all the rest of the nation, fell under the condemnation of two bad terms: they were both "profane and doers of evil"; the first involving a lack of religious sensibility and the second a sense of ethical discrimination. To top it all off, to hear these members of the ancient people of God speak, the surprising thing was that nothing they said gave evidence of stemming from the mouth of a people that belonged to the Lord: "every mouth spoke folly." Is it to be wondered at that the prophet reiterates: "For all this his anger is not turned away, his hand is stretched out still"?

c. Because of Prevailing Wickedness There Will Be Civil War (vv. 18-21)

As the chapter progresses the reader gets the feeling that this passage is very close to Amos 6:4-12 — similar conditions, a similar net-result predicted.

9:18-20 18. For wickedness burned as a fire
and devoured thorns and thickets;
and it has kindled the undergrowths in the forest,
and they roll upward as thick columns of smoke.
19. By the overflowing of the wrath of the Lord of hosts the land was scorched,
and the people had become as food for the fire.
A man turned against his brother, nobody was spared.
20. They carved off on their right hand and still were hungry;
They devoured on the left and still were not satisfied.
Each devoured the flesh of his own arm,

21. Manassah Ephraim and Ephraim Manasseh;
Both together attacked Judah.
For all this his anger is not turned away, his hand is stretched
    out still.

The nation's wickedness is the subject under consideration. In the first two verses the picture of a devastating
fire is used to describe the prevailing wickedness. Different aspects of such a fire are considered. It is seen raging
in "thorns and thickets." It rages in "the undergrowths of
the forest." It spreads like a regular forest fire. Thick columns of smoke rise and roll upward. There is something
frightening about the tremendous power and sweep of such
a fire. So wickedness blazes on powerfully. An added
feature appears in v. 19; it is the wrath of God which is
the point where this fire starts. God's anger is itself a fire.
Now it sweeps more like a prairie-fire over the land. It
engulfs the people and catches them unawares. Then of a
sudden it becomes apparent that the prophet is not describing disaster in general, but under the fire he is depicting civil war, as the last line of v. 19 indicates: "A man
turned against his brother, nobody was spared."

Verse 20. Civil war now expressly dominates the picture
down to the end of the chapter. The fire-figure is abandoned. Men are depicted as standing knife in hand, slash-
ing out in every direction, trying to get something to appease
their hunger. They cut on the right and on the left. Nothing satisfied their ravenous hunger. In fact, in a very
extreme form of comparison they are described as each
"devouring the flesh of his own arm." No man, even in
the extreme frenzy of hunger would think of doing a thing
like that. But that is actually what civil war does. It
lead men on to destroy themselves. Like as when two
brother tribes, Ephraim and Manasseh begin to assail one
another, as seems to have happened in the last days of the
Northern Kingdom. And then, as if their misery were not
enough, they launched attacks on Judah, the Southern Kingdom. Some of all this is portrayed in II Kings 15:13-16, 25,
30; cf. also Hos. 7:3ff., 8:4. Conclusion: the same dread
refrain.

Notes

Verse 1. The word *'artsah* has an old case ending which in this instance serves as a kind of accusative. Cf. *KS* 372 c.

Verse 2. The subject *ha'am* stands forward for emphasis (*KS* 341 f).

Verse 3. To read *lo* for *lo'* (the negative) is still the simplest solution of the problem of this verse, as was long recognized by the Jewish marginal reading (*Keri*). *Simchath* is a construct before a preposition (*KS* 336 w; *GK* 130 a).

Verse 6. *Pele'* is also a construct (*KS* 337 c). *Yullad* is a prophetic perfect like all the perfects in the whole section. Over against *Procksch* it must be remarked that even if the plural of *'el gibbor* appears in Ezek. 32:21 in an entirely different connection, this hardly warrants whittling down the idea of the divine nature of this Child in Isaiah.

Verse 7. Does the *le* at the beginning of the verse tie what follows back to the four names, or is it the beginning of an entirely new sentence? The German tradition basing on *Luther* claims the former; the English tradition, based on *KJ* version, the latter. The latter would seem to deserve the preference. It avoids a long and cumbersome sentence structure, and makes good sense.

That this whole passage should be a dynastic oracle or should be based on one, as some claim in connection with the ideas commonly advanced about the enthronement-of-Yahweh festival, contributes little if anything to the real interpretation of the passage. Besides, not an ascending monarch but a newly born child is under consideration here, as *Herntrich* rightly indicates.

Verse 8. When *shalach* and *naphal* appears in sequence without a *waw* conversive, this is due to the fact that synonymns are being used. Cf. *KS* 370 c.

Verse 10. The last verb *yesakhsekh* is controlled by the *waw* conversive of the first verb in the verse, though it is separated from it. *KS* 368 h.

Verse 14. Two extremes used to cover also all that lies in between — on this construction, which is so very common, cf. *KS* 92 c.

Verse 18. "'Columns of smoke," apparently an adverbial accusative (*KS* 332 k).

Verse 20. Some would alter *zero'a* ('arm') into *re'o* ('his neighbor'). The original is the more violent and colorful figure.

Albrecht Alt wrote an essay (*Festschrift*, Alfred Bertholet, JCB Mohr, Tuebingen, 1950, p. 29 ff.) in which he attempted an approach to this chapter that deserves consideration. After painstaking textual reconstruction, skillfully done but not entirely convincing, he arrives at the point of the four names of 9:6, drawing attention to the fact that according to Egyptian records in the time of the Middle Kingdom, a king, on the day of his accession to the throne would be given five "great names" by the deity. *Alt* indicates that this standing custom in some way may have influenced the ceremonial that prevailed when a descendant of David took the throne. Then he attempts to prove that the state of the text suggests that originally there was a fifth compound in the Isaiah text of 9:6. He quite correctly points out also that the text suggests that only *one* name is in reality ascribed to the child by Isaiah ("his name shall be called") and that the four names really constitute the totality of the child's well-rounded character. But still more important he suggests that the policy or program of this "child's" reign is being set forth in the four names and adds the suggestive thought that the whole passage as to its form may be regarded as a herald's pronouncement (*Heroldsspruch*) made to the Northern Kingdom (Israel, 8:23) as well as to the Southern (Judah). These suggestions deserve to be mentioned and cannot be lightly dismissed. We do not feel however that our basic approach, used above, should be reworked into this pattern.

In the same article, *Alt*, following *Fohrer's* suggestion maintains that the expression, which we have above translated "Sea Road," really refers to the Assyrian province of *Du'ru*, which at that time lay along the Mediterranean, west of Galilee. This conclusion is based on a study by *Fohrer* of the Assyrian documents from the time of Tiglath-pileser. Considering the fact that the name of the road that ran along the Sea of *Genneseret*, "Sea Road," or *via maris*, first originated in the days of the Crusaders, Alt's suggestion at least deserves attention.

Chapter X

d. Because of Social Injustice There Will Be a Day of Reckoning (10:1-4)

The piece that began with 9:8 is continued and concluded with this section. The chapter-division is unfortunate at this point. In justification of this approach we point to the fact that, like the three preceding sections, this one also closes with the refrain: ". . . his hand is stretched out still." We refuse, however, to stretch this approach so far as to reach back into Chap. 5 and take vv. 24-25 and add them here merely because of the refrain used. This would be the type of interpretation which lets subjective opinions determine what the author should have said rather than to respect what he has said.

In one respect this new section differs from the three that preceded. In them the whole nation was under indictment; here one class of persons is under attack. On the whole it seems most likely that the words in question are being addressed to Judah, or to be more specific, to the judges and courts of Judah.

10:1-4 1. Woe to those who decree unrighteous decrees, and the recorders who keep writing burdensome ordinances
2. who crowd away the needy from justice,
and who rob the poor of my people of their rights;
that widows may become their spoil,
and that they may make orphans their prey.
3. And what will you do on the day of reckoning
and at the time of ruin when it comes from afar?
To whom will you flee for help
and where will you leave your wealth?
4. Save that they will crouch among the prisoners
and fall under the slain.
For all that his anger is not turned away,
his hand is stretched out still.

197

On the word "woe" see 5:8. It introduces pronouncements of judgment.

In this chapter we find ourselves in the field of litigation
and lawsuits. Those who are appealing to the law to insure
or recapture their rights address themselves to the judges
and lawyers. But these are doing the very opposite of that
for which they have been installed in office. The "decrees,"
or decisions, they render are "unrighteous"; the "ordinances"
they publish are "burdensome"; a heavy weight laid on
the shoulders of those who already have been wronged.
We seem to witness the process of the courts from the
point where verdicts are rendered down to the point
where they are cast in written form. The whole of court-
machinery is grinding out iniquity and injustice. Where
(v. 2) courts were set up to safeguard the rights of the
ones otherwise helpless, here the result is that they are
"crowded away from justice" rather than helped to obtain
it. And so "they are robbed of their rights." The ones
thus wronged are described as "needy" and "poor," and
to be more specific, "widows," and "orphans." This is a
deplorable state of affairs touched upon elsewhere by the
prophet (see 1:23 and 5:23) but nowhere as fully as here.
That these latter are made the prey and the spoil of their
oppressors involves the figure of a strong wild beast pouncing upon its victim. Surely sins like these cry out to high
heaven for vengeance.

Verse 3. The prophet addresses himself to those who
have perverted justice, in a sharp attack. He calls to mind
the "day of reckoning." He assumes that they know in
their inmost conscience that such a day is inevitable. It
is practically a part of the old law written in the hearts to
admit the ultimate dawning of that day. What can be
done when it approaches? Hosea used a similar approach
in 9:5. For the guilty it spells ruin, overthrow, just judgment. When this ruin is described as coming from afar,
this is merely another device for indicating that it appears
to tarry long in its coming. It may also be likened to a
storm that hovers long on the far-distant horizon and as
a result appears more ominous. The question, "To whom
will you flee for help?" implies that for sins of this sort,

stubbornly adhered to, there is a sort of inevitable punishment. The second half of the question reflects on the unholy gains that were acquired by the perversion of justice: where can one leave it in safe deposit, as it were, to be picked up at a later date? For this use of "leave" see Gen. 39:6.

Verse 4. There would be only one course to follow (ironically indicated by the clause introduced by "save that"). The words might be translated: "They may crouch under the prisoners." In that case a pitiful scene is introduced: Prisoners, awaiting sentence, crouch in abject fear in a small prison, some lying hopelessly on the ground, others huddled above them. Or, if you want a choice of two evils, they may be likened to people who seek, of all places, to take refuge among the corpses on the field of battle. No other courses are open for criminals of such black guilt. Could a more dismal prospect be imagined?

The prophet concludes with the now familiar refrain. With this sharp indictment Isaiah, at least for the present, drops the role of Cato the Censor.

5. Woe unto Assyria! (10:5-34)

a. Boastful Assyria Has Misconstrued Her Special Assignment from God (vv. 5-11)

It will serve a good purpose to recall that this, too, is a part of the Immanuel Book (chaps. 7-12). A glowing Messianic prophecy was interrupted beginning with 9:8ff. and continuing to 10:4. All this intervening material was not misplaced nor had the prophet forgotten toward what goal he was moving. All this material that came after 9:8 reminded the nation that she was in no wise ready for the glorious days of the Messiah, the Child of the Four Names. It also now reminds the guilty nation that there will be some unhappy dealings with God's scourge, the Assyrian. All this dovetails together very appropriately and logically if one will but take time to enter sympathetically into the prophet's thoughts. Here, over against the prevailing trend of our times, it may also be suggested that the text of the book as it stands, though there are obvious difficulties here and there, is not in a hopeless state nor in need of multiple corrections and adjustments. Accepting the current critical treatment of the text would only leave the reader and the exegete in a state of having very little respect for the normative character of the prophetic message, in fact often with a feeling of condescending sympathy for a patchwork of very dubious value.

10:5-10 5. Woe unto Assyria that is the rod of my anger; and unto the one in whose hand my fury was a staff.
6. Against a godless nation I send him,
and against the people of my wrath I give him orders,
that he may rob the spoil and take the plunder,
and that he may trample them down like mire in the streets.
7. But that is not what he thinks nor is that his intention.
But he is minded to destroy and cut off nations not a few.
8. For he says: "Are not my captains all of them kings?
9. Is not Calno like Carchemish? Is not Hamath like Arpad? Is not Samaria like Damascus?
10. Just as my hand found the kingdoms of the idols
whose graven images excelled those of Jerusalem and Samaria,
11. shall I not also do to Jerusalem and her idols,
as I did to Samaria and her images?"

Verse 5. On "woe" see v. 1.

As we see v. 5, there are two separate and distinct approaches, or two analogous but different figures. The first figure represents the Lord's anger as personified and as having Assyria in its hand as a rod to be used for chastising Israel. God, or his anger, are the agent; Assyria is the instrument of punishment. The second figure is much like this but with an original turn to the idea. Here Assyria is the agent, and God's anger is the instrument that Assyria wields. But here, of course, the thought is that the Lord has put his wrath into Assyria's hand, but in either case God is the active agent and Assyria is a tool in his hand. On the translation of 5b see the *Notes*.

God is the speaker at this point. He has just defined the relation of Assyria to himself. Now he goes on to show against whom he has delegated the Assyrian. It is a "godless nation." Nothing indicates whether North or South Israel is meant. Going back as far as 8:1ff. we venture that

Northern Israel is primarily under consideration. "Godless" here bears the older meaning of "profane." At the same time, in line with v. 5, they are designated "the people of my wrath." The mission of the Assyrian is to devastate, spoil and plunder, all of which activities are but part and parcel of the activities of war. But the thoroughness with which Israel is brought low is indicated by the expression that they are to be trampled down "like the mire of the streets." Assyria is not out after skirmishes; she engages in all-out war with all its devastations.

Verse 7. In Hebrew the first part of this verse reads thus: "But this is not what *he* [special emphasis] thinks." The passage seems to reflect both on the past and the present; for some of the Assyrian activity lies in the past; more of the same is still currently going on. According to II Kings 18:25 the Assyrians had some conception of the fact that God wanted them to act as his punitive agent against Israel. But haughtily they brushed this knowledge aside and substituted their own preference in the matter. Thus their preference was that they "were minded to destroy and cut off nations not a few." Lust of conquest dominated their thinking. Typical imperialistic ambitions were in control at the helm. His pride had gotten the better of him.

Verses 8, 9. A sample of the thinking of the Assyrian king is submitted at this point. He indicates what computations have led him to arrive at the conclusion that none of the cities that he is minded to take will be able to resist effectually. His thoughts run over conquests made, comparing them with conquests planned. Geographically he moves from the northeast to the southwest. Carchemish on the Euphrates was taken; he expects to invest Calno in northern Syria with equal success. Hamath on the Orontes was taken; he expects to capture Arpad, the key to Syria, without difficulty. Damascus had been overrun; why should not Samaria be brought to fall with equal ease? All this points to the fact, first that Samaria, the northern kingdom, is primarily under consideration, and secondly that the final destruction of Samaria (722 B.C.) had not yet occurred.

Verse 10. The Assyrian's proud line of reasoning continues. Since it does not run as some commentators anticipate, much fault is found with vv. 10 and 11. Yet they present a very logical progression and effectively represent the thinking of the Assyrian king. First of all he represents his advance as being basically one of combat with the deities of the nations conquered, a typical point of view of religious heathen of days of old. A victory was a demonstration that your gods were stronger than the gods of your enemies. When the king says his "hand found the kingdoms of the idols" that means that his military power conquered them. But according to his thinking it was a struggle first of all of gods versus gods. Quite properly he links Jerusalem and Samaria together as in a class by themselves over against all others. Though he may not have understood the distinctive features of the religion of Israel, he knew that this nation was in a class by itself. Whether he knew that officially their religion abhorred idolatry we cannot say. But all the others mentioned made more of images than Israel did and had more of them. So he claims that their "graven images excelled (in quality, numbers and value) those of Jerusalem and Samaria." So, finally, he comes to a climax: his ultimate objective was Jerusalem. Samaria had already been vanquished a number of times. All that remains was to "do to Jerusalem and its idols" as he did to Samaria and her images. The logic is clear and convincing. His pride is superb. But he has made his reckoning without his host. Naturally such vaunting calls for an answer at the hands of the prophet, which answer now follows.

In this passage v. 10 is not an intrusion (*Fremdkoerper*, as *Procksch* sees it) nor metrically unacceptable. We do not yet know enough about Hebrew meter to render such judgments. The simple logical and reasonable progression of thought is the best defense of the entire passage.

b. Delayed Judgment Will Strike This Haughty Conqueror (vv. 12-14)

10:12-14 12. And it shall come to pass when the Lord will have concluded all his work on Mount Zion and in Jerusa-

lem, "I shall visit judgment upon the fruit of the pride of the heart of the king of Assyria and upon the haughty spirit of his eyes. 13. For he says: 'By the strength of my hand have I made achievements and by my wisdom, for I am clever.
I have removed the boundaries of peoples,
and have plundered their stores,
and like a mighty one I have brought low those who sat on thrones.
14. And my hand has found the wealth of the peoples like a nest,
And as one gathers eggs that are left, so have I gathered all the earth;
and there was none that flapped a wing or opened a mouth or chirped.' "

We entitle this section "Delayed Judgment" because some other task first had to be performed by the Assyrian and then the Lord would take him in hand to judge him. Furthermore, in the middle of v. 12 there comes a transition from indirect to direct discourse without any formal announcement — a feature of Hebrew style which was quite common. Attention now centers on Jerusalem and Zion, as was so frequently the case with Isaiah. The Lord had a work to do there. Exactly what form it would take, is not here discussed. Chapters 36–38 describe it at length. It involved a great threat against the safety of the city and a most striking deliverance, after the city had been all but ruined. When that work will have been brought to an end, then God can take the pride of Assyria in hand. By a unique sentence structure — a long succession of "of"-phrases — "fruit *of* the pride *of* the heart *of* the king *of* Assyria" — the "the puffed up pride of the king about ready to burst," as *Delitzsch* describes it, is colorfully portrayed. But the object of God's attack is the "pride" and the "haughty pride" of the nation and the king.

Verse 13. The words here used may sound very boastful, almost more so than that with which any mortal would be ready to charge the king. But any one who has read the boastful style of the record of the victories of the Assyrians, as recorded on the monuments, will find at this point that the prophet is skillfully reproducing this bombastic style. Success is attributed to the strength of his hand and to his own wisdom and cleverness. He describes how, quite autocratically, he has shifted international boundaries (cf. II Kings 17:24ff. for a case in point) and how he has plundered stores that the nations laid up for themselves. In fact the translation we have used — "like a mighty one" — could mean "like a bull," and this could be a reference to the mighty bull-colossus which was a symbol of the might of Assyria. So then, like a bull the king stormed in fiercely upon men sitting on thrones and overthrew them.

Verse 14. To this, one grand figure is added, bold in its imaginative approach. The nations are eggs in the big world-nest. He, the king, went out on a plundering expedition to gather such eggs. When the mother bird saw him approach she always fled. So that all he found was abandoned eggs, which he then gathered in, completely unmolested: "there was none that flapped the wing or opened the mouth or chirped." With playful ease he did his conquering. This is proud boasting to the nth degree.

c. For Her Arrogance Assyria Will Be Burned Out as by a Forest Fire (vv. 15-19)

The progression of thought is very easy and natural. If, as just shown, Assyria's judgment may be delayed momentarily, ultimately it will come, with the devastating force that is described in this section. Besides, what this section offers is not to be pictured as made up of "mixed metaphors and confused ideas." Rather, the picture is clear and easily grasped. True, at times there is a rapid change of figure, which need not, however even be characterized as "mixed metaphors."

10:15-19 15. May the ax boast itself against him that chops with it?
or the saw magnify itself against him who saws with it?
as though the rod were to sway him that lifts it up,
or as though the staff lifted up the one who is not wood.
16. Therefore the Lord, Yahweh of hosts will send a wasting sickness among their well-fed soldiers;
and under their glory he will kindle a kindling like the kindling of fire.
17. And the Light of Israel will become a fire, and his Holy One a flame;
And it shall burn and devour their thorns and briers in one day.

18. And also the glory of their forest and fruitful land will it
    consume soul and body.
And it shall be as when an ailing person wastes away.
19. And what is left of the trees of their forest will be so few that
    any lad may be able to write them down.

The arrogant tone seen in the preceding section is still
being described, but at the same time the utter futility and
folly of this arrogance is being revealed. Seldom have figures been employed more effectively. What could be more
preposterous than for the ax to be of the opinion that it was
controlling the wood-chopper? What could be more silly
than for the saw to insist on its independent operation over
against the woodsman that sawed with it? Or to carry the
absurdity farther, a man lifts a rod, but the rod could
hardly be of the conviction that it was swaying the man.
And then comes the climax, if we rightly understand that
the one "who is not wood" may be a reference to the Almighty. Then Assyria, the staff, thinks it is manipulating God
himself. To such extremes proud arrogance can mislead itself.

Verse 16. So then the Lord will inaugurate a procedure
whereby this proud nation will be made to feel its frailty
very painfully. He, who has other armies besides Assyria
at his beck and call, will send "a wasting sickness among
their well-fed soldiers." This could have been what the angels of the Lord brought when he smote in the camp of
the Assyrians in one night 185,000 men, as we read II Kings
19:35. Not without reason some hold that this may have
been a swift striking bubonic plague that was used by the
Lord's angel. But whether we see a general figure or such a
specific allusion matters little in this case. It has been remarked that the second half of the verse with the almost
repetitious use of the root "to kindle," especially in the Hebrew, produces a kind of onomatopoeic effect that enables
one almost to hear the crackling of the flames as they burn.

Verses 17, 18. With a single change of figure the Lord,
here called "the Light of Israel," is thought of as the fire
himself, because it is he that controls and sends it for judgment. The parallel statement has it that the "Holy One

[will be] a flame." Those that are consumed by this holy fire are found to be in two classes. There are, first of all, "their thorns and briers." In the light of the second group, who are described (v. 18) as "the glory of their forest and fruitful land," it would appear that the metaphor involved describes the lower levels of society among the Assyrians as the "thorns and briers," and the higher levels as the "glory of the forest." Nor should the expression used in this connection "soul and body" strike us as out of place. This was a popular expression for "the whole man." In other words, complete destruction is indicated. With a rapid change of figure, but quite without confusion of thought, the idea suggested in the first half of v. 16 about "wasting sickness" is here used again: "and it shall be as when an ailing person wastes away." The Assyrians will be found to be as frail as other mortals. Sickness will sweep away their sturdy warriors. Again, whether this be taken literally or figuratively matters little. The net result is the same: The arrogant will be brought low.

Verse 19. One further aspect of the figure of the proud Assyrian forest is played up for a climax. Of the mighty men that made up the state and the army so few will be left as would be the trees that are left after a devastating forest-fire: "any lad may be able to write them down." You do not have to be able to count up to high figures for this purpose.

d. After the Disaster of God's Judgment a Remnant of Israel Will Return to Him (vv. 20-23)

The critical approach is much concerned about viewing this piece at least as being quite isolated (cf. *Procksch*) and out of context. Yet, what is more natural than to explore what will be Israel's lot after the judgment of God has struck and eliminated the threatening oppressor. This passage tells how Israel will react.

10:20-23 20. And it shall come to pass in that day that the remnant of Israel and the escapees of the house of Jacob shall no longer lean on him that smote them. But they will sincerely lean upon Yahweh, the Holy One of Israel.

21. A mere remnant will return — a remnant of Jacob — unto
the Mighty God.
22. For though your people, O Israel, were like the sand of the
sea,
only a remnant shall return,
the appointed destruction will usher in a flood of righteousness.
23. For the Lord, Yahweh of hosts, is making a destruction, even
as he has appointed, in the midst of the whole earth.

Verse 20. As has been remarked, this prophecy (the part
that preceded and what now follows) is not utopian in spirit.
It does not usher in a golden age. There will be only a
"remnant" and "escapees" surviving the calamity. But at
least they will have learned a lesson. They will no longer
be leaning on the help of neighboring nations, whom in times
past they frequently called to their assistance —Syria, Assyria, Egypt and Babylon. All these turned from helping
them, to smiting them, when the supposed helper found it
to his advantage to turn upon his ally. Now after the bitter lesson was learned, "they will sincerely lean upon Yahweh." Officially the nation (Northern Kingdom and Southern kingdom) always leaned upon Yahweh. Oftentimes
there was little sincerity about their allegiance. Now that
will be changed.

Verse 21. But the word that echoes through this passage is "remnant." A promise and a threat are to be found
in that word, the promise that some will turn back; the
threat that they will be a meager lot. When they return
to the "Mighty God" they will discover that he is mighty to
help, in fact, is their only hope. When it is stressed that this
remnant will "return," here, too, there are two possibilities
that seem to be in the prophet's mind. The first emphasis
seems to be on repentance, the second on the hope of return from the Captivity that inevitably will come.

Verse 22. The more ominous side of the word just spoken
is spelled out first a little more clearly. The Hebrew only
says "a remnant," but it clearly means "a mere remnant,"
as our translation also indicates. The second half of the
verse has its difficulties. Our translation understands it as
follows. "The destruction" that will come when the Assyrian armies overflow the land is "appointed" in the sense

that it is definitely decreed or appointed beforehand how long it shall last and how far it will go. But still the most notable thing about it will be the fact that it is all "righteousness." It will not go one step further than men deserve; it will at the same time serve to help realize God's wholesome purposes. In the destruction God's righteousness shall be abundantly in evidence.

Verse 23. To this last thought v. 23 attaches itself very directly. The point is that the destruction made by the Lord of hosts is of broad scope. It is part of his vast plan which is world-wide in scope. Besides all of it is carefully planned in advance: it is a destruction "even as he has appointed in the midst of the whole earth." Men need not have fears about a blind justice, that strikes indiscriminately and viciously and cannot be understood nor accounted for. Come it will, but it will be righteous and serve to carry out God's major purposes.

e. *Zion Will Be Delivered When Assyria Topples* (*vv. 24-27*)

The message of the previous section as to both its parts is of sufficient importance to warrant having it spelled out in greater detail. That the prophet now does, offering first a word from Yahweh himself, then an explanatory prophetic word of his own.

10:24-27 24. Therefore thus says the Lord, Yahweh of hosts: "O my people, who dwell in Zion, be not afraid of the Assyrian, who ventures to smite you with the rod, and will lift up the staff against you as the Egyptians did. 25. For in a very short time, anger will be full grown and my fury against the destruction they practiced." 26. And Yahweh of hosts will wield a scourge against them like when he smote Midian at the rock Oreb, and his rod will be over the sea and he will lift it up as he did against Egypt.
27. And it will come to pass at that time his burden will move off from their shoulder and his yoke from your neck, and every yoke will be broken because of fatness.

It is best to class this as a piece of prose.

Verse 24. First comes a word of reassurance, which Israel would stand much in need of when the Assyrian crisis was at its height, for this crisis was extremely acute. When the Lord addresses Israel as his people, that indicates his love for them. When he adds "who dwell in Zion" the emphasis appears to rest on the fact that Zion is dear to the Lord also as the place of his habitation. Therefore he will also love those that dwell there and love the sanctuary found there.

The Assyrian, indeed, will be painfully smitten by the rod of God's hand. But we have translated the verb involved as a conative, "venture to smite." For the intention of the Assyrian will be deadly. But it shall not be realized. The descriptive phrase "as the Egyptians did," reminds the hearer that the Egyptian taskmasters did treat the Israelites very cruelly. But at the same time there is a kind of wholesome double meaning about the expression. Egypt attempted to destroy Israel by the rod of the taskmaster, but the attempt was futile. The more they were oppressed the more they flourished.

Verses 25, 26. The first part of verse 25 is unusually difficult. We believe that it yields a very acceptable sense that fits well into the context. For the anger that will "be fully grown" is certainly the Lord's anger at the pride and presumption of the Assyrians. As their sins mount higher so does the anger of the Lord, till it has reached its climax. With this the second half of the verse agrees very well. For his fury will also become full grown against the destruction they practiced. They were indeed sent as a rod of punishment against Israel, but they cruelly overdid their part, enough to arouse God's wrath. Here the Lord indicates that his wrath will have to come into play. With this thought v. 26 agrees well, explaining the preceding verse more fully. Giving a different turn to the scourge-idea which had appeared earlier in the chapter, the prophet indicates that the Lord, who controls the whole host of created things in heaven and in earth, will use some available agency as a scourge that he will wield against Assyria. It will then be effective against the world-power Assyria as it once was in days of old against the swarms of invaders that overran Israel in the days of Midian, where at the rock Oreb a Midianite chieftain came to a great overthrow. See Judg. 7:25. Another way of stating it is that he will act as he did in the days of the Exodus, stretching his rod — for that is what the rod of Moses actually was — over the sea and bringing deadly destruction on the embattled hosts of Pharaoh. See Exod. 4:2ff. and 14:16.

Verse 27. The deliverance aspect of this great work of the Lord is drawn a bit more fully in this verse. Since the burdens of the taskmasters of Egypt are still in the mind of the prophet, he adds verse 27.

From the idea of a burden the prophet passes quite naturally to that of a yoke, which is proverbially burden-some. But the last sentence has caused commentators no end of trouble. We hardly agree with those who describe it as utterly senseless. Though we cannot be too sure what is meant, the thought would appear to be that Israel is likened to a stocky ox with a yoke upon his neck. So sturdy and strongly developed does the ox get to be that by the bulk of his muscular development of the neck muscles he virtually bursts the yoke he bears and so becomes free. All this is part of God's reassurance for Israel that she shall assuredly become free from the yoke imposed by Assyria.

f. The Strategic Assyrian Advance That Almost Took Zion Described in Terms of Bulletins from the Front (vv. 28-32)

10:28-32 28. He has come to Ayath —
he has passed by Migron —
he has stored his baggage at Michmash —
29. they have crossed the pass —
"Geba is a lodging-place for us" —
Ramah trembles —
Gibeah of Saul has fled. —
30. Utter a shriek, inhabitants of Gallim —
hearken, O Laisha —
O poor Anathoth! —
31. Madmenah is in flight —
the inhabitants of Gebim seek refuge. —
32. This very day he is at Nob to halt momentarily;
he will shake his fist at the mountain of the daughter of Zion,
the hill of Jerusalem.

The transition in thought from the preceding section to
the one now before us is well put by *Koenig*, who suggests
that the happy time of deliverance just described will come
about for those who are true to Yahweh no matter how near
the invading Assyrians may come, and they will come dangerously close. This threatening approach is here described
in a kind of war-bulletin style (*Scott*), if compared with
Judg. 5. At the same time this is more in the nature of a
poetic phantasy. For this is not the exact route that the
Assyrians took when Jerusalem was threatened, but the
threat was as acute as the one here described. Besides,
this section reads like a number of bulletins direct from
the front line of advance — short, snappy reports. Again
the whole is cast in a verb form that is the equivalent of
the historical present — the writer is vividly describing an
event that lies in the future. Then it has also been noted
by those particularly at home in the geography of the Holy
Land, Like *Dalman*, whom *Procksch* follows — that the route
here described is not the usual and direct route coming
down from the north toward Jerusalem but a side route
along which an enemy may steal unobserved, which fact
has led some to describe the attack here outlined as a sneak
attack. The first two verses (28-29) give a progress report;
v. 30 gives rather the personal reaction of the speaker.

The starting point is Ayath, some ten miles almost due
north of Jerusalem. The successive names, if plotted, mark
an almost direct line due south. Most of these places can
be identified with a fair measure of certainty, except Gallim and Laisha. For further identification with present-day
names see the more recent commentaries (or *Oesterley* and
Robinson, A History of Israel, vol. 1, p. 396). The last-mentioned spot is Nob, from which eminence the city of Jerusalem may be seen, as Jerome, referred to by *von Orelli*,
remarks. In addition there is an inimitable play on words
running through the whole section, an effect that cannot
be reproduced by translation without undue distortion. The
whole account reflects the panic that seized town after
town as the relentless foe advanced.

As for details — after Ayath is passed and Migron, the foe,

facing the difficult pass of Michmash, finds it expedient to store his baggage there, the same old pass where Jonathan clashed with the Philistines (cf. I Sam. 14:1ff.). Night comes on the advancing army so they decide to lodge at Geba. Ramah, hearing of it, trembles. From Gibeah, also famous by association with the early history of Saul, they flee before the enemy arrives. Dramatically the writer summons Laisha to shriek with fear at the thought of what will befall her. Anathoth's fate wrings an exclamation of sympathy from the prophet. The others flee ahead of the advancing enemy.

Verse 32. At Nob, quite possibly Mt. Scopus of a later date, the enemy forces halt to catch their breath. In a threatening gesture the hand is being waved over the city — we should prefer to say, the fist is shaken — the city is within grasp and all but taken when the account is significantly interrupted. That is as far as it ever got. The danger was acute. The fall of the city was imminent. Her doom was sealed. Yet that last step never became a reality.

g. Yahweh Will Cut Down the Proud Assyrian Forest (vv. 33-34)

10:33-34 33. Lo, the Lord, Yahweh of hosts, will lop off the crown of the branches with an awful crash,
and the lofty of stature will be cut down,
and they that are high will be brought low.
34. And the thickets of the forest will be struck down with an ax,
and Lebanon will fall at the hands of the Majestic One.

In the previous section everything took place on the field of battle. Now the terminology of the forest prevails. Assyria is that forest. Yahweh is the woodsman. The mighty and proud trees are seen to crash one after the other. Blows of the ax have taken the place of the din of battle. The net result is the same: Assyria will meet with a catastrophic overthrow.

The last title used for the Lord — "the Majestic One" — occurs also in Punic for the gods of that land (Phoenicia).

Notes

Verse 1. We have sought to catch the force of the Piel participle (*mekhattebhim*) by translating it "keep writing."

Verse 2. To have the indefinite *yethomim* with *'eth*, the sign of the accusative, is rare. Cf. *GK* 117 d.

Verse 3. In *leyom* the *le* is temporal, *KS* 331 f.

Verse 4. Between the first two words of the verse we assume that the *yodh* is written but once (haplography). Therefore we read the verb as *yikhra'* and translate it "will crouch." To get a few Egyptian gods into the picture by textual correction is far-fetched.

Verse 5. Usually the last clause of the verse is reconstructed as though it called for a complete rearrangement, But no unity of approach seems to satisfy, About three different approaches are currently in use. Our translation above, "Woe unto the one in whose hand . . .," seems to make good enough sense.

Verse 6. *'ashallechennu* may be classified as a *yaqtul durans*, i.e., in the sense of "I keep on sending." (*KS* 157 b).

Verse 7. The *ki* of the second half of the verse is adversative — *KS* 372 e.

Verse 10. In explaining the *min* comparative before "Jerusalem" and before "Samaria" it should be noted that the point of comparison is not stated, as being more or less obvious from the context. This allows for being both more excellent in quality or workmanship, being splendid idols, or they were more numerous. See *KS* 308 c.

Verse 13. The initial *ki* in this case may be construed as "namely." *KS* 373 a.

Verse 14. The subject of the infinitive *'esoph* is to be thought of as indefinite, "as *one* gathers." *KS* 299 h.

Verse 16. To strike *Yahweh tsebha'oth* merely for metrical reasons is unwarranted.

Verse 18. By the use of *kabhodh* ("glory") a kind of superlative is produced (*KS* 309 g).

Verse 19. *Yikhtobh* is an imperfect expressing the thing that is potential. Therefore: "*may* read." *KS* 186.

Verse 22. Here the initial *ki* is concessive. (*KS* 394 a). On *shoteph* with accusative see *GK* 117 z.

Verse 28. *Ba'* equals a historical present (*KS* 133).

Verse 27. In an attempt to find a more acceptable meaning for the last three words of this verse the commonly accepted conjecture is *'alah mippeney Rimmon*, "he has gone up from Rimmon" (*RSV*). This is ingenious but not necessary.

Chapter XI

b. The Messiah of the Line of David and His Great Work of Salvation (Chap. 11)

Isaiah here resorts to one of the most effective contrasts possible, a contrast that could easily be lost sight of due to the chapter-division that is found at this point. The preceding chapter had depicted the downfall of the Assyrian military strength in terms of the cutting down of a mighty forest. After the ax of divine judgment had crashed in among the trees, nothing but stumps was left standing all over the vast mountain-side. So the imposing might of empire collapses. But God's way of working his purpose is to use the small, the weak, and the insignificant. But, adhering to the same general pattern just employed, there will be an insignificant stump in Israel, the house of David, or Jesse, fallen upon evil days and become very unimportant. This stump God will enable to bring forth a live shoot, which will develop into a tree actually bearing fruit. This tree of lowly beginnings is the Christ of God. In other words, that which is imposing collapses; that which is insignificant is capable of producing the greatest possible results.

All of this is still a part of the general theme, "Through Judgment to Salvation." Chapter 9 had shown what judgment was still to befall Israel. From 10:4 on, the judgment upon Assyria was under consideration. Now the more positive note of the salvation that is to come is distinctly heard and the Messiah again appears as the great agent of this salvation.

This chapter may be outlined as follows:

(1) The Messiah's Equipment (vv. 1-3a)
(2) His Manner of Doing His Work (vv. 3b-5)
(3) The Transformation to Be Wrought Even in the Realm of Nature (vv. 6-9)

(4) A Description of His Work in Terms of What He Can Do for Israel (vv. 10-16)

G. A. *Smith* has a rather attractive way of showing how these parts are integrated; he presents them as three great ideals: "the perfect indwelling of our humanity by the Spirit of God; the peace and communion of all nature, covered with the knowledge of God; the traversing of history by the divine purposes of redemption."

Though the promised Messiah is the dominant figure in the chapter it should be noted that though the child-concept with reference to him clearly stands out, there is as yet no allusion to the Child which is the son of a virgin, nor is there even a faint reference to the Child-of-the-Four-Great-Names. Nor is there any need of such references. The alert mind recognizes enough of continuity in observing that in each of the three cases involved we are dealing with a child.

It may also be pointed out that the figure of the Messiah is, as frequently, cast in a heroic mold, gigantic and towering, heroic and powerful. He has a vast work to do and is equal to the task.

There is the critical problem whether we dare regard this chapter in its entirety as stemming from Isaiah himself. The approach that has most followers at the present, has very grave misgivings especially about vv. 10-16. We shall deal at length with that issue in the Notes at the conclusion of the chapter.

(1) The Messiah's Equipment (vv. 1-3a)

11:1-3a 1. And there shall go forth a shoot out of the stump of Jesse,
and a sprout from its roots shall bear fruit.
2. And the spirit of Yahweh shall rest upon him —
the spirit of wisdom and understanding,
the spirit of counsel and heroic action,
the spirit of knowledge and of fear of Yahweh.
3a. And his delight shall be in the fear of Yahweh.

Verse 1. First, the person under consideration is identified. The identification offered presents a natural mystery to the hearer of that day; for no prophetic word is fully clear before its fulfillment. The picture involved as such presents what is left of a once mighty tree after it has been cut down — a stump. This stump in turn stands in obvious contrast to the vast number of *dead* stumps that cover the ground after the vast Assyrian forest was hewn down by the Almighty (chap. 10). Here the difference is that the stump is not dead. Obviously, the reference is to the royal house of David, called in this case, "stump of Jesse," because, at the time involved, the glory that inhered in the name of David will have been lost and the family will have sunk to the level at which it stood when Jesse bore the honor of the clan. All of this is another way of saying that a time will come when the illustrious Davidic family will have lost its luster and will have returned to its status of an average undistinguished family (cf. Amos 9:11). Such was the family of Joseph and Mary at the time when Jesus appeared on the scene. First, human glory must be brought low and human achievement appear as nothing. Then God can take over. Another way of stating the case is: "a sprout from its roots shall bear fruit." This marks a later stage of the development. First the family is proved to be dead; out comes a shoot (cf. 53:2; Rev. 5:5). Then the shoot is proved to be healthy; it develops into a tree capable of bearing fruit. Since the word for "sprout" is *netser*, this word may have furnished the basis for the thought that Matthew presents when (Matt. 2:23) he notes that it was indicated by the prophet that the Messiah should be called a "Nazarene." This appears to be the only passage that the writer had in mind.

Verses 2, 3a. Now comes the new feature that distinguished the latest offspring from the line of David: he is divinely equipped. All of his equipment is mediated through the spirit of Yahweh, with which he is endowed in superlative measure, not intermittently but perennially (for the spirit "shall rest" i.e., abide, on him). Cf. Judg. 6:34; I Sam. 11:7; II Sam. 23:2.

It hardly seems permissible to think directly in this instance of the Third Person of the Holy Trinity. For the *personal* character of the spirit was not yet so clearly revealed in the Old Testament. So we are compelled to think of that unique divine power which emanated from the Almighty and could enable men to do divinely-imposed work effectively. Therefore, this individual from the line of David has divine power in superlative measure. We cannot in New Testament times divorce our thinking from the personal spirit of God. But the Old Testament did not as yet fully reveal such truth.

Now the various gifts that the Spirit imparts are enumerated. The term "spirit" occurs seven times. If the first use of it in the first line of v. 2 is taken as the equivalent of a sturdy stem and the next six gifts are thought of as the branches that went out from the central stem, we are fully justified in the conclusion that the traditional seven gifts of the spirit are here thought of as endowing the Messiah. Each gift is rich in meaning. The seven-branched lampstand of the Tabernacle of days of old may be the type that furnished the illustration involved.

Now the individual gifts that this illustrious descendant of David will enjoy are enumerated. First comes the gift of "wisdom." The rich connotation that this term bears in Old Testament usage demands that we take it to mean a rare capacity for comprehensive judgment coupled with the ability to put to practical use the insight that is enjoyed. Basically this is in the sphere of the intellect, but it does not imply mere theory. In the same general area lies the gift of "understanding." The root meaning here involved points in the direction of being able to decide between various possibilities with which a person may be confronted and to choose the most advantageous course under the circumstances. Or this might also be regarded as the ability to solve problems. Obviously these first two gifts belong together.

The next two gifts of the spirit also constitute a pair: "counsel and heroic action." The first of these implies ability to devise an adequate plan for the situation that is being confronted, or to plot comprehensive strategy (cf. 9:6). For to understand the problem that is being encountered and to see its many-sided complexity does not yet guaranty a solution that is practical. But here again, to devise a plan is not the solution. There must also be the ability to execute the plan devised. For this purpose the other gift mentioned comes into play, "heroic action." The familiar translations usually call this "might." But the root-meaning implies that the particular form of might that a person qualified to inaugurate victorious action displays is under consideration. This is the gift that makes heroes (Hebrew: *gibbor* vs. *gebhurah*.)

So far the emphasis lies largely in the field of capacity to act. But such action to be successful in the long run must have deep roots. These roots are: "the spirit of knowledge (of Yahweh) and of fear of Yahweh." The parenthetical addition "of Yahweh" is implied in the Hebrew construction but was added with care to clinch the fact that both attributes are directly in relation to Yahweh, Israel's covenant God. "Knowledge of Yahweh" reaches deep. It means quite a bit more than insight into the nature and attributes of the Lord. It involves an embracing love that takes hold on the one known, refusing to let him go. Hosea already had some insight along these lines: Hos. 2:20; 4:1, 6; 6:6. But even such traits can hardly appear alone. So the companion to such knowledge is "the fear of Yahweh." That is, so to speak, the deep tap-root of the ruler's character: reverence for God and becoming humility. In fact this last attribute is of such far-reaching importance that an explanatory clause is appended to indicate its fundamental importance, namely the word of v. 3a: "and his delight shall be in the fear of Yahweh." All thinking and action will be in total submission to the divine will of him who commissioned this ruler to act for him. Such yielding of his own will to the higher demands will not be burdensome and unpleasant but rather a matter of sheer "delight." The verb used implies that this attribute constitutes the very air that the person involved breathes.

Add up these seven gifts of the spirit and the net result, as has been frequently pointed out, is the *Perfect Ruler*. It is from this point of view that this portrait is to be viewed. He stands in sharp contrast to the disappointing rulers that were encountered on the throne of Judah in Old Testament days. They were very unsatisfactory. This one leaves nothing to be desired.

(2) His Manner of Doing His work (vv. 3b-5)

11:3b-5 3b. He shall not judge according to what his eyes see,
nor decide according to what his ears hear.
4. But he shall judge the lowly with righteousness,
and shall decide for the meek of the earth with equity.
And he shall smite the earthly-minded with the rod of his mouth,
and with the breath of his lips he shall slay the wicked.
5. And righteousness shall be the girdle round his loins,
and faithfulness the girdle round his waist.

Verses 3b-5. These verses represent a kind of sampling of
the deeds this perfect prince will do. Many more deeds in
many other areas of activity could have been added. The
emphasis lies on the perfect fulfilment of his duties. The persons singled out as the recipients of the benefits of his reign
are the lowly and the meek. If they get their rights, every one
else surely will. For that is the acid test of impartial administration of duties, not to overlook the unimportant people.
But this ruler has a heart for them and will champion their
cause. He is enabled to do this the more perfectly (v. 3b)
by the fact that he is not dependent upon inadequate
sources and media of communication. He sees more than
eyes — his own or those of his servants — can detect. He
knows more than informers — mercenary or upright and official — can supply for him according to what they have heard.
Having all knowledge at his disposal his decisions are the
more comprehensive and correct. But all this activity of his
is embraced in the one verb "judge." That signifies all the
activities of effective rule, according to Old Testament usage
of the verb. "Decide" then means the official verdict that is
ultimately pronounced.

But (v. 4b) he shall also know how to deal effectively
with the wrong-doers, here called "the earthly-minded"
and the "wicked." With amazing ease he will dispose of
them where they deserve to be disposed of. One word of his
suffices and they are consigned to befitting punishment, or,
to use the Hebrew idiom, he "smites them with the rod of
his mouth." And if they deserve the death penalty, he shall
slay them with the same effortless ease, by "the breath of
his lips." Note that where most translations say smite "the

earth" (4b) we have translated "earthly-minded" because the parallel term "the wicked" requires this.

So this brief description is summed up in a comprehensive statement in v. 5. His entire reign is described as marked by "righteousness" and "faithfulness." The former is all-embracing, like a broad girdle about the loins of a man. It holds everything together. As flowing garments are prevented from entangling a man in action by the broad girdle that holds these garments compactly in place, so the course of righteousness that he pursues never entangles him in contradictions or subsequent difficulties. He remains so true to the obligations that his relation to Israel demands. Of the same sort is the effect of his "faithfulness." Since he can always be depended upon to do what should be done, all things are completed when they should be and difficulties cannot develop later because of oversight. By its very brevity this description is most effective. One senses that much more could have been offered by way of detailed explanation.

(3) The Transformation to Be Wrought Even in the Realm of Nature (vv. 6-9)

11:6-9 6. A wolf shall lodge with a lamb,
and a leopard shall lie down with a kid;
and a calf and a lion and a fatling together.
And a young lad shall lead them.
7. A cow and a bear shall graze together,
and their young shall lie down together,
and a lion shall eat cut-feed like an ox.
8. The nursing child shall play at the hole of the asp,
and the weaned child shall place its hand on the den of the great viper.
9. Men shall not hurt nor harm in all my holy mountain;
For the earth shall be full of the knowledge of the Lord as the waters cover the sea.

Verse 6. Not only shall men be governed well in the realm of this great prince; the perfection of his administration is to extend even into the realm of nature, which through man's sin was made subject to vanity. There are somewhat similar passages to be found elsewhere in the prophets, in some of which vegetation is said to be involved as well as the animals that are found everywhere over God's earth. Cf. Hos. 2:20-22; Isa. 30:23-26; 65:25; Ezek. 34:25ff.

Verse 7. Arrangement by pairs — one formerly wild, one tame — prevails throughout the passage. Two traditionally hostile creatures are now pictured as living on the friendliest of terms; wolf and lamb, leopard and kid, then calf and lion and fatling. Besides, (v. 7) cow and bear, then their young ones, then lion and ox. All these engage in the friendliest contacts and live at utter peace. Into the midst of the picture a child is placed, one of tender years, and is represented as leading this motley crew of beasts out into pasture single-handed and without the least bit of trouble. All ferocity is gone; nature is no longer red in tooth and claw. The statement about the lion eating cut-feed, may be nothing more than highly poetic language. Cf. Rom. 8:19ff.

Verse 8. All this is climaxed in v. 8 by describing two of the youngest of children, the one still nursing and the other just weaned, as playing out of doors and finding the hole that marks the entrance to the hideout of the most poisonous of small serpents. If the child in question plays there or even thrusts its hand into the hole, the mother, on discovering what is happening, need not come running in deadly terror at what might happen, but can calmly let the child go on with its harmless play. For all of nature has been reduced to perfect harmony. Every discordant note, every element of danger and disaster has been extracted.

Verse 9. This verse calls for careful balance of evaluation. The "holy mountain" is perhaps best taken to refer to the temple hill, though the words could allow for a reference to the entire land. But we prefer to limit the meaning to what seems the more obvious. For the Lord's holy hill, that is his sanctuary in Jerusalem, which had so often been the object of the attack of hostile foes, shall no longer be disturbed by such threats. For the note of harmony prevails throughout this now-redeemed world. Therefore this center at which hostility so often directed its attack shall be delivered from such dangers. This is mentioned as a striking instance of the overall change. But to remind the reader that the change extends much farther, the line is added that indicates that the whole earth is involved. And that which shall prevail throughout the whole earth is this potent factor called "the knowledge of the Lord." Such knowledge will be the powerful leaven that penetrates deeply and alters all things that are amiss. Nowhere shall any hurt or harm be done.

Surely we have thus far witnessed nothing of this transformation of nature. Its achievement shall be saved up until the days of the second coming of Christ, when there shall be a new heavens and a new earth, wherein dwelleth righteousness. That is, where all will be right.

A later use of the two halves of v. 9 must be briefly examined. If Isa. 65:25 uses the first half of v. 9 in reference to what *beasts*, rather than *man*, will not do, that is not necessarily determinative for the original meaning of the passage. It just shows that there are comprehensive words that may be variously used. However Hab. 2:13 uses the second half of the verse much like our own passage. But the whole of v. 9 is laid into the mouth of Yahweh himself. Thereby the whole section, vv. 1-9, becomes a word of Yahweh.

(4) A Description of His Work in Terms of What He Can Do for Israel (vv. 10-16)

11:10-12 10. And it shall come to pass in that day that the root of Jesse which stands as an ensign to the peoples — him shall the nations seek out, and the rest he gives will be an honor.

11. And it shall come to pass in that day that the Lord will again stretch forth his hand to redeem the remnant of his people who are left over, from Assyria and from Egypt and from Pathros and from Ethiopia and from Elam and from Shinar and from Hamath and from the coastlands of the sea.

12. And he will raise up a signal for the nations,
and he will assemble the outcast men of Israel,
and gather together the scattered women from Judah from the four
   corners of the earth.

These verses describe the first phase of the work that he will do in behalf of Israel — namely the return of the exiles. Though the prophet is about to center attention on what the Lord will do for his own people, he would not create the impression that Yahweh's only concern is for Israel. So in a transition verse that describes his overall work in more universal terms he shows how this Perfect Ruler, by the outstanding perfection of his personality will attract peoples from far and near. Him they shall "seek out" for the purpose of worship, as the verb often suggests. This function is tied up with the fact that he stands as a signal, or "ensign to the peoples," to rally them from far and near, this famous descendant of Jesse's. And they that come shall have the experience that the rest that this One gives to the weary conscience will be an honor and a most desirable thing to be sought after. So this verse does not stand here as a misplaced item, to be reconciled with difficulty to the context in which it appears. It prevents narrowing the thought about this great Ruler's work unduly by concentrating only on Israel.

Verse 11. This verse is usually taken to indicate that the passage as such must be post-exilic because it speaks of the return of captives or deportees, which would be relevant only if there were numerous captives to bring back. But a comparison of a number of pertinent passages in connection with almost all the localities mentioned will indicate that a larger measure of deportation, due to the fortunes of war and other mishaps, had been going on for some time. On Egypt compare Hos. 9:3, 6; Isa. 7:18. On Pathros, which is Upper, or Southern, Egypt, see Jer. 44:1. On Ethiopia, compare Isa. 18:1ff. In connection with the coastlands of the sea Joel 3:6ff. may be compared. So then the reference is first of all to a bringing back of men, that would be much welcomed now that the prophet speaks, and would be most welcome in days to come where it would be more of a necessity. That the Lord is said "to *again* stretch forth his hand" seems to reflect on a similar mighty work of his when he addressed himself to the task of delivering his people from Egypt in the days of Moses and Aaron. When a remnant is referred to as the object of God's attention that seems to imply nothing more than that, though some will perish in captivity, there still will be a sizable contingent left to deliver.

Verse 12. The manner in which the Lord will do his work is now described in a somewhat colorful way. He raises a signal for the nations (cf. 49:22) on an elevation. People see it from afar and follow its suggestion. "Israel" in this connection would seem to imply the entire people. Even if they had been sold in the slave market of the most extreme lands of the earth, God still would have concern for them and bring them back.

Another phase of what the Lord intends to do for Israel is set forth in vv. 13-14.

11:13-14 13. Then Ephraim's jealousy will cease,
and those in Judah who manifest hostility will be cut off;
Ephraim will not be jealous of Judah,
and Judah will not be hostile against Ephraim.
14. But they will swoop down upon the shoulder of the Philistines to the west,
and together they will plunder the people of the east;
Edom and Moab shall come under the power of their hand,
and Ammonites shall submit to them.

It has been suggested that these verses deal with the physical Israel, which is reasonable to assume; also that in them the honor of Israel is more central than the honor of the Lord — a claim that may also be accepted as reasonable. But neither of these observations makes these verses trivial or unimportant. For, first of all, the matter of healing the inner division between Israel and Judah which had been an irritating thing ever since the days of Solomon, certainly was an objective worthy to acknowledge as important. Hosea 1:11 had referred to it; Ezekiel was to make an issue of it (Ezek. 37:15ff.) It must be admitted that after the return from Exile the division never occupied the prominent place that it once had. But that meant leaving ancient antipathies behind and dropping traditional hostilities. What follows is not so much prediction of national victories, for the Philistines and Edom and Moab gradually faded out of the picture. So the passage is another way of saying, Side by side will they fight every foe they encounter. And in so far as Israel returned to the Lord, in so far this inner unity is in evidence. Promises of purely physical success are nowhere given to Israel. "The shoulder of the Philistines" is the low-hill ridge that leads down to the Philistine coastal plain. All the words really say is: For the chastened people of God there will be success in all defensive measures wherever they turn. "This is no common war" *von Orelli* remarked.

The last two verses give a still clearer account of the return at least in more colorful terms.

11:15-16 15. And Yahweh shall utterly destroy the tongue of the sea of Egypt,
and will wave his hand over the River with the glowing heat of his breath;
and will smite it into seven brooks,
and he will enable men to cross over with their shoes on.
16. And there will be a highway from Assyria for the remnant of his people that are left,
As there was for Israel when they came up from the land of Egypt.

Verse 15. This passage is highly poetic, woven together out of concepts of the rich past of the people of God, especially of the days of the Exodus and the Occupation of Canaan. As a "tongue" of the sea confronted the children of Israel on their flight from Egyptian bondage, so the present difficulty is thought of as being much of the same pattern. Again the Lord will remove the obstacle — in this case "utterly destroy" it (the verb implies: "put completely under the ban"). Two actions of the Almighty blend in the next line: a gesture of command coupled with an effective blast from the lips of God drying up the waters that lie across their path. That will make this deliverance more wonderful than the one at the Red Sea. Putting it figuratively once again, one broad stream that would have been unfordable is broken up into a number of little rivulets through which men will be able to wade almost dry-shod, at least they will not need to remove their shoes.

Verse 16. Totally abandoning this approach, the return of the scattered ones of Israel is now thought of as taking place along an easy highway, a concept common enough in Isaiah (cf. 40:3, 4; 42:16; 49:11; 35:8). A different attitude is taken over against the Wilderness wanderings that Israel had to make under Moses. Now, in retrospect, these wanderings are thought of as having taken place along a well-built highway; for did not the Lord make a way for his people on this occasion? All this then illustrates how effectively the Perfect Ruler will be able to do every aspect of the work that shall fall to his lot. If there seems to be a bit of the coloring of the return from the Babylonian Exile in all this, that is not to be wondered at, for Isaiah had much to say in this area and also supplied much that was calculated to help Israel when those days came. *Fischer* aptly remarks: "The idea of a new Exodus like the one from Egypt appears here for the first time; it is then resumed in Jer. 16:15f.; 23:7f. (cf. 31:8, 9) and is developed at great length in Isa. 40-55."

Notes

We shall in this case give particular attention to the more critical approach, especially that part of it which seeks to demonstrate that vv. 10-16 must be of a date later than Isaiah's. We shall give occasional attention to conjectural emendations, which are, in this chapter, too, for the most part none too constructive and too highly subjective to have much solid value.

To begin with, ideas like that of *Duhm*, that the chapter as such is to be attributed to Isaiah the Old man — such opinions are mere whims and fancies.

Then, quite a bit is made of the possibility that the passage as a whole should be regarded as stemming from the occasion of the anointing of Hezekiah as king of Judah, so that the one who moved before the eye of the writer was none other than the young king of Judah about whom the prophet expresses exuberant hopes. Then, since the Davidic house had such remarkable promises of a glorious future, there was seen dimly behind the young king the figure of the coming Messiah. So the passage would be secondarily Messianic. In fact it is even claimed that something is lost if the chapter be limited to Christ. We cannot help but believe that such an approach adds little but in reality takes much away. For in the last analysis what is said about the king to be anointed would hardly be anything other than extravagant court flattery, attributing more to the king than could rightfully be expected; unless perchance Judah hoped in every king that came to the throne to see the Messiah realized ultimately — a hope the existence of which is easily assumed and hard to prove with any degree of certainty.

To give the later post-exilic date to the passage, it is among other claims held that the language of v. 1 about the "stump" obviously refers to "the stump as an existing fact," and: "the fall of the stump belongs to the past" (*Gray*). We claim that from its context the verse becomes a reference to the future. Claims to the contrary must be supported by more than bold assertion.

Verse 3. The first three words are not, as is now quite commonly claimed, "meaningless." They are not to be dismissed as bearing an obvious dittography on words found in v. 2. By usage and according to context they constitute a very meaningful conclusion to the first two verses, emphasizing the great importance of the fear of the Lord in the make-up of this Ruler.

Verse 4. If in this verse the word for "earth" is construed to signify, as the parallelism suggests, "the earthly-minded," then all need of substituting *'arits* ("bully") for *'eretz* is lost.

Verse 9. To go on the assumption that we have here a "royal accession liturgy" it is found that the text of this verse hardly agrees with this assumption. So this verse is classified as a later addition, partly from Isa. 65 and partly from Habakkuk. The assumptions that are being made need not agree with the text, but the text must conform to assumptions that are made about it.

Verse 10. If for this whole passage (vv. 10-16) the claim is made that the burning hope for the future that it expresses represents fifth or fourth century faith that the enemies would be overthrown, are not pronouncements about the power of faith of one age over against another age most precarious? There is good evidence that there was strong hope of victory in Isaiah's day; whereas the evidence may be read to mean that the post-exilic centuries suffered from extreme weakness of faith. Then, because the purpose of v. 10 in this connection has not yet been noted, the verse as such is faulted as being metrically unclear and stylistically clumsy. The likelihood is that the verse is prose, and therefore as poetry quite unacceptable.

Verse 15. To substitute *hecheribh* ("dry up") for *hecherim* ("banish") merely loses a more colorful verb for a less colorful one.

On the subject of a return from Assyria *Fischer* remarks: "We have no historical record of a return from Assyria. It is to be noted here and elsewhere that many prophecies both of weal and of woe are *conditional* as to their fulfillment; depending on the attitude of those of whom they are spoken, they either are fulfilled or remain unfulfilled."

Chapter XII

i. *Praise for the Great Day That Is to Come* (*Chap.* 12)

It is interesting to observe how the thought-patterns of days of old keep recurring. At the close of the previous chapter Israel's deliverance had been described in terms of the experience of the Exodus — water crossed to escape the pursuer. On that occasion (Exod. 15) a great hymn of praise to Yahweh was sounded. When the new Exodus occurs a new hymn must be sung. In a very practical manner the prophet not only suggests the propriety of such a hymn, but even composes it for the use of his people. There are really two aspects of the hymn. *Koenig* has rightly called it "a prayer and vow of thanks on the part of redeemed Israel." As soon as these two obvious parts of a hymn of praise are detected, the claim that there are two separate hymns becomes rather futile. Nor is it feasible to draw any conclusions from the fact that the first two verses are cast in the form of the second person singular, whereas the last two appear in the second person plural. These are merely two familiar forms of the so-called "ideal second person."

At the same time it must be admitted that Chap. 12 constitutes an "effective finale" (*Procksch*) for the whole section (chaps. 1-12). But again to say that the impossibility of Isaianic authorship is demonstrated by the psalm-like character of the chapter (*Herntrich*), is to use purely subjective opinion as the ultimate criterion of verdicts. A writer with the versatility of Isaiah, having, no doubt, heard many a psalm in his day, would quite naturally fall into a style like that of psalm poetry. Or, that the same writer expects a definite reference to some contemporary historical event and denies authorship to Isaiah because such reference does not appear, is quite inconclusive. None appear more apodictic than *Ewald*, who simply remarked on this score: This chapter "cannot be from Isaiah." He did not even stoop to answer the gainsayer. Verdicts are often poor arguments.

Similar hymns, commonly attributed to Isaiah, would be found 25:9; 26:1-6; 27:2-5; compare also 14:3ff. Isaiah often gets swept away with feelings of great wonder and praise at the great works Yahweh will do for his people.

The following may serve as an outline of this magnificent hymn:

Praise for the Great Day That Is to Come.

(1) A Resolve on Israel's Part to Offer Such Praise (vv. 1-2)

(2) A Summary Description of the Blessings of That Day (v. 3)

(3) An Exhortation to Offer Such Praise (vv. 4-6)

12:1-6 1. And you will say on that day:
"I will praise thee, O Yahweh, that though thou wast angry with me,
yet thine anger was turned back and thou didst comfort me.
2. Lo, God is my salvation; I will trust and not be afraid;
For Yah Yahweh is my strength and my song;
and he has become my salvation."
3. And with joy you will draw water from the wells of salvation.
4. Also you will say in that day:
"Praise Yahweh, call upon his name;
make known his deeds among the peoples.
Call to mind how exalted his name is.
5. Sing unto the Lord for he has done marvelous things;
make this known in all the earth.
6. Exult and sing for joy, O you inhabitants of Zion;
For great in your midst is the Holy One of Israel."

(1) A Resolve on Israel's Part to Offer Such Praise (vv. 1-2)

Verse 1. The song is introduced by the words, "And you will say in that day." The implication is that what God has done will so deeply impress God's people that they will be moved spontaneously to utterance of praise. Oftentimes when such a situation is encountered then men feel they ought to be accomplishing their task with much greater

fervor than they feel at the moment. That results in words
of a resolve like: "I will praise thee, O Yahweh." In this
case, however, since the chastened people of God are speaking, they cannot help but reflect on how the Lord was first
obliged to take them in hand with severity and in anger. It
is quite obvious that the nation is not thanking God for having been angry but rather that his anger is now turned
away. In a sense, it must be admitted, they can understand
and appreciate that God did vent his anger on them. But
the object of thanks is rather that this anger is now "turned
back and thou didst comfort me." Only profound penitence
can speak thus. Often when God's anger has achieved its
purpose, he proceeds to comfort in a twofold sense, first, by
bestowing pardon to the penitent; then, by granting manifest tokens of his gracious love, that is to say, any blessings, physical or spiritual, that his wisdom sees fit to grant.
On God's turning from anger see: Ps. 30:7; Isa. 26:20;
54:7f.

Verse 2. The whole experience of such a sort opens up
new insights into the nature and being of God. In this case
this experience is summarized in the statement, "Lo, God is
my salvation." Not my judge, not my avenger! Immediately the outcome of this new insight is indicated: "I will
trust and not be afraid." This is just the kind of utterance
that one would expect from Isaiah, the strong Old Testament
exponent of faith. Every new experience with God calls for
a proper reaction. In this case that reaction is trust, or faith,
and the banishment of fear. But the deeper insights that
grow upon God's people are so deep and rich that they
deserve to be summed up in different ways to display
their many-sidedness. So the hymn proceeds to add a splendid quotation from days of old, taken from the song that
Israel sang, epitomizing its experiences at the crossing
of the Red Sea (Exod. 15:2): "Yah, Yahweh, is my strength
and my psalm, and he has become my salvation." The order in which achievements are attributed to God is not the
historical one. For first men must experience the "salvation" of God — God must help them in their sore need. That
is mentioned last, for the reason that we often give the results first and the cause last. But from the moment that

one is consciously aware of the fact that God has effectively helped, one instinctively falls back on him and he becomes the source of one's "strength." When that has taken place the next level to which we mount is making him one's "psalm," or the subject of one's praise. But note how in this quotation everything centers about Yahweh: he is all in all. (cf. also Ps. 118:14).

(2) A Summary Description of the Blessings of That Day (v. 3)

Verse 3. At this point the prophet momentarily interrupts his psalm and reminds them that they are to sing it, that again and again they will avail themselves of the new-found privilege of drawing on God's salvation. He presents this thought in highly poetic fashion by likening it to a man's drawing fresh water, as his need requires, from a fountain that has been made accessible. But each attempt made in that direction is made "with joy." He sees his people again and again falling back on God to receive at his hands the help that they so sorely and continually need.

Some would make this verse appear as an attempt to instruct Israel to let the very drawing of water in the course of day's regular chores be done with thanksgiving (*Scott*). Helpful as such a course of action might be, the context hardly suggests such an interpretation. More to the point is the approach of *Delitzsch* to the effect that this is a prophetic word foretelling how Israel will avail itself of a newly-discovered privilege. It might also be to the point to compare such Scriptures where Yahweh is likened to a fountain put at Israel's disposal to meet her specific needs. Compare in this connection: Jer. 2:13; 17:13; Ps. 36:9; 87:7.

(3) An Exhortation to Offer Such Praise (vv. 4-6)

Verse 4. And now the prophet, having first addressed himself to each individual in Israel, addresses himself to the nation as a whole, using plural imperatives. This part of the psalm partakes of the nature of an exhortation. Additional ways in which praise and thanksgiving may be expressed are touched upon. God's favors have been rich;

they call for rich praise. In this verse, four verbs follow.
In Hebrew the first two clauses are made up of two words;
the third, of three; the fourth, of four. Being swept along
by praise increases the writer's eloquence as he progresses.
The first summons is to plain praise. The second dwells on
the public proclamation of God's character as Israel has
come to know it. For that is what the expression, "call upon
his name," actually means. For which reason Luther always
translates it: *Prediget seinen Namen* (Preach his name).
The third statement expands this thought with distinct emphasis upon the idea that peoples are to be made to know
the deeds of God that Israel has experienced. This is the
Old Testament note of evangelism. The last statement has
to do with *recalling* what God has done. Favors received, so
soon recede from the mind of the recipient. A conscious
effort must often be made not to let them fade into oblivion.
When the exalted nature of his name is referred to, "name"
always implies "character," for all that Israel has beheld
has raised her sights about the greatness of her God.

Verse 5. The "marvelous things" which are to be commemorated in songs to Yahweh are more specifically deeds
done on a high level of action, far above the poor level
that man can attain. Again comes the summons to see to it
that these blessings that Israel received are to be made very
widely known. The Old Testament keeps reiterating that
God's ultimate goal in his dealings with Israel is the
salvation of the nations. Though active evangelism was not
yet the order of the day, Israel was still to make the most
of every evangelistic opportunity that came its way, in a
sort of anticipation of the Great Commission.

Verse 6. The verbs used toward the end of the psalm
involve more intensive forms of expression of joy and gladness; "Exult" literally means "raise shrill shouts." "Sing for
joy" could be rendered "exult." Praise is to gain momentum
as it goes along. For the present there is no thought of
how the nations might react to what they hear. It is only
the "inhabitants of Zion" that are being spurred on and
helped to do their part. But most appropriately the psalm
ends on the note, not of what man should be doing, but on
the note of the greatness of God: "For great in your midst is

the Holy One of Israel." The prophets were far more preoccupied with their God than with man and his minor
achievements.

Notes

We would at this point dwell more at length for once on the
subject of authorship of this chapter by Isaiah and the feasibility
of such a contention. In addition to the general approaches indicated above we would append briefly a brief review of terms
used by Isaiah that *Koenig* has assembled to show that the vocabulary is that of Isaiah. Where the refrain had been heard in 9:
11, 16, 20; and 10:4, "his anger is not turned away," such a refrain
almost demands that the dissonance be resolved as it is here
in v. 1, "thy anger was turned back." Again the verb *saghabh*
(v. 4) had been met with in 2:11, 17; 9:10. Its appearance
here argues for distinctively Isaianic vocabulary. In the next verse
(5) *ge'uth* appears; at least the same root appears in 2:12, and
the word itself in 9:17. Again, *tsahali* in v. 6 echoes the same verb
in 10:30. And "the Holy One of Israel" has appeared repeatedly
since 1:4.

Fohrer's contention is that Isaiah does not yet operate with
the thought-pattern *Vorher-Nachher* (first judgment — then deliverance) as do the more eschatological prophets of a later date.
All Isaiah knows is unrelieved judgment. That is an extreme position that can be maintained only by removing from Isaiah all
that you subjectively feel he should not have said.

Verse 1. In "you will say" the second person merely reflects
the indefinite subject. See *KS* 324 b.

Verse 4. The expression, "praise Yahweh," construes Yahweh in
the dative — a case where the accusative construction is replaced
by the dative. See *KS* 289 h.

Verse 5. "Sing unto the Lord" in our idiom requires a preposition "unto." Hebrew construes the verb with a direct object (*KS*
211 g).

Verse 6. "Inhabitants" is a singular feminine for a collective
noun and so refers to the total population. See *KS* 255 d.

ORACLES OF JUDGMENT

Chapter XIII

II. ORACLES OF JUDGMENT (Chaps. 13-27)

A. WORDS OF JUDGMENT AGAINST INDIVIDUAL NATIONS, (Chaps. 13-23)

These eleven chapters may be subdivided as follows:

1. Against Babylon (13:1-14:23)
2. Against Israel's Immediate Neighbors (14:24-17:1 ff.);
3. Against Distant Neighbors (chaps. 18-21);
4. Against Jerusalem and Tyre (chaps. 22-23).

If these oracles are all to be dated as written at one time, it would seem that the only specific indication of time to be found within them is the one of 14:28, which refers to the year that King Ahaz died (715 B.C.). They would all then seem to be later than this date, and so comparatively late in the ministry of Isaiah.

Chapter 13 may be subdivided as follows:

a. The Summoning of Warriors for an Assault (vv. 2-3);
b. The Description of the Assembled Host (vv. 4-5);
c. The Terrors of the Day of the Lord (vv. 6-8);
d. The Destruction Wrought by the Day of the Lord (vv. 9-16);
e. The Medes — God's Agent for the Overthrow of Babylon (vv. 17-19);
f. The Total Desolation of Babylon (vv. 20-22).

Other chapters of Scripture similar to Chap. 13 are the following: Isa. 21 and 47; Jer. 50:1-51:58.

1. Against Babylon (13:1-14:23)

13:1 1. The burden of Babylon, which Isaiah the son of Amoz did see.

The major issue which must be settled in connection with chap. 13 is whether the heading, which attributes the chapter and presumably the one that follows directly to Isaiah, is reliable. The words involved are: "The oracle concerning Babylon which Isaiah the son of Amoz saw." The prevailing attitude denies the possibility of Isaianic authorship.

The reasons for rejecting the possibility of authorship by Isaiah are chiefly the following. The Medes are mentioned in 13:17 as the agents of God's judgment of Babylon; yet the Medes were not yet on the scene at this time, having come into prominence shortly before the fall of Babylon (538 B.C.), therefore perhaps almost a century and a half after the time of Isaiah's activity. Secondly, in v. 19 Babylon is designated as "the glory of kingdoms, the splendor and pride of the Chaldeans." In Isaiah's day this was not yet the case, but Nineveh was the ranking capital city and outranked Babylon by far. Since Nineveh did not fall until 612, thus allowing for Babylon to achieve prominence, it is claimed this oracle must date at least after 612. Aside from other minor arguments that could be adduced, these two are commonly regarded as demanding that this chapter and the next be ascribed to some later anonymous writer.

It will be noted that one positive and one negative assumption are involved in this conclusion. The one is that prophets can only pronounce oracles that are in keeping with the state of knowledge and affairs prevailing at a given point in history. In other words, their pronouncements have a relevance to what they and every one else of their day knows. They speak in the light of prevailing contemporary knowledge. The second assumption grows out of this first one: long-range prediction is not to be thought of as possible or likely. Prophets did not predict, for that would have violated the ordinary laws of human knowledge and insight.

We maintain that, from the point of view of the prophets, prediction is, when it pleases the Almighty to grant it to men, not only possible, but at times definitely claimed by the prophets as being characteristic of some of their messages. In fact (see Isa. 41:21-29) the issue at which the idols may be detected over against the true God, is just this, that Yahweh is able to make known the future in advance and does so, at times, long in advance.

So then there are several arguments that weigh heavily in the scales in favor of authorship of this chapter by Isaiah. First, headings like v. 1 were not rashly employed. Nor is it in harmony with the well-known care of the writers and editors of the sacred Scriptures to make unsubstantiated claims. It will not satisfy as explanation to make the claim: someone once thought this chapter dated from Isaiah — but we now see he was mistaken.

In the second place, the chapter has the brilliance of language and of thought that is commonly associated with Isaiah. In that respect it resembles Chap. 21, in which, of course, the same issue is raised as in this chapter.

Thirdly, that Assyria would be replaced as leader in the struggle for world-supremacy by Babylonia, which would then in turn be the conqueror of Jerusalem and Judea, is already accepted in Isaiah's day as something revealed by God. See Isa. 39 and II Kings 20:12-19. If Babylon's rise was foreseen, what would make it seem so strange that its fall should also be predicted?

Another point of view should be borne in mind: From Gen. 11:9 onward down to the Revelation of John (14:8), Babel, or Babylon, becomes a kind of symbol of wickedness and unwholesome, hostile pride, or as *G. A. Smith* says: ". . . (she remains) in fact or symbol the enemy of God and the stronghold of darkness. . . . Babylon represents civilization; she is the brow of the world's pride and enmity to God." For Isaiah to foresee this and to speak in terms of God's reckoning with this attitude comes closer to the issue involved than to reckon in terms of dates and historical pre-eminence. In fact, and this seems to be commonly overlooked, Babylon's fall is not presented here as tracing from the wrongs she may have done to God's people or in history generally but as something that grew out of her pride (cf. v. 19). In chap. 14 it must be admitted that Babylon's brutal conquests are under consideration, but there the subject is not Babylon but her king.

With all these considerations in mind we are ready to accept the statement of v. 1 as correct.

The word for "oracle" (*massa'*) demands brief consideration. By and large "oracle" may be the best translation. But the debate is not yet closed on this subject. A number of scholars, like *Procksch*, still favor the translation "oracle of doom," i.e., *Schicksalsspruch*. This is in line with the familiar "burden" (KJ), *Luther*: *Last*. Etymologically either possibility may be allowed for. Yet in some cases like Lam. 2: 14, "burden" is not feasible. In any case, the word reappears in Isa. 14:28; 15:1; 17:1; 19:1; 21:1, 11, 13; 22:1; 23:1. All these are words of doom, and so "burden" was not so inappropriate after all. The passage Jer. 23:33 does not demand that the interpretation of the word as "burden" is necessarily wrong. The attitude of those that put the question to Jeremiah was wrong, not necessarily the etymology as such.

13:2-8 2. On a bare mountain, raise a banner, cry aloud to them; wave the hand that they may enter in at the gate of the nobles.

3. I have given commandment to my consecrated ones;
I have summoned my mighty men, my proudly exulting ones to execute my anger.

4. Hark, a tumult on the mountains after the fashion of a huge crowd;
hark, a noisy assembly of kingdoms, nations gathered together.
Yahweh of hosts is mustering a host for battle.

5. They are coming from distant lands from the end of the heavens,
the Lord and the weapons of his indignation, to destroy the whole land.

6. Wail, for the day of Yahweh is at hand, as destruction from the Almighty it will come.

7. Therefore all hands will be slack, and every man's heart will melt.

8. They will be dismayed; pangs and anguish will take hold of them.
They will writhe like a woman in travail.
They will look dumbfounded at one another,
their faces will be fire-red.

a. *The Summoning of Warriors for an Assault (vv. 2-3)*

The description is marked by a certain vagueness at the outset ("The apocalyptic loves the anonymous" — *Procksch*): there is a big stir and commotion; presently it becomes apparent that the day of the Lord has come. After the chapter has run more than half its course things appear in sharper outline: an assaulting army of Medes and a city that has been ravaged, Babylon. As the scene opens, vigorous efforts are being made to assemble an army. We do not learn from what source it is being recruited. We cannot identify even those who do the assembling. But first a banner is raised, rather, commanded to be raised on a bare mountain where it will be visible from afar. As the ones who have caught the signal come within hailing distance, they are summoned by a loud cry. They are further urged to make haste for the assembling of the forces, by a vigorous waving of the hand. At that point the description seems to move far ahead to the final purpose of all this commotion. The forces that are assembling become aware of the fact that they are to "enter in at the gates of the nobles." Before this can be done the city involved must first be conquered. That it is a city of no mean importance appears from the fact that its gates seem to be famous, at least they are called "gates of the nobles." It could even be that this description of the gates refers to the ones conquered in a half-sarcastic manner.

Verses 2, 3. By way of further throwing light on what all this action involves, the Lord himself is introduced as speaking. This whole procedure up to this point may be summed up in his own description of it: "I have given commandment to my consecrated ones." He has work for them to do; they are under orders to execute some mandate of his. All this is part of the language of "holy war." For the Hebrew has a special idiom for getting a war under way: they "sanctify a war," an expression which *KJ* used to render "prepare war," and *RSV* describes as "declare war." But when a war is allowed to generate, men are under orders from the Almighty to wage it, and so they are "consecrated" for a specific task. The Lord further defines what he is doing in the words: "I have summoned my mighty men, my proudly exulting ones to execute my anger." The mighty warriors are his; he is putting them to use. They are conscious of their strength and confident of success, and are therefore called "proudly exulting ones." But now we come to the deepest root of the venture: some men or nation have roused his anger, which he purposes justly to execute. The warriors summoned are the instruments he employs. So much for the summoning of the warriors.

b. The Description of the Assembled Host (vv. 4-5)

Verses 4, 5. Those who have obeyed his summons and have come together are a motley crew. On the mountains — as we learn from what follows, very likely the mountains of Media — there is a tumult which can be heard afar off. The tumult is that which would normally emanate from "a huge crowd." This crowd is not made up of persons from one nation only; they are "a noisy assembly of kingdoms." Such assemblies are never quiet and restrained. He who gave the initial orders of v. 2 is now identified. It is "Yahweh of hosts" and he is "mustering a host for battle." Those participating may have no sense of being involved in a project of Yahweh. They may have no intention of executing his will. But such is the case nevertheless. The description of the host continues. They are "coming from distant lands." Apparently the nation which is doing the assembling is utilizing various national groups that have been previously conquered and are now compelled to furnish contingents for the army of the conqueror. For that matter they may be said to be "coming from the end of the heavens." And so the army marches on to whatever goal they may be led. But they are "the Lord and the weapons of his indignation to destroy the whole land." In these descriptive terms the land that is to suffer is not yet identified. All this is spoken from the point of view of the enlightened prophet. The nations do not see the Lord as leader of their host. They do not recognize that they are tools in God's hands (cf. for a similar thought 5:26 and 10:5).

c. The Terrors of the Day of the Lord (vv. 6-8)

Verse 6. Now it becomes apparent that the day of the Lord is somehow involved, a time demanding that God act. This day usually involves some measure of divine judgment. The scene again remains somewhat vague. They whom disaster will strike are not identified. They will be pointed out later. But for the present, persons are summoned to "wail" because this dread and terrible day is about to break upon them, the day being further described as "destruction from the Almighty" — a phrase with a play on words in Hebrew which is partly captured by a translation such as "destruction from the Destructive." All of this is reminiscent of words of Joel, viz., 1:13 and 1:15–2:1.

Verses 7, 8. They whom this day and its judgments will strike are now described as to the total effect that shall result. "All hands will be slack" for there will be no purpose in trying to resist the inescapable. "Every man's heart will melt," we are also told. The impact of the judgment will be so great that courage will fail every man that beholds it. This last thought is further unfolded in v. 8. The worst form of consternation will assail the victims of Yahweh's wrath: "they will be dismayed." The description moves over into terms so commonly employed for a painful experience of the most extreme sort, the figure of a woman in travail, shot through with torment and twisting in anguish. Sheer terror will stare forth from every face, when one man beholds another. Lastly, "their faces will be fire-red." With equal propriety it could have been said that faces would be pale with fear. For a wide range of emotions will race across the features of men, so that one moment they will be pale, the next, flushed to the extreme.

Up to this point the poetic rhythm of the Hebrew has been in the pattern of 3:2. From vv. 9-22 it will follow the pattern largely of 3:3.

d. The Destruction Wrought by the Day of the Lord (vv. 9-16)

13:9-16 9. Lo, the day of Yahweh comes harsh with wrath and fierce anger to make the earth a desolation and the sinners within shall be destroyed out of it.

10. And as for the stars of the heavens and their constellations, they will not give their light.
The sun will be dark when it rises, and the moon will not give its light.

11. "And I will punish the earth for all its evil, and the wicked for their iniquity.
I will put an end to the pride of the arrogant, and the haughtiness of tyrants I will bring low

12. I will make the plain fellow more rare than fine gold, and the important fellow than the gold of Ophir.

13. Therefore I will make the very heavens tremble, and the earth will be shaken out of its place,
through the wrath of Yahweh of hosts, and on the day of his fierce anger.

14. And like a frightened gazelle, or like sheep that none gather, each man shall turn to his own people, and each man shall flee to his own land.

15. All who are found [in Babylon] will be thrust through and all who are caught will fall by the sword.

16. And their little children will be dashed in pieces before their very eyes;
their houses will be plundered and their wives ravished."

As noted above the description of destruction that is to be brought on by the great host assembled according to vv. 1-8 will be part of the events of the "day of the Lord." Thoughts of the final judgment blend in this description with thoughts of the immediate destruction of Babylon, even as in the eschatological discourses of our Lord in Matt. 24 and parallels. In the description that follows, all nature is pictured as giving its aid to support the work of the Almighty in terrifying the nations. At times some pleasant aspects of the day of the Lord are noted in the Scriptures. Not here. The day will be "harsh with wrath and fierce anger." What the great day will achieve will be "to make the earth a desolation and the sinners within shall be destroyed out of it." Though the emphasis seems to lie on the world-wide aspect of what transpires, in the last analysis what befalls Babylon is under consideration, as shall presently become obvious.

Verse 10. The old world-order of this physical universe

will perish. More particularly it will already seem to the Babylonians when their empire falls that the heavenly bodies are falling. "And as for the stars of the heavens and their constellations, they will not give their light": the very stars themselves and the larger groupings of them, long familiar to men (like Orion), apparently shall go down to ruin. Though the sun rises, it will appear to give no light; so too the moon. Apparently the actual happenings of the last day and the subjective impressions of the Babylonians when their city falls, all blend into one. Similar passages are Joel 2:10, 31; 3:15; Matt. 24:29.

Verse 11. From this point on, Yahweh is represented as speaking and interpreting what he is doing. In his words too there is the blend of the universal with the particular (Babylon). The earth will be punished for what it has done, "and the wicked for their iniquity." Here it becomes quite clear that Babylon has amassed guilt by her misdeeds so that the overthrow that befalls her is fully deserved. It also becomes clear at this point that the distinctive nature of Babylon's sin was pride of empire: for 11b reads: "I will put an end to the pride of the arrogant, and the haughtiness of tyrants I will bring low." Such was also the spirit of Assyria (cf. 10:7-11) and of Moab (cf. 16:6). All worldly empires become inflated with a sense of their own supreme importance.

Verse 12. In this verse two words for "man" are used, apparently in the sense that the first refers to the "plain fellow" and the second to the "important fellow" — both will become such a rarity that they would be likened to precious gold, which is a rare article in any case. So few shall be the remnants of the once very populous Babylon.

Verse 13. When so vast a structure as the universe is to be destroyed, the description must involve more than a few basic statements. So the account goes on. The heavenly bodies as such were under consideration in v. 10. The basic reason for it all followed in v. 11. Now comes a description of the destruction of the very heavens. They shall tremble visibly and their firm structure will be shaken. Even the good old solid earth "will be shaken out of its place" (cf. 24:18-20 and Jer. 4:24). Both these results are traced back to the same cause: "the wrath of Yahweh of hosts" and "his fierce anger." Man's sin may be the ultimate cause, but the Lord's wrath called forth by sin is the active cause, a factor that all the prophets strongly stress.

Verse 14. From here on to the end of v. 16 the interest centers on how all this will affect men, particularly, of course, in the great old city of Babylon. Men shall scatter to the four winds. Two figures are employed to describe what happens. Men shall be like "a frightened gazelle," a rather timid creature in the face of danger, or they will be "like sheep that none gather." Sheep possess no gift for gathering themselves when they are once scattered. So shall "each man turn to his own people and each man shall flee to his own land." Again cf. Jer. 50:16; 51:9. "Every man for himself" will be their motto on that day. All sense of solidarity shall have been destroyed. They will deem themselves fortunate if they can save their own skin.

Verse 15. The feature here mentioned hardly applies to the whole world. We have, therefore, inserted in the translation the ["in Babylon"]. Should anyone, in spite of the general flight that will have taken place, still be left over within the city, hiding somewhere in the ruins, he "will be thrust through" by the first soldier of the enemy that finds him.

Verse 16. One last bloody and tragic touch is added, the one that refers to the fate of the "little children." They will be dashed to pieces before the very eyes of their parents. When once the fury of war is unleashed the most extreme forms of cruelty are the order of the day, no matter how inhuman they may be. The Scriptures mention this type of cruelty repeatedly (cf. Hos. 13:16; Nah. 3:10). The rest that is mentioned goes without saying: "their houses will be plundered and their wives ravished." The last of these indignities was particularly repulsive and is also mentioned as typical in Deut. 28:30; Zech. 14:2.

But up till this point, all is vague, lacking specific identification of who inflicts the punishment and upon whom it is inflicted.

e. The Medes — God's Agents for the Overthrow of Babylon (vv. 17-19)

13:17-19 17. Lo, I am stirring up the Medes against them,
who pay no regard to silver, and as for gold, they
take no delight in it.
18. Their bows will shatter young men,
and on the fruit of the womb they will have no mercy;
and on children they will not look with pity.
19. And Babylon, the fairest of the kingdoms, the proud glory of the Chaldeans
shall be as Sodom and Gomorrah when God overthrew them.

Verse 17. Here a suddenly clear identification of the spoilers becomes possible: it is the Medes. Yet with the enlightened view of history characteristic of the Old Testament, it is not the Medes as entirely independent agents who are acting. God has a hand in all history and also in this development. As in 10:5 God used the Assyrians against Judah, now he uses the Medes against Babylon; "Lo, I am stirring up the Medes." Jeremiah 51:11 also mentions the Medes as agents. In Isaiah the Medes are mentioned rather than the Persians who were the major conquerors under Cyrus the Great, 538 B.C. The Persians were not yet recognizable in Isaiah's day as a major force in history. When the Medes are described as men "who pay no regard to silver, and as for gold, they take no delight in it," the thought appears to be that they are a wild, untamed horde of men, who are so strongly motivated by thoughts of revenge because of all that they in their day have suffered at the hands of the Babylonians, that silver and gold by way of plunder become secondary considerations. Such a burning sense of revenge is almost unheard of in the annals of nations.

Verse 18. Medes and Persians are known to have had bows as their chief weapon. This description reckons with that fact. Now those are listed against whom these bows will be used with particularly devastating effect: young men, fruit of the womb, and children. The second of these would seem to refer to the unborn children who are destroyed together with their pregnant mothers. Mercy and pity will be out of the question in these tragic events. Cf. also Amos 1:13; II Kings 15:16.

Verse 19. Finally there comes an unmistakable identification of the nation against whom all the woe thus far referred to will be directed — Babylon. It was granted to the prophet to foresee that, as Nineveh was the jewel and queen among the nations in his day, so Babylon would rise to succeed Nineveh, and would also have achieved unique fame among the mighty kingdoms of the world, "Babylon, the fairest of the kingdoms, the proud glory of the Chaldeans." Whether this pronouncement about the greatness of Babylon and her drastic overthrow was partly predictable by an enlightened statesman who had followed the course of empires need not concern us greatly. There may have been a blend in what the prophet said, of human prognostication, fortified and enlightened by divine revelation. In any case Isaiah was sure of the ultimate outcome. To use a classic comparison: it would be "as Sodom and Gomorrah, when God overthrew them." No overthrow was ever more complete and lasting.

Though the first impression that the reader is apt to receive on reading these words and the rest of the chapter, is that the overthrow was total and instantaneous, this is not actually said. Nor does history teach it to have been so. Rather, as *Delitzsch* summarizes the actual outcome: "Cyrus allowed the city with its two encircling walls to continue to stand. Darius Hystaspes, who had to conquer Babylon a second time in 518 B.C., laid low the walls with the exception of some thirty yards. Xerxes completely destroyed the glorious temple of Bel. When it was finally conquered by Seleucus Nicator (312) it lapsed into ruins progressively in the measure that Seleucia rose in strength. When Strabo lived (born 60 B.C.) the city was a total ruin."

Now for a graphic description of

f. The Total Desolation of Babylon (vv. 20-22)

13:20-22 20. It shall not be inhabited nor dwelt in from generation to generation.
No Arab will pitch his tent there. No shepherds shall make their flocks to lie down there.

21. Beasts of the desert shall lie down there.
their houses shall be full of howling creatures.
Ostriches will dwell there, and satyrs shall dance there.
22. Jackals will howl in its palace,
and more jackals in their pleasant mansions.
Its time has almost come and its days shall not be prolonged.

Verse 20. That a city once so renowned, glorious and powerful should experience so total an overthrow is well nigh unbelievable. But so it happened. Though a great conqueror like Alexander the Great saw an unusual potential in this ancient capital, neither he nor any other ever attempted a rebuilding and restoration of the city. There is something awesome about such complete desolation, when it continues century after century. Somehow even the wild Arabs will avoid the place and refuse to pitch their tent there. No shepherd of any racial background will make his flock lie down on this accursed ground.

Verse 21. From this point on the precise identification of the "beasts of the desert" that do lie down there becomes difficult. We shall not venture to clear up this difficulty. In addition to those translations that we have attempted, some think that perhaps it refers to other creatures, like hyenas and owls. But ruins haunted by these repulsive creatures shall be the characteristic mark of the place. The "satyrs" mentioned would appear to have been, in the popular imagination, desert-demons of the appearance of goats — se'ir means — "longhaired ones" (cf. Lev. 17:7). Here they would seem to represent any unholy creature which the common thinking of men is wont to associate with desert spots. The word of the Savior in Matt. 12:43 might be thought of here.

Verse 22. Sounds as well as sights repel the chance onlooker. In place of the usual word for "palaces" the Hebrew changes it by shifting a single vowel, so that the term reminds one of a "widowed," deserted place.

The description closes with a reminder that it will not take until the far distant future until these changes all take place: "Its time has almost come and its days shall not be prolonged."

Notes

Verse 1. For "the oracle on Babylon" the Hebrew has the construct relationship: oracle of Babylon, in place of the preposition (*KS* 336 d).

Verse 2. The Hebrew coordinates clauses "and they shall come in" for "that they may come in." Cf. *KS* 345 l.

Verse 3. For "to execute my anger" the original has a plain dative, "for my anger," *le* expressing relation (*KS* 332 qw).

Verse 7. "Hands" — dual for plural, because the dual is so commonly used on itmes appearing in pairs. See *KS* 257 d.

Verse 9. The Hebrew says "harsh *and* wrath" — the *waw concomitantiae*, which, of course, here means "harsh with wrath. The verb "shall be destroyed" is really active, "he shall destroy"; at the same time it marks a transition from the infinitive construction to the finite verb (*KS* 413 d.).

Verse 10. "Their constellations" is the plural of a proper noun ("Orion") which in this case means: Orion-like groupings of stars. (Cf. *KS* 264 f.).

Verse 11. That *tebhel* appears without article is due to the fact that it is a noun in process of developing into a proper noun (*KS* 293 b).

Verse 20. "Be inhabited" and "dwelt in" are two instances of intransitive verbs being used passively (*KS* 98).

Verse 22. "Will howl" as plural subject with singular verb, the singular being used as the frequent form when the verb stands first (*KS* 348 n).

Chapter XIV:1-23

The heading appearing over Chap. 13 covers this chapter as well. Looking at the core of the chapter, vv. 3-21, we can be more specific and entitle this chapter, as some do, "The Tyrant's Overthrow."

A brief glance at the outline of the material of this chapter (i.e., vv. 1–23) will help us to get our bearings quickly.

g. The Overthrow of Babylon in Relation to God's Gracious Purposes for Israel (vv. 1-2);
h. Israel's Taunt Directed against Babylon's King (vv. 3-21)
   (1) Introduction (vv. 3-4a);
   (2) The Fall of the Oppressor Signifies the End of All of Babylon's Cruelty and Oppression (vv. 4b-6);
   (3) The Song of Exultation That Greets This Overthrow (vv. 7-8);
   (4) Sheol's Reception of the Shade of Babylon's King (vv. 9-15);
   (5) The Estimate of Babylon's King Made by Those Who Behold His Corpse Lying Unburied on the Field of Battle (vv. 16-21);
i. God's Verdict with Regard to the Whole Empire of the King of Babylon (vv. 22-23).

From this it appears that there is a kind of prologue as well as a sort of epilogue. Both are in prose. Both serve a very good purpose and do not necessarily at all give the impression that they are later editorial additions. For if the editor could sense the propriety of such additions, or setting for the poem, similar insight could be deemed reasonable in the mind of the original writer himself. Nor can the fact that prologue and epilogue are both prose make them to be inappropriate for the poetic core of the chapter. The style of Biblical writers has much flexibility.

Now the important issue comes to be: is the larger poem as such to be referred to some one particular king of Babylon, and if that be the case is the chapter written in retrospect after this king has been overthrown? If that were the case, authorship of the chapter by Isaiah would be utterly out of the question. But to begin with, as we shall indicate later, it is not a single historical figure that is meant when the king of Babylon and his fate is described. The king of Babylon is a kind of symbol of world power in general and of the power of Babylon in particular. In fact there is something eschatological about the whole subject. The chapter seems to be cast in terms of the *ultimate* overthrow of the powers and rulers of this world, as even *Fohrer* admits, writing in 1960.

Let us define our position a bit more fully. The possibility and even the likelihood of the captivity of Israel (or Judah) and the final overthrow of her captor and so the return of the people of God from captivity is clear to the prophets and the people in Isaiah's time, for Hezekiah sees the inevitability of the captivity and the fact that it will not delay much longer (cf. Isa. 39:7f); and Micah sees the same outcome plus the return from captivity, as Micah 4:10 clearly indicates. If Israel's captivity is foreseen and the return, it is but one short step to the insight that the original captor of Israel, Babylon, must be overthrown before Israel can be restored. *Fischer* also says rather aptly: "We are here dealing with a prophecy."

It is at this point where the opening words of our chapter fall into clear focus.

g. The Overthrow of Babylon in Relation to God's Gracious Purposes for Israel (14:1-2)

14:1-2 1. For the Lord will have mercy upon Jacob and will again choose Israel and will give them rest in their own land; and aliens shall join themselves to them and shall associate themselves with the house of Jacob. 2. And peoples will take them and bring them to their proper place, and the house of Israel will take possession of them for themselves in Yahweh's land as male and female slaves; thus taking captive those that were their captors, and dominating their oppressors.

Verse 1. It will hardly do to ignore the first word of the Hebrew text (*ki* — "for") as *RSV* does. That discards the connection that is indicated. Chapters 13 and 14 constitute a unit. After the total and enduring overthrow of Babylon has been indicated it is now shown how this is part and parcel of Yahweh's plans with regard to his people: Babylon is cast to the ground that Israel may be raised up. The language of these first two verses has points of contact with passages such as 49:22f.; 56:6-8; and 61:4-9. The next step, then, after Babylon is laid low is that the Lord's mercy will again be manifestly directed toward Jacob and Israel, terms used interchangeably for variety's sake. He had "chosen" them once, as Deut. 7:6f. indicates. He will direct his active and loving choice toward them once again, as Zech. 1:17 expresses the same thought. That he "will give them rest in their own land" is merely a paraphrase of the idea of captivity: Yahweh will himself terminate this captivity. No nation enjoys "rest" while pining away in a foreign land.

After Israel will have been restored to its own land it will become apparent that other nations will change their attitude toward Israel. Resident "aliens" who had had some opportunity to learn what Israel stood for and had been in somewhat friendly relationship with Israel shall advance one step closer. They will "join themselves to them and associate themselves with the house of Jacob." Formal acceptance into the congregation of Israel is what they will seek. They will want to be full fledged proselytes; all of which is just another way of saying that the privilege of being an Israelite is so great that they would like a part in it.

Verse 2. Now this first step is followed by a second, which is drawn in somewhat more idealized coloring bordering on hyperbole. When such over-generous help is given to Israel, the prophets will hardly have insisted that what they predict will actually occur according to the letter. What we have is an emphatic and colorful way of expressing how deeply Gentiles will appreciate how much they owe to God's chosen nation, Israel. Peoples did not literally "take them and bring them to their proper place," but they did in more instances than we might suppose help the children of Israel on their way as they returned from the captivity. So also the next verse indicates in a striking way how the roles of the two parties were reversed: how the slaves became free, and the free, slaves; how the captives became captors and *vice versa*. We need not even admit with *Fischer* that this process is described in a manner "starkly mundane" (*stark irdisch*). Nor need we follow *Procksch*, who claims that this is "typically Jewish in the racial sense." *Delitzsch* had caught the spirit of it all far better when he had already in his day remarked: "To be ruled by the people of God is in the eyes of the prophet rare good fortune, and to let oneself be ruled by them is freedom." For no active enslavement of Gentiles by Israel is in any way indicated. Gentile submission is sought by them (i.e., the Gentiles) and is purely voluntary. Isaiah 2:3 is an analogous passage and still more directly similar is Zech. 8:20-22. For the whole passage compare also 49:22 ff.; 60:4 ff.; 61:5 ff.

h. Israel's Taunt Directed against Babylon's King (vv. 3-21)

(1) Introduction (vv. 3, 4a)

14:3-4a 3. And it shall come to pass when Yahweh will have given you rest from your grief and your turmoil and from the hard service with which you were made to serve, 4a. then you will take up this taunt against the king of Babylon and you will say:

Verses 3, 4a. In point of time these words take Israel past the actual return. For the return as journey involved much of "grief," "turmoil" and "hard service." When all this will have been replaced by "rest," then there will be leisure for an occupation such as taking up a "taunt." The spirit of this poem rises to a higher level than cheap taunt at the expense of a fallen enemy. It is primarily a striking way of expressing how strange and marvelous the ways of the Lord are with regard to the mighty of this earth. For what follows is "one of the most remarkable poems of the Old Testament" (*Scott*). But the expression "the king of Babylon" must first be carefully evaluated. There actually are three possibilities of interpretation. The writer could have had a certain king of Babylon, a historic personage, in mind. Or he could have been describing the imperial power of Babylon as such by the use of this term. Or it could be, as we already indicated in connection with Chap. 13, that the name "king of Babylon" has become a kind of symbol of the forces hostile to God and his people. We incline toward the last of these interpretations. This is about what *Jamieson*, *Fausset*, and *Brown* had in mind with the expression "an ideal representation of Babylon."

(2) The Fall of the Oppressor Signifies the End of All of Babylon's Cruelty and Oppression (vv. 4b-6)

14:4b-6
4b. "How the oppressor has ceased,
the boisterous raging ceased!
5. Yahweh has broken the staff of the wicked,
the scepter of rulers,
6. that smote the peoples in wrath
with smiting incessant,
and trampled down nations in anger
with persecution unrelenting."

This section would be summed up in the above statement.

We have tried by the arrangement of lines to indicate what the Hebrew rhythmic pattern is like. The poem is in the form of the typical lament with a 3:2 cadence, a slightly longer line followed by one just a bit shorter — limping alone in a sad measure. Nor is this pattern adhered to with utmost rigidity. That is apparently what *G. A. Smith* had in mind when he labelled this a "simple and even rude piece of meter." Efforts therefore should not be made to improve upon the piece by making it conform to our notions of what Hebrew poetry should be. We therefore reject practically all conjectural emendations currently made on the text. Besides there is an elegiac note about the whole piece. No gloating, but abundant sadness! As a whole the poem reminds of Ezek. 31 and 32, where a lament is sung on Pharaoh, king of Egypt.

Verse 4b. Big empires are impossible without strong pressure on the recalcitrant to submit. Therefore the Babylonian king is first described as the "oppressor" — no article being used in Hebrew, to hint at the thought that *all* op-

pressors come to the same end. The form of activity that
the oppressor engaged in is described as "boisterous raging."
Both the person and his activity are now come to a full
halt. The wild confusion of maintaining the empire has
stopped.

Verses 5, 6. But all this did not simply collapse of itself.
It is now distinctly claimed that, no matter what gods Babylon may have had, Yahweh, the God of Israel, exercises
full control over all nations and kings, so that it was by his
special control that the "staff of the wicked, the scepter of
rulers" was broken. Yahweh treats these mighty rulers, who
often considered themselves divine and were so acclaimed
by their people, like wilful children who must have their
toys, which they are abusing, taken from them and broken
— a powerful figure! What tyranny lay behind the administration of the affairs of empires is well indicated by
the use these rulers were making of their toy scepters: with
their scepters they "smote peoples in wrath with smiting incessant." These are the efforts to keep the rebellious under
total domination. Or to develop the picture more fully, in
the process they "trampled down the nations in anger with
persecution unrelenting." These verses reflect the huge sigh
of relief that went up from the dominated nations when
the controlling power was broken.

(3) The Song of Exultation That Greets This Overthrow (vv. 7-8)

14:7-9   7. "The whole earth is at rest and quiet,
            they break forth into singing.
  8. Even the cypresses rejoice over you,
      the cedars of Lebanon:
  'Ever since you lie asleep
      no woodcutter has come up against us.' "

Verses 7, 8. Rather bold imagery — the whole earth, that
is, all that dwell on the face of the earth, not only heave a
great sigh of relief, but they break forth into one loud song
at the death of the tyrant. What a tyrant he must have
been, or better: how tyrannical must have been the administration of his kingdom. The idea of breaking forth into
singing is a characteristic form of statement of the prophet.

Cf. 44:23; 49:13. But more than human rejoicing is involved. By a unique turn of thought the very trees themselves are represented as sharing in this common joy. Again this is a thought repeatedly found in Isaiah. Cf. 35:1f.; 52:9; 55:12. Cypresses and cedars are mentioned, perhaps because they were the trees most commonly sought by foreign invaders. It is a well-known fact that one after the other of the nations that invaded Syria and Israel slashed away at the cedars of Lebanon in particular, because they made choice timber for lasting construction. Babylon must have ravaged Lebanon beyond all others that went before. In the statement, "no woodcutter has come up against us," obviously the added thought to be supplied is, woodcutters that raged against us on the scale of the Babylonians.

(4) Sheol's Reception of the Shade (or Specter) of Babylon's King (vv. 9-15)

14:9-15   9. "Sheol from beneath is stirred
  to meet you as you arrive.
  She rouses up the shades to meet you,
   all the rams [princes] of the earth.
  She makes rise from their thrones
   all the kings of the nations.
10. They all begin to speak,
  and they all say with regard to you:
  "You too have become as weak as we are,
   you are like one of us.
11. Your pomp has been brought low even to Sheol,
  plus the sound of your harps.
  Underneath you worms are spread as your bed,
   maggots are your covering.
12. Oh, how you have fallen from heaven,
  you brilliant Morning Star!
  How you have been cut down to the ground,
   you who overpowered nations!
13. You however said in your heart:
  'As high as the heavens will I climb;
  above the stars of God
   will I erect my throne.
  And I will take up my dwelling on the mount
   of the Assembly,
   in the remote regions of the north.

14. I will scale the heights of the cloud,
   I will make myself like the Most High.'
15. In truth, you will be thrust down to Sheol,
   into the recesses of the pit."

Verse 9. Sheol is the region of the dead; all men go there
after this life. Sheol is an insatiable monster, in a sense.
It is a kingdom of shades, or specters, in another sense. Job
3:13-19; and 26:6 are similar to our passage. Men still exist
there, but they are reduced to the consistency of shadows;
they have no more reality than that. They may be stirred
from their slumber and apathy. But they can be roused only
to make a few remarks. Then they lapse back into inaction.
All of this is a highly poetic way of saying that there is a
Hereafter, but we know very little about it. The Hereafter
is an area on which for the most part the Old Testament
had very incomplete revelation.

So here there is a momentary flutter of commotion among
the departed spirits as the king of Babylon is being given as
much of a reception as men ever got. A ripple of interest
and action sweeps over the assembled shades. These
"shades" again (Hebrew: *repha'im*) are "the weak or
flabby ones." When these shades are said to be "beneath"
that is in keeping with an almost universal conception that
since the departed are laid in the grave, their habitation
may be regarded as being primarily "beneath." But the
"shades" involved are also designated, perhaps a bit
ironically, as "rams," which here means something like bell-
wethers. *Procksch* regards the whole sketch as marked by a
certain "gruesome beauty." In a half-ironic way these kings
are thought of as still having some sort of throne even
down in Sheol; for they "rise from their thrones."

Verse 10. The shades even have the capacity of speech.
All, in fact, are moved to express their sentiments, which
are unanimous to the effect that this greatest of monarchs
(his much-vaunted empire) has become like all the rest.
Death, the great leveler, has brought this about. The one-
time eminence is completely erased. One thing that we
might have expected fails to find expression. Nothing is said,
in any of the words spoken, about a judgment, or about re-

wards or punishments for deeds done in the past, as *Smith* rightly points out. That is a deeper-going insight that comes to light later. After an indication in general about the equality of the shades, the contrasting fate of Babylon's king, with what he once was, is drawn in somewhat heavy and repulsive detail.

Verse 11. The point of departure in this verse is the remembrance that the great monarchs of days of old spent much time and wealth on feasting and drinking. All the "pomp" that marked these banquets is now a thing of the past. So, too, the music that was customarily heard there — "the sound of harps." Where the ones who took part in the banquets used to repose on luxurious couches and draped themselves with expensive coverings, now the couch will be worms, and the covering maggots. The Sheol concept here blends with the grave concept, unless Sheol must also be thought of as crawling with worms and maggots continually.

Verses 12, 13. The first impression at this point is that the shades of Sheol are speaking as in the previous verse. Yet the verse could be an exclamation of the prophet. In the next four verses we have what some are pleased to describe as a "descent into hell" rather than an anticipated ascent into heaven. (*Hoellenfahrt aus Himmelshoehen, Fischer*). As background figure perhaps we should think in terms of the fall of a meteor. Whether the language is clearly mythological is pretty much a matter of dispute. *Procksch* and *Fischer* claim that the evidence is still inconclusive; *R. B. Y. Scott* and *Fohrer* take the opposite view. In any case the identification of "morning star" (Hebrew, *helel*) with the god of Nippur (*Ellil*) is quite questionable. But the king of Babylon, as a symbolical personage, is viewed as already having come to a disastrous overthrow. So sure is the prophet that this overthrow will occur. In fact, the greatest possible overthrow that can be conceived of is from the heights of heaven to the depths of Sheol. There was a time when Babylon "overpowered nations"; now she is "cut down to the ground." The figure of a felled tree is substituted for that of a fallen star. But, oh, what an overthrow! An analysis is made of the thoughts that had once animated the proud king. In his inmost mind he had harbored ambitions to climb as "high as the heavens." Or, what amounts to the same thing, he was ready to erect a throne above the very stars of God. These were bombastic words and high-vaulting ambitions. Reduced to prose they meant he was going to rise as high as any being, mortal or divine, had ever risen apparently. Echoes of the ambitions of the men who built the original tower of Babel (Gen. 11) are heard here (*Mauchline*). Equally much to the point is *Delitzsch's* remark that a measure of "self-deification after the manner of the devil and as a forerunner of the Anti-Christ" are to be found here (cf. Dan. 11:36 and II Thess. 2:4). It is also proper to detect a veiled allusion to Gen. 3:5 ("Ye shall be as gods"). Also Ezek. 28:13ff. and Ps. 48:2 may be compared. In v. 13 the language becomes quite mythological, especially in the reference to "the mount of the assembly," which was the Semitic counterpart to Mount Olympus of the Greeks and lay "in the remote regions of the north."

Verse 14. The vaunting speech goes on, rising to still more boastful heights. On his own — how he can do it remains an unanswered question — he purposes to scale these unattainable heights; and — still on his own — he intends to make himself "like the Most High." Thoughts of Dan. 4 in reference to Nebuchadnezzar comes to mind at once. Pride seldom mounted higher. On this note end the reflections of the Babylonian monarch.

Verse 15. The prophet cannot but render a verdict concerning such an attitude: "In truth you will be thrust down to Sheol, into the recesses of the pit." It might even be well to translate as *Procksch* does: ". . . you *must* be thrust down. . . ." Such heaven-storming defiance challenges God to act, and he will.

(5) The Estimate of Babylon's King Made by Those Who Behold His Corpse Laying Unburied on the Field of Battle (vv. 16-21)

The scene shifts at this point. No longer are the departed shades of Sheol speaking. We find ourselves transported to some imaginary field of battle where the corpse of the king of Babylon is thought of as lying unburied.

14:16-21 16. "They that see you shall closely scrutinize you
they shall carefully ponder over you:
'Is this the man that made the earth to tremble,
who shook kingdoms?
17. who made the earth like a desert,
and tore down her cities?
and did not let his prisoners go home?'
18. All the kings of the nations, yea, all of them, lie in state,
each man in his grave.
19. But you, you have been cast forth tombless
like a despised branch,
in a welter of corpses, of bodies pierced with the sword
who go down to the stones of the pit as a trampled carcass.
20. You will not be united with them in burial,
for you have ruined your land,
you have slain your people.
May the offspring of the wicked
nevermore even be mentioned.
21. Make ready to slaughter his sons
for the guilt of their fathers.
Let them not rise up (again) to possess the land
and fill the face of the world with cities."

Verses 16, 17. When we reach v. 19 we discover that an entirely different approach prevails. But we are definitely back on earth, back on some imaginary field of battle. Since no one particular king appears to be under consideration, and since poetic fancy has free play, the emblematic figure of the Babylonian king may be poetically thought of as suffering the indignity of lying unburied on a field of battle. It is immaterial whether this ever happened or not. The contempt with which the ruler of once-mighty Babylon would be treated is the point. Passers-by stop and study closely what they see. They reflect carefully. They are moved to exclaim: "Is this the man that made the earth to tremble, who shook kingdoms?" There he now lies, brought as low as the corpse of the meanest soldier. He certainly never dreamed that he could fall so low. At one time he possessed power (v. 17) to devastate ruthlessly; he could overthrow and bring to complete ruin even mighty cities.

He took prisoners and never let them return to their homeland.

Verses 18, 19. By contrast, other monarchs less mighty than he enjoyed greater honor after their death. It is as though the speaker began to reflect and said *all* others enjoyed a better lot, yes, on closer reflection, he could not recall of ever having heard of a single exception — "yea, all of them." Where we translated "in his grave" the Hebrew really says, "in his house." But the Babylonian monarch alone is (v. 19) "tombless." A number of derogatory comparisons are made. He may be likened to "a despised branch," which could well mean a worthless sucker. Where the Hebrew goes on with a rather colorful expression, claiming that he lies "clothed about the slain" that might be covered by our translation "in a welter of corpses," dead bodies lying in a disordered tangle. To make this a bit more colorful, they are said to be "bodies pierced by the sword," or are even in the category of "trampled carcasses." When it is also said of them that they "go down to the stones of the pit" that could be a reference to the fact that bodies of men who had died ignominiously were buried under a heap of stones which by-passers threw upon them to make a kind of stigmatized memorial. Of this practice we find indications in Josh. 7:26; 8:29b; and in II Sam. 18:17. To find in the expression a reference to graves lined with stones seems to lack clear evidence. Another analogous case of a monarch of a later date spoken of as lying unburied is Jehoiakim (Jer. 22:18ff.).

Verse 20. This statement seems to grow out of the fact that the monarch depicted, whether real or fictitious, was never one with his people during his lifetime, therefore he also shall not be united with them in death. Behind expressions such as these is an unformulated belief that the spirits of the departed are gathered into a common dwelling place after the end (cf. Gen. 23; 50:25; Exod. 13:19; Josh. 24:32). This monarch will be denied such a privilege. He has "ruined [his] land" by the disastrous wars he had fought. He had slain, that is, virtually "slain [his] people" in those same wars, which took so large a toll of lives on both sides. The last statement of the verse is either a prediction or a wish. We slightly prefer the latter. The king is thought of as so dishonored a character that even his descendants live under the shadow of this disgrace. So much so, that later generation will disdain even to mention father and children.

Verse 21. This verse is a kind of malediction. At least it involves the idea that if such things as here recorded should come to pass they would be nothing more than just retribution. One need not claim that these words are "rife with a terrible hatred" as *Procksch* would have it. At least a parallel to the first thought expressed is the case of the sons of Zedekiah, who were slain before their fathers eyes after the capture of Jerusalem. In any case Babylonian monarchs did such things. It need not appear too strange if a like fate were to befall them. The next line merely expresses the thought that it is devoutly hoped that rulers of this type may never occupy the throne either "to possess the land" or to "fill the face of the world with cities" as they expand their empire by bloody conquests and build new cities as monuments of their so-called achievements.

i. God's Verdict in Regard to the Whole Empire of the King of Babylon (vv. 22-23)

14:22-23 22. "And I will rise up against them," says Yahweh of hosts, "and I will cut off from Babylon name and remnant, offspring and offshoot," says Yahweh of hosts. 23. "And I will make it to be occupied by hedgehogs — water marshes; and I will sweep it with the broom of destruction," says Yahweh of hosts.

These two verses finalize the two preceding chapters. It is now no longer the king of Babylon who is under consideration, but his whole empire. The divine verdict about this realm is being reported. It is as though God had long remained inactive. Now he bestirs himself and rises from his throne to take the task of punishing guilty Babylon in hand, "I will rise up against them." Total overthrow and extinction is threatened. Sooner or later this will come to pass. For Yahweh "will cut off from Babylon name and remnant, offspring and offshoot." The Hebrew uses at this point two pairs of alliterated nouns, something like the familiar English expression "kith and kin."

Verse 23. Besides, in the place of man who is expelled from the area, there will be unattractive creatures like hedgehogs, and in the place of an attractive landscape, "water-marshes," left over somehow from the old irrigation canals that used to function so well in conjunction with the two great rivers and make the farm-land so productive. All the glory will be, as it were, swept away "with the broom of destruction." An ominous word of doom! With good reason *Fischer* calls these two verses "a concluding affirmation." To call them "prosy and without color" (*Fitch*) is quite unwarranted.

Notes

Verse 4. For "boisterous raging" *KJ* has the translation "the golden city." The word involved is *madhhebhah*, a difficult term whose root, if it were Aramaic, could mean gold; and thus the *KJ* version arrived at this unique meaning.

Verse 6. *Makkath* stands in the construct state before a preposition (*be*), a rather common construction in Hebrew (*KS* 336 y).

Verse 9. "she rouses up" is actually an infinitive form (cf. *GK* 113 h).

Verse 11. *She'ol* in this case is used as an adverbial modifier (*KS* 330 c).

Verse 12. The word *ben* (*son* of the dawn) is clearly used to express some form of relationship, according to the very familiar pattern (*KS* 306 h).

Verse 17. The noun *bayethah* is of the so-called pregnant construction (*KS* 213 b).

Verse 21. For the word "of their fathers," which is in the plural, the Septuagint already suggested that the singular *'abhihem* might be read, concentrating attention more on the one figure, the king of Babylon, who has thus far been under consideration. To let the text stand as the Hebrew has it, makes for a somewhat broader thought. At the close of the verse, some propose the reading *'iyyim* (ruins) for "cities." One thought is as acceptable as the other.

In 1959 Gottfried Quell (*Festschrift* fuer Friedrich Baumgaertl, Erlangen, p. 131 ff.) attempted to set forth an approach briefly suggested by Albright in 1934 to the effect that vv. 4b-21 was originally "a Canaanite epic" which the author of Chap. 14, a clumsy, illiterate prophet (the author of 14:1-3 and vv. 22-23) took over almost verbatim and made the mythological material refer to the king of Babylon. The essay is done with great skill and lively imagination. The illiterate prophet is berated, belittled, and denigrated; but finally it is conceded that he still was a true Yahweh prophet. Even as the treatment of this prophet borders on the fantastic, so, almost line for line, too much is read into Chap. 14. Our understanding and appreciation of the prophet Isaiah is not appreciably furthered by this approach. In principle, the thought as such is feasible that some such Ugaritic poem could have been reworked and made Yahwistic instead of Baalistic and so become a colorful addition to the words of Isaiah.

Chapter XIV: 24-32

2. Against Israel's Immediate Neighbors (14:24–17:1ff.)

a. Assyria (14:24-27): The Lord's Unalterable Purpose in Regard to Assyria

Let it suffice in regard to the many possible dates for this passage that have been suggested that the passage may have been uttered some time before 701 B.C., when the great overthrow of Assyria occurred on the soil of Palestine (Isa. 37).

It is quite commonly conceded that the passage bears the stamp of being authentically from Isaiah. Men are equally ready to grant that it belongs to the grandest of the things Isaiah ever wrote, showing particularly the marvelous concept that the prophet had of the universal aspects of history and how all things lie in the hand of Yahweh when the fortunes of the nations are being considered. *Scott* has expressed it well: "Here Isaiah's message that Yahweh is Lord of history and that his purpose is the finally determining factor in what happens, comes to clear expression."

When we look at the broader context we note that a striking word against Babylon precedes. Historically it would seem that this word against Assyria should precede the pronouncement against Babylon, for in point of time, Assyria fell before Babylon. However *Vilmar* has rightly pointed out that Babylon was the kingdom that in a very special way gave expression to defiance of Yahweh and his purposes; she is the epitome of the spirit of the ungodly world; whereas Assyria is merely a paler copy of the same attitude.

But for that matter it must be noted that 14:28-32 also in point of time should stand before 14:24-27, for Philistia suffered her severe reverses before Assyria did. But again it may be pointed out that Assyria as the pale shadow of

Babylon falls into that category and is so placed by the side of this great world monarchy.

Much ado is made of the fact that the essence of the oracle against Assyria appears already in Chap. 19. Therefore it is concluded that Isaiah should have appended this to the preceding oracle. But there is always the possibility that a prophet like Isaiah made many pronouncements on a given subject. To insert the one before us (14:24-27) immediately after the word against Babylon and as the forerunner of the smaller nations, whose doom is pronounced, also makes very good sense. Topical arrangements allows for several possibilities. Besides, chronological arrangement must not always control the issue.

Fohrer provides a somewhat wholesome perspective when he suggests that because Assyria had proved itself to be an unwilling and useless tool in the hands of the Almighty, he proceeds to break this instrument of his hands, as it deserves.

To broaden the perspective still more we may note that it is not inappropriate to class Assyria as among Israel's more immediate neighbors, like Philistia, Moab, Damascus, which immediately follow, because Assyria was making almost perennial invasions into Palestine, just as though she were a near neighbor of hers.

14:24-27 24. Yahweh of hosts has sworn, saying:
"Indeed, as I have devised it, so shall it be;
as I have planned, so shall it stand";
25. that I will break Assyria in my land,
and trample him down upon my mountains.
And each man's yoke shall be removed from him,
and his burden shall be removed from his shoulder."
26. This is the purpose which has been devised with regard to all the earth,
and this is the hand which is stretched out over all the nations.
27. For Yahweh of hosts has formulated his plan. Who can bring it to naught?
His hand is stretched out. Who can turn it back?

There are other instances where the inviolability of God's pronouncement is set forth by the use of an oath by himself — 62:8; Amos 4:2; 8:7; Jer. 51:14. Over against the unstable and feeble things of the world it must be made clear that there is an unalterable purpose on the part of the Almighty, especially with regard to certain judgments of his that divine justice must bring to pass. Such is the situation with regard to Assyria. God works with definite purpose and with adequate planning. At least that much must be expected of all true rulers. Much more is this the case with regard to the Lord. At the time this word was spoken Assyria may have appeared to be far from a final overthrow. In the eyes of the Lord the matter looked otherwise.

Verse 25. In this case the clear purpose is "to break Assyria." Thinking back to the idea that a nation is an instrument in God's hand, we can well understand that the worthless instrument may be broken in pieces and cast aside. The concept is a grand one, emphasizing the omnipotence of the Almighty. To be a bit more specific, the Lord has determined to do this breaking in no other place than in his own land and upon the mountains of the land of his people — the land which the Assyrians had so often invaded and defiled. There will he "trample him down." The figure changes to the idea of grinding under foot the object that has offended, and leaving it behind, utterly useless and helpless. Since, however, the imperial designs of nations cannot be achieved without laying heavy burdens upon the shoulder of each member of the dominated nation, this overthrow of the Assyrian will result in the removal of such yoke and burden from all individuals. A mighty sigh of relief rising from the breasts of all will mark the occasion, says the colorful language of the prophet.

These two preceding verses cover the Lord's pronouncement. Verse 26 appears rather as a summation and comment on the part of the prophet. For the prophet indicates the broader scope of this plan that God has. Though, on the face of it, it involves only Assyria, nevertheless since Assyrian domination was world-wide, these events will affect all the earth and so the hand "is stretched out over all the nations." This statement describes a sort of gesture. Before the Lord fetches his mighty blow he raises his hand for the blow, a figure used by Isaiah several times also in reference to God's judgments on Israel (9:7–10:4).

Verse 27. Summing up the thought of the irrevocable

nature of the Lord's decisions, the prophet asks the question, Who could venture to oppose the Lord on any matter where he has reached a decision? None apparently saw the doom of Assyria as Isaiah did. But he was O so right!

b. Philistia (14:28-32)

Again a number of dates for this oracle have been suggested. To us it seems most reasonable to follow the approach outlined so well by *Procksch*. Since Shalmanezer died about 722 B.C., before the capture of Samaria had been concluded, Sargon took the siege of that city in hand and brought it to a close. Then, in order to establish himself firmly on the throne, he had to hurry back to Babylon and overcome opponents that would have challenged his right to the crown. In the process he did suffer a defeat near Babylon in 721. However, while his hold on the throne still seemed uncertain, a coalition was formed against him, headed by the king of Hamath to the north and including Damascus and what was left of Samaria, and Hanno, king of Philistia. It was during this time that Philistia seemed strong and destined to play an important role, that Isaiah indicated that her doom was sealed and her future very uncertain.

14:28-32 28. In the year when king Ahaz died, this was the oracle:
29. Rejoice not, O Philistia, all of you,
that the rod of him that smote you is broken.
For from the root of the serpent shall go forth a viper,
and its fruit shall be a flying serpent.
30. And the very lowliest of them shall have food,
and the poor shall lie down in safety.
And I will kill your root with famine
and what is left of you shall men slay.
31. Wail, every gate; cry out, every city;
O thou whole Philistia, dissolve in fear.
For from the north comes a smoke,
and there is not a straggler in his ranks.
32. And what answer shall one give to messengers of nations?
That the Lord has established Zion,
and in it shall the poor of his people find refuge.

Verse 28. But a few passages are dated according to the years of the reign of Judah's kings. Cf. 6:1; 20:1. Isaiah clearly remembered the date of this oracle. Whether we are to draw the conclusion that the oracle came after Ahaz was dead, or merely that both events transpired in the same year must remain unresolved.

Verse 29. But the point at issue was that Philistia, one of the nations that had in its day caused Judah much suffering, should not feel that now success and prosperity are coming her way. The reference to the breaking of the rod that smote them does not require that a particular person is to be thought of, but merely that one instance of oppression has just been terminated. This event caused the Philistines to dream of a grander future. For this momentary relief does not herald prosperity but rather a succession of further evils. The point of the comparison seems to be that after this momentary relief, things will not get better but worse. For that is the unquestioned meaning of the sequence: serpent, viper, flying serpent. Two possibilities of interpretation may be submitted as alternatives. Either these three point to a succession of Assyrian monarchs: Shalmanezer V, Sargon, Sennacherib; or to a succession of rulers of Judah, beginning with Hezekiah, who actually did smite the Philistines after they had achieved temporary independence (cf. II Kings 18:8). In fact, it could be that the three serpents are successively applicable to several situations that will arise, one always worse than the other. The old Jewish interpretation that the "flying serpent" referred to the Messiah has least to recommend it. The "flying serpent" may be a term from mythological origin, but in itself is as harmless as any reference to dragons that we might in good conscience make in our day. This by no means implies that Biblical terminology sanctions mythological views.

We may here add the fact that pronouncements against the land of Philistia are quite common in Scriptures. See Amos 1:6-8; Zeph. 2:4-7; Jer. 47; Ezek. 25:15-17; Zech. 9:5-7.

Verse 30. This verse is only then understood when the contrast involved is noted, namely that the possessive before "root" is emphatic. So then the first half of the verse refers to the advantages that Judah will enjoy; the second half to the utter destruction that will befall Philistia. When it shall go so badly with the Philistines, even the lowliest of the low shall not lack food in Israel, and the "poor" shall enjoy safety, the latter being, according to later Biblical usage, the *godly* poor. The words, "will men slay," could be so translated as to refer to "hunger" viz., what is left of you shall hunger slay. In any case the passage clearly says that all will be well with Israel; nothing will go well for Philistia.

Verse 31 now defines exactly what form the impending calamity will take. At the sight of it "every gate and every city" are bidden to wail and cry out. This refers, of course, to the *people* living in the cities and moving about within the gates. To call the threatening calamity a "smoke" coming from the north is figurative and poetic language referring to the invading army which comes from the traditional point of invasion in the land of Syria, the north (*Procksch* calls the north *die Wetterecke Palestinas* — i.e., the corner from which storms are wont to break). The smoke mentioned may be that of the camp-fires of invaders or the smoke that billows up from towns that are being reduced to ashes. "Smoke" is a more colorful and ominous way of stating the case. The last clause ("there is no straggler in his ranks") reminds of the well-trained character of the invading armies and their stern military discipline. Cf. 5:26-28.

Verse 32. Two possibilities of approach are involved in this verse, each leading to about the same result. It could be a specific reference to Philistine emissaries who come to Jerusalem, seeking, as they actually did, Hezekiah's participation in the uprising that Hanno of Gaza was organizing against the Assyrians. Or the messengers could be thought of as being men sent from different nations after the disastrous defeat of the Assyrians who were massed against Jerusalem in Hezekiah's day. The outside messengers would then be men sent to verify whether that disastrous defeat actually took place in the striking manner that some claimed. Whoever the inquirers were, the answer has the same meaning. It is a confession of faith to the effect that Zion has been established by the Lord; therefore the Assyrians had not been able to capture the city. Or else, Zion has the Lord as her ally and protector and does not need the defense that comes from alliances with other nations. So that all the poor (i.e., again; the pious poor) and the weak who make up the nation and seem so helpless over against the powerful Assyrian military machine, shall actually "find refuge" in Zion, which may also be thought of as an impregnable stronghold.

So this last verse is in the nature of a confession of faith. *Fohrer* has aptly claimed that the substance of this answer is, "We believe." So an oracle against a neighbor nation terminates in a mighty confession of faith, calculated to induce others to make it their own.

As a further item of background it must be noted that the oracles against outside nations involve a moral issue, which is sometimes taken for granted, as in this case. The moral issue is that the Lord is bringing judgment upon these outside nations either because of their wrongs done against the natural law, of which all men are conscious in some degree, or because of wrongs done to God's people. That the Philistines had inflicted all kinds of injustice upon Israel in the course of the years is only too well known.

Notes

Verse 24. The perfect *hayethah* is clearly a case of the use of the prophetic perfect. See *KS* 129.

Verse 25. "Trample him down" as finite verb continues the construction which in the previous verb was still an infinitive of purpose. Such transitions are common. See *KS* 413 d.

Verse 30. "The lowliest of them" achieves a superlative sense by the unique Hebrew device of saying "the firstborn of the lowly." Cf. *KS* 309 a. Therefore there is no need of altering the text to read: "They shall have food on my pasture" i.e., *bekhori*); nor is the literal rendering of the *RSV* acceptable.

Verse 31. The singular without article (gate, city) particularizes the issue somewhat like "*every* gate" and "*every* city." The absolute infinitive *namog* ("dissolve") takes on an imperative sense and may be used for the imperative in asyndetic construction. Cf. *KS* 217 a and *GK* 113 bb. *Bodhedh* without article represents another case of particularization.

Verse 32. The singular verb "shall one give" is a typical case of the use of an indefinite subject in Hebrew. See *KS* 324 d.

Chapter XV

c. Oracle Concerning Moab (15:1–16:14)

This oracle has been aptly described by *Procksch* as *das Schmerzenkind der Exegese* (almost: the problem child of exegesis). Certainly they go too far who overplay the difficulties of the passage and assert that it is of "little meaning" to the present-day reader. We at least would insist that this applies only to the *casual* reader. Equally extreme is the opinion that we have here "a perfect jungle of oracles." Add to this the assertion of some that the text is extremely uncertain, you have so strong an indictment of the Oracle as to make a reader question whether it was a wise providence that had this piece incorporated in the Sacred Scriptures. Without doubt these two chapters have their difficulties, in fact more than their average share of them. But careful study of these words can be very rewarding and well worth the effort that may be put to it.

To begin with, it may be helpful to trace the relations that prevailed historically between these two nations — Israel and Moab — during the centuries of their contact with one another. After Moab had caused the Israelites no little trouble during the first centuries of their dwelling in the land of Canaan, it was Saul who subdued them first and David who made the subjugation stick. After the division of the kingdom, Moab came under the domination of the Northern Kingdom till Ahab's day, when they asserted their independence (II Kings 1:1; 3:4ff). Jehoshaphat subdued them without battle, but Israel lost control of the trans-Jordan area in Jehu's day, giving way to the Syrians (II Kings 10:32ff.) Moab vented its spite on Israel from this time on in various ways. When Jeroboam II regained all the old territory down to the Dead Sea, Moab will have been subdued without a doubt (II Kings 14:25). Still periodically Moab did invade Israel (II Kings 13:20), and no doubt it had been able to reclaim or repossess cities in

Reuben and Gad that had in days of old belonged to them. This situation still prevailed when Tiglath-pileser and his Assyrian hosts overran the Northern Kingdom. Such was the situation as Isaiah found it in his day. Sargon may already have captured Samaria (722 B.C.).

But to explore the possibilities of more recent developments a bit more fully; it seems that Sargon directed a major campaign against the Arabians (715 B.C.). To reach Arabia he swept through the length of Moab from the north, devastating her larger cities and murdering and plundering as he advanced. This is the situation that these two chapters largely have in mind. But a sequel should not be overlooked. It appears that in 713 Moab joined a coalition against Assyria headed by the city of Ashdod to the west, and so incurred further displeasure on the part of the Assyrians, with whom Ashdod and Jerusalem and Moab had entered into treaty relationships. This violation of the treaty irritated Assyria and may have brought on the prediction that judgment would strike Moab to the full within the space of three years, as indicated in 16:13f.

Commentators are far from being agreed that the above-pictured situation is the one that was involved. Some favor the days of Joash; others move the time down after the Exile, and so on.

However a major question is: May these two chapters be ascribed to Isaiah? A majority of writers say No. *Skinner*, for example, lists the following factors as militating against the very possibility of Isaianic authorship: the "elegiac strain of this passage, its outflow of purely human sympathy towards the cities of the calamity, its poverty of religious ideas, and its diffuse and labored style." These factors he claims "stamp it with a character foreign to (Isaiah's) genius." Subjective impressions enter so largely into determining questions such as these that we feel each of these arguments may easily be met by due consideration of the unique subject matter involved as well as by the fact that quite a number of terms and expressions used are typically those of Isaiah. It is not however our intention to inspect the details of this issue. We merely add that some hold that the original for these chapters was a piece written by a native

Moabite, which was freely taken over by Isaiah and later reworked again by Jeremiah. For the strange situation prevails that Jer. 48:29-38 covers much the same ground, however does not run parallel to Isa. 15:8–16:5.

On the subject of the pattern of the meter followed in this oracle, too much uncertainty prevails to allow for any solid verdict.

But the major item of concern for the entire Oracle is whether we have here "prediction or lament." Expositors are divided into two camps, the more recent trend being to classify the chapter as a lament, or an elegy, over what has befallen Moab. As far as grammatical forms are concerned, we are faced by that peculiarity of the Hebrew language, that the language does not know tenses as we are familiar with them. So the first verbs that appear in v. 1 are so-called perfects. But it so happens that the perfect is used both to describe or narrate what occurred in the past as well as, in other instances, to refer strongly to the future (prophetic perfect). If a man be inclined to discount prophecy, or merely to hold that it was resorted to far less frequently than we were wont to suppose, he will incline, even before the evidence is examined, to the idea that we have here a lament over events that have already transpired. If he feels that predictive prophecy was a rather common form of pronouncement on the part of the prophets, he may incline equally much to the impression that Isaiah is foretelling what will presently befall Moab. There seems to be at least three instances where the future is indicated: 15:9; 16:2, 12. This would seem to give prediction the preference, as far as forms go. There is nothing unnatural as far as that goes to have prophets lay claim to superior revelation, especially in regard to the future. Such oracles are not to be considered suspect, or they that hold to such interpretation as less open to the truth. The prophet then may be thought of as seeing the horrible future that will befall Moab unfold itself before his eyes with all the horrors of bloody warfare and searing drought.

We offer this outline:

1. Cruel Invasion and Drought for Moab (15:1-9)

2. The Appeal for Asylum Addressed by Refugees to Judah (16:1-5)
3. Indication of Further Affliction, Especially of Moab's Grape Culture (16:6-12)
4. An Epilogue Fixing the Time of the Disaster (16:13, 14)

We have let the outline include Chap. 16 because both chapters comprise a unit. We preserve almost throughout the past, or perfect, tense, to give the flavor of the Hebrew. In the original language the tragedy has practically already occurred.

15:1-9 1. Yea, by night Ar was laid waste, Moab destroyed; Yea, by night Kir was laid waste, Moab destroyed.
2. She went up to the sanctuary
and Dibon [went up] to the high places to weep;
Moab wails over Nebo and over Medebah.
Every head is shaved; all beards are cut.
3. In their streets they have girded on sackcloth;
On their housetops and in their squares all of them weep, collapsing in tears.
4. And Heshbon and Elealeh cried out,
their voice was heard as far as Jahaz.
Therefore the warriors of Moab cried out in distress,
each man's soul trembled.
5. My heart cries out for Moab
her fugitives have come to Zoar, to Eglath Shelishiyah.
Yea, at the ascent of Luhith, men go up weeping;
Yea, down the road to Horonaim, they raise a cry of destruction.
6. Yea, the waters of Mimron have become waste places;
yea, the grass [around] is dried up, vegetation is done for;
green things have not sprung up.
7. Therefore the remainder that they have gathered and whatever they have laid up in store
they carry away over the Poplar Brook [going to Edom].
8. For the outcry has gone all around the borders of Moab;
their wailing extends to Eglaim, their wailing to Beer-Elim.
9. Yea, the waters of Dimon are full of blood,
and I shall appoint for Dimon even more distress,
for the escapees of Moab, a lion, also for the rest of the land.

We append a map at this point, (p. 277) for the whole chapter is so deeply involved in geographical references that without a mental picture of the geography the reader must remain bewildered. Some of the places indicated are

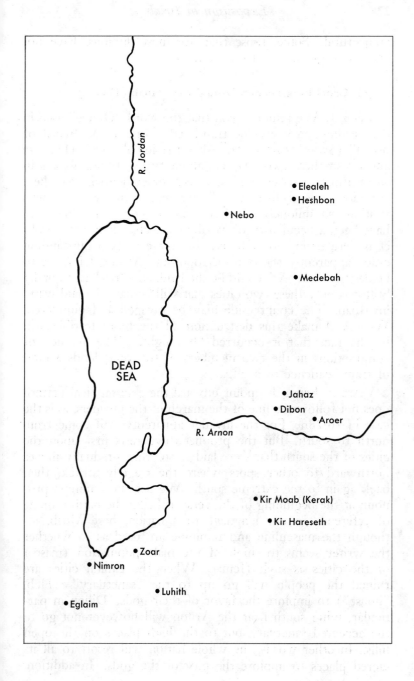

conjectural. Some, those that are most dubious, have not
even been given a spot on the map.

(1) Cruel Invasion and Drought for Moab (15:1-9)

Verse 1. We remind again that the word "Oracle" used in
the heading, may also be translated "burden" or "word of
doom" (*Schicksalsspruch*). Also, the initial "yea" (Heb. *ki*
appears in these two chapters about twelve times, always in
the affirmative sense, not the causal, or evidential. Nowhere
else does this stylistic peculiarity appear in the prophet's
writings so uniquely. It has been surmised that this may
have been a peculiarity of Moabite speech, which the prophet is here trying to embody. In any case two outstanding
cities, apparently the two metropolises (Ar and Kir), are to
be destroyed. ("Ar" could be the land, and "Kir" its capital.)
Still it is only these two cities that will actually be laid waste
in Moab. The countryside may be ravaged and plundered.
What will make this destruction all the more terrible will
be the fact that it occurred "by night." The absence of
conjunctions in the two members of the verse lends a kind
of tragic cadence to it all.

Verse 2. From this point onward the geographical pattern
does not follow the line of the march of the invaders, as is the
case in 10:28ff. For the invader apparently will come from
north to south. But the prophet's eye rests first upon the
cities of the south that were laid waste, then gradually moves
northward to other spots where the tragedy struck, then
back again to the extreme south. We use the feminine pronoun at the beginning of the verse as being the natural mode
of reference in our language to a nation, here Moab, although the masculine and feminine are used as to whether
the writer seems to think of the male population (masc.)
or the cities as such (fem.). When the capital cities are
ruined the people will go up to the "sanctuary" (Heb.
"house") to implore the favor of their gods; Dibon in particular, lying south near the Arnon will however not go to
the accepted sanctuary but to the high places on the open
hills. In other words, the whole nation will resort to all its
sacred places to implore the pity of the gods. In addition,

some measure of lamentation will be involved over places that were hit hardest by the invasion, places like Nebo and Medebah farther to the north. Following accepted practices of lament, those who engage in it, with typical Oriental demonstrativeness, will have shaved their heads and gashed their beard, customs that prevailed almost universally in days of old to express grief (cf. in general Ezra 9:3; II Sam. 15:30; Jer. 14:3f.; Lev. 13:45; Micah 3:7; Gen. 37:24; I Kings 21:27; Isa. 3:24).

Verse 3. In the streets of the cities that have not been destroyed will be evidence of the fact that the nation is suffering grievously and is giving vent to its bitter grief. Wherever you go on the streets you will see men with typical vestment of those who lament — sackcloth on the bare skin. Making public display of their grief, as Orientals are often wont to do, they will even shriek out their lamentation from the housetops, carrying on to the point where they exhaust themselves over it all and "collapse in tears."

Verse 4. It is not to be wondered at that the prophet knows the location of cities and places in Moab so well that he makes no attempt at indicating their location. The land lay just across the River Jordan and the Dead Sea from Israel. So up more toward the north, two cities, frequently mentioned together because they lay near to one another, Heshbon and Elealeh, make such a loud outcry that the sound reaches down as far as Jahaz, almost to the River Arnon. This may be poetic hyperbole, but the impression grows that Moab is going to be most grievously afflicted when the disaster strikes. To indicate still farther the intensity of the nation's grief, it is stated that even her courageous men, her "warriors," will cry out aloud in their distress and add to the universal outcry. These men will display no heroism; rather their soul shall tremble, "each man" of them.

Verse 5. The speaker in this verse would appear to be the prophet himself. He is not oblivious to the great grief of the neighboring nation; he is not unsympathetic. His "heart cries out for Moab." For a similar thought see 16:9, 11. There is no vindictiveness on the prophet's part, no gloating. — The flood of the fugitives has swept southward. In mind the prophet follows them. They will get to the southern end of the Dead Sea (see Gen. 19:20-22), where also lay, the to us unknown place, Eglath Shelishiyah. There also seems to have been located a steep ascent that had to be climbed, called Luhith, where the prophet envisions them as mounting as they weep bitter tears. Then follows on their route the descent of Horonaim. Cry after "cry over the destruction" that has befallen all the land is foreseen by the prophet as sounding from the lips of these refugees.

Verse 6. The context would seem to indicate that Nimron lay to the south, near the other places just mentioned. Once the "waters of Nimron" may either have been famous or plentiful. Then the spots will count as "waste places." The grass all around will be "dried up" and "the vegetation done for." These statements point to the fact that a drought appears to have capped the climax of the calamities then prevailing, for three parallel statements are made on this score; the third: "green things have not sprung up." The affliction of the land and the people must be thought of as most terrible. So the prophet predicts that it will be.

Verse 7. The fugitives are still in flight and have reached the southernmost border of the land. There is still the Poplar-Brook to cross. Then they will have reached asylum in the land of Edom. One further touch may be introduced here. Of all that they once possessed there is now only a "remainder" which they hastily gathered before they took to their heels. It involves but a little "whatever they have laid up in store." These pitiful remnants they are seen carrying with them as they wade across the stream.

Verse 8. One summary statement appears now: the outcry ringing out and echoing over the land reaches the border all the way around the land: "The outcry has gone all around the border of Moab." A *nation* is shrieking! It may be that the remaining half of the verse refers to places that lie in the extreme north. Then the impression created would be this: a wave of crying and shrieking rolls over the length of the land northward until it hits the last border of the land.

Verse 9. Where the previous item in the account struck the *ear* the one that now follows meets the *eye*. After the Assyrians have gone through the land ravaging and pillaging and murdering, they have left behind, for example, by the city of Dimon, water stained red with human blood. This seems to have motivated the choice of the name Dimon for Dibon referred to above (v. 2). For Dimon means "Bloody" (in Hebrew *dam* means "blood.") Somehow the prophet seems to understand that Dibon's lot is going to be still heavier. She may have been deserving of greater punishment. Therefore the word of the Lord indicates "even more distress" is in store for her. The text speaks rather vaguely, like: More will follow (a neuter plural noun being used). That it will be a cruel and evil lot appears from the statement: "For the escapees of Moab, a lion, also for the rest of the land." We shall not attempt to make the term "lion" yield a more specific sense, as though it perhaps referred to the lion of Judah (Gen. 49:9) or, perhaps to the Assyrian lion. We are content to let the term designate a dangerously hostile force.

The closing line, "also for the rest of the land [a lion]" seems to indicate that all that has been prophesied concerning Moab's affliction does not exhaust the full tale of it.

Notes

Verse 1. The *ki* used so frequently in this chapter is to be translated in the affirmative sense "yea"; cf. KS 351 c. *Lel,* "night" used twice in the same construction, is without doubt in the absolute state (*KS* 337 y). On the asyndeton, used twice in the verse, see *KS* 374 b.

Verse 2. "She went up to the sanctuary" reads in the Hebrew: "She went up to the *house.*" Some treat this as utterly meaningless. But in the parallel member "high places" appears. So the "house" referred to is the sanctuary. Therefore to change the text to read "the daughter of Dibon" (*RSV,* etc.) is quite unnecessary. The adverbial expression "to the high places" appears without the preposition, as happens so frequently. See *KS* 330 c. The form *yeyelil,* appearing with a double prefix, is explained *GK* 70 d.

Verse 3. There is disagreement in number in the Hebrew text, which reads: "In *his* streets *they* have girded." This grows out of the flexibility of Hebrew syntax and readily adjusts itself. See *KS* 249 c.

Verse 5. The expression "they raise the cry," is a typical instance of the use of an indefinite subject used in the vague sense of "*men* raise." See *KS* 324 d.

Chapter XVI

(2) The Appeal for Asylum Addressed by Refugees to Judah (16:1-5)

We have here the second turn of thought in the Oracle concerning Moab. The prophet advises the bewildered Moabites as to what they should do in the present emergency. He even suggests the words they should use in appealing to Judah for help. Then he goes on to indicate why this appeal of theirs is very timely, and even invites Moab to share in what is the unique hope of Israel, or Judah, for the future. In brief he suggests that Moab implore the help and pity of Judah.

16:1-5 1. Send lambs, a gift worthy of territorial rulers,
from the rocky country by way of the wilderness to the mount of the daughter of Zion.
2. Like fluttering birds, like startled nestlings,
so shall the daughters of Moab be at the fords of the Arnon.
3. [You inhabitants of Zion] give advice; grant our request;
make your shade as deep as night at high noon;
hide the neglected ones, betray not the fugitive.
4. Let my [i.e., Moab's] neglected ones sojourn among you.
Be a hidingplace for them from before the face of the destroyer.
Of a truth, the oppressor [of Judah] has come to an end;
destruction has ceased;
he that tramples under foot is vanished out of the land.
5. And a throne will be established in steadfast love;
and a man will sit on it in faithfulness in the tent of David,
a ruler and one who seeks justice and espouses righteousness.

The point of view that prevails in this section practically amounts to this: Help for Moab can be found only with Judah under the present circumstances. The prophet is speaking. He counsels Moab to appeal to Judah. The form of the appeal involves that first of all a substantial token of submission, which is at the same time a strong plea for help, be offered in the form of the kind of tribute that had long been the standard pattern for Moab to follow: "Send lambs." When we compare II Kings 3:4 we observe that this form of tribute in previous days had run up into amazingly large figures. When Moab asserted its independence from Israel the giving of this tribute was interrupted. Now, says the prophet, resume it. In the language of diplomacy in those days, substantial tribute was the token of submission and allegiance. The prophet does not dictate how large the number of sheep sent is to be. Moab has been sorely pressed; it may not be able to equal its former contributions. Therefore: "send lambs," but, at the same time make it "a gift worthy of territorial rulers." The mode of procedure is sketched out to make the issue clearer: "the rocky country" is the plateau of Moab itself; "by way of the wilderness" means the southern portion of Judah through which the sheep must be driven to reach "the mount of the daughter of Zion."

Verse 2. This verse is half-parenthetical. It indicates how bewildered and confused all the Moabites were. Above (chap. 15:4), it had been indicated how pandemonium had seized the Moabite *warriors*. This verse reminds that the *women* had panicked also. They were as helpless as "fluttering birds" and "startled nestlings." Their panic seems to have reached its height at the "fords of Arnon." This verse then indicates how much in need of simple concrete advice all Moabites were. So the verse is not out of place. It need not be moved back after 15:8, as present-day fashion suggests.

Verse 3. The prophet now lays the very words that the Moabites are to use in their very mouth. He spells out the course of procedure for a badly frightened and bewildered people. At this point we have inserted an explanatory parenthesis to indicate that the word of the prophet is addressing itself to the people of Moab. They are to appeal to Judah to tell them what to do. They are to say: "Give advice." Judah has good counsel and will freely give it. By this approach Moab throws itself upon the mercy of its brother nation. The next part of their appeal is difficult to assess. *RSV* says "Give counsel." Others suggest: "function as umpire." The most usable translation seems to be: "grant [our] request." The request then follows and it amounts to this: grant asylum to the refugees; hide them; protect them. Or, as here worded: "Make your shade as deep as night at high noon." For the term "shade" frequently connotes protection. It is true, the sheltering of fugitives may involve some risk. Judah is being asked to take that risk. With this agrees the further spelling-out of what the Moabites are pleading for: "Hide the neglected ones, betray not the fugitive."

Verse 4. To indicate that the Moabites are still speaking in the first half of this verse we have inserted in the translation the possessive "Moab's" after "my." That so many different aspects of their plea are being presented is due to the fact that the need was great, the dangers were many, the afflictions were countless. In other words the many pleas are an indication of the extremity of the need of the poor Moabites. So then vv. 2-3a were the words of the emissaries of Moab addressed to Judah.

Following a pattern that appears dozens of times in the Scriptures (note especially Ps. 2) the speaker in a given piece may change without any outward indication that such a change has taken place. The attentive readers are expected to detect that such a change has occurred. So in the middle of v. 4 the prophet, who had spoken in vv. 1 and 2, resumes his words and now begins to tell of a new situation that prevails as far as Judah is concerned, a situation which will allow the people of Judah to entertain the request of the Moabites favorably. Something had occurred, somewhat like what occurred a dozen years later when Sennacherib's expedition of 701 B.C. came to a disastrous end: all pressure on Judah was removed. Or, as the text states it: "Of a truth, the oppressor has come to an end, destruction has ceased; he that tramples under foot is vanished out of the land." Once again, apparently Judah was not so involved with the mighty forces of Assyria as to cause her to be under pressure. That is virtually an affirmative answer to the request that Moab has just been told to address to Judah.

Verse 5. Now comes the intriguing fifth verse, which has long been regarded even as far back as the time of the *Targum* (which practically represents the earliest Jewish tradition), as a Messianic passage. A sudden high-point is reached in the prophet's words to Moab. The fact that Moab has come to take refuge under the wings of Judah makes the prophet very sympathetic toward this brother nation, inducing them to say: You are coming to seek relief from us; we will cooperate and give you a share even of the best that our heritage and tradition have to offer — our Messianic hope. This then is one of the not infrequent passages in the prophets where the truth concerning the Deliverer from Israel is not withheld from those of other nations. The language of the verse is so typically Messianic that this aspect of the case becomes immediately apparent if only passages such as Isa. 9:6 and 11:1-10 and Amos 9:11 are compared. To attempt to limit this word to some flourishing state of the nation Judah as a reward, or the like, for what she has graciously done for Moab, fails to do justice to the passage.

This, then, is what these words seem to indicate for Moab: Israel has a throne with a future, not like the unstable thrones of even the most imposing of the powerful nations round about on every hand. This one will be established by virtue of the "steadfast love" which the Lord has so graciously held out to his people. The throne does involve "the tent of David"; that is to say, the Davidic line, which ever since II Sam. 7 enjoyed a divinely appointed distinction and an eternal destiny. In fact, the future prospects of this unique throne involve "a man [who] shall sit on it in faithfulness" to a degree never displayed in the rule of any earthly monarch. He shall, at the same time, uphold and achieve the highest ideals that rulers could aspire to, for he "seeks justice and espouses righteousness."

To find this Messianic hope offered by Judah to be shared with Moab indicates as strongly as can be done that the Messianic expectations were not vague and tenuous; not fantastic dreams that never took root in the thinking of the nation.

(3) Indication of Further Affliction, Especially of Moab's Grape Culture (16:6-12)

It has often been assumed that in the words of this section, more particularly in the words of v. 6, Israel is giving a negative answer to the pitiful plea of the Moabites. Such is hardly the case. The prophet is again speaking, but now in the name of all Israel as well as in his own; and even as Chap. 15 was a prophetic prediction of disaster to befall Moab, this word is the continuation of that approach, indicating that because of faults deeply imbedded in Moab's own character and attitude her afflictions are not yet at an end. But that which is now described will affect one of the chief and famous products of the land, the culture of the vine. It could be at this point where the criticism that the Oracle suffers from a "poverty of religious ideas" sets in. Deep moral attitudes are not in the forefront of the prophet's thinking but grape culture. Still it must be conceded that not every last word of the prophet has the same measure of depth as he is known to reach at some times. Still more, it is quite proper to indicate that a proud nation is about to be afflicted at a point of which she was inordinately proud. But that is just the major point that is being made: Moab is guilty of a very unseemly pride. She shall pay the penalty for it.

16:6-12 6. We have heard of the pride of Moab — he is very proud —
of his arrogance, his pride, his haughtiness; his boastful talk is not right.
7. Therefore Moab shall wail over Moab, every last one shall wail over the raisin-cakes of Kir Hareseth;
moan for them, ye utterly stricken ones.
8. For the fields of Heshbon lie wilted, the vine of Sibmah;
the lords of the nations have trampled upon its red clusters,
which reached to Jazer and strayed to the desert;
its shoots spread abroad and crossed the sea [Dead Sea].
9. Therefore I will bitterly weep over Jazer, over the vine of Sibmah;
I will drench you with my tears, O Heshbon and Elealeh.
For the battle-shout has fallen on your fruit and harvest.
10. And joy and gladness are taken away from the fruitful field;
and in the vineyards men neither shout nor cry for joy.

No treader treads out the wine in the presses;
I have put an end to the vintage-shout.
11. Therefore my soul moans over Moab like a lyre,
and my heart over Kir-Heres.
12. And it shall come to pass when Moab presents itself
and wearies itself upon the high-places,
and comes to her sanctuary to pray, she will achieve nothing.

So then, at this point the prophet is speaking and expressing sentiments that the nation of Israel shares with him. It is even possible that the previous words of this Oracle had been spoken sometime before when Moab's attitude was more wholesome. But now an unseemly pride has taken possession of her. This pride could have been the result of the overthrow of Samaria in 722 B.C. Moab felt unduly elated over the fate of her one-time rival and gave every evidence of the fact that she had not attempted to subdue such feelings but gave free rein to them. The exact form of this pride is not here indicated. In a parallel passage Jeremiah (48:42) indicates that this was that it had "magnified itself against the Lord." Such an attitude can never be harmless. By heaping terms — "arrogance . . . pride . . . haughtiness . . . boastful talk" — the prophet indicates how really extreme this pride of Moab was. Using the same root three times, the prophet makes his words more effective (something like: hauter, haughtiness, etc.).

Verse 7. It is as though the thought "God resisteth the proud" were inserted after this verse. When he does that, Moab will have abundant reason for wailing over Moab, "every last one of the people," because the affliction shall be universal throughout the nation. From this point on to the end of v. 10 attention centers on the effects of it all on Moabite grape-culture. The prophet might have chosen any other area of life, ruined cities, ravaged fields, fleeing inhabitants (as in chap. 15), the desolate appearance of the whole land. He prefers to center attention on one item only, an item that played a large role in Moabite life, and of which the Moabites may have been excessively proud. So he begins with the famous raisin-cakes of Kir Hareseth, which no longer can be raised or exported. Over them Moab must lament as over a part of her lost glory.

Verse 8. There follows a look out into the vineyards themselves. At Heshbon they lie wilted and neglected. So also "the vine of Sibmah," which may have been exceptionally choice. They lie wilted thus because military leaders with their armies have marched roughshod over them as they advanced, caring nothing for their value. Rather colorful is the way of stating it: "The lords of the nations [the commanders of the various national units making up the Assyrian army] have trampled upon its red clusters." Letting his poetic fancy run on a bit, the prophet describes how prolific the grape culture of the Moabites had been. Speaking as though grape culture were the only fruit of the land, he describes it as advancing even to the fringe of the land; then its vines begin to run out even into the dry desert; then they keep spreading out till they have thrown a bridge over the Dead Sea and are beginning to grow over on the Judean side of the Sea. Of such fruitful vines you might say: They can never be destroyed. But they will be.

Verse 9. Such a setback is not regarded with indifference by the prophet. He bemoans this particular loss of the nation almost as though it were a loss suffered by his own people. He weeps over vines destroyed even as they do; weeps even copiously ("drench") over Heshbob and Elealeh, apparently another major center where grapes were raised. The last line of the verse may be construed as a sort of play on the word *heydad*. In Israel and in Moab it was the peculiar shout raised by those that trod out the grapes in the wine-press. As each foot was stamped into the wine-press, this word gave the accompanying shout, which was quite naturally a very joyful and exuberant one. Not the treader's shout, but the *heydad* of the military, as they plunged from one devastation into another, will be the sound heard all over the land.

Verse 10. This is spelled out a bit more fully now. Every joyful shout will be terminated from the fruitful fields and the vineyards. Glum silence shall reign everywhere. The treaders will not shout because they will have nothing to tread out. The Lord himself has thus put an end to the vintage shout.

Verse 11. The prophet must have been deeply touched over the doom he had to proclaim on Moab, for again he indicates how it affects him. Deep inner waves of sympathy swept over him as mournful music sweeps over a lyre, his soul being as it were the musical instrument. The figure is expressive of deepest inner sympathy. Some would construe this verse as an utterance of the Lord. But even as v. 9 more aptly refers to the prophet so does this verse.

Verse 12. One more thought to give expression to the inescapability of this doom for Moab: even last minute appeals to the gods for mercy cannot avert the inevitable. If the whole nation were to present itself at the public shrines and were to engage in toilsome and wearying petitions to the gods ("wearies itself") the upshot of it all would be "she will achieve nothing." The prophet sees that the doom is irrevocable.

(4) An Epilogue Fixing the Time of Disaster (16:13, 14)

16:13-14 13. This is the word which Yahweh spoke concerning Moab in times past. 14. But now Yahweh says: "In three years like the years of a hireling, the nobles of Moab shall be brought into contempt together with all her great multitude. And what is left shall be small and weak, not much at all."

Verses 13, 14. It seems best to construe these two verses as being nothing more than making the time of the fulfillment of the doom on Moab more precise. Two chapters had indicated that doom would come, leaving the time factor quite indefinite. Perhaps something happened after some time had elapsed, which indicated to the prophet that the time for the fulfillment of his Oracle must be within a space of three years. And that this time limit is not to be extended is indicated by the expression "years of a hireling." Usually the man who hires himself out for service to another computes the time down to the very day. So precise is the time limit in this case. Although this is the way this expression is usually construed there is another possibility which may be entertained. "Years of a hireling" are toilsome years. Therefore after three toilsome years are past Moab's doom will have been sealed. In any case high and low, "nobles" and "the great multitude," will be "brought into contempt"; that is, proven to be utterly ineffective. Yet this does not spell total extinction. It does mean that what is left "shall be small and weak, not much at all." What a sorry prospect for Moab, for the nation once so proud!

Notes

Verse 1. There is no need whatever to change the pointing of the text from the imperative ("send") to the indicative ("they have sent," *RSV*). By making such a change, the lively style of the writer is lost together with the note of counsel given by Israel to Moab.

Verse 2. The preposition in the phrase "at the fords of the Arnon" is passed by in the Hebrew because the preceding word ends with the same letter as this preposition (*be*). Cf. *KS* 330 l.

Verse 3. Note the chiastic arrangement in the last line of the verse. Cf. *KS* 339 f.

Verse 4. In the statement "he that tramples under foot is vanished" we also have an instance where the subject is singular but the verb plural. Cf. *KS* 346 l.

Verse 8. The reverse construction appears here — subject, plural; predicate, singular. *KS* 348 k.

Verse 9. The construction "I will drench you with tears" offers a double object in Hebrew. *KS* 327 n.

Verse 10. Another case of the use of an indefinite subject appears here: "Men neither shout nor cry out." Both verbs are third person singular masculine, like the German *man*. *KS* 324 a.

Verse 14. By heaping related terms in the last line, an effect is produced which is the equivalent of a superlative. *KS* 309 k. Whether the term "hireling" (*sakhir*) refers here to the laborer in the fields and so is used in a more general sense, or whether it refers to one hired for military service and so refers to a mercenary soldier is not yet settled. Since the expression appears repeatedly in Scripture it seems to refer to a man hired for wages in the more general sense.

Chapter XVII

d. *Damascus-Ephraim (Chap. 17)*

Apparently this oracle was originally spoken while Damascus was still standing. Damascus fell into Assyrian hands in 732 B.C. *G. A. Smith* expresses the sentiment of most writers when he says that this, "one of the earliest and most crisp" of Isaiah's prophecies, was written about 734. In his book, Isaiah is, of course, interested in a higher point of view than mere historical consecutiveness. Therefore to fault this piece as being out of order is merely an indication that one is expecting something from the prophet that he is not concerned about giving.

Still it should be noted — and most writers fail almost entirely to take note of this issue — that the fall of Damascus did not actually take place after the pattern which is here outlined. It never was completely ruined, nor did it pass off the scene. So that the "ruin" the prophet speaks of is rather to be interpreted in the sense that Damascus became a mere ruin of her former self. She was stripped of her power and her importance. She descended to the level of an Assyrian province after her capture by that nation. The spirit of this prophecy was clearly fulfilled if not the letter.

Authorship of the chapter by Isaiah is quite generally conceded by writers, with some fluctuation of opinion on one or the other part of it. The geographical sequence runs somewhat as follows: after Philistia (chap. 14:29ff.) to the west, and Moab (chap. 15) to the east, comes Aram, or Syria, to the north. Parallel passages on the same subject are: Amos 1:3-5 and Jer. 49:23-27.

The history of Damascus prior to the days of Isaiah runs briefly as follows. Since about the year 1000 B.C. she had become the head of the Syrian state and had occupied a position which made her a keen rival of Assyria through the centuries. This rivalry came to an end in 732 B.C. with the capture of the city by her ancient competitor. She never again attained the prominence which had once been hers, though she ranks among the ancient cities of the East, with a very long and continuous history.

Though the title given to this chapter would seem to indicate that Damascus alone is under consideration, yet, according to the historical pattern of that time the fortunes of Samaria and Ephraim were so intimately tied up with old Damascus that the mention of the one involuntarily brought to mind the future of the other. Isaiah had already made mention of the alliance that existed between the two states in 7:1. II Kings 16 may also be compared. So, starting with Damascus, Isaiah moves over to the analogous subject of Ephraim, the Northern Kingdom.

We divide the material of this chapter as follows:

(1) The Fate of Syria-Ephraim (vv. 1-6)
    (a) The Fall of Both Predicted (vv. 1-3)
    (b) How Low Israel Shall Be Brought (vv. 4-6)
(2) The Return of Some to the Lord (vv. 7-8)
(3) The Desolation Caused by Forsaking the Lord (vv. 9-11)
(4) The Unexpected Collapse of the Seemingly Victorious and Successful Invader (vv. 12-14)

(1) The Fate of Syria-Ephraim (vv. 1-6)

17:1-6 1. The Oracle concerning Damascus
Behold, Damascus will be a city no longer,
yes, she shall be a ruin, a heap of stones.
2. The cities of Aroer will be forsaken;
they will serve for flocks,
which will lie down there and no one will frighten them away.
3. So that the bulwark will be removed from Ephraim
and the kingdom from Damascus;
and what is left of Syria will become like the glory of the children of Israel.
Oracle of the Lord of hosts.
4. And it shall come to pass in that day that the glory of Jacob shall be brought low;
and the fatness of her flesh shall grow lean.

5. And it shall be as when a reaper bunches together standing
grain
and his arm reaps the ears;
and it shall be as when one gleans ears in the valley of Rephaim.
6. Indeed, there will be left in him [i.e., Jacob] only a gleaning
like the beating off of olives,
two or three berries in the treetop,
four or five on the fruitful branches,
says Yahweh, the God of Israel.

(a) *The Fall of Both Predicted* (vv. 1-3)

Verse 1. Doom on Damascus is pronounced first. As representative of the whole nation of Syria she functions here as capital cities so often do (synecdoche, part for the whole). The Hebrew uses prophetic perfects for a vivid reference to the future. One might conclude from the first statement ("city no longer") especially when the next line describes her as "a ruin, a heap of stones," that total and perpetual ruin of the material city is what the prophet is predicting. But as pointed out above, since this did not come to pass exactly in that form we are forced to construe the statement as referring to the ruin of the city's prestige.

Verse 2. The reader's first reaction to the statement of this verse is apt to be that the thought of v. 1 is continued. However, "the cities of Aroer" lie in the land of Israel; two of them in particular are found: one in the tribal territory of Gad (Num. 32:34), the other farther north in land that once belonged to Ammon (Josh. 13:25), later to Israel. So after a brief announcement of the fall of Syria comes a prompt announcement of the ruin of at least parts of Israel. This ruin will be so complete that the land swept clean of inhabitants will serve for pasturing flocks, with so few people left that flocks, once they have lain down, will not be disturbed by any one.

Verse 3. This verse now speaks of both victims of the judgment of God. Since Israel and Syria had made common cause, it is not to be wondered at that the prophet treats them jointly from the point of view of judgment, as already noted above. The removal of "the bulwark" from Ephraim would seem to imply that the breaking of the strength of Damascus will remove the buffer-state that had so often served to shield Israel from the wrath of Assyria. At this point our interpretation of the whole section about Damascus is buttressed by the statement that "the kingdom" is to be removed from Damascus. Apparently this refers to the loss of her one-time great sovereignty. The next statement throws both parties into a common lot. For when it is said that what is left of Syria "will become like the glory of the children of Israel," it is more than likely that the statement is ironical. Israel's glory will have vanished; so will Syria's. The word translated as "oracle" at this point is not the same as that used in the chapter heading. Here it means "pronouncement"; there it meant partly "word of doom."

(b) *How Low Israel Shall Be Brought* (vv. 4-6)

Since the next three verses concern themselves particularly with the subject how low Israel will be brought, it seems essential to indicate that "Jacob" here without a doubt is merely another term of reference for the Southern Kingdom, and thus a synonym for Judah. On the basis of 2:5 and 8:17, where the context seems to indicate such a meaning, *von Orelli* concludes that now in these verses Judah's unhappy lot is depicted in addition to that of Israel. Apparently the passages referred to, form too slight a foundation for the conclusion reached. We regard "Jacob" as a synonym for "Israel" chosen merely for the sake of variety. Israel's distressful lot is represented in three distinct figures: first it is like a wasting sickness, then like gleaning a field of grain, lastly like stripping an olive tree of its berries.

Verse 4. It should also be noted that in this verse, as well as in vv. 7 and 9, the phrase "in that day" appears, marking a division of thought in each instance. This phrase is, as usual, a vague measure of time referring to something merely future. So the first point is that Israel's one-time glory will be a thing of the past, even as a wasting disease may cut down the fatness of healthy man till he has withered away to skin and bones. Not a very attractive sight. So Israel will lose territory and prestige.

Verse 5. The second comparison takes us out into a wheat

field where both the reaper and the gleaner have passed by and left practically nothing. The description is rather colorful. The reaper is visualized as reaching into the standing grain with his hand, grasping together the ears of grain as such, then cutting them off with the sickle, leaving most of the straw standing. Then comes the gleaner and picks up what little the generosity of the reaper may have intentionally left behind. Israel's land will get a double going-over. There is some likelihood that, when the "valley of Rephaim" is mentioned, which lay southwest of Jerusalem, a broad and fertile plain, that there the inhabitants of Jerusalem, like Isaiah may have witnessed the scene deacribed many a time.

Verse 6. Then the figure changes to one perhaps almost equally common in Palestine, that of beating off olives. It matters little whether beating was the customary mode of reaping olives or whether shaking of the tree was first resorted to and then the beating of the branches with rods to bring down what was left. The point of the comparison is that when men get through with the olive tree precious little may be found on it: "two or three berries" near the top, and "four or five on the fruitful branches." It is not the remnant idea that prevails here. There is no emphasis on the fact that *some* will be left, but on the fact that exceedingly *few* will survive the calamity. All this was literally fulfilled in the fall of Samaria in 722 B.C. A statement attributing the whole pronouncement to Yahweh himself rounds out this part of the oracle.

(2) The Return of Some to the Lord (vv. 7-8)

17:7-8 7. On that day man will look to his Maker
and his eyes will regard the Holy One of Israel;
8. and he will not look to the altars, the work of his hands,
nor will he regard that which his fingers have made,
either sacred poles or sun-pillars.

Even as the time-designation is of the vaguest sort ("on that day"), so the individual involved is not too accurately specified. Is the Israelite meant? Or does "man" perhaps refer to "mankind" in general? The latter would be the most likely approach. The two verses almost amount to a general statement of principle: when God judges men, now or at any time, there always will be some that give heed and let themselves be drawn to repentance. By this approach we are relieved of the necessity of finding some historical occasion where a significant return of men took place in Israel's history. The type of reaction described in this passage is in terms of the situation then prevailing in Israel. On the whole this vague reference to "man" has an analogy with several verses in Chap. 2, namely vv. 9, 11, 17, 20.

Verse 7. Man is only too much inclined to disregard God and give no thought to him. Left to himself he can often cheerfully overlook God for a long space of time. When calamities strike then men bethink themselves. Then they look to their Maker; then people in Israel will again regard the Holy One of Israel.

Verse 8. One thing that Israel needed to abandon or forget was its altars that were symbols of cults foreign to Israel's God. The passage II Kings 16:10ff. offers a flagrant example of how far Israel is known to have gone in the wrong direction under the leadership of an unfaithful king. Such altars had no divine warrant for their use and construction as did the altars of the true worship of Yahweh; they were the work of men's hands. But just because they were of a man's own invention they often claimed an interest that was never given to the altar of the true God. For man did then "regard that which his fingers had made." Two further implements of heterodox worship are listed here: "sacred poles," or Asherahs, which often marked schismatic shrines; and "sunpillars," Phoenician symbols of Baal; or perhaps, as some translate the word, "incense altars." Objects of foreign cults may have been many and various. But they all were symbols of apostasy at the same time, and would, under the stress of adversity be recognized as such and abandoned.

(3) The Desolation Caused by Forsaking the Lord (vv. 9-11)

This passage is much like vv. 4-6; it also describes how low Israel will be brought.

17:9-11 9. In that day his cities of refuge will be like a deserted spot of a forest or of a hilltop,
which men deserted because of the children of Israel
and it will become a desolation.
10. For you have forgotten the God, who is your salvation
and the Rock, who is your refuge, you have not remembered.
Therefore, though you plant pleasant plants
and set out slips for an alien god;
11. though you hedge them about carefully in the day when you
     plant them;
and make them sprout on the day when you sow them;
yet the harvest will flee away in the day of sickness and incurable
     pain.

Verse 9. Strong cities, which ordinarily might have been used for purposes of refuge in days of calamity (not the technical "cities of refuge" of which Israel had six for cases of accidental slaying) will in this time of distress be nothing better than those ruined cities that the Canaanites left behind in the days when Israel came in to occupy the land. Here and there in the forest or on a hilltop such an old, ruined fortress might have been standing, but it was no longer of any use to any man. It was a "desolation."

Verse 10. Going to the root of the matter this verse points out that the basic evil that brought on all such desolation was nothing other than that they had forgotten God, of whom alone it can be said that he is the "salvation" of his people. Or to use parallel terms, they had abandoned the Rock, who was their only "refuge." For thus the two terms — God of your salvation and Rock of your refuge — are to be interpreted. Two cases of appositional genetives. "Rock" in such connections as these denotes a solid ground where one may stand out of the reach of danger. Cf. Deut. 32:18 and Ps. 18:2. From here on the reference seems to be to what ancient writers called little "Adonis gardens," named for their use in the worship of the Greek Adonis, a private cult that achieved great popularity. Women particularly would plant little flower pots, or baskets with pleasant plants, or set out little slips for this "alien god," and give these objects of their private devotion most assiduous attention. Very likely some measure of sympathetic magic was associated with what they did. They sought to promote the growth of vegetation, or even perhaps the resurrection of the dead Baal (who during the dry season had expired) by the use of these cult devices. They even used hothouse-plant methods to promote quick growth and sprouting, yet, though they did all this, the results would not be forthcoming. They would harvest no tangible results but they would have "a day of sickness and incurable pain," figuratively speaking. In other words, everything that they would have sought to forestall would come upon them. With this solemn threat Isaiah forewarned his generation.

(4) The Unexpected Collapse of the Seemingly Victorious and Successful Invader (vv. 12-14)

17:12-14 12. Alas, the roar of many peoples,
like the roar of the sea do they roar!
and the uproar of nations,
like the uproar of great waters do they roar.
13. The peoples roar like the uproar of great waters.
But he will rebuke them one by one and they will flee far away.
And they will be driven away like the chaff on the hilltop before the wind,
and like tumbleweeds before the storm.
14. And at eventide, lo and behold, there is terror;
before morning comes they are no more.
This shall be the portion of those who plunder us,
and the lot of those that spoil us.

From 17:12 to 18:7 may be regarded as "a prophetic soliloquy." It has no connection of a direct sort with what preceded. Yet there is a deeper inner connection. To close with v. 11 would have been a negative conclusion. The outstanding thing about the judgment that befell particularly the Northern Kingdom would have overlooked that striking instance of divine judgment on the Assyrians. So the prophet lets that disastrous overthrow of the enemy be the concluding observation that he makes. The same subject is treated in 14:24-27 and 29:5-8.

Verse 12. This verse as such is a "magnificent piece of sound," as G. A. *Smith* rightly says. In the original Hebrew it is very onomatopoeic. The great concourse of "peoples" very likely refers to the vast multitude of the Assyrian armies

with contingents from many nations, although the make-up
of the Assyrian army is hardly the prime consideration.
But large armies are bound to be a vast sea of sound
and fury. Their commotion alone is enough to frighten
any beholder. No more fit comparison could be found than
the roaring of the waves of the sea, or the "great waters."
Whether this comparison involves a conscious thought of
ancient mythological descriptions from epic myths of days
of old may justly be questioned. Too much is being read
into mythological possibilities, interpretations that would
have amazed the very prophets had they heard what
is claimed to be the background of their thinking.

Verse 13. But though the invading Assyrians make a loud
commotion, the Almighty has the last word. "He will rebuke
them one by one" — the reference being to what he did
when the angel of the Lord smote the camp of the Assyrians in one night (Isa. 37). In fact, so thoroughly does he
rebuke that he may be said to take up these opponents of
his "one by one." Result: "like chaff on the hilltop before
the wind" so shall they be dissipated, of like "whirling
tumbleweeds before the storm." Both comparisons stress
the utter ease with which seemingly invincible forces are
scattered by the Lord's might.

It should be noted that there is a very general tone
about all that is being said. Assyria is not mentioned. One
might almost say that the prophet is laying down general
principles. Times come when the enemies of God's people
storm and rave and rant. The future of the church looks
very precarious. In one of the many ways that the Lord
may utilize, he "rebukes" the foe. The grave danger dis-
solves then and there. In other words, this general truth is
here expressed. The prophet has a broader perspective
than the immediate situation confronting Israel in those
days.

Verse 14. Just how God interfered, or will interfere, is not
related here (*Procksch*). But an effective summary account is offered. The danger becomes acute, as it did in
the night when Israel fled out of Egypt, or when they were
encamped by the Red Sea with Pharaoh's chariots advancing against them (Exod. 12:29-31). But "before morning

comes they are no more." That certainly happened in the case of the Assyrians under Sennacherib. Such a lot — the prophet generalizes again — will befall all who attempt to plunder and spoil those whom God has chosen for his own.

Notes

Verse 1. The unusual words for "ruin" i.e., *me'i* (with an initial *m*) perhaps to make an alliteration and parallel to *me'ir* of the first clause.

Verse 2. "Aroer" is an appositional genitive to "cities," a struction explained in *GK* 128 k.

Verse 5. This verse offers one of the many instances where the construction begins with the infinitive (*'esoph*) and goes over into the finite verb (*yiqtsor*). See *KS* 413 d.

Verse 6. The sentence begins with a masculine singular verb soon to be followed by its subject in the feminine plural. This is explained by the preference of the Hebrew in beginning with the masculine form of the singular, as the more usual form. See *KS* 348 i and *GK* 145, 7.

Verse 13. We have translated *galgal* as "tumbleweed" which term seems to carry the simplest connotation. It could be rendered "whirling dust." Some demand that this must be a reference to the stems of the wild artichoke. *KW* says *Artishoken-stengel*.

Chapter XVIII

3. Against Distant Neighbors (Chaps. 18-21)

a. Advice to the Ethiopian Envoys (Chap. 18)

This is a chapter in regard to which one could adopt too negative an attitude by dwelling too largely on the difficulties — which it must be admitted are many — and proceeding, as e.g., *Gray* does, to point out that four major questions may be propounded with regard to the chapter, questions which will be extremely hard to answer in a definite way. However there is a consensus of opinion with regard to the general purpose of the chapter on the part of most commentators. If this consensus is rightly accepted one may even arrive at the verdict that *Procksch* renders: "This glorious bit of revelation is to be classed among the best and most profound utterances, done with prophetic artistry."

Nothing too definite can be offered with regard to the metrical structure of the chapter. For though a certain pattern does obtain, here, as in most other instances, we would have to resort to too many alterations to allow us to arrive at anything sure.

As brief historical background we would fit in the following: Ethiopia (called "Cush" in the Scriptures) lay immediately south of Egypt, its northern boundary being about at the First Cataract. Thence it extended south with southern boundaries not too clearly marked. About the year 714 B.c. Shabako — called So in the Scripture (II Kings 17:4) — managed to take the Egyptian crown and set it on his own head, thus establishing the Twenty-fifth Dynasty. The power of Ethiopia continued until 633, when a native Egyptian, Psammetichus, again recaptured the crown and put an end to the power of Ethiopia.

The somewhat detailed description that is given of the

Ethiopians suggests that they and what they stood for were still a novelty and called for a bit of colorful information for the hearer, or reader. At the same time this description does not transcend the bounds of good taste. In fact, it may be said to have been spoken with a measure of diplomatic skill, calculated to win the good will of the envoys of the Ethiopians in the face of a firm dismissal which was being given them by the prophet. For it is now commonly agreed that the substance of what the chapter sets forth was spoken by Isaiah to Ethiopian envoys who had come to the court of the king of Jerusalem. They were either seeking to induce Judah to enter an alliance with Ethiopia against Assyria or at least the Israelites were being stirred up to oppose Assyria.

In a sense the burden of Isaiah's words is that the rescue of the Lord's people is near. Therefore it behooves Judah to wait patiently for the Lord and not to seek help from any other source. Therefore either side of the issue may be stressed by the title given to the chapter, either "the dismissal of the Ethiopian ambassadors," or "the impending overthrow of the Assyrian power." A related chapter is Isa. 20. The tone of the chapter before us may be contrasted with that of Chap. 28-31 where the "Egyptian negotiations" are denounced in a spirit "of fierce indignation" (*Skinner*).

We would outline the contents of the chapter as follows:

a. Advice to the Ethiopian Envoys

(1) The Situation Described in Diplomatic Language (vv. 1–2)
(2) An Invitation to the World to Watch What Transpires (v. 3)
(3) How God Purposes to Deal with the Assyrians (vv. 4-6)
(4) The Future Submission of Ethiopia to the Lord (v. 7)

(1) The Situation Described in Diplomatic Language (vv. 1-2)

18:1-2 1. Ah, land of the buzzing of wings,
    which is beyond the rivers of Ethiopia,
2. which sends envoys by way of the Nile

in papyrus boats over the face of the waters.
"Go [back] you swift messengers to a people tall and sleek,
to a people feared then and now,
to a nation energetic and all-subduing,
whose land is cut through by rivers.

We shall not minimize the difficulties of interpretation
encountered in this chapter. Let it suffice by way of illustration that the word used for "buzzing" according to the
dictionary allows for four different meanings and the word
for "envoys" for three. On all the many possibilities involved *Gray* in the ICC may be consulted. Still the
context usually cuts the possibilities down to the point where
a translation like the one we offer is pretty well substantiated.

Verse 1. The initial "ah" is not to be rendered "woe" for
it is hardly more than a "particle of salutation." A country
is being apostrophized. When it is further described as being "a land of the buzzing of wings" this is without a
doubt a reference to the fact that Ethiopia abounded, as it
still does, in a very great number of insects, far more so
than the land of Israel. It is further described as lying
"beyond the rivers of Ethiopia." At first glance such a statement may seem to involve an absurdity. But very likely it
is a perfectly reasonable statement, which conveys the
thought that this country has some notable rivers (note:
the White Nile, the Blue Nile, and the Atbara) beyond
which it extends southward with vague boundaries. These
two statements serve to acquaint the uninformed Israelite
concerning this land which is newly come to men's attention.

Verse 2. Now a word about the envoys. They have
been sent as an official delegation and, we conclude, have
just now appeared at the court of the king in Jerusalem.
They came along the Nile (Heb. "sea") as the natural ar-
tery of traffic for men en route from Ethiopia to Jerusalem.
Their means of transportation was "papyrus vessels," light
and portable, at places of portage. These vessels were constructed of the famous papyrus reed, which abounded along
the Nile, which were woven together and the vessel made

watertight by the use of pitch. We need not assume that
after the envoys left the Nile waters that they continued
across the corner of the Mediterranean in these flimsy vessels. A colorful reference to this unusual craft added sufficient freshness to the account.

Now consider the prophet's message to these men. We
freely admit that the text does not say that Isaiah addressed them nor that he addressed them by the use of the
following words. But to operate with this deduction does
serve as a good working-basis for the understanding of
what follows and is in no wise out of keeping with the tenor
of the passage. This view is quite commonly accepted in
our day. Having access to court circles and being a man
of some standing by virtue of the fact that he was the
Lord's prophet, Isaiah may not have stepped beyond the
boundary of his authority if he, as is here the case, tactfully
and firmly addressed these Ethiopians after they delivered
their message. He says "Go," which in such a context
means: Go back home. He compliments them on their
efficiency: they were "swift messengers" as was required of
men in such a calling. They were to go back to their people
"tall and sleek," as Herodotus had in his day remarked
about them at a later date, "the tallest and most beautiful
of mankind." "Sleek" is a word difficult to render. Among
the possibilities are "bronze-skinned," or "satin-skinned."
They must have been commanding figures. The people as a
whole are admitted to have a reputation which made them
to be "feared." Perhaps the distance at which they lived
lent enchantment to their reputation. Then the nation is
said to be "energetic and all-subduing" which adds not a
little to their fame. The description closes with a reference
to the fact that the land is "cut through by rivers." There
is something gracious about admitting what a good name
this nation has and has long had (cf. the phrase "feared
then and now" which can with equal propriety be rendered
"feared far and near"). The envoys themselves are com-
plimented on their efficiency and appearance. But they are
firmly dismissed by the prophet. If this dismissal seems
abrupt, for the third verse already addresses the nations
and no longer the envoys, the vv. 4-6 give an explanation

which shows why the prophet could not do otherwise than he did. True, the whole account is somewhat compact, but not bewildering or incomprehensible.

(2) An Invitation to the World to Watch What Transpires (v. 3)

18:3 3. All you inhabitants of the world
and you who dwell on the earth,
you should look as when an ensign is raised on the mountains;
you should listen as when a trumpet is blown.

All this is, of course, introductory to vv. 4-6. By addressing all the inhabitants of the world the prophet, perhaps in the presence of the Ethiopian envoys, makes it clear that tremendous issues are involved in something that is about to happen, something that is calculated to startle the whole world. The last two clauses of the verse indicate with what care the whole world should "look" and "listen" when these things begin to transpire. They should look as nations did in days of old when signals, or ensigns, were raised on mountain tops, calling peoples within a given area to assemble at some point of meeting. Or, they should listen as men listened to the signal-trumpet that was blown by heralds perhaps for the purpose of gathering men for the battle.

(3) How God Purposes to Deal with the Assyrians (vv. 4-6)

18:4-6 4. For thus the Lord said to me:
"I will look quietly in my dwelling-place,
like the shimmering heat above the sun,
like a dew-cloud during the heat of harvest."
5. For before the harvest is ripe, when the blossom is over,
and the flower becomes a ripened grape,
then will a man cut the vines with pruning hooks
and the branches he will hew away, yea, cut away.
6. (But) they will be abandoned together to the birds of prey from the mountains
and to the beasts of the earth.
The birds of prey will spend the summer upon them,
and the beasts of the earth shall spend the winter upon them.

Verse 4. Two things are not said, but they lay in the air at that time and were involuntarily thought of by them that heard the prophet: one was that the Assyrian threat against Israel pervaded the air: the Assyrian hordes or their well-trained armies might come at any moment. The other was that the Lord was apparently doing nothing about it, aside from predicting their disastrous overthrow through his prophet. Twice already in major pronouncements the prophet had dealt with this subject, viz., in 10:5-34 and in 14:24-27. Not to relate what is here said to the Assyrian crisis and its outcome would be sheer folly. But note also how the prophet is wont to make a clear distinction between such words as the Lord gave him and his own reflections which he based on these words. Here vv. 4-6 are a direct divine pronouncement.

The chief point of comparison is the quiet, unobtrusive way the Lord lets situations ripen out. His attitude seems to be one of quiet observation. What else befits the Almighty, who has all things completely under his control? Calm serenity pervades his rule. His attitude is marked by a divine poise which reminds us how sure he is of the outcome and how completely he has it under control. The world situation is likened to a field of grain which is slowly maturing. The shimmering heat that pervades the field seemingly even stronger than the heat of the sun and the dew-cloud (perhaps, the night-mist) that adds its effect during the night, both in their own way represent the Lord or his activity. He is the silent influence that brings things to maturation. But high enthroned, watching each step, there is the Lord. All things rest in his hands.

Verse 5. The process of ripening is traced through in somewhat colorful details. The harvest is the obvious goal toward which things are moving. The time of blossoming in the fields, preferably the figure is that of a vineyard (cf. 5:1ff.), is past. The flower is moving in the direction of becoming a ripened grape. A few more steps in the process are involved. There may be dangling vines and loose shoots that unnecessarily absorb strength from the vine. They will be trimmed and hewn away together with every useless branch. Now comes the long-delayed intervention of the Lord of hosts. Verse 6 marks the sudden change of pace, the unexpected turn of events. Put aside all such questions as: Does the vineyard represent the Assyrians? Does it, like Chap. 5, represent Israel? That is the side of the question that is not developed.

Verse 6. In the background of the reader's mind should be the thought of the Assyrian and his fate. He had expected one kind of harvest, easy picking, in fact (cf. 10: 10). Over against that the Lord was expecting another kind of harvest (cf. Rev. 14:14ff.). In any case, the figure used in vv. 4-5 is completely dropped. The Assyrian host is thought of and its fate is depicted in terms of innumerable corpses all over a field of battle which no one takes in hand to bury but where scavenger birds and beasts have their day. When it is said that these creatures spend summer and winter upon the carcasses of men, that implies quite naturally that they are devouring carrion flesh. Everyone knows that such carcasses do not lie available for devouring for the space of a whole year. Nor is the intention to assign one season to the birds, the other to the beasts. This is merely a poetic way of saying that birds and beasts will feed on the dead for a long while because they are so many. According to Chap. 37 apparently there were more dead bodies than the Israelites could conveniently dispose of. Note that in the above approach we have treated vv. 4 and 5 as protasis and v. 6 as apodosis.

(4) The Future Submission of Ethiopia to the Lord (v. 7)

18:7 7. At that time a gift will be brought to the Lord of hosts by a people tall and sleek, and by a nation feared then and now, a nation energetic and all-subduing, whose land is cut through by rivers, to the place of the name of the Lord of hosts, to Mount Zion.

Verse 7. It appears at once that this verse is prose. It looks to future times. As usual the future is not defined whether it be the immediate future or the remote. More than likely both are thought of as involved. Thinking of the more immediate effect, it could well happen that some in Ethiopia watched developments as they took place round about Jerusalem, and when the disastrous defeat of the Assyrians occurred, this news penetrated also to their land and induced some to acknowledge the Lord. Think of the

Ethiopian eunuch (Acts 8). The thought as such is voiced
also in II Chron. 32:23; Ps. 68:31; and Zeph. 3:10. The rest
of the verse is a repetition of the terms of v. 2 in describing
the nation of the Ethiopians. The words there used were in
the nature of a sincere compliment. They are the same here.
The only added thought is that the gifts brought in token of
submission to the Lord will be brought to the place of
God's revelation, Mount Zion. So one aspect of the universalism of Isaiah has again found expression. The whole
chapter has a unique charm and an attractiveness all its
own.

Notes

Verse 1. The word for "beyond" (*me'ebher*) is changed by some
to read *ma'abhar*, i.e., "ford." This change is unnecessary, because
the text makes good sense as it stands.

Verse 2. Though the subject of the preceding verse is *'eretz*
(fem.) the participle, "the one that sends," i.e., *hashsholeach*,
takes its masculine gender not from this noun but from the nearer
one, *kush*, which is masculine. In support of the view that the
words that we have translated "then and now" do constitute a
time clause see *KS* 387 c.

Verse 3. The word for "world" [*tébhel*] has no article, for as
KS points out (293 b) it is in process of becoming a proper noun.
We would prefer to use a passive infinitive in place of the active
kinso'. The impersonal construction seems to lie behind this active form. See *KS* 215 a.

Verse 4. Further indications by way of example of how the
prophet frequently distinguishes between the message the Lord
gave him, and his own reflections may be found in 1:3 f; 8:16;
9:2; 10:26; etc.

Verse 5. The statement "the flower becomes . . ." involves a
feminine subject (*nitstsah*) but the verb is masculine (*yihyeh*).
This is due to the fact that the subject follows the verb, which
frequently starts with the masculine as the more obvious likelihood. Cf. *GK* 145 q. Besides the verb *yihyeh* marks the transition from the infinitive construction (*tom*) to that of the finite verb.

Verse 7. It is claimed that the first *'am* without a preposition
like "by" (Heb. *min*) involves an impossible construction. Basically this looks like one of those many passages where the *m* is
passed by because of the preponderance of the same letter at that
point. See *KS* 330 l-p. Besides immediately following is word
'am again, this time preceded by a *min*.

Chapter XIX

b. The Oracle Concerning Egypt (Chap. 19)

This is a chapter of exceptional breadth and glory of outlook! At the same time it is a chapter of many difficulties and one whose authorship by Isaiah has been sharply called into question. Sometimes the whole chapter is denied the great prophet. More commonly at least the second half of the chapter (vv. 18-25) is presented as something that Isaiah the son of Amoz could not have written.

The reasons for questioning Isaiah's authorship are several. First of all the style is said to be below par: Isaiah could not have written pieces like vv. 1-4 where the name of Egypt appears seven times. Here men seem to overlook that the subject matter under consideration is Egypt, a fact which almost necessitates the frequent use of the name. Or it is said that where vv. 1-4 deal with the area of political matters, vv. 5-10 concern themselves with physical problems, then in 11-15 the writer returns to the political. It almost seems as if the rigid canon of literary composition were being laid down that when a writer begins to treat one aspect of a case he must confine himself exclusively to that issue. Or it is pointed out that no reasons for God's judgments on Egypt are set forth. But may it not be assumed that these reasons are obvious — one heathen nation was much like every other? Or lastly, it is claimed that material that Ezekiel and Deutero-Isaiah use appears quite frequently. But it must be remembered in the case of Ezekiel's material it is just as likely that the process was the reverse: Isaiah was the originator; and as far as Deutero-Isaiah was concerned, this merely presents another argument against the acceptance of this dubious author.

But more effective than these minor arguments is the one that *von Orelli* has used so effectively and that has hardly even been deemed worthy of notice by those who are more critically minded, namely the argument that after the elaborate preparations that Yahweh undertakes with the Egyptians for their correction, nothing is done in the sequel to follow through on these preparations of the Almighty: everything is allowed to run out into the sand by Isaiah's presentation. For Isaiah to stop short with vv. 1-17 would have been abortive writing, building up to a great possibility and letting the matter drop. Much more might be said on the subject, but we have at least touched on the major issues.

But as we indicated in our opening words there is something of a grand and universalistic outlook to the chapter. The narrow confines of Israel are left behind. The sharing of the nations in the wealth of Israel is sketched rather attractively. A broad outlook is characteristic here as so often elsewhere in the message of this great Old Testament prophet.

It should also be noted at the outset that a somewhat ideal point of view is sketched in the last part of the chapter, a spirit of perfect peace and harmony between Assyria, Egypt, and Israel. As far as the totality of these nations was concerned this result was never achieved. But in the area of spiritual realities men of these three nations did achieve a measure of unity that was real and satisfying. The prophet well knew that he was sketching out the net result in overly glowing colors, which were dictated to him by his enthusiasm for the good cause.

If the question be asked why so much attention is given to Egypt by the prophet it may very properly be noted that the fortunes of Israel had been very deeply interwined with those of Egypt at three different times of her history in particular: in the days of the Patriarchs; in the days of Solomon; in the last days of the history of the kingdom of Judah where alliances with Egypt were frequently the topic at issue between these two nations. Chapter 18 practically belongs under consideration here because Ethiopia was virtually part of the kingdom of Egypt.

The following outline may guide us in our study of the chapter:

(1) God Corrects Egypt (vv. 1-17)

   (a) God's Judgment in the Form of Civil Strife and Tyranny (vv. 1-4)
   (b) The Disastrous Failure of the Nile to Overflow (vv. 5-10)
   (c) The Collapse of Egyptian Wisdom (vv.11-15)
   (d) Judah a Terror to Egypt (vv. 16-17)

(2) God Restores Egypt (vv. 18-25)

(1) God Corrects Egypt (vv. 1-17)

   (a) God's Judgment in the Form of Civil Strife and Tyranny (vv. 1-4)

19:1-4 1. The oracle concerning Egypt.
Lo, the Lord will ride upon a swift cloud
and will come to Egypt.
Then the idols of Egypt will quake before him;
the courage of each Egyptian will melt within him.
2. And I will incite one Egyptian against another,
and they will fight, brother against brother, and neighbor against neighbor,
city against city and kingdom against kingdom.
3. And the spirit of the Egyptians will be emptied out,
and I will confound each plan.
And they will resort to idols and sorcerers and mediums and wizards.
4. And I will give the Egyptians over into the hand of a fierce master;
and a powerful king will rule over them.

Verse 1. Scenes like this one are always colorful: the Lord comes in person to execute judgment on Egypt. His chariot is the cloud (cf. also Ps. 18:10; Nah. 1:3; Dan. 7:13). In fact the very expression: He "will come" has something ominous about it; for it is frequently used to connote his coming to judge (cf. Ps. 96:13). His coming to one place does not deny his omnipresence; it merely makes his action center on that one place. At his fierce and holy presence all beings may well tremble. The prophet begins by listing first the seemingly most exalted of all that are affected by his coming — the "idols" of Egypt, from a root meaning: "the nothings." Supposing them for the moment to have some kind of existence, there they are at his sight, trembling and ridiculous in their weakness. This reminds us of what James says about the demons (James 2:19). Another over-all effect of the appearance of the Almighty is that "the courage of each Egyptian shall melt within him." They all in some way will be confronted by the Lord, but they will not be able to endure his presence. The Lord is so much above all, above so-called gods and above men, great and small.

Verse 2. When civil or other strife comes between men it may, if it be the judgment of God, be said to have been incited by him (cf. also 9:11). Such disturbances certainly come as a just judgment from God. Here such intestine discord is pictured as is known to have prevailed in Egypt before the Ethiopian dynasty took over, which was about Isaiah's time. Here it is vividly described as involving Egyptian against Egyptian, brother against brother, and neighbor against neighbor. Ordinary bonds of attachment and loyalty no longer count in times of upheaval. So the description goes on listing "city against city and kingdom against kingdom." This last category may describe the traditional division of the land in districts called "nomes," as the Greek translators render at this point. In any case, we have a picture of wild confusion.

Verse 3. The next aspect of the case that is delineated involves the idea of utter lack of constructive planning. The intelligence (here called "spirit") necessary for devising adequate plans for Egypt is here thought of as having been poured out of a vessel leaving it empty. What plans they may happen to make, the Lord will confound, each one of them. Finding themselves incapable of devising what needs to be devised, the men of Egypt will fall back upon what, to Isaiah's way of thinking, is the utmost of futility: "they will resort to idols and sorcerers, unto mediums and wizards." Though various other translations of the terms used could be offered and defended, there is no question about the area in which these counsellors move and what sort of characters they are. All lies in the area of the occult and the manifold forms of humbug and chicanery to which men have been known to resort when they are at their wit's end. In any case, Egypt was notorious for various classes of professionals of this sort, as is obvious from the stories of Moses at Pharaoh's court (see Exod. chaps. 7-9). As little as court magicians of those days could avail, so helpless will they be again in these latter times.

Verse 4. Such times of anarchy have in all periods of human history only too often resulted in the rise of tyrants and demagogues making capital of man's confusion and inducing men to surrender themselves with blind obedience to the master planners that they claim to be. The text does not clearly indicate whether the "fierce master" in question will be a foreigner or a native. Opinions are just about evenly divided. It could be that some Assyrian conquerer should be thought of, for Assyria did shortly conquer Egypt. In any case the "powerful king" that will rule over the Egyptians seems to be identical with the "fierce master." But all this civil strife and tyranny will be God's judgment on Egypt, which is here revealed by the mouth of the prophet and described as being "utterance of the Lord, Yahweh of hosts."

(b) *The Disastrous Failure of the Nile to Overflow* (vv. 5-10)

19:5-10 5. Then also the waters of the Nile will fail,
and the stream will be parched and dry.
6. And I will make the channels foul;
the streams of Egypt will get low and dry up;
the reeds and rushes will rot.
7. The meadows along the Nile and at the mouth of the Nile,
together with all that is sown along the Nile will dry up,
be scattered and be no more.
8. The fishermen will groan and grieve,
all that cast the hook into the Nile;
and they that spread out the net on the face of the waters will
languish.
9. The men that work in combed flax shall be at their wit's end,
and the men that weave white cotton.
10. The pillars [upper classes] will be crushed,
and the wage earners will be heavy of heart.

Verses 5, 6. Already in the days of Joseph it can be noted how disastrous an experience it was for the land of Egypt to have the practically annual inundation of the land by the Nile to fail. Though the word used for the river (*ye'or*) means only "stream," in Egypt the only stream that counted was the Nile. See the same use of the word for Nile in Ezek. 32:2; Nah. 3:8. Successive aspects of the failure of the inundation to come are described. First, "the waters . . . fail." Then "the stream is parched and dry." Then "the channels" become foul. Then all the minor rivulets throughout the land "get low and dry up." Following this "reeds and rushes will rot." In this connection (v. 6) the name used for "Egypt" (*matsor*) which is a play on the regular word used for the land (*mitsrayim*) really means at the same time "siege," for Egypt will really be in a state of siege.

Verse 7. The first word of the verse has its difficulties. It could mean "bare places" (*RSV*). This could be meant in the sense of places bare of trees and shrubs. This could signify, as *von Orelli* suggests, "meadows." In this somewhat detailed way of describing every last portion of the land, the fields where grain is usually sown are mentioned last as a kind of climax. There the sad story is that which was sown may spring up but ultimately it will be "scattered and be no more." The whole country, in other words, will become a disaster-area as far as the growth of vegetation is concerned.

Verse 8. Another class of men will suffer badly. They are the fishermen, whether they fish with hook or with net. With waters reduced to a minimum, the catch of fish, on which the Egyptians depended so largely for the meat-portion of their diet, was disastrously curtailed. The groans and complaints of the fishermen and their languid attitude are well described in this verse.

Verse 9. Another area affected by it all is the garment industry. Flax for linen goods failed to come up. And cotton also was a failure. So here men are at their wit's end as to what to do to supply the clothing-needs of the nation.

Verse 10. To sum it up, all classes of society are equally involved, whether it be the "pillars" (the term in this connection seems to imply the more well-to-do groups), or the people who work for their wages day by day, they all stagger along under their heavy burden, not knowing what to do to alleviate the distress.

At this point the prophet moves over into another area which may well be considered, when the calamities befalling a land are so many. This is an area where the Egyptians were famous in days of old, the ability to provide wise counsel for all manner of situations. Cf. I Kings 4:30.

(c) *The Collapse of Egyptian Wisdom* (vv. 11-15)

19:11-15   11. The princes of Zoan will be sheer fools.
   As for the wise men, the counsellors of Pharaoh,
   their counsel will be stupid.
How can you say to Pharaoh: "A son of wise men am I, and a
   son of ancient kings"?
12. Where, pray, are these wise men of yours?
Let them make it known to you,
and men will discern what the Lord of hosts has planned with
   reference to Egypt.
13. The princes of Zoan act foolishly,
the princes of Memphis have been beguiled.
Those who are the cornerstone of the tribes have duped the
   Egyptians.
14. The Lord has mingled within her a spirit of warped judgment;
   ment;
they have made the Egyptians stagger in all their doings,
as drunkards stagger about in their own vomit.
15. And there will be nothing left for Egypt to do,
which head or tail, palm-branch or reed could do.

Verse 11. Different classes of those who are supposed to be especially gifted with wisdom are enumerated as being incapable of furnishing the needed words of wisdom. There are, first of all, "the princes of Zoan," a famous city on the northeast border of Egypt, also called Tanis, a name which sometimes, as here, stands for all Egypt, being the part nearest for contact with Israel. Princes are thought of as men who traditionally have some ability to devise good plans for emergencies. But in this emergency of the failure of the Nile to inundate, neither they nor the so-called "wise men," nor even the professional "counsellors of Pharaoh" are able to devise a helpful solution. You just cannot provide an adequate substitute for all that the Nile provided for this ancient land. All of these may at other times have advertised their traditional capacity, claiming to have had wise men as their ancestors, or claiming to be descended from kings famous from days of old. That still does not make them equal to this emergency.

Verse 12. The prophet speaks a challenge: Can any of your reputed wise men come up with a plan that clears up for the people what the Lord of hosts, who, of course, has all things under control, is actually doing?

Verse 13. The lack of understanding on the part of "the princes of Zoan" is manifest. The same holds true with regard to the "princes of Memphis," which lies to the southern tip of the delta. By giving two termini, one north, one south, the prophet says in effect: Throughout the length and breadth of the land there is not a wise man who can cope with the existing emergency. In fact, to carry the thought one step farther, "the cornerstone of the tribes" that is to say, the strong leaders on whom the structure of the state rests have not produced solid counsel but have done no more than "duped the Egyptians," by whatever counsel they did offer.

Verse 14. Now it comes to light that, according to the lofty point of view of the prophet, these things do not just happen. They come to pass by the control and permission of the Almighty Lord of hosts, the ruler of all nations. He has, as it were, given the nation a staggering potion to gulp down, which has warped their judgment, or, according to the root meaning, produced a state of dizziness. The whole nation is in effect staggering around in its uncertainty, or to change to a more expressive figure, they are drunkards who "stagger about in their vomit"; not a very edifying scene to contemplate. So utterly at loss and unable to help itself will the nation of Egypt be when the Lord takes it in hand. There just simply is nothing (v. 15) that anybody in the land of Egypt can do to set things right. Men, high and low, all will be equally helpless. For these two extremes are indicated by the expression "head or tail, palm-branch or reed." Cf. 9:14.

(d) *Judah a Terror of Egypt* (vv. 16-17)

19:16-17 16. On that day the Egyptians will be as timid as women, and tremble and be afraid of the hand of the Lord, which he is swinging over them. 17. And the land of Judah shall become a cause for dizziness; whenever one calls Judah to mind, they will be afraid because of the plan of the Lord of hosts which he plans against them.

Verses 16-17. The subject of how God corrects Egypt is still under consideration, even though in these two verses the poetic structure of the presentation is abandoned and the rest of the chapter is prose. What makes the prophet's approach unique is that what is set forth pictures once-mighty Egypt as all atremble at small and insignificant Judah. But that is only a secondary consideration. The main cause for fear on Egypt's part is that she recognizes that in all that is befalling her it is in reality the hand of the Lord of hosts which, with threatening gesture, is swinging over her and coming down in heavy blows on her back (cf. 11:15). The first part of v. 17 might be rendered freely: At the mere mention of Judah, Egypt is filled with consternation. For when the Egyptians think of Judah this will immediately bring the God of Judah to mind and Egypt will be apprehensive: What new evil has the Lord of hosts devised against us now? Some sense of Yahweh's rule over the destinies of all nations will have been brought home to them and they will wonder, What is he planning now? It may well be believed that a measure of understanding of some of these issues may have seeped down into the mind of the nations that had dealings with Israel.

It cannot be denied that this section (vv. 16-17) can with some propriety be regarded as a transition piece which opens the new field of thought: How God restores Egypt (vv. 18-25).

(2) **God Restores Egypt** (vv. 18-25)

The subtitle of this portion could be: The Fruits of God's Chastisement of Egypt. A number of items are listed here without any attempt to bind them together into any sequence. We have, then, a loose enumeration of a group of results that God achieves in dealing as he does with Egypt.

19:18-25 18. On that day there will be five cities in the land of Egypt, speaking the language of Canaan and swearing allegiance to the Lord of hosts. One of them shall be called the City of Destruction.

19. On that day there shall be an altar to the Lord in the midst of the land of Egypt and a pillar to the Lord at its border. 20. And it shall be a sign and a witness to the Lord of hosts in the land of Egypt. When they cry out to the Lord because of oppressors, he will send them a deliverer and a champion and he will deliver them. 21. And the Lord will reveal himself to the Egyptians and the Egyptians will know the Lord of hosts on that day and they will worship him with sacrifice and offerings, and will vow vows unto the Lord and perform them. 22. And the Lord will smite the Egyptians, smiting and healing, and they will return to the Lord. When they make supplication to him he will heal them.

23. On that day there will be a highway from Egypt to Assyria, and Assyria will come to Egypt and Egypt to Assyria, and Egypt will engage in worship together with Assyria.

24. On that day Israel shall be the third party with Egypt and Assyria, a blessing in the midst of the earth, 25. whom the Lord of hosts will have blessed, saying: Blessed be Egypt my people, and Assyria, the work of my hands, and Israel, my inheritance."

Verse 18. The first of these results announces that some in Egypt will be converted. In fact there will be a sizable nucleus of cities, five in number. Whether this refers to Jewish colonies, of which there were a number in Egypt from the sixth century on or whether this is a reference to cities of native Egyptians who find and acknowledge the Lord, is almost impossible to determine. By Christ's time there were a million Jews in Egypt according to Philo. Beginning shortly after the Babylonian Captivity, Jewish groups did form in the land. They may have been the centers of interest that served as nuclei around which some Egyptians also clustered. "Five" is a modest round number. These beginnings in Egypt were modest, to say the least. But it is significant that they were there at all. Their "speaking the language of Canaan" — i.e., Hebrew — almost compels us to think in terms of such as were born Jews. The fact that they "swear allegiance to the Lord of hosts" points in the direction of their open avowal of their faith in him. That then means that the narrow boundaries that had once confined the people of God to a limited territory will be broken. God's people will spill out beyond these limits, even into a culture rated highly in days of old and be able to maintain itself there. Only it strikes the reader as strange that of these cities one "shall be called the City of Destruction." No truly satisfactory explanation of this statement has yet been offered. By a very slight change in the writing of one consonant this could be construed as a subtle play on words; for then a name that was originally the "City of the Sun" (i.e., Heliopolis — Greek *helios* means "sun") would be referred to as a city in some way distinguished by "destruction. This destruction could be conceived of as the destruction that this city brought upon idolatrous temples and images after the knowledge of the Lord, the God of Israel, came to its inhabitants. In any case, such a thought is not out of harmony with the general tenor of the passage.

Verse 19. Following the line of thought just begun, a further development in the land of Egypt will be that "in that day" — a very vague designation of future time — there will be both an altar and a pillar to the Lord, the one in the midst of the land, the other at its border. The presence of an altar argues for the presence of an established sanctuary. This could well be a prediction of what happened in 160 B.C., when Onias IV, the Jewish high priest, being compelled to flee the land, sought and received permission from the Egyptian monarch, to build a temple "like that in Jerusalem" (Josephus, Ant. XII.9, 7) and even pointed the king Ptolemy to this passage for authority to do as he did. About the "pillar to the Lord" we know nothing as a historical reality. But pillars generally, like the ones at the temple at Jerusalem (I Kings 7:15ff.), were familiar appurtenances of established worship among all nations in antiquity. So then, altar and pillar served as "a sign and witness to the Lord of hosts in the land of Egypt." More is meant than that there were enclaves of Jews in the land. For v. 20 goes on to say that in time of necessity, they will both cry unto the Lord and be heard by him, and nothing limits that statement to some little groups of Jews in the land, especially in the light of v. 22 immediately following. The thought rather seems to be — since the language seems to be bor-

rowed from the Book of Judges (see 6:7) — the Lord will
deliver these one time opponents of his people even as he
so often delivered the Israelites when they cried out because of foreign oppressors.

Verse 21. As already indicated, the above interpretation is
demanded by this verse. For every deliverance that comes
in answer to prayer is a revelation of the Lord given to those
whom he delivers. Result: They who have gone through
such an experience "will know the Lord of hosts" with that
intimate knowledge of experience that the verb "to know"
demands in Hebrew. Experiences of that sort imperatively
demand public recognition, which the Egyptian are here
represented as offering, and offering it in conformity with
vows so to do, which they made in the day of trouble.

Verse 22. This is not at variance with this thought, though
at first it would appear to be so. It is merely an original
way of saying that the Egyptians, being objects now of the
care of their heavenly Father will experience that care in
the form of chastisements. They too will have sinful ways
in evidence in their lives as all God's children do. They will,
therefore, become the objects of God's correction. He will
smite them with the tender concern of the Father, but the
two things "smiting and healing" will always go together.
Whenever they are smitten and then "make supplication
to him, he will heal them." When the affliction has drawn
them to see their deep need of God in all their life, God
will restore them and heal their unbelief and disobedience.
So the fact that God sets them right is viewed as one of the
great achievements of God upon Egypt in times to come.

Verse 23. An entirely new thought appears here as a further result to be achieved by the manner in which the Lord
will deal with Egypt. History indicates in an amazing way,
now that the facts of the case have been brought to light
more fully through the contributions made by archaeology,
how there was traffic back and forth over the bridge called
the land of Israel, made by Assyrians passing on to the south
and the Egyptians moving northward. Practically in
every case the issue was the waging of wars. But the prophet envisions a future where there will be use of the same
bridge by the same nationalities; but now the purpose is

not to be what it was, but joint worship of the same God. The contact between the two will be that of blessed fellowship.

Verse 24. Even that bold thought is to be outdone by another which is here sketched. Though in times past Israel merely lay in between these two mighty neighbors as an insignificant second-rate power, now she shall be on an equality with them: she will constitute the third party in this "triple entente." In fact, only as she rises up to fulfill this function will she actually achieve her true destiny. For already to Abraham it was promised that in him "all the families of the earth will be blessed" (*RSV* margin). When Israel binds these two mighty powers together into allegiance to the Lord, all this will have become true and Israel shall be the mediator of the great, divine blessing. How many other nations may also be involved in the course of time is not stated in this passage. Enough that these three shall be unified in so holy a pursuit.

Verse 25. This thought is expanded a bit more fully now when God's pronouncement on the subject is presented showing what each of the three allies contributes to the alliance. Egypt is said by the Lord to be "my people," a name which was once (Hos. 2:3) an honorable title reserved for Israel. But Egypt will have risen to the level where Israel once stood. Assyria, on the other hand, will be aptly designated as "the work of my hands" (see 64:8), implying that they were lovingly fashioned out of a shapeless lump into a vessel of honor. For Israel the honorable title is reserved that was indicated as being hers already in Mosaic times — "my inheritance" (cf. Deut. 4:20). On this high level, with each of the three great nations of Isaiah's time distinctly exalted and honored in a unique alliance of a spiritual sort, the chapter comes to an abrupt conclusion. All narrow limitations of race and creed will be stripped off and a momentary glimpse is offered of the goal toward which the Lord is leading the nations, with Israel in a spot of focal importance.

More is involved in the matter of the fulfilment of this passage than what has thus far been indicated. Only as the gospel came to the land of Egypt and land of the Near East did these things become realities. In those early centuries the church, especially in the land of Egypt, made notable contributions to the glory of the Savior's name, even as did the church of the whole area of North Africa. If much of this was later annulled by the Mohammedan conquests, the fact still remains that once a flourishing Christian church was in these lands and showed forth the glorious things of which this prophecy speaks.

Notes

Verse 4. That *'adhonim* is a kind of majestic plural and is to be construed as a singular, appears also from the singular form of the adjective "fierce." Cf. *GK* 124 i; *KS* 253 h i.

Verse 8. On the use of *mashlikhey* in the construct state before a preposition, see *KS* 277 m and 336 w.

Verse 10. Since *shathah* in the sense of "pillar" for "upper classes" is a bit unusual, it still seems to be far preferable to the line of thought suggested by the translation "brewers," especially since this leads to introduce the whole industry of brewing with textual changes appropriate to such an interpretation.

Verse 12. The initial word *'ayyam*, "where are they," is a case of the proleptic use of a pronoun; its antecedent follows. See *KS* 340 l.

Verse 14. *Ruach 'iw'im*, the second word being a plural of potency, would convey the thought of a very strong delusion, or even "warped judgment." See *KS* 262 f.

Verse 15. The expression "head or tail," marking as it does the two extremities, is the unique Hebrew way of expressing the totality. *KS* 92 c.

Verse 16. The text does not really say "as *timid* as women." It just says "as women." Obviously this is a generic plural and women, over against men, are commonly thought of as the more timid sex. See *KS* 264 a.

Verse 20. The expression, "a deliverer and a champion," is an obvious case of *hysteron proteron*. For first, the one in question must champion the cause of the people; then comes the deliverance.

Verse 23. The *'eth* before the last word *'ashshur* is not the sign of the accusative but the preposition "together with."

Chapter XX

c. *Isaiah — a Sign and a Portent (Chap. 20)*
(A Warning against Rating Egypt too Highly)

The chapter-sequence is significant. Egypt had just been represented in a most favorable light. But that development lay far in the future. The Egypt contemporary with Isaiah was not the Egypt that he had described in the second half of Chap. 19. In fact, the Egypt of Isaiah's day may correctly have been described by *G. A. Smith* as "a big-mouthed, blustering power, believed in by the mob." Political alliance with her was to be discouraged. That is what this chapter aims to do, and that by a unique device, whereby the prophet himself, in the manner in which he walks about for the space of three years, becomes an object lesson.

A brief sketch of the historical situation of those days is almost a necessity at this point. The threat of the great power of Assyria loomed big on the horizon. Just at this time in the area of Palestine, the city of Ashdod in the land of Philistia was the center of the anti-Assyrian movement, backed and egged on by Egypt, who cheerfully promised her help in case of a showdown. Attempts were being made to enlist Judah, and also Moab and Edom for that matter, in the coalition which was being formed. At first the Assyrian monarch, Sargon II, had sought to regulate the situation by deposing Aziru, king of Ashdod, and replacing him by his brother, all this by remote control from Nineveh. But Aziru was removed by the people of the city and a certain Yamani was made king. Apparently Yamani was pro-Egyptian.

Then Sargon sent his Tartan (i.e., the "commander-in-chief" mentioned in v. 1), who promptly took Ashdod, Yamani fleeing to Meluhha, perhaps an area in Ethiopia. But the king who reigned there, perhaps Shabako, delivered him over to Sargon in a kind of extradition proceedings. But Egypt refrained from acting in this crisis, in which she might be said to have been morally responsible. But all the while Judah, which had never been too strongly enthusiastic about the whole coalition of the anti-Assyrian forces, discreetly withdrew, as did also Moab and Edom; and so no very serious consequences developed as far as she was concerned. This much at least Isaiah, by word and example, was able to achieve.

Shall we immediately deny authorship of this chapter to Isaiah, because it is written in the third person? Shall we ascribe it to disciples of his, of whose existence we know (see 8:16)? That is not necessary. As indicated in our treatment of Chap. 7, the use of the third person by writers in referring to themselves was common enough in days of old.

On the question, whether an actual occurrence is recorded in this chapter, some are inclined to rate it with Jer. 25:15ff. where the thing enjoined upon the prophet never actually was carried out nor could it be. In this case the objection is the utter impropriety about having a venerable prophet go about the streets of Jerusalem stark naked. But, as we shall show, this extreme procedure need not be attributed to the prophet.

At this point we may briefly inject the notice that these were days when Ethiopia was closely allied with Egypt, with an Ethiopian monarch on the ancient throne of Egypt. And both these nations were confederates, at least in name, of Judah.

We may also insert a reminder here that the chapter, being preoccupied with other issues, does not report when and under what circumstances Isaiah returned to wearing a normal type of dress.

We may also take note of the historical fact that when Sargon sent the Tartan to take Ashdod, the Assyrian forces did not follow through on the success they had. They did not at this time go down and inflict the penalty on Egypt and Ethiopia, of which this chapter speaks. The conquest of Edom, we are told by the historian, did not come till the days of Asarhaddon (681 B.C.) and Ashurbanipal (669).

But this need not disturb us, for the prophet had not said that all these events would take place in one campaign. He merely predicted the total outcome.

To round out the picture still more fully we should take note of the fact that the party that favored closer contact with Egypt was rather strong in Jerusalem already in Isaiah's days, as 30:1-5 and 31:1-3 abundantly indicate.

Lastly, we find no adequate ground for labeling v. 2 (or also v. 5) as a later addition, made somewhat clumsily by some editor or annotator. The chapter displays coherence and is not marked by obscurity. It is brief but not unclear.

20:1-6 1. In the year that the commander-in-chief came to Ashdod (when Sargon, king of Assyria, sent him) then he made war against Ashdod and took it. 2. Now at that time the Lord had spoken by Isaiah, the son of Amoz, as follows: "Go, and loose the hairy mantle from your loins, and take your shoes from your feet." And he did so, walking without his outer garment and barefoot.

3. Then the Lord said: "Just as my servant Isaiah has gone without his outer garment and barefoot three years as a sign and a portent against Egypt and against Ethiopia; 4. so shall the king of Assyria drive away the captives of Egypt and the exiles of Ethiopia without their outer garments and barefoot, boys and old men, with buttocks uncovered to the shame of Egypt. 5. Then men shall be afraid and ashamed because of Ethiopia, their hope, and because of Egypt, their pride. 6. And they that live in the coastlands shall say on that day: 'See, what has become of our hope to which we fled for help, to deliver us from the king of Assyria; and we, how shall we escape?' "

Verse 1. One thing should not be demanded of the writer of this chapter, namely that he furnish us with an exact historical time-table of the successive steps involved in this episode of his life. He, for example, does not date the event by indicating the year in the reign of Hezekiah when this took place. It is sufficient for his purposes to indicate that this happened in connection with the coming of the Tartan against Ashdod. Even as the account does not date the coming of the original command to Isaiah, so the word of explanation of what Isaiah was doing is not dated, i.e., vv. 3-6. The average reader has no trouble

about the point involved. Things that make the word difficult would be, for example, to claim that only after three
years of strange behavior on the part of the prophet did the
word of explanation come to clarify what was happening.
Certainly the text does not aim to give such an impression.

The first verse serves, headline fashion, to indicate an
event and its outcome: Sargon saw that the trouble-spot,
Ashdod, required attention; he sent his Tartan to take the
matter in hand; the Tartan came, made war against Ashdod and took it. To Isaiah's contemporaries there was no
need of further historical background. In some connection
with this event, either while the Tartan was on the way, or
when he arrived at Ashdod, or after Ashdod had fallen,
Yahweh gave orders to Isaiah, which at the same time the
prophet passed on to his people; for the words, he "had
spoken by Isaiah," in a case like this must involve that the
word was first spoken to the prophet giving him directions,
and then was transmitted by the prophet to the people as
a message from the Lord to them.

Verse 2. The orders received by Isaiah were: "Go, and
loose the hairy mantle from your loins, and take your
shoes from your feet." Since all information with regard to
the dress of the ancient Israelites is given quite casually in
the Scriptures, we know comparatively little on the subject.
The word for hairy mantle is *saq*. This, being a somewhat
coarse material, was sometimes worn by prophets to give
proof of the fact that they were not men to pamper their
bodies (see Zech. 13:4; Mark 1:6). At the same time it was
the material used for the garment worn in times of mourning, be it mourning over the dead or mourning over some
calamity, physical or spiritual. Note the many instances
where it serves as a mourning garment — Gen. 37:34; II Sam.
3:31; I Kings 20:31f.; 21:27; II Kings 6:30; 19:1, 2. In this
passage both points of view might appear together. It was
Isaiah's prophetic garb; it was also the garment of mourning that he had put on with a view toward the calamities
that were about to befall. When he was ordered to take it
off, that still left the typical undergarment, a kind of tunic.
Out of doors and in public men were not wont to go about
dressed so unconventionally. For to appear thus, meant that

a man did offend against prevailing customs, not against moral decency (*Delitzsch*). At the same time it meant: "after grief comes disgrace." The claim that Isaiah, therefore, went about for a period of time stark naked can hardly be maintained. But it certainly was a striking sight to behold a venerable prophet of the Lord go about in such unconventional dress and also barefoot. It cannot be denied that such procedure loudly called for an official interpretation. This interpretation would appear to have been given by the prophet at once. Why should a man go through a strange pantomime which said nothing to anybody?

Verse 3. When we translate the next "and" of the Hebrew text as "then," we meant it in the sense that the very next thing that the Lord did was to provide the required public interpretation of this strange act. Though cast into the form of a word spoken directly by the Lord about Isaiah, nothing stands in the way of conceiving of these words as spoken in that very form about himself in the third person. This marks a high measure of objectivity on the part of the prophet. He is acting merely as the Lord's "servant" at this time. He is not trying to attract undue attention. However to remove the difficulty caused by the tense of the pronouncement, "has gone . . . for three years," — which would necessitate the assumption that the word was after all spoken after Isaiah had thus strangely carried on for three years — note that the Hebrew perfect, here used, can also express what was done in the past but somehow still reaches over into the present, and would therefore in our language be translated as a present. If the phrase, "for three years" is added, this is merely a condensed way of saying: This act begins now; I want it to continue for the space of three years. In other words this symbolic act, or "sign and portent," was to grind a certain truth into the consciousness of the people by continual repetition. The truth to be impressed must have been of unusual importance or one that would in the nature of the case be driven home very slowly. The temper of the minds of the men of Judah was so unready for the reception of this truth. To this then is added the further information that all that is being done serves as a sign "against Egypt and

against Ethiopia." What this implies is unfolded in the
next verses. For other instances where prophets resorted to
symbolic acts, see Hos. 1-3; I Kings 11:29-31; (22:11);
Isa. 8:1-4. On "my servant" cf. Amos 3:7; Num. 12:7.

Verse 4. In very brief and pointed fashion the meaning
of Isaiah's "sign and portent" runs thus. Isaiah symbolizes
what shall be done with the captives from among the
Egyptians that the king of Assyria will drive out of Egypt
as captives and out of Ethiopia as exiles. Meaning, of
course, that both Egyptians and Ethiopians will be taken
captive and exiled, and all of them will be stripped of
their outer garment and be barefoot, as was proverbially
the case with captives and exiles. Among the further hardships of war encountered will be the dragging away even
of those who are too young for military service and those
who are too old. As slaves they may still command some
lesser price. And in addition some degree of shameful treatment will befall these exiles. Some will be stripped even of
their undergarment (leaving perhaps some kind of loin
cloth, though even this bit of decency was not always practiced) so that they went "with buttocks uncovered" — involving the highest measure of disgrace for some of the
peoples of antiquity, or of present-day nations. So would
Egypt be put to shame, proud old Egypt mentioned here
alone, for she had by far a more famous history than did
the newcomer on the scene — Ethiopia. We remind again
that this did not take place at once but was delayed several
decades as to its fulfilment.

Verse 5. Now all this is applied to Israel and her confederates, who had built such high hopes on help from ancient Egypt and the then-dominant Ethiopia. Fear shall
possess them, because Ethiopia will be openly set forth as
impotent. At the same time they will be ashamed of themselves for having made so terrible a blunder. Ethiopia was
their hope; Egypt was their pride. How mistaken can
men be? What is here stated as a general result that shall
be experienced on every hand, is now in v. 6 specifically applied to the confederates that had been mustered by Ashdod.

Verse 6. They that express their frustration and disappointment are described as being "they that live in the coastlands," which would refer primarily to Philistia, where the counter-Assyrian movement was centered. But the expression is vague enough to include nations adjacent to them, Judah, Moab and Edom. Their admission is a sad one: "See, what has become of our hope to which we fled for help, to deliver us from the king of Assyria." It ends on a cry of despair, "and we, how shall we escape?"

All this comes as an afterthought. It does not appear that Isaiah had much success in preaching the defeat of Egypt and Ethiopia. The most that dare be claimed is that he may have dampened the ardor of some for the coalition that Ashdod was trying to bring about at that time. Judah may have participated less enthusiastically than the rest.

Notes

Verse 3. On the use of *halakh* as a past that reaches over into the present see *GK* 106 q.

Verse 4. The word for "uncovered" (*wachasuphay*) should perhaps be read as the construct of the plural (*wachasuphey*) Cf. *GK* 87 g.

Chapter XXI

d. Concerning Babylon, Edom, and Arabia (Chap. 21)

The matter that strikes the attentive reader first in coming to this chapter is its unusual difficulty of understanding, its vagueness. The picture is not drawn in sharp outlines. As one finally begins to apprehend what is being set forth a certain colorfulness and dramatic quality becomes quite obvious. But it is one of those Scriptures that must be mulled over quite a bit before it begins to talk to the reader.

The issue is much the same as in Chap. 13. But the fact that the writer comes back again to the same subject shows that it occupied quite a place in the thinking of the book, assuming for the moment that Isaiah may not have written this chapter. Though, as our caption indicates, three nations are involved, the last two really seem to come into the picture only in so far as they are involved in the downfall of the first. So the fall of Babylon dominates the picture.

It may help somewhat, if we note at the outset that the writer presents his material neither as a historian nor a reporter. Rather he has something in common with the writer of ballads. He plunges his reader into the midst of a given situation. As the situation develops, the reader begins to catch glimpses of what it is and where he is going.

The following outline for the chapter may be used:

(1) The Vision of the Seer (vv. 1–10) — Babylon
(2) The Watchman Episode (vv. 11-12) — Edom
(3) The Fleeing Caravans (vv. 13–17) — Arabia

It should also be noted that our chapters (21-23) run parallel with 13 to 20; also from this point of view, that the scene moves from the east toward the west, in the one case beginning with Babylon and ending with Tyre, and in the other beginning at the same point and ending with Egypt.

May this chapter be attributed to Isaiah, particularly the first part of the chapter? Most writers are in agreement that it should not be. Parts (2) and (3) perhaps could; not (1). Though we have to admit that there is some force in their arguments, we still feel that there is enough strength in the counter-arguments to offset this basic claim. Since the negative arguments alone are listed so freely in present-day commentaries we shall not offer them here. But the major arguments for the possibility of authorship by Isaiah are here briefly set forth.

There are obvious similarities with Isaiah's style, though this argument is seldom conclusive. Furthermore, it should be noted that if the period had been that when Cyrus was about to conquer Babylon (*ca.* 540 B.C.) and not to mention the Persians as the nation that was particularly involved in this conquest, is most unreasonable. Elam and Media are mentioned but not the leading conqueror.

True as it is from one point of view that in Isaiah's day Assyria was the world power and Babylon had not yet made notable conquests, yet it is also true that she was an outstanding city and that from the time of the tower of Babel onward, Babel Biblically ranks as the exponent of antigodly world-power, and continues in that role down to the time of the last book, Rev. 18:1ff.

It indeed has been contended that no event lends itself so readily to the fall of Babylon here described as the fall under Cyrus (539 B.C.), yet a number of earlier dates have been suggested and are by no means impossible. Sargon II conquered the city in the days of Isaiah (710) and Elamites and Medians may well have helped him. Sennacherib made a similar conquest in 701.

But the major objection still seems to be that, should the writer have had Cyrus' conquest in mind, he lived too long a time prior to that event (more than 150 years) to reckon with an event so distant in the future. Rather it is thought that only as historical situations become living issues for men, do prophets begin to take them in hand. We are ready to concede that ordinarily such is the case. But the situation with regard to Babylon is different. Though she was not yet the dominant power that Nineveh was, it could well have been that in the light of Gen. 11 Babylon's future potential for world leadership may have been anticipated by many. She had a long history going back to the most ancient times (note Gen. 10:10, where already Babylon is regarded as primary among kingdoms). So we see the reference involved need not be to an early overthrow shortly after the times these words were spoken, but it may have been a case where the event is recorded as inevitable, but the exact time is left in the very vague future.

That a sympathetic attitude over against the one to be overthrown is to be noted in this chapter (especially vv. 3 and 4) and that the same attitude appears in other chapters of this book, like 15:5 and 16:9, 11, merely indicates that often the prophets were far from hostile to those whose defeat they had to foretell. But in itself such sympathy is not a development in a later age.

(1) The Vision of the Seer (vv. 1-10) — Babylon

21:1-10 1. The oracle concerning the wilderness of the sea.
As storms in the Negeb tend to sweep along,
so shall it come from a terrible land.
2. A hard vision has been told me:
"The treacherous one continues to deal treacherously;
the destroyer continues to destroy.
Go up, O Elam; besiege, O Media.
All the sighing she has caused I bring to an end."
3. Therefore my loins are full of trembling;
pangs have seized me like the pangs of a travailing woman.
I am bowed down because of what I have heard;
I am dismayed because of what I have seen.
4. My mind wanders, shuddering has overwhelmed me.
The twilight that I longed for has become anxiety to me.
5. Men set the table, they spread the rugs;
they eat, they drink.
Arise, O you princes; grease the shield.
6. For thus has the Lord said to me:
"Go station a watchman;
let him tell what he sees.
7. When he sees riders, horsemen in pairs,
riders on asses, riders on camels,
then let him listen attentively, most attentively."

8. Then he cries out: "A lion!"
Upon a watchtower, O Lord, I am standing by day continually,
and upon my post I am stationed every night.
9. And, behold, there came riders, horsemen in pairs.
And one answered and said:
"Babylon is fallen, is fallen:
and all the images of her gods has he dashed to the ground."
10. O my threshed and winnowed people!
What I have heard from the Lord of hosts, the God of Israel,
that have I made known to you.

Verse 1. The opening title according to the following context must refer to Babylon. But by itself it is not immediately clear why this should be an apt designation of Babylon. "Wilderness" sometimes means a desolate area (see Hos. 2:5; Jer. 2:31). Besides, in Assyrian cuneiform inscriptions the land of Babylon is sometimes referred to as a "sea," apparently because it was cut through by so many irrigation channels and was full of swamps. Also, the first part of the title — "wilderness" — is indicative of what the land will be after the judgment implied in the following has befallen her. Yet here we should observe at once that if the writer has destruction and overthrow of the city in mind, that certainly did not happen for some time to come. Cyrus, for example, did not destroy anything. He just took the city without bloodshed. Ultimately in the course of the centuries Babylon became a howling wilderness. Another way of explaining the meaning of "wilderness of the sea" is to begin with the earlier times when the area where the city was to stand was mostly covered by the sea, before dikes and dams and alluvial deposit had furnished an area for the building of the city. Both explanations seem to yield almost the same result. In any case the title was a bit enigmatic, containing a veiled allusion to what the writer has in mind, as is also the case with other headings such as 18:1; 21:11; 29:1; 30:7.

Now the oracle begins. It speaks of a storm coming from the Negeb, a name now again employed for the southern part of Palestine, seemingly indicating that the writer was familiar with the Palestinian scene and a native of that land. These storms appear to have swept along with a singular fury. So the form of calamity that will befall Babylon will be in the nature of a terrific storm. Concerning this storm it is also indicated that it will come from "a terrible land." The reference seems to be to the Medians, who are about to be mentioned (v. 2). The passage 13:17f. contains a similar reference to these barbarian people, their cruelty and lack of pity.

Verse 2. It is no doubt partly for this reason that the prophet now designates what he has to reveal as a "hard vision" for it deals both with calamitous things and with things hard to understand. This vision is summarized in the Hebrew in four words, the sense of which is caught in our translation: "The treacherous one continues to deal treacherously; the destroyer continues to destroy." The auxiliary verb, "continues," had to be inserted to catch the force of the Hebrew participle, which connotes ongoing action. We already have a typical riddle of a statement. Who is treacherous? Who is the destroyer? Answers to these questions are far from uniform. It could be the avenging Medians. It could be the cruel and unjust inhabitants of the city Babylon. We much prefer to think of the latter. When powerful empires are built much treachery and destruction goes into the process. Babylon will have been guilty of her share by the time her empire stands. In that brief indictment the reason is indicated why Babylon must fall. Her accumulated guilt demands it.

This being the case, the rest of the verse calls upon the avenger to do his work. This avenger is definitely known; really there are two of them, Elam and Media, being countries that lay east and north of Babylon. The former is summoned to "go up," the verb being used to express the idea that in importance the place to which they were to go (Babylon) occupied a more prominent position than did the attacker. The second verb ("besiege") indicates that a city is involved. In this indirect way the picture gradually begins to emerge.

Verses 3, 4. Now for two verses the subjective physical reaction of the prophet to the fact that he receives a prophetic message is pictured for us, all in all a description of heavy physical involvement of pain and anguish. Since nothing indicates what it was that particularly afflicted the prophet so painfully as alarming factor, it would seem that the very act of being the recipient of revelation deeply shook the prophet, as happened to Daniel when a rare disclosure of the future was granted to him. See Dan. 10. Such revelations seem to put a unique physical and mental strain on the recipient. It might be said, since persons in such situations encounter God in an unusual way, man's human nature shrinks and cringes at near contact with the Almighty. We believe this approach to be better than to think of sympathetic suffering on the prophet's part in expectations of the afflictions that will befall Babylon. For, to tell the truth, Babylon suffered precious little when she fell under Cyrus.

In vv. 3-4 the terms involved may be translated variously, but with practically the same general result. Without trying to evaluate precisely what measure of physical or mental distress each term entailed we shall briefly note the total impression according to our translation. Trembling that shakes the very loins is involved. Even an acute physical pain like that of a woman in childbirth. The writer is both bowed down and dismayed. Receiving such divine disclosures of the future puts a mighty strain on the receiver. It even (v. 4) unsettles the mind, shakes his body with painful shudderings, and seems to make the evening, when darkness falls and when man may be inclined to relax from the day's strain, to be a fresh anxiety because the original shock of the experience still dismays one whenever the thoughts revert to it. Some types of revelation as received by prophets must have been far from delightful experiences.

One point of contrast according to the broader context should not be overlooked here. Different approaches to revealed truth may be made. When later in Chaps. 40–55 the overthrow of Babylon becomes the subject of consideration, the writer is exultant over the prospect that this conqust spells deliverance for captive Israel. Therefore a jubilant tone pervades these chapters. Here everything is different. It is not so much the contents of the message as the experience of being granted a revelation that stirs and shakes the prophet.

Verse 5. Having injected his personal experience (vv. 3-4) the writer now comes back to the impending siege that v. 3 had announced and describes the attitude of those who are about to undergo this siege. In a general way v. 5 indicates that the siege and capture of Babylon will come utterly unexpected. Those within the city, instead of being on their guard and ready for an attack, are living along in a state of complete security. Nothing is farther from their thoughts than an attack by the enemy. Tables are set for feasts; rugs are spread for banqueters to lie on; the feast begins, men eat and drink. Into the midst of the festivities comes the call to arms: "Arise, O princes." Only one of the preparatory measures that they should have taken care of is here quickly commanded — "grease the shield," a precautionary measure that could make the blow of the sword glance off ineffectively. Though the scene described would not necessarily imply an exact description of actual events but could be a colorful description of the careless attitude of those about to be vanquished, it appears that it also describes what actually took place, as Dan. 5:30 briefly records. Other sources give the details. Xenophon tells (Cyrop.VII, 5, 15) how Cyrus diverted the protecting waters of the Euphrates at night while the Babylonian forces were actually feasting in their security, and so marched in and took the city practically without a single stroke of the sword. But v. 5 as such merely indicated that total security marked the expectation of the city that was to be taken.

Verse 6. The second phase of the prophet's vision runs from v. 6 to v. 10. Where the first phase had indicated at least the possibility of the overthrow of Babylon, the second phase predicates its actual occurrence, for it culminates in the statement of v. 9: "Babylon is fallen." What these verses then appear to describe is how the fall gradually came to pass from the angle of the prophet. It almost becomes necessary to assume that a watchman is posted, let us say at the eastern fringe of the land of Judah, on some watchtower to keep a check on developments. Apparently this watchman must be thought of as having more than ordinary keenness of vision: he is able to look clean across the desert to the land of Babylon and see forces on the move. But stationing such a watchman would seem to indicate that developments in the situation involved are coming very soon and are of such moment as to demand that they be reported promptly. The scene is analogous to one where newspaper reporters are stationed at a given point to be in readiness to pick up and transmit important news as it is in the making. Here instead of a reporter you have a "watchman," who is to be stationed (v. 6). He is to report as soon as developments become apparent. Verse 8, however, seems to identify the prophet himself with the watchman. Still it is a matter of almost complete indifference who the watchman is. As *Binns* indicated, the "figure of the watchman is used to make the message more vivid." But the watchman has orders to promptly report what he sees. To bring the prophet's "other I" into the picture only tends to confuse things.

Verse 7. In particular the watchman is to be on the lookout for "riders, horsemen in pairs, riders on asses, riders on camels." These would be thought of as putting in their appearance perhaps on the eastern horizon. Two possibilities suggest themselves. These riders could have been scattered remnants of Babylonians in flight; for their city has fallen. Or these various riders could be the enemy that attacked, or was about to attack, Babylon. Even merely catching a glimpse of these is indicative of the fact that things are happening out there, things that have been predicted. "Asses" have been found to have been used by the Elamites (cf. "Elam" v. 2) and "camels" by the men of Media (again v. 2). So the conclusion is that the attackers are going into action. But from that point on the watchman as such is to listen as intently as he can.

Verse 8. When the appointed watchman cries out "a lion," that, being perhaps traditional shepherd-language (cf. 15: 9; Jer. 50:44-46) — the cry of alarm, when the lion attacked the flock — this indicates that the predicted attack on Babylon is under way. So much for the instructions under which the watchman was operating. The rest of the verse indicates that the prophet considered himself as being just such a watchman, that he was on the alert day and night, scanning the horizon carefully, ready to report the first indication of activity in the area that was to be watched.

Verse 9. As soon as the item that he was to watch for became apparent, it was time for the announcing of the fatal message about Babylon. This message is, with a solemn iteration: "Babylon is fallen, is fallen." This announcement could be referred to a capture of Babylon in Isaiah's day. It would cover perhaps the fall of the city in the famous capture by Cyrus. It could be a reference to the final overthrow of the center of ungodliness in the last days. Here, of course, only the instances of Old Testament fulfilment can be involved. But the New Testament still uses the terminology of this passage in Rev. 18:1f., in reference to the end of days. An additional item of some color is that covered by the second half of the verse: "All the images of her gods has he dashed to the ground," the subject of the verb being implied as God himself.

We seem to have here a typical case like the ones that Isa. 41:26f. refers to, where God is able to foretell the future — a thing he alone can do — and as he foretold so it came to pass.

Verse 10. This verse, too, has its difficulties of interpretation. It actually says no more than: "My threshed one, my winnowed one." It might be a reference to Babylon, which, whether judged or not, is still God's, and so could be referred to as "*my* threshed one." So God might express pity over the one whom his justice had to judge. But if one bears in mind that in several other passages Israel is referred to as having been threshed by God, in one instance even on the threshing-floor of Babylon (Micah 4:12; Jer. 51:33), it would seem more to the point to let these words be an exclamation of sympathy for Israel who had been harassed by the enemy before God intervened in their behalf. Of sympathy, we say, in the sense of rejoicing over the relief that Israel will experience at Babylon's overthrow. But in concluding this vision the prophet expresses the thought that he has withheld nothing of what the Lord in this connection made known to his prophet. It was a matter of true stewardship of the prophetic office to make known all that God had made known for the good of his people. The prophet asserts that he has discharged this obligation.

(2) The Watchman Episode (vv. 11-12) — Edom

This is an oracle against Edom, a fact hidden in the caption by the significant word Duma. Oracles against Edom are common enough in the prophets, cf. Obad. 1-21; Amos 1:11, 12; Jer. 49:7-22; Ezek. 25:12-14; 35; Mal. 1:2-5. Edom on her part was the spiteful neighbor, always venting her spite on Israel. But nothing of the spirit of retribution speaks through the words here recorded. In fact the prophet seems quite sympathetic to this old brother-nation.

Yet this word like the others in this chapter has a certain riddle-like quality about it, a double meaning of terms in the title.

21:11-12 11. The oracle concerning Duma.
Some one is calling out to me from Seir:
"Watchman how far is the night along?
Watchman, how far the night?"
12. The watchman answers.
"Morning has come, but again night.
If you want to make inquiries, make them;
come back again!"

Verse 11. That Edom, or Seir, is involved appears clearly from the second line of v. 11. "Duma" which is a kind of mystery-name for Seir, signifies "silence," in the sense that silence is the major symptom pervading an area that has been utterly destroyed (cf. Ps. 94:17; 115:17). In that sense this is an oracle indicating destruction. This destruction, however, ties up with Babylon's overthrow, although this is merely implied. But the vagueness, or indefiniteness, is one of the major marks of this oracle. We cannot identify the person that calls from Seir; we cannot identify the watchman that answers. In fact, it has been rather appropriately said that this "very indefiniteness is the message" (*Fitch*) of the passage as a whole.

A voice is heard directing an inquiry to some watchman,

whose primary business it is to keep alert for dangers developing during the night and among other things, to keep track how the night is progressing. "Night" as here used would seem to signify the night of misery. So, paraphrasing what is here said, someone is inquiring whether the misery that will strike Babylon and concurrently afflict Edom is soon to pass over. The petition has something pathetic about it, an effect that Luther caught with unusual beauty in his almost untranslatable translation: *Hueter, ist die Nacht schier hin?* ("Watchman isn't the long night soon over?") The repetition of the question indicates the painful anxiety of the questioner.

Verse 12. The watchman cannot give much satisfaction. It would seem that at the time when he answers there was momentary relief, but nothing enduring. A new wave of misery struck again. This is what his words seem to mean: "Morning has come, but also night." The issues involved have not been settled. Things will worsen before they get better. Beyond that the watchman is not in possession of any definite information. The questioners may come again later and ask.

So all we have in this oracle is a vague indication that when Babylon's evil day comes other nations will also have to suffer.

(3) The Fleeing Caravans (vv. 13-17) — Arabia

The far-reaching effects of the destruction that hits Babylon will be noted even out among the isolated caravans that travel across the Arabian deserts. This is indicated by the following oracle, which also has something of the air of mystery about it and somewhat reluctantly yields its meaning to the inquiring mind.

21:13-17 13. The oracle concerning Arabia.
In the thicket at evening you will spend the night, you caravans of Dedanites.
14. You inhabitants of the land of Tema bring water for the thirsty ones;
  meet the fugitives with the bread they need.
15. For they have fled from the sword, yea from the drawn sword;
  sword;

from the bent bow and from the impact of the war.
16. For thus the Lord spoke to me:
"Within a year, like the years of a hireling,
all the glory of Kedar will be at an end.
17. And what is left of the bows of the sons of Kedar will be
precious little; for Yahweh, the God of Israel, has spoken."

Verse 13. There seems to be an intentional ambiguity about the heading of this piece. After the word "oracle" stands a word that very likely is intended to be translated "concerning Arabia." That same word is at once repeated and in this new connection is to be translated "at evening," a meaning which it may well bear. The title then indicates that the oracle as a whole has to do with the broad area of Arabia, for whose tribes the name "Kedar" is later used in v. 16. More precisely, "caravans of Dedanites" are involved. Again we are plunged into the midst of a given situation, "at evening." Making all permissible surmises we arrive at the conclusion: certain caravans of Dedanites, who were neighbors to the Edomites (cf. Ezek. 25:13; Jer. 49:8; see also Gen. 10:7 and 25:3) are being warned not to stay on their usual desert trails for they are not safe. The marauding enemy, perhaps Assyrians, are on the loose. They are ravaging right and left. Therefore the caravans of Dedanites are to go aside into the thickets far back from the trail and hide there, spending the night.

Verses 14, 15. Apparently the next step of the advice given is a word directed to the people of a town near where the Dedanites have fled into the thicket, the town Tema, in northwestern Arabia. These good people are dramatically being appealed to to provide the hiding caravan with water and bread. It may be that the caravan had to continue in hiding for a time till their food and drink supply ran low. The situations were so fraught with peril even for caravans, which ordinarily are not too much disturbed by the fortunes of war which sweep from land to land but fail to disturb the trails through the desert. These disturbances are described in v. 15: The sword is drawn and may be used against them; the bow is bent with the same threat; and the impact of the war is keenly felt.

Verses 16, 17. A prose epilogue concludes this last oracle similar to the prose epilogue of 16:13f. In it the prophet indicates that he has been speaking by the word of God, not merely giving certain cautions which grew out of apprehensions that filled his mind. The first point being made is that the power of Arabia will be at an end within a year; in fact, a precisely computed year, as would be the year of a man who has hired himself out to toil for another precisely one year and no more. Or, to state the thing more poetically: the bows of the sons of Kedar (that means: the bow men) will be very few in number; they will have suffered so badly because of the misfortunes of war. "The God of Israel" who rules the destinies of all nations is the one with whom this oracle originated. It is, therefore, a word entirely true; it will be fulfilled.

Notes

Verse 1. For the infinitive *lachaloph* a governing verb is to be supplied, like *hayu*, making a kind of periphrastic conjugation, allowing a thought to be added on a bit loosely. Cf. *KS* 339 y and *GK* 114 o. The verb *ba'* represents not so much a past as an anticipative future (*KS* 133 a).

Verse 2. The noun *'anchathah* means most likely "all the sighing she has caused" and so is a subjective genitive suffix.

Verse 5. "Princes" as noun has the article, but is still in the vocative. *KS* 290 e.

The expression "Grease the shields" especially if the verb be translated "anoint" might seem to allow for the interpretation: dedicate them for a holy war. But the parallel passage II Sam. 2:21 does not allow for such a meaning.

Verse 9. The verb *wayya'an* is a clear case where the general subject "some one" is called for. *KS* 324 d.

Verse 11. The same construction, just noted in v. 9, also appears here (*KS* 324 n).

Verse 12. The verb *shûbhu* would seem to be that adverbial use of the chief verb in a unique Hebrew construction, making it the equivalent of the adverb "again." To find a reference to repentance here is quite far-fetched.

Verse 17. *Qésheth*, bow is obviously used here in the collective sense (*KS* 349 e).

Chapter XXII

4. Against Jerusalem and Tyre (Chap. 22-23)

a. Oracle Concerning Jerusalem (Chap. 22)

After Israel's immediate neighbors (14:28–17:1ff) and her more distant neighbors (chaps. 18–21) have been reflected upon, Jerusalem herself comes in for consideration. But this chapter, like the preceding, is fraught with unusual difficulties, difficulties that have to do chiefly with the sequence in time. Every commentator must speak with becoming caution at several points along the route as he moves through this chapter. The text itself is not in half as bad a shape as some would have us think, though difficult, too, at certain points.

Together with the majority of commentators we are inclined to set the time of the chapter at about 701 B.C., when, according to II Kings 18:14-16, Sennacherib had advanced against Jerusalem and demanded a heavy tribute, which somehow Hezekiah was able to amass and so buy off the attacker. Everything in this passage points to the need of making a break between vv. 16 and 17, when momentarily at least, Sennacherib, respecting the terms of the tribute, withdrew his forces from before Jerusalem. With v. 17 then comes the next threat from the Assyrians, which however, in point of time lies after the time of our chapter. So the first part of the chapter already reflects the hilarious joy over the withdrawal of the siege troops from around Jerusalem's walls. The very learned defense that *Procksch* makes for the date of 713, after a treaty of defense had been concluded with the king of Ashdod, does not carry sufficient conviction. Nor does *Fischer* with his date of 722 seem to meet the needs of the situation.

We proceed to offer an outline for the chapter:

(1) Unseemly Jubilation at a Critical Juncture in History (vv. 1-4)

(2) The Inevitable Judgment Brought On by This Unseemly Attitude (vv. 5-7)

(3) Further Evidence of This Unseemly Attitude — Efforts at Self-help (vv. 8-11)

(4) The Unseemly Jubilation Again Described — Failure to Repent (vv. 12-14)

(5) The Demotion of Shebna, the Royal Steward (vv. 15-19)

(6) Shebna's Replacement by Eliakim, a Conditional Replacement (vv. 20-25)

One matter that is difficult to settle, especially in the first fourteen verses is the over-all time of these verses: Is it past, present, or future? At the outset we seem to have regular perfects followed by converted imperfects — the usual style of Hebrew narrative relating a past event. Yet we feel, for reasons that will be indicated later, that this pattern is broken in vv. 5-7. Then with v. 8 the text goes back, abruptly we admit, to the narrative of the past.

Candor compels practically all commentators to admit that no approach, smoothly as we may seem to make it appear worked out in an outline, really meets all the difficulties and is entirely satisfactory,

Many find it quite helpful to draw attention to the fact that in two sections a sharp contrast is in evidence between the attitude of the people on the one hand and the prophet on the other, in reference as to how men should react to the prevailing situation. Isaiah is sharply at odds with the behavior of the people of Jerusalem. The areas where this contrast stands out are vv. 1-4 and vv. 8b-11.

(1) Unseemly Jubilation at a Critical Juncture in History (vv. 1-4)

22:1-4 1. The oracle concerning the valley of vision. What is it with you, that you have gone up, all of you to the housetops?

2. You who are full of noises, O turbulent city, an exultant town? Your slain are not slain with the sword, nor dead in battle.

3. Your chiefs have altogether fled; they were bound without an arrow being shot;

all of you who were found were made prisoners together,
even when they had fled far away.
4. Therefore said I: Let me alone that I may weep bitter tears;
make no effort to comfort me over the destruction of those who
    belong to my people."

Verse 1. "Oracle" has been the heading of a number of recent chapters (13, 15, 17, 19, and 21; 1, 11, 13, in the sense of a prophetic pronouncement with overtones of doom. But "the valley of vision" is a perplexing expression, originating, it would seem, from the statement in v. 5, where it also refers to Jerusalem. But though almost all men are agreed that it is a designation of Jerusalem, the question is: In what sense is this appropriate? Is it to be tied up with the thought of people being on the housetops perhaps with the intent of viewing the stars for idolatrous purposes (cf. II Kings 17:16)? Or does the idea of vision involve the thought of inspection, let us say, of sacrificial victims again perhaps for purposes of idolatrous worship? Or is the idea of vision to be thought of as being the equivalent of looking out afar on the nations as Isaiah has just done in his oracles respecting the various nations that lie about Israel? Or shall we, perhaps, reduce it to its simplest denominator that the city was the place where Isaiah was given the visions to see all that the Lord granted to him? We, ourselves, incline toward this latter opinion. The term "valley," by way of synechdoche, part for the whole, is one prominent part of the city. For where there are mountains there must be valleys, and the prophet's dwelling may have lain in one of the valleys, thus making this designation quite appropriate. As expression, it still remains an enigmatic description of Jerusalem. So much for the title of the chapter.

The chapter plunges the reader at once into a certain situation: practically every one of the inhabitants has gone up on the housetop for a better view of whatever it is that at the moment demands attention.

Verses 2, 3. The excitement of the hour has produced noisy clamor that echoes all over the city. For the prophet apostrophizes the city: "You who are full of noises, O turbu-

lent city, an exultant town." Excitement appears to be at
fever pitch. Taking the event before us that was above
indicated, the occasion for all the excitement might have
been the unexpected withdrawal of the Assyrian forces.
The population is wildly jubilant over this withdrawal. But
the prophet at once indicates that all this jubilation is improper and unwarranted. Men are shutting their eyes to
certain things that happened that might well cloud their
joy. Some disgraceful and humiliating things had happened in connection with the siege of the city by the Assyrians, things listed in the second half of this verse and in
v. 3. The puzzling expression: "Your slain are not slain
with the sword," at least involves something less honorable
than the usual death on the battlefield. It could be, comparing 28:1, that they were overpowered by wine and so
were easily disposed of by the enemy, when they should
have been physically alert. As v. 3 goes on to say, the
chiefs did not put up a valiant fight: they fled in the hour
of battle. Without even shooting an arrow in their own
defense, they were taken captive. And besides, they were
even taken prisoners in cases where they had seemingly
made their escape and "had fled far away." The troops
certainly did not cover themselves with glory in the encounter, and the people should have been thoroughly
ashamed of them. Instead, they rejoice wildly as though
their troops had distinguished themselves. Perhaps a certain notice that appeared on records left by Sennacherib
may throw some light on the case. He indicates that Hezekiah's mercenary troops deserted in the moment of crisis.
But all this ignominy the nation glibly passes by. They
think they have occasion for rejoicing.

Verse 4. But what are the prophet's thoughts in this
situation? Verse 4 seems to reflect what he repeatedly said
to the inhabitants of the city round about him, when they
looked askance at him because he would not share their
hilarity. He felt that the time called for bitter tears of
grief over his deluded people. He wanted to weep in solitude, not rejoice with the multitude in its wild extrava-
gance. And if any may have felt sorry for him because he
refused to share their attitude and felt he needed some com-

fort from them, such comfort he felt he must repudiate. There just was no comfort to be had about a misguided people such as they were.

(2) The Inevitable Judgment Brought on by This Unseemly Attitude (vv. 5-7)

Here we encounter one of the major difficulties of this chapter: How does this piece tie up with what precedes and with what follows? Leaving it stand in the past tense, as most translations do, would produce an almost impossible situation as far as coherent sequence of parts is concerned. We therefore regard this piece as being cast in the form of what is known as the prophetic perfect, which means, it must be construed as a prediction of the future. Our reason for this approach, a reason which almost makes it imperative to construe the passage as future, is the first line of v. 5. For when expressions like this occur — "The Lord of hosts has a day" — they invariably refer to the future. God's day is always a future matter (*Gray*). In other words, the prophet sees what Israel by its misguided happiness, which in this case is very sinful, will bring down upon its own head. First comes a general description of the nature of this impending day: it is a day "of tumult, downtreading and confusion." The Hebrew nouns in this case combine a unique alliteration with a noun formation that simply cannot be reproduced in translation but is most striking and effective. This confusion will center upon Jerusalem, here called "the valley of vision." In the next line the vision seems to portray the enemy already before the city walls directing siege-operations with loud calls of mutual encouragement that echo back from the hills that surround the city. The enemy are industriously trying to demolish a portion of the city walls with huge efforts and clamor. This is the first part of the impending disaster that the prophet sees in his vision.

First let us submit a translation that embodies the future idea.

22:5-7 5. For the Lord, the LORD of hosts, has a day of tumult, downtreading, and confusion in the valley of vision;

of tearing down of the wall and shouting reechoing to the
mountains.
6. Specifically, Elam will take up the quiver
together with chariots manned with warriors, also readied riders,
and Kir will uncover the shield.
7. And so it will come to pass that your choicest valleys will be
full of chariots,
and the horsemen will take their post at the gate.

Verse 5 already has been partly expounded. Note that the
capitalizing of LORD in this case marks the difference between the general term for "lord," applicable to God or man,
and the specific proper name Yahweh, which we, together
with *RSV* usually render "Lord."

Verse 6. Now to be a little more exact, by means utterly
dark to us, unless it be specific revelation by the divine
Spirit, the prophet sees in a vision certain contingents of
foreign troops of the besieging Assyrian army. Men from
"Elam" (which lay east and north of Babylon, cf. 21:2)
are seen getting their bows ready. They were renowned
bow men. Chariots bearing fighting armed men are seen
in the field. Cavalry men, or "readied riders" appear. Warriors from Kir (an Assyrian province near Media; cf. II
Kings 16:9; Amos 1:5) are preparing for battle by taking
the protective covering off the shield. This is a part of the
picture as the prophet sees what Judah and Jerusalem must
face. But even that is not all.

Verse 7. Lifting up his eyes the prophet sees the vision
taking on broader proportions. The fine valleys round about
Jerusalem are full of chariots bearing down upon the city,
a wild and alarming spectacle. And tight up against the
city gate the horsemen will have taken their post. With
that future in prospect, how can men be light-hearted and
rejoice?

(3) Further Evidence of This Unseemly Attitude — Efforts at Self-help (vv. 8-11)

22:8-11 8. And he took away the covering of Judah.
But Judah looked at that day to the weapons of the
"house of the forest."
9. And you saw that the breaches of the city of David were many;
many;

and you collected the waters of the lower pool.
10. And you counted the houses of Jerusalem;
and you pulled down houses in order to fortify the wall.
11. And you made a reservoir between the two walls for the
    waters of the old pool;
but you did not look unto him who brought it about;
nor did you regard him who shaped it up long ago.

Verses 8, 9. Though nothing indicates it, except the unusual progression of the thought, we seem to be under necessity of regarding the Hebrew perfects again as plain historic past tenses. Even so, the first line of v. 8 is not immediately clear. We take "the covering" to be, so to speak, the veil of ignorance (cf. 25:7). The Lord did something that took the blindness away from the eyes of the rejoicing population of the city. Somehow they saw that this was not a time for hilarious joy. The obvious conclusion that so many prophets preached so clearly and so forcibly, they however failed to draw, namely that the situation called for sober repentance. Instead when they began to see with what they were confronted they thought only of defensive measures to ward of the impending attack. But the unfortunate thing was that all devices resorted to were purely on the human level. Divine aid was not invoked. The need of it never seemed to occur to the people. Their efforts in this direction are enumerated. We see the almost feverish activity with which the city bustled. The fact that so many things have to be taken in hand, seems to point to indifference and carelessness that had prevailed during a longer period of comparative safety. Now all the weaknesses become apparent at once. Were there sufficient weapons available? They looked to "the house of the forest," built by Solomon in his day as an armory for rather expensive weapons (cf. I Kings 7:2-5; 10:17, 21). Then they cast their eyes in the direction of the fortifications of the old fortress, the southeastern section called "the city of David." There the breaches were seen to be many and dangerous. Then there was the matter of providing an adequate water supply for the time of siege by the enemy. Somehow they saw to it that the waters of the lower pool were collected and stored more effectively. Unfortunately no exact information is available as to the ancient pools and walls of Jerusalem. All we are able to arrive at is the general picture.

Verse 10. Time did not allow for the quarrying of stones from the near-by hills of Jerusalem. They had to resort to more drastic measures. The houses of the city were counted and listed. How many could be spared in the present emergency? The materials of those that could be spared were used to fill in the breaches in the walls. The Hebrew says they made the walls so high they could not be scaled.

Verse 11. And the water-problem? At one convenient point, presumably to the south near the later Pool of Siloam, or in the lower Tyropoeon Valley, where there already were two walls, a reservoir was constructed for the "waters of the old pool." But in their mad haste to get everything done in quick order, no time was left for looking to him who controls situations like this and alone can extricate those that have become entangled in their complications. The prophet's way of stating the case indicates how strongly he believes in the total control of the Almighty in every human situation, and that faith demands that his help be earnestly sought. Or, as the second statement of this case has it: This is a clear indication of the divine foreknowledge, in which the prophet believed so strongly and which men must recognize, if they would know and understand what the Lord of hosts does. For his plans are not only for a day, and hand to mouth: They reach back into time immemorial. Cf. 45: 21, the Lord is almost thought of as plastically shaping the future as he shaped the clod of earth when he created man (the same verb is used in both passages).

(4) The Unseemly Jubilation Again Described — Failure to Repent (vv. 12-14)

22:12-14 12. And the Lord, the LORD of hosts on that day called to weeping and lamenting;
and to shaving of the head and to the girding on of sackcloth.
13. But, lo, joy and gladness, slaying cattle and killing sheep; eating meat and drinking wine;
[saying] "Let us eat and drink, for tomorrow we die!"

14. But the Lord of hosts has long revealed himself in my ears: "Surely, this sin shall not be expiated for you till you die," says the Lord, the LORD of hosts.

Verse 12.   The Lord's calling of men to weeping, and so forth, need not here necessarily be thought of as going audibly by way of the voice of the prophet, though that possibility must be readily conceded. The situation as such, in the light of all that Israel had heard from her prophets, demanded of the common-sense insight of the average Israelite, that he adopt an attitude of true repentance, which would give expression to itself in various possible forms. Some might weep and lament aloud that they had sinned against their God. Others, with Oriental demonstrativeness, might even venture to shave their heads and gird on the traditional sackcloth, the garment of the penitent. But all this was conspicuous by its absence. No one gave tokens of having taken God's deliverance seriously to heart.

Verse 13.   Instead, there was every manifestation of giddy joy, as though a great achievement had taken place, where in reality the achievement was entirely negative: the enemy had for the moment withdrawn, and that as before shown (vv. 2-3) under rather inglorious circumstances. And how did this untimely celebration express itself? Chiefly in intemperate feasting as though their belly were their god. Of the meager stock of cattle and sheep that were left, some had to be slain. Meat reserved for important festivities, had to be eaten. Wine had to be drunk. And still there was no background of true happiness for it all. Their joy might have seemed to come into the category of a kind of gallows-humor, for they were saying: "Let us eat and drink, for tomorrow we die." They could not even be serious in the face of possible death. Apparently they did not need to be told how desperate was their case. So men act when they have become dull to higher values (cf. I Cor. 15:32). But for Israel to take such an unworthy attitude in the light of the many opportunities for a more enlightened approach is quite unpardonable. This Isaiah expresses in the next verse.

Verse 14.   But an answer for this sort of attitude was already long at hand from the Lord. Isaiah had been given this response in one form or another and had transmitted it to his people very faithfully: "Surely, this sin will not be expiated for you till you die." In other words, pardon is out of the question. The people by this time will not and cannot repent. Should we resort to New Testament terminology? Shall we describe this as being another definition of the sin against the Holy Spirit? It may well be. It should be noted, of course, that the clause, "till you die," does not imply that after death, or by death, expiation could be achieved. More to be point would be the observation that this divine pronouncement carries with it a certain measure of indignation on the part of the Almighty. It is spoken in strong and justifiable anger (*zornerschuettert* — *Procksch*).

(5) The Demotion of Shebna, the Royal Steward (vv. 15-19)

22:15-19 15. Thus the Lord, the LORD of hosts said to me: "Come! Go to this steward, to Shebna, who is over the palace: [and say]
16. 'What have you here, and whom have you here that you are here hewing out a tomb for yourself? He is hewing out this tomb on the height, and is carving out a habitation for himself in the rock.
17. Lo, the Lord will hurl you violently and grasp you forcibly;
18. He shall wind you up entirely and hurl you like a ball into a spacious land; there you shall die, and there shall be your magnificent chariots — you are a disgrace to your master's house! 19. And I will thrust you down from your station and tear you from your post.' "

Verse 15. This is the only instance of the denunciation of an individual by Isaiah. Other instances are recorded in the Scriptures: see Amos 7:16-17; Jer. 20:1-6; 28:15-17. *Skinner* calls this, perhaps a bit too colorfully, "A Philippic against a Parvenu Politician." As to rank and station, that of "royal steward" (literally "steward over the house") ranked among the highest of cabinet officers. Yet, though this was merely a political post, there seems to have been some deeper involvement in this case, which made the sharp rebuke by the Lord himself imperative. The reference "this steward" carries in the demonstrative "this" a somewhat derogatory note. The man was apparently a parvenu; he had come up from the ranks; he aspired to prominent station. But, as has frequently been suggested, he may also have been of that party at court who so strongly favored alliance and closer cooperation with Egypt, a policy Isaiah so deeply abhorred (30:1-5).

Verse 16. In any case, it appears from this verse that the steward in question was busily engaged in hewing out a tomb for himself, a piece of foresight that many a good man engaged in during his lifetime, but which in this case apparently, involved, some unwholesome aspirations, so that especially after his death the man involved would have an honored resting-place among the socially elite. But neither as far as property holdings, nor as far as social connections were concerned, was Shebna eligible for the honor in question. He was, therefore, to be addressed accordingly: "What have you here, and whom have you here?" At this point, after being charged with doing a highly improper and unworthy thing, the address goes over into the third person, again a derogatory approach, discussing the man objectively with himself. Apparently also the fact that Shebna was aspiring to hew it out "on the height" was a further indication of the man's vain ambitions, which did not agree well with the truly noble aims which should have marked a man of his responsibility. With all this may be tied up the possibility that Shebna was a foreigner, an Aramaean, as the form of his name might seem to indicate.

Verse 17. That the wrong he did was not minor appears from the strong pronouncement of punishment that is spoken against him. The Lord himself will take him in hand with a drastic sort of treatment which is described here figuratively in the following terms: He will be violently hurled away, after having been forcibly grasped and rolled up into a tight ball so as to be capable of being hurled all the more conveniently. The exact sequence of the steps in the process is not strictly observed (the figure of *hysteron proteron*). But the total effect is clear: the man is to be totally disposed of and effectively removed from his position of prominence. The "spacious land" into which he is to be hurled would appear to be Babylon, the land of captivity. There he will encounter the fate of so many: he shall die in a foreign land, a fate regarded as a great misfortune by the Jew (cf. Amos 7:17; Hos. 9:6). It even could have been that in the process of being led into captivity, he may have been transported in those very chariots with which he surrounded himself in Jerusalem, as a mark of his aspiration to high office (cf. II Sam. 15:1ff.). In the Hebrew the original expression "chariots of honor" makes the word "honor" stand immediately next to the noun "disgrace," marking a striking contrast. For aspiring to be so great, but in a wrong way, the man would have become a disgrace to the very court of the king of which he had become so important a member.

Verse 19. It is God who thrusts him down and tears him up from his post. His offense must have been peculiarly obnoxious to warrant such strong condemnation.

By way of sequel we note that Shebna appears twice. Later on in the book he is still holding a high post, but not as high as previously (cf. 36:3 and 37:2). So there is the possibility that he took this rebuke of the prophet to heart, was demoted, but still was found worthy to occupy a lower post of honor at court. When he appears there he has been replaced by Eliakim, of whom the next section speaks.

(6) Shebna's Replacement by Eliakim, a Conditional Replacement (vv. 20-25)

22:20-25 20. And it shall come to pass in that day, I will call my servant Elaikim, the son of Hilkiah; 21. and I will vest him with your robe and bind him with your girdle, and put your power in his hand, and he will be a father to the inhabitants of Jerusalem and to the house of Judah. 22. And I will lay upon his shoulder the key of the house of David, and he shall open and none shall shut, and he shall shut and none shall open. 23. And I will drive him in as a firm spot; and he shall occupy a seat of honor for his father's house. 24. And should the whole weight of his father's house hang themselves on him, all offspring and offshoots, all the little dishes, all the little pots and big pans; 25. at such a time, says the Lord of hosts the peg, ever so firmly fastened, will give way; it will be cut off and fall down. And the entire weight that clung to it will be cut off. For the Lord has spoken."

Verse 20. But the Lord has a replacement ready for Shebna, the Eliakim referred to above. He is called by the honorable title of "my servant," used in reference to men who
consciously did their task and lived their lives as servants of
the Most High (cf. II Sam. 3:18; Isa. 20:3; Amos 3:7). If
he also is said to be the son of Hilkiah, this cannot, of course,
be the same Hilkiah mentioned in Jer. 1:1, the father of
Jeremiah.

Verse 21. Whether an actual investiture with special
official garments took place by way of induction into office
is not necessarily settled by the statement here used, for
"vest" could be used figuratively. But the more likely interpretation is that actual clothing with special garments
was the mode of symbolizing induction into office — robe
and girdle. To Eliakim then will be transferred all the power
that Shebna had wielded; and, since the post seemed to
involve authority for good over many people, it is said of
him that he will be "father to the inhabitants of Jerusalem
and to the house of David." This could imply that Shebna
had been so engrossed with plans for self-promotion that he
had failed to do his duty faithfully in reference to the individuals for whom he was appointed.

Verse 22. A more emphatic way of conveying the thought
that great responsibility was to be vested in Eliakim was the
giving to him of "the key of the house of David." The key
symbolized that the man had responsibility for the safety of
the royal palace and had access to all its secrets and treasures, which he was to guard carefully. Whether by way of
induction into office an actual key was put into his safe-
keeping, to be carried about as a symbol of authority, or if
at that time the terms were merely figurative, will be difficult to determine. The key, as has been properly remarked,
need not necessarily have been of great size, so that it had
to be shouldered as would be a musket. For "to lay upon his
shoulder" could again very aptly in itself be an expression
conveying the thought of transfer of authority. In any case,
it does signify the latter thought and is so used elsewhere
(see Matt. 16:19; and Rev. 3:7), where it is even used in
reference to Christ. This latter use, however, does not yet
imply that there is something Messianic about our passage.

It merely allows for some measure of Messianic use of the terms. But the note is yet added that there is something final about the acts of the incumbent in office: when he opens no man dare venture to interfere; when he shuts none dare open without his permission. All of which is indicative of an unusual measure of authority and responsibility.

Verse 23. Though the whole word spoken at this time seems to have been addressed to Shebna, informing him of his own lot as well as of the destiny of Eliakim, it would appear that the more detailed statement is for the benefit of Eliakim, to whom the word was, no doubt, communicated in some form or other. From that point of view the statement not only indicates the honors that shall be laid upon the new steward but also the large measure of his responsibility. Summing up the measure according to which men shall depend on him, there stands the statement that he shall be "as a peg in a firm spot." Many, apparently, will have occasion to lean heavily on this man and so his position will be one of unique distinction. This thought is also covered by the second figure here used: "He shall occupy a seat of honor for his father's house." His position shall reflect honor on all the nearest of kin. The expressions used hardly seem to carry farther than that. To try to make the "peg in a firm spot" to be, in the figure, the main peg of a tent, and "the seat of honor" the place by this peg reserved for an honored guest, seems both far-fetched and of little avail, if it could be established as the true meaning.

Verse 24. At this point the familiar translations and interpretations create an unnecessary difficulty. They treat this verse as a continuation of the prediction of what shall happen to Eliakim after he comes into office. But then the unusual situation is met with that a man is solemnly pointed out as the Lord's choice for a vacant post and then he is immediately discarded, being taken to task for nepotism, the undue favoring of his own relatives when it comes to giving positions of prominence in connection with his office. Since such a dual attitude toward one man seems unreasonable it is common procedure to label vv. 24-25 as later additions made in the light of what developed afterward in Eliakim's case. So the passage stands discredited.

The difficulty is easily solved by a somewhat more sympathetic approach which gives the Biblical writers credit for consistency. In the light of what the passage says, v. 24 can and should very properly be treated as a conditional clause, a construction that the Hebrew syntax very definitely allows for. Then these verses become a warning for Eliakim concerning a danger that he will soon face in his new office. His relatives shall swarm in upon him seeking patronage. If he yields to their demands, his office will crash down upon his head to the ruin of all those that sought to attach themselves to him, as well as to his own ruin. The whole crew of those who will crowd in on him seeking appointment to office is colorfully described by a number of colorful terms that show the impropriety of such goings-on: "the whole weight of his father's house . . . all offspring and offshoots, all the little dishes, and little pots and big pans." We have, especially in rendering the last statements under this head, departed a bit from the literal rendering to catch the force of the ironic statements that cover such undignified procedure. The statement stays in the category of kitchen utensils.

Verse 25. The figure is most appropriate, for it allows using the previous figure of the peg, on which all these utensils are hung. The peg cannot bear the weight of it all, even though it was originally (v. 23) driven "in a firm spot." But all this mess is too much even for the firm spot. The whole lot of them with the peg crash to the floor with a loud clatter. Or, to change the figure, all of them "will be cut off," a phrase repeated twice over.

So the words for Shebna and Eliakim are tied in with the Oracle concerning Jerusalem because they were contemporary and a direct outgrowth of the then prevailing crisis.

Notes

Those who are strongly minded to correct and improve the text of this chapter because of its seemingly deplorable state of preservation, resort to a very large degree of emendations. But, as is frequently the case, the poetic structure is quite dubious. There is also a slight variation of the versions, especially the Septuagint.

These facts are exploited to an extreme measure and a feeling of great uncertainty assails those who approach the text with these presuppositions.

We do not deny that a few minor corrections of the text might rightly be considered, since the text must always be critically examined. But in spite of some difficulties of interpretation, the text by and large is in good state of preservation.

Verse 2. The expression "slain with the sword" involves the construct relationship, where the noun in the construct state expresses the means involved (*GK* 128 x).

Verse 3. "Without an arrow being shot" is a free translation of a very concise construction, where the words literally read: "without the bow." The above paraphrase seems to catch the point. (See *GK* 119 w)

Verse 4. The Hebrew uses the expression "the daughter of my people." The word "daughter" is a feminine used collectively. At the same time the genetive is a genitive of apposition (*KS* 255 e).

Verse 6. In *we'eylam* the conjunction *we* involves the so-called *waw explicativum*, being the equivalent of our "namely," or "specifically."

Verse 7. By the use of the noun "choicest" a kind of superlative is created (cf. *KS* 309 f; *GK* 128 r).

Verse 8. In *wattabbet*, the *waw* is a recognized form of introducing the apodosis, and is here to be translated as the adversative, "but." See *KS* 415 t.

Verse 14. The initial *waw* here is not the form used with the so-called *waw*-conversive construction with the imperfect of the verb. So here the verb comes to mark that which has long been going on, a matter that we tried to catch by translating "has *long* revealed himself," (*KS* 367 h).

Verse 17. The expression "hurl you violently" consists of two nouns in Hebrew — "the hurling of a man." At least the words may aptly be translated thus. We believe that means what our above statement suggests. For "man" *gébher*, signifies man in his strength.

Verse 24. The expression "offspring and offshoot" employs in the original a masculine and a feminine plural. This is an acknowledged device for signifying the whole scope of the terms involved. See *KS* 309 e.

Emendations

Verse 6. To read *rakhabh 'aram parashim*, i.e., "the Aramaeans mounted horses" is the type of emendation that could not be disapproved of, though it is not necessary.

Chapter XXIII

b. Oracle concerning Tyre (Chap. 23)

Does this chapter come limping along as a kind of a afterthought, or perhaps as some sort of supplement? The approach of *Delitzsch* has much to commend it: the second major power that Isaiah knew — after Babylon (chaps. 13 –14) is Phoenicia. Babylon heads this section (chaps. 13– 23), Tyre closes it.

The text is not without its peculiar difficulties. *Procksch* resorts to about twenty-five textual emendations. Such an approach, if warranted, would shake any man's confidence as to the reliability of the conclusions arrived at, if not of the whole interpretation of the passage. *Mauchline* still rightly insists: "the general sense (of the passage) is not seriously in doubt." Admitting difficulties of interpretation does not give warrant to resorting to changes of the text at every difficulty encountered.

One of the major difficulties is whether we have materials here from two major sources, one dealing with Tyre, the second with Sidon. This problem can be magnified far beyond that which is warranted. In fact, Tyre, Sidon, and Phoenicia, all come into the picture. But the simple explanation of the problem involved might well be simply this, that these are three ways of describing one and the same object of concern — the land of Phoenicia, which may be referred to by its own name or, by synecdoche, by the one or the other of its two prominent cities, of which Sidon first enjoyed the supremacy, Tyre, after the glory of Sidon had waned.

Much of the chapter may be classified as marked by a meter of some five beats to the line, except vv. 17 and 18.

As to authorship, again there is wide diversity of opinion. Some would deny it all to Isaiah. Some would grant him vv. 1-14. A few would add the last part, too, but with cer-

359

tain reservations. For us the arguments that question whether it is to be attributed to Isaiah fail to carry conviction. For *Fohrer*, who claims nothing is Isaianic, the chief determining factor is that the religious content of the chapter is sparse. Who can demand that a writer always have a generous measure of religious thought in what he writes? The influence of Yahweh in controlling the historical outcome as far as Phoenicia is concerned is dominant, according to v. 9. What more is necessary?

But what time is involved as far as the overthrow of Tyre in particular is concerned? Dates suggested range from *ca.* 720 B.C. to 700, even to the time of Nebuchadnezzar (*ca.* 588) and down to the time of Alexander (332), when the island stronghold also fell into his hands. The problem is complicated by the fact that there were two Tyres, Tyre on the mainland and Island-Tyre, a half mile off-shore and extremely difficult to take. Shalmaneser took the mainland Tyre, so did Nebuchadnezzar. Only Alexander succeeded in taking Island-Tyre. But in the instances preceding his capture of the old stronghold the power of Phoenicia was largely broken or at least made ineffective. Perhaps most difficulties are met by taking *von Orelli's* remark seriously that the fall of Tyre took place *gradatim*, i.e., by successive stages.

We should note at once that, in our interpretation of the chapter, the very difficult verse (v. 13) has a prominent place. For it says specifically that it was the Chaldeans that reduced Tyre to a ruin. So this would point to the capture of the mainland-city of Tyre by the Chaldeans under Nebuchadnezzar. To all intents and purposes that was the capture of the city that sealed its destiny. Tyre was all but completely subdued when the fortress on the mainland was taken.

This may be the point at which a brief notice concerning the land of Tyre should be inserted. The country was surprisingly small. We are told that it was approximately 140 miles in length and at no point more than 15 miles in width. So it lay wedged in between the mountains and the sea. It could not develop agriculture to any extent, not even remotely enough to supply the needs of the inhabitants of

the land. Therefore this enterprising people took the only
other course open to them; they turned to the sea and became the greatest maritime nation of days of old. One cannot help but admire their enterprising spirit. They built
sea-going vessels, whole fleets of them. They sailed the seven
seas, at least as far as men dared go in that day, passing
around to the west coast of Africa, around to India, up to
Britain; and they completely dominated the Mediterranean.

Israel presented a complete antithesis to all this. She was
little acquainted with commerce, "as little . . . as it was possible for a civilized nation to be," says *G. A. Smith.* Yet
though this chapter tells of the doom of Tyre, there is clear
evidence that the prophet appreciated the "grandeur of the
commerce" of this bold nation of mariners. This is even more
the case with Ezekiel, who deals with the fate of Tyre in
Chaps. 26–28.

The outline of this chapter is simple. It falls into two
parts:

(1) The Fall of Tyre (vv. 1-14)
(2) Her Restoration (vv. 15-18)

(1) The Fall of Tyre (vv. 1-14)

23:1-5 1. Howl, O ships of Tarshish;
for Tyre is destroyed so that no house is left, nor any
harbor.
From the region of Cyprus it is revealed to them.
2. Be still, O inhabitants of the coastlands, you traders of Sidon;
they that crossed the seas filled thee [with goods].
3. On many waters her revenue was the grain of Shihor, the
harvest of the Nile.
4. Be ashamed, O Sidon, for the sea has spoken (the refuge of
the sea) saying:
"I have not travailed, or brought forth children;
nor have I raised up young men, or brought up virgins."
5. When a report comes to Egypt, they will be distressed, as when
the report about Tyre came.

Verse 1. In a dramatic apostrophe the ships of Tarshish are
addressed, as the embodiment of the power and prestige
of Phoenicia. These ships are bidden to "howl," expressing
their amazement and distress over the sad news which is

just beginning to be broadcast over the Mediterranean area: "Tyre is destroyed." The destruction is so complete that "no house is left" for the former inabitants, "nor any harbor" for the ships to put into. The place where these the mightiest sea-going vessels of antiquity, as it were, hear the news of Tyre's overthrow, is the region of Cyprus, where either in one of the harbors of that island, or from a vessel that they pass at that point the news is conveyed to them. This apostrophe could also be thought of as being, by metonomy, addressed to the sailors on these Tarshish ships.

Verse 2. Next the inhabitants of the Mediterranean countries are addressed by the prophet. They are bidden "Be still." This implies the thought of being reduced to complete silence by sheer astonishment. The "coastlands" spoken of (*KJ*: "isles") are the much indented shores of the countries surrounding the Mediterranean. For, to an extent, all these countries are going to be affected by what befalls Tyre. Another class of persons is brought into the picture, men who are going to be more directly disturbed by all this, the "traders of Sidon," who go about selling the wares that have been transported by the Phoenician vessels. When they are described as having "crossed the seas," this strongly recalls how many-sided was the activity that mercantile Tyre controlled. The ones that are spoken of as having been "filled with goods" by these traders are the various cities that were lived in by the inhabitants of the coastlands.

Verse 3. The picture of the intense commercial activity involved in the Phoenician ventures is rounded out a bit more fully when some further items that engaged the attention of those who roamed about "on many waters," are reflected on. There was the immense grain supply of the ancient granary of the world, Egypt, that was transported by these Tyrian merchants. Their "revenue," or we might say, the source of their revenue, was "the grain of Shihor," Shihor being the western arm of the Nile at its delta, where perhaps ships took on loads of Egyptian grain to carry them far and near. This grain is also described as "the harvest of the Nile," because the Nile's inundation was the source of Egypt's fertility. The middleman between the Egyptian grain resources and the nations much in need of grain was

Tyre, who had actually thus become "the merchant of nations." Perhaps the grain trade was the heaviest of all branches of trade. Other items of export are not referred to in this prophecy.

Verse 4. If now Sidon is again spoken of, this is merely one of the three designations (see above) used for the Phoenician land, used for variety's sake. Perhaps after the sailors and the coastlands had been appealed to, now a word is addressed to what is left of the afflicted country itself. Her inhabitants are asked to "be ashamed." Here this is nothing more than the very opposite of being proud. It means: Hang your head in shame, shame over the tremendous loss of inhabitants. This shame is thought of as brought on by a remark that the sea makes. The remark comes as a result of the fact that where Phoenician traders were merchants, and traders were strewn all over the Mediterranean, now they will become so few that the sea will claim she never had any such children: she neither 'travailed, or brought forth children," nor "raised up young men or brought forth virgins." This lament of the sea is highly poetic and at the same time unique. Nowhere else in Hebrew poetry does anything quite like it appear.

Verse 5. Three classes have been called on to express their grief in vv. 1-4. It is quite appropriate to bring a fourth class into the picture, the land of Egypt itself, which will be strongly affected by all that befalls the nation who was her grain-exporter. In Egypt men "will be distressed." When the statement is added, "as when the report about Tyre came," this seems to indicate successive stages of the conquest of Phoenicia, confirming what we mentioned in the introduction to this chapter that the conquest came about *gradatim*, by degrees. This verse speaks specifically about the report of the fall of Sidon that comes to the ears of Egypt. That report will cause grief like that which struck the land when Tyre was reported to have fallen. The "distress" spoken of seems to trace back to the fact that in times past when the Eastern countries made a move toward the west, Tyre was always a kind of bulwark that stopped invasions before they ever hit Egypt. That outpost will now be gone.

What now follows in vv. 6-14 may be regarded as an evaluation of the fall of Tyre and Sidon.

23:6-14 6. Pass over to Tarshish; howl you inhabitants of the coastlands.

7. Is this your jubilant city whose beginning dates from days of old,

whose feet used to carry her far away to sojourn?

8. Who planned such a thing against Tyre, the bestower of crowns,

whose merchants were princes, whose traders were the honored of the earth?

9. The Lord of hosts planned it to desecrate the most magnificent pride,

and to make contemptible all the honored of the earth.

10. Flow over your land like the Nile, O daughter of Tarshish; there is no restraint any more.

11. He has stretched out his hand over the sea,
    he has made kingdoms tremble.

The Lord has given commandment concerning Phoenicia
    to destroy her strongholds.

12. And he said: "You shall no more be jubilant,
    O ravished virgin daughter of Sidon.

Up, cross over to Cyprus; but even there you will find no rest."

13. Lo, the land of the Chaldeans, this was the people.

It was not the Assyrians that appointed her [Tyre] for the wild beasts.

They set up the siege-towers; they razed her palaces;
    they made her a ruin.

14. Wail, O ships of Tarshish,
    for your stronghold is laid waste.

Verse 6. That Tyre is being addressed at this point becomes evident from v. 8. The command to pass over would appear to be spoken to the inhabitants of the city, as, or just before, the siege begins. They who cannot fight should flee now, while they still can. It is reported that when Alexander began to besiege the city the old people and the women were evacuated over sea to Carthage, a Phoenician colony. Tarshish most likely was located in Spain on the Guadalquiver; and called Tartessus by the Romans. Whether at any time a similar evacuation to Tarshish occurred we do not know. The suggestion to "howl" is meant no doubt in the sense of "wail," and implies a kind of lament over the sad lot of the city. Naturally the "inhabitants of the coast-lands" all around the Mediterranean had an interest in the city with whom they had traded so much and so long.

Verse 7. A few of the glories and achievements of Tyre are here enumerated, glories which are quite out of keeping with her impending calamities. She was once a "jubilant city," proud and boastful of her achievements. She had a long and famous history. She was known to be very ancient; her "beginning dates from days of old." Herodotus tells that her priests claimed in his day that the city was already 2300 years old. Josephus records an analogous claim, when he states that the city was founded 240 years before the building of the temple of Solomon. It is doubly painful when an ancient city tumbles in ruins. Another notable achievement of Tyre was the founding of colonies like Carthage, Tarshish, and others, especially in the Mediterranean area. In different suitable spots where her feet carried her she settled down, or "sojourned." Her colonies were her strength and glory. Witness how Carthage could even rival powerful Rome.

Verse 8. The prophet feels there must have been greater forces working at the overthrow of such a city, than what the eye saw. So he asks: "Who planned such a thing against Tyre?" The vagueness of the expression "such a thing," especially in the Hebrew, carries an undertone of the ominous. A few more achievements come into the picture. Tyre is called "the bestower of crowns," because after colonies were extablished and had stable government, the mother city, so to speak gave her daughter a king and crowned him. It is no mean achievement to bestow crowns. Besides, Tyre built up a kind of aristocracy of merchants — "whose merchants were princes." Her traders were men in reputation for solid attainments — "whose traders were the honored of the earth." A city with such a record seems to be too solidly established to be readily overthrown. Some greater force must have been at work in this tragedy.

Verse 9. The prophet now names this force. It was none other than the Lord of hosts. Not a native Tyrian deity; for the Lord God of Israel is the God of all the nations and King of kings. Nor did he merely let this calamity transpire.

He actually "planned it." And both his purpose and his motives were quite proper, even necessary. Tyre had done such wonderful and impressive things that she had grown rather proud of her greatness. She had become guilty of a "magnificent pride." And such pride is always blameworthy. It exalts itself against the Lord and thrusts him aside. Therefore God designs to "desecrate" such pride and make it to appear as the reprehensible thing that it is, the mother of all sorts of iniquity, as Isaiah had pointed out earlier in his book. See 2:11, 17; for "the Lord alone will be exalted." When the successful grow proud, they grow corrupt and self-sufficient. The only way to bring them down to their proper level is "to make contemptible all the honored of the earth" who have come to trust in their own devices and no longer need the Lord. The language of vv. 8-9 is significantly that of Isaiah.

Verse 10. The prophet is still explaining what actually happened when Tyre fell, or all that is involved in her fall. He can do this by pointing out some of the consequences in the region of distant Spain, in Tarshish, to be more precise. It would seem that the colony (Tarshish) had been restrained and restricted by the mother-city (Tyre) in such a way that her free operation and government were hampered. This unwholesome restraint is now at an end. Tarshish feels free to expand and move about as she pleases, as freely, in fact, as the unimpeded waters of the Nile move over the land in the annual inundation of Egypt.

Verse 11. Since the effects of Tyre's overthrow will be felt so widely, it would appear that as a result the prophet is reminded again of the fact that the whole disaster did not happen without the Lord's approval. So he comes back to that subject and again evaluates what happened. Isaiah frequently represents the Lord as stretching out his hand to make a certain move, the very moment when he lifts up his hand being an ominous one (cf. 5:25; 9:12, 17, 21; 10:4). In this case the area in which he is about to make his influence felt is "the Sea." For the maritime empire of the Phoenicians is involved. In fact, historically speaking, this was a time of upheaval, where "he has made kingdoms tremble." Indeed, the Lord is looked upon as the one who in sovereign

power controls all the affairs of the nations. In this case it
is as though he had given a specific command with regard
to Phoenicia "to destroy her strongholds." To make the
matter more colorful, even the command that he gave in this
connection is reported (v. 12). To the city that had ex-
ulted in her past achievements, Sidon (by way of variety,
rather than Tyre) is told that she shall no longer have
occasion to exult over her successes, whether in commerce or
in war: "You shall no more be jubilant, O ravished virgin
daughter of Sidon." Her lot is likened to that of a poor virgin who had been raped, and keenly feel the shame of it.
As in v. 6, the people of the city that has fallen or is about
to fall, are given the suggestion that they flee over the sea,
in this case to Cyprus, where another of her colonies was
to be found. Somehow, however, the prophet knows that
even by such flight she "will find no rest." Further disaster
of some sort will follow hard on the heels of the fugitives.

Verse 13. Now comes the verse that constitutes the major
crux of the chapter. Some despair of making anything of it
(like *Box*) and omit it completely. Others emend it so radically that it has no semblance to the Hebrew text. In any
case men are at least impelled to make the assertion that
the difficulties are "insuperable" (*Skinner*). Still, we believe if it be taken at its face value and an honest effort be
made to extract its native meaning, they that do so will
arrive at an unforced and reasonable interpretation. The
verse indicates who the agent is that will bring about this
tragic overthrow of Tyre and Sidon, as already indicated
in the introductory remarks on this chapter.

It is almost as though the prophet had said: The Chaldeans did it. Instead, where he seems to have been thinking
in terms of what *land* it was from which this destruction
came, he says: "the *land* of the Chaldeans, this was the
people." Where perhaps at the time when he first uttered
his prophecy the thought that would have come to the
people of Israel would have been that the Assyrians were
the ones who would seem likely to undertake a project
like overthrowing Tyre, Isaiah makes it very clear: "It was
not the Assyrians that appointed her (Tyre) for the wild
beasts." This last reference indicates that for a time at least

the overthrow is to be so complete that no man will dwell on the site of the ancient city. She will be reduced to the level of being a habitation for wild creatures (cf. 13:21f.). Where this remark referring to the Assyrians was more parenthetical in nature, the rest of the verse goes on, speaking of the Chaldeans and telling that they set their war machinery in motion: "set up their siege towers, razed her [i.e., Tyre's] palaces [or bastions] and made her a ruin." Furthermore such a thought that the Chaldeans were the nation destined to achieve certain notable results is quite in keeping with other remarks of the prophet (see 13:19 and cf. 43:14; 47:1, 5; 48:14, 20). Certainly it is in no sense out of place to indicate who the agent will be that achieves the overthrow of Tyre, or Phoenicia.

Verse 14. The section ends as it began in v. 1: "Wail [or, howl], O ships of Tarshish." Only the reason assigned for wailing in this case is a kind of paraphrase of the statement previously used: "for your stronghold is laid waste."

It should yet be indicated that where the point of view in the text seems to be that of retrospect, people looking back on what has already transpired, it should not be forgotten, that the use of the past tense in Hebrew often is what we call the "prophetic perfect" — a past that is the equivalent of a very assured future. The event in question has practically taken place. So, though we used the past tense as the Hebrew did, this whole passage should be regarded as a prophecy which tells of the impending overthrow of Tyre.

(2) Her Restoration (vv. 15-18)

This piece is prose, except for the little ditty that constitutes v. 16. We indicate at once that we cannot accept the approach which suggests that the tone of the piece (15-18) is rather ironic, whereas it was quite sober in vv. 1-14.

23:15-18 15. And it will come to pass in that day Tyre will be forgotten seventy years, like the days of one king. At the end of seventy years it will happen to Tyre as the song of the harlot has it:

16. "Take the harp, go about the city, you forgotten harlot;
Play well, sing much, that you may be remembered."

17. And it shall come to pass at the end of the seventy years,

the Lord will remember Tyre, and she will return to her business, and she will play the harlot with all the kingdoms of the world upon the face of the earth. 18. And her income and her hire will be dedicated to the Lord. It will not be stored up or hoarded; but her income shall procure abundant food and choice clothing for those who dwell before the Lord.

Verse 15. Nothing could be gained by determining the dates involved in the seventy years here mentioned as the period when Tyre lies waste. For she never really passed off the scene completely until modern times. Seventy is often a number with a significance primarily symbolic. Cf. Jer. 25:11f.; 29:10; and Dan. 9:24. If seven be the mark of a work of God and if ten signifies a measure of completion, seventy means a period during which God will have achieved his purpose in a given direction. Seventy years then means: Tyre will lie waste till her devastation has achieved it purpose in the divine disposition of things. The somewhat unusual expression "like the days of one king" had perhaps best be taken in the sense *Delitzsch* suggests, "a space of time whose conditions remain the same." While *one* king reigns there usually is no major changes in policy; things flow along smoothly, more or less in one uniform pattern. Now comes a rather unique quotation, indicative of the wide variety of the material that the prophets found they could utilize from the literary point of view. It is a ditty that perhaps might have been sung in the taverns frequented by sailors. It still constitutes a very suggestive way of bringing home the truth that is to be set forth. The ditty is a part of the piece called "The Song of the Harlot." It constitutes a suggestion how a forgotten, derelict, old harlot might seek to rehabilitate herself in her old occupation. She might take up a harp and start strumming an accompaniment to her little piece. She might wander up and down the streets advertising her wares. She is bidden to play well and to sing much. Perhaps she could bring herself to the attention of her former customers. This little ditty does have a touch of biting sarcasm, but that is limited to v. 16.

Verse 17. The point is soon grasped. The prophet makes it himself. The Lord will restore Tyre after his corrective work on her is done. Will she have been effectually corrected? Far from it. As soon as she is back on her feet she will go back to her former sinful ways. For, according to this lesson that the prophet is teaching, a city or a nation prostitutes itself when it lives for the sake of making profit. She cheapens and debases her whole existence. For the pursuit of wealth unleashes the basest tendencies in man, for "the love of money is the root of all manner of evil." If that is all that a nation lives for she becomes a harlot for the nations with whom she deals. All of them drop down to a low level of existence. They put the stain of filthy lucre on themselves. So Tyre "will return to her business" (literally: her hire). As she did before, she will do "with all the kingdoms of the world upon the face of the earth." "She will play the harlot." How could living solely for profit for one's self be described more aptly? There can be something noble and impressive about commerce. Almost invariably there is something base and debasing. This is the language of prophecy concerning commerce in Hosea, Micah and Ezekiel; and it reaches over into the New Testament: see Rev. 17:5; 18:3, 11-13.

Verse 18. In approaching this somewhat difficult verse we do well to abandon all notions like those of *Fohrer* to the effect that we have here an instance of a "perverted piety." Much more helpful is *G. A. Smith's* interpretation that we do not have a reference here to Tyre's "conversion, but something close to it." The passage speaks of a time when Tyre will begin to mend her ways. To dedicate the proceeds of harlotry to the Lord was analogous to what most nations in antiquity did, especially when the women sacrificed their virginity to some deity, and dedicated the proceeds to the deity, or were themselves temple prostitutes. Such practices were roundly forbidden in the law of Moses (Deut. 23:17f.). But Tyre at least will come to recognize what a debasing thing her commerce could become and would like to give token of her better intentions by giving of her wealth to the Lord. Something of that spirit is indicated by the passage Ezra 3:7 (cf. 1:4) when the city furnished materials for constructive work in Israel after the captivity, much as Hiram did in David's day. Some godly souls were found in the same city in New Testament days (see Acts 21:3f.). All this is analogous to what the Gentiles the world over will do in the Messianic age, according to Isa. 60:5-7; Hag. 2:8f.; Ps. 45:12. Here the means contributed to the Lord will serve to feed the hungry and clothe the naked. It is, to tell the truth, merely told what men of Tyre will do. There is no approval involved, either spoken or implied. There may even be a touch of rebuke. When men take ill-gotten gains and devote them to charity, is not condoned here.

Notes

Verse 1. The verb (howl) is masculine, the noun subject (ships) is feminine. This is explained (*GK* 110 k) as being due to the fact that when commands are given the first form that comes to mind is used, here the masculine without regard for grammatical correctness. The *min* in *mibbayith* and *mibbo'* produces a compact expression which is the equivalent of a negative result clause (*GK* 119 y).

Verse 4. The expression "the refuge of the sea" is hard to explain. Does it perhaps mean that what the sea says, may also be thought of as having been said by Sidon? The negative before *gidddalti* must be thought of as extending its influence to the next verb (*romanti*); see *GK* 152 z.

Verse 6. It is interesting to observe that the *Septuagint* substitutes Carthage for Tarshish, which may be regarded as a means whereby their translation is made contemporary. For apparently in their day Carthage was the Phoenician city to which refugees would have been transported.

Verse 7. The imperfect *yobhiluha* in a past context must describe frequent or habitual conduct; therefore "used to carry" (*Skinner*).

Verse 10. If emendations must be made, here is one that, following the lead of the *Septuagint*, might serve a purpose. *'ibhri* could perhaps have been written for *'ibhdi*, "till thy soil." But that approach is not very helpful. Phoenicia had precious little soil to till. The word *mézach*, which we have rendered "restraint" (*BDB*) originally does mean "girdle." *Koenig* thinks in terms of a dike that keeps out flooding waters. But to think in terms of free and unrestricted movement throughout one's land seems to be a good thought in the context, as we have construed the expression above.

Verse 11. The indefinite "he" (in the suffix of *yadho* and as the subject of *natah*) is used by way of anticipation, the anticipative use of a pronoun. That it refers to the Lord becomes apparent in the second half of the verse. The form *lashmidh* is a hiphil infinitive, *hashmidh,* with *le.* In combining the two the *h* is elided, almost like the article, (*GK* 53 q).

Verse 12. In the expression "daughter of Sidon" we have a genitive of apposition (*GK* 130 e).

Verse 16. *Phillips* offers an interesting and telling rhymed version of the Son of the Harlot:

> "Take up your harp,
> Mix with the throng,
> Harlot forgotten by men.
> Use all your art,
> Sing us your song,
> And you'll be remembered again!"

Verse 17. Many versions render much like *RSV*: "she will return to her hire." This is not clear. *Phillips,* whom we follow, has it: "she will return to her business."

Chapter XXIV

B. WORDS DEALING WITH GLORIOUS CONSUMMATION (Chaps. 24–27)

1. The Universal Judgment (Chap. 24)

The next section of the book of this prophet covers Chaps. 24-27, and concerns itself with the general subject of the consummation of all things from several points of view. For a while it had become quite the rule to speak of these four chapters as the Apocalypse (of Isaiah). But this mode of designation has again been dismissed as inadequate, Scott even going so far as to charge that there is "no real justification for the use of this designation. Many prefer to follow the lead of *Delitzsch*, who would prefer to call it a grand "finale," such as may close a major musical composition, and in which a number of preceding themes are made to re-echo and blend together into one harmonious whole.

Also in the case of these chapters the possibility of the authorship by Isaiah has been called into question. The majority at present are ready to attribute it to a later period. *Procksch* finds as conclusive evidence to uphold this view the fact that the sharp outlines of thought characteristic of Isaiah are missing here. But is it not true that many features of passages that describe the judgment to come fail to appear in sharp focus due to the inability of man to fully comprehend the still-veiled future? Others claim that the judgment of the world is a concept that is foreign to the pre-exilic prophets. But aside from begging the question, this claim is obviously the outgrowth of a prejudging of what prophecy can or cannot take as its subject matter in a so-called process of development. Subjective opinions enter too largely into the making of such conclusions.

We give a brief word on the possible meter of the passage as a whole. It must be admitted that to an extent, sevens or double threes prevail. But where they are arrived at by omission or alterations of the text, the wish is again father to the thought. It is better to agree that a certain type of rhythm does prevail to a certain extent, making a highly rhythmical prose. But the writer refuses to be bound by a rigid pattern. Whether it be prose in a higher strain or pure poetry may yet be debated.

Where the majority of commentators reject the possibility of authorship by Isaiah, they are almost totally unable to arrive at any unanimity as to the time that should be assigned to these chapters. This is indicative of a definite weakness of their entire position. We prefer to let the possibility of Isaiah's writing stand. No fixed time within his ministry, however can be determined.

Chapters 24-27 have this in common, that like so many other passages that deal with a future judgment they are marked by a certain mysterious twilight (*Helldunkel, Fischer*). Even in the process of unveiling the future it does not seem to lie within the power of man to discern it with any larger measure of clarity. The adjectives used by *G. A. Smith* are in place when he asserts that "the language is imaginative, enigmatic, and paradoxical." It is also to an extent true what this same writer claims as being the general impression that these words make on the layman, at least when he reads casually: it is an impression of destruction that is "weary and unintelligent." But this is merely another way of saying that this is one of the chapters on which laymen need some measure of help from those who are in a position to interpret intelligently.

But are there not after all a few indications that clearly point to a later date than that of Isaiah's days? Does not the passage 26:18 point to a time where losses of one sort or another have brought population figures so low that the passage may be thought of as expressing "a desire for growth in population"? That interpretation is merely one of several that could be extracted from the passage. Or does not 27:8 and 10 point definitely to the exile? It does in *R.S.V.* translation. But other translations, like *Phillips*, indicate that such an interpretation is merely a possibility, not a conclusive argument at all.

Though some of these arguments can be expanded at

great length at least a comparison of the following passages indicates that the thoughts of these chapters have much in common with ideas developed elsewhere by Isaiah: cf. 24:13 with 17:6; cf. 24:16b with 21:2 and 33:1; cf. 24:20 with 1:8 and 19:14; cf. 25:4b with 4:6 and 28:2; cf. 27:2-5 with 5:1ff. We are quite familiar with the argument that says such similarity may be traced to the fact that a later disciple became deeply imbued with the style of his master, so that he even used his vocabulary. But it should not be lost sight of that such similarity is even more readily understood as stemming from the fact that the good master wrote both series of passages himself.

By way of summary it may yet be indicated that the general theme of these chapters is "the day of the Lord." Besides, all the instances where the past tense it used, may well be classed as being what the Hebrew grammar calls "prophetic perfects," perfects that should be translated as lying in the future, that is simple futures or a translation may be used like: "The Lord is about to. . . ."

We offer a somewhat more detailed outline of the chapter under the caption of the *Universal Judgment.* In support of the claim that this judgment is universal, note already in the first six verses how often the word "earth" occurs as the object against which the judgment is directed.

a. The Judgment as Such (vv. 1-13)

    (1) The Lord Administers It (v. 1)

    (2) It Is Universal and Thorough (vv. 2-4)

    (3) Its Cause — the Pollution of the Earth by Man (vv. 5-6)

    (4) Every Agency That Contributes to Gracious Living — Like Wine — Will Be Removed (vv. 7-9)

    (5) An Example of Judgment — a Typical City (vv. 10-12)

    (6) The Thoroughness with Which the Judgment Will Be Administered (v. 13)

b. The Glorification of God by the Remnant Who Survive the Judgment (the prophet cannot share any optimistic outlook as yet) (vv. 14-16)

c. How Complete and Inescapable the Judgment Will Be (vv. 17-20)

d. After Disposing of the Rivals to His Greatness (angels and princes) the Lord Will Reign in Glory on Mt. Zion (vv. 21-23)

a. *The Judgment as Such (vv. 1-13)*

24:1-13 1. Lo, the Lord is about to empty the earth and lay it waste;

he is about to turn the surface of it upside down
and to scatter its inhabitants.

2. The same fate will befall people and priest, the slave and his master;
the maid and her mistress, the buyer and the seller;
the lender and the borrower, the creditor and the debtor.

3. The earth will be utterly emptied and completely plundered;
for the Lord has spoken the word.

4. The earth will grieve and wither away;
the world will languish and wither away;
men of high standing among the people of the earth will languish;

5. seeing that the earth under its inhabitants had become polluted;
for they had transgressed the laws, changed the ordinances;
and had broken the covenant of ancient times.

6. Therefore a curse will devour the earth,
and its inhabitants will pay the penalty;
therefore the inhabitants of the earth will be consumed by fire,
and but few mortals will be left.

7. The juice of the grape will mourn, the vine will languish;
all who were merry of heart will sigh.

8. The sound of the tambourine will be stilled;
the noise of the exultant will cease;
the sound of the harps will be stilled.

9. No more will men drink wine with singing;
strong drink will be bitter for those who drink it.

10. The empty city will be broken down;
every house will be closed so that men cannot enter.

11. An outcry because of lack of wine will be in the streets;
all joy will reach its eventide;
all gladness of the earth will depart.

12. All that will be left in the city will be ruins;
every gate will be battered into ruins.

13. For thus it will be in the midst of the earth among the peoples,
as when an olive tree is beaten,
or at the gleaning of the grapes when the vintage is over.

(1) The Lord Administers It (v. 1)

Verse 1. A scene of judgment on the broadest possible scope is depicted, a judgment that lies entirely in the future. The Lord is the one who presides at the judgment, even for that matter, disposes of it all alone in his own sovereign authority. In v. 1 the figure seems to be that of a man cleaning a dirty vessel: the bowl is the earth; men are the filth in it that must be removed. With consumate ease, the Judge picks up the vessel, turns it upside down, and empties it. Where the Hebrew uses the idiom of "turning the face" upside down (which is far more meaningful than "to twist its surface, *RSV*) we used the word "surface" for "face" to cover our own point of view. In the process all the inhabitants are scattered. Where may they stand when the Almighty deals thus with the earth? One must catch the grand imagery of the prophet.

(2) It Is Universal and Thorough (vv. 2-4)

Verse 2. To convey the thought that there will be none who are exempt from the judgment — for the Lord is the omnipotent Ruler of the universe — six classes of persons are grouped in pairs, taking a person of one class and listing the natural counter-part. "People and priest" (cf. Hos. 4:9) is a pair that moves in the area of religion. "Slave and master" operates on the level of extreme social distinctions. "Maid and mistress" belongs in the same category. "Buyer and seller" takes us into the vast field of business transactions. "The lender and the borrower, the creditor and the debtor" moves over into the area of more involved financial transactions. But these last terms do not indicate a late period in Israel's history where trade and business were replacing agriculture and crafts. For these basic forms of business transaction prevail even in the simpler economy to quite an extent.

Verse 3. This verse rounds out the first picture by reiterating the thought that this judgment is all-inclusive. The dirty vessel will have no remnants of filth clinging to it; the emptying and the plundering will be utter and complete. All this is another way of saying that after many preliminary and minor judgments will have been experienced on the earth, they will be climaxed by a judgment that brings all judgments to a close. This judgment is the apex of judgments. It is at this point that the inevitability of it all is indicated by one of the formulas that the prophets offer from time to time to indicate that a future event is utterly inevitable: "for the Lord has spoken the word." Behind the events of history lies the powerful creative word of God that makes history to come to pass as it does.

Verse 4. Leaving the figure of the dirty vessel, the prophet now speaks in terms of a mighty blast that has gone forth from the mouth of the judge, like a devastating hot wind (sirocco) that blows from the desert. As a result the earth as a whole grieves and withers away; or the inhabited world (for that is the meaning of *tébhel*) languishes and withers away. But not only the material world as such but the very people in it will pass away under the same judgment: "Men of high standing among the people of the earth" will feel the same effects. At some point in history the impotence of man as a creature of God will be openly displayed. This final judgment will be the occasion.

(3) Its Cause — the Pollution of the Earth by Man (vv. 5-6)

Verse 5. But we are not to imagine that such results come about in an arbitrary way. A moral order prevails in an earth where human beings are to be found. Judgment comes to avenge and to rectify grievous moral disorders. That disorder may be described as a pollution, which the people on the face of the earth have dropped down upon it making it vile and in need of a thorough cleansing (cf. Jer. 3:9; Num. 35:33; also Gen. 6:11). Or, since the measure and evidence of man's misdeeds is the divinely given law or the ordinances, it was the breaking of these that ultimately brings on the judgment of God. Or, that which is wrong with the earth may still be defined in other terms. There was a "covenant of ancient times" (this is a more serviceable and accurate translation than "everlasting covenant") that had been set up between God and men. One may here refer to Gen. 9:9, 12f. as a formalized expression of the terms on which God deals with men since the times of the great flood. One may also adduce at this point Rom 2:14ff. as a reference to the natural law written on man's heart and functioning even where there has been no specific revelation as was granted to Israel. Basic insight into fundamental moral issues granted by God to man makes man responsible and answerable to the Judge, so as to be without excuse.

Verse 6. Still further aspects of this great all-inclusive judgment are touched upon. Men by their polluting misdeeds have brought down upon this earth a "curse" which devours nothing less than the earth itself. Curses spoken by men are almost without exception futile and ineffective. The curse pronounced by God blasts the earth with its fierce fire. Or, to underscore the complete justice of all acts of God in judgment, it may also be stated thus: its inhabitants will pay the penalty." Not that laws operate automatically; but in the moral order of the universe God functions with total justice and deals with men as they have fully deserved. Letting the figure of the fire come to its full force, we find it finally described as consuming "the inhabitants of the earth." When the scene closes on the note that "few mortals will be left," this seems to clash with the concept of the universality of the judgment which has been stressed till now. But apparently the author is not so much concerned with total consistency or mathematical accuracy. He does want to express in some way the thought that some constructive results can come out of the judgment.

(4) Every Agency That Contributes to Gracious Living — Like Wine — Will Be Removed (vv. 7-9)

Verse 7. A few more aspects of the judgment may be brought in to round out the picture. Every aspect of gracious living that may seem to help to make life attractive will also be removed from the scene. Both in this verse and in v. 9 the loss of the fruit of the vine is dwelt on at length (patterned after Joel 1:10f.). This need not be considered as an indication that at the time the people of Israel were altogether too much given to the use of wine. But wine is considered from the point of view of being an exhilarating agent, not necessarily a reprehensible use, if due moderation be observed. The "juice of the grape" would seem to refer to the juice within the skin of the berry while the clusters still hang on the vine. The blasting effect of the judgment will cause this juice to dry up. The plant as such, the "vine," will languish, too. "All those who were merry of heart will sigh," apparently over the loss of the wine and the vine. There is no need of putting a critical construction on these words for a land where wine was practically a necessity, though occasionally an abused gift.

Verse 8. Harmless, merry feasts seem to be thought of as one of the losses occasioned by the judgment. Happy shouts and gay music are not neccessarily something evil. They may be thought of, as we often think of them as parts of gracious living.

Verse 9. Again the point of view of v. 6 comes to the forefront. It is assumed that some persons may escape the judgment. Should they have wine left to drink, in those dismal times there will be no singing accompanying the drinking of the wine. In fact, all strong drink will have lost its charm and "be bitter for those who drink it." Judgment casts its gloom on every aspect and activity of life.

(5) An Example of Judgment — a Typical City (vv. 10-12)

Verses 10, 11. Another illustration of the completeness and nature of the anticipated judgment is offered. Take any city. The language used is vague. For what city is "the empty city," or "the city of chaos" (*RSV*) or "the city of confusion" (*KJ*)? Any representative city may be thought of, perhaps a famous capital like Nineveh, perhaps Babylon. But why call it "an empty city"? To tell the truth, for all its imposing grandeur, any metropolis really is quite empty of true values. Most of its imposing aspects are hollow or shallow. Therefore these cities cannot continue in greatness; they cannot last. Therefore it is quite proper to make the claim that any such city "will be broken down." To carry the picture a bit farther, "every house will be closed so that men cannot enter." Two possibilities are involved in this statement. It either means that the ruins in evidence on every hand are piled high as to virtually obstruct the entrance into every house — a mild hyperbole. Or it could mean that they who are left in the destroyed city have barricaded the entrance so as to prevent brigands and marauders from forcing an entrance. A sorry picture when all that can be said of once famous cities is that they are dismal heaps of barricaded ruins. This is practically what v. 12 says. But first v. 11 draws attention to the fact that every last indication of what might be joy or gladness will be stamped out in the course of the judgment. Some will lament that not a decent drink of wine is to be had anywhere in the city. Joy as such will have faded out, or to employ a more colorful figure, it "will reach its eventide." Or to resort to still another figure: "All gladness of the earth will depart." Gladness has picked up its belongings and has moved away. We would say that gloom hangs over the whole dismal city.

Verse 12. Only a man who has seen a thoroughly ruined city can appreciate this verse: "All that will be left in the city will be ruins." The gates will present this gloomy sight in a most striking way, for they were the centers of city activity in days of old.

(6) The Thoroughness with Which the Judgment Will Be Administered (v. 13)

Verse 13. To conclude the dismal description, this verse resorts to a comparison that first reminds us that a world-wide situation is being thought of ("in the midst of the earth among the peoples") and that very little of even the least value can still be found anywhere. For it is all like as when "an olive tree is beaten." If you recheck on the tree the olives still to be found are negligible in quantity. Or if a similar check be made on the grapes "when the vintage is over." Any search made will not even be worth the effort. An effective way of pointing up the thoroughness with which the judgment did its work. The same figure was used in 17:5f. with a little more of detail but with the same general purpose.

b. The Glorification of God by the Remnant Who Survived the Judgment (vv. 14-16)

24:14-16 14. These will lift up their voices and will shout for joy;
over the majesty of the Lord they will exult from the West.
15. Therefore glorify the Lord in the East,
and in the coastlands of the sea, the name of the Lord God of Israel.
16. From the ends of the earth we have heard songs: "Glory to the righteous!"
But I said: "I pine away, I pine away; Woe is me!
The treacherous will deal treacherously;
the treacherous will deal very treacherously."

This portion consists of a glorification of God by the remnant, apparently, who have survived the judgment, a glorification in which the prophet is not yet able to join, for there are not sufficient grounds for such optimism.

Verse 14. The reader quite naturally is puzzled as he begins to read. Who are the "these"? The simplest answer is to go back to the nearest noun that could serve as antecedent. Some "peoples" are referred to in v. 13, who apparently constitute the remnant after the divine judgment has done its work. These people will recognize the constructive purpose that lay behind the great destructive work of judgment. They will see that one result of even a well-nigh universal judgment is that the righteous will be vindicated and by such vindication the "majesty of the Lord" will be openly displayed in the earth. But for the present this glorification is thought of as arising only "from the West." The reason for this geographical distinction is that in the next verse God's praises are thought of as arising from the other geographical extreme, the East. By touching both limits, according to a common approach that the Hebrew idiom makes, all that lies between is included. So this becomes a mode of indicating that world-wide praise will arise when men begin to see God's comprehensive constructive purposes in judgment. This is the scope also of the following statement of v. 15: "and in the coastlands, the name of the Lord God of Israel." The area referred to is the entire Mediterranean region, the usual meaning of the term "coastlands."

Verse 16. Now the burden of the songs of praise of the remnant is revealed. It is, "Glory to the righteous." Though it might seem most natural to translate the word involved as "the Righteous One" (*RSV*), especially in a song of praise, we still much prefer to let it refer to righteous men as such, who have maintained their integrity and have faithfully held to the Lord God of Israel. These will be thought worthy of mention, for they will be the only ones who will survive the great judgment. A similar point of view, where the word "righteous" again refers to a class of men appears in 26:2.

But it would seem that this praise on the part of the remnant is a bit premature. For that is the way in which we construe the exclamation that follows. It as as though the prophet would erect a safeguard against a hasty optimism when men begin to see at least some of the constructive purposes behind divine judgment. It is as though the prophet said, Do not soon become too optimistic about how men react. Many of the seemingly positive reactions to God's judgments are hasty, superficial, and soon erased. So in his grief over this prospect the prophet exclaims: "I pine away"! The sin and the sinners that he saw round about him were so deeply involved in their wrong conduct that they would go on, in spite of all that the judgment might have taught them, in their evil course and run into destruction. In other words: "The treacherous will deal treacherously, the treacherous will deal very treacherously." This impenitent attitude of theirs pains him deeply and impels him to exclaim : "I pine away, I pine away; woe is me!"

It must be admitted that v. 16 is extremely difficult to interpret, especially if one considers current translation. *KJ* renders it: "My leanness, my leanness," a meaning which the words involved may well bear, but which may be construed to mean as *RSV* does, in a masterful translation: "I pine away." For further possibilities see the *Notes* at the end of the chapter.

c. How Complete and Inescapable the Judgment Will Be (vv. 17-20)

24:17-20 17. Terror, pit, and trap will be upon you, O inhabitant of the earth!

18. And it shall come to pass that he who flees from the rumor of the terror will fall into the pit;

and he that clambers up out of the pit will be caught in the trap.
For the windows of heaven will be opened,
and the foundations of the earth will tremble.
19. The earth will be utterly broken down;
the earth will be utterly broken asunder;
the earth will shake exceedingly.
20. The earth will reel badly like a drunkard;
it will sway violently like a watchman's hut.
Her transgressions will lie heavy upon her;
she will fall and not rise again.

Verse 17. This section of the chapter forcefully indicates how much the idea of universal judgment was upon the writer's mind. In vv. 1-13 he had already dealt comprehensively and effectively with the subject. Having turned to a feature that would occasion at least some praise (vv. 14-16) he cannot but come back again to the picture of judgment, which so completely occupies his mind. The final judgment is a vast and comprehensive thing. But as for v. 17 as such, the prophet, by a striking alliteration, which we have only partly reproduced in translation, indicates how the judgment may be described as three terrible monsters rushing in upon man, so to speak. The first is sheer "terror." How this reaction may seize upon men at times of great disaster is only too clear. When the next calamity is described as the "pit," the comparison is borrowed from the language of hunting or trapping. But by adding this figure to the first the thought is advanced: There simply is no escape from the prevailing evils. And should one manage to clamber out of the pit, he is caught in a trap hidden under leaves; and so the dangers that threaten are inescapable. As v. 17 concludes this is the lot facing every "inhabitant of the earth." The basic figure here used appears also in Amos 5:19 and Jer. 48:43f.

Verse 18. This verse adds two other forms of description to clinch the point. Thinking back to the days when another universal calamity involved the earth, and the form that destruction took, the prophet, borrowing the terminology of that disaster, says that "the windows of heaven will be opened" (Gen. 7:11; 8:2). Or, to think in terms of the unleashing of the terrible forces of nature, Isaiah brings in by way of comparison a mighty earthquake: "the foundations of the earth will tremble." Only they who have lived through such an experience will understand the terrible terror that grips the human heart on such an occasion.

Verse 19. But since this appears to be a description of the final judgment, something in excess of familiar earthquakes is here brought into the picture. That the ultimate of judgment is involved is indicated by the use of phrases which practically demand the use of all-inclusive adverbs, "utterly, utterly, exceedingly." Attaching this verse in thought for a moment to v. 1 we might think of the Lord as shaking the vessel in his hands with the utmost of violence.

Verse 20. But even these extreme statements are not to be thought of as having done full justice to the case in hand. So, continuing along the same line, or perhaps even outdoing what has already been said, the writer describes the earth as reeling badly as might a drunkard, or as swaying violently in a strong wind-storm, as a fragile watchman's hut out in the open field might sway after it is abandoned, or is about to collapse entirely. The mental picture that the prophet had of the judgment and that caused him to dwell so insistently on the over-great terror of the event must have been overpowering. It still reminds us that men may be much inclined to underestimate the scope of this great event.

By way of concluding this part of the picture, the author reverts to the cause of it all, which he had dealt with in a preliminary fashion in vv. 5-6. There is a deep moral cause for such a judgment. This cause is the "transgressions" of mankind, which lie heavy upon her. Their mass has become more than man can live under or God can tolerate. The judgment must strike. There is a note of finality about the conclusion of the verse and the section: "[The earth] will fall and not rise again." This is the last judgment of this present world-order.

But one is not to become engrossed in the negative, or punitive, aspect of this judgment. There are higher considerations. There will be a glorious consummation. Of this the last section speaks.

d. After Disposing of the Rivals to His Greatness, the Lord Will Reign on Mt. Zion (vv. 21-23)

24:21-23 21. And it will come to pass in that day, the Lord will punish the host of heaven in heaven,
and the kings of the earth upon the earth.
22 And they will be gathered together as prisoners are gathered in a pit;
and they will be shut up in a prison.
And after many days they will be tried.
23. And the pale moon will be ashamed [red in the face],
and the sun confounded.
For the Lord of hosts will reign on Mount Zion and in Jerusalem,
and before his elders glory will be manifest.

Verse 21. Still judgment! But now the more glorious aspects of it, especially in so far as the passage notes how high and mighty they are that are subject also to the judgment of the Lord of hosts. Something of an insoluble mystery is involved here, the same mystery of which I Cor. 6:3 speaks when it reminds men of the church that they shall judge angels, or when Rev. 20:10 speaks of Satan being cast into the lake of fire and brimstone, and the many kindred passages that could be adduced. For the victims of judgment now being referred to are "the host of heaven." In seeking to determine who these are, it hardly seems appropriate to begin with the idea set forth in Job 4:18, where the Lord is spoken of as charging his angels with error. For that passage is highly poetic and not adapted for determining the precise doctrine of Scripture. Of course, the expression, "host of heaven," as such could refer to the stars. Here that use of the term seems out of place. It could also refer to fallen angels, who certainly would be more suitable candidates for the judgment of God than any others. To think in terms of the guardian angels of the nations — referred to in Dan. 10:13f.; also in Ecclus. 17:14 (17); but not in Ps. 82:1ff — would in this connection again be somewhat dubious. Are we justified in supposing that these mighty guardian angels might have failed properly to administer the obligations laid upon them in this unusual assignment? A very strange angelology would result from such an approach. Better by far to think of the fallen angels, who, even after their fall were granted some measure of freedom of action, as Christ's clash with the demons and their remarks clearly indicate (Matt. 8:29, etc.), but whose judgment is nevertheless inevitable. Therefore we identify the "host of heaven" with the "powers of evil which have been activating the course of evil upon the earth" (*Fitch*). But it should not be forgotten that these are mighty potent forces, as *Milton* in *Paradise Lost* is wont to portray them, as do also the Scriptures themselves. They constitute one class against whom the Lord will display his sovereign power in a manner downright glorious. Then there are, as second class, "the kings of the earth upon the earth." No matter how mighty they may have been, or what epithet of greatness may have been appended to their names, they must submit to the judgment, for it is universal. It may be that when it is asserted of the first group that they will be judged "in heaven" and of the second, that they will be judged "upon the earth," that this indicates two consecutive phases of the judgment in two different locales; one in the heavens where these beings moved about, the other on earth where kings reigned and sinned. For it is involved in this form of statement, yea, in the very nature of judgment, that misdeeds that call for judgment have been perpetrated. It certainly would be quite an easy thing to furnish indictments one after the other, of the rulers that reigned mightily upon the earth. Their mistakes and crimes in many a case were of major proportion.

Verse 22. An earlier procedure before the final judgment seems to be spoken of here. Perhaps we have only a measure of rhetorical detail involved here. Or are there successive stages in the final judgment? Who would venture to pronounce with finality on these issues. As the sequence here given runs, first, all those who are to stand trial, angels, kings, and perhaps all others involved, are to be "assembled together as prisoners are gathered in a pit." This part of the description might be no more than a human device calculated to make clear that there will be successive stages in the procedure involved. Then after all these have been gathered, "they will be shut up in prison." A kindred thought is to be found in Rev. 20:1-3, 7-9. We would be asking silly questions if we inquired where a prison large enough to hold this vast assembly could be found. But the concluding statement of the verse does definitely seem to suggest that the successive steps mentioned will actually be taken. And so all these will be tried only "after many days." The purpose of such a delay seems to elude us, for some of these great impending events will hardly be understood by any man until they transpire. But the judgment is inevitable.

Verse 23. Even the heavenly bodies will be involved in the universal judgment, as also the words of Jesus indicate (Matt. 24:29). In this case their lot will be that they fade out, for "the very powers of heaven will be shaken." Only here the figure used implies their being abashed that they have such a pale light over against the superlative brightness of the glory of the Lord which will predominate over all things on that day. For now comes the climax toward which the whole scene has been building up: "The Lord will reign on Mount Zion and in Jerusalem." All inferior forms of rule and authority must bow out before him who has "all authority in heaven and on earth." True, here the prophet does not see the broadest implications of the Lord's dominion, for he centers it in Jerusalem, and more particularly in Zion. Yet his statement is not erroneous for Zion is the center historically from which his rule does emanate. That such rule is a particular manifestation of great glory, as the Revelation of John and other Scriptures abundantly indicate is the note on which this passage closes. The language describing this phase of the case is borrowed from Exod. 24:9-11, where the elders of Israel, together with Moses, on the mountain of Sinai witnessed a particular manifestation of divine glory and lived to tell of it. All the redeemed will be witnesses of what the elders saw in their day, as it is described in Matt. 25:32: "When the Son of man shall come in his glory and all the angels with him. . . ." This is the crowning aspect of the great judgment, the universal judgment, as Isaiah saw it in his day. The thought expressed is kindred to that found in Ps. 104; Isa. 4:5f; 60:19; Ps. 29:9; 86:9.

Notes

Verse 4. It may be noted that *tebhel* has no article, which is an indication that the word is being treated as a proper noun, even as English usage sometimes capitalizes and writes "West" (cf. v 14). Cf. *KS* 293 b. The first two verbs ignore the customary *waw* consecutive construction, being synonymns (*KS* 370 h).

Verse 5. The subject of this verse being identical with that of v. 4 in a "verbal sentence (*Verbalsatz*) makes this to be a circumstantial clause (therefore "seeing that . . ."). Cf. *KS* 362 n.

Verse 9. The *be* in *bashshir* marks accompaniment (*KS* 402 s).

Verse 10. "Empty city" literally says in Hebrew: "city of emptiness," or "city of *tohu*." The word *tohu* first appears in Gen. 1:2, describing the initial state of the earth as being "empty." Here the same basic thought seems to prevail in the sense that big cities of this world are void of true abiding values. But *tohu* is also used as a designation of idols, who are vain things (cf. I Sam. 12:21). But this translation is far-fetched in this context. The expression could mean "the city of confusion" or "the wasted city," thinking in terms of what the city involved is going to be. But that seems a most stilted way of expressing oneself. *Mibbo'* involves a *min* of separation, which is the equivalent of an infinitive clause of result (cf. *KS* 406 n and *GK* 119 x).

Verse 16. In this verse *razi-li* is very difficult. Both *KJ* and *Luther* favor what the root could mean: "my leanness," which says nothing to the present-day reader. The translation "my mystery" merely perplexes and can produce only an artificial meaning. *RSV* is most commendable by way of interpretation.

Verse 17. The alliteration referred to above runs thus in the original: *pachadh, waphachath, waphach.*

Verse 18. For "windows of heaven" the Hebrew has "the windows from on high." The word *marom* (high) however is frequently used for "heaven."

Verse 19. *Ro'ah* as absolute infinitive *kal* is quite abnormal but so formed to agree with the vowel pattern of the following verb (cf. *GK* 67 o). Besides, it is a *kal* absolute infinitive used with a *hithpolal* verb, a construction which is not too uncommon (*GK* 113 w).

Verse 22. The *min* of *merobh* is a *min* temporal (*KS* 401 f).

Verse 23. We heartily disagree with those who see similarity in the second half of this verse and the so-called "accession psalms." Or an indication that here Jahweh "mounts his throne in triumph." *Malakh* may mean "becomes king" but never could Israel believe that Yahweh had abdicated.

P. Lohman, in *ZATW* 1917-1918 (pp. 1-58) offers a very learned article, treating Chaps. 24-27 as though we could even now determine what individual lyrical units originally made up these chapters, and attempt to show how they were then pieced together by later redactors. This essay abounds in unproved and unprovable assumptions and contributes little to the constructive interpretation of these chapters.

Chapter XXV

2. A Song of Praise for the Universal Judgment (Chap. 25)

In this chapter the broader context should not be ignored. The materials of the whole book have not been thrown together carelessly. Our chapter follows upon the account of the universal judgment. If a song of praise follows, even without an indication that the song is related to such a judgment, the obvious conclusion is nevertheless that God is being praised for this judgment. We claim this in spite of the fact that the occasion for the praise offered appears to be the overthrow of an ungodly city. For the city's overthrow and the world's judgment are the same subject regarded from two different points of view.

A certain typical prophetic vagueness pervades the chapter. Differently stated, the song in question does not aim to be so specific as to be applicable only to one given historical situation. It has therefore been called "an ideal account." It may be said that it reflects the whole attitude of the "alien world toward Israel" as well as "God's judgment upon it." The church of God may sing this song with perfect propriety at the final judgment. For the issues will be the same then as at any time prior to that judgment.

Although the prevailing trend is to interpret the chapter as not stemming from the pen of Isaiah, it appears to us that they who claim that "the obscurities have not nearly been cleared up," and that, therefore, it behooves all to refrain from making "final or dogmatic opinions" on this issue are in the right.

It will not be out of place to remind ourselves that, for that matter, Chaps. 25–27 "stand in the front rank of evangelical prophecy" (G. A. Smith). The aspect of the "evangelical" that is under consideration is, in this case, the clear hope of eternal life reflected in v. 8.

Quite frequently in songs of this sort — which Isaiah, by the way, delights in providing for his people to encourage them the more to offer due praise — a sort of "introductory rubric" is offered like, "It will be said on that day" (cf. 25:9; 26:1; 27:2). The absence of such a rubric signifies nothing in particular.

One problem that should at least be briefly touched upon is the question: Does this song (vv. 1-5) interrupt the sequence of things? For in 24:21-23 the effects of the judgment are under consideration, even as they are in 25:6-8. Our song then could be regarded as an intrusion, as has been very frequently claimed. However, who are we to determine at this time how long a writer in days of old may dwell on a given subject? Who are we to lay down the rules for him, demanding that he dare not be moved at a given point to break forth into song because he is deeply touched by the subject he has in hand. And who may decree that, having given vent to his feelings, he may not with perfect propriety resume the subject that had been under consideration.

We present an outline for the chapter.

a. Praise of God for the Overthrow of the Ungodly City That Had Oppressed His People (vv. 1-5)
b. The Good Things That God Has Prepared for His People (vv. 6-8)
c. The Overthrow of Moab, a Typical Enemy of God's People (vv. 9-12)

a.   *Praise of God for the Overthrow of the Ungodly City That Had Oppressed His People (vv. 1-5)*

25:1-5   1. O Lord, thou art my God,
I will exalt thee, I will praise thy name;
for thou hast done marvelous things,
plans formed long ago were carried out in utmost faithfulness.
2. For thou hast made of the city a heap,
of the fortified town a collapsed ruin;
the citadel of aliens that it is a city-unit no longer;
never will it be rebuilt.
3. Therefore powerful peoples will give honor to thee;
towns of ruthless nations will fear thee.

4 For thou hast become a place of refuge for the lowly,
a place of refuge for the poor in his distress,
a refuge from the storm and a shade from the heat.
For the angry threatenings of the ruthless are only like a rainstorm beating against a wall.
5. Like the burning heat of the sun on parched ground thou
art wont to quell the noise of strangers, —
yes, like the burning heat quelled by the shadow of a cloud,
so the triumph-songs of the ruthless are subdued.

Verse 1. The nation Israel is the speaker throughout this song. It might have been a little more to the point to translate: "O Lord, who art my God, I will exalt. . . ." For a separate point is not being made of the fact that the Lord is the speaker's God. That thought is merely being injected by way of indicating why the speaker turns to God. However, a certain exuberance of the spirit of praise is in evidence when thought is piled upon thought ("exalt," "praise"), and when the things achieved by God are enumerated as being so many and so varied, as these five verses indicate. First, quite naturally, come several summary statements, such as: "Thou hast done marvelous things." The point is that God's comprehensive judgment is a very marvelous achievement, causing the thoughtful to marvel endlessly at the magnitude of the achievements involved. Note similar thoughts expressed in Exod. 15:11; Isa. 9:6. Another effective statement of the case follows: "Plans formed long ago were carried out in utmost faithfulness." May we say with reverence: God engages in long-range planning; his plans have been well thought through and long thought through. Yet the literal translation of the phrase involved, "from afar off," could also imply the thought that his plans seemed remote in the sense of difficulty of achievement. In any case, when the judgment is carried through, a carefully-contemplated objective will have been reached. And, since these plans were transmitted to men, it is important to note that God kept the promise that was implied, and so the meaning of the expression "in utmost faithfulness" becomes apparent.

Verse 2. The negative part of the universal judgment is treated first. "Thou hast made of the city a heap, of the fortified town a collapsed ruin." The question immediately raised by this claim is: What city? The statement is vague, perhaps intentionally so. The writer does not refer to any city in particular, because any representative city of the long list of historical metropolises may be thought of. They all are exponents of the spirit of worldly, godless empires; they all stand in opposition to the city of God; they all are doomed to be overthrown. Nineveh or Babylon could serve as excellent examples of what the prophet had in mind. Their greatness had been challenging. Their hostility to the people of God had been strongly in evidence. They were reduced to a "heap" and a "ruin." To see these "citadels of aliens" fall "never to be rebuilt" displays the magnificent power of God in a very striking fashion.

Verse 3. When centers of world-power fall into ruins, nations cannot help but understand what the Lord is doing. Besides, they are impressed by what they see. So v. 3 lists the positive results that grow out of the understanding of the judgment that God has wrought. The "powerful peoples" referred to are the Gentile nations as such, who play the part of onlookers and are not totally devoid of spiritual understanding. They see that the God who directs the destinies of all nations has acted, and they "honor" him for it. Besides, over against the towns that fell are towns still standing that beheld the tragic overthrow of the centers of wickedness, and they "fear" the Lord as a result. Join "honor" and "fear" together, as has been aptly remarked, and you have worship. So, just as Israel should praise God for his judgments, so will the nations, according to the measure of insight that they possess.

Verse 4. The listing of positive achievements continues. When mighty cities that are the heads of empires fall, then the oppression that these cities and empires engaged in come to an end. The poor folks that were oppressed get relief. Various names are employed to describe these persons: "the lowly," and "the poor." When used with reference to people within the people of God these terms are usually the equivalent of "the godly." Concern for such persons is characteristic of the Lord God of Israel. Kindly thoughts for those who suffer social wrongs are often expressed by the Scriptures. It was the revealed religion of the Old and New Testaments that taught men such concern. The afflicted had taken refuge in the Lord; they found that in due time he truly became for them "a place of refuge." The oppression that had been suffered is described by two terms, "storm" and "heat." We still employ the same figures. Only now it is shown that by the overthrow of the tyrant powers these forces of evil became ineffective: "for the angry threatenings of the ruthless are only like a rainstorm beating against a wall." This comparison is usually faulted as being difficult, if not impossible, to understand, and so textual emendations are resorted to. We believe the force of the comparison can be readily caught if an "only" be inserted. The outbursts of passion, or "the angry threatenings," by which the ruthless express their rage become quite futile when the Lord has set about to deliver his own. They do as little damage as the average storm, beating against a normal wall, does by merely washing the face of it. The threatenings of the storm were fierce; the net effect was nil. We regard this as an effective comparison.

Verse 5. This is another effective and comforting description of the relief that the Lord affords to those poor afflicted people that make him their "place of refuge." The heat-figure of v. 4 is explored. What before was described as the "angry threatenings of the ruthless" is now described as "the burning heat of the sun on parched ground" or, as "the noise of strangers." For, on the one hand it can become very uncomfortable, like extreme heat, and, on the other, it usually involves some form or other of boisterous and noisy demonstration. But as relief from burning can be effected by "the shadow of a cloud" and much relief is experienced by the one who had suffered from the heat, with equal ease and effectiveness he can relieve them that place their hope in him. So the catalog of things to be achieved by the judgment of the Almighty is brought to an effective conclusion by the assertion that "so the triumph-songs of the ruthless are subdued." The Hebrew merely says "songs" but without a doubt their "triumph-songs" of exultation over the achievement of their ungodly plans are

meant. Once they shouted with fierce and ungodly glee.
When God is done with them, they and their shoutings
will be quite subdued. A tremendous sigh of relief runs
through this passage. Many are the oppressions that stem
from the domination which "the city" practices. But the
Lord will deliver those that are afflicted thereby. Then
will they praise him with songs like this, provided long in
advance by the pen of the prophet.

The positive side of vv. 4-5 still moved in terms of relief
from evils and so was half negative. Now, vv. 6-8, comes
a listing of the good things that God has prepared for his
people, but it, too, will revert to the negative, in a sense, in
v. 8.

b. The Good Things That God Has Prepared for His People (vv. 6-8)

25:6-8 6. And the Lord of hosts will make for all peoples a
feast of delicacies on this mountain, a feast of wine well
aged, of delicacies rich in marrow, of wine poured off clear from
its settlings. 7. And he will destroy on this mountain the veil that
veils all people, the blanket that blankets all people. 8. He will
swallow down death forever. And the Lord Yahweh will wipe
away the tears from all faces; and the disgrace of his people he
will remove all over the earth; for the Lord has so promised.

Verse 6. The blessings of that new day are now described
in terms of a feast, a rather common figure in the Scriptures.
The guests are "all people." Apparently they are come to
worship the Lord, for the feast takes place "on this mountain," which, of course, is Zion. The feast then is a sacrificial feast, as in Ps. 22:26f. The New Testament takes up
this figure and develops it more fully; see Matt. 8:11;
22:2ff.; Luke 14:15ff. The Hebrew expression used is "feast
of fat things" (*RSV*). Since the East in days of old
rarely had meat in its diet, fat was especially prized as a
delicacy. That accounts for our above translation. We
might have said with *Kissane*: "rich viands." In any case,
this is clear, that all who come to worship are regarded
as the Lord's guests. The wall of separation between Israel
and the Gentiles is no more. Some of the items on the
menu for the feast are described to lend color and interest

to the picture. If the wine is stressed first as being particularly good, that may be due to the fact that a feast is called a *mishteh*, "a drinking," but without any unwholesome connotation. The wine is well aged and therefore at a peak of good flavor. The delicacies are rich in marrow, for the nutritive quality of marrow was rated rather high by the ancients and bones left from a meal were often broken open to get at the marrow and eat it. The second reference to the wine shows merely the care with which, as it were, the Lord prepared this feast: "wine [was] poured off clear from its settlings," being allowed to age long, but guarded in the pouring so as not to make it murky.

Verse 7. The second item mentioned is the removal of a veil from all peoples. This activity also is associated with "this mountain," that is to say, applies only to those who have come to acknowledge and worship the true God. The "veil" could be the symbol of mourning, as it sometimes is: see II Sam. 15:30; 19:5; Jer. 14:3; and that interpretation would bring this statement in line with the second half of v. 8. But the New Testament reference to the veil, found in II Cor. 3:15, rather would suggest that the veil and the blanket signify ignorance. For as *Fischer* puts it: "The knowledge of Yahweh will be the noblest joy of the nations . . . and they too will see his glory." When two figures are used (veil and blanket) it would seem to argue for a state of dense blindness before these obstacles are eliminated.

Verse 8. No particular pattern is being followed in the enumeration of the blessings bestowed on the nations. Just a chance assortment of good illustrations is being sought. But the blessing now mentioned startles us as presenting a point of view which is entirely new, "He will swallow down death for ever." We have kept the verb used in the Hebrew (swallow) for its color. Some versions say "destroy," which is, of course, what is actually meant. With so little having been said on the subject of the hereafter in the Old Testament Scriptures the sudden advance in insight marked by this passage is downright overwhelming: just one concise and pregnant statement. The ancient foe of mankind will be utterly disposed of. Who till now would have dared to hope that? But here it is, boldly and unmistakably set forth. Paul quotes it with a slight variation in I Cor. 15:54. Some feel, strangely even *Kissane*, that the statement can refer to nothing more than the life of the Jewish state. But *Mauchline* appears to be much nearer to the full truth involved: "This is surely the hope of immortality." There is more material on this score in the Old Testament than many suppose. Cf. also Hos. 13:14. Isaiah 65:20 begins to point in this same direction. So does Dan. 12:2. In the New Testament we may yet refer to Rev. 7:17 and 21:4.

Now follows one of the tenderest passages of the whole of Sacred Writ: "And the Lord, Yahweh, will wipe away tears from all faces." That the Lord himself should stoop to engage in such apparently trivial service may be the most amazing aspect of this statement. The thought appears again in Rev. 21:4. But it should not be overlooked that the statement has such a broad sweep that it covers all tears, because they will be wiped "from all faces." The Lord's concern for the pains and sufferings of men hardly could be stated more aptly. In this area, too, the distinction between Jew and Gentile will be no more. The immediate reference of the final statement of blessings conferred does limit itself primarily to the chosen people: "and the disgrace of his people he will remove all over the earth." For the instances had been many where jibes like, "Where is your God?" were hurled at the children of Israel. But the time will come when Israel shall be vindicated and no longer suffer such shame. This implication applies more or less to all who are the true children of God. But it appears clearly that death, tears, and shame will be overcome. So the Lord has promised: "for the Lord has spoken."

The song now continues with special reference to Moab (vv. 9-12).

c. The Overthrow of Moab, a Typical Enemy of God's People (vv. 9-12)

25:9-12 9. And it will be said on that day: "Lo, this is our God for whom we have waited that he might deliver us. This is the Lord, we have waited for him. Let us be glad and rejoice in his deliverance." 10. For the hand of the Lord will rest upon this mountain. And Moab will be trampled down on its own

soil, as straw is trampled down in the dung pit. 11. And though
he spread out his hands in the midst of such a situation as a
swimmer spreads out his hands to swim, yet he [the Lord]
will bring low his pride in spite of the clever strokes of his
hands. 12. And the steep fortifications that make up your walls
he shall bring down, lay low, and thrust down to the earth, even
into the dust.

Verse 9. It might have been more to the point to list v. 9
above separately as the resumption of the hymn of vv. 1-5,
and then to treat vv. 10-12 as a development of the theme,
the overthrow of Moab. In any case, this explanation indicates the course that the thought of the last part of the
chapter takes. Quite obviously the enumeration of the
great things that the Lord will achieve in the final judgment
calls for jubilant praise of God. So v. 9 follows here most
appropriately. The particular form, however, that this
praise takes is emphasis on the fact that the people of
the Lord were obliged to wait long till the objectives of
the Lord were finally brought to pass, but they were not
disappointed. The word used for "wait" involves the idea
of a measure of suspense, of tense waiting. But now the
"deliverance" has come. Now then is the time to "be glad
and rejoice." Such rich gifts as just enumerated cannot be
received without a large measure of the praise that is due
unto his name.

Verse 10. The first line of v. 10 could well be regarded
as still continuing the hymn of v. 9. An additional instance
of God's favor toward his people is inserted into the picture: his hand rests upon this mountain (Zion). Since the
context refers to a blessing or to an act of approval, we
must consider the gesture referred to perhaps as expressing
a friendly attitude of fellowship, or as involving his helping hand that will always be in readiness for the needs of
his people. This might be regarded as the opposite of that
use of the hand referred to in the refrain-like statement
(9:12b, 17b, 21b; 10:4b). Here the hand of God's grace,
there the hand of judgment.

Now comes the sudden and unexpected reference to the
doom of Moab. Is this a harsh discord? Does the prophetic word suddenly drop to unworthy levels? Is there

some "unexpected animus" involved in these verses? We think not. But we do have here a strong, objective statement of a doom that will befall a guilty nation due to the judgment of God. Are divine judgments something of a reprehensible and inferior work of the Almighty? No. Neither is there any unwholesome gloating over the fate of an enemy manifested in these words. Such sentiments are ascribed to the writer without a trace of justification. The judgment of Moab is a stern necessity. Besides it is very likely that Moab is merely thought of as a representative nation of all those that expressed wicked hostility against the people of God. One aspect of the divine judgment is to give to every man according to his deeds. What Moab was known to have done to Israel in times past is referred to in II Kings 24:2; cf. Zeph. 2:8-10; Ezek. 25:8-11. Such enemies will be completely crushed by the judgment of God, being trampled down — and if you want a colorful figure — "as straw is trampled down in the dung pit," or dung-heap.

Verse 11. We believe that this verse does not continue the figure just used. In fact, the above translation "dung-pit" rather than "dung-heap" is merely made to provide water for the swimming mentioned in this verse. It is very questionable whether the Israelites in days of old had dung-pits of such huge proportions that a man could swim in them. But does not this verse indicate that the man representing Moab is thought of as swimming "in the midst of it"? Not necessarily. The "it" in this phrase may be used rather loosely, as we have indicated: "in the midst of such a situation." By such an approach the lack of propriety of having the Lord thrust a man back into black waters of a dung pit is avoided. Rather, we have the plain figure of a man trying to escape from pursuit by swimming and finding himself thrust back into the water. However cleverly he may make his strokes, his attempts at escape will avail nothing. The Lord will bring low his pride. Moab shall not escape when the Lord takes in hand her punishment, which is long overdue. The figure is unusual and striking but not far-fetched.

Verse 12. A completely different figure now takes the place of the one just used. Moab is thought of as a strongly-walled city. These walls, however, can avail nothing against the mighty blows that the Lord directs against them. Complete demolition of them is indicated by the three verbs used, "bring down, lay low, and thrust down," and by the added modifying phrases "to the earth, even into the dust." Moab's doom is final and complete. Even as the blessings bestowed are superlative so the judgments inflicted are to be final. No gloating, no berating, no unholy glee; just an impartial recording of facts.

Notes

Verse 1b. In our translation we have used the verb *'asíthah* twice for smoothness in translation. The last two words, being of the same root, express a sort of superlative, "utmost faithfulness."

Verse 2. Even though the Septuagint has it, it is hardly necessary to change *zarim* ("aliens") to *zedhim* ("insolent"). The point is, a city of non-Israelites is being referred to. We have also translated the word usually meaning "city" to "a city-unit" because a "citadel" could never constitute more than one of the units of a city. The figure is metonymy, the whole for the part.

Verse 6. The second *hallot* is written thus in place of the usual passive, *hallut*, merely to secure a correspondence in sound. Cf. *GK* 72 p.

Verse 8. This verse also has become famous by its use in I Cor. 15:54, where Paul uses the version, "Death is swallowed up in victory," giving the verb in the passive, and taking the more Aramaic meaning of *nétsach*, "victory." The meaning of the passage certainly has not been materially altered by this free translation.

Verse 12. We regard the genetive found in the expression, "the high fortifications of his walls" as being an appositional genetive, and have therefore translated, "the steep fortifications that make up your walls," which we deem to be a bit clearer.

Chapter XXVI

3. A Hymn Glorifying the Works of God Done for His People (Chap. 26)

How far does this "song," or hymn, extend? Some feel it covers only vv. 1-6. Some would extend it to vv. 1-10. Then some are inclined to let it run from v. 1 to v. 19. We agree with the last-mentioned group.

The outline may indicate what we have in mind and how the hymn is made up of various elements.

a. Praise for the Strong City (vv. 1-6)
b. Prayerful Reflection on God's Judgments (vv. 7-15)
c. The Prayer of Hope (vv. 16-19)
d. Exhortation: The Nation Must Wait Quietly for God's Constructive Judgments (vv. 20-21)

The theme of the chapter is indicated by the above caption. Some would have it to be: God's Righteousness (*Koenig*) or, The Vindication of the Lord (*von Orelli*). If we would like a more colorful statement it is even feasible to formulate the theme as being The Tale of Two Cities.

A definite rhythmical pattern appears on closer study. As *Procksch* states it, in vv. 1-3 six accents make up a line; in vv. 4-5a, we have five accents, also in vv. 5b-6; then in vv. 7-19 there are six tristichs (i.e., verses with three lines) having seven accents per line. That something of this nature is in the picture cannot be denied. But to make the whole portion really conform to this pattern requires too many clever manipulations of the text, where the controlling factor is the meter — the text being violently forced into the Procrustes bed of the meter — a procedure which the Hebrews can hardly be shown to have conformed to and which allows for altogether too many arbitrary cases of treatment of the text.

Though the prayer, which covers almost the entire chapter, breathes a warmth and an intimacy, it will hardly do to ascribe to it "a passionate force which stands quite without equal in the Old Testament" (*Procksch*).

The factors of time and circumstances under which the chapter came into being are extremely difficult. Nothing in the text points definitely to an event in the history of Israel or Judah. One might rather say that the prophet is reflecting on the broad lessons of sacred history as contrasted with world history, thinking particularly of the works of the Lord done for his people. Piecing these works together, it is as though an overall pattern begins to emerge which calls for resounding praise of God and invites further prayerful reflection, and ends on a note of clear hope.

Furthermore, since repeatedly in the preceding two chapters the thought of the overthrow of a mighty city had occurred and since there was another city which was upheld by God, it is as though the prophet were contrasting the two cities, showing the imperishable nature of the one and the sure doom of the other. This is practically the same theme that has appeared frequently in sacred literature, most brilliantly set forth by Augustine in "The City of God." So we could be justified from this point of view in again suggesting as title, "The Tale of Two Cities."

It might also be suggested at this point that some commentators have discovered throughout the chapter a closely-knit sequence of thought, which is of obvious design and at the very outset overthrows any claims about a kind of patchwork pattern resulting from having unskilled editors piece together unrelated items. *Skinner* very appropriately uses the expression "concatenated structure" to describe the close consecutiveness of thought that is in evidence throughout the chapter.

a. Praise for the Strong City (vv. 1-6)

26:1-6   1. In that day this song will be sung in the land of Judah:

We have a strong city; he appoints salvation as its walls and bastions.

2. Open the gates that the righteous nation may enter in, they who keep the faith.

3. [The man] of steadfast purpose thou dost keep in perfect
     peace, for he trusts in thee.
4. Trust in the Lord forever, for the Lord God is an eternal rock.
5. For he has laid low those that dwell on high, the lofty city;
     he brings it low, yea, brings it low to the ground;
     he levels it to the dust.
6. The foot tramples upon it, the feet of the poor,
     the steps of the lowly.

Verse 1. We are transported into the midst of a particular situation, which is of such a sort that only as the thought
develops do we find a statement as to what is actually happening. Even the opening phrase ("in that day") is not
immediately clear as to whether it looks forward or backward. In the light of v. 5 it seems to appear rather obviously that the fall of a certain city is specifically under
consideration; in fact, its fall gave rise to this hymn of
praise. So it would be safe to claim that "in that day"
looks back upon this particular event. When the song to be
sung is limited to "the land of Judah" the reason appears to
be that in that land dwell the people of God, who are wont
to praise him when he does mighty things for them. So the
initial point of this "song" is that the fall of one city
strongly reminds God's people of the invincibility of another. This one is often called Zion, and as the city of God
represents what he is building for his people for all eternity.
A statement follows at once, which indicates the source and
nature of this strong city of which they boast: not ordinary
walls and bastions (i.e., outworks projecting from the major wall) but salvation, i.e., deliverance granted by God, is
the force that makes it strong. A meaningful equivalent for
"salvation" would be "victory" — as the word may also be
translated in this context. Or, recasting our entire approach
to the figure, it is as though the master-builder of the strong
walls of God's city is none other than the Lord himself.
The knowledge of that fact breeds sound assurance. It even
stimulates him who reflects on this matter to burst forth
into song.

Verse 2. We might regard this verse as connected with
the preceding by the idea that this strong city whose walls
have thus been firmly grounded and built by the Lord him-

self, still lacks inhabitants. There is always room in the kingdom, or the city, for more men. So they who already dwell there are called upon to open the gates readily for others to enter in, particularly "the righteous nation" or, as they are also described, "they who keep the faith." Two qualities of the true people of God are here stressed: they are marked by righteousness and by dependability, or steadfastness, here called "faith." The emphasis on being righteous had already appeared in 24:16. They are a particularly honored class. If "birds of a feather flock together," then the righteous ought certainly to be strongly drawn to one another. To regard this verse as addressed to angels is somewhat far-fetched; or to see those who are invited in to be returnees from the captivity.

Verse 3. The hymn still is thinking in terms of the blessings enjoyed by those who are citizens of this marvelous city. These men who, if any do, deserve the designation of "righteous," are now described as men who enjoy a rare measure of peace and composure, first of all because they are marked by "steadfast purpose" but primarily because they trust in the Lord. The Lord maintains and upholds them continually. This thought has been given classic formulation in the translation stemming from the King James Version: "Thou wilt keep him in perfect peace whose mind is stayed on thee." In a literal translation it would read as follows: "The steadfast purpose thou dost keep in peace, peace, for he trusts in thee." Such an idiomatic statement just has to be subjected to certain changes. In the classic version, previously cited, this word has been a guide and stay to many a Christian. The verse has kinship with Ps. 112:7f.

Verse 4. Building on the last thought, that such a person trusts in the Lord, the hymn proceeds to exhort men to put their trust in the Lord, not for a day or days, but "forever." For such trust cannot be misplaced. It has the surest possible foundation: "the Lord is an eternal rock." Since he cannot waver neither will the man who is "stayed" on him. (Cf. Deut. 32:4.)

Verse 5. Still in a closely-knit sequence of thought the hymn proceeds to offer substantial evidence as to how firm a foundation is the Lord. One of his mighty acts is brought into remembrance: he brought a lofty city low. It was one of those cities which bore the stamp of its pride clearly upon it. It was "lofty," i.e., eminent and famous and presumably strong, if not near-invincible. Its overthrow, attributed not to any national foe but directly to the Lord himself, was complete; it was brought low, yea, down to the ground, yea, it was levelled to the dust.

These then are the two opposing cities, the one of v. 1 and the one of v. 5. They are respectively the personification of the principle of righteousness and of the principle of evil. In connection with v. 1 the writer may involuntarily have had the image of Zion before his mind's eye. In the second case it may have been Nineveh or Babylon, concerning which it was certainly true that when she was finally destroyed, her overthrow was complete and lasting, as it is to this day. One should not insist that some actual historical event must have taken place before the prophet could have penned these lines. Eternal verities are being expressed. The thought involved had been prepared for by the statements found in 24:10-12 and 25:3, in thoughts of as general a character as we have here. Besides, 25:12 has even supplied the terminology of a part of our verse; which suggests the thought that, according to this latter passage, one might also with some measure of propriety think of Moab as a symbol of the "lofty city." The second half of the verse, by the way, offers a change of tense in the original, which brings the work of overthrow into a kind of progressive action which keeps going on continually. God's overthrow of the principle of wickedness is continually progressing.

Verse 6. The concluding verse of this section rounds out the picture of the total overthrow of the lofty city by showing us a quick glimpse of the ruins of it, and the "poor" and the "lowly" walking across the rubble-heaps. They survived; the city did not. They outlived the city which had seemed so mighty, if not almost impregnable. The terms used imply nothing in the nature of an unholy or unwholesome attitude on the part of the poor and lowly. It is simply a powerful and drastic way of indicating what it is that endures. It should, of course, not be overlooked that both terms used are titles which apply to the lowly persons who have held unswervingly to their God, so that the terms used are synonymous — godly and righteous. To claim outright that therefore only Jews are being thought of, presses the point too far.

b. Prayerful Reflection on God's Judgments (vv. 7-15)

26:7-15 7. The way of the righteous is level;
            straight is the path of the righteous; thou dost make it smooth.
8. Yea, in the way of thy judgments, O Lord, we have waited for thee;
the desire of our soul is for the remembrance of thy name.
9. My soul has longed for thee in the night;
yea, with my spirit within me have I sought for thee.
For when thy judgments strike the earth, the inhabitants of the world have always learned righteousness.
10. If favor is shown the wicked, he does not learn righteousness;
in a land of much rectitude he acts perversely,
and fails to see the majesty of the Lord.
11. Lord, thy hand is uplifted, they fail to see it.
They shall see it and be confounded.
The zeal for the people and the fire of thy wrath against thy enemies shall consume them.
12 O Lord, thou wilt ordain peace for us;
for also all that we have achieved thou hast wrought.
13. O Lord, our God, lords other than thou have dominated us.
We will acknowledge only thee and thy name.
14. They are dead, they will not live; they are shades, they will not arise;
that is why thou hast visited and destroyed them, and wiped out all remembrance of them.
15. Thou hast added to the nation, O Lord,
thou hast added to the nation;
thou hast glorified thyself;
thou hast widened out the limits of the land.

Verse 7. The judgments of God are an intriguing and instructive subject. They invite reflection. They become the next item that is considered in this hymn, on the basis of what was said in the first section about the overthrow of the lofty city. Hymns can become prayerful reflection.

They may even, as is the case in this verse in particular, take the language of wisdom literature (cf. Prov. 4:26; 5: 6, 21). Looking both backward and forward to get the exact setting of v. 7, we must construe it to mean that the way that the righteous travels through life becomes level as a result of the just judgments of the Lord that serve to remove obstacles and dangers from his path. There may be other purposes and motivations for the Lord to bring a judgment upon the earth, but the welfare of the "righteous" is a major factor in dictating what he does. This repeated emphasis on the righteous (cf. also v. 2) and what God does for them shows how important these men are in God's sight. When the going gets rough, he himself smoothes the way for them. Let it be noted that, since the whole hymn breathes the spirit of prayer, it follows, in the nature of a smooth transition, that the statement, without further explanation just veers over into direct address of God: "Thou dost make it smooth."

Verse 8. This verse indicates that the normal way for God to act is "in the way of [his] judgments." The righteous know that and expect it. They wait for the Lord to perform his judgments. The parallel statement adds the thought that there even is an intense longing in the inmost heart of the godly that God would, in his own time, act in the manner in which they know him to act. That is the "name," or reputation, that he has established; and from this point of view his saints love to recall what he performs. *RSV* quite aptly translated at this point that this is the Lord's "memorial name."

Verse 9. The thought just set forth is developed a bit more fully. It becomes obvious here how strongly God's own often must have longed for divine intervention. For the "night" here spoken of apparently is the night of affliction, as the word is also used in 21:11. The whole inner man (soul and spirit) shared in this eager longing that God might act. It was a sort of outreach for God (I "have sought for thee"), not merely a calm philosophical reflection, not merely sober investigation; but an eager, impassioned search that looked for results. But that, in the last analysis, the necessary results cannot be achieved unless a divine judgment happens, is clearly understood and accepted as foregone conclusion. It is stated, again somewhat in the form of statements found in the wisdom literature, as follows: "When thy judgments strike the earth, the inhabitants of the earth have always learned righteousness." It takes a divine judgment to jar them loose from their hold on unrighteousness.

Verse 10. Continuing, still in the tone of pronouncements in wisdom literature (cf. Eccl. 8:11; Ps. 10:5, 6), the song indicates why the Lord must follow the course of judgments in dealing with the sons of men. "Favor" will not work, except perhaps in a limited sense. If the Lord resorts only to kindly treatment in dealing with those who oppose him, these men "do not learn righteousness." This expression here would seem to mean: they do not change radically for the better. Sharp treatment is the only type that secures results. Without severity, the wicked, "in a land of much rectitude, acts perversely." That is to say, even in a land where righteousness is known and approved, as it was in the land of Israel, even there kindly treatment of the wicked fails to make an impression on them. The wicked are unimpressed; they "fail to see the majesty of the Lord." These are some of the sober reflections that make up a large part of this song.

But these thoughts are developed a little more fully.

Verse 11. At this point devout reflection turns into direct address of God. All along these thoughts had been thought through as in God's presence. When the Lord's hand is said to be "uplifted," this is to be thought of as a gesture that implies that a blow is about to be delivered. That has to be the Lord's characteristic pose over against the wicked. His hand is, as it were, continually uplifted to bring down the blow of judgment upon their heads. But the wicked remain totally unaware of the danger that menaces. But it cannot always be so. A sharp disillusionment must come; "They shall see it and be confounded." A rude awakening awaits them. In time they will be fully ripe for the judgment. Then what happens may be thus described: "The zeal for the people and the fire of thy wrath against thy enemies shall consume them." A similar thought is expressed in 9:7 and 37:32. But though the Lord may appear slow to act and all too deliberate in his judgments, he has a deep and true "zeal for the people." God does not maintain his cause in a half-hearted manner. There is besides "the fire of [his] wrath against [his] enemies." God's wrath is no idle figment of the imagination. It even will "consume" them. At this point the reflections upon the Lord's judgment come to an end. But it must be admitted the song offered many a constructive thought on the subject of divine judgments.

Verse 12. The hymn goes on in a word of direct address to the Lord and outlines the positive result that is achieved by God's judgment for the righteous. What the Lord appoints for them is "peace." The word here is taken in that comprehensive sense of total welfare and success. This thought briefly brings to mind all helpful things that were achieved by the nation through the centuries. Yet, to tell the full truth of the matter, the nation must confess its inadequacy and the Lord's sufficiency: "All that we have achieved thou hast wrought." Such confessions God's people are always ready to make.

Verse 13. The backward look over the nation's history continues. There were those painful experiences when the foreign oppressor dominated the nation and ground it under his heel, as happened so often during the days of the Judges and in the last years of the monarchy: "Lords other than thou have dominated us." Those were, so to speak, passing episodes. Under such domination Israel would recall more strongly than ever that she had only one Lord, and acknowledged only his name and will continue to do so, as she now states in a solemn vow.

Verse 14. Continuing the backward look on the lords that dominated God's people in the past, the nation reflects on what their lot has been. They may have loomed big and invincible in their day. But they had to meet the common lot of all the children of men: "They are dead, they will not live; they are shades, they will not arise." Death, the great leveller, has taken care of them. Implied in this statement is the conviction that the wicked have no future to look forward to. This again is part of the Old

Testament heritage, which in the area of the future life showed very few gleams of light, sometimes none at all. But just because they, though wicked, were only frail mortals, God punished (or "visited") them in death, "destroyed them and wiped out all remembrance of them." So, historically speaking, the Lord met one major danger that so often threatened his people. This negative achievement is gratefully recalled.

Verse 15. But there are also positive achievements that deserve to be recalled. One of these is that numerically the nation has been strengthened. Since this seems to have been done by "widening out the limits of the land," perhaps the nation is here reflecting on all territorial expansion that she had been blessed with in the course of her history. For surely it was no trivial gift from God to have Israel's holdings expand from the very meager foothold that she had in the land in the days of Joshua, until the time when she came into full control in the days of David and Solomon. Whatever questionable procedure here and there may have been involved in the process, the overruling providence of God, without a doubt, was active. The entire verse has an analogy in 9:3.

c. The Prayer of Hope (vv. 16-19)

26:16-19 16. O Lord, in distress they sought thee;
they poured out prayer when thy chastening was upon them.
17. Like a woman with child, when she comes to the time of her delivery, writhes and cries out in her pangs,
so were we because of thee.
18. We were with child, we writhed;
we have, as it were, brought forth wind.
We have not wrought deliverance in the earth;
no inhabitants of the world came to birth through us.
19. But thy dead shall live; my bodies shall arise.
Awake and be jubilant, O dwellers in the dust,
for thy dew is the dew of light;
and the earth shall bring the shades to birth.

Verse 16. But there was still so much to be achieved. The backward look was not too reassuring. There had been so many instances of distress in bygone days that it became difficult to take a hopeful attitude in looking to the future. So the nation had recourse to "prayer." The word used here generally refers to muttered incantations and the like. Softly-whispered prayer might be a good interpretation. When God's "chastening was upon them," they were profuse in their intense but not too confident prayer. Israel's past history, in spite of all that God did for his people, was not one grand victorious march through the centuries. Many a subdued hope was to be encountered. In fact, often these were very trying days. The nation had a destiny, but she seemed so far removed from achieving it. It is this thought that is under consideration in the next two verses.

Verses 17, 18. In spite of brave hopes that appeared in the prayerful reflections of vv. 7-15, there also was good ground for a much more pessimistic appraisal of the past. The nation in this context might well be likened to a woman with child. Pregnancy may be a painful and distressing experience, especially as it comes to a climax. So it was with Israel, or Judah. She writhed and cried out in her pain. Finally when the hoped-for result was due, all that the experience had produced was — wind. In her entire history up till this time, the nation, the people of Israel, produced nothing that was of general and substantial benefit to the nations of the world. She had a high destiny in this respect. The results achieved were negligible. Continuing in the figure used: "No inhabitants of the world came to birth through us." Without figure it could have been stated thus: We produced nothing tangible. At this point with v. 18 the hymn touches the lowest point of its outlook. All is gloomy despair. But by one of those sudden and inexplicable changes of mood, from the lowest depth to the noblest height, the hymn suddenly comes with a breakthrough of truth that is downright amazing and makes a zenith point of eschatological hope. Inspiration granted him a sudden flash of insight at which we can only marvel.

Verse 19. It is as though the Lord had made a major investment in his saints. At least, he had an abiding interest in what befalls them. So, though they were dead, they still were *his* dead. Being thus related to the Lord of life, it is most reasonable to expect that they will share in his endless life: "*Thy* dead shall live." By one of those startling turns of thought, in which the Hebrew mind delights, the same group are now called "*my* dead bodies," the nation speaking through the prophet. The nation has a deep concern for her children, though they have been claimed by death.

This new insight, startling and novel in the Old Testament, is just exploded on the scene. It is true that this does not predicate a universal resurrection of all mankind. It would seem to confine itself to the possibility of the resurrection of the godly in Israel only. But even that much insight is a startling advance for those days. Nor is this to be understood to mean that the *nation*, almost extinct in the Babylonian Captivity, will survive this ordeal as a nation and come back again to have a separate national existence in the land of Palestine. Hosea 6:2 and Ezek. 37 may think in such terms quite properly. But we have here an actual indication of the hope of the resurrection. Silence about the resurrection of the rest of mankind does not deny such a possibility.

Such a prospect is not to be viewed with cool detachment and imperturbable equanimity. They who were above and had been brought low, even down to the dust, are now exhorted: "Awake and be jubilant, O dwellers in the dust." Apparently these "dwellers in the dust" are to be thought of as the dead bodies that now have the prospect of rising again. The dust referred to is the dust of death — "unto dust thou shalt return" (Gen. 3:19). The statement is highly poetic when the dead are exhorted to be jubilant. But by virtue of the impending resurrection this is not impossible. The new life that is held in prospect is now described in another figure as "dew," and a "dew of light" at that, which is to say, an invigorating dew. For a similar thought see Hos. 14:5. The letters of the word "light" may be construed, as they quite properly are in II Kings 4:39, as meaning "herbs." But that would be a bit meaningless here, though both *Luther* and *KJ* render it thus. One further turn of the thought is added by the use of another figure: "The earth shall bring shades to birth." The "shades" are the departed ones who live a meager, drowsy, shade-like existence, if this deserves to be called an existence. But impossible though it seems to be, these shall return to a full life and experience a sort of second birth. This thought is at this point in strong contrast to the hopeless conclusion of v. 18. So the prayer (vv. 1-19) comes to a climax in a blaze of glorious revelation concerning the resurrection of the dead. This aspect of the case still required some amplification in the fuller truth that Jesus declared: "*All* that are in the graves . . . shall come forth" (John 5:28).

d. Exhortation: The Nation Must Wait Quietly for God's Constructive Judgments (vv. 20-21)

26:20-21 20. Come, my people, go into your rooms,
and shut the doors behind you;
hide yourself for a brief moment until the wrath is past.
21. For the Lord will come forth out of his place
to punish the inhabitants of the earth for their guilt.
And the earth shall disclose the mass of blood shed upon her;
and shall no more cover her slain.

Verse 20. Is this exhortation a part of the hymn that began with v. 1? It could well be. Exhortation or instruction may appear in hymns. In any case, there is an inner connection between the section that ended with v. 19 and these last two verses. A glorious hope emerged in v. 19. But that hope is not to be realized at once. In some manner it was disclosed to the prophet that some time must elapse before it can be realized. During that time the nation should adopt the course here outlined. By the way, these last two verses are best attributed to the prophet himself, not to the Lord (*Procksch*), for the Lord speaking would hardly use the form of address found in v. 21.

The exhortation begins with a kindly "Come," as exhortations often do. It is not yet a time of celebration, or of joy over ambitions finally realized. It is a time of waiting, in fact, of retirement into solitude ("go into your rooms"); a time of shutting out the noisy world and its turmoil. And it may be described as a time of quietly retiring off the scene, going underground, as it were, and biding God's time. This could be a reference to what the New Testament calls the "great tribulation" (Rev. 2:22; 7:14). Since it calls for retirement only for "a brief moment" it could be likened to the course of action enjoined upon the Israelites on the night when the avenging angel went abroad through the land of Egypt (Exod. 12:23-27). For there is a time of "wrath" involved, which is another way of again referring to the necessity of judgment before the purposes of the Lord can be achieved.

Verse 21. This verse now tells more precisely what the Lord must take in hand before some of his more glorious purposes can be completed. What now follows is a description of one phase of the great last judgment. There are many more aspects to it than the one here described, but this one is important too. A startling event will take place ("lo"). To achieve his purpose the Lord will appear on the scene or, "he will come forth out of his place," which is heaven, "to punish the inhabitants of the earth for their guilt." We know that he shall punish all the unforgiven sins of men, but it would appear at this point that the particular guilt that is under consideration is that described in the words following. There is the unsettled score of blood shed upon the earth, oftentimes the blood of the innocent, about which God did nothing and man did nothing. But if it be true that innocent blood cries out for vengeance to high heaven, as a very early record carefully notes (Gen. 4:10; cf. also Ezek. 24:7f.; Job 16:18), then this one item alone will call for very specific action of God, action in regard to which the Lord certainly will not be remiss. In some manner quite unknown to us, the "earth shall disclose the mass of blood shed upon her" — and it must surely be an amazing total — "and she shall no more cover her slain" as she has done through the ages, soaking up the blood of victims and then gradually wiping out the stain by the attrition of weather. Exactly how God will go about this stupendous task of divine judgment the prophet himself apparently did not see at this time. But all this is one more instance where God's mills grind slowly but grind exceedingly fine. On this note, one of reassurance in regard to the achievements of God's justice, the hymn may be said to close quite effectively.

Notes

The high number of Notes, comparatively speaking, that are about to follow indicate the manifold difficulties of this chapter.

Verse 2. For the word "faith" the Hebrew has a plural, a common way of expressing a high degree of the quality under consideration — called the plural of potency, or potential plural; cf. *KS* 262 f.

Verse 3. "He trusts" is covered in the Hebrew, according to form, by a passive participle, but as to meaning is construed as active. Cf. *GK* 50 f; *KS* 235 d.

Verse 4. The expression "Lord God" in Hebrew runs thus: *Yah Yahweh*, the first being a short form of the name of the covenant God of Israel, a combination occurring besides only in 12:2. Here it is preceded by what grammarians call a *beth essentiae*, cf. *BDB* p. 89 a.

Verse 5. Does the language of this verse contain mythological terminology, indicative of the primeval contest with chaos? All its statements could just as well be figurative language which every man could easily understand without cumbering the thought with mythology.

Verse 7. "The way of the righteous" in the original reads: "The way *for* the righteous," a dative construction, which, to tell the truth is one of the accepted equivalents of a genitive. See *KS* 286 c.

Verse 8. For "the remembrance of thy name" the Hebrew has "for thy name and for thy remembrance," a sort of hendiadys, which is best rendered as we have just quoted it.

Verse 9. We have here an instance of a sort of double expression of the subject for purposes of intensification: "My soul, I have longed" which could also be rendered: "With my soul I have longed." Cf. *KS* 325 o-p. At the end of the verse we have inserted an "always" to indicate that a gnomic aorist, or perfect was used.

Verse 10. The negative *bal* represents a more refined form, or may be said to be poetic usage. Cf. *KS* 352 d.

Verse 11. *Qin'ath 'am*, literally "zeal of the people" is an objective genetive and naturally means "zeal *for* the people." See *KS* 336 d.

Verse 14. Of the two possibilities of translation we finally chose the one which reads: "They are dead, they will not live; they are shades. . . ." The other possible rendering is: "The dead will not live, the shades will not arise." This second form appears too much as a generalization. The first ties up the verse with the preceding, and refers to the "lords" there mentioned.

Verse 16. The verb *tsaqun* has an archaic *nun* attached. See *GK* 72 o. In regard to the emendations attempted upon the text of this verse we may do well to quote *Kissane*, who indicates concerning "the many emendations" that "none (are) entirely satisfactory," as is so frequently the case with emendations.

Verse 18. For "deliverance" the Hebrew again uses the plural. Cf. the note on v. 2. The verb translated "came to birth" is simply *naphal*, which is used of beasts *dropping* their young in birth. It also might be used of human beings to express the idea of giving birth. In any case the expression still has some difficulty. The same verb is used, apparently in the same sense at the conclusion of v. 19.

Verse 21. To express the idea of "a mass of blood" the Hebrew simply uses the plural of the noun "blood," as is already the case in Gen. 4:10.

Chapter XXVII

4. The Overthrow of the Kingdom of This World vs. the Prosperity of Zion (Chap. 27)

This section of the book rounds out the subject which has been under consideration since Chap. 24. Everything pointed to the glorious consummation of history. But in history two forces were running parallel, the world and the people of God; or, as previously indicated, the two cities, the one destined to continue into eternity, the other destined to overthrow. First the emphasis lay on the universal judgment (chap. 24). Then followed an exuberant song of praise for this judgment (chap. 25). But on the positive side there followed a hymn glorifying God for the works that he had done for his people (chap. 26). Now, touching both sides of the question, after the overthrow of worldly powers has again been briefly indicated, the rest of the chapter indicates how Zion, the eternal city of God, will enjoy rare prosperity (chap. 27).

When we come to the question of authorship of the chapter it must be admitted that direct evidence for its being written by Isaiah is not overwhelming. On the other hand neither is direct evidence to the contrary. So also merely an impression is being recorded when it is claimed that we have here a "late imitator of Isaiah." *Fischer* concedes that the chapter could stem from Isaiah. Details involved will be examined as we go along.

Closely tied up with the question of authorship is that of the time of composition of the chapter. Here conclusions range all the way from Isaiah's time down past the fall of Jerusalem, to Alexander, even down to the age of the Maccabees. However we shall attempt to show, in connection with v. 11, that the city there referred to as having fallen but recently could be Samaria (722 B.C.), a date which lies well within the time of Isaiah's ministry.

418

As to the question of the sequence of material we shall attempt no rearrangement of verses, like making 26:20, 21; 27:1, 12, 13 a unit and removing vv. 2-11 from their present place. For such rearrangements usually stem from not having sought diligently enough for the inner connection of thought embodied in the prophetic book as such, as well as from unwholesome and unwarranted changes of the text to produce a smoother flow of thought, a method by which almost anything can be proved at times. Neither is the text, which does offer some difficulties, so bad as to allow for claims such as: ". . . in most of the chapter either the text is corrupt and unintelligible, or the thought of the writer is expressed obscurely and in a very remarkable manner" (*Gray*). Allowing room for the proper functioning of textual criticism, we claim that by and large an understandable and enlightening text lies before the reader, deserving our highest respect and veneration.

We suggest the following outline:

a. Overthrow of the Mighty World-powers (v. 1)
b. Another Song of the Vineyard: God's Kindly Protection (vv. 2-5)
c. The Fruitful State of the Vine in the Last Days (v. 6)
d. God's Purposes in Dealing Gently with Israel (vv. 7-9)
e. God's Stern Dealings with the "fortified city" (vv. 10-11)
f. The Gathering of the Scattered Children of Israel (vv. 12-13)

a.   *Overthrow of the Mighty World-powers (v. 1)*

27:1 1. On that day the Lord with his well-tempered, great, and strong sword will punish Leviathan "the fleeing serpent" and Leviathan "the winding serpent"; and he will slay the dragon that lies by the sea.

Beginning, for the moment, with the third of the above forces that are to be destroyed, it is important to observe that elsewhere (Ezek. 29:3; and 32:2) the same term for "dragon" is used, clearly in reference to Egypt. So the last creature typifies a powerful nation of that time. By analogy the first two may rightly be thought of as emblematic of great nations. Since then the other two are each described first as "Leviathan." They must have quite a bit in common. A good bit of similarity prevailed between the Assyrian and the Babylonian empires in days of old, the latter taking over the role of the former after the fall of Nineveh. We admit at once that such an approach involves a measure of prophetic foresight on the part of the writer, for Babylon's star had not yet appeared in the heavens. But still it can be shown that Leviathan, as such, in Biblical usage, can refer to a powerful beast (even though the language has a touch of the mythological), as later on it became common usage in Daniel to refer to empires by the figure of beasts. The descriptive adjective "fleeing" aptly refers to the Tigris River (on whose banks Nineveh lay) with its swift current; and "winding" in like manner correctly describes the course of the Euphrates, along whose banks Babylon lay. So this could be a verse that refers to the big world-powers of those days: Assyria, Babylon, and Egypt. Establishing a kind of parallelism, the sword of the Lord has *three* qualities ascribed to it, with the result that there are three forces available ready to deal with three empires that are on the scene. These three attributes of the sword are "well-tempered" (or hard), "great," and "strong." We have already conceded that the language may have a touch of the mythological in it: a great beast slain in a primeval conflict, as Marduk slew Tiamat in a pre-creation struggle. But to what extent such language was in those days consciously mythological will forever be shrouded in doubt.

Besides, just because it can be shown that Leviathan in popular usage did refer to some kind of fabulous creature, and also that certain heavenly constellations were described by terms like these, still all this hardly erases the underlying concept of great nations representing the kingdoms of this world, which on their part are hostile to the kingdom of God and must ultimately be dealt with by him.

This first verse of Chap. 27 is a transition verse. From one point of view it rightly may be regarded as concluding Chap. 26, showing that there is more to the divine judgment than the avenging of innocent blood. For this reason some treat 27:1 as the conclusion of the previous section. It may

however, with equal propriety, be regarded as introducing
Chap. 27, as we have done.

b. Another Song of the Vineyard: God's Kindly Protection (vv. 2-5)

27:2-5 2. On that day there will be a delightful vineyard —
sing of it!
3. I, the Lord, am its keeper;
regularly do I water it;
day and night do I guard it lest anyone should harm it.
4. Wrath have I none [against it].
O that I might be given thorns and briers,
I would proceed against them in warlike fashion;
I would burn them up at once;
5. unless men lay hold of my protection,
or make peace with me, yea, unless they make peace with me.

A vineyard song had already appeared in 5:1-7. In that
instance the emphasis lay on the fact that God would have
to take measures against an unproductive vineyard. Here
by way of contrast the side of the case that is examined is
God's kindly protection of his vineyard. Here as there the
vineyard is "the house of Israel" (5:7). But here, besides,
the emphasis lies on the far-distant future— "on that day,"
implying a great future day when the Lord's work will come
to a climax. The result of having a "delightful vineyard"
comes from the care that the keeper bestows on it. Especially the fact that he checks and removes all forces that
might harm the vineyard. For the present the emphasis
lies on the fact that whatever hostile forces there are, they
will not get the better of the vineyard. Therefore it is a
thing of enduring value. We could say in New Testament
terminology: "The gates of hell shall not prevail against
it." And this quality alone, not dwelling on others that
could be enumerated, could well make the vineyard a subject worthy of a song —"Sing of it!" It is true that the Hebrew is most abrupt, but, we would say, abrupt by way of
exclamation: (literally) "On that day, a pleasant vineyard;
sing of it." All is clear, though concise. This hardly calls for
the criticism: "Even the most helpless writer would not
stammer thus."

Verse 3. How kindly the Lord is disposed toward his vineyard is given in some detail. Watchmen were a regular adjunct of a vineyard, at least in the days when the grapes were ripening. Here the Lord makes it clear that such menial duties in reference to the vineyard are not beneath his dignity: "I . . . am its keeper." He has assumed the added responsibility of watering it "regularly" or at stated intervals, not "every moment" (*RSV*), for no vineyard requires that much watering. But he who "neither slumbers nor sleeps" does let his watchful care run over day and night. Never for a moment is his concern for that which he has planted relaxed. It is implied that there continually are those who would "harm it."

Verse 4. What the eye saw of God's providential dealings in the interest of his vineyard did not always square with this claim of continual providential oversight. For Israel had often been assailed from the days of her youth. This calls for some specific reassurance from the Lord, which he gives in a statement which disavows the contrary: "Wrath have I none [against it]." We have added the phrase in brackets as a thought that is implied in the context. Not only may it sometimes have seemed as though the Lord were neglectful of his vineyard; it might even appear, because of the deep unworthiness of his people, that he was abandoning them, because of his wrath against them. This thought is here categorically denied. It might help a bit to catch the distinct flavor of the thought by translating: I harbor no resentment against my own.

The rest of the verse explains this. The "thorns and briers" referred to are types of the enemies of God's people. The wish is expressed that the Lord might encounter those that are known to oppose his own; he would proceed at once against such "in warlike fashion," as men behave when the dangers and necessities of war are upon them and drastic measures are called for. Staying within the figure of the thorns and briers, the assertion is made that these undesirable items would be burned up at once. God has often demonstrated, when an emergency arose and his people were threatened, that he is deeply concerned about their delivery, and that all opposition must melt before him. Cf. II Sam. 23:6-7; Isa. 10:17.

Verse 5. The beginning of the verse presents some problems in translation, which seems to make the sequence of thought a bit obscure. But there seems to be good warrant for rendering the beginning by a concessive "unless." For the impression is not to be created that a relentless attitude would be maintained by the Lord against his enemies, no matter what might happen. The enemies are largely the heathen. But they, too, are candidates for admission into the kingdom. Therefore this possibility is explored a bit more fully. If then such persons were to cast themselves upon his mercy and desist from enmity against his own; (or, to rephrase the situation: "unless men lay hold of my protection"), they will be spared. The reference involved seems to be that of claiming asylum in an emergency at God's altar in the hour of danger. Two examples may be cited: I Kings 1:50; 2:28. Such an attitude might also be described in the words: (unless they) "make peace with me," that is, come to terms, which involves primarily, desisting from their unwholesome enmity. The repetition of this latter clause may involve a kind of sad emphasis, indicating how really necessary it is to come to terms with the Lord, or else —. So ends the vineyard-song in this context, with emphasis on God's kindly attitude toward his vineyard, all visible evidence to the contrary.

c. *The Fruitful State of the Vine in the Last Days* (v. 6)

The Lord had been the speaker almost throughout the vineyard-song. Now the prophet speaks. Besides, the figure has changed. Now Israel is thought of as a tree.

27:6 6. In days to come Jacob shall take root;
Israel shall blossom and sprout;
and they will fill the earth with fruit.

The hopeful outlook for the people of God of the future! The tree's roots are thought of as becoming firmly implanted in the soil; then the tree blossoms profusely and sprouts, as healthy trees do in spring. Finally fruit is produced in such abundance by this one tree that the whole earth is filled with it. Two subjects are used in this connection: Jacob and Israel. As *Fischer* remarks, this parallel use of of the two names is characteristic of Isa. 40–49 in describing the whole of the people of God. This does not necessarily equate these two names with the Northern and the Southern kingdoms. That one nation should produce marvelous results of so striking a nature that the whole earth is abundantly blessed as a result is in keeping with things predicated of the people of God elsewhere in the Old Testament, beginning with Gen. 12:3.

d. God's Purpose in Dealing Gently with Israel (vv. 7-9)

27:7-9 7. Has he [God] smitten them [Israel] as hard as he smote their [Israel's] oppressors?
Or was he [Israel] slain with the slaughter of those slain by him [God]?
8. Only by driving her away, or by dispersing her, didst thou use to strive with her [Israel].
He removed her by his harsh wind on the day of the storm.
9. Therefore on this condition will the guilt of Jacob be expiated —
and this will be the only return that he expects for the removal of her sin —
that she [Israel] make all the idol-altar stones like pulverized chalk-stones;
no Asherim or sun-pillars [or, incense-altars] will remain standing.

God's purposes, as our heading indicates, are being examined: what has he in mind with regard to his people when he deals kindly with them, as he so manifestly does? Not all the divine objectives are reviewed. The one specially reflected on is the removal of idolatry and its appurtenances. But first it must once again be clearly set forth that God actually did deal very kindly with Israel throughout the course of her history. To establish this fact the prophet raises a question, which points very definitely in the direction that his thinking is taking. The question seems to be purposely put in such a form as to challenge further reflection. Pronouns seem to be used ambiguously. But certain conclusions emerge gradually as one reflects further on the matter. We have attempted to indicate the reasonable conclusions that may well be arrived at, conclusions which are surely in harmony with the goal of the entire passage. Our mode of indicating these conclusions was to insert brackets indicating subject and object, and the like.

The point then is this: God surely smote Israel's oppressors much more severely than he smote his own people. Considerations of merit are not brought into the discussion. Nor is the approach one that suggests unseemly partiality on the Lord's part. One thing surely is clear: the Lord did show an unusual measure of kindness to his people. Some were slain in the process of treatment that he had to use, but even then measures of extreme rigor were avoided over against Israel, as the second half of the verse indicates. (For similar thoughts cf. 28:24-29; also Jer. 24:25.)

Verse 8. The Lord did have to "strive" with his people in the course of their history. A certain, almost habitual, pattern was discernible in the Lord's dealings with Israel. Repeatedly groups of them were taken by the enemy, "driven away" and "dispersed," until the climax came in the Assyrian captivity for the Northern Kingdom, which, as we hope to show in connection with v. 10, may already have taken place. Deportation, however, was not yet extinction, which latter fate in the course of historical events did befall numerous nations of antiquity. As for Israel, he merely "removed her by his harsh wind." But even in that treatment kindness was discernible. Some of the thoughts here set forth are not limited to Isaiah. See also Jer. 18:17.

Verse 9. But all this kindly treatment of Israel had a direct purpose, and this purpose was to have Israel's guilt expiated. A response on Israel's part was expected which would make such expiation possible. This response in itself would not be anything meritorious, but, in the nature of the case would be so natural and normal a reaction that Israel could not do otherwise than manifest it, and God could not do otherwise than expect it. Expect it, he did, and at the same time it could be regarded as "the only return that he expects." And this return was that Israel make a clean and complete break with everything that has to do with the idol-cults that were so often slipped into by the children of Israel. A basic order in the Book of Deuteronomy covered the case: 16:21. Later statements indicate that the issue had never been totally overlooked (see II Kings 18:4; 21:7; Jer. 17:8). But in the end no man and no nation can serve two masters. So the prophet asserts that the nation would have to make a thorough work of completely destroying those items which were the center and core of idolatry — the "idol-altars." Sacred poles and pillars that surrounded such altars would naturally have to be dealt with in the same fashion. They could not "remain standing" (cf. 17:8). The thoroughness with which the whole task was to be carried out is indicated by the statement that when the people were done with the altars, all that would be left would be "pulverized chalkstones."

e. God's Stern Dealings with the "fortified city" (vv. 10-11)

27:10-11 10. For the fortified city lies desolate,
an abandoned and forsaken habitation like the wilderness;
there the calf grazes, there it lies down, and destroys its branches.
11. When its [Jacob's] boughs have withered, they are broken off;
women come along and make a fire of them.
For they are a people totally without understanding;
therefore their Maker has no pity on them;
he that formed them shows them no favor.

For the interpretation of these two verses much depends on the identification of "the fortified city." Is this one of the two met with repeatedly in Chaps. 24–27? If so, is it the "city of chaos" (24:10)? Cf. also 25:2; 26:5ff. On the other hand, the whole approach to the problem of the city could be determined by the interpretation of the chapter up to this point. If the material is attributed to Isaiah, then the city will be one recently desolated. So rather than refer it to Carthage, or the capital city of Moab, or to Jerusalem — the more common of the attempted interpretations, we feel that the determining factor in this case could be that its people are referred to as being "totally without knowledge" (cf.

Deut. 32:6). Such a description would not be given for any city of the Gentiles, for Gentiles could not well be blamed for being without knowledge. But the people of God can be held accountable. With this approach we seem to be pointed in the direction of Samaria which fell during the time of Isaiah's ministry (722 B.3.) and very readily would have come to mind for the readers or hearers of Isaiah's message.

These two verses would then constitute an example to the contrary, in opposition to what had just been said in vv. 7-9 dealing with God's kindly treatment of his people. Here then is an instance where kindly dealing had to give way to stern dealing because they who had received divine mercy had not made a wholesome return by cleansing themselves from the things that made them tainted in the sight of God. This city, Samaria, is pictured in all its desolation after the Assyrians had done their cruel work upon it. Where there had been a prosperous and thickly-populated community there was now "a forsaken habitation like a wilderness." The city had become pasture land and the calf grazed there and rested there. When its "branches" are said to be destroyed, the pronoun does not appear to have an obvious antecedent. It may be that the picture has shifted and the city is now being thought of as a tree whose foliage is being destroyed.

Verse 11. This picture is continued in this verse, and a possible antecedent for the "its" could be Jacob, as we have indicated by adding it by way of brackets. A further step in the devastation of the city could then be that branches of the dead tree wither, are broken, are gathered by women who need faggots for fire. Then comes the deeper cause for all this — already indicated above — the people are "totally without understanding." By inserting the word "totally" we have tried to cover the unique emphasis of the expression used for "knowledge," a plural, calculated to refer to a higher level of knowledge, in fact a kind of superlative. This is the higher discernment that would be encountered among the people of God. They are the ones who in a significant sense could describe the Lord as their "Maker." If it is then said of him that he "has no pity on them" and "shows them no favor" the point is that they have forfeited the grace of God, to which they offered no fitting response while it dwelt in their midst. These verses may be said to constitute the dark background of this chapter. But since the flourishing state of the people of God is a major issue in the chapter, it appears readily that the next note may well be a note that dwells on the hopeful outlook.

f. The Gathering of the Scattered Children of Israel (vv. 12-13)

27:12-13 12. And it shall come to pass on that day the Lord will hold a threshing from the ears of grain of the Euphrates to those of the Brook of Egypt. And you will be gathered together one by one, O children of Israel. 13. It shall come to pass in that day that a great trumpet shall also be blown, and they who had strayed in the land of Assyria shall come, also those who were scattered in the land of Egypt, and they shall worship the Lord on the holy mountain in Jerusalem.

Verses 12, 13. To get the full measure of these two verses at once, it should be noted that two areas from which God's scattered people are to be gathered are under consideration, the area once covered by the domain of David and Solomon — from the Euphrates to the Brook of Egypt — and then the area that lay beyond these confines, both to the north and the south — Assyria and Egypt. From Israel's own traditional territory (cf. Gen. 15:18; I Kings 8:65) people will be gathered like kernels are in a threshing. From the second area they will be gathered by being summoned with a trumpet call. The point is, God's fatherly care for his own will appear in this that the scattered ones will be most faithfully gathered and made a unit again. Their unity however will express itself in their united worship at the sanctuary in Jerusalem. The scene is highly idealized. It may refer to the return from Babylonian captivity. It may yet point to a great future gathering. In any case, it emphasizes that the people of God have a great future awaiting them. The reference to Assyria could well have been written shortly after the fall of Samaria, when the major number of the deportees apparently had been carried off to Assyria (cf. II Kings 17:6).

Though one traditional way of assembling people was by raising an ensign, or "signal" (5:26), the use of the trumpet for such purposes is also indicated in the Old Testament: see Joel 2:1; Ps. 81:3. The New Testament knows of the same device: see Matt. 24:31; I Cor. 15:52; I Thess. 4:16.

The unique character of the threshing here referred to in v. 12 is this that the verb used implies beating out grains with a stick, a more painstaking mode of procedure, indicative of the Lord's personal concern for his own.

Notes

Verse 1. Since Leviathan, according to Job 3:8, was used to refer to some heavenly body, the attempt has been made to let its use in this verse also point in that direction, with the result that three comparatively insignificant constellations have been thought of as referred to: Serpens, Draco, and Hydra (*Burney*). So the whole verse is made to be purely mythological allusion. This seems to be a desperate attempt to produce mythological material and is hardly convincing.

Verse 2. At this point a slight textual emendation seems to suggest itself, one that is almost universally accepted in our day. Instead of the expression *kerem chemer* ("a vineyard of wine") which is more or less meaningless, a lead, first suggested by the *Septuagint*, is followed, viz., to take for the second word *chemer* the word *chemedh* "desire," a change which involves merely a sharper angle in the writing of the last letter. We accept this as a reasonable and commendable emendation.

Verse 3. The word *liregha'im*, which *RSV* translates "every moment" involves one of those plurals which does not signify "every" but "many." See *KS* 74.

Verse 4. The expression *mi yitteneni* usually is a typical way of introducing a wish ("Would that"). In this instance the expression is not yet smoothed down to that level but is half wish and half of the literal meaning, "O that I might be given." Cf. *GK* 151, a.b.

For "Proceed against them" the Hebrew has "against it." Apparently the thorns and briers are regarded as a unit.

Verse 5. The initial *'o*, usually translated "or" should be taken in this instance as meaning "unless." See *GK* 162 a.

Verse 8. *Besa'se'ah* could be a pilpel infinitive (from *su'*) and would then mean, as we have rendered it "by driving away." It was formerly construed as being a repetition of the word *se'ah*, a Hebrew measure containing two and one-half gallons. It would then be rendered "by measure measure" which could signify "measure by measure" (*RSV*), which could mean "moderately." See *GK* 55 a.

Verse 9. The phrase *bezo'th*, "in this" could be used proleptically here, in the sense of "on this condition" — involving that the condition is about to be mentioned. In the statement, "that she [Israel] make all her idol-altars" the Hebrew uses the masculine pronoun, where we have set a "she." This was done because in the preceding verses, the feminine pronoun was used in referring to the nation. A nation may be conceived as a masculine entity, for strength, or as a feminine entity, for productiveness. Hebrew does not strive at strict consistency.

Verse 11. "Understanding" appears in what is known as the amplificative plural, to mark a strong degree of the quality involved (*GK* 124 e).

Verse 12. The word *shibboleth* may mean either "stream" or an "ear of corn." We believe the latter meaning is involved here.

THE BOOK OF ZION

Chapter XXVIII

III. THE BOOK OF ZION (Chaps. 28-35)

A. ZION'S PRECIOUS CORNERSTONE (Chap. 28)

With this chapter the climate of the book changes. We are no longer in the area of universal judgment. Zion is the dominant thought. The prophet's thoughts center about the glorious future of this citadel of God. For this reason, perhaps, no more appropriate caption can be given to Chaps. 28-35 than "The Book of Zion" (*von Orelli*). On the face of it, it might seem very much in place to let the thoughts of "Woe" dominate the scene, for in this section almost every chapter begins with a "woe" (cf. 28:1; 29:1 and 15; 30:1; 31:1; 33:1). So *Delitzsch* called this "The Book of Woes." But this is a more formal peculiarity; it fails to penetrate more deeply into the subject under discussion.

There is ground for believing that these chapters were spoken or/and written during the reign of Hezekiah. Another prominent issue that keeps appearing in this general area is the issue of alliance with Egypt. That was the outstanding and popular political trend at the time. Sometimes the issue lies in the background, sometimes it is specifically lifted into the foreground. In any case it is a serious and dominant trend.

As far as our particular chapter is concerned the title we have used above may be as appropriate as any: Zion's Precious Cornerstone. Though this stone, as such, is mentioned only in v. 16, yet it is the center around which the rest of the thoughts cluster. These thoughts are pitched on so high a level that *G. A. Smith* is moved to make the claim with regard to this chapter that it is "one of the grandest of all prophecies." It certainly is Isaiah at his best. To a very large extent there is agreement among commentators that this chapter must be ascribed to Isaiah. To fix the precise year is difficult, but many incline to the year 725 B.C.

Those who concentrate attention on the possible meter that prevails in the chapter have their difficulties. They admit that the meter is not easy to determine. In vv. 1-4 double lines with seven accents can be noted to an extent. Then the lines of vv. 7-13 have five or seven accents, and so forth. Some attempt to rearrange the verses to obtain better coherence. One suggested pattern runs as follows: 7–13, 16, 17a, 14, 15, 17b–22. We hope to demonstrate that the coherence in evidence in the present sequence of verses is good and meaningful.

It would make the whole approach more dramatic if we at least accepted the reasonable suggestion that at v. 7 the prophet may be thought of as breaking in upon an assembly, held perhaps in one of the chambers of the Temple, where policy was being determined with regard to the alliance with Egypt, but many of the participants were under the influence of alcohol — a most disgusting spectacle. The prophet launches into a virulent attack. All this would serve to dramatize the issues rather strongly, but unfortunately all rests upon too flimsy a foundation to be susceptible of any proof.

We submit a brief outline of the contents of the chapter:

1. The False Crown of Glory vs. the Right Crown (vv. 1-6)
2. The Doom of Judah's Dubious Security vs. the Solid Endurance of the Lord's Project (vv. 7-16)
3. A Further Announcement of Doom: The Lord Will Do a "strange" Work (vv. 17-22)
4. A Parable Illustrating How Judiciously the Lord Does His Work upon His People (vv. 23-29)

1. The False Crown of Glory vs. the Right Crown (vv. 1-6)

28:1-6 1. Woe to the proud crown of the drunkards of Ephraim, and to the fading flower of its glorious beauty
which lies at the head of the rich valley of those overcome with wine!
2. Behold, the Lord has at his disposal a strong and mighty one;

as a downpour of hail, a storm of destruction, as a downpour of
  water sweeping along mightily,
so will he forcefully dash things to the ground.
3. The proud crown of the drunkards of Ephraim will be trampled
  under foot.
4. And the fading flower of its glorious beauty,
which lies at the head of the rich valley,
will be like the first-ripe fig before the summer,
which, as soon as a man sees it, while it is still in his hand, he
  swallows it.
5. On that day the Lord of hosts will be a glorious crown
and a diadem of beauty for the remnant of his people;
6. and a spirit of justice for those that administer justice,
and might for those that turn the tide of battle at the gate.

Verse 1. Was this piece spoken before or after the fall of
Samaria in 722 B.C.? Aside from the forms of verbs that are
used, which we shall examine in the *Notes*, the decisive argument seems to be that "woes" are usually pronounced with
reference to things that are yet to come. Therefore, with
the great majority of commentators, we regard this as spoken
while Samaria still stood. The style is somewhat bombastic, intentionally so, whether the first verse be read in the
original or in any translation. The bombast reflects the pride
of the inhabitants. Samaria, built by Omri, father of Ahab,
lay on a pleasantly rounded hill, some 340 meters high, at
the head of a fertile valley. The city with its walls might
well be likened to a crown, "a proud crown" in fact, because
its people were proud of its location and of its strength. Into
this first figure blends a second one, perhaps a mixed metaphor, likening the city to a flower, a "fading flower." Blended
together, this amounts to a chaplet of wilting flowers crowning the city hill. It may be described as "fading" because
to the experienced eye of the prophet the decline of the city
has already begun. The rich, or fertile, valley, at whose head
the city lies, constitutes a part of the city's glory. But the
conclusion of the description brings a glum note into the picture: It is a city of those "overcome with wine," or, as previously stated: it was the crown "of the drunkards of Ephraim." Cf. Amos 6:4-10; Hos. 7:5-7. A wealth of description
is packed away in this first verse.

Verses 2, 3. The implied indictment of v. 1 is that the city is ripe for judgment. Note: the name of the city has not been mentioned; but the evidence points exclusively in this one direction. Being then ripe for judgment, the city will find that the Lord, who dispenses all judgment that befalls his people, has in readiness a force adequate for this purpose, like unto "a strong and mighty one." He will, when the time comes, dash to the earth everything that is ready for the judgment. Three comparisons are used to indicate the utter effectiveness of the agencies that will be employed to bring low the proud and debauched city. The force striking the city, which was, as is historically clear, nothing other than the armies of Assyria, may be likened first to a mighty "downpour of hail"; secondly, to a force of wind that is "a storm of destruction"; and thirdly a mighty rain, "a downpour of water, sweeping along mightily." Any one of these elemental forces can effect an utter destruction of anything that stands in its path. Summing up, these forces "will forcefully dash things to the ground." As a result (v. 3) "The proud crown of the drunkards of Ephraim will be trampled under foot." It surely will be a sorry spectacle, when like a garland of flowers that are torn from a drunkard's head, the wreath lies trampled into the mud or dust. So uninviting a spectacle will the city present after its tragic downfall.

Verse 4. The above description of the doomed city is in part repeated. The "proud crown" idea is dropped and the "fading flower" kept. Again, what some would call a sort of mixed metaphor is resorted to: The flower, meaning the city, is likened to a "first-ripe fig." But since the "fading flower" already has conveyed to the hearer or the reader the idea of the city of Samaria, to liken this city to a fig hardly confuses anybody. Let the captious take exception. But these "first-ripe figs" were the ones that ripened in June rather than in fall, and were eagerly desired because they were so sweet in flavor. But the point of the comparison is really not how fast the man who finds it gulps it down, but rather the *eagerness* with which he lays hold on it. So will the Assyrians eagerly reach forth to capture this prized city of Samaria. This approach agrees better with the facts of history. For the Assyrians had to besiege the city three years before it capitulated.

Verse 5. Up to this point the chief item under consideration really was the "crown" — Samaria, indicated by the order of words in Hebrew, which put the word "crown" immediately after "woe." Verse 5 now indicates that this experience will teach at least some men to center their attention on the true crown of Israel, "the Lord of hosts." He truly will be a glorious crown to those who give him the place of supreme importance in their lives.

Another special title is here introduced by way of synonym — "a diadem of beauty." But not all will allow themselves to be taught this lesson, only "the remnant of his people," a concept with which Isaiah operates rather frequently. See 4:2; 10:20f.; 11:11, 16; 37:32. At least God's judgment upon the proud and dissolute city will not have been without some constructive results. This is spelled out a bit more fully in the next verse.

Verse 6. This verse implies rather than states certain results, namely, that the severe judgment on Samaria will bring some to their senses. They will repent and turn back to the Lord, both in Israel and in Judah. Those who have thus been brought to their senses will be motivated by higher principles. Just a few illustrations are submitted. Those whose business it is to "administer justice" will be controlled by a "spirit of justice," as such officials should be. Other penitent leaders who help defend the city in days of assault, will be granted by the Lord, whom they now serve, "might," courageous strength for battle, so that when perhaps the attackers have even penetrated through the city gate and seem to be about to capture the city, these servants of the Almighty will boldly stem the surging tide of battle and drive the attackers back out through the city gates and so prove themselves deliverers of God's people, like the heroic "judges" of days of old.

2. The Doom of Judah's Dubious Security vs. the Solid Endurance of the Lord's Project (vv. 7-16)

28:7-16 7. But these also reel with wine,
and stagger about with strong drink.

Priest and prophet reel with strong drink,
and are overpowered by wine.
They stagger because of strong drink and reel over the vision;
they totter as they render the decision.
8. For all tables are full of filthy vomit;
no clean place is left.
9. "Whom will he teach knowledge,
and to whom will he make the message clear?
Babes just weaned from milk? those taken away from the breasts?"
10. For [all we hear is]: 'precept upon precept, precept upon precept;
line upon line, line upon line;
here a little, there a little.' "
11. Yea, with stammering lips and with a foreign tongue he will speak to this people,
12. he who said to them: "This will bring rest;
give rest to the weary; this is the refreshing."
But they would not listen.
13. Therefore the word of the Lord will be for them:
"Precept upon precept, precept upon precept;
line upon line, line upon line;
here a little, there a little;"
so that they may go their way and stumble backward,
and be broken and snared and taken.
14. Therefore hear the word of the Lord, you scoffers,
who rule over this people here at Jerusalem:
15. Because you have said: "We have made a covenant with death,
and with Sheol we have a contract;
a sweeping scourge, when it descends, shall not fall on us;
for we have made lies our refuge, and falsehood our shelter."
16. Therefore thus says the Lord Yahweh:
"I am about to lay in Zion a stone, a tested stone,
a precious cornerstone, solidly embedded."
He who believes shall not panic!

This section of the chapter may be said to extend as far as v. 22. We have preferred to let it extend only to v. 16, and to make vv. 17-22 a second pronouncement of doom. In any case, the doom announced in vv. 1-16 is contrasted with the solid endurance of that which the Lord has established. Man's flimsy work perished; the Lord's building endures.

Verse 7. This is the point at which (as indicated above) the prophet might have broken in upon an assembly of those who were making policy for the nation and may have discovered that they were drunk even when they were de-

liberating on matters of state. For a moment we are inclined
to have difficulty over the "these" here under consideration.
Since the word may have been spoken with a gesture in the
direction of those who stood before the prophet, it could
have been clear to those who first heard it. In any event, v.
14 clearly indicates that the people, particularly the ruling
classes of *Judah*, are here under consideration. The emphasis has shifted from Samaria to the Southern Kingdom. If
there are "drunkards of Ephraim" there are also drunkards
of Judah. Just about every one before the prophet on this
occasion must have been tipsy, reeling with wine and staggering about with strong drink. The verbs are heaped up
to indicate every state and degree of inebriation. "Priest and
prophet" particularly, are involved, the priest as the official
expounder of the law of the Lord (see Lev. 10:9) and the
prophet as the man professionally appointed to receive messages for the people from the Lord. Such weighty obligations require a clear mind. But here both "reel with strong
drink and are overpowered by wine." In fact, things have
come to so sorry a pass that they stagger in the very process
of making a solemn pronouncement. For the obligation of
the priest cf. also Deut. 33:10 and Mal. 2:6. There must
have been some very unworthy characters among the ad-
visors of King Hezekiah.

Verse 8. The extent to which drunkenness prevailed is indicated rather graphically by the repulsive appearance of
the very tables at which these state-counsellors sat. There
was not a table on which the vomit of the drunkard was not
to be found. In fact there was not even a "clean place"
left on any table top.

Verse 9. This verse appears to express the reaction of the
assembly to the correction of the prophet. They counter
with sarcastic remarks. Perhaps the prophet had used simple statements to penetrate through the fog of their drunkenness, so they come back with the scoffing words here
given. Paraphrased the verse might run thus: "He's trying
to impart knowledge of God's purposes and to give us messages he claims to have heard from God; who does he think
we are? sucking infants and newly weaned children?"

Verse 10. This is one of the strangest words in prophetic

literature, especially the first half: all "a" sounds, are practically monosyllables: *tsaw latsaw, tsaw latsaw, qaw laqaw,
qaw laqaw*. Men are at a loss to determine whether this is
supposed to be the heavy-tongued stammering of the drunkard, or the infantile patter of the babes, or, for that matter,
whether it is supposed to be idle chatter (German: *Kauder-
welsch*). We incline to the view that it is sarcastic talk,
done in monosyllables to make the simplicity of the prophet's
message ridiculous. He is represented as spelling something
out that they have long understood; he's been playing the
part of the pedantic pedagogue; they are amused at the
fact that he seems to treat them like simpletons. He is doling
out his instruction in small doses: "precept upon precept, line
upon line."

This might serve to give a cue to the last expression: "Here
a little, there a little." The prophet is trying to teach them by
giving a bit of instruction at a time: he is spelling out his
message. Since this verse apparently is direct discourse,
which is not even formally introduced in any way, we have
ventured to preface it with a bracketed: "all we hear."

Verse 11. These sarcastic words just heard from the lips
of those whom the prophet has sharply corrected, call for a
retort. The prophet gives them a very sharp one. They
represent the Lord's prophet as stammering? Let them take
note of the fact that the Lord himself will speak unwelcome
sounds to them which may also in a way be likened to
"stammering lips," and to a "foreign tongue." That is to
say, in a language in which they were not accustomed to hear
them speak. What they were wont to hear from him as he
addressed his people was, in times past, gentle words and
kindly speech. Such a word of gentle approach now follows, somewhat difficult to determine as to its import.

Verse 12. Many are the interpretations that have been
offered for this verse. Perhaps the best approach is that suggested by 30:15, indicating that an attitude of quiet trust
in the Lord will impart strength to them that cultivate it.
For the evil days prevailing are likely to impart a sense of
fear and apprehension. Here we may let ourselves be reminded that throughout this section the alliance with Egypt
as a possible remedy for the current ills is being strongly

warned against. Its counterpart is a firm trust in the Lord.
Only in this latter approach will there be rest. The prophet
has been imploring the leaders to provide this rest for the
people; "this is the refreshing." But this was the course that
was consistently being rejected, or as the prophet says: "They
would not listen." So then, kindly words of guidance were
persistently pushed aside. Well and good! Let them hear
words of an opposite sort.

Verse 13. With telling sarcasm the prophet gives them
such hard words and aptly enough casts them into the very
form that they had employed for their scoffing remarks. If
they mocked the elementary simplicity that they thought
they had detected in the word of the Lord, it will be as
though they heard the Lord himself say what they scoffingly
charged his prophet with saying. Perhaps it will be such
elementary truths as: "The soul that sinneth, it shall die,"
or some analogous words of doom. As a result of what that
word of judgment pronounces, they will "go on their way
and stumble backward and be broken and snared and taken."
Assuming all this to have been originally an encounter between rebellious leaders and the prophet, we see Isaiah at
his best, withering in his scorn and effective in quick retort.

Verse 14. But he drives home the word of rebuke still
more sharply. Beginning at this point, the prophet very
obviously takes issue with the trend that favors a political
alliance with Egypt. But since Judah's leaders have resorted
to scoffing remarks, and since scoffing, as *Skinner* has well
remarked, is "the last degree of ungodliness," Isaiah virtually
thunders this word at those "who rule over this people here
at Jerusalem."

Verse 15. He lays bare what their boastful attitude is.
They were so sure of the efficacy of their procedures when
they entered into an alliance with Egypt, that they made
bold to claim: "We have made a covenant with death, and
with Sheol we have a contract." In other words, this famous
alliance of theirs which they have made with Egypt is supposed to furnish them security even against death and
Sheol. For this reason they seem to be calling it "a covenant
with death" and "a contract with Sheol." To try to interpret
these expressions as involving some actual covenant made

with death and the hereafter, only makes the issue more complicated, and would seem to point in the direction of necromancy, and the like. By "covenant with death" they merely mean we have taken out insurance against death; death cannot harm us, neither can Sheol. Or abandoning all figurative language, it is as though they were claiming: We have taken all necessary measures to insure our safety and that of the state.

That a grave danger is threatening they admit. They call it "a sweeping scourge," and apparently have in mind the forces of Assyria which are sweeping along and blasting every opposition that crosses their path. But they are so sure of the protection that Egypt apparently had so vaingloriously promised that they maintained: That "scourge, when it descends, shall not fall on us." Figurative language throughout, characteristic of the veiled language in which treaties secretly made are couched! The verb "sweep" had already been used (8:8) in reference to the Assyrian battle-forces. But there the figure was that of water rushing along mightily. Here it refers to a scourge descending powerfully on the back of the one smitten.

The prophet has a bit more to add, which is not by way of direct quotation but rather as a form of words that they would have used about their secret devices if they but understood a bit better what they are doing and saying: "[You say]: "We have made lies our refuge and falsehood our shelter." Nobody would consciously and deliberately do that, but they, in effect, have done it. For apparently already then diplomacy and secret treaties were a bundle of lies and a fabric of falsehood, and both of these are notoriously unreliable. The prophet here ruthlessly tears from their face the curtain of self-deception behind which they have been hiding.

Verse 16. Now we come to the most glorious word of the chapter. After the spurious and deceptive issues confronting the nation have been pointed up for what they are, what is more natural than to draw emphatic attention to what really counts, or to what really affords a firm foundation. The Lord himself is about to provide a solid foundation for his people and their future. The figure of a building to be erected is

employed. Its location is Zion. A proper stone to mark the
corner is to be laid, thus providing the guiding lines for the
whole outline of the structure. This stone will not soon
crumble, in fact cannot crumble at all. It has been subjected
to all requisite tests. It is of the finest material. It will be
solidly imbedded. God is providing this foundation because
man cannot. Yet he so desperately needs something solid.
But what does this stone represent? How is it to be interpreted? The answers are numerous. Most of them are
shadings of one and the same basic thought. The claim that
this solid base is "the prophetic message," certainly is very
appropriate, (*Koenig*), for God's contact with his people is
by way of the word of his prophets. Or it may even be a bit
more to the point to label this stone as "the Messianic salvation" (*von Orelli*). Much along the same line, though
not so much to the point, is *Skinner's* claim that the stone
is the symbol of "God's relation to Israel (which) is the stable
foundation of all of God's work in the world." This would
include thoughts such as those of *G. A. Smith* that the stone
represents the fact of "God's assurance that Jerusalem is inviolable." Others quite naturally connect this passage with II
Sam. 7, about the enduring character of the throne of David.
Still, "the Messianic salvation" seems to be the best interpretation. For in that salvation the Messiah himself is included. And this would account for the consistent approach
of the New Testament in referring the passage to Christ as
its fulfilment. See Matt. 21:42, 44; Luke 20:17; Acts 4:11;
Rom. 9:33; Eph. 2:20; and I Peter 2:4-6. The passage must
have burst upon the hearers and the readers of that day as a
bright and glorious light. The many words of one sort or
another concerning the great work that the Lord would perform, must have prepared the minds of the people of God for
the possibility of an adequate understanding of this word.
The statement that follows virtually invites men to build on
this foundation: "He that believes shall not panic." In reality the good thing promised is usually stated: ". . . he shall
not make haste." We believe our translation, though entirely
new, as far as we know, catches the distinctive thought in the
idiom of our day. The calm poise of the believer is under
consideration. Frantic unrest was the mark of all who en-

gaged in the customary expedients. Not so the man who builds of the foundation God provides. (Cf. 26:3.) Verse 16 beautifully enriches the concept of the Messianic kingdom as developed by Isaiah and marks the role faith plays in it.

3.   A Further Announcement of Doom: the Lord Will Do a "strange" Work (vv. 17-22)

28:17-22 17. "And I shall make justice the measuring line and righteousness the plummet.
And hail will sweep away the refuge of lies,
and water shall flood away the hiding-place."
18. And your covenant with death will be cancelled out;
and your agreement with Sheol will not stand.
When the sweeping scourge descends,
you will be trampled down by it.
19. As often as it descends it will take you.
For morning by morning it will descend, by day also and by night.
Merely to hear a report will be sheer terror.
20. For the bed is too short to stretch out on it;
and the coverlet is too narrow to roll one's self in it.
21. For the Lord will rise up as on Mount Perazim;
he shall quiver with anger as in the valley of Gibeon,
to do his work — strange is his work —
and to achieve his task — alien is his task.
22. And now stop your scoffing, lest your bonds be made stronger.
For news of a destruction fully determined has come to my ears,
from the Lord God of hosts upon all the earth.

Verses 17, 18. These words go on the assumption that the Lord's work is being carried on the new basis which he himself has just described in v. 16. Not only will there be a secure foundation but the standards of measurement will be in keeping with how the Lord's work in his kingdom should be done. There, for example, "Justice will be the measuring line," by which all acts of his and of his people will be governed. "Righteousness will be the plummet," or the plumbline, by which the test will be made whether a deed deserves to stand. The inferior material will be swept away as utterly inadequate. "The refuge of lies" — that is to say the covenant with Egypt — will be swept away as by a fierce hail-storm. "The hiding-place" — the shifty diplomacy of the day behind which they were taking refuge — will be washed away, as with a severe flood. That "covenant with death" — as they called it — will be ruled out, or "cancelled out," as ineffective and inadequate. Their "agreement with Sheol" (cf. v. 15 again) "will not stand." They thought they had found means to invalidate "the sweeping scourge" — the Assyrian. Instead, the covenant with Egypt will be so ineffective that whenever a blow threatens from the Assyrian, the people of Judah will be "trampled down by it." Again we have what would be described technically as a mixed metaphor. But the issue is perfectly clear. Each blow of the scourge will utterly smite them to the ground.

Verse 19. The vivid description of the impending doom goes on. Cf. II Kings 18:13. Still thinking in terms of the scourge of Assyria as descending again and again, its frequent blows are predicted as coming "morning by morning," "by day also and by night." So frequent will be the rumors of fresh attacks and they shall all be so ominous that "merely to hear a report will be sheer terror." We believe so to construe the word "report" in this context does better justice to it.

Verse 20. The prophet resorts to a new figure to describe the situation that will then prevail, that of a bed. Not like our use of a kindred figure or making your bed and then being obliged to lie in it. This bed will be too short. The bed, however, is the inadequate preparations that were made for the Assyrian emergency. They will not help in the situation for which they were designed. Or to slightly vary the figure, they have a coverlet against the cold of an emergency, but the coverlet "is too narrow to roll one's self in it."

Verse 21. Finally the doom that is being described is seen to be of such a sort that the Lord himself has a direct hand in it. He will appear on the scene, as he once did in the interest of the children of Israel when, in David's day, they lay in battle with the Philistines at Mount Perazim, which was between Jerusalem and Bethlehem. (cf. II Sam. 5:19-21). Then he intervened to save. Or his appearance could be compared with his intervention at Gibeon, northwest of Jerusalem, in fact, on two memorable occasions (see Josh. 10:12 and II Sam. 5:22f.). Then, too, he appeared that he might help his own. But now, though he will be deeply stirred to intervene, even "quiver with anger," the strange difference will be that he will vent his wrath *on his own* and so may be said to be doing a work which is both "strange" and "alien" to his character, as he is known to his people. This statement is marked by a certain vagueness, which makes it all the more ominous. But the prophet is sure that he will not have been misunderstood by his people.

Verse 22. So he concludes with a strong warning. The basic attitude of the leaders of Judah seems to have degenerated to the point where the Word of the Lord merely induces scoffing when it is heard. Peremptorily he commands them to stop their scoffing (cf. v. 14), and threatens a worsening of the disasters already upon them unless they give heed. The "stronger bands" referred to could well be the tightening of the Assyrian yoke upon Judah's neck. In fact, what is impending is nothing less than "destruction" now fully "determined" by the Almighty. The prophet, in continual touch with his Lord, has heard the news concerning this destruction. And the disaster involved will strike more than Judah. It is designed for "all the earth." Thus concludes the double pronouncement of doom.

4. A Parable Illustrating How Judiciously the Lord Does His Work upon His People (vv. 23-29)

28:23-29 23. Give ear and hear my voice;
hearken and hear my speech.
24. Does the plowman, who readies his land for sowing, plow continually?
Does he keep breaking up the soil and harrowing it?
25. Or rather, when he has smoothed the surface, does he not scatter black cummin
and sow other cummin?
and put in wheat in rows and barley in its proper place,
and spelt as its border?
26. His God has always instructed him as to proper procedure;
he teaches him.
27. For black cummin is not threshed out with a threshing sled,
nor is the cart-wheel rolled around on other cummin.
But black cummin is beaten out with a rod,
and other cummin with a staff.
28. Is grain for bread crushed?

No, men do not keep threshing away at it,
nor does a man drive his cart-wheels and horses over it;
he does not crush it.
29. This all comes from the Lord of hosts.
He is wonderful in counsel and great in wisdom.

Verse 23. Doing a "strange" work, the Lord might be
misunderstood by his people. So he lets the prophet provide a parable in which he makes plain what he is doing.
The parable is not provided with an interpretation, because
its point can be very readily grasped. It hardly can be called
a fair appraisal of the parable to claim that "the precise
point of the analogy is somewhat obscure" (*Skinner*). There
might be some uncertainty about some details of explanation but its general import leaves no doubt as to its overall
purpose. It begins in the language of wisdom literature,
reminiscent of Gen. 4:23 and Ps. 49:1.

Verse 24. The plowman without a doubt represents the
Lord himself. He is depicted as working after the manner
of a farmer who tills the soil, sows and reaps certain crops
and threshes out the resultant product. The first point is
that in breaking up the soil he does not go on without a
change in procedure, plowing and plowing, harrowing and
harrowing, endlessly. The point already made is that the
Lord is indeed preparing Israel that it may bring forth, let
us say, the fruits of righteousness. But where a kind of breaking up of the soil of the nation has to be done — this may involve the preparatory work done by his judgments, to make
men's hearts ready for doing good works — the preparation
of the soil as such does not go on endlessly. Discretion is
used by the tiller of the soil.

Verse 25. Equal discretion is used in the matter of sowing
the various crops, grain and other seeds, that were customarily raised. The farmer is no dunce; he knows proper procedure. The technical terms of agricultural products, or
seeds, may not be entirely clear to us in our day. The overall picture does not as a result become unclear. The minor
seeds are the two types of cummin mentioned. The major
bread-grains are wheat and barley and perhaps spelt. Some
of these are so sown as to edge off the sowed area; others

cover the major part of the same area. It could be that
wheat was in some way "put in rows." That matters little.
The Israelite farmer did not farm quite as our farmers do.
But prepare the soil he did, and sow he did in a sensible
fashion. This knowledge of his and the procedures used
may well be traced back even to God himself (v. 26) as
something done according to some kind of implanted in-
stinct. At least what he does is dictated by common sense
and makes good sense. For this part of the parable the inference is also from the lower to the higher. How much more
may Israel expect that when the Lord works the soil of his
people Israel, he, too, will use good sense and proceed according to modes of working that are entirely reasonable.

Verse 27. The same approach is used in regard to threshing procedure. The lighter products, the two kinds of cummin mentioned, were usually threshed out by beating with a
stick or staff. Harsher methods would have crushed so much
of the crop as to be unwise procedure. But for the grains
used for daily bread, the kernel being harder and the ear
often much tougher, a different approach commended itself.
There was, first of all, the threshing-sled; flat boards with
insets of stones or metal on the surface to break up the ears
of grain. Then there were threshing-carts whose wheels
might have similar insertion to make their wheel-surface
sharper. And then there were the hoofs of the threshing-
oxen used for the same purpose by driving these creatures
round and round on the grain to be threshed out. Every
farmer had sense enough to recognize that these methods
had to be adapted to the nature of the material being
threshed out. The foolish use of methods is strongly denied
as being simply too unreasonable to think of. And the implied conclusion? God the Lord displays no less sense in
working upon his people than the husbandman working on
his grain?

Verse 29. Where this verse seems at first only to indicate
that the farmer's wisdom in these matters is so basic a need
that it may indeed be traced back to the Lord himself, the
last line of the verse is entirely back on the subject of God's
work done on Israel. It is not only reasonable, it not only
makes good sense when carefully inspected, it is, as he is,

"wonderful in counsel and great in wisdom." This concluding analogy, or parable, apparently was necessary for those who, living right in the thick of a very complex situation, needed assurance that the Lord would not deal too severely with his recalcitrant people.

Notes

Verse 1. In the phrase "flower of glorious beauty" a participle, "fading," is inserted after the initial noun which is in the construct state. See *KS* 321 b.

Verse 3. The verb "will be trampled" appears in the plural, which suggests reading the word "crown" as a plural, which may be done without changing a letter of the text.

Verse 4. The final *h* of *'othah* should be read without a *mappiq;* see *GK* 91 e. The expression *yir'eh haro'eh*, verb plus corresponding participle, is a typical way of expressing the indefinite subject, "any one." See *GK* 144 e.

Verse 9. Where the Hebrew construct "weaned of" would cover the case, sometimes, as here, an additional preposition is inserted "weaned of from." Cf. *KS* 336 w.

Verse 10. The bracketed ("all we hear") merely supplies what the ellipsis has taken for granted.

In the Hebrew the letters *tsaw* and *qaw* are consecutive in the alphabet and taken together constitute the letters of the root *tsuq*, which means "distress." Could it be that this verse with its unusual build-up is trying to indicate this? We believe the suggestion is too clever to accept.

Verse 12. At the end of the verse the form *'abhu'* has a redundant *aleph*. Cf. *GK* 23 i.

Verse 14. The Hebrew uses the expression "men of scoffing" with "men" used merely as a relation-word. For this reason we felt it was unnecessary to translate it. See *KS* 306 n.

Verse 15. In the form *yebho'enu* the verb is thought of as containing the preposition "on." Cf. *KS* 22.

Verse 16. The form *yissadh* might be allowed to stand if an implied relative pronoun were prefixed to it. It seems simpler to take the consonants and give them the vowel-points of the active participle *yosedh*, as the principal versions do. The expression "a tested stone" could also be rendered "a stone of testing" implying that men are tested by him. We prefer the former of the two possibilities.

Chapter XXIX

B. GOD'S STRANGE DEALINGS WITH ZION
(Chap. 29)

To indicate that there is a coherent development of thought discernible, note that in the preceding chapter after Samaria had been under consideration under a somewhat enigmatic and intriguing name ("Crown"), now it is Jerusalem which is under consideration, also under a unique descriptive aspect, also challenging and intriguing, "Ariel." The two capitals, no doubt, often were held side by side from various points of view.

Most commentators are agreed that this oracle could have been spoken shortly before Sennacherib's advance against Jerusalem, anywhere from 705-701 B.C., depending on the interpretation of v. 1. In fact, if v. 1 reflects on the end of the church year, as it may, it could even have been spoken at the festival that appears at that time, the Festival of Tabernacles. This, at least would allow for the possibility that it was spoken before the assembled throng of worshippers in the Temple.

This would explain one feature that appears in the chapter — the indictment of formalistic worship, similar to, but much briefer than a similar indictment appearing in 1:10-15.

They who view the present state of the text with deep misgivings will, often chiefly for reasons of meter of the poetry — a very uncertain criterion — suggest the following appraisal and rearrangement: (the verses enclosed in parenthesis are to be regarded as later additions): 1-4, 5b, 6-8, 5a, 10, (11-12), 13-16, (17-18), 19-20 (21), 22-24.

The question whether the whole chapter is to be ascribed to Isaiah, as usual, leads to a division of opinion. There is obvious material that bears kinship with portions found elsewhere in the acknowledged material that comes from him. To the contrary critical arguments on certain verses do not seem to carry much weight. Therefore we concur with writers like *Fischer*: "This prophecy bears the stamp of a genuine work of Isaiah."

Naturally we reject the opinion of those who regard vv. 17-24 as comprising two "eschatological supplements."

We prefer to outline the contents of the chapter as follows:

1. Jerusalem's Grave Distress and Startling Deliverance (vv. 1-8)
2. Total Lack of Comprehension on People's Part (vv. 9-12)
3. The Cause of the Nation's Blindness — Formalistic Worship (vv. 13-14)
4. Denunciation of the Pro-Egyptian Politics (vv. 15-16)
5. The Glorious Future Transformation (vv. 17-24)

1. Jerusalem's Grave Distress and Startling Deliverance (vv. 1-8)

29:1-8 1. Woe to you Ariel, Ariel, the city where David encamped;
add year to year, let the festivals run their cycle.
2. Yet I will cause distress for Ariel,
and there shall be moaning and bemoaning;
yea, she shall be to me a veritable Ariel [altar-hearth].
3. And I will encamp against you round about,
and besiege you with entrenchments,
and raise up forts against you.
4. And you shall speak from way down on the ground, and your words shall issue forth from down in the dust;
and your voice will be like that of a ghost,
and your speech shall twitter from down in the dust.
5. Nevertheless the multitude of your enemies will be like fine dust;
the multitude of the ruthless will be like wind-driven chaff.
6. And in an instant suddenly you will be visited by the Lord of hosts,
with thunder and earthquake and tremendous noise,
with storm-wind and storm and with the flame of devouring fire.
7. Like a dream, a night-vision, so shall be the multitude of the nations who go to battle against Ariel.
yea, all who go to battle against her and her fortress, and distress her.
8. And it will be as when a hungry man dreams,
and, lo, he is eating.
Then he awakes and his hunger is not stilled.
Or it will be as if a thirsty man dreams and, lo, he is drinking.

Then he awakes and, lo, thirst still leaves him faint.
So shall the multitude of all the nations be who go to battle
    against Mount Zion.

Verse 1. The "woe" introduces a threat-oracle: distress that is about to befall Jerusalem is announced. The one involved is "Ariel." The prophet does not define this enigmatic term. It could mean "the lion of God" and seem to describe Jerusalem as a brave, lion-like man, as the term apparently is used in II Sam. 23:20 and Isa. 33:7. But this approach involves grave difficulties in the interpretation of v. 2. The other possible meaning is "the hearth of God." Since it is plain from what follows that the subject under consideration is Jerusalem, the thought that this city is the hearth of God is meaningful from this point of view: This is the place where God's home, or hearth-fire, is among his people. In v. 2 this thought will be amplified a bit by permissible interpretation. The prophet inserts a word of guidance as to what he has in mind when he defines Ariel as "the city where David encamped," or, so to speak, had his and his army's headquarters and later even permanent residence. Cf. II Sam. 5:6-9. This is a subtle reminder that Zion became so important only because of the unique promise that David received from the Lord (II Sam. 7).

The second part of this verse indicates that Jerusalem, or Zion, is also being thought of as the place of the worship of Israel. There the years rolled by with their catalog of sacred festivals. Since these festivals are spoken of as "running the cycle," or making their round, it could well be that the prophet is indicating that only one more year will elapse before what he is about to predict will actually come to pass. Since this event apparently was Sennacherib's invasion (701 B.C.) this would date the prophecy as about 702. But when they as people are encouraged to observe their festivals, this already points in the direction of what is stated in vv. 13-14 that routine observance has become the order of the day (cf. Amos 4:4-5).

Verse 2. In spite of their meticulous worship, which cannot turn aside divine displeasure but rather rouses it, "distress for Ariel" is what the Lord has appointed. Verse 2 is in a measure adversative to v. 1. The coming disaster will bring with it "moaning and bemoaning" (as *Cheyne* so aptly translated the expression). In fact, Ariel will actually become in a very striking sense "a veritable altar-hearth." At this point we *translated* the term Ariel to make the issue clear. As the altar-hearth was also a spot marked by dripping blood of the sacrifice and by the fierce fire that burned atop it all, such will be the spectacle that Jerusalem will present, or could present in the evil day; "could" — for this extreme of disaster was averted. The *Targum* paraphrased rather well: ". . . as an altar is surrounded with the blood of holy sacrifices round about on a feast day." Note that the approach of this verse is that the attacker is none less than Yahweh himself, an approach that is continued in the next verse.

Verse 3. The figure of an attack is expressed a bit more clearly in this verse. The Lord represents himself as even encamping for a prolonged siege against the city round about. *He* places the entrenchments; *he* raises up the forts. Something must be sadly amiss when the Lord takes such an attitude over against his people. This necessary assumption remains and will be articulated a bit later.

Verse 4. The fate of this now proud nation is depicted a bit more in detail. Zion will be brought low, but she will have been cast to the ground with such violence and will be in so very weakened a state that what she utters comes as spoken from "down on the ground," and her "words will issue from down in the dust." Elaborating the thought still farther, that voice of hers will "be like that of a ghost," perhaps speaking through a medium, indistinct and unnatural, even with a kind of twittering or mumbling sound. The point is the extreme humiliation and weakening that the nation will suffer. As usual in threat-oracles, a certain vagueness as to the nature of the historical fulfilment involved marks the passage. What they imply rather than say is what adds to the ominousness of the pronouncement.

Verse 5. Now follows one of those surprising and utterly unmotivated changes from the minor to the major key, a transition that takes us by complete surprise. Because we did not expect this turn of thought does not impugn its genuineness. God's grace can never be categorized and rationalized by us. Still a point is being made, that namely, an unexpected and most surprising turn of events will transpire. So it comes to pass that the actual course that events took in that unusual attack, or siege, that Sennacherib set afoot against Jerusalem, is exactly reflected by this startling turn of the thought. There was, as usual, a "multitude" of the enemies, the Assyrian host. They were famous for their ruthless efficiency. But somehow they became "like fine dust," which the wind can blow completely away. Or they may be likened to the "wind-driven chaff," which is about as weak for resistance as any material can be. In this statement the enemy is described by the use of the expression "the multitude of the ruthless."

Verse 6. As much as the attack was engineered by the Lord, so will be this strange deliverance when it takes place. And it came "in an instant suddenly." No one had dared anticipate anything like the overthrow of the Assyrians that took place in that one memorable night (II Kings 19:35-37). Another effective way of describing what happened is to say that they were "visited by the Lord of hosts." This expression, which can be used either in the positive or negative sense, here definitely conveys the thought of a gracious visitation: God comes in person, takes the difficult situation in hand himself, and with his own right arms works a wondrous deliverance. But the rest of the verse adds the appropriate color in that it depicts the divine intervention occurring, as is so often the case in the Old Testament, by means of a tremendous storm. The component elements of that storm are specified: "thunder and earthquake and tremendous noise, with stormwind and storm and with the flame of devouring fire." Add to the storm and the black clouds, earthquake and lightnings, and the picture with all its majesty becomes rather vivid. The overpowering majesty of the Lord of hosts is reflected in this type of visitation. To have this depicted as offsetting the danger that threatened Zion is sheer genius and not a belated, more or less clumsy, insertion by a late nameless writer. *Scott* points out that threat-oracles love this "piling up of words" in their conclusion. Analogous to this passage is the approach of Isa. 30: 27-33.

Verse 7. Now follow two references to dreams from two very different points of view. This verse represents Israel as being the one that has the dream, an ugly dream dominated by the sight of "the multitude of the nations who go to battle against Ariel." They will indeed "go to battle against her and her fortress and distress her." Somehow the account at this point seems to keep hanging in midair. It stops with distress for Zion. But the enemy did not achieve a victory. The whole ugly dream or night-vision never got beyond that stage. The inconclusiveness of v. 7 is meaningful. Note that this verse again brings into play the term "multitude," which in the original signifies a huge noisy crowd. Our passage uses the word four times. The attacking forces must have swarmed over practically the entire land of Judah.

Verse 8. Now comes the totally different use of the figure of a dream. In v. 7 the man who dreamed was Israel. Now it is the Assyrian. He is the "hungry man." What he aims to devour is Israel. In the dream he already sees himself eating. How boldly the Assyrian Rabshakeh asserted his convictions about the inevitable fall of the Holy City (II Kings 18:19-25). "Then he awakes and his hunger is not stilled." What a disillusionment it must have been when their plans turned into complete ruin! The second half of the verse merely uses the figure of thirst for the dreamer. It took faith and inspiration by direct divine intervention for a prophet to speak thus. It is true that only after the event had occurred in the unique manner in which it did, that the full light of Isaiah's meaning dawned on his countrymen. Then it was as clear as the light of the sun, as the concluding words of this section summarized it all: "So shall the multitude of all the nations be who go to battle against Mount Zion." Zion's inviolability could not have been asserted more positively, inviolable only so long as she holds to her Lord.

2. Total Lack of Comprehension on the People's Part (vv. 9-12)

29:9-12 9. Stop and be confounded; blind yourselves and be blind.
Be drunk but not with wine; stagger but not with strong drink.

10. For the Lord has poured out upon you a spirit of deep sleep;
and he has closed your eyes — the prophets,
and has muffled your heads — the seers.
11. And so the vision of all this has become for you like the words
   of a sealed book,
which one gives to an educated man, saying: "Please read this,"
and he says: "I cannot, for it is sealed."
12. Or the book is given to an uneducated man with the words:
   "Please, read this,"
and he says: "I do not know how to read."

Verse 9. The first part of this verse, though expressed as a command, depicts what the people of Judah did when they heard the preceding pronouncement (vv. 1-8). They stopped short in their tracks with a look of utter incredulity upon their face. The message gave them pause but it induced no understanding because it was not received with faith. The rest of the verse indicates the intensification of their lack of understanding as being something which they themselves caused. For the blindness of unbelief makes men increasingly less perceptive of the truth. But they themselves are at fault. Therefore the prophet says: "Blind yourselves and be blind." The hardening of one's own heart leads deeper into the divine judgment of hardening. Or the distressing consequences may be described as being like unto a state of intoxication, or a blind staggering about, though the immediate cause in this instance is neither wine nor strong drink.

Verse 10. Following through on the description of the unhappy state of the nation, the prophet now represents the Lord as himself taking a hand in intensifying their blindness. They that prefer to be blind shall experience to the full what that means. The figure changes. The Lord is represented as pouring out upon the nation "a spirit of deep sleep," which makes them totally oblivious to their perilous situation. The case is somewhat analogous to that of the Pharaoh of Moses' time, who first hardened his own heart, and then finds himself in a state where the Lord has intensified his frame of mind. Here two more descriptive phases of the people's state are added: "He has closed your eyes. . . and muffled your heads." How totally unable to meet an emergency poor Judah must have been as a result of this judgment!

However, the prophet has a very specific application of this thought in mind. The "eyes" of the people are their "prophets." The guiding "heads" are the "seers," merely another word for prophets. The reference may be to the professional prophets, or even perhaps to all prophets, good or bad. They will be denied any guiding visions that might have helped the people in the impending emergency. The whole verse is reminiscent of 6:6-9. There is such a thing as the judgment of blindness, or hardness of heart spiritually.

Verses 11, 12. Two illustrations of the situation about to be created are now given. Verse 11 would seem to indicate how the educated people, under the judgment of hardening, will react to it all; v. 12, how the uneducated will behave. The reference to the "book" that is involved may be to the book of the messages which the prophet had delivered to the people and which was available, but would be of little help, considering their perilous spiritual state. 8:16 could be still another reference to an existing book of messages from Isaiah. The first instance then applies to the possible use of a sealed book, being given to a man capable of reading, but unable to read in this case; for the book is tightly sealed. The second instance refers to an illiterate person to whom a book is given with the request that he read it, but he must reply: "I don't know how to read." So the prophet's messages from God will not benefit this people one whit as long as they continue in the state of hardening into which they have passed.

3. The Cause of the Nation's Blindness — Formalistic Worship (vv. 13-14)

29:13-14 13. And the Lord said:
"Because this people draw near with their mouth,
and honor me with their lips, but their heart is far from me,
so that their fear of me has become a commandment of men
  learned by rote;
14. therefore I will again deal with this people in a wonderful
  way,
marvelous and wonderful;
so that the wisdom of her wise men shall perish,
and the understanding of men of understanding shall hide its face."

Verse 13. Though no connection is traced between vv. 12 and 13 nonetheless an inner connection is to be established. One is almost compelled to assume that the intended connection of thought is that the formalistic worship of the nation has brought about the state of blindness and hardening in spiritual things that has just been described.

The expression "draw near" in this case plainly signifies public worship. One can hardly help thinking of the reformation that Hezekiah in his day undertook in regard to corrupt and heathenish practices that had crept into the worship at Jerusalem (cf. II Kings 18:4ff.). Since this reform was set afoot by decree from the king, that is by royal edict, the response of the people may have been quite formal, going through all the motions of true religion but not expressing its vitality. Whatever its occasion, there it was — a thing offensive to God, as externalism always must be. The outer obeisance was there; the heart was far from the Lord. The reverence (or "fear") that should have been in evidence was in obedience to a commandment set forth by men and "learned by rote." True religion must go deeper. This outward kind of religion is most offensive, being another form of hypocrisy. In fact, it calls for some corresponding action on the part of the Lord.

Verse 14. The action that God will take is now described. Where true worship also begets wisdom, false worship destroys effective wisdom. In bringing the judgment of folly to replace wisdom down upon the heads of this nation God may be said to be dealing with this people "in a wonderful way, marvelous and wonderful." For it is a marvelous thing when wisdom and understanding are withdrawn from a people and they become fools. As a result no one will know how to act in an emergency; no one will be capable of coping with the difficulty encountered. This is not the approach that reasons with men to demonstrate to them the folly of the course they have elected to follow. It simply announces the judgment that they have incurred and fully merited. Such an approach is calculated to shock men out of following a course of action that men are never too eager to remedy. Note how Paul uses v. 14 in I Cor. 1:19.

4. Denunciation of the Pro-Egyptian Politics (vv. 15-16)

29:15-16 15. Woe to them who try to go deep away from the Lord to hide their schemes,
and say: "Who can see us and who knows us?"
16. O what perversity! Is the potter being counted as the clay?
so that the product says to its manufacturer: "He has not made me!"
and the pottery says to the potter: "He does not understand!"

One might well be at a loss as to what unholy "schemes" are being denounced at this point, if it were not for the fact that the adjoining chapters make it clear that there was a pronounced pro-Egyptian trend in international politics much in evidence in those days (cf. 28:15-22; 30:1-5). What v. 15 then indicates is that they who were involved in this kind of international scheming and plotting were doing it largely in secret, trying to veil their machinations from the eyes of the prophet whose opposition to such devices was well known, and apparently also from the eyes of the Lord himself, as though such a thing were possible. The covenants involved in this case were not arrived at openly. But, strange as it may seem, the persons involved thought that they had kept their schemings hidden even from the eyes of the Lord. The issues apparently needed no more specific identification than we have here. They were immediately clear to Isaiah's hearers. However when men said: "Who can see us and who knows us?" this does not necessarily demand that they actually made such a claim in the hearing of men. This was what their attitude practically said at that time. Obviously such a statement is a denial of the very omniscience of God.

Verse 16. Similarly this verse adds up to a denial of the omnipotence of God by Isaiah's statement working under cover. Very properly Isaiah labels such an attitude as "perversity" in an impatient exclamation. He draws the obvious conclusions that grow out of such an attitude. The "potter" (the Lord) actually is being counted as no more than the "clay." The Lord is a being of manifest limitations: he cannot cope with these schemers. Or, to reduce the issue to a more extreme absurdity, "the product is saying of its manu-

facturers: 'He has not made me.'" The situation is most
ridiculous. For all that man, the creature, amounts to over
against God, the creator, is a piece of pottery. Dare such an
article challenge him that made it? Or could he presume to
go even one step farther, as these politicians are doing, and
say: "He does not understand," which is another way of
claiming: Our enterprises are too deep for him. (cf. Rom. 9:
20)? All the thinking of this class of men is brushed aside
as the trivial thing that it is with the exclamation, "O what
perversity!" With this brief but effective indictment the
subject is dropped for the present. It will be resumed later.
The figure of the Lord as potter is found also in 45:9; 64:8;
Jer. 18:4 ff.; Job 10:9.

5. The Glorious Future Transformation (vv. 17-24)

29:17-24 17. Is it not yet a very little while till Lebanon shall
be reduced to a fruitful field,
and the fruitful field shall be counted as a forest?
18. And on that day the deaf will hear the words of a book,
and after gloom and darkness the eyes of the blind will see again.
19. And the meek shall find new joy in the Lord;
and the poor among men shall exult in the Holy One of Israel.
20. And all the ruthless shall come to an end,
and scoffers cease,
and all who devise evil shall be cut off;
21. who in trying a case make a man appear as an offender,
and lay a snare for the man who reproves in the gate,
and turn aside for a mere trifle him who is in the right.
22. Therefore thus says the Lord, who redeemed Abraham, concerning the house of Jacob:
"Not shall Jacob now be ashamed nor his face again grow pale.
23. For when his children see what my hands have done in their
midst,
they shall sanctify my name;
and they shall sanctify the Holy One of Jacob,
and shall reverence the God of Israel.
24. Also they that err in spirit will acquire insight,
and the fault-finders shall accept instruction."

This section describes two different phases of the glorious
transformation — vv. 17-21 and vv. 22-24.

The opening phrase as to the time when this is to come

to pass ("a very little while") does not necessitate that the prophet himself and the people were led to expect that the items about to be enumerated actually would have to come on the scene within the next few years. We believe that the expression is indicative of time as it is measured on the divine clock. Measured by the Eternal One the time will be short. That does not yet demand that the prophet and his contemporaries were definitely aware of this aspect of the time-factor. In any case, there will be surprising changes of a most unexpected sort.

Verse 17. This verse describes two such changes, moving in opposite directions. "Lebanon," in the light of 10:34, would seem to be a type of the great Assyrian empire, again about to be reduced to a level of weakness, or to be more specific, "reduced to a fruitful field." In other words, what was an impressive stand of trees (Lebanon usually appears with this connotation)will be reduced in appearance to the ordinary type of vegetation that appears in a "fruitful field." In one word, Assyria will be brought low. The other aspect of the case is the very reverse. That nation, which presented a very ordinary level of achievement among the nations, namely Israel, is to move from her ordinary status to the standing of a "forest." The term "Lebanon" might have been used here, but it would have been out of place to declare that Israel shall acquire the standing of one of the great world-empires. For the world-powers were of a very dubious distinction. They do not represent the acme of high achievement in the Scriptures. A far more suitable comparison, in the very language of the prophet, is that of the vineyard (cf. 5:1-7; 27:2-5). Summing up: What seems impressive among the nations will be sharply reduced in stature; what looks unimpressive will be far more highly esteemed. All this implies the eschatological future.

Verse 18. Another unique and startling reversal of situation will be that at least in some measure physical defects will be healed. So for one, the deaf man will hear again. That not ordinary sounds are indicated as being heard by him but rather "the words of a book," would seem to imply that the same book, which was hinted at in v. 11 is again under consideration, namely the book of the prophet. In other words, the newly-acquired gift of hearing will be utilized for the noblest conceivable purpose, hearing the message from God, as it appears written in the book of the prophet. In like manner the "blind," having long been consigned to "gloom and darkness" will be able to strip off his defect and "will see again." It is not claimed that all deaf people and all the blind will have this experience, but marvelous cures will occur. The passage may even imply that when the Messianic Age has reached its consummation then all physical defects will be a thing of the past. For that will be a time when there will be a world "wherein dwelleth righteousness," that is: where all things are right. Somewhat analogous is 30:26b.

Verse 19. The sampling of areas where God's transforming work takes place continues. We come to the area where the rights of God's own people are to be restored to them after having often been denied them. God's own are here designated by two terms, "the meek" and "the poor." Comparing passages like Amos 2:6f; Isa. 11:4; 14:30; cf. 32, we find that the term "meek" customarily is used by the prophets (and also by the Psalms) as a description of godly souls who have no strength to stand up for their own rights but commit their case into the Lord's hands. The term "poor" is practically used the same way (cf. Matt. 5:3-5; 11:4f.; Luke 6:20).

Verse 20. Still another area is taken in hand. Two classes of troublesome people are referred to as becoming extinct, either in isolated instances or even ultimately by way of total extinction. They are the "ruthless" and the "scoffers." Here the "ruthless" are most aptly thought of as foreign oppressors who again and again have played the role of tyrants over weak Israel. This was always a galling experience, but it shall come to an end. Equally disturbing oftentimes to the faithful was the behavior of the "scoffers," these anomalies among the people of God, who in spite of all the Lord had done in the midst of Israel, made light of him and of those that put their trust in him. A third group is referred to as to "be cut off." They are "all who devise evil." The verb used would apply to such who studiously address themselves to the pursuit of any purpose, here an evil one. Their

complete devotion to evil is their chief characteristic. Such
may expect that the Lord will, sooner or later, "cut them
off." Their devotion to what is bad is the very caricature of
what God designed man to be. Examples of their manner of
operation are given in v. 21.

Verse 21. All three instances here cited lies in the domain
of the law courts. These courts, or the presiding judges,
were to be the unwavering exponents of right and justice.
When they became corrupt that was a grievous weight on
the minds of all right-thinking people. So correction of the
malfunctioning of justice may indeed be thought of as a
notable achievement among the many great transformations
wrought in the Messianic Age. One thing calling for reform
listed here is, in trying a case, to "make a man appear as an
offender," when he was the one whose rights should have
been upheld. The second case has to do with a judge, or as
he is here described, "the man that reproves in the gate,"
the verb used referring specifically to the major function of
a judge. Subtle devices are resorted to in order to bring
such a man into difficulties and so undermine his reputation
for integrity. The third case refers to those who "for a mere
trifle," we might say "a technicality," turn aside "him who is
in the right." All such things as make men smart by their
very injustice shall also be overcome in the great transformation. So the great transformation has been effectually
described from a number of different angles.

Verse 22. Now comes the second description of the transformation vv. 22-24. It concerns itself with a change of attitude on the part of those who have begun to believe in the
Lord and in the marvelous manner of his working. This
description is introduced as also being a solemn pronouncement of the Lord. It is recalled, first of all, that it is the same
one that once "redeemed Abraham" and so has a standing
record for redemption. It appears best to think of God's call
to Abraham in his still unredeemed state when he dwelt
"beyond the river" in Mesopotamia. Joshua 24:2f. speaks of
this. From this ancestor came the "house of Jacob (cf. 2:5),
a nation once redeemed from Egypt and now again to be
redeemed in the great transformation. For many were the
times when Israel's history did anything but reflect the fact

of her being a redeemed and chosen people. Often the adversaries did and could taunt her with the question: "Where is now thy God?" (Ps. 42:3, 10) and Israel had to stand there ashamed, and at loss for an answer. That situation is to be ultimately remedied in the work that God proposes to do. The parallel expression has it: "nor shall his face again grow pale." For in more intense shame the blush gives way to extreme paleness.

Verse 23. What makes the difference is that God's work done in Israel's behalf will then be so manifest that it will supply all needed apologetic. Then God's children will see what his hands have done in their midst and all misgivings and criticisms shall completely collapse. Instead they will "sanctify (his) name," that is, openly acknowledge his well-established reputation for faithfulness. When two more expressions follow which are much in the same vein, it becomes apparent that the point at issue is that the direct relation to God will now be so clear, so firmly grounded, and so thoroughly apprehended that it will be the soul of the new attitude that prevails throughout the nation. These two statements are: "they shall sanctify the Holy One of Israel" — a favorite title for the Lord in Isaiah — and "they shall reverence the God of Israel," not make disparaging and critical remarks about him in a querulous spirit.

Verse 24. Rounding out the description of the better attitude prevalent among the nation, the word of the Lord adds that two classes of misguided souls will take a more wholesome attitude, those that "err in spirit" and the "fault-finders." Deeper insight will be given to those who had been erring in their whole approach; and instead the fault-finders will admit that they themselves were at fault and have much to learn, and so they "shall accept instruction."

So it has been noted that the whole chapter hangs together well and comes to a very suitable climax.

Notes

Verse 1. The word "city" (*qiryath*) stands in the construct state being followed not by another noun but by a sentence (*GK* 130 d). The verb "encamped" could grammatically be construed as meaning that at one time David encamped *against* this city. But to translate "where David encamped" is more contextual.

Verse 2. The *ke* before the last word, Ariel, is here obviously an example of the *kaph veritatis* (*KS* 3388) and so we have ventured to translate "a veritable altar-hearth."

Verse 3. It is true that the *khaddur* "in a circle," i.e., "round about" is a bit unusual, but we do not believe that that gives warrant to the textual changes that result in a *kedavidh* ("like David").

Verse 5. We have construed the last three words of this verse as the first part of v. 6, a perfectly permissible departure from the Masoretic text-order.

Verse 8. We find the somewhat unusual use of the word *nephesh*, which here must mean "hunger" or "appetite."

Verse 10. Quite commonly the words "prophets" and "seers" are regarded as glosses. But to us they appear as so essential to the right interpretation of the text as to warrant considering them as normal parts of the text, nouns in apposition.

Verse 13. *Niggash* ("draw near") may be regarded as a sort of gnomic aorist and so express the habitual: "they habitually draw near."

Verse 14. *Yoseph*, like the form in 38:5, may be regarded as a participle from *yasaph*.

Verse 15. The participle *hamma 'amiqim* appears in that unique adverbial use which is described in *KS* 399 n.

Verse 16. *Haphkekhem* (written *KW* as *hophkekhem*) is an infinitive used as an exclamation in a very concise ellipsis, meaning Oh, how perverse you are! *GK* 147 c.

Verse 18. *Me'ophel* meaning "from darkness," is the equivalent of an adverbial clause of time: "after gloom . . . is ended." *KS* 401 f.

Verse 19. The expression "the poor among men" constitutes a sort of superlative. *GK* 133 h.

Verse 21. The word *dabhar* could be taken as meaning a "trifle," but if Exod. 18:16 be compared it may appear that the word here signifies "a case" tried before a law-court.

Verse 23. Literally the verse begins: "For his [i.e., his children] seeing." "His" in this case is used collectively, and therefore "his children" can stand in apposition with it. *GK* 131 o.

Verse 24. *Ruach* is an accusative of specification (*KS* 336 h): "those who err in respect to spirit."

Chapter XXX

C. AGAINST THE ALLIANCE WITH EGYPT (Chap. 30)

This is also a part of the "Zion Book." That this is the case appears less obviously than in the preceding two chapters, but v. 19 is a clear indication of the entire trend involved.

The time when this message was delivered is commonly taken to have been somewhere between 705 and 701 B.C. as the Assyrian crisis was coming to a head.

The core of the message is high-level prophetic thinking, as v. 15 in particular shows. A very excellent delineation of faith and its nature is there set forth. But as to the issue which gave occasion to this pronouncement, it is the same as was the case in 29:15, the seeking of an alliance with Egypt, an issue which was more or less dark in Chap. 29 but now is dragged forth clearly into the open and called by name. But still that negative of which the prophet is against stands out only secondarily. *Luther* already remarked rightly with regard to this chapter: "The prophet admonishes to have faith and fear the Lord."

As usual, attempts at reworking and emending a good text which has difficulties but may be said to have been transmitted with fine care, are again much in evidence. Briefly it may be pointed out that quite commonly vv. 6-7, 18-26, 27-33 are regarded as later additions by a hand other than that of the prophet. We shall attempt to show what a coherent development of thought can be traced throughout the chapter. This, in itself, is a strong defense of the unity of the chapter and of the feasibility of attributing it to Isaiah as author.

In determining the pattern of the outline of the chapter we can hardly go along with *Kissane*, who finds the chapter to consist of eight strophes and eight verses each. But the progression of thought may be indicated by the following outline.

1. Denunciation of the Proposed Alliance with Egypt (vv. 1-5)
2. The Futility of This Alliance (vv. 6-7)
3. The Utterly Wrong Attitude of the Nation and the Ultimate Outcome (vv. 8-14)
4. A Basically Sound Attitude and Its Consequences (vv. 15-26)
5. The Lord's Judgment on the Nations, Especially on Assyria (vv. 27-33)

To sum it up, we have here a most constructive approach to the problem of international politics. Though cast in a form adapted to the specific needs of that day it still contains invaluable lessons of abiding value over against the deep-seated inclination always to seek alliances with foreign nations when the going becomes difficult.

1. Denunciation of the Proposed Alliance with Egypt (vv. 1-5)

30:1-5 1. Woe to those children [of mine] — oracle of Yahweh —
who manifest their rebelliousness by making a plan that comes not from me,
and contrive an alliance that comes not from my spirit,
that they may add sin to sin;
2. who proceed to go down to Egypt without inquiring of me,
and to seek refuge in the protection of Pharaoh,
and to seek shelter under the aegis of Egypt.
3. But the protection of Pharaoh shall become your shame,
and the shelter under the aegis of Egypt, your disgrace.
4. For his [the king of Judah's] princes have been in Zoan,
and his messengers have reached Hanes.
5. But every one will come to shame over a people that cannot profit them,
that has neither help nor aid, but only shame and disgrace.

Verse 1. Men might not be inclined to brand a political trend by so harsh a name as Isaiah uses "rebelliousness."

But he had raised the same charge before in 1:2-4 (cf. also Hos. 4:16). The Israelites are children of God. Their first concern, if they are minded to live up to their high destiny, should be to do that which is in harmony with the will of their God. But that issue is not being raised. They could not claim that their plan originated with Yahweh, or had his sanction. Or to restate the case, they may be said to "contrive an alliance that comes not from [his] spirit." Two possibilities for ascertaining the exact meaning of "contriving an alliance" present themselves. One meaning of the verb could be "to weave a weaving" — indicating the complex and intricate nature of that which is being planned. Equally possible is the other meaning of the root, which suggests that they "pour a libation" as a sort of prayer asking for divine sanction, or blessing. Either approach yields almost the same result. The point is that in all these machinations God has been left out; his spirit has not been consulted. For a similar rebuke see Hos. 8:4. When the prophet adds: "that they may add sin to sin," certainly does not describe their avowed intention, but it is a correct statement of what the nation's procedure amounts to in the end. Every step in the policy the nation is following adds to the measure of their guiltiness.

Verse 2. Now the prophet becomes a bit more specific. It would appear that this word was spoken just at the time when the news began to be circulated that an important delegation had left on an embassy to Egypt. But that step — the prophet keeps on reiterating — had been taken without previously inquiring of the Lord whether such an approach met with his favor. Whether these ambassadors were conscious of it or not, clearly stated, their approach meant that they were "seeking refuge in the protection of Pharaoh," and "shelter under the aegis of Egypt." Since the words used were usually associated with making the *Lord* one's refuge and seeking *his* shelter, it becomes clear that human help is being substituted for divine protection. All this certainly adds up to "rebelliousness" (v. 1). The Pharaoh involved was of the Twenty-fifth dynasty. It may have been Shabako (714-700 B.C.). It may be that his nephew Tirhaka was involved. It is even possible that one of these was in Zoan and the other in Hanes (see v. 4) and that both had to be contacted in the course of the conferences that were involved.

Verse 3. In any case, the outcome is going to be the very opposite of what was hoped for. "Protection?" "Shelter?" No; but "shame" and "disgrace." That on which they pin their hopes will prove their undoing. Historically it is now known that the Twenty-fifth dynasty was very weak.

Verse 4. This verse may be an exact indication how far the diplomatic transactions had progressed. The princes of Judah had made contacts. They had come to Zoan, in the northeastern part of the Delta of Egypt and nearest to the borders of Judah, where Tirhaka was in control, ruling in conjunction with his uncle, Shabako. They may also have journeyed down even as far as Hanes (which may have been the Heracleopolis Magna, fifty miles upstream from Cairo, where Shabako himself had his court. The mention of the two towns reached may have been designed to indicate how far the Ethiopians had penetrated in controlling Egypt at the time. All this is, however purely conjectural, since we lack detailed historical information on these points. The prophet's contemporaries may have understood very well what he was saying.

Verse 5. The prophet keeps repeating how vain these diplomatic efforts to get assurance of protection, really are. He goes so far as to claim that "every one" involved "will come to shame over a people that cannot profit them." Egypt has been greatly overrated. She may have been strong once. All that remains of her greatness is the name. She herself seems to think herself strong. Others may rely on her. All are laboring under a sad misconception. The prophet repeats: All that can be expected is "shame and disgrace." Egypt cannot give "help or aid."

2. The Futility of the Alliance (vv. 6-7)

30:6-7 6. An oracle on the Beast of the South.
In a land of distress and anguish — lioness and lion belong there; the viper and the flying serpent —
they carry their wealth on the backs of young asses,

and their treasures on the humps of camels,
to a people that cannot profit them.
7. For the help of Egypt is vain and empty.
Therefore I have called her "A Big-mouth that is a Do-nothing."

Verse 6. The utter uselessness of this alliance has already been touched upon in the preceding verses. Now a special issue is made of it. This is presented under the caption: "An Oracle on the Beast of the South." This Beast of the South is not Arabia (*Procksch*) just because the creatures about to be named are thought of as being characteristic of Arabia rather than of the wilderness on the way to Egypt. Numbers 21:6ff. and Deut. 8:15 indicate that quite an assortment of dangerous creatures inhabited the desert through which the children of Israel had to come in days of old. Even if "the flying serpent" is mentioned, that need not be taken as Biblical warrant for the conception that there are flying serpents. It could be that the prophet is listing real and fabulous creatures that men are inclined to associate with this wilderness. The point is that the ambassadors that were delegated to go down to Egypt were ready to take big risks and encounter grave dangers to accomplish what they deemed a necessary mission. So highly did they rate Egypt's help. For aside from the dangerous creatures to be encountered the land itself is "a land of distress and anguish." The prophet sketches out the picture a bit more in detail: the caravan in which they went is described. Young asses and camels seem to make up the beasts of burden involved. They transport the wealth and treasure that are being offered the Egyptians as tokens of good will and sincerity. But the futility of it all comes in the concluding clause, "to a people that cannot profit them." All this treasure is so much water down the drain.

It may yet be suggested that the name for the "Beast of the South" is Behemoth, a plural form to indicate the excessive size of the creature, which usually was thought of as being the hippopotamus — a designation particularly appropriate for Egypt, in whose waters the hippopotamus is found, a thought that is further developed in v. 7.

Verse 7. The prophet keeps harping on one string: "the

help of Egypt is vain and empty." He had to keep reiterating, because the opposite opinion had taken such firm root
in Israel's thinking. He finally epitomized his point in a
telling statement of extreme brevity. What his statement
means is clear enough, except that it is almost impossible to
translate. Literally it says "Rahab who sits still" (*RSV*). *Von
Orelli* gives a translation that could be rendered "Agitator
of Inactivity." We attempt a new approach: "A Big-mouth
that is a Do-Nothing." In this sort of compound name
ráhabh is the first word. It means "the noisy one," the "boisterous." She talks much, is long on words but ineffective in
action. When Isaiah says: "Therefore I have called her" it
would appear that this unique title for Egypt is of his own
coinage. It may have been a telling label that finally summed
up his whole position very effectively.

3. The Utterly Wrong Attitude of the Nation and Its Ultimate Outcome (vv. 8-14)

30:8-14 8. And now go, write it on a tablet before them
and note it in a book,
that it may be for a time to come as a witness forever.
9. For they are a rebellious people, lying children,
children who have been unwilling to hear the instruction of the
Lord;
10. who have said to the seers: "See not!"
and to the prophets: "Do not prophecy to us right things!
speak to us smooth things; prophecy illusion.
11. Depart from the [right] way; turn aside from the [right]
path;
leave off speaking before us about the Holy One of Israel!"
12. Therefore thus says the Holy One of Israel:
"Because you have despised this word,
and have put your trust in oppression and crookedness, and rely
on them;
13. therefore this iniquity shall be to you like a crack in a high
wall, threatening collapse, and already bulging out —
whose collapse comes all of a sudden.
14. And its breaking is like that of a potter's vessel, shattered so
ruthlessly.
that among the sherds there cannot be found a fragment big
enough
to rake fire from the embers, or to scoop water out of a puddle."

A rather telling description as to where the fault in this matter actually lies: not somewhere outside the nation but strictly within their own hearts and in their utterly wrong attitude to their God and his word.

Verse 8. To see the nation right as effectively as possible Isaiah is bidden by the Lord to commit his indictment to writing, and that in a twofold form: on a tablet and in a book. The prophet had resorted to the use of a tablet once before (8:1-4). That tablet also had contained a single compound name. This suggests that the inscription on the tablet in the present instance may have consisted only in the telling designation given to Egypt. The book, or scroll, put forth at the same time may have contained the entire contents of Chap. 30. Another very attractive approach is that the tablet may have embodied the entire fifteenth verse of this chapter, which is the high point of the prophet's positive instruction. Both tablet and book are to serve the purpose of perpetuating this important revelation given at this time, and at the same time testifying against the nation and revealing its unwholesome attitude. Some (*von Rad*, et al.) see here an indication of the writing out of the entire message received by Isaiah up until this time.

Verses 9, 10. At this point they are exhorted to look within, no longer outside itself. The basic difficulty is not something external; it lies in their own hearts: they are "a rebellious people, lying children, children who have been unwilling to hear the instruction [or law] of the Lord." This is an indication of the fact that the rebelliousness that marked the nation on its march through the wilderness in Mosaic days, is still their distinguishing badge. God may speak; they do not want to be instructed. In fact, either in attitude or in actual words, they have told their seers: "See not!" They have tried to silence their prophets. Or if the truth has sometimes been bluntly spoken, they are not concerned whether it is right or not. What they want is words that are "smooth," flattering, pleasant to listen to. For that matter, they will cheerfully abide by "illusion" rather than hear the truth. One wonders how far people may stray from the truth. It should, of course, also be remarked that no one may have been so desperate actually to make these demands on the prophets. But in effect, that is what Israel's attitude at least amounted to.

Verse 11. To round out the picture, this was, in effect, nothing less than asking a man who is on the right road, to leave it and take a wrong one. For what they are concerned about is not either right or wrong, but the comfortable, the delightful, the beguiling, that which sounds pleasant. In fact, to bring this to a climax, they want nothing less than to be left alone regarding "the Holy One of Israel" and his rightful demands, which, in the goodness of his heart, he makes upon his people. This last request is nothing less than a blasphemous insult of the Almighty. In bringing all this clearly out in the open the prophet has laid his finger on that which is Israel's real trouble. For further instances where Israel attempted to silence the prophets sent with a message from God see: Amos 2:12; 7:11, 13; Micah 2:6; Jer. 11:21; cf. also I Kings 22:8-13.

Verse 12. In the thoughts just expressed in v. 11, the Holy One of Israel has been summarily dismissed. He refuses to be dismissed. He steps up with a word of doom that indicates that he is still fully in command of the situation. He gives another summary statement of what they have done when he says: "You have despised the word." When the Lord grants his word to men he is bestowing his choicest treasure. When men reject the word offered, they are guilty, of the most heinous misdeed. If the word, however, is despised, something must be substituted for it. Israel's substitute was "oppression and crookedness." In this context it would seem that "oppression" refers to the methods to which they resorted to raise the tribute to be paid to Egypt to enlist her help. "Crookedness" on the other hand may be a telling description of their entire policy in international politics. But certainly these two are poor substitutes for the word of the Lord.

Verse 13. So the prophet once again has to become a messenger of doom. In doing this, he uses a new descriptive term for the recent embassy that was sent down to Egypt: he calls it "their iniquity," and likens it, in a rather colorful figure, to "a crack in a high wall" which by its very presence in the wall is "threatening collapse and already bulging out." The crack is there. How soon it will prove the collapse of the wall remains to be seen. The wall is thought of as showing obvious signs of strain. The "collapse comes all of a sudden." Such effective comparisons tend to discredit what deserves to be discredited. The prophet certainly was not deficient in producing an effective attack on the vulnerable position of the pro-Egyptian party, and its policies.

Verse 14. This verse carries the preceding illustration to an effective conclusion, by adding an analogous figure, that of a broken "potter's vessel," that has been shattered so ruthlessly that a sherd large enough for any practical use, can no longer be found, a use like raking fire from embers or scooping water from a puddle. By this time the prophet has fully demonstrated how utterly futile is the prevailing policy of the nation.

4. A Basically Sound Attitude and Its Consequences (vv. 15-26)

30:15-22 15. For thus says the Lord, the Holy One of Israel:
"If you return and wait calmly, you will be rescued;
if you remain quiet and maintain confidence, you will be strong."
16. But that you did not want; but you said: "Not so;
we shall fly to the attack on horses": So you shall flee.
Again: "We shall ride on swift steeds." So your pursuers shall be swift.
17. A whole thousand of you shall flee at the threat of a single person;
or, You shall flee if five men threaten you;
till you are left like an abandoned flagpole on the top of a mountain,
like an ensign on a hill.
18. Therefore the Lord waits to be gracious to you,
and therefore he exalts himself to show mercy to you.
For the Lord is a God of justice;
Blessed are all they that wait for him!
19. Yea, you people of Zion who dwell at Jerusalem, you will not keep on weeping; he will surely be gracious to you at the sound of your cry for help; when he hears he will answer you.
20. The Lord will indeed give you bread of short measure, and water of scant allowance; but not will your teacher hide any more, but your eyes shall see your teacher. 21. And your ears will

hear a word spoken behind you, saying: "This is the way, walk in it," when you might turn to the right or turn to the left. 22. And you will regard as unclean your gold-covered and silver-covered graven images and molten images. You will scatter them as filthy things. You will say to them: "Get out!"

This section may be divided into two parts, the first running from vv. 15-18. The title we have given indicates the same thing by its two parts: attitude and consequences. *G. A. Smith* rather aptly says that vv. 15-18 deal with the subject "not Alliances but Reliance."

Verse 15. With this word an instructive, comforting word of gospel-import begins. The prophet constructively defines the course the nation should substitute for its pro-Egyptian policy. The Hebrew says: "In returning and waiting . . ." which is best covered by a sentence structure in English which begins with a conditional clause: "If you return . . ." as *Luther* also construes his translation. "Return" happens to be the word usually used for repentance. In this case that thought may be associated with the word in a secondary sense. Primarily it means to turn aside from the unwholesome policy that controls the thinking of the nation, in short, the alliance with Egypt. After this is abandoned then it behooves the nation to "wait calmly." There are times when the danger threatening is beyond man's ability to control the situation. All that is left is to wait on the Lord. Such a situation prevails in this case. This is further spelled out as involving to "remain quiet and maintain confidence." If this approach be used, the nation will be ultimately "rescued" and at the same time will "be strong." For seemingly passive reliance on the Lord is not weakness; it is actually strength. A great word of faith, like to that spoken in 7:4!

Verse 16. But this attractive and inviting approach of faith is exactly what the nation did not want; they flatly rejected it: "Not so!" A dashing cavalry or chariot charge; that caught their fancy. By a bit of play on words Isaiah indicates that upon that which they rely will turn into the very opposite for them: they want to "fly" but will "flee." They, themselves, want to be "swift," but it is their pursuers who will be "swift" in the pursuit. This clearly involves an allusion to the chariots and horses of the Egyptians in which they put their trust. Cf. also 31:1.

Verse 17. Another way of looking at their defeat is that couched in the terminology of the holy war. In that connection the Lord had once promised Israel that with a minority they could overcome any majority. See Lev. 26:8; Deut. 32:30; also Josh. 23:10. Now the reverse of that promise is to be the order of the day. A single man shall hurl a threat at them and rout a thousand. Or if the odds be equally extreme, five men might threaten and put the nation to flight, the rout being so complete that all that might be left where the army stood would be some abandoned banners or flagstaffs on a hill.

Verse 18. Since this unwholesome attitude of dependence on human resources for the present is so strong, the Lord as yet cannot display his gracious attitude toward the people; he must wait. Presently he will exalt himself, that is, rise up victoriously to the attack and thus show mercy to his own. But that time has not yet come. And until their attitude as a nation becomes what it should be, the Lord cannot help, for he is "a God of justice." Certain principles of right and wrong, of repentance and returning, are involved. Certain standards have to be met and they have not yet been met. So for the present, whether the nation likes it nor not, she must wait until the Lord's time has come. But even so: "Blessed are all those that wait for him!" Cf. Ps. 2:12. Comforting God's people with a clear look to the glorious future is met with also in 65:17-25; Amos 9:13-15; and Joel 3:18. This is developed at greater length in the words following, vv. 19-26.

Verses 19, 20. The thought set forth here would hardly apply to the entire nation, who have just been depicted as manifesting a most unwholesome attitude. It, therefore, must be the remnant who are addressed here. In that sense the title given ("you people of Zion, who dwell at Jerusalem") must be meant. Zion once again is the spot where the hope is centered. The grace that is promised is first defined as "you will not keep on weeping." The end of the period of sadness is promised. For a situation will arise when it will be possible for the Lord "to be gracious at the sound of [their] cry for help." So the Lord delights to do for his own. When it is said, "When he hears he will answer you" is meant in the sense of, As soon as he hears. A list of favors that God will bestow now follows to show how kindly he will be disposed toward his own. But introducing this list is a brief statement to the contrary, reminiscent of v. 18, which also said that he could not show mercy at once. Verse 20 is meant in the concessive sense, which we have sought to indicate by inserting a concessive "indeed." That means, though "bread of short measure and water of scant allowance" will be their lot, that shall not prevail indefinitely. Rising to the higher level of things, one of the mercies that will again be in evidence will be that their God-given teachers, prophets like Isaiah, will no longer be obliged to hide from the dangers that threaten them, but will step out into the open and freely speak their message. This throws a unique light on the situation in which God's prophets sometimes found themselves.

Verse 21. When it is now said that their "ears will hear a word" it implies both that prophets can again speak without let or hindrance and the people will actually hearken to what is said and do it. In brief, the people will enjoy wholesome guidance. This is portrayed in an effective figure, in which the directing word is heard "behind" the hearer. The figure would be one taken from the use of draft-animals which have the driver coming or sitting behind them and indicating what turns are to be made and when, and the beast readily follows. This all implies a docile attitude of the "people of Zion" over against the word of the prophet.

Verse 22. The remnant will take a further step in the right direction. Hezekiah, king of Judah, had indeed instigated a reform (II Kings 18:4), but all such addictions as idolatry usually have deep roots. In private many a man may have retained some idol of his in hiding and so a harmful deposit of the old sin was still festering. Now when the better day dawns, the nation will of its own volition complete the reform begun by the king and will take idols that had cost them quite a bit, even if they were only covered with gold and silver plating, and throw them out and defile them, making further use impossible. That the old sin of idolatry had been quite firmly ingrained in the nation's life appears from the rather frequent references to the subject that appear (2:8, 18-20; 10:11; 27:9; 31:7; 1:29; 17:10).

30:23-26 23. And he will give you rain for the seed with which you sow your ground and bread as the produce of your soil, which will be rich and fertile. Your cattle will graze on that day on broad pastures. 24. The oxen and the asses that work the ground shall eat fodder mixed with salt, which has been winnowed with shovel and fork. 25. And on every high mountain and on every exalted hill there shall be irrigation ditches flowing with water on the day of great slaughter when the towers will fall. 26. Also the light of the moon shall be as the light of the sun; and the light of the sun shall be seven times as bright as now, like the light of the entire seven days [of the week] on the day when the Lord binds up the hurt of his people and heals their wounds.

Verses 23, 24. Here the description of the blessed consequences of the basically sound attitude of the remnant continues with special emphasis on the physical aspect of the case. For with Israel the physical and the spiritual were not sharply separated and contrasted with one another. The description is somewhat idealized, especially toward the end. The first part portrays an agricultural people abounding in blessings as they go about their various pursuits. Rain, so very essential a commodity in the many dessicated areas of the Near East, is described as coming when the sown seed needs it most; the seed will sprout and the land will be fertile. Cattle shall enjoy all the pasturage they need. As far as stall-feeding is concerned, whenever it is resorted to, the fodder shall be of the choicest sort, well mixed with salt content and by the use of every helpful device known.

Verse 25. The mountains and hills, usually bare of vegetation, will be supplied with some, here unnamed, sources of water, which will allow for the terraced hillsides to be irrigated by irrigation-ditches. It is then assumed that they will flourish with vegetation. At this point a kind of sigh injects itself in the otherwise glorified account. Contemporary with the paradise-like state of things, which already will have begun, there will be reminders of the evil age just coming to a close, when it is said that in part it still will be a "day of great slaughter when the towers will fall." Armies still will be fighting here and there. Cities and embattled towers still will be in a state of siege and will be in process of demolition. In other words, echoes of vv. 12-15 again will be heard. The coming of the days of blessing will be gradual; the overcoming of the days of war and affliction will be gradual. So v. 25b is not an impossible thought "most unsuitable" (*sehr befremdlich, Procksch*) at this point.

Verse 26. In addition, the new order of things is portrayed in terms of a remarkable intensification of glorious light, with the emphasis not on its blinding intensity but on its glorious nature, somewhat like 60:20. Hyperbole marks the whole description. The pale light of the moon is to take on the brilliance of the sun, the light of one day of sunshine is to be the equivalent of an ordinary entire week of seven days. We can hardly rethink these thoughts without being reminded of an intense glare, which is certainly not what the prophet intends. That everything written is here to convey the thought of great blessings for God's children is indicated by the concluding clauses, that this will be done "on the day when the Lord binds up the hurt of his people and heals their wounds."

5. The Lord's Judgment on the Nations, Especially on Assyria (vv. 27-33)

30:27-33 27. Behold, the name of the Lord comes from afar; his anger burns and heavy are the banks of clouds. His lips are full of indignation and his tongue like a consuming fire. 28. His breath is like a sweeping torrent, reaching up to the neck, to shake nations in a sieve of destruction, and place on the jaws of peoples a halter that leads them astray. 29. You shall sing a song as in the night when a holy festival is observed, and have gladness of heart as that of a man who walks to the sound of a flute to go to the mountain of the Lord, to the Rock of Israel. 30. And the Lord shall cause his glorious voice to be heard and the descent of his arm to be seen in storming anger and with a flame of devouring fire in a driving shower of rain and hailstones. 13. For the Assyrians will be filled with terror at the sound of the Lord's voice, who shall smite them with the rod. 32. And it shall come to pass that with every blow of the appointed rod that the Lord lays upon him, there shall be timbrels and harps; and he will make terrible war upon him with bran-dished arm. 33. For already for a long while a place of burning has been readied; this too is prepared for the king, a deep funeral pyre with much wood is prepared; the breath of the Lord like a torrent of brimstone will kindle it.

A judgment scene of unusual grandeur is portrayed. There are many like it in the Scriptures. God manifests him-self in a storm and in fire. In the first two verses two pictures blend into a powerful scene of action, that of a storm and that of an angry man breathing fire and destruc-tion. There is something reminiscent of the Sinai incident in evidence (Exod. 19:16ff.), but also of passages like Isa. 29:6; Deut. 33:2; Hab. 3:3f.; Judg. 5:4-5; Ps. 18:7ff.; 50:3-5. The whole description is pervaded by a deep feeling of awe on the part of the writer. But it would be improper to impute to the prophet something of a "gloating exultation" (*Skinner*). For though later on some measure of gratitude may be expressed that the Lord has vanquished his danger-ous foes, there is no unholy glee over the fate of the wicked.

Verse 27. What the prophet sees in particular is "the name of the Lord (coming) from afar." The expression "name of the Lord" always means the full revelation of himself that the Lord has granted to men. In the fulness of his divine being he appears on the scene for judgment. His anger is hot, for the wickedness of men has been great and it clamors for divine intervention. He seems to be enshrouded in such a way that it must be said: "heavy are the banks of clouds." To us it may seem improper, but the bold figure here has it that his anger expresses itself as a hot breath of indignation flaming forth from his mouth to consume "the enemy and the avenger."

Verse 28. The second figure replaces the first. The judg-ment sweeps along like mighty waters, "a sweeping torrent reaching to the neck" and actually flooding over the nations on the face of the earth. A third and fourth figure blend into this picture which is marked by an exuberance of imagina-tion. What is being done with the nations may be likened to the work of a mighty man who puts the nations into a sieve of vast proportions, but not for separation or cleansing what is in the sieve, but to shake them together for de-

struction in wild confusion. Imagine: all the wicked on
the face of the earth in one huge siege, being battered to
death. Or, to note the last figure, a halter is to be attached
to the jaws of the peoples, a halter that might also very
properly be called a halter of destruction, for it tends to lead
the peoples away to their doom.

Verse 29. Till now the judgment, which is specifically designed for the Assyrians, would seem to appear as a universal
judgment, for v. 28 mentioned "nations" and "peoples."
These terms could indeed be generic plurals and the description would then still be in reference to this one nation. But
now, in a highly colorful way, the overthrow of the hosts of
Assyria is pictured very dramatically, with the same exuberant use of figurative description that we have already noted.
But undeniably there is something glorious about a scene
of this sort, even as the Lord himself, in depicting the last
Great Judgment (Matt. 25:31ff.), begins by stressing the
glory of the transaction. That aspect of the case was also
detected by the Old Testament prophets. So in this case,
they who witness what God does in his inimitable, glorious
way, will be moved to praise the Lord for what he does.
They will sing words of solemn and sober praise, similar to
the songs sung when certain festivals, perhaps particularly
the Passover festival, were celebrated. The gladness of heart
naturally would not be over the fate of the enemy but over
the deliverance of God's people. For it will be noted that
the prophet particularly stresses that a typical example of
such joy would be that of a man, who "walks to the sound
of a flute to go to the mountain of the Lord, to the Rock of
Israel." God is in his thoughts. The Rock of Israel is being
praised. The "mountain of the Lord" is this worshipper's objective. Note the propriety of the name chosen for God in
this connection — "the Rock of Israel." The emphasis lies on
the sure and immovable foundation that the Lord provides
for all that put their trust in him. Also see for the use of
this splendid title II Sam. 23:3; Isa. 17:10; Deut. 32:4, 18, 37.

Verse 30. The description of the glorious judgment continues in this verse, still under the aspect of a furious storm,
in which the Lord himself appears on the scene. When he
causes his glorious "voice" to be heard, the reference is to

thunder, as is also the case throughout Ps. 29. The lightning, on the other hand, may be regarded as "the descent
of his arm" as each bolt strikes "with a flame of devouring
fire." To complete the picture of devastating forces being unleashed, the words are added: "in a driving shower of rain
and hailstones."

Verse 31. From this point onward the reference to the
Assyrian is explicit. The bold Assyrian forces are pictured
as "filled with terror," not with bold courage, as each thunder
crashes. For in the midst of this scene of confusion the Lord
himself is seen as he "smites them with the rod." It may
have been, as is commonly assumed, a swift pestilence
which wiped out the Assyrian hosts on the soil of Israel, but
the enlightened seer detects the Lord himself at work,
tracing, as usual, the effect back to its primary cause.

Verse 32. This scene is dwelt on a bit more at length, for
there was something superb about the action involved on this
occasion. The prophet uses a certain boldness, that he, no
doubt, knew could easily be misunderstood, but could also
be construed rightly and properly by the chastened "people
of Zion" (v. 19). Blow after blow is falling on his enemies,
demolishing their mighty host. The destructive force is called
"the appointed rod" (or, "the staff of punishment" *RSV*)
indicating that the Lord availed himself of some agent of
destruction that the prophet as yet is not able to identify, but
which II Kings 19:25 has designated as "the angel of the
Lord." But the bold imagery of this description indicates
the reaction of God's people as they witness what transpires.
As each blow of deliverance falls "there shall be timbrels
and harps." That this scene was not enacted literally must
be obvious to every thinking man. But that the essence of
what transpired is nevertheless graphically caught is indis-
putable. And we still believe that the "people of Zion" may
have shared in the scene with a certain holy and reverend
joy and awe, especially when in the morning of the next day
the people of the city went out and "behold, these were all
dead bodies" (II Kings 19:35). Then it became most obvious
that the Lord had "made war upon him [the Assyrian] with
brandished arm."

Verse 33. Somehow the prophet seems to sense that with

some great mass-destruction impending, a tremendous task of disposing of the dead bodies would confront the delivered people of God. That aspect of the case now calls for a bit of consideration, which is given in the usual grand style of the prophet. It may be said that the Lord has also foreseen this eventuality and taken the steps requisite for coping with it. Speaking in strongly anthropomorphic language, it is as though he had long been gathering wood for a tremendous funeral-pyre, has stacked it up well and deep (for the cremation will have to be a most tremendous one). Provision is also made for the disposal of the body of the Assyrian "king." This does not necessarily involve that the prophet definitely expected that the body of this great nation's king would lie among the dead. It is merely a colorful way of stating that the king himself will somehow definitely share in this drastic overthrow, as II Kings 17:37 in its own way indicates. Highly dramatic and poetic descriptions like the one in question, must not be pressed too sharply according to the letter. But the rest of the dramatic action pictures the Lord himself as kindling the fire of this huge pyre by his own breath which kindles the wood "like a torrent of brimstone." On that final note, stressing the divine enactment of the judgment, the chapter closes.

Notes

Verse 2. Though we translated ". . . without inquiring of me," the original has: "without asking my mouth." The same expression occurs in Josh. 9:14; Gen. 24:57. Add to this the fact that in Exod. 4:16 the same idiom refers to the one who acts in a sort of prophetic capacity, the whole situation adds up to this: They did not consult God's prophet about this dubious project. Since he himself is speaking, the only translation left in our idiom is the personal pronoun "me."

Verse 7. The initial *waw* here according to the context carries an explicative force. See *KS* 360 d.

Though the second last word *hem* is plural, though referring to Egypt, this is due to the fact that the many who make up this boastful and inactive nation are being thought of. Cf. *KS* 346 p.

Verse 10. The word *nekhochoth* uses the feminine to express the abstract concept of "right things," a frequent way of covering an abstract idea (cf. *KS* 245 d).

Verse 12. The infinitive *ma'oskhem* is the equivalent of a clause of cause. See *KS* 403 c and *GK* 61 d.

Verse 13. The participle *nophel* is determined as to the time involved, by its context, so that it does not here mean "falling," but "about to fall," or, "threatening collapse." *GK* 116 d.

Verse 14. The clause *lo' yachmol* ("he will not pity") is rightly regarded as merely the equivalent of an adverb (*KS* 361 q).

Verse 15. *Beshubhah* — "in returning" — uses an impersonal construction, where we would say "in your returning." *KS* 106.

Verse 16. The initial *waw* in this case is clearly adversative. See *KS* 360 c.

Verse 18. *Yarum* presents a difficulty. But this form still may be translated "he exalts himself," though this must be a reference to the future, as the first clause of the verse is. A textual correction *yiddom* might be accepted in the sense: "he holds still."

Verse 19. The last word *'anakh* is a perfect (*'anah*) with suffix used in a futuristic sense. See *KS* 129.

Verse 20. Though we may well translate (with *RSV*): ". . . bread of adversity and water of affliction" this seems to mean, as *Gorden* has aptly put it: "bread of short measure and water of scant allowance."

verse 24. The participle *zoreh* (*pual* without the *m* preformative, *GK* 52 s) needs to have a subject supplied out of the context. See *KS* 324 n.

Verse 26. The article stands before "seven days" being the article of total familiarity (*KS* 297 b) and referring to the familiar seven days of the week.

Verse 27. "Heavy are the banks of clouds" is a very difficult expression. *RSV* translates similarly "in thick rising smoke."

Verse 33. The phrase "for the king" has its difficulties. For if taken literally it seems to list the Assyrian king among those slain on the battlefield. The vowels might be changed so that it reads (*RSV* m): "for Molech," the Moabite god. But why should he be remembered in this context?

Chapter XXXI

D. A DENUNCIATION OF THE COVENANT WITH EGYPT AGAINST ASSYRIA (Chap. 31)

A great variety of themes suggested for this chapter could be listed at this point. There is no basic disagreement among writers as to what the subject actually is. It could even be described as a Sketch of a Prevailing Crisis. It has been labelled "Egypt and Assyria." Whereas most of these approaches ring a somewhat negative note, they are usually agreed in this that they feel that Chap. 31 again offers in brief what was already set forth in Chap. 30. This already led *Luther* to remark that the prophet treats of the subject of the futility of help from Egypt almost to the point of boring the hearer. But he also remarked that the emphasis involved was due to the precariousness of the prevailing situation. *Von Orelli* takes our chapter together with the one that follows and arrives at the more positive theme, "The Blessed Transformation to be Wrought by Divine Grace."

We insert our outline at this point.

1. The Futility of the Help Expected from Egypt (vv. 1-3)
2. Yahweh Will Campaign against His Misguided People but Will Deliver the Remnant (vv. 4-5)
3. A Call to Repentance (vv. 6-7)
4. The Overthrow of the Assyrians (vv. 8-9)

As far as form is concerned, this chapter may be classified as the last Woe of the series beginning with 28:1. As far as the meter of vv. 1-3 is concerned, it may be regarded as made up of three double three-accent lines followed by one pair of five-accent lines. From v. 4ff. on the problem is not so simple. *Procksch* admits, no unanimity prevails as to the classification of the meter.

1. The Futility of the Help Expected from Egypt (vv. 1-3)

31:1-3 1. Woe to those who went down to Egypt for help and to rely on horses;
and put their trust in chariots because they are many,
and in horsemen because they are numerous;
but did not look to the Holy One of Israel,
nor inquire of the Lord.
2. Yet he also was wise and brought disaster;
and did not turn back his words;
and will arise against the house of evil-doers
and against the help sought from those who work iniquity.
3. And the Egyptians are men and not God;
and their horses are flesh and not spirit.
And the Lord will stretch forth his hand,
and the helper will stumble and he who is helped will fall;
and all of them will perish together.

Verse 1. The time is farther advanced than in Chap. 30. According to the tense of the verbs involved (which we expect to examine in the *Notes*) the prophet is referring not to things which are in process of happening, but to things that have already taken place. Men "*went* down to Egypt for help" and "*went* down to rely on horses." This was their avowed intention. By this time every one in Judah may have heard of what transpired. Some reports that have come down to us would indicate that Egypt had fabulously large resources of chariots and horsemen. Israel had none, or at best, very few. The Assyrians also appear to have been very well equipped in this direction. So the chariots, which were "many," and the horsemen, which were "numerous" were the items on which they had centered their entire confidence. But the Lord was left entirely out of the picture: they "did not look to the Holy One of Israel." Such a look would have been evidence of faith. But this is the prophet's point: they had no faith. The issue is the same as that dwelt on in 22:8-11 and 30:15ff. In the expression "look to the Holy One," the verb "look" — as *Calvin* already pointed out — conveys the thought of having confidence. So the issue is this: The nation took the position: What we need is chariots and horsemen from our strong neighbor in the South. We ourselves can supply the needed infantry. So we will be equipped to meet the impending threat of mighty Assyria.

Verse 2. Now follows what may be classified as the great understatement of the Scriptures. As to the tense used in our translation ("was") see the *Notes*. If the past tense be correct, then the prophet is not expressing a generally-accepted truth so much as reflecting on the nation's entire past experience. It is true that this is the first time in the sacred Scriptures that wisdom is ascribed to God. But the truth as such was most abundantly known in Israel. Yahweh knew how to meet crucial issues in the past and was always equal to emergencies. Israel's history bore abundant testimony to this fact. There seems to be a mildly ironical note in the prophet's manner of stating the case, coupled with sharp rebuke. At this point, where perhaps a positive thought would have been anticipated by the hearer, a sudden turn to the negative sets in: he "brought disaster." He can, of course, deliver; but when his people proved recalcitrant, he "brought disaster" by way of shaking them out of their wrong approach and driving them to bethink themselves. Cf. Amos 3:6. The point is that such measures often become necessary but they are always totally under divine control. He who can so effectively handle these complicated issues of history is the One whose help is to be sought and the whole problem entrusted to his ability to handle it adequately. Because of Israel's sad failure to look to him, the threatening aspect of the situation has to be well weighed, and in the present instance it amounts to this, that he "will not turn back his words," namely the threats that he has pronounced against his faithless people. They need not expect that in spite of their infidelity they will accomplish an easy victory. First some sharp judgments must take place. He "will arise against the house of evil-doers," that is, the very people of Judah themselves; and "against the help sought from those who work iniquity," that is, the Egyptians, whose aid was so eagerly sought. Their entire enterprise will encounter opposition from the Lord. This is the clear sketch of the present crisis that the prophet gives Judah. It is important to note, as this statement indicates, that Israel's concept of history was that both victory and defeat, progress and setbacks, are always fully under Yahweh's control as he moves forward to achieve his purposes.

Verse 3. The point under discussion is of such importance as to call for more ample treatment. What was the mistake that was being made when Judah's ambassadors went down to enlist Egyptian help? The explanation is cast in the form of a concise epigram. This word draws praise from practically every commentator. It is the epitome of diplomatic insight and of practical political wisdom. When the unenlightened mind seeks help from some one nation as the only possible source of deliverance then men are forgetting that there is only one who is God and that any aggregate total of people of any nationality cannot muster strength comparable to that of the Almighty. There is the possibility that the word may be translated: "The Egyptians are men and not *gods*." But going one step farther, as far as those much vaunted horses and chariots of Egypt are concerned, "their horses are flesh and not spirit." Again, a most weighty pronouncement! Its truth is so obvious as to seem commonplace. "Spirit" in this context carries the connotation of "source of power." "Spirit" is quite commonly a synonym for *power*. God is *all* power. "Horses" — so eagerly sought after in the present crisis — are "flesh," a term which in the Old Testament regularly connotes frailty and evanescence. What has Israel done? Of the two possible sources of strength, she has abandoned the one that has solid merit and has built her whole future in the present emergency on that which is palpably inadequate.

The contrast expressed in the first line of the verse is also reflected in words such as Hos. 11:9; Num. 23:19; cf. also Ezek. 28:2, 9. In the second line of the verse it is not actually *said* that God is a spirit, but it is most definitely implied. So the level of John 4:24 is not quite reached in this classical pronouncement of the Old Testament.

The prophet proceeds to show what the Lord will do to drive home the truth involved and to make it still more apparent to Judah. The Lord will take a hand in the present crisis, or, to speak more nearly in the language of the Scriptures, "the Lord will stretch forth his hand." The purpose of the hand being stretched forth is to fetch a blow at an ad-

versary, in this case, two adversaries — Egypt, "the helper,"
and his own people Israel, presumably "the one who is
helped." And as far as all the grand schemes are concerned,
which were being concocted in those days, they shall all fail
and both these nations shall suffer reverses at the hand of
the Assyrians. This, then, is the same message that was set
forth by the prophet in 30:1-7. But obviously, under the circumstances, where Judah was so strongly determined to stake
everything on Egypt's help such prophetic instruction had
to be dinned in men's ears almost *ad nauseam*.

2. Yahweh Will Campaign against His Misguided People but Will Deliver the Remnant (vv. 4-5)

31:4-5   4. For thus the Lord said to me:
"Just as a lion or a young lion growls over his prey,
against whom the whole band of shepherds is called forth,
at whose shouting he is not terrified
nor gives way because of their noisy multitude —
so the Lord of hosts will come down to campaign against Mount
Zion [the Temple] and against its hill [the city].
5. Like hovering birds so shall the Lord of hosts shield Jerusalem.
shielding, delivering, passing over, and saving."

Verse 4. It is almost impossible to determine whether the
assertion, "for thus the Lord said to me," belongs to the
preceding verse or should be attached to v. 4, as its initial
statement. We have kept it in the latter place, following the
tradition of the Hebrew text.

The difficulty that has vexed those that sought to ex-
pound these two verses is that v. 4 seems to breathe hot
and v. 5 seems to breathe cold. Or, are both figures designed to express some gracious act? Or, is the tone of the
first ominous and the tone of the second conciliatory? Commentators, therefore, are divided into two camps. *Luther*
appears to be on the right track when he paraphrases: "You,
O Israel, are my prey. . . ." It must be admitted that the
figure is unusually bold to liken the Lord to the lion that
crouches over the prey he has just seized and is about to
devour. The addition of the words "a young lion" serves
the purpose of making the picture that of a lion in the prime

of its strength and therefore all the more fearless. Lions were common enough in those days, having their lair in the thickets of the Jordan (see I Sam. 17:34-37; Amos 3:12). When a lion had seized a sheep and was about to devour it, an alarm would be raised by the shepherds and all would congregate at the point where the lion crouched, seeking by a wild outcry to intimidate the beast. All the lion does in such a case is to growl and keep on tearing his prey. He does "not give way because of their noisy multitude." If the words then following say: "So the Lord of hosts will come down . . ." apparently it is meant in the sense that the lion in the figure used represents the Lord. Judah is the prey he has seized, or as the latter part of the verse says, he comes "to campaign against mount Zion and against its hill." Those who are described here as the "whole band of shepherds," are all who are desperately trying to interfere with his corrective endeavors that are directed against his people, efforts apparently so harsh as to warrant using the figure of a lion about to devour his prey. Some think that the "shepherds" represent "the mob of politicians and treaty mongers" among the people of Judah (*G. A. Smith*). *Luther* identified the Assyrians with the shepherds, as the ones who were trying to dispose of the people of Israel in their own way. One might accept both interpretations, for both represent forces that attempt to interfere. In any case, when the Lord will take his people in hand for judgment in this present crisis, no one, individual or group, will stop him. The Lion will not "give way because of their noisy multitude." He has a "campaign" on against both the sanctuary and the Holy City. A play on words lies hidden here, for the verb "*campaign*" and the name "Lord of *hosts*" involve the same root. Because he is the Lord of hosts he will campaign fearlessly against his people as the circumstances demand.

Verse 5. But the sudden turn from the fearful and dreadful to the gracious is intentional and calculated to startle. For in the dread invasion of Sennacherib, described by Isaiah in Chaps. 36 and 37, presented this very kind of experience. Assyria invaded and ravished the land terribly: all seemed lost: Jerusalem alone still was to fall. Then came the very sudden turn of events for the better, the sudden retreat of the Assyrian host, and the total deliverance of Judah and Jerusalem. See 37:35; 38:6.

Verse 5. So did the Lord "shield Jerusalem." The heaping of verb-forms indicates the many-sidedness of this help: "shielding, delivering, passing over and saving." In the original there is a subordination of some of these activities in a manner which we seem utterly unable to reproduce, but which does not materially alter the case. Significant is the verb "passing over," being that very verb used in Exodus in the account of the first Passover. Marvelous as was the deliverance from Egyptian bondage so shall that of Jerusalem be in these latter days.

At this point many commentators insist on it that there hardly can be any doubt that vv. 6-7, or at least v. 6 must be classified as a later addition by some other writer or copyist. Also at this point we much prefer to regard the entire chapter as directly from the hand of Isaiah. *Kissane* has provided strong support of this contention, aside from other pertinent arguments, by showing that vv. 5-7 present a pattern that appeared also in 30:19ff., namely: pardon (v. 5); conversion (v. 6); and renunciation of idolatry (v. 7).

3. A Call to Repentance (vv. 6-7)

31:6-7 6. Turn back to him from whom the children of Israel have deeply revolted. 7. For on that day [of deliverance] every one will cast aside his idols of silver and his idols of gold, which your hands have made for you — a sin!

Verse 6. Since a deliverance is coming and in reality only those can be said to share in it who have sincerely repented, also from this point of view this interjected call to repentance is logically defensible, and even most appropriate. Nor is its effectiveness impaired by the fact that the verse begins in the second person and then suddenly switches over to a very objective approach in the third person. Such mobility of approach is most common in Hebrew and not to be measured by our language rules and patterns. The second part of the verse does indicate the need of repentance in that it shows how extreme the measure of departure has been, or how deeply they have revolted. The prophet was concerned for their soul's salvation. Why should he not voice his concern?

Verse 7. Since now idolatry had taken such a firm hold on the people, the prophet cannot but reiterate that the evidence of true repentance will be total renunciation of the idols, even to the point of casting them aside as something cheap and unworthy of the people of God. All the more so since they are nothing more than the work of man's hands. The same approach appeared in 30:22; see also 2:20 and 17:7f.

But the next two verses also make up a part of a very logical sequence. It had been intimated that the Lord would inaugurate a great deliverance for his people (v. 5). After having suggested preparation for this event in the form of sound repentance, is it not very much in place to indicate the exact nature of this deliverance, which is in reality the overthrow of the Assyrians?

4. The Overthrow of the Assyrians (vv. 8-9)

31:8-9 8. And the Assyrian will fall by a sword — not of man and a sword — not of men — will devour him.
And he will flee from the sword,
and his young men will be put to forced labor.
9. And his strong rock will pass away in terror,
and his princes [officers] shall desert the standard in panic — utterance of Yahweh, whose fire is in Zion and whose furnace is in Jerusalem.

Verse 8. The theme of the overthrow of the Assyrians has been set forth repeatedly (cf. 10:12; 14:25; 30:31-33). One special aspect of that defeat is stressed here — the fact that primarily it will not be a military disaster, or one that will take the form of a defeat on the field of battle. A mysterious "sword" is described negatively as not being "of man" (or "of men," the second term apparently appearing only to complete the parallelism), a sword that remains a mystery to this day. For though in 37:36 the agent is described as the angel of the Lord and the slaying that he did, many still incline to the opinion that the agency employed may have been a swift-acting form perhaps of bubonic plague.

In any case the defeat came not via the ordinary channels. It must be born in mind that this part of the verse describes the agent God employed. Apparently in the second half of the verse the "sword" referred to has to do with the sword of men, such as soldiers would use on the day of battle. So the claim of this part of the verse is to the effect that the well-equipped Assyrian forces will not be able to stand up victoriously against the enemy's sword, but shall suffer reverses on the field of battle and be taken captive and "be put to forced labor" as captives generally were in days of old. For ultimately, after the reverses suffered in Judah, the forces of Assyria were defeated and the empire collapsed (fall of Nineveh, 612 B.C.).

Verse 9. This collapse is described a bit more at length in this verse. The passing away of "his strong rock" presents some difficulties. It could refer — to indicate two of many possibilities — to the king of the nation, who, usually being a vigorous monarch, was the strength of his people. The term could refer to "the elite of his army," for the Assyrians had a well-equipped and trained military force, the best of those days. Assuming that the army then may have been the nation's "strong rock" it is here pictured as "passing away in terror," i.e., passing off the scene too frightened to offer any resistance. Or, as the parallel statement has it, "his princes shall desert the standard in panic."

The concluding statement of the verse assures the reader that this pronouncement is nothing less than a pronouncement of Yahweh himself. The appended relative clauses may be construed to mean that Yahweh's sanctuary is in Jerusalem, and it is implied that he will rise up in defense of that which is his very hearth (cf. 29:1), or "Ariel" — the hearth of God. "Furnace in Jerusalem" may again be nothing more than the parallel statement rounding out the description. To seek to discover some special significance, other than the reference to God's hearth, in this expression seems to yield only a stilted exposition.

Notes

Verse 1. When we translate "went down" not "go down" it is because *wayyibhtechu* indicates that a narrative about the past lies before us. The *yishsha'enu* merely continues the further explanation who they are who went down to Egypt, persons namely who went "for help and to rely on horses." Cf. *KS* 413 f g.

Verse 2. In *wegham* the *we* is adversative, contrasting two parties that may lay claim to wisdom. See *KS* 360 c.

Verse 4. Though *'asher* could be reproduced by a "when" or "if," (cf. *BDB* 83 b) it appears better to let it remain a plain relative (cf. *KS* 390 d).

Verse 5. At first glance it seems inappropriate to use the plural ("birds") in showing what Yahweh is like. But this is a case where the plural merely indicates that the point of the comparison (*tertium comparationes*) belongs to the whole group (*KS* 264 b).

Verse 6. The elliptical form of the statement is rather bold in that it passes by the *min* which seems essential for the proper statement of the case. See *GK* 138 f N.3.

Verse 8. The negative clearly limits itself to a single noun in this case — a "no-man" — *GK* 152 a. In the expression "flee from [the] sword, the article is omitted. Some call this the "emphatic indetermination." See *KS* 293 d and *GK* 125 c.

Verse 9. The *lo* in the last line is a dative of interest. *Ks* 36.

Chapter XXXII

E. THE NEW REGIME (Chap. 32)

We are still in the Zion Book. Though Zion is not mentioned by name, indubitably it is at Zion where the New Regime, here described, is to be located.

For the moment, the anti-Egyptian approach is dropped by the prophet. Still, there is a rather apparent progression of thought. If Chap. 31 ended on the note of the disastrous overthrow of mighty Assyria, by way of contrast this chapter shows how the people of God shall arise and recover from their overthrow and by the grace of God take a new lease on life, an approach already indicated by *Luther* (see also *Delitzsch*).

Though the authorship, in part or in whole, by Isaiah is strongly questioned by some — *Procksch* claims that the assumption of it leaves a man somewhat uneasy — *Bewer*, we believe rightly, maintains that such claims are "without altogether cogent reasons." *Fischer* advances the same claim, as do others.

As to the time within Isaiah's ministry, when these oracles were proclaimed, opinions vary somewhat — if such questions can ever be answered with any finality. The words in which the ungodly women are denounced (vv. 9-14) are usually assigned to an earlier period because of their similarity with 3:16ff., which is usually thought of as spoken early in the prophet's career. Again the claim is made that the last part of the chapter (vv. 15-20) with its view of the glorious future must have been spoken as a part of the prophet's most mature thinking.

The metrical pattern, as far as it has met with some measure of approval, may consist of the following arrangement: vv. 1-8 may be arranged in four strophes, each with six half-lines; vv. 9-14 consist of three strophes, each with four lines and four accented syllables per line; vv. 15-20 has two strophes, each of three lines with three or four accents per line (*Procksch*). As usual quite a bit of manipulation of the Hebrew text has to be resorted to in order to make this pattern work.

Our outline is influenced by *Vilmar*, and runs as follows:

1. Described in Terms of a Good King and a Good Government (vv. 1-8)
2. Preceded by a Painful Judgment (vv. 9-14)
3. Inaugurated by the Outpouring of God's Spirit (vv. 15-20)

It will be noted at the outset that we do not take the second part of the chapter to be denunciation of ungodly women, though on the face of it that would appear most logical and see mto agree with the manner in which the section opens. But a bigger subject than that is involved.

1.   Described in Terms of a Good King and a Good Government (vv. 1-8)

32:1-8   1. Behold, a king will reign in righteousness,
and princes will rule in justice;
2. and each of them will be a hiding-place from the wind,
and a shelter from the storm;
as streams of water in a dry place;
as the shadow of a mighty rock in a weary land.
3. And the eyes of them that look will not be closed;
and the ears of them that hear will be attentive.
4. And the mind of the rash will have insight and knowledge;
and the tongue of the stammerers will be quick to speak clearly.
5. No longer shall a fool be called noble,
nor a knave be spoken of as honorable.
6. For a fool will continue to speak folly,
and his mind will produce wickedness;
by practicing profaneness and speaking impious things against Yahweh;
by leaving the craving of the hungry unsatisfied —
he deprives the thirsty man of drink.
7. As for the knave — his knaveries are evil;
he plots wicked devices, to destroy the oppressed with lying words,
even though the poor man speaks uprightly.
8. But the noble devise noble things,
and stand up in support of noble things.

Verse 1. At once we are thrown into the midst of the question whether the "king" is the Messiah. At *Luther's* and *Calvin's* time these men themselves advanced the clear-cut claim that a contemporary of the prophet's was under consideration — King Hezekiah. In our day *Fischer* joins them; his verdict is: hardly the Messiah. *Maclaren* cannot abandon the Messianic implications. *Wade* says: It "may be styled a Messianic prophecy." *G. A. Smith* uses guarded terms when he says: ". . . it is evident that in this verse Isaiah is not thinking of the Messiah alone and particularly." We take a similar position. This word refers to the times contemporary with the prophet, but by type it reaches beyond those immediate possibilities.

If "A New Regime" is being described the prophet's conviction clearly is that a true change for the better must take its beginning at the highest levels of government: first the king; then the princes; then the minor officials; then the people. The importance of the king's attitude is reflected in the Book of Proverbs (see 16:10-15; 20:8, 26, 28). Since we are not interpreting this verse as directly Messianic we cannot be disturbed by the observation that the image of the king is quite a bit paler than that presented in 9:5f.; and 11:1ff.; or for that matter II Sam. 23:2. For these passages are without question Messianic and are done in the richest colors. Now the outstanding mark of a good ruler is, as these other passages just cited also indicate, to "reign in righteousness." Such a rule is the embodiment of everything good and noble. For the better days that would come upon Judah, such a rule was imperative; under the Messiah's jurisdiction the same holds true. The next step in the process of rehabilitation will be that the king be supported by princes that exercise their princely function "in justice." It may be that the two virtues under consideration may be distinguished as follows: Righteousness covers the principles involved — justice is the application of the principles to the individual cases that come up for consideration. How all this will work out for the rank and file of the people of Judah is now indicated (v. 2) by a number of colorful descriptions of the blessings of good government.

Verse 2. The reader of the Scriptures in the King James

Version will be puzzled at the radically different approach, which begins: "And a man will be . . ." over against our rendering: "And each of them will be . . ." In every way the newer translation deserves the preference (see *Notes* for further discussion). And so v. 2 refers to both halves of v. 1: king and princes shall govern effectively and in harmony, and so by their joint and effective rule they will be for their subjects all that is now described in the rest of the verse. In regard to the *KJV Scott* very properly remarks that "nowhere is the music of the *KJV* more notable."

Where oftentimes in the past the administration of government left much to be desired, that shall all now be changed, in the better days, which, in the providence of God, are bound to come sooner or later. These rulers then will be first of all "a hiding-place from the wind," the wind of adversity that fiercely whips the poor traveller. Also there will be "a shelter from the storm," when the rains of trouble threaten to wash the poor victim away. Again, when men shall well nigh perish from thirst, good rulers shall help them in their trouble as "streams of water in a dry place" can save the life of a poor man lost in the desert of affliction. Most colorful of all is the last benefit mentioned: These rulers shall be "as the shade of a mighty rock in a weary land." In the blinding sunlight of great trouble "shade" can often be a life-saver. Many is the traveller who has found it so. To then cower in the shade of a rock standing up in the desert has saved more lives than one. Just rule can be so refreshing for upright men. Thus far then in this chapter — good rulers and the attractive benefits of good rule for good subjects have been described.

Verse 3. This verse describes the removal of spiritual disabilities in terms of removal of physical defects. By way of background for this verse those earlier statements found in the book concerning God's judgment of hardening the nation's heart must be considered. This verse then claims that these disabilities, once threatened and actually inflicted, will be cancelled out. The blind eyes will receive sight; the deaf ears will again receive power to function effectively. But the higher achievement involved will include that eyes will be able to discern spiritual truth and reality. Ears will again

be able to hearken when God speaks and distinctly understand what was spoken. So the organs for spiritual apper-
ception will rightly fulfill their mission.

Verse 4. A higher step of achievement will be attained
and attainable according to this verse. Here "insight and
knowledge" are at stake. When men went their own sinful
way, no deeper realities were perceived. Speaking clearly
and well the truth of God was all but impossible. Men stam-
mered around over each utterance. Both these defects will
be overcome. For the ill-advised and rash utterances of the
past, the pronouncements of true wisdom will be substituted.
And those who have this new and better insight will be able
to speak it effectively.

Verse 5. When true values were unknown the true designation of men and values was lost as well. A "fool," who had
no practical knowledge of God, could sometimes be classed
as among the "noble," in a tragic confusion of terms; and
so, too, "a knave" could be mistaken for an "honorable" man.
Men will know better in this better age than to be guilty of
such folly.

Verse 6. In this picture of the better days that are to
come, the fool and the wicked man are not completely absent, but all issues will have been cleared up so thoroughly
that it will be like two utterly diverse groups camped over
against one another and totally separated from each other.
The "fool" will be a fool and all men will know him for such.
His words too will be quite in keeping with his basic attitude.
All that his "mind" (Heb. "heart") can produce will be
wickedness. At some length the involved forms of wickedness, like a kind of nest of vipers, is described as unwholesome and utterly incapable of producing anything sound:
he works "by practicing profaneness and speaking impious
things against Yahweh, by leaving the craving of the hungry
unsatisfied — he deprives the thirsty man of drink." It will
be noted that first his impious attitude toward the Lord is
described, then his unkind treatment of his fellowman. The
wrong relation to God begets an unwholesome relation to
man.

Verse 7. This clearing-up of issues is described still more
fully, dwelling upon the incorrigible nature of ingrained

wickedness. Not that God could not have changed their heart; but these "fools" did not want to be reborn. Both terms, "fool" and "knave," have deep moral connotations. Folly sits not in the head but in the inmost core of one's being. By a clever little pun in the original (cf. "knave" and "knaveries") the doer and the deed are stamped as "evil." All his thinking and planning is devious and crooked so that oppression is consistently practiced even on the man whose case is sound and his speech upright. In other words, the extreme of sin produced the extreme of perversion of a man's basic rights. If the prophet seems to spin this part of his presentation out at too great length (*Skinner* speaks of the prophet's "labored didactic style") it may well be that the confusion which had prevailed in Isaiah's time was so extreme, that to have it all cleared up deserved a longer description because of its fundamental importance.

Verse 8. But clearly marked as the "fool" will be, so, too, will the man who is "noble." By the use of this term the prophet apparently does not limit himself to a certain class in society, men who stand in positions of rule and authority only, but includes all right-thinking, godly men. Still in the light of the two first verses of the chapter "princes" may have been chiefly under consideration. A notable feature of the "New Regime" will be the noble man who devises noble things. *Luther* gives a uniquely clever rendering: *Aber die Fuersten werden fuerstliche Gedanken haben,* "Princes shall have princely thoughts." Apparently an abundance of men of this type will be available. They then will "stand up in support of noble things," so that high-principled thinking and living will be the order of the day in this group, and good men who do good will be strongly supported and upheld in what they do. Noble thinking and living shall be the order of the day.

2. Preceded by Painful Judgment (vv. 9-14)

32:9-14   9. Rise up, you careless women, hear my voice; you complacent daughters, give heed to what I say.
10. A bit more than a year, you complacent ones will tremble; for the vintage will fail and the fruit harvest will not come.
11. Tremble, you careless ones; shudder, you complacent ones.

Strip and make yourselves bare, and gird sackcloth on your loins.

12. Beat upon your breasts for the pleasant fields, for the fruitful
vine;

13. for the soil of my people which springs up in thorns and
thistles,

yea, for all the houses where gladness prevailed, for the city of joy.

14. For the palace will be forsaken,

the noise of the city will be abandoned;

Ophel and the Watchtower will become dens forever —

a joy of wild asses, a pasture for flocks;

It certainly would not be utterly wrong to give this section a title like "Frivolous Women Warned of Disaster"
(*Scott*). But the *Targum* already regarded it as directed
at the princes. Besides, there is justification for regarding
the passage, from v. 12 on, as addressing itself to the men of
Judah. There appears to be some agreement that the passage is genuine from Isaiah. A parallel, definitely scoring the
women only is to be found in 3:16ff.

Verse 9. As to structure this verse has some analogy to
Gen 4:23 and Ps. 41:1f. If a specific occasion were to be
visualized one might venture to conceive of at least the first
verses as addressed to women present at some public celebration of the Festival of Tabernacles, when dances and
general festivities were the order of the day (cf. Judg. 21:
15ff.). Into the rejoicing of the day cuts the shrill denunciation of the prophet. But it still will have to be admitted that
not a syllable of the text gives actual warrant for such an
approach. On general principles Amos 4:1 and 6:1 may be
compared. As to context, it may be admitted that "the usual
three stages" (*G. A. Smith*) are in evidence: "sin in the present, judgment in the immediate future, and the state of
blessedness in the latter days."

The reason we preferred not specifically to mention the
women of Judah in the caption for this section was chiefly
this, that women cannot take a position like this without
its being a position held more or less generally by all people
of the nation. However, "careless" and "complacent" they
were, lolling about at ease and in luxury. Actual concern for
the deeper needs of the nation was farthest from their
thoughts in spite of all warnings that the prophets might

have spoken. "Rise up" conveys the thought: Start up from your luxurious and indolent living. There are times when being merely careless is downright criminal.

Verse 10. The exact source of the trouble that shall come upon Judah is not stated. But certain disastrous consequences will be only too much in evidence. When the news of the disaster strikes the ears of the women they will be seized with a fit of severe trembling. For the present the shocking news only involves that "the vintage will fail and the fruit harvest will not come" — cause sufficient for grave alarm among any people. Cf. also 16:7ff. Both grape-harvest and fruit-harvest will fail. It seems to be intimated that this disaster will come as an accompaniment of war, as it so often was the case.

Verse 11. Again they are commanded to do what they will automatically do when the disaster strikes: "tremble. . . shudder. . . ." That they should again be described by the terms "careless" and "complacent" apparently indicates a most reprehensible measure of carelessness in the face of grave evils that should the rather have induced serious alarm. The rest of the verse bids them go through the acts that were commonly the lot of prisoners of war. The better style and material of garments were not allowed them, but they were to cover their nakedness with coarse sackcloth and be ready to take over the most menial tasks. Captivity was to be their obvious lot.

Verse 12. Apparently all fields that had borne crops were to present such a spectacle of devastation and ruin that a man — and the men are actually addressed at this point by the use of a masculine participle form — might well go through the actions customarily resorted to by persons who are lamenting a grievous disaster, by beating their breasts in despair. Lament over the soil which supplied the physical wants of men but is now covered by thorns and thistles, will be a natural and common thing in that evil day. But the ruin will extend farther. "Houses where gladness prevailed" will, in their ruined state, be further cause for public lament and grief; so, too, the city that could in its better days have been described as "the city of joy." It seems most natural to think here in terms of Jerusalem as the chief and representative city, as is clearly the case in the next verse.

Verse 14. Separate causes for lament, according to this verse, will be certain features of this city that will count as spectacles of grief. The palace, usually the center of business and excitement, will be "forsaken." The noise and bustle, that mark the thriving city, will be "abandoned." Besides Ophel, the southeastern hill of the city and the Watchtower (location unknown) will in what traces of walls still remain standing, be nothing more than "dens forever" (note the relative use of the term "forever" in this context — noted already by *Luther*). Whatever activity there is on these sites will be confined to the presence of animals like "wild asses" and "flocks." The whole picture is one of total desolation for what was once bustling activity. And all this will not come in some very distant future. The prophet is very specific — it will be in "a bit more than a year" (v. 10). All of this is a very pointed threat, enough to startle any complacent citizen, and especially the ones who perhaps more than others helped breed the attitude — the women of Jerusalem.

3. Inaugurated by the Outpouring of God's Spirit (vv. 15-20)

32:15-20 15. until the Spirit is poured upon us from on high,
and the wilderness becomes a fruitful field,
and the fruitful field is reckoned as a forest.
16. Then justice will dwell in the wilderness,
and righteousness will abide in the fruitful field.
17. And the result of righteousness will be peace,
and the fruit of righteousness, quietness and confidence forever.
18. And my people will dwell in peaceful habitations,
and in safe dwellings and in quiet resting places.
19. And there will be hail when the forest comes down,
and the city is laid utterly low.
20. Happy are you who sow beside all waters,
who let the feet of the ox and the ass roam freely!

Verse 15. Somewhat inappropriately this new section begins in the middle of a sentence. That a new turn of the thought is here to be found is obvious. But rather than find fault with the case in hand we might also regard it as a very effective transition. Without changing a letter we might substitute for the "until" the translation "at last" (see *Notes* and so a new turn of thought would have been effectively introduced. In any case we have here one of the rather numerous references to the time when it will please the Lord to make a radical change for the better by giving his Spirit in generous measure. See Isa. 44:3; 54:13; 60:21; Ezek. 36: 26; 39:29; Joel 2:28; Zech. 12:10. Yet it should be noted that in hardly a one of these passages is there a clear statement to the effect that this spirit is a person. The usual connotation of these Old Testament approaches is that God's spirit is the index of divine power. This usage is not yet the New Testament terminology where the Spirit is the Third Person of the Holy Trinity. But this is exactly the point involved: a new influx of divine power will be abundantly bestowed. For the verb "pour out" is intended to convey the idea of generous bestowal. As for the rest of the passage shall we subscribe to the criticism of G. A. *Smith* that vv. 15-20 are "luminous rather than lucid"? We shall have to admit that the last two verses are not too easily interpreted. But otherwise the passage glows with a bright light indicative of the great things to be achieved by the Spirit in the latter days. It may yet be remarked that there is something of a clash between vv. 14 and 15, but that ought rather to be described as a sharp transition from the picture of severe judgment to one of superior blessedness.

The first blessing to be derived from the generous gift of the Spirit will be in the area of the land as such. As groundwork for the life of a people richly gifted with the Spirit there will be a redeemed land, where the "wilderness" the steppe-like area where flocks could find scant pasturage — will be transformed to the level of being "fruitful field," and the fertility and productiveness of the "fruitful field" will be stepped up to the point where it produces prolifically, even as a "forest" might. This is another way of describing a redeemed and reclaimed world of nature.

Verse 16. Now the thought turns to the *people* who inhabit this better land. They shall manifest certain fundamental virtues that mark the people of God as a new and different people. As here used, "righteousness" is basically respect for God's law, whereas "justice" may be defined as "respect for the rights of others" (*Kissane*). These two will be abiding characteristics of the people of that new age (note the use of the two verbs "dwell, abide"). If it is further asserted that these two virtues will dwell in the "wilderness" that is, of course, the open country where shepherds and nomads roam, whereas the "fruitful field" is the habitation of the farmer who cultivates the soil. Somehow in this description the city-dweller is not specifically mentioned. But that omission may be regarded as secondary and unimportant. In other words then all areas of life will share in the blessings of the happy times that are to come.

Verse 17. One thing grows out of the other. The outpouring of the Spirit will have a chain of beneficent results: enhanced fruitfulness (v. 15), the universal prevalence of basically right conduct (v. 16), and now the by-products of righteousness (v. 17). These by-products are "peace . . . quietness and confidence forever." How sweet this promise must have sounded to the ears of those who had known the turmoil and fury of war.

Verse 18. The blessings that center about the homes and dwellings of God's people are now pictured from the point of view that these habitations will be "peaceful," i.e., have all those things that make for complete, entirely satisfactory existence. Besides, homes will be "safe" and "quiet," for the Lord will abundantly bless them who walk consistently in his ways. The whole scene bears the stamp of an idyllic existence, perhaps much like that of our first parents in paradise.

Verse 19. In trying to cope with the difficulties of this verse we may do best if we follow through on certain leads that the book of the prophet has offered in the earlier chapters. So the idea of "the forest coming down," or being hewn down, has clearly appeared in 10:18, 33f. and there clearly was a reference to the overthrow of the Assyrian world-power by the power of the Almighty. So, too, the concept of an unnamed city being "laid utterly low" appeared in 24:10; 25:2f.; and 26:5, and, as we have already shown in each of these cases the reference appeared to be to the capital of the Assyrian empire, Nineveh. When the forest is hewed down and the city is laid low, this drastic overthrow of the insolent world-power will be marked by the fact that "there will be hail." Hail may be most uncomfortable, but usually is not deadly. So the by-products of the overthrow of Assyria will involve some discomforts for the people of God. So, then, before the blessed age of the Spirit comes there will be a measure of affliction troubling them. The age of blessings will not come immediately.

Verse 20. This last verse appears to be the most difficult of all. So many interpretations have been suggested by commentators. All we can do is to suggest a reasonable possibility. It would appear that the land where the people of God dwell is so abundantly watered that practically everywhere where men may be inclined to sow, there will be the prospect of a successful yield of grain. A nation faced with such a prospect is richly blessed and to be called "happy." The last line perhaps signifies that all crops will grow in such profusion (hyperbole!) that both ox and ass need not be carefully watched over to keep them away from where the fields of grain are flourishing. The comparatively light damage that they can do to bumper crops will be too trivial to be concerned about. So these creatures will be allowed to "roam freely" as they may be inclined.

Notes

Verse 1. In vv. 1-5 *Kissane* makes the first four verses conditional ("if" etc.) but apparently nothing in the construction would suggest such an approach.

The *le* before *sarim* may be regarded as exponent of the subject, which is not common but possible and most in keeping with the trend of the thought. *KS* is doubtful; see 271 a-d.

Verse 2. *'Isch* is distributive "each" — cf. *KS* 75.

Verse 3. The verb "be closed" is best thought of as coming from the root *sha'a'*, "to be smeared over."

Verse 5. For *nadhibh* KJV offers the translation "liberal" which however in our day carries entirely unsuited connotation.

Verse 6. The word *nephesh* here carries the rather unusual meaning of "appetite," or "craving."

Verse 7. The verb "plots" (*ya'atz*), being a perfect, is best construed as a gnomic aorist in the sense of "always plots." *KS* 126. The *be* in *bedabber* carries a concessive meaning, *KS* 405 b.

Verse 10. The imperative *chiredhu* ("tremble") is masculine though obviously construed with a feminine subject, according to the general rule: begin masculine if the gender of the subject has not yet been disclosed (*KS* 205 c).

Verse 11. The three imperatives, beginning "strip," etc., are unusual and difficult forms (cf. *GK* 48 i and 110 k).

Verse 12. The masculine plural form of the participle is best allowed to stand as addressing itself to the men of the day, as *Bewer* has well pointed out.

Verse 15. A possibility suggested above is to read the consonants *'dh* with an *o* rather than an *a*, i.e., "at last" for "until." This is feasible though not necessary.

Chapter XXXIII

F. ASSYRIA'S FALL; JERUSALEM'S INVINCIBILITY (Chap. 33)

The titles suggested for this chapter run a wide gamut of possibilities, all the way from "Our God Is a Consuming Fire" (*G. A. Smith*) to "A Prophetic Liturgy" (*Scott*). This difference of approach is largely due to the great variety of thoughts packed away within this chapter. Without evaluating the many possible approaches we shall content ourselves with the fact that an old theme of Isaiah's is again brought to the fore: One mighty foe shall fall; God's people shall endure. Or: "Assyria's Fall; Jerusalem's Invincibility."

What time suggests itself as most likely for the dating of this pronouncement by the prophet? Many are of the opinion that the year is still 701 B.C., as it was in Chap. 32. Only this chapter is a few months later. II Kings 18:14-17 is the passage to compare. One city after the other in Judah had been taken. Hezekiah attempted to put the Assyrians off by the payment of a sizable tribute, straining Judah's financial resources to the uttermost. Apparently the terms proposed had been accepted; the tribute had been paid. Apparently Sennacherib then broke the covenant he had made and demanded Jerusalem's surrender after all. But in between these two events falls our chapter, i.e., between vv. 16 and 17. Nor will it be necessary to concede that some verses like 15 and 16, also 20-24 should be regarded as later additions made perhaps by some disciple of the great prophet. The whole chapter does present a logical and natural progression of thought. Nor are we impressed by the claim that Chaps. 33–35 present a style and content supposedly different from the genuine words of the great prophet. Many points of contact with other valid words of Isaiah will be indicated. Besides, the whole matter of style is one where subjective impressions play too large a role to allow for quick criticism.

So, for example, because navigable streams are mentioned in v. 21 some conclude that the use of such a figure is downright impossible unless the writer had been living in proximity to such streams, that is to say, in Babylonian exile.

We therefore reject the two other approaches as to the dating of the chapter, such as the time of Alexander (*ca.* 300) as being quite without substantial evidence; and the other area of dating, 162 B.C., when Lysias destroyed the temple fortress, or 160, when Alcimus slaughtered many of the Hasidim, violating a covenant made with them (see I Macc. 7:5-20).

It is freely admitted (*Procksch*) that the chapter does present a unit picture, though the figures do change in rapid succession. But again we question the criticism that the eschatological picture cannot match the grandeur of the great apocalypse of Chaps. 24–27. Even if Chap. 33 did not rise to the more sublime heights of the earlier apocalypse, must a writer always move on the same high level? Besides, this impression of the lower level of this chapter is in this case being strongly overstressed.

We will have to concede that some measure of obscurity is met with in the chapter and that "the vague shadows of the eschatological figure" are by their very obscurity perhaps made "more effective." But that concession amounts to no more than admitting that sometimes painters paint in sharp outline and sometimes in outlines that are less sharp.

We must also briefly take note of the fact that a trend has come to the fore which makes of the chapter primarily "a prophetic liturgy," (cf. *Gunkel, ZATW*, 1924, pp. 177-208). This conclusion is based chiefly on the fact that there is a change of person in the chapter; and that sometimes God is addressed, and again he speaks by the word of his prophet. Similar liturgies are said to be found in Micah 7:7-20; Ps. 12; 20; 60; 85. Though it may be granted that some of these passages could be construed as having a liturgical pattern, the mere possibility of some kind of responsiveness does not yet stamp them as actual liturgies. Poetry allows for a large measure of flexibility — apostrophe, injected prayers, imaginary conversations, dramatic appeals, etc., without necessitating a liturgical form. Besides if it be allowed that such a chapter is a liturgy, one has only detected the mold into which the passage has been poured. That observation has but little to do with the appreciation of the passage as such, whose message may be equally effective whether its form is noted or not. Solid proof for the presence of a liturgy in this instance is still wanting.

It may freely be conceded that there are echoes of the Psalms running through parts of the chapter, as in vv. 2, 10, 14ff., 24. Furthermore v. 6 is reminiscent of Prov. 1:1-7.

Attempts to rearrange certain verses, even if done by so sober as writer as *Fischer*, lie in the area of subjective preference. The author in question suggests, toward the end of the chapter, the following sequence: 21, 23a, 22, 23b.

We submit an outline of the chapter.

1. Assurance That Assyria Will Be Overthrown (vv. 1-6)
2. The Pitiful State to Which Israel First Will Be Reduced (vv. 7-9)
3. God's Intervention, Overthrowing Assyria and Sustaining the True Israelites (vv. 10-16)
4. The Crisis in Retrospect (vv. 17-19)
5. The Magnificent Security of God's Holy City in the Future (vv. 20-24)

1. Assurance That Assyria Will Be Overthrown (vv. 1-6)

33:1-6 1. Woe to you, you devastator,
but you yourself have not been devastated;
and to you, you treacherous one,
but men have not dealt treacherously with you.
When you have had your fill of devastating, you will be devastated;
when you have reached the ultimate of treachery, you will be dealt with treacherously.
2. Lord, be gracious unto us; for thee have we waited.
Be their arm [support] every morning,
yea, our salvation in a time of distress.
3. At the noise of the tumult, peoples will flee;
at thy rising up, nations will be scattered.
4. And your booty will be gathered up as locusts plunder,
as grasshoppers scurry, so shall men scurry upon the prey.

5. The Lord is exalted, for he dwells on high;
he will fill Zion with justice and righteousness.
6. And he will be the steadfastness of our times,
a treasure-trove of much salvation, of wisdom and knowledge.
The fear of the Lord is his treasure.

Verse 1. Some adversary is about to be overthrown. We believe that nothing fits the facts in hand better than the thought that this adversary is the Assyrian. We appear to be transported into the midst of the situation described in II Kings 18:14-17. The invasion had begun, Assyrian forces were swarming over the land of Judah. At the walls of Jerusalem they halted. Hezekiah paid the stipulated tribute. The Assyrians withdrew. Then they changed their mind, violating the covenant, or treaty, just made, and again they were before the walls of the Holy City. This first verse may be thought of as thrown into their teeth from the walls of the city by Isaiah himself. He pronounces a Woe on the truce-breakers. They have devastated Judah badly by this time; they have proved themselves exceedingly treacherous. Isaiah charges them on these two counts. He indicates that there is a divine retribution for them that deal cruelly and faithlessly. This retribution takes the same form that the original misdeed took: the devastator will be devastated; the treacherous one will be dealt with by treachery. God will allow both forms of misdeed to go on till the miscreant has had his fill. Then he will intervene with his just punishment. This is not merely a general assumption but a specific prophecy. No one could of himself foresee this outcome, but the enlightened eye of the prophet is given to see it. The verse runs along a line of thought similar to 21:2 and 24:16.

Verse 2. The present emergency is beyond human correction. Therefore it calls for prayer. Leading his people in a prayer calculated to meet this emergency, Isaiah the prophet speaks the next two verses. By the use of the petition "be gracious" the prophet implies that there is no merit on the part of Israel that could make this nation deserving of God's help. But at the same time there must have been a goodly contingent of the people who still had some measure of allegiance to the God of Israel and could truthfully say: "for thee have we waited." So far prophet and people are praying together. Now the prophet turns to intercession: he prays *for* his people in the words: "Be their arm every morning." Such swift breaks in grammatical construction from the use of the first person to the use of the third are far more common in Hebrew speech than with us. The text does not need to be altered to conform to the pattern we might have used ("our arm" *RSV*). "Arm" here quite naturally signifies "support." The plea is that for each day as it comes a fresh measure of God's gracious help is implored. So the Lord himself will be the salvation of his people "in a time of distress."

Verse 3. It is not immediately apparent in this verse what the situation is: What "tumult"? What "noise"? The second half of the verse would indicate that God's intervention is being described: he rises up, and at his taking the matter in hand the nations will be scattered. This suggests that "the noise of the tumult" is the thunderous sound of his voice as he rises up to encounter the enemy (cf. 30:30). Then it is that the peoples flee. This aptly describes the scattering of the Assyrian forces when the angel of the Lord, perhaps through the agency of a swiftly working and deadly plague, smote the camp of the Assyrians. It was as though he had thundered at them. It was as though he had in person risen up to confront them. They fled and were scattered. As to the Lord's rising up, Num. 10:35 may have been in mind.

Verse 4. As far as historical sequence goes, this verse describes the next step that took place in the camp of the Assyrians. As to form, there is again a swift change of person. The prayer is concluded. The prophet now addresses Israel. What they gather is called "your booty." That is to say, the booty that will now fall to your lot after the Lord has so significantly intervened. A vast amount of plunder must have fallen into Israel's hands after the panic and retreat of the Assyrian host. The plunderers are described as falling upon the spoil as locusts, who, when they fall upon vegetation devour it greedily and in haste. The second comparison serves the same purpose. The point of the comparison is the greedy haste in falling upon that which is being gathered up. Note well, as the text describes it, it was a plundering without a preceding engagement on the field of battle.

Verse 5. But the prophet does not remain long on the lower level of thought where the victors fall hungrily upon the plunder. He reassures Israel by interpreting for his people what the entire incident reveals. The Lord God of Israel had by it all achieved new glory and is the more greatly exalted in the grateful appreciation of his saved people. Any true glory that man may ascribe to him he fully merits "for he dwells on high," he is in his very nature already exalted far above what human thinking may ascribe to him. Another aspect of the case is added at this point. Yahweh's exaltation will express itself also in this that, having now saved his people, he will proceed to make of them a people worthy of the name they bear. He will do this in and for the city that the prophet loves so dearly and for which he has such high hopes, Zion. High principles ("justice") and irreproachable conduct ("righteousness") will abound in that city, or, as the prophet puts it, Zion will be filled with these splendid manifestations of their loyalty to the God who so significantly delivered his people.

Verse 6. The prophet goes on in his reassurance of all that has been achieved for Israel. The Lord, whom they had more or less taken for granted and worshiped in routine fashion, will now be for them even the one who alone can give steadfastness to times and nations, he will be "the stability of our times (*KJ*). More than that, his people will prize him so highly that he will be regarded as "a treasure-trove of salvation, of wisdom and knowledge." He will be able endlessly to deliver them and grant them salvation no matter how many times dangers may encompass them. For the difficult situation, where they as people might not know where to turn, he will provide the wisdom needed and the knowledge that passes human insight. In fact, it all will be summed up in this: "The fear of the Lord is his [i.e., Israel's] treasure." This "fear" is the reverence that is always basic for a right attitude toward God. In these words the prophet seems to have the catalog of attributes in mind that he attributed to the Messiah in 11:2. He begins with the first two and hastens on to the last. He would seem to imply that both the Ruler (Messiah) and his people will be marked by the same noble attributes.

2. The Pitiful State to Which Israel First Will Be Reduced (vv. 7-9)

33:7-9 7. Lo, the valiant ones have cried without;
the ambassadors of peace have wept bitterly.
8. The highways lie devastated;
the wayfaring man has disappeared;
covenants have been broken; cities are lightly esteemed;
man counts for nothing.
9. The land mourns, yea, languishes;
Lebanon is ashamed and wilted;
Sharon has become like a wilderness;
Bashan and Carmel shake off their leaves.

Verse 7. On the difficulties involved in the word rendered "valiant ones" see the *Notes*.

A sad state of affairs in the land is being described. From the second half of the verse it may appear that the "valiant ones" and the "ambassadors" are two names for one group. They could have been the men who were detailed to attempt transactions with the Assyrian ambassadors about concluding some kind of agreement. This verse takes us to the moment where the impossibility of achieving some understanding first becomes apparent. Sturdy soldiers, in the anguish of heart, cry out with a loud shriek of pain. Ambassadors are not ashamed to be seen out on the streets shedding bitter tears. They know how desperate Israel's situation is. From this point on the prophet takes us out here and there in the land to give us a vision of the pitiful state of affairs.

Verse 8. Somewhat like Judg. 5:6 there is a situation so desperate that no man ventures to do any traveling. No travellers are to be seen on the highways: "the wayfaring man has disappeared." Covenants on which men were ready to build their hopes have so little value in the eyes of powerful conquerors that they are cheerfully broken. Cities are nothing more than one more obstacle to be cleared out

of the path of the invader. What if there be one more or
less ruined city? And as to human lives, they count for
nothing. Life was cheap in those days when Assyria was out
to make its conquests: "man counts for nothing."

Verse 9. And as for the appearance of the land itself, it all
looks as if, together with the people that inhabited it, it were
steeped in deep mourning and were languishing wherever
you turned. It would seem that the prophet had the ravaged
state of Judah in mind — a most sad spectacle. Three of the
most fruitful areas are mentioned in succession, each being
described as being in a pitiful state instead of in flourishing
abundance: they are "wilted," "like a wilderness," and are
said to "shake off their leaves." A sorry spectacle indeed!

What the prophet thus describes, no doubt, was an actual
sketch of the land as it appeared at this juncture.

3. God's Intervention, Overthrowing Assyria and Sustaining the True Israelites (vv. 10-16)

33:10-16 10. "Now will I arise," says the Lord,
"now will I lift myself up, now will I be exalted.
11. You will be pregnant with chaff, you will bring forth stubble;
your breath is a fire that will consume you.
12. And peoples will be burned to lime,
as thorns cut down will they flare up in the fire."
13. Hear, you who are afar off, what I have done;
and you, who are near, acknowledge my might.
14. The sinners in Zion have begun to be in dread;
trembling has seized the godless.
Who is there among us who can dwell with a devouring fire?
Who is there among us who can dwell with eternal flames?
15. Only he who walks very righteously and speaks very uprightly,
who despises the gain won by usury,
who draws back his hand from taking a bribe,
who stops his ears from listening to plots involving bloodshed,
and shuts his eyes from looking [with pleasure] on evil.
16. He shall dwell on the heights;
his place of refuge shall be the mountain-fastnesses;
his bread shall be given him; his water shall be sure.

Verse 10. Just when things have come to a kind of climax
of distress, the Lord himself will intervene. This is pictured
as though he had been inactive, sitting idly by and watch-

ing the situation build up to a climax. When the time is fully ripe for action, the Almighty arises to his feet, and takes steps demanded by the new emergency, steps that will greatly exalt him in the sight of all men.

Verse 11. He is represented as still speaking and addressing the Assyrians as to the futility of all their bold plans with regard to the kingdom of Judah. Apparently great things for Assyria were in the making, but they shall amount to no more than if a woman were pregnant with so useless a thing as chaff, and then, at the hour of birth, brought forth no more than stubble — what a ridiculous anticlimax! Assyria's breath, or "rage," as the term could also be translated, rages against Judah, will set Assyria herself on fire, producing the very opposite effect of that which was contemplated. Very rarely did a project ever turn out as adversely for the planners as did Sennacherib's plans against Judah. Assyria's overthrow was sheer disaster. We have construed these words as spoken by the Lord himself. Perhaps it would be equally feasible to regard them as spoken by the prophet apostrophizing the enemy. Figures similar to one covering this verse are to be found in 59:4; 26:18; and Ps. 7:14.

Verse 12. This verse concludes the Lord's pronouncement. So great a conflagration, or disaster, will be involved that it may rightly be described as "*peoples* [being] burned to lime." This expression implies a most thorough burning, as appears from Amos 2:1. Or again, this mighty, invading army shall be disposed of as readily as thorns cut off will flare up in a quick, crackling fire and soon burned out.

Verse 13. In anticipation of the fact that the evidence of defeat and overthrow in this case will be so startling and convincing that all must be impressed by it and the news be flashed abroad among all nations of the earth, the Lord summons all, both those afar off as well as those near at hand (Judah) to take note of what he has done and to acknowledge his might. Not merely the striking defeat should be noted, but he as well who brought it about, Yahweh, the God of Israel. Isa. 34:1 speaks in the same vein.

Verse 14. Not only those who are strangers to the Lord should take to heart what he has done, but also those of his own people who have denied him by their sinful ways. They should be moved to repentance at what transpires. They are addressed as "the sinners in Zion," men who have lived *among* the people of God but not *like* them. God's display of his just power and wrath on the enemy should induce them to tremble. In fact, the prophet announces this happy result as actually taking place already: they "have begun to be in dread; trembling has seized the godless." A wholesome reverence and fear has taken hold of them, a result not noted in II Kings 18 and 19, but a valuable supplement to this historical account. In the second half of the verse the feelings that induced this wholesome fear are described. These sinners began to understand, what is so abundantly set forth elsewhere in the Scriptures, that "our God is a consuming fire," or "eternal flames." The questions posed are more than rhetorical questions, for they are answered in some details in vv. 15 and 16.

Verse 15. These verses bear a striking resemblance to the list of godly characteristics that are listed in Ps. 15 and 24:3ff. This does not eliminate them as genuinely written by Isaiah himself, who could have known them for the psalms of David, that they claim to be in their very heading. Here as there, plain, homely virtues are listed as being in evidence in the life of a man who knows what sort of God the Holy One of Israel is. If even the elementary qualities of the second table of the law are not in evidence, let no man presume to come into the holy presence of this God. A very broad area of conduct is indicated by the first two requirements, "to walk very righteously and speak very uprightly." That covers the entire conduct of a man and all that he says; both are offered as presenting a very high level of wholesome conduct that will make it apparent to all observers that such a man's religion is not vain. The remaining sins that are listed as being abhorred have to do with kindly dealings with one's fellow men. For the sins that are shunned are usury, bribery, bloody plots, and secret delight in evil deeds. All such lists of virtues, whether stated negatively or positively, are always to be regarded as a fair sampling to which many more details might be added. Typical areas of godly living are described in brief.

Verse 16. Godly conduct is not without its rewards. Godliness, also in the Old Testament, does not merit salvation. But it does keep a man from doing those things for which divine justice might have to take him to task. It allows the Lord to bestow his blessings upon such a one. A few of such basic blessings are here listed. Such a one will not be driven to the depths of disaster: "he shall dwell on the heights." He will be like the one who has a safe refuge high in the inaccessible mountains, in a fortress well stocked with necessary food and drink, figuratively speaking. Luxuries are not promised, but necessities.

This entire answer that is given in vv. 15 and 16 may indeed be regarded as spoken by the Lord himself, outlining what kind of conduct meets with his good pleasure. Nothing indicates that the priest is the one who gives this answer in a sort of liturgy designed for occasions where men might raise the question. Nor will we regard these last two verses as a bit too pedantic for the great prophet, or as failing to rise to high levels of prophetic thoughts. Such criticisms are too purely subjective in character to be taken seriously.

4. The Crisis in Retrospect (vv. 17-19)

33:17-19 17. The king in his glory shall your eyes behold;
they shall see a broad expanse of land.
18. Your mind will muse on the terror [that was]:
"Where is he that counted? Where is he that weighed the tribute?
Where is he that counted the towers?"
19. The insolent people you will see no more,
the people of obscure speech you cannot understand,
of ridiculous pronunciation you cannot grasp.

We draw attention to the fact that in vv. 17-19 seven accented syllables make up the line.

Verse 17. We are momentarily perplexed by the abrupt introduction of the "king" without any hint as to his identity. The matter is further complicated by the fact that in the original the noun "king" stands without the article — "a king," unless the word in this instance has the status of a proper noun. In that case it could refer to Yahweh himself or to the Messianic King of whom Isaiah has so much to say. They who take special note of the fact that the

words "the king in his glory" belong together, incline mostly
to the opinion that none other than Hezekiah is meant, who,
according to 37:1 at the time of crisis in Judah, did not present a very glorious picture in torn garments and sackcloth.
That shameful humiliation will be at an end. He will again
appear in worthy apparel, manifesting the glory that should
mark the man on Judah's throne. However, comparing v.
22, which is part of the more immediate context, we note
that the prophet unmistakably describes Yahweh himself as
the king of Judah. The point then is that the events that
transpire in the land of promise will be a new revelation of
the Lord's glory that the nation and other nations shall
see clearly revealed. A new sense of the glory of the God
of Israel will be borne in on them. We incline to accept this
interpretation. By so doing, however, we do not exclude
the possibility of Messianic undertones. For the passage does
seem to look forward to the great achievements of the Messianic age. But in granting this possibility we do not yet
accept the interpretation that the "king" himself is the Messiah. But even as the eyes rest with delight on the Lord
the King, so shall the outlook of men not be hampered by
the machinery, tools, and men-of-war cluttering up the
land. The eyes shall range freely in every direction and "see
a broad expanse of land."

Verse 18. Now comes the actual retrospect. Those thrill-
ing and startling days of the Assyrian campaign will come to
mind, after the danger is a thing of the past. The "mind"
(Heb. "heart") will occupy itself with the unique events of
those days, more particularly with the striking personages
that were in the land in those days. There was the man
that counted the items of spoil that had been taken. Then
there was the official who weighed the tribute that was
brought to the victor; money was *weighed* in those days; it
was not coined money made to be conveniently counted.
Then there would be the foreign official who "counted the
towers," perhaps for the purpose of making an assessment as
to how many should be broken down in the process of de-
militarization. All these personages had vanished off the
scene. Besides (v. 19) the "insolent people," i.e., the conquerors were no longer strutting about. The whole army of

the invaders with their speech hard to understand and most strange as to its pronunciation would have left the scene. Though the Assyrian tongue was kindred to the Hebrew Semitic, yet it presented such notable differences that it seemed almost like an utterly foreign speech. This then was the backward look after the enemy had been disposed of.

5. The Magnificent Security of God's Holy City in the Future (vv. 20-24)

33:20-24 20. Look upon Zion, the city of our appointed festivals!
Your eyes will see Jerusalem, a quiet dwelling place, a tent not to be moved.
Never will its stakes be torn up nor its cords be torn.
21. But there in majesty, the Lord will be on our side.
It will be a place of broad rivers and streams,
where no oared galley shall attempt to go,
no gallant ships pass by.
22. For the Lord is our judge, the Lord, our lawgiver,
the Lord our king; he will save us.
23. Now indeed your rigging hangs loose;
it cannot hold the mast firmly in its socket;
the ensign is not spread out.
But the time will come when prey shall be divided in abundance;
even the lame shall seize much prey.
24. And no inhabitant shall say, "I am sick."
The people that dwell therein will be forgiven their iniquity.

Verse 20. The point of view is the same as it was in the preceding section — what will things be like when the invasion is completely beaten back? Attention is fixed on the holy city. In a rather unique reminder it is called "the city of our appointed festivals." The festivals were one of the things that gave this city a fine distinctiveness. If one will regard it after the Lord has disposed of the enemy that threatened it, he will find it to be "a quiet dwelling place," not the place of hectic turmoil that it had been in invasion days. Or to use a figure borrowed from nomadic life, it might be likened to "a tent not to be moved," practically a permanent dwelling. All the troublesome unrest of taking down the tent almost day after day and finding a fresh place to pitch it night after night, all this will be entirely out of the question. Undisturbed peace shall be its attribute, now that it is on the Lord's side.

Verse 21. But even so, it will not be the city that will be its own strength and defense. The Lord who shall dwell within that city will be on their side, the Lord "in majesty." For there is something majestic about the rest of the Lord even as about his works and his acts. Now the prophet lets his thoughts roam into new and different fields. He thinks of the holy city in terms of some of the mighty cities in days of old, like Thebes in Egypt (Nah. 3:8), that lay by the side of mighty streams, which served as their protection. Other Scriptures take the same approach: see Ezek. 47:1-12; Zech. 14:8; Ps. 46:4. For streams of water were a blessing valued much more highly in days of old. Though the prophet knows well that the terrain round about Jerusalem makes mighty rivers an impossibility, yet he lets his fancy play and pictures such broad streams as utterly preventing oared galleys and gallant ships from attempting a naval attack upon the fair city. They will not even "pass by."

Verse 22. Now the thought of the Lord's presence within his city is more fully elaborated. He is there in various capacities. He will be "judge" — one of those charismatic personalities that wrought deliverance in Israel. He is there as a helpful "lawgiver" who helps regulate wholesome life among the people by just laws. He is there as "king," the constant ruler and head of his own. In all these capacities they rightly say: "he will save us." No nation could ever utter such a boast. *Scott* boldly claims that this verse is a "shout" serving as a response in the liturgy, so bolstering his approach that this is a prophetic liturgy. This verse with even greater propriety may be regarded as a calm, sober reflection (note the introductory "for"). Nothing indicative of a liturgical response is to be found in this verse.

Verse 23. Leaving the glorious future for the moment, the prophet dwells on the inglorious present, the spectacle that Judah presented at the time this message was originally spoken. In doing so he again reverts to nautical terminology, only now, the city itself is the big ship. But everything is in a condition of unpreparedness. The city is not ready for a big conflict. Figuratively speaking "the rigging is hanging loose." Though the next clause is difficult, it could mean that the loose rigging is unable to "hold the mast firmly in its socket." How utterly unready for an engagement at sea is the vessel whose mast is not even held firmly in place! Add to that "the ensign is not spread out" as ensigns are wont to be when the battle is about to be undertaken. These observations seem to be injected to recall the fact that if a victory came about it was not due to the superlative preparedness of the city. Everything was unsatisfactory as far as human preparation was concerned. But in spite of all this, strangely "the time will come when prey will be divided in abundance." In the unexpected situation that developed, "prey" played a large part, when the Assyrian camp was suddenly evacuated in a disastrous panic and flight. For the present the prophet cannot be too specific. He himself could not visualize exactly what would happen. He concludes this approach with the added claim that "even the lame shall seize much prey," the lame a type of the physically deficient. Even he shall carry away a rich plunder.

Verse 24. The unique situation of the days when Assyria shall be freely plundered by Israel is still under consideration. Where ordinarily in moments of danger and difficulty men may plead incapacity due to temporary illness and say: "I am sick," no such excuse even will be thought of on the unusual day of Assyria's disastrous flight. All will hasten to spoil, of which there will be so much and it will be so easy to acquire.

But all this might be thought of as moving on a cheap and mercenary level — everybody intent on plunder and nothing else. By concluding the sketch with a trenchant remark as to the deepest values that shall be in the forefront in those days, the prophet proves himself a true prophet, a man of deep theological convictions. This significant statement runs thus: "The people that dwell therein will be forgiven their iniquity." That is what really took place as a result of the intensive activity of the prophet to make spiritual issues uppermost in Israel's experience of that day. This word ranks on a par with the weighty pronouncements of other great men of God; see Ps. 103:3; 32:1; Micah 7:18;

Jer. 31:34. On this point our chapter is a most valuable supplement of Isa. 37 and of II Kings 18, neither of which happen to record this valuable spiritual reaction. Coming last, this statement brings the chapter to an effective conclusion. Having been chastened by the Lord in these trying experiences and having been made aware of the fact that the nation deserved no deliverance from the hand of the Lord, yet they had learned in the day of adversity to implore God's mercy, and the Lord had graciously heard them. The final reaction then very properly could be said to have been a new experience of divine pardon.

Notes

Verse 6. The phrase "of much salvation" is an attempt to catch the unique force of the feminine abstract plural, which really says "salvation." Cf. *KS* 262 e. "Wisdom" is actually in the construct state, apparently to tie it closer together with "knowledge," though an "and" intervenes. See *KS* 337 s and *GK* 130 b.

Verse 7. We have rendered *'ar'alam* as "their valiant ones." The word seems to be built on the *'ari'el* (God's hearth") of 29:1, which, if compared with II Sam. 23:20, leads to the conclusion that the basic term may be a collective "heroes," or "valiant ones." Though the abstract noun thus used would not be possible with us, it still seems to make good sense in Hebrew. The final *m* of the form could be prefixed to the next word making it a *pi'el* participle and the usable translation "Ariel cries out" would result.

Verse 10. "Lift myself up" is actually a *hithpo'el* form. See *GK* 54 c.

Verse 11. "You will bring forth" does not stand in the usual *waw* consecutive construction because synonyms are involved. See *KS* 370 h.

Verse 15. "Very righteously" and "very uprightly" in Hebrew are plural nouns used adverbially to express a high measure of the quality referred to. Cf. also *KS* 330 s.

Verse 18. Because "count the towers" does not in any wise indicate for what purpose they are to be counted, some have conjectured *meghadhim* (treasures) for *mighdalim* (towers).

Verse 20. *Yissa'* is a case of the use of the impersonal verb, usually rendered best in English by a passive (*KS* 324 d).

Verse 24. "Their iniquity" strictly speaking is a kind of accusative of specification ("be forgiven with respect to their iniquity"). Cf. *KS* 336 h.

Chapter XXXIV

G. THE DESTRUCTION OF ALL ENEMIES OF GOD'S PEOPLE (Chap. 34)

Quite obviously Chaps. 34 and 35 belong together. They supplement one another. No writer seems to have stated this more aptly than *Fischer* when he gives them the title, *Endgericht und Endheil* (Final-judgment and Final-salvation). Let it now already be noted that this is a characteristic of Isaiah: he loves to view the final outcome. He does so in Chap. 12, which brings a major portion of the book to a conclusion. He does so again in Chaps. 24–27, with a more extended treatment on both aspects of the case. So then also in Chaps. 34 and 35. He loves to bring things to a conclusion; he loves to sound the note of victory and of salvation completely achieved — always, however, against the dark background of the just judgment on the wicked, who are the enemies of God's people.

In this instance practically the entire first half of the book is brought to a well-rounded conclusion, leaving room for the historical interlude of Chaps. 36–39.

We must deal briefly with the question of date and authorship of these two chapters. *Procksch* very confidently asserts that the two chapters involved are material appended at a much later date than the days of Isaiah, and adds that this is "universally acknowledged" (*allgemein anerkannt*). Even *Fischer* feels compelled to acknowledge that to try to maintain the authorship of these two chapters by Isaiah, unless one also maintains that Chap. 13 and Chap. 40–66 are from Isaiah, is rather difficult.

We believe that we have indicated above, in connection with Chap. 13 that such a view is not so untenable. We have, at the opening of this chapter shown that Chaps. 34–35 are quite in the pattern that Isaiah likes to follow. It is also quite possible that Zeph. 2:13f. and Jer. 50:39, could be regarded as based on 34:11-15, both being, by the way, pre-exilic prophets. The grounds for Isaiah's authorship are as substantial as those which deny this possibility.

We must briefly allude to one criticism. With varying degrees of intensity the accusation is raised against this chapter that it "explodes into flaming hatred" against Edom (*Procksch*). We maintain that such interpretations are carried into the chapter, but cannot be shown actually to reside within the material here set forth.

It might be true, on the other hand that, as the same author claims, this chapter lacks some of the poetic grandeur of conception that marks Chap. 13. But who would demand that all that a poet writes must of necessity always reach the same high level of poetic treatment? Rhetoric was always a secondary matter in the writing of the prophets.

We offer our own outline for the chapter, much like that of many other writers.

1. A World-wide Judgment Predicted (vv. 1-4)
2. A Particular Example of This Judgment — Edom (vv. 5-7)
3. The Total and Permanent Desolation of Edom Predicted (vv. 8-12)
4. The Scene That Its Capital City Will Present in the Future (vv. 13-15)
5. The Inevitability of This Judgment Asserted (vv. 16-17)

It might be in place at this point to get one aspect of a proper approach into the picture, put rather aptly by *Scott*, who claims that this chapter demonstrates how God "deals with the implacable opponents of his righteous purposes." In other words this chapter is not an instance of an extreme nationalism running rampart, or of hatred boiling over and splashing on people odious to Israel. Verse 8, as we shall indicate when we come to it, guards against such unjust interpretation.

1. A World-wide Judgment Predicted (vv. 1-4)

34:1-4 1. Come near to hear, you nations;
and give close attention, you peoples.

Let the world hear and all that fills it,
the earth and all that comes out of it.
2. For the Lord is full of wrath against the nations,
and furious against all their host;
he has put them under the ban of destruction,
he has given them over to slaughter.
3. Those that are slain among them shall be cast out;
as for their carcases — their stench shall rise;
the mountains shall dissolve from their blood.
4. All the host of heaven shall melt away;
and the heavens shall be rolled up like a scroll,
and all their host shall melt away,
as the leaf wilts from off the vine,
like the wilting of the fig tree.

Verse 1. The poet deals in tremendous concepts. What he is about to say involves the "nations" — the Hebrew term refers to those who usually manifest hostility toward God's people — and the "peoples," i.e., the various nationalities. He visualizes them as being within the sound of his voice and summons them, not to witness what is to be done, but to hear an important forecast concerning their future prospects, prospects of doom. The same all-inclusive call appears in 41:1 and 49:1. In Amos 3:9 the nations are invited to see a unique spectacle by way of contrast. But since in the concept of the Hebrew people the whole world — people and fruits of the field and all the earth produces together with the heavenly bodies — is one vast complex of interrelated things that tend to make up one unit-world, the "world and all that fills it" as well as "the earth and all that comes out of it" are also made to hear the same summons to have their future foretold. This is the approach that appears at its best when it is said that the Lord will create "a new heaven and a new earth." The conception that Yahweh is in full control of the whole of creation also shines through 33:13.

Verse 2. What is about to happen is now traced back to the Lord's "wrath" and his fury. Both have grown to huge proportions and can, as it were, no longer be restrained. They are directed against the "nations" — again that note of hostile attitude on their part. But the Lord's decisions are made and are now being revealed. They amount to this:

"he has put them under the ban of destruction," like the wicked Canaanites of old (cf. Lev. 27:28f. and Josh. 6:17, 21), and "has given them over to slaughter." It goes without saying that the causes that stirred the Lord to wrath are right and justifiable, and they do not happen to be mentioned in this connection. Again we point to v. 8 as covering this aspect of the case later.

Verse 3. Now a horrible scene is painted by the prophet. Dead bodies of slain men lie about on every hand with no man left to bury them. It is not necessarily asserted that in a total war every one of the men that make up these nations shall be put to death. One possible aspect of the case is offered for consideration. As the bodies decompose, an awful stench arises (cf. Ezek. 39:11ff.). Then the picture becomes still more gory and gruesome: so much blood has been spilt that the rivers thereof melt away the very mountains of the earth — hyperbole as extreme as the tongue or pen of man can make it.

Verse 4. But things are also represented as taking place on a cosmic scale, as is also the case in 13:10; 24:21-23; 51:6; 65:17; 66:22; and Joel 2:30f. Where "the host of heaven" in 24:21-23 may well refer to superterrestrial beings, here the reference seems to be to the stars themselves, even as in the following line "heavens" would seem to refer to the physical heaven that envelopes this earth. This latter again — in a colorful figure — "shall be rolled up like a scroll" and, no doubt be put away or vanish away (cf. Rev. 6:13; Matt. 24:29 in the very words of Christ himself). As far as the heavenly bodies are concerned, they shall wilt away as "the leaf wilts from off the vine, like the wilting of the fig tree." This whole world-order, which seems so firm and so positively established shall be seen to be quite evanescent before the Lord, the Judge.

2. A Particular Example of This Judgment—Edom (vv. 5-7)

34:5-7 5. When my sword has drunk its fill in the heavens, lo, it will descend on Edom, on the people I have doomed for judgment.

6. The Lord has a sword that will be glutted with blood and
   smeared with fat,
with the blood of lambs and goats,
with the fat of the kidneys of rams.
For the Lord will have a sacrifice in Bozrah
and great slaughter in the land of Edom.
7. And wild oxen will fall down with them,
and young steers and mighty bulls.
Their land will drink its fill of their blood,
and their soil will be drenched with fat.

Verse 5. As already indicated, Edom stands here merely
as a representative nation, the name being almost symbolic. For the unnatural and unrelenting hate that the
world has for the people of God was exemplified by the
nation that was closest of kin to Israel — Edom. Always
and everywhere Edom appears as hostile to Israel and seeking to do her harm. So she deserves special punishment,
but she is still representative of all. Edom will not be the
only nation on whom divine judgment descends. The discourse for a moment in this verse takes a turn to the first
person: God himself is speaking. He describes himself as first
letting his sword make devastating strokes in among the
heavenly bodies until they are fully destroyed. The sword
is poetically said "to drink its fill." Then it descends on
Edom, "the people [says the Lord] I have doomed for judgment." God has been patient. Edom's doom has long been
under advisement. The fact that the Lord has an instrument
of judgment may be doubted by some, but the fact is solemnly asserted — "The Lord has a sword." This sword appears at the moment here described as already having done
a very gory work and so being "glutted with blood and
smeared with fat." When it is asserted that this blood and
fat come from lambs and goats and rams, these being the
creatures that make up the flocks of smaller animals, it would
appear that the Lord's wrath is not directed against harmless
animals as such but against the common run of people in
the land of Edom. Similarly, in the next verse, wild oxen
and young steers and mighty bulls could well represent the
important element in the population of the land. At the
same time the idea of a sacrifice on a grand scale plays into

the picture, a figure to be found also in Zeph. 1:7f.; Jer. 46:10; 50:27. For now it appears that the victims in this sacrifice are the inhabitants of the Edomite city of Bozrah ("the Lord will have a sacrifice in Bozrah."). The identity of this city has not yet been precisely established. It could be the old Petra, it could be the present-day *el-Busere,* which lies some twenty miles to the southeast of the Dead Sea and may have been the capital (cf. Amos. 1:12; Jer. 49: 13, 22; Isa. 63:1). But the picture is concluded in bloodiest terms: the land will drink as much blood as it can possibly absorb and so their soil will have its fill of the fat oozing out from the carcases.

It cannot be justly claimed that the writer revels in the prospect of what shall befall Edom. He is making the point that it will be an awful judgment that awaits these that have so insistently harmed and troubled the people of God and so defied the Lord himself.

There follows another aspect of this judgment.

3. The Total and Permanent Desolation of Edom Predicted (vv. 8-12)

34:8-12 8. For the Lord has a day of vengeance
and a year of requital to avenge the cause of Zion.
9. And its [Edom's] streams shall be turned into pitch
and its soil into brimstone,
and her land shall become burning pitch.
10. Night and day it shall not be quenched;
its smoke shall go up forever.
From generation to generation it shall lie waste;
no one shall pass through it forever and ever.
11. But the jackdaw and the porcupine shall possess it;
the longeared owl and the raven shall dwell in it.
He will stretch over it the line of desolation,
and the plummet of emptiness.
12. As for her nobles — there shall be no kingdom that they can proclaim;
and all her princes shall be nothing.

Verse 8. Though this section of the chapter dwells primarily on the subject that Edom's desolation is to be permanent, it begins with an explanation why the Lord will let so terrible a judgment befall this land. If the event as such is described as "a day of vengeance," this already implies that the vengeance is just, for it comes from the Lord. But then it is more precisely described as being designed as "requital to avenge the cause of Zion." With an unrelenting hatred Edom had gone on year for year, venting its spite on the people of God. Such misdemeanors cannot go on unrequited. God ultimately takes them in hand, and it is pure justice when he does so.

Verses 9, 10. Having inserted this explanation, the prophet proceeds to describe what the land of Edom will be like after God's judgment has descended upon it. It shall present a scene of desolation very much comparable to that which marked the old cities of Sodom and Gomorrah after the Lord had destroyed them. Again some measure of poetic hyperbole characterizes the picture. To state the case graphically, the streams of the land are to be "turned into pitch and its soil into brimstone," both highly combustible, and so when ignited they will keep on burning, the whole territory being like "burning pitch." It is even expressly said (v. 10) that this burning is to go on "night and day," and that it "will not be quenched." In the parallel statement its smoke is pictured as rising "forever." Then as if to indicate that a high measure of hyperbole prevails in the language used, the area is pictured as lying waste "from generation to generation." Apparently the language employed is not to be measured with scientific accuracy, for it cannot burn and lie waste at the same time. So, too, the concluding statement of the verse is not being pressed according to the letter when it is said that "no one shall pass through it forever and ever." For men have passed through this area again and again since those days and still do, though they all confess to its desolateness.

Verse 11. So, too, it would be quite improper now to point back to v. 9, which had filled the picture with perpetual fire, and now claim that here it is asserted that certain forms of animal life will be found there after all. But the verse is to be compared with Isa. 13:19-22, where dismal-looking and dismal-sounding creatures are said to inhabit an area which has been visited by God's judgment. We shall not quarrel over the exact translation of the names of the creatures here enumerated. Among them the "raven" seems to be about the only one on whose description all seem to agree . But by the use of still another figure its total repulsiveness is further described. The "he" in the sentence appears to trace back to the "Lord" as antecedent in v. 8. The "confusion" and the "emptiness" referred to are the famous terms used in Gen. 1:2 to describe the chaotic condition that prevailed before God's guiding hand shaped the materials he had created and made them a well-ordered world. The "stretching of the line" referred to is usually associated with construction efforts. Here it indicates planned and systematic destruction calculated to bring about a condition resembling the chaos that reigned over the newly formed earth.

Verse 12. This verse departs from the physical features of the desolate area and the dismal creatures that inhabit it, and turns for the moment to the consideration of one human element that might be reckoned with — the "nobles" of the land. When it is asserted with regard to them that "there shall be no kingdom that they can proclaim" the reference appears to be to the fact that the rulers of the land did not obtain office by heredity, as was the case in some monarchies. Edom was a people who chose their kings in regular election, and then proclaimed the man chosen to be the king. That process is no longer to continue. There will be no nation and no kings to elect. *R.S.V.* arrives almost at the same result by a very different translation of v. 12a: "They shall name it No Kingdom There." For either translation v. 12b fits equally well: "All her princes shall be nothing." So the land is described after the hand of the Lord had descended in judgment upon it.

The next verse opens a section that takes us into a typical city of the land of Edom, perhaps Bozrah itself. For when "palaces" are mentioned we are no longer out in the open country.

4. The Scene That Its Capital City Will Present in the Future (vv. 13-15)

34:13-15 13. Thorns will spring up in her palaces,
weeds and thistles in her strongholds;

and it will be a haunt for jackals
and an enclosure for ostriches.
14. And the creatures of the desert shall meet with jackals,
and desert-demons shall call to one another.
Yea, there the night-hag [Lilith] will repose,
and find for herself a resting-place.
15. There the arrow-snake will nest and lay her eggs,
and bring forth and hatch her young under her protection.
There also will the vultures gather, each with her mate.

Verse 13. Again we are confronted with the vexing problem of the flora and the fauna of Palestine. The various types of weeds mentioned are variously translated, as are the creatures that are now mentioned as also inhabiting the deserted cities. We shall by-pass the problems involved and follow the more commonly accepted translations. The palaces and strongholds must certainly be in a state of utter ruin if they can be inhabited by the creatures here mentioned, and abound in the weeds which will be found there. Among the beasts mentioned in v. 14 are those which, for want of exact knowledge, merely can be labelled as "creatures of the desert" and "jackals." For some reason not known to us the impression prevailed in days of old that deserted areas were the favorite haunt of demons and all kinds of evil spirits, a thought even voiced by the Savior himself (Matt. 12:43). It could be that since such beings love to destroy and make desolate, they love desolation. Among beings of this sort Lilith is mentioned, a term which some have associated with the root of the word "night," which fact has given rise to the translation "night-hag," which we too have used for want of a better term. In reality, as expressed by most authorities, the term would rather have an Accadian root and should be rendered as some kind of storm-spirit. So everything that makes a place odious and detestable may be said to congregate in this area.

Verse 15. Among these creatures two more types of being are brought into the picture, "the arrow-snake" (a term which also is variously translated) and the "vultures" — birds that feed on dead carcases. Not an attractive thing is to be found in the entire description of the land after it has been visited by divine judgment.

5. The Inevitability of This Judgment Asserted (vv. 16-17)

34:16-17 16. Search and read from the book of the Lord:
not one item shall be missing.
None shall be without her mate;
for the mouth of the Lord has so commanded,
and his Spirit, it has gathered them.
17. He has cast the lot for them,
they shall possess it forever;
from generation to generation they shall dwell in it.

Verse 16. The prophet looks ahead to the time when all this shall actually come to pass. At that time a book will be available known as "the book of the Lord." All that will be found in this book is not said. It may contain many words known to have been written by inspired men of God and even may be thought of as also containing Chaps. 1–33 of Isaiah's book. It is not the book of life, which is referred to elsewhere (cf. Mal. 3:16; Ps. 139:16). To this accessible book men should turn and read and make a comparison. They will find that not one item of what the prophet has enumerated "will be missing." This claim does not merely have in mind the various types of desert creatures which are said to inhabit the land of Edom. It covers the entire sweep of the prophecy. For when the prophet makes assertions like these, "the mouth of the Lord has so commanded, and his Spirit, it has gathered them," it is a good indication of the consciousness of the authority of their message which animated the prophets and also of the fact that God's Spirit watched over the preservation of these words from on high.

Verse 17. Another claim as to the authority of the message delivered follows: God has cast the lot over Edom and his lot involves an inevitable outcome. He has, with care, measured out all these things beforehand, or as here said, "his hand has apportioned it with the line." Seemingly at this point the prophet, with the picture he has just presented still vividly before his minds eye, thinks back upon all that wretched company of detestable creatures that he has enumerated as inhabitants of the desolate land and adds the comment that "they shall possess it forever; from generation to generation they shall dwell in it." As to the general impression that the land makes on men of more recent date, the following quotation from *Delitzsch* may indicate: "The land has never attained to its former level of civilization but swarms with snakes. Only wild crows and eagles and flocks of kattabirds (?) fly about the mountains and the sterile highlands."

Notes

Verse 2. *Procksch* points out that in Isaiah's book the words for "wrath" and "be furious" (*qetseph* and *chemah*) do not happen to appear, and concludes therefore that this verse cannot come from Isaiah. But the single use of a word can never provide such a proof. There are words which a man may use but once in the course of a book. The verb "he has given" appears without being linked to the preceding clause by a connective, a procedure which often is followed when synonymous verbs are used.

Verse 3. For "the slain among them" the Hebrew has "their slain." The pronominal suffix is the equivalent of a partitive genitive (cf. *KS* 37).

Verse 4. The verb *nagollu* would normally in the Niphal use an *a* rather than an *o*. This exception is covered by *GK* 67.

Verse 5. *Kissane* uses a strong argument for reading instead of "Edom" *'adham*, which means "man," or "mankind," and so arrives at the conclusion that this passage does not refer to Edom at all, but speaks in terms of a universal judgment. The reference to Edom in v. 6 is then also branded as an insertion of a later date. He hopes thus to counter the argument that Isaiah could not have written the chapter. But for his treatment of Edom he has no textual grounds or manuscript evidence, and even less cause for his treatment of v. 6.

Verse 6. The form *huddashnah* is a Hothpael (cf. *GK* 54 h).

Verse 8. The word for "requital" (*shillumim*) is an intensive plural and so merely a stronger form. See *KS* 261 e.

Verse 13. Though "thorns" is plural, the verse begins with a singular verb, as is so commonly the case in Hebrew. See *KS* 348 n. The word for "palaces" as to construction is an accusative of specification. *KS* 328 b. As to the word for "enclosure" we much prefer to read *chatser* for *chatsir*, which would mean "grass."

Verse 15. At this point *Procksch* would rearrange the verses with the sequence 15, 17, 16. But after the allusion to the "book" in v. 16, v. 17 may well come as an afterthought.

Chapter XXXV

H. A PROPHECY OF THE FLOURISHING STATE OF GOD'S PEOPLE IN THE FUTURE (Chap. 35)

Chapters 34 and 35 stand in sharp contrast to one another. We, writing in our day, would be inclined to do what *Luther* does in his translation — insert a strong adversative like "but" at the beginning of v. 1. Edom, the symbol of all the enemies of the people of God, faces a grim prospect of desolation; but the land of the people of God, yea, the people themselves have a most hopeful prospect for the future. *Procksch* rather aptly has remarked that the contrast is like "Inferno" v. "Paradiso" — to borrow terms from Dante.

As to poetic pattern, it has been suggested that we have in this chapter two nearly equal halves (vv. 1-6a and 6b-10) each of five double verses with four accented syllables each. Some deviation from the pattern must be allowed for.

For the same reasons that are advanced why Chaps. 40–66 should be attributed to an author other than Isaiah, this chapter is by rather general consent described as dependent on Deutero-Isaiah (cf. 43:16ff.; 48:21; 49:9ff.). We merely remind the reader that it is extremely difficult in any case to determine in which direction the borrowing went. Chapter 35 could have been the original. Even more dubious is the claim that Chaps. 34 and 35 could not have come from the same hand (*Scott*). Why not? Does diversity of material demand diversity of authorship? Can he who wrote one chapter of doom never write a chapter of hope?

The claim that we have here a poem that may be likened to a "choral Symphony" and that this is appropriately reflected by the "melodious language" of the King James Version must be cheerfully accepted. The same claim may be made for *Luther's* translation.

Two more helpful titles may be submitted. *Fischer* uses

as caption "Blessed transformation of Land and People" (*Wandlung zum Heil.*). *Ziegler* goes so far as to use the heading "The Messianic Salvation." We quote this last title because there can be no doubt that the Messianic Age is in the picture. In fact, such glorious sketches of the future always include the Messianic.

We submit the following outline:

1. The Impending Transformation of the Land of Judah (vv. 1-2)
2. The Attitude of Assurance To Be Cultivated (vv. 3-4)
3. Relief from Manifold Physical Disabilities Predicted (vv. 5-7)
4. The Highway for the Safety of God's Pilgrims (vv. 8-10)

1. The Impending Transformation of the Land of Judah (vv. 1-2)

35:1-2 1. But wilderness and dry land shall exult;
the desert shall be jubilant and flourish.
2. Like the crocus it shall blossom abundantly;
yea, it shall be jubilant with joy and singing.
The glory of Lebanon shall be given to it,
the splendor of Carmel and Sharon.
They shall see the glory of the Lord
and the splendor of our God.

Verse 1. Nothing points in the direction that the "wilderness" and "dry land" referred to lie far off. In fact, the offhand way in which they are referred to seems to point to something familiar to all, and therefore is to be sought in the land of Judah itself. An area which was under the blight of God's displeasure will, it is here promised, in the course of time be turned into a veritable paradise. In a vivid personification the area is even represented as giving vent to its joy over its transformation by jubilant shouts and exultant cries. The desert mentioned (the Arabah) is really the deep cleft on the Jordan valley which runs down through the Dead Sea and on to the Gulf of Aqabah, a very barren and inhospitable region. In other words, the transformation will be as striking as can be.

Verse 2. The change involved is further described as being like unto bare land that suddenly becomes covered all over with crocuses (the exact identity of the plant involved is a bit dubious). It could be the anemone. To an extent such a transformation of the landscape does take place when spring comes in Palestine, when the fields are for some weeks covered with a carpet of flowers. Again, in a colorful personification, the land itself is described as being "jubilant with joy and singing." Three comparisons are employed in order to make the scene still more attractive. Three regions famous for fertility and beauty are alluded to: Lebanon, famous for its fragrant cedars; Carmel noted for its mighty oaks; and Sharon, celebrated for its flowers and rich pastureland. In the statement, "They shall see the glory of the Lord," the sentence order in Hebrew puts unusual emphasis on the pronoun "they," that is to say, the people of Judah contrasted with the people of Edom, of whom the preceding chapter made mention. By making these barren areas so abundantly fruitful the Lord shall reveal his own glory and his splendor. New insight into the glory and majesty of God will come to his people as a result of what he does for the land. Note, too, how the prophet identifies himself with those that have this experience. He says this will reveal the splendor of "*our* God." He hopes to share in this experience. As a whole the passage has some analogy with 4:2, 29 and 32:15.

2. The Attitude of Assurance To Be Cultivated (vv. 3-4)

35:3-4   3. Strengthen the weak hands,
                and make firm the tottering knees.
4. Say to those who are panic-stricken: "Be strong, fear not; behold there is your God — with vengeance shall he come; with divine recompense he shall come and shall save you."

Verse 3. Obviously discouraged people are under consideration, not necessarily "exhausted prisoners." Any one who hears the message of the great change of the land that is impending should take this message of hope and assure others by the use of it. There is no need of speculating at

length who is to do the encouraging. "Weak hands" signify lack of courage to go on. It points to men who see no
purpose in living. Even so, "tottering knees" applies to those
who have lost all capability of going forward with assurance. All such are to change their whole outlook on life
and take hold of life and its problems with confidence. On
the basis of what the Lord will do, life should take on fresh
zest.

Verse 4. Men, whom disaster had made "panic-stricken"
or apprehensive of future calamities, are to "be strong and
fear not." All this seems like a kind of prelude to the words
that Jesus used on one occasion to describe his ministry:
"The poor have the gospel preached to them" (Matt. 11:5).
But the essence of the assurance that is to be given all these
dispirited people is not the external changes that will take
place, but the God who stands behind the transformations
that are impending: "Behold your God." It is as though when
he is pointed out to them they see their God in action.
But there will be two distinct aspects to the work he is
about to do. On the one hand, "with vengeance shall he
come." They who have opposed him and fought him off
and have done harm to his people and his kingdom shall
find that vengeance awaits them, just, divine retribution. This
is the judgment-aspect of his work. But the attractive side
of his work is that "with divine recompense he shall come
and save you." His saints will be recompensed for what they
have suffered in his name. A great salvation awaits them,
so great that they ought to march forward with great courage
and high expectations.

3. Relief from Manifold Physical Disabilities Predicted (vv. 5-7)

35:5-7   5. Then shall the eyes of the blind be opened,
and the ears of the deaf shall be unstopped.
6. Then the lame man shall leap like the hart,
and the tongue of the dumb shall sing praises.
For waters shall break forth in the wilderness,
and streams in the desert.
7. And the parched land shall become a pool,

and the thirsty ground, springs of water.
In the haunts of jackals, where they lie, grass will become reeds
and rushes.

From times immemorial a great variety of physical ills has
plagued the children of men. A perfect state of the future
cannot be envisioned without the removal of all such ailments. This text holds in prospect for the children of God
that the outstanding disabilities of this sort will be removed
by God's gracious providence, implying that they shall all
vanish off the scene; implying also that not only they who
are in the land of Judah shall have a share in this deliverance. Or shall we interpret all these physical ills that are
mentioned as being merely symbols of the greater spiritual
disabilities that are going to be vanquished? The best approach seems to be that he who can and will banish the
ills that plague the body will not fail to do as much for
the spiritual being of man. By themselves vv. 5-7 specifically
refer to physical deliverances.

Verse 5. Blindness shall be no more. This note has been
rung before by the prophet (cf. 29:18ff.; 30:20ff.), and is
quoted again by our Savior in Matt. 11:5ff., as proof that
the Messianic Age had come. The removal of deafness is
referred to next.

Verse 6. This recital continues by referring first of all to
the lame man, whose cure is described so drastically by the
assertion that he shall be granted so complete a restoration
that he shall be able to leap like the hart. So, too, the
tongue of the dumb shall not merely be enabled to speak
with some measure of difficulty but shall be able to engage in
the most blessed use of the tongue — singing the praises of
the Lord. From this point on to the end of the next verse,
the emphasis is on the abundance of water, which in Bible
lands was always regarded as a most outstanding blessing,
because there was almost always a dearth of it. The "wilderness" — already referred to in v. 1 — shall, as it were, have
artesian wells spring forth. So also the desert, similarly referred to in the same verse, shall be overrun by streams.
Continuing the description (v. 7), in the parched land there
not only shall be more water but actual pools on every hand,
and the thirsty lands shall see springs of water. If previously

the jackals, creatures that are wont to dwell in desolate spots, could find a bit of grass to make their haunts, vegetation shall become so lush that reeds and rushes shall be found in these and in many other areas. There appears to be a reference here to 34:13, written by the same prophet.

4. The Highway for the Safety of God's Pilgrims (vv. 8-10)

35:8-10 8. And a highway shall be there and a road;
and it shall be called the Holy Way.
and an unclean person shall not pass over it;
but it shall belong to those.
He that passes along this road, though inexperienced, shall not err therein.
9. No lion shall be there,
and no ferocious beast shall come upon it;
they shall not be found there.
But the redeemed shall walk there.
10. And the ransomed of the Lord shall return;
and they shall come to Zion with jubilant songs;
everlasting joy shall be upon their heads.
Joy and gladness shall overtake them,
and sorrow and sighing shall flee away.

Verse 8. Roads in the Holy Land in days of old were mere trails. Here an added feature is to be found in the landscape — a highway, a concept with which the book of Isaiah loves to operate (see 40:1ff.; 41:17ff.; 43:14f.; 48:21f.). This "highway" shall both ease the way over ravines and difficult places but shall also serve perfectly as a "road," leading them that use it directly to their destination. But it will be different from all other roads in that it shall bear the name "the Holy Way." It will be reserved for holy uses, as shall presently be defined more closely. In some way, not further described, "an unclean person" shall be barred from using it. This obviously includes the Gentiles, but perhaps also the unredeemed among the children of Israel. "It shall belong to those," i.e., to the ones who are about to be referred to in this context as standing in a special relation to the Lord. But it will be a road so clearly built that no one using it will ever "err therein." A man cannot lose the way on this highway, as one so readily could on the trails of old,

especially if they led through desert places. The persons just
referred to as using the road but not getting lost should
not be described by the translation "fools" (*K.J.* and *R.S.V.*).
For though this is the more common meaning of the Hebrew
word used, in this context it refers to the "inexperienced,"
i.e., to people who have not used the road before.

Verse 9. To the perfect nature of this highway also belongs the fact that all dangers involved in travel will be
eliminated. As an example, the presence of wild beasts rang-
ing on this road shall be done away with. "No lion shall
be there; and no ferocious beast shall come up on it." The
means that shall be used to bar these creatures from access
to the road we are not told. Poetry does not require precise
specifications before it makes its point. Enough to say:
"they shall not be found there."

But the ones for whom the highway is reserved are first of
all "the redeemed." The emphasis carried by the root involved in this word is on the fact that he who redeems the
persons involved is under some obligation to do this favor for
them. Here we might well think of the covenant obligation
under which the Lord put himself by making Israel his covenant people.

Verse 10. But the second descriptive term used for these
is "the ransomed of the Lord." This describes them as delivered by an act of free choice. But both terms taken together convey the thought of a thorough-going redemption.
Both these classes shall "walk there" and "return," and "shall
come to Zion with jubilant songs." Where they come from is
not said. Since the previous chapters repeatedly referred to
deportations of the disobedient, return from captivity would
seem to be involved here. We might even venture to suggest that return from any estrangement might well be
thought of. But Zion is their goal, and Zion represents the
embodiment of all the blessings that God has prepared for
his people. Since they who are coming are aware of this,
"jubilant songs" are upon their lips. The final phase of God's
redemptive work for his people seems to be involved here, or
at least included. For this reason, the redeemed are further
pictured as having "everlasting joy upon their heads." Joy
shall be their crown of glory, or, if you will, the halo that

crowns their head. They no longer will be like those who have not yet arrived at this holy city, figuratively speaking. They need not pursue joy; "joy and gladness shall overtake *them*." The negative side of the experience will be that "sorrow and sighing shall flee away." No note of disharmony shall mar their lives from this point on. Cf. the same word 51:11.

So the prophet has again brought a major section to a close with a triumphant hymn, as he had done in Chap. 12.

Notes

Verse 1. Some would insist that the verbs used here are to be taken in the optative sense (as the imperfect well may be), following the example of the *Septuagint*. However we prefer the future which appears to be more positive, as is the tone of the entire chapter. The very first verb appears to be carrying a superfluous *m*, by dittography from the following word *midbar*.

Verse 2. Following the *Kittel* text, we have taken "like the anemone" as the beginning of the verse. But we prefer the translation "like the crocus." Biblical botany is still shrouded in some difficulty. The expression "jubilant with joy and singing" is made up in the Hebrew of two absolute infinitives, perhaps chiefly for variety. *Gilath* carries an old feminine ending (cf. *KS* 337 s).

Verse 4. The very last word, the verb *yosha'akhem* is to be emended to read *yoshi'akhem* (*GK* 65 f.).

Verse 7. The word *ribhtsah*, "her lair," which we have translated, "where they lie" because of the feminine singular suffix, which often represents the collective idea (*KS* 348 g), stands in apposition to the noun "haunts."

Verse 8. Following the example of the *Septuagint*, many are inclined to insert the adjective "clean" before "highway." This indeed would be in the spirit of the context, but may also be regarded as an instance of the freer use of the text by the Greek translators. Again the words "and a road" could be an instance of dittography. But it still makes good sense, for it indicates that the highway definitely leads to a goal. *Ges. Buhl* suggests *'ewilim*: *ratlos*, *hilflos* (perplexed, helpless).

Verse 9. For "ferocious beast" the Hebrew has "ferociousness of beasts," the abstract rather than the concrete.

Verse 10. Because this verse appears again in 51:11 does not yet warrant the quick conclusion that since Chap. 51 is exilic, or post-exilic, Chap. 35 must be of the same late date. The argument may with equal propriety be reversed: both may be from Isaiah.

HISTORICAL INTERLUDE

Chapter XXXVI

IV. HISTORICAL INTERLUDE (Chaps. 36-39)

Various titles are given to these four chapters. *Koenig* captions them: "Historical Background for Isa. 29, 30, 31." *Scott* uses the heading "Isaiah and Hezekiah — a Narrative." *Procksch* titles Chap. 36, "Sennacherib before Jerusalmen."

The date of the event recorded is almost without question the year 701 B.C., which 36:1 designates as the fourteenth year of Hezekiah. For many now agree that Hezekiah's reign ran from about 715-687. This would agree with the date of this campaign as 701 and with the fifteen years added to his life, according to 38:5, assuming, of course, that Hezekiah's sickness and the events of Chap. 36 fall in about the same year, as Isa. 38:1 seems to indicate. This campaign of Sennacherib began in 703, when he proceeded against, and subdued, Merodach Baladan of Chaldea. It continued into 702, when Sennacherib subdued Armenia, and came to a conclusion in 701 in the event here narrated. See Pritchard, *Ancient Near Eastern Texts*, p. 287f. For further facts on the problem of chronology see the *Notes* at the end of this chapter.

A. The Assyrian Invasion and Delegation Sent to Jerusalem (Chap. 36)

An interesting chapter brilliantly written! There is a parallel chapter to be found in II Kings 18, in fact, II Kings 18-20 runs parallel with Isa. 36-39, with a few significant additions in either case. Isaiah has as additional material the passage 18:9-20, Hezekiah's psalm after his recovery; whereas II Kings 18:14-16 is missing in Isaiah. In addition there are certain minor textual differences as to phrases and expressions used, which show that some revision of the original was undertaken.

This raises the question, Which of the two accounts is the original? The preponderance of opinion in this case seems to be correct; namely, the account in II Kings is the original. The chief argument in support of this contention is the fact that certain expressions distinctive of II Kings appear in the account. Therefore it appears most likely, since II Kings was not completed until at least the thirty-seventh year of the exile of Jehoiachin (II Kings 25:37) which is about 560 B.C., that some later editor will have added these chapters (36–39) to the previous part written by Isaiah. There is, of course, always the possibility that both books (II Kings and Isaiah) may have used a third source. Another difficulty involved in the supposition that Isaiah wrote these chapters lies in this, that the death of Sennacherib is reported in Isa. 37:38, which occurred in 681, at which time it is hardly likely that Isaiah would still have been alive.

The chapter may be outlined as follow:

1. The Commander-in-chief's Meeting with a Committee of Hezekiah's Officials (vv. 1-3)
2. The Assyrians' Demand That Jerusalem Capitulate (vv. 4-10)
3. The Request of the Jewish Officials That the Transactions Be Conducted in Aramaic (vv. 11-12)
4. The Assyrians' Insolent Refusal Coupled with the Request of Immediate Surrender (vv. 13-21)
5. The Report of the Royal Commissioners Presented to Hezekiah (v. 22)

1. The Commander-in-chief's Meeting with a Committee of Hezekiah's Officials (vv. 1-3)

36:1-3 1. Now it came to pass in the fourteenth year of King Hezekiah, that Sennacherib, king of Assyria, came up against all the fortified cities of Judah and took them. 2. And the king of Assyria sent the commander-in-chief from Lachish to Jerusalem to King Hezekiah with a great army and he took his stand by the conduit of the upper pool on the highway to the Washerman's Field. 3. And there came forth to him Eliakim, the son of Hilkiah, the steward of the palace, and Shebna, the secretary, and Joah, the son of Asaph, the chancellor.

Verse 1. This account is to be supplemented by that which II Kings 18:14-16 reports, which apparently was a part of the same campaign. For there it is stated that Sennacherib required of Hezekiah a very sizable tribute, which Hezekiah gathered and submitted, even stripping the gold from the doors of the temple. Without a doubt the understanding was that upon payment of this tribute, Hezekiah would have secured immunity for Jerusalem. But somehow Sennacherib changed his mind, repudiated the agreement, and proceeded a second time against Jerusalem and demanded the surrender of the city, as our passage in question tells. Isaiah 33:7f. may be a reference to the disappointment caused by the breaking of the covenant by the Assyrian monarch. Why Isaiah does not report the first transaction and the payment of the tribute we can only guess. It even might have been that he did not care to report an event which seemed to reflect unfavorably upon Hezekiah. In any case, the report of II Kings and that of the book of Isaiah do not stand in conflict with one another.

What our account reports is that Sennacherib was completely successful in his Judean campaign: he took "all the fortified cities of Judah" — except, of course, Jerusalem, as the account indicates. All this agrees with the inscription of the Annals of Sennacherib (Pritchard, *op. cit.*, p. 287f.,) which contains the famous statement how he made Hezekiah a prisoner in Jerusalem "like a bird in a cage." It may be that the event recorded in Isa. 37:9 was already in the making, and that the advance of Tirhakah, king of Ethiopia, induced Sennacherib to send his commander on this occasion to try to intimidate Hezekiah, so that the Assyrians might not come into a position which would have compelled them to fight on two fronts simultaneously.

Verse 2. The emissary sent by the Assyrian king is called Rabshakeh in most translations. This is, however, as is commonly conceded, not a proper name but a title, which might correspond to our "commander-in-chief." He brought a "great army" along to impel Hezekiah not to dare to refuse too readily. Headquarters for the Assyrians at the time were at Lachish, some twenty-five miles southwest of Jerusalem.

This commander then took his stand, perhaps somewhat pompously, "by the conduit of the upper pool on the highway to the Washerman's Field." This conduit is supposed to have been somewhere along the north wall of the city. It should be added that the group representing the Assyrian king included "the Tartan and the Rabsaris" (II Kings 18:17). The location involved is the same one that is mentioned in Isa. 7:3 as the spot where Isaiah encountered King Ahaz of Judah as the king was making preparations for the impending attack by the combined forces of Syria and Ephraim *ca.* 734 B.C.

Verse 3. The representatives of King Hezekiah were also three in number, Eliakim, Shebna and Joah. It may have been thought to be poor policy for kings in person to engage in diplomatic transactions of the kind here involved. Still, the three Hebrew representatives were men of high rank and station. Apparently Shebna was already demoted at this time, as Isaiah had predicted in 22:15ff., possibly not yet demoted to the extent that seemed to be held in prospect in Isaiah's prediction. For each of the descriptive titles given these three officials we do not seem to know the exact equivalent. "Steward of the palace" — a kind of major domo — was no trivial post. "Secretary," or scribe, would seem to imply that the official keeping of minutes of transactions was a part of his responsibility. The term "chancellor" coming from a root that signifies "remembrancer" might seem to indicate that some duties involved in protocol fell to his lot. In any case, the men involved were worthy dignitaries of the realm.

Now follows the speech of the commander-in-chief. We need not assume that we have here a word for word record of what was said. Apparently a competent historian summed up and arranged the words spoken, in an effective and able way, even as it is known to be the case that Greek historians rather freely reported outstanding speeches made on special occasions. That which almost immediately impresses the reader is the fact that the speech was put very effectively. You might, from one point of view regard the arguments advanced as irrefutable. His points, one after the other, are telling and effective.

2. The Assyrians' Demand That Jerusalem Capitulate (vv. 4-10)

36:4-10 4. And the commander-in-chief said to them: "Say now to Hezekiah, 'Thus says the great king the king of Assyria: On what do you base this confidence that you have manifested?'" 5. I have said: "The strategy and might for war [against me] amount to mere words. Now tell me on whom have you put your confidence, that you have rebelled against me? 6. Behold, you have put your confidence in this crushed reedcane, in Egypt, which, if a man lean on it, will run into his hand and pierce it. So is Pharaoh, king of Egypt, to all who put their confidence in him. 7. But if you say to me, 'We have put our confidence in Yahweh, our God,' is not he the one whose highplaces and whose altars Hezekiah removed and said to Judah and to Jerusalem: "Before this one altar you must worship?" 8. Come now, make a wager with my lord, the king of Assyria; let me furnish you with two thousand horses, and see if you on your part are able to furnish enough riders for them. 9. How then can you hope to repulse one of the least of the captains who serve my lord? Also you have put your confidence in Egypt for chariots and horsemen. 10. Furthermore, do you imagine that without Yahweh I have come up against this land to destroy it? Yahweh said to me, 'Go up against this land and destroy it.'"

As to form we have here a *Botenspruch*, a messenger's pronouncement.

Verse 4. A scornful and disdainful attitude marks the utterances of the Rabshakeh. For his own king he always uses the proper title; in reference to Hezekiah, he consistently omits it. He speaks, however as an intermediary, not as a plenipotentiary, and recognizes those whom he addresses as being of the same rank and station. So what he says is to be relayed to Hezekiah. It should also be noted that the key-word of his speech is the expression "base your confidence." Some measure of confidence must have been displayed by the Jews. The Rabshakeh is attempting to demonstrate that this confidence of theirs is based on sand, for he keeps playing on this one idea, using the verb at least six times.

Verse 5. The word for "I have said" comes from the mouth of the great king, as the end of the verse indicates. The ambassador is so completely identifying himself with his master's thinking that he speaks in his name, and in his person. The statement in which the king quotes himself is difficult. By inserting the words "against me" we feel we have clarified the statement, following *Koenig*. The people of Judah do have some "strategy" that they purpose to follow and they have gathered some "might" for war against the Assyrians, but it seems that the Rabshakeh has some secret information that much of this preparation has not yet passed beyond the stage of "mere words" as to what they hope to achieve. Their intentions, in other words, are bold and brave. Their resources are quite limited. No doubt the Jews knew this only too well, and so the first argument of the envoy was a telling one.

Verse 6. Next comes the issue of allies: with whom is Judah affiliated? Answer: with Egypt, a name once famous for military power and achievement. Judah leans heavily on Egypt. Everyone knows that to be the case. But quite sarcastically the envoy likens Egypt to a "crushed reed-cane" (*Gray*), perhaps a papyrus reed. Skilfully this figure is built up into another colorful argument. For what is most likely to happen is, that if one leans strongly on this already crushed reed, it breaks completely and runs into a man's hand, not helping him but wounding him. Perhaps Assyria by this time already had clashed with Egypt in the battle of Eltekeh, not far from Lachish, in which battle Egypt had been worsted. Therefore the commander-in-chief sums up his argument: "So is Pharaoh, King of Egypt, to all who put their confidence in him." Incidentally in the second half of v. 5 the Rabshakeh had made a strong point from the fact that the misplaced confidence of the Jews in Egypt had led them to make the grievous mistake of "rebelling" against the Pharaoh. For from his point of view the only reasonable attitude for a little state like Judah to take was to submit and pay tribute to so renowned an empire like the Assyrian. The Egyptian Pharaoh on the throne at that time was Shabaka, under whom it is commonly assumed Tirhakah (Isa. 37:9) was fighting. At this point the words of the king which were being quoted come to an end.

Verse 7. Since the Rabshakeh is pulling the ground out from under the feet of the Jews, he now moves on to show that their religious confidence that they have, cannot be of any benefit to them. He well knows that they were ready to take the attitude that they would put all their confidence in Yahweh, their God. But this attitude had its severe defects. Had not Hezekiah recently, in the course of his reforms (II Kings 18:4), removed all the high places, where Judah had been wont to worship Yahweh? With the strong adherence which the common people had for these traditional places of worship they might have thought Hezekiah's reforms a precarious thing, in spite of the fact that Deuteronomy (12:26) demanded that in due course of time high places be abandoned and one central sanctuary be allowed and only one. So the rank and file of the people might have been impressed by the arguments the Rabshakeh advanced. We inserted the word "one" in the king's order, to make the issue involved stand out the more clearly.

Verses 8, 9. Another point: half sarcastically the envoy addresses a challenge to the committee of the Jews: he is ready to make a bet, or "wager," with them. We are not quite sure how he means the words, "let me furnish you." Perhaps this is only a hypothetical statement, meaning: If I were to furnish you. . . . It can hardly be regarded as a promise that he will furnish the horses if they can furnish the riders. The Rabshakeh is making the Jews aware of their limited resources. They do not even have enough cavalrymen to ride on two thousand horses. And from this he draws his conclusion (v. 9): You are virtually unable to offer reasonable opposition to "one of the least of the captains who serves my lord." The case of the Jews was really desperate. Here he adds as a kind of afterthought, the argument that for resources in this department of warfare, they are again relying on Egypt to furnish whatever "chariots and horsemen" they may need. He pursues this argument no further because he had just demonstrated how ineffective Egypt actually is.

Verse 10. Now comes the argument that caps the climax, the religious argument. It is surprising how well informed the commander-in-chief is in regard to the religious state of affairs in the land. He knows who the God of the Jews is; he knows what his attitude is toward his faithless people. But we confess to being somewhat puzzled as to how he

means the authorization that he has for coming against the
people of Israel when he claims that he is not coming without a mandate from Yahweh, in fact, even claims to have
this mandate directly from Yahweh. It may well have startled the people to hear this envoy say words that agreed
with those their own prophet Isaiah had been trying to tell
them. Is it possible that words spoken by Isaiah in reference
to the historical aspect of this Assyrian crisis had actually
somehow penetrated through to Sennacherib and his
envoy, words like 5:26ff.; 7:18ff.; 10:5ff.; 28:11ff., 17b.? This
does not seem too likely. It may be a better approach
to say that all this man was claiming was that indirectly,
through the course of events, he could regard himself as
doing what he is doing with divine sanction, because the
Jews had been far from faithful to the Lord their God.
But to Hezekiah's ambassadors and to the people on the wall
this must have been a startling claim that Yahweh had incited him to take this course and make this attack. We can
almost see them writhe under the impact of it.

3. The Request of the Jewish Officials That the Transactions Be Conducted in Aramaic (vv. 11-12)

36:11-12 11. Then Eliakim and Shebna and Joah said to the
commander-in-chief: "Please speak to your servants
in Aramaic, for we understand it; and do not speak Jewish to us
in the hearing of the people who are on the wall." 12. But the
commander-in-chief said: "Has my master sent me to speak
these words to your master and to you, and not rather to the
men who are sitting on the wall, that they together with you
may eat their own dung and drink their own urine?"

Verse 11. It is known that by this time Aramaic had become the language of diplomacy throughout the Near East.
On the other hand, the language of the Hebrew people
here appears under the designation of "Jewish" because after the fall of Samaria (722-721 B.C.) the ones that were
left in the land were practically only from Judah, from which
the name "Jewish" is derived. The common people, that is
those who held no government post, were acquainted only
with their own Jewish language. The Jewish ambassadors

felt that some unwholesome propaganda was falling upon the ears of these folk and so they besought the envoy to refrain from speaking in Jewish. Quite likely this demand was made in a subdued voice so that the people sitting on the wall might not catch the direct cause for the embarrassment of their own ambassadors.

Verse 12. The Rabshakeh's reply is intentionally coarse and undiplomatic. He takes the position that he is, of course, trying to influence the thinking of the common people by what he is saying. He says in effect: I am using propaganda pressure on these men intentionally and my king instructed me to do this. I want them to hear my words. Then he concludes as crudely as ever a diplomat could have, trying no doubt to humiliate King Hezekiah's men and to embarrass them. The margin of the Hebrew Bible suggests somewhat more refined expressions that may be substituted for these unmentionable things in the public reading of the Scriptures. So, for example, they suggest the expression "water of the feet" for "urine."

4. The Assyrians' Insolent Refusal Coupled with the Request of Immediate Surrender (vv. 13-21)

36:13-21 13. Then the commander-in-chief stepped forth and called out in a loud voice in Jewish and said: "Hear the words of the great king, the king of Assyria: 14. thus says the king: 'Do not let Hezekiah deceive you; for he cannot deliver you. 15. Do not let Hezekiah make you put your confidence in Yahweh, saying: "Surely, Yahweh will deliver us; this city will not be given into the hand of the king of Assyria." 16. Do not listen to Hezekiah, for thus says the king of Assyria: Make a peaceful settlement with me and come out to me; and eat each one of you of your own vine and fig-tree, and drink each one of you water from your own cistern; 17. until I come and conduct you to a land like your own land, a land of grain and wine, a land of bread and vineyards. 18. Beware, lest Hezekiah mislead you, saying: "Yahweh will deliver us." Has any of the gods of the nations delivered his land from the hand of the king of Assyria? 19. Where are the gods of Hamath and Arpad? Where are the gods of Sepharvaim? 20. Did they deliver Samaria from my hand?'" 21. And they kept silence and never answered him a word, for the king's orders were: "Do not answer him."

Verse 13. To make his words more effective by being bold, if not brazen, the Rabshakeh "stepped forth," and, instead of lowering his voice or speaking in Aramaic "called out in a loud voice." When he begins by drawing attention to the fact that he has words from "the great king, the king of Assyria," apparently he is attempting to make the Hebrews feel that their own king is of an inferior order and not to be classed as on the level with the monarch of such an empire as Assyria.

Verse 14. His very first word works in the same direction: it is an attempt to belittle King Hezekiah; he is the one who is obviously deceiving his people when he tried to induce them to resist the Assyrian monarch. Insultingly, this envoy claims: "He cannot deliver you."

Verse 15. Again that key-word of the Rabshakeh's first speech comes to forefront, viz., "put your confidence" in Yahweh. On the face of it, it would appear that what the commander-in-chief quotes Hezekiah as saying is a very good and pious sentiment: "Surely Yahweh will deliver this city." But the Rabshakeh hardly meant it that way, nor did Hezekiah originally. There is something just a little too glib about the statement. *Procksch* caught the actual force of the claim rather well when he translated it: *Yahweh wird uns schon helfen,* that is to say: Don't worry; everything will come out all right. Micah 3:11 may well be thought of as a good parallel. The statement reflects not so much faith but unwarranted confidence. The covenant-position of Israel was being exploited by an attitude of confidence that presupposed that all was well between God and his people: they had given no cause for offense. Yet the very opposite was true. When the king now says: "This city will not be given into the hands of the king of Assyria," he has not yet humbled himself in the sight of the holy God. Later on when a different attitude was displayed by king and people, then Isaiah could make claims like this one of Hezekiah with true propriety and in a wholesome way.

Verse 16. The Assyrian envoy goes on to quote from his majesty, the great king of Assyria. The words presented sound like a gracious invitation, but the hard fist under the soft kid-glove appears very shortly. This "peaceful settlement" referred to is nothing other than the demand for complete and unconditional surrender. With every evidence of clever propaganda, this envoy practically represents the state into which they will pass if they but surrender on the spot, lay down their arms and come out to the Assyrians, as being an ideal state of affairs. They can go right on enjoying the fine privilege of "eating from their own vine and fig tree" — a situation which is repeatedly referred to in the Scriptures as the epitome of an ideal state (cf. I Kings 4:25; Micah 4:4; Zech. 3:10). Another colorful item indicative of peace and contentment would be that each one will drink the water from his own cistern.

Verses 17, 18a. Now comes the brutal truth: they will face deportation. When the Assyrians will have disposed of other issues connected with the present campaign and are ready to go back to their own land they will take the people of Judah along as deportees. But that experience, again in terms of clever propaganda, is represented as though it were an experience to be coveted by any normal man. The Jews will be taken from their own fine land to a land just as fine, "a land of grain and wine, a land of bread and vineyards." In other words: Don't dread deportation; it's a happy experience. The contrast with the next verse shows the extent to which clever distortion works in propaganda. For what follows says in effect: Deportation is not the grave danger you face, but being misled by your king to believe that "Yahweh will deliver you."

Verse 18b. Now the religious issue is explored somewhat more fully. First a general statement is made: "Has any of the gods of the nations delivered his land from the hand of the king of Assyria?" As far as the historical evidence is concerned this claim was practically true. No land had been able successfully to withstand Assyria; ergo: the gods of all these nations had been weaker than the gods of Assyria. Though, to tell the truth, not the power of the Assyrian gods but that of the king of Assyria is praised, after the pattern of world-conquerors of all times. But it should be noted that at this point a historical inaccuracy creeps into the picture: the achievements listed are made to sound as though it was

Sennacherib who conquered the areas mentioned, where in reality these were the conquests of his predecessors.

Verse 19. For Hamath was conquered in 720 B.C. and Arpad in 740, whereas Sennacherib first came to the throne in 705. But smooth propaganda glosses over matters of this sort. Hamath lies north of Jerusalem about 250 miles, on the Orontes River and Arpad about 100 miles still farther north. The location of Sepharvaim has been thought of as lying between the two, and may be identical with the Sibraim mentioned in Ezek. 47:16.

Verse 20. Now the Rabshakeh comes nearer home when he refers to Samaria, which fell 722-721. The statement is somewhat condensed. It does not spell out the obvious that Samaria was the capital of the sister kingdom to the north, and also somewhat vaguely, lets the "they" refer to the Samaritan gods. On this note the second section of a clever address ends.

Verse 21. It is difficult to determine at this point whether the silence referred to in this verse is that of the king's ambassadors from Judah, or the people. II Kings 18:36 specifically says it was the people. This passage in Isaiah may intend to say that both parties kept silence. In any case, the king's orders, apparently to ambassadors and people were: "Do not answer him." We incline to the opinion that in spite of the silence of all after the speech was finished, the Rabshakeh felt some satisfaction that he had made quite an impression on his audience, as no doubt he had.

5. The Report of the Royal Commissioners Presented to Hezekiah (v. 22)

36:22 22. And Eliakim, the son of Hilkiah, the steward of the palace, and Shebna, the secretary, and Joah, the son of Asaph, the chancellor, came to Hezekiah with torn garments, and told him the words of the commander-in-chief.

Verse 22. With a certain measure of circumstantiality the complete names and title of the three representatives of Hezekiah are here mentioned, after the pattern of other literatures, like the Greek in the case of Homer, as having come to their king, Hezekiah, to report what happened in the conference with the Assyrian deputies. Significant is the fact that they came with "torn garments," which was a way of giving visible expression to deep emotion particularly of a painful sort. The elements of truth in the Rabshakeh's speech, as well as the fact that they had accomplished nothing in the interview, had disturbed them deeply. All this sets the scene for the next chapter.

Notes

Verse 2. Lachish is the modern Tell ad-Duweir.

Verse 5. As the Hebrew text now stands the first word of the verse is "I have said" — *'amarti*. This does not fit into the text, in the opinion of some as another reading offered by some twenty manuscripts, *'amarta* — "you have said." The fact that a textual form reads more smoothly does not necessarily stamp it as the more acceptable form. In this case the difference is slight. Besides, in this case the customary meaning "say" perhaps should yield to the other feasible meaning of "think."

Verse 8. In the expression "the king of Assyria" the word "king" already in the genetive here by way of exception carries the article. For further treatment of the subject see *KS* 303 d and *GK* 127 f.

Verse 11. Some would like to delete the words "Shebna and Joah," on the assumption that only one of the ambassadors will have done the speaking. However, it is readily imaginable that each in his own words helped to present this plea to the Rabshakeh.

Verse 16. The word that we have rendered "peaceful settlement" is *berekha*, usually signifying "blessing." Here it may mean the way of arriving at a blessing. So we have translated it as we did. *RSV* simply renders it "peace."

Chapter XXXVII

B. FURTHER TRANSACTIONS AND THE DISASTROUS OVERTHROW OF THE ASSYRIANS (Chap. 37)

The contrast in thought between this chapter and the preceding is well caught by G. A. *Smith*, who says: "We pass from Rabshakeh, posing outside the walls of Zion, to Hezekiah prostrate within them." Aside from this, the chronological sequence from Chap. 36 goes on uninterrupted into Chap. 37. So *Delitzsch* says quite aptly that this chapter deals with the "Second Assyrian Attempt to Force the Surrender of Jerusalem."

Here might be the place to indicate how much this chapter is in keeping with the note so frequently sounded by the prophet that a very serious clash with Assyria will be faced shortly by the people of God. A mere listing of the number of instances where the subject has been treated thus far will serve our purpose. Cf. 6:11-13 (a typical instance where the Assyrian is not mentioned by name); 5:26; 7:18; 8:8; 10:28; 30:29-33; 29:1-8; 30:19-26; 32:14. All these passages are more or less veiled and unclear. They almost demand that the prophet make the issue clearer, as he finally does in Chaps. 36–37. Either the prophet intentionally clothed this part of his message in the form of an intriguing mystery to invite further reflection, or at first he himself did not see the issues any too clearly.

Men are far from being agreed that Chap. 37 is the logical continuation of Chap. 36. So for example it is claimed that 37:8-20 "is almost certainly a later version of 36:1–37:4c." *Procksch*, who takes about the same view, adds that this is "one of the saints-legends, drawn on a golden background, lifeless and lacking in the spirit of true history, whose value lies chiefly in the pronouncements of the prophet that have been inserted." Quite aside from this, the other problem that appeared in the previous chapter still calls for attention:

558

Does the parallel account of II Kings 19 constitute the original account or is it built on Isaiah's account in the chapter before us? We shall not attempt to answer the latter question; to do so would take us too far afield. But we do claim and hope to substantiate in a measure that one coherent account, logical and without contradiction, lies before us, an account that has unassailable value in the form in which it stands in the Isaiah text.

We venture to use as title for this chapter the caption, Further Transactions and the Disastrous Overthrow of the Assyrians. We use the following subdivisions:

1. Hezekiah's Request for Isaiah's Intercession (vv. 1-5)
2. Preliminary Reassurance: Sennacherib Will Depart and Perish (vv. 6-7)
3. The Beginning of a Change in the Situation (vv. 8-9a)
4. A Supplementary Attempt by Rabshakeh to Secure Hezekiah's Surrender — the Blasphemous Letter (vv. 9b-13)
5. Hezekiah's Prayer for Deliverance from the Assyrian Host (vv. 14-20)
6. Isaiah's answer to Hezekiah — a Word from the Lord (vv. 21-29)
7. A Reassuring Sign: Normal Agricultural Procedure Will Be Resumed by the Third Year (vv. 30-32)
8. Jerusalem Will Not Be Attacked (vv. 33-35)
9. The Startling End of the Assyrian Campaign (vv. 36-37)

1. Hezekiah's Request for Isaiah's Intercession (vv. 1-5)

37:1-5 1. And it came to pass when Hezekiah heard it, he rent his clothes and put on sackcloth, and went into the house of the Lord. 2. And he sent Eliakim, the steward of the palace, and Shebna, the secretary, and the senior priests, clothed in sackcloth, to the prophet Isaiah, the son of Amoz, 3. that they should say to him: "Thus says Hezekiah: 'This is a day of distress, of rebuke, and of blasphemy; for children have come to the point of birth and there is no strength to bring them forth. 4. Perchance the Lord your God will hear the words of Rabshakeh, whom his master, the king of Assyria, has sent to defy a living God, and will administer a rebuke because of the words which the Lord your God has heard; and perhaps you will lift up your prayer for the remnant that is left.'" 5. And the servants of King Hezekiah came to Isaiah.

Verse 1. The king expresses his consternation in the same manner as his ambassadors did, who rent their clothes to give vent to the extremity of their distress. The king goes one step further — he "put on sackcloth" — the typical garment of the penitent. Then he takes an additional significant step — he "went into the house of the Lord." For it had been understood, since the days of the dedication of the Temple that it was the divinely appointed place for public intercession (I Kings 8:33, 34). Whether he accompanied his prayers with a sacrifice (cf. Joel 1:13,14) must be left as an open question.

Verse 2. Then he sends a delegation of prominent officials to Isaiah the prophet. The fact that such outstanding officials were sent, points to the high esteem in which the prophet was held at that time. In the group were Eliakim (cf. 36: 3) and Shebna and the senior priests, still clothed in sackcloth. Sending to the prophet of the Lord is a tacit admission that the policy pursued with royal sanction till now, was abandoned, the policy of soliciting the help of Egypt against Assyria. So the note of penitence comes indirectly into the picture. The obverse of this new attitude is faith in the living God, a feature tacitly admitted but not expressed in so many words. That Shebna should have participated in the delegation, would seem to indicate that the prophet's rebuke (22:15ff.) had not been without effect. *Skinner* goes so far as to claim that this feature of the story indicated "the completeness of Isaiah's moral victory."

Verse 3. The *Botenspruch*-idea (the typical message of an emissary) determines the form of this message, as the formal opening indicates — "thus says Hezekiah." How disastrous the situation is, appears from the triple description of the nature of the day, "a day of distress, of rebuke, and of blasphemy." The tenseness that pervaded the atmosphere of the city is well expressed by these terms. For the third term some prefer the translation "rejection." The statement involved could even have been a proverbial saying for a day of harsh and bitter experience. The whole city sighs under the burden of what has transpired. That there is a change, a basic change of attitude, is evidenced by the statement: "The children have come to the point of birth and there is no strength to bring them forth." This statement expresses the thought that there is some faith on Israel's part that the Lord is their helper, but not enough faith to take a hopeful attitude. The pro-Egyptian policy at least has been abandoned. As to the figure employed see Hos. 13:13.

Verse 4. The opening term ("perchance") is an admission that divine help is not deserved. When the king speaks of God's hearing the words of Rabshakeh, this does not mean that the Lord, despite his omniscience, may have failed to hear; but here the verb "heard" implies taking due note of and being ready to act accordingly. Such an attitude may be hoped for because Rabshakeh was, in the last analysis, sent to "defy a living God." By the use of the indefinite article ("a") Hezekiah is hardly admitting that there are other living gods. Rather the opposite. This is merely a unique way of asserting with what kind of God Sennacherib is actually dealing, in contrast to the gods of the heathen, who are all of them fictions of the mind and non-entities. So the hope is that this living God will "administer a rebuke," because his divine sovereignty has been challenged. The king makes bold to ask that the prophet make intercession for the nation. We believe that the "perchance" of v. 4a carries over into the second half of the verse, and have thus inserted a "perhaps." It may well be that the word "remnant" here does not refer to the select group of those whom God keeps for himself, but merely for those who are still left in the city, which has suffered a serious measure of depopulation. But for intercession for the people of God by a man of God, Israel had ample warrant; some of these instances, of course, from times later than those of Isaiah (see Gen. 20:7; Num. 21:4ff.; Jer. 15:1; Amos 7:1ff.; Jer. 14:1ff.). This intercession is asked for rather modestly. The nation had not given too close heed to the prophet's words of guidance and might well have deserved a refusal. This then is the message with which the delegation comes to Isaiah (v. 5). It is not said that they delivered their message; but that they did so is too obvious to call for a special statement to that effect.

2. Preliminary Reassurance: Sennacherib Will Depart and Perish (vv. 6-7)

37:6-7 6. And Isaiah said to them: "Thus shall you say to your master: 'Thus says the Lord: Do not be afraid because of the words which you have heard, with which the lads of the king of Assyria have reviled me. 7. Lo, I will put a spirit in him, so that when he hears a certain report, he will return to his own land, and I will cause him to fall by the sword in his own land.'"

Verse 6. One might almost say that Isaiah was several steps ahead of the delegation that had come to see him. He already may have made intercession in behalf of the city and its people, both of which he sincerely loved. God already has given him an answer to their request, or has intimated to the prophet that he will grant him the message when he is asked for help. His whole approach to the problem is marked by a certain dignity. The answer again is cast somewhat in the form of a certain *Botenspruch* (cf. v. 3 *supra*). It is to be transmitted directly to the king. It squarely meets all the needs of the case in brief. It is a word from God — "thus says the Lord." The first thing needed in this emergency is courage ("do not be afraid"). Though the term used for those who had comprised the Assyrian delegation could be translated "servants," it happens to be a word which connotes a certain immaturity in this case, and so may be translated as "lads," or even as "young chaps," of the king of Assyria. So he says in effect: Do not be disconcerted by what these lads have boldly proclaimed. It was all in the nature of words that "reviled" the Lord Most High.

Verse 7. For the present one item that belongs to the impending developments is proclaimed by the prophet. Further aspects will be revealed later. The one here touched upon is that God will "put a spirit in him." This, of course, is further explained as involving that he will practically panic when a certain report reaches his ears, and will return to his own land, leaving unfinished the task of taking Jerusalem. But the translation "spirit" is inadequate. We shall note a few alternate translations which will help convey the idea involved: it could be "resolve," or "impulse," or "craven fear," or "foreboding," or even "despair" (*Verzagtheit*, as *Luther* renders it). In any case it will be the very antithesis to the overweening boldness that has found an echo in the words of his delegation, headed by Rabshakeh. The climax of his fate will come when God will "cause him to fall by the sword in his own land." For the present this brief indication of Sennacherib's disaster rather than the overthrow of the city is sufficient. This does not clash, as is frequently claimed, with the actual development in the area of Palestine or near the borders of Egypt where the judgment of the angel of the Lord struck the Assyrian camp. Two things are asserted for the present: God will take a hand in the case by instilling a spirit of craven fear so that Sennacherib beats a retreat; and then in his own land the great monarch shall be assassinated. The rumor from his own land that is referred to may have been the news of some uprising in Babylon, which demanded immediate attention. Various commentators remark that such a situation actually developed (e.g., *Fischer*).

3. The Beginning of a Change in the Situation (vv. 8-9a)

37:8-9a 8. And Rabshakeh returned and found the king of Assyria fighting against Libnah; for he had heard that he had left Lachish. 9a. For he [the king of Assyria] had heard that Tirhakah, king of Ethiopia "has gone forth to fight against you."

Verse 8, 9a. According to the previous chapter, Rabshakeh's last harangue had met with a total lack of response, indicating that he had failed to achieve his purpose to intimidate the men of Hezekiah. So the narrative, having told us what was transpiring within the city walls, now goes on to tell us what Rabshakeh did. He goes back to his master, possibly leaving a contingent of troops encamped about, or near, Jerusalem. But word has reached him that Sennacherib has moved up north from Lachish, about ten miles, to fight against Libnah. This move seems to have been made because Sennacherib felt it to be more necessary at the moment to have Libnah under control should the Ethiopian forces come up to encounter him. The report had reached him that

Tirhakah was actually advancing against him. A perfectly natural anachronism appears here. Tirhakah was not yet king of Ethiopia, since he first came to the throne *ca.* 688 B.C. So for the present the siege of Jerusalem is out of the question.

4. A Supplementary Attempt by Rabshakeh to Secure Hezekiah's Surrender — the Blasphemous Letter (vv. 9b-13)

37:9b-13 9b. So, when he heard it, he sent messengers to Hezekiah saying: 10. "Thus shall you say to Hezekiah king of Judah: 'Do not let your God in whom you trust deceive you, when he says that you will not be given into the hand of the king of Assyria. 11. Lo, you have heard what the kings of Assyria did to all lands by destroying them utterly. And should you be delivered? 12. Did the gods of the nations which my fathers destroyed, deliver them — Gozen, Haran, Rezeph, and the people of Eden, who were in Telassar? 13. Where is the king of Hamath, and the king of Lair, of Sepharvaim, of Henah, and Ivvah?'"

Verse 9b. At this point the objection has been frequently raised that this account could hardly be historical, because an emissary who had just dealt with a group in person, demanding their submission, would hardly resort to the use of a letter to achieve the same purpose shortly thereafter. But such an approach overlooks the fact that diplomats resort to all manner of devices. When a direct conference failed to achieve its purpose, a letter, with strong propaganda content could well be utilized to soften up a group that at least had been deeply impressed by the first conference.

Verse 10. As we learn from v. 14, the messenger sent bore his message not by word of mouth but by a letter, the contents of which is here briefly summarized. In his propaganda approach the king of Assyria makes the issue a religious one in dealing with a people who are more religious than the average. He begins boldly by asserting that their God in whom they trust is deceiving them, when he lets them be told that they "will not be given into the hand of the king of Assyria." The Assyrian king has all the evidence of recent history on his side. Israel is familiar with this evidence.

Verse 11. There are all the lands that recently have been overrun by the Assyrians and there was not a single one of the gods of the nations who could stop them. The God of Israel had never gotten his people very far along the road to strength and success. Why should he be able to do so now? So the very proper and most logical conclusion seems to be: "And should you be delivered?"

Verses 12, 13. Here the king of Assyria throws in for good measure a number of good illustrations, cases of cities and lands with whom the people of Judah were quite familiar. His "fathers" (i.e., his predecessors) had destroyed whatever nations they assailed, and none of the gods of the lands involved could deliver them. The examples cited here may be briefly identified and located. Gozen, is the Assyrian Guzana, in Mesopotamia; Haran, a bit farther north in the same region; Rezeph, west of the Euphrates, a little to the south of Gozen; Eden identical with Bit-adini, a strong state in Mesopotamia, Telessar, quite a bit farther to the north, beyond Carchemish; Hamath, in the same general area on the Orontes; Arvad, a bit farther to the south on the Mediterranean; Sepharvaim must have lain near Riblah; Henah and Ivvah, presumably in the same general area. Apparently some of the more recent successes of the Assyrians are being listed. In Gozen, by the way, the captives of the Northern Kingdom had been settled, according to II Kings 17:26. The location of Lair is unknown.

5. Hezekiah's Prayer for Deliverance from the Assyrian Host (vv. 14-20)

37:14-20 14. And when Hezekiah had received the letter from the hand of the messengers and had read it, he went up to the house of the Lord; and Hezekiah spread it out before the Lord. 15. And Hezekiah prayed to the Lord and said: 16. "O Lord of hosts, God of Israel, who art enthroned above the cherubim, thou art the God, thou alone, over all the kingdoms of the earth; thou hast made the heavens and the earth. 17. Incline thy ear, O Lord, and hear; open thy eyes, O Lord, and see, and hear all the words of Sennacherib, which he has sent to revile a living God. 18. Of a truth, O Lord, the kings of Assyria have laid waste all lands and their own land, 19. and have cast their gods into the fire; for they were not gods, but the work of man's hands, wood and stone, and so they destroyed them. 20. And now, O Lord our God, save us from his hands, that all the kingdoms of the earth may know that thou alone art the Lord."

Verses 14, 15. We already have referred to the fact that in reality the message from Sennacherib was transmitted in a letter. Hezekiah read it and at once went up to the house of the Lord and "spread it out before the Lord." This was not an act calculated to reveal something to the Lord which he might have overlooked, but rather was in the nature of a symbolic act. He laid both his prayer and the letter before the Lord.

Verse 16. The manner in which God is addressed is noteworthy, "O Lord of hosts, God of Israel." Since the word "hosts" in the first title is best referred to the entire host of created things, the title used aptly expresses that all things are completely under divine control, also this present emergency. The second title indicates that this omnipotent ruler stands in a special relation to Israel, a relationship which he himself initiated. This leads to further glorification of the Lord: he is enthroned above the cherubim. This claim in the first place grows out of the fact that the nation knew that in his own sanctuary God was known to be enthroned above the cherubim of the ark of the covenant, which was a reflection of the greater truth, no doubt, that in the heavenly sanctuary also it was the cherubim who upheld his throne. Such a unique divine enthronement befitted him who is the only God and Lord of all. His unique and sole claim to deity is expressed here in unequivocal terms. Israel knew that there was no other God. Therefore, all things in heaven and on earth stood under his total control — also the existing emergency. From every point of view the address to the deity was most appropriate. This whole concept is further clinched by the well-known fact that the very heavens and the earth were his own divine handiwork, and so entirely under his governance.

Verses 17, 18. When the Lord is invited to hear and see what Sennacherib has done by way of reviling the living God (again really as above: "*a* living God") Hezekiah's concern is for the honor of the Lord. It must be conceded (v. 18) that the kings of Assyria have made the conquests that they claim. They virtually have "laid waste all lands," wherever they came, bent on conquest. And here, as the Hebrew text stands, a unique turn of the thought appears, for he asserts that these kings have also laid waste "their own land." This indeed could mean that in their eager pursuit of conquests by war, such heavy tax burdens and levies had been laid on their own land as well nigh to ravage and ruin it. The same thought already had appeared in 14:20. But this thought is inserted half parenthetically, and is followed through no farther.

Verse 19. What is stated, however, is that which Sennacherib might have said himself: The Assyrians have "cast into the fire" the gods of the conquered nations; and that they could do "for they were not gods, but the work of man's hands, wood and stone, and so they destroyed them." It took a good measure of faith to make such a statement in the face of all the success that the Assyrians had had in their conquests.

Verse 20. All this leads up to the prime issue in this prayer, that God might save his people from the hands of the enemy. Hezekiah had been driven to see that there was no other help. But it is not mere desperation that drives him to this petition. There is still concern for the Lord's honor. The point ultimately to be made is that "all the kingdoms of the earth may know that thou alone art the Lord." That is to say, that he is the only Yahweh that exists.

6. Isaiah's Answer to Hezekiah — a Word from the Lord (vv. 21-29)

37:21-29 21. Then Isaiah, the son of Amoz, sent to Hezekiah, saying: "Thus says the Lord, the God of Israel: Because you have prayed to me concerning Sennacherib, the king of Assyria,
22. this is the word that the Lord has spoken concerning him:
> She will despise you and mock you,
> > the virgin daughter of Zion;
> behind you she will wag her head,
> > the daughter of Jerusalem.
> 23. Whom have you reviled and insulted?

> Against whom have you raised your voice,
>> and lifted your eyes in pride?
>
> Against the Holy One of Israel.
>
> 24. By your servants you have mocked the Lord,
>
> for you have said: With the multitude of my chariots
>
> I have gone up to the heights of the mountains,
>> to the remote regions of Lebanon.
>
> I have felled its tallest cedars,
>> its choicest cypresses;
>
> I have penetrated to the remotest heights,
>> its garden-like forests.
>
> 25. I have dug wells and drunk water,
>
> I have dried up with the soles of my feet
>> all the streams of Egypt.
>
> 26. Have you not heard
>> that I undertook it long ago,
>
> from the days of antiquity;
>> and I shaped it up,
>
> and now have brought it to pass?
>> And it was for the purpose of overthrowing
>
> fortified cities so as to be heaps of ruins.
>
> 27. And their inhabitants, shorn of strength,
>
> were dismayed and confounded;
>
> and they have become herb of the field and green grass,
>
> grass on the housetops,
>> like a field of grain not yet headed out.
>
> 28. Your sitting down and your going forth,
>> as well as your coming in have I known,
>
> and your raging against me.
>
> 29. Because your raging against me
>> and your arrogance have come up into my ears,
>
> I will put my hook in your nose
>> and my bridle in your mouth;
>
> and I will make you to go back by the way
>> by which you came.' "

Verses 21, 22. It is true that above (v. 4) Isaiah's prayers for this crisis had been solicited by the king. However, the prophet was not summoned into the king's presence. It therefore would appear that, as *Procksch* remarks, Isaiah came under divine impulse, and because in some way, not indicated, the king's prayer had become known to him. To be more exact, he *sent* the message that follows by some servant of his own. He indicates to the king that the communication that he is sending is, in effect, God's answer to his prayer. God has made a solemn pronouncement. The whole is cast in the form of a kind of "taunt-song." Whether Isaiah had it all written out at the time, or whether he later gave it the poetic form in which it now appears is impossible to determine. But the communication begins on a high note of triumphant defiance, which is all the more remarkable if the existing circumstances are considered. It seems much better, as the Hebrew verb form most certainly allows, to translate the verbs as futures. For in the depressing circumstances that prevailed at the moment, Judah was doing anything but "despising and mocking" the king of Assyria. The point is that the time will come when she will do this. Isaiah's taunt-song is prepared for that day of victory. At that time it will appear that she is "the virgin daughter," that is, the unsubdued one. She even will go so far as to dare to "wag her head" behind the king as he beats an ignominious retreat — wagging the head being a gesture of contempt (cf. Ps. 22:7; 44:14; 109:25; Lam 2:15; Matt. 27:39). When the expression "daughter" of Jerusalem is used, it is a figure of speech for the entire population of the city.

The rest of this song (vv. 23-29) falls into two parts. Verses 23-25 describe what the Assyrians have done and what sort of attitude they have manifested. Verse 26-29 shows the counter-move that God will make over against the presumptuous plans of the Assyrians.

Verse 23. To begin with, the words of Rabshakeh and later those of the king himself, which he sent in his letter to Hezekiah, were directed against Yahweh himself; he has been reviled and insulted. But here Yahweh is designated as "the Holy One of Israel," to remind men that he is high above those commonly designated as gods, and in fact the Only One and the Most High.

Verse 24. The boastful strain of the utterances of the Assyrian are again much in the style of the monumental inscriptions that have come down to us from Assyrian sources. Such inflated pride against the Lord is commonly described by the term *hybris*. The king and his court set the pace; his "servants" readily and arrogantly adopted the same attitude. The first object of pride was the vast multitude of chariots with which he had appeared on the scene, even over very difficult terrain, "the heights of the mountains, to the remote regions of Lebanon." There, for purposes not indicated, the Assyrians "felled its tallest cedars, its choicest cypresses." Even where the forest was at its best ("its garden-like forest") and the going most difficult ("its remotest heights") he yet made his way. None may ever before have achieved this feat.

Verse 25. There is another area in which the Assyrian forces gave evidence of their great numbers. Using a very strong hyperbole, he claims first of all that where wells were filled in to hamper the conqueror (cf. II Chron. 32:2-4) he promptly dug them again, or dug new ones and drank water as he needed it. Such trifles could not arrest his victorious advance. Or, on the other hand, he represents his troops as being so numerous that when they approached the many arms of the Nile delta, merely by wading through, they dried up all the streams of Egypt. How boastful can you get? It matters little that strict historical accuracy is not to be met with at this point. It is well known that Sennacherib (705-681 B.C.) did not himself penetrate down into Egypt. It was Esarhaddon (670 B.C.) and Ashurbanipal (668) who achieved this feat. But all this was part of the movement which Sennacherib started. He even may have made proud boast in anticipation of what he would do in the land of Egypt.

Verse 26. Now God takes this monarch to task. To show how little such a mighty sovereign like Sennacherib amounts to, God challenges him by drawing to his attention the fact that all this which is now transpiring, is only quite secondarily the work of Sennacherib. It is primarily Yahweh's project, which he had in mind for a long while, then put it in motion, shaped it up and now has finally brought it to pass. Though it is not expressly said here — it had been said clearly enough 10:5ff. Assyria is merely the tool that God employs for his own purposes. These purposes are outlined as involving the "overthrowing of fortified cities so as to be heaps of ruins." God foresaw this dreary outcome as far as Israel was concerned and saw the necessity of proceeding just in this manner.

Verse 27. His plan further involved that "inhabitants

[of these cities] shorn of strength, were dismayed and confounded." This was most obviously the case at the moment
Isaiah's message reached Hezekiah; but all this was a part
of God's plan devised long ago. How utterly the dwellers
in these cities were to be made a spectacle of weakness and
helplessness is also shown to have been a part of this plan
of God of long standing. For all they would amount to would
be that "they have become herb of the field and green grass"
— both of which are notoriously short-lived. Or to vary the
figure slightly, in the present crisis they amounted to little
more than "grass on the housetops, like a field of grain not
yet headed out." Apparently the thought involved in this
last comparison is that the field in question is trampled under
foot and ruined before it produces any grain. So shall Judah
be down-trodden by the conqueror. Or in keeping with the
figure previously used, it might be better to think of the ver-
dure of the fields as withered by a hot sirocco blowing from
the desert and destroying all that it strikes, by the evening
of that day. The hyperbole involved aptly expresses the
success in overthrowing cities and peoples, as it appears from
the conqueror's point of view.

Verse 28. But Yahweh has this arrogant one under continual surveillance: he knows what his tool is doing in every
move that he makes. When the king sits down to rest; when
he goes forth bent on some new project; when he comes in
having accomplished what he set out to do — God always
knows exactly what he is doing. Of all this, of course, Sennacherib was completely unaware. But one thing more was
known by Yahweh, as he here tells him: "your raging against
me." From its lofty pinnacle of faith, where Israel stands,
she sees and understands all this, whereas the Assyrian king
is practically doing no more than running his head against a
wall.

Verse 29. Now comes the climax of the well-deserved
treatment that shall be Sennacherib's lot. Because of his
raging (here mentioned a second time) and his arrogance,
which in this instance was directed against God and not
against the enemy on the local scene, God is going to act
in such a way as to make it abundantly clear that the situation is entirely under his control. He shall deal with the

Assyrian as he deserves. The description that follows may well have been borrowed from the forms of cruel treatment that the Assyrians were wont to use in the case of captives taken in war. God will put his hook in the king's nose and his bridle on his mouth (or lips). Then, of course, the king must go as he is led. But the course that the Lord has determined for him is that he go back by the way he came, not as a great conqueror but as the one who cannot escape going the way God leads him. His return, it is implied, will not be in triumph but in disgrace.

7. A Reassuring Sign: Normal Agricultural Procedure Will Be Resumed by the Third Year (vv. 30-32)

37:30-32 30. And this shall be a sign for you: This year men shall eat what grows from spilled kernels; in the second year that which springs up from the same; then in the third year sow and reap, plant vineyards and eat of their fruit. 31. And the surviving remnant of the house of Judah shall again strike root downward and produce fruit upward. 32. For from Jerusalem shall go forth a remnant and a band of escapees from Mount Zion. The zeal of the Lord of hosts will achieve this.

Verse 30. The "taunt song" addressed Sennacherib. Now beginning with v. 30 Hezekiah is addressed: a "sign" is indicated for him. This does not mean an occurrence of a miraculous character. Rather it is to be construed about as follows: The course that things take will serve as an indicator of what is to be expected. Or, you can measure the time that developments will take by the following schedule of growth of the things of the field. The use of the word "sign" appears to be much the same in Exod. 3:12, about Moses worshipping the Lord at the mountain where the Lord appeared to him. That experience would confirm that the word of the Lord was true. Though the nouns used in this connection are somewhat difficult, one is almost compelled to arrive at conclusions such as: The first year from now you will not yet be able to reap what is sowed because you will not be able to sow this year. What springs up from spilled kernels that the enemy spilled in devastating your fields is all that you may expect. The year following the disorders of war will still be so troublesome that sowing will be out of the question. Whatever springs up from spilled kernels of the preceding kernels will again be all that you dare expect. Only for the third year will there be regular sowing and reaping. All of which in effect amounts to this: The present disorders will continue till the third year. Don't expect relief before that. When planting vineyards and eating of their fruit is brought into the picture besides, it would seem that indirect reference is made to passages like Deut. 28:30; Amos 5:11; Micah 6:15; Zeph. 1:13; Jer. 6:12, which all regard it as a special blessing from God when you are enabled to reap the fruits of your toil, you and not your enemy, or conqueror.

Verses 31, 32. So much for the physical aspect of things. Over and beyond that the nation Judah shall make a new happen. "For from Jerusalem shall go forth a remnant" — an idea already advanced by the prophet at the close of Chap. 6. Some survivers shall always be left. But by calling them "remnant" the prophet indicates that they shall not be too numerous. A future is still to be expected, but not too glorious a one at the outset. But the nation of God's people does not face extinction. As a guarantee there is added the pledge: "The zeal of the Lord of hosts will achieve this." God is zealous for his cause. That serves as guaranty; not men's strenuous efforts, not man's perseverance (cf. 9:6).

8. Jerusalem Will Not Be Attacked (vv. 33-35)

37:33-35 33. "Therefore thus says the Lord regarding the king of Assyria: He shall not come into this city, neither shall he shoot an arrow into it, or come before it with a shield, or build up a ramp against it. 34. By the way he came, by the same he shall return; and he shall not come into this city, says the Lord. 35. For I will protect this city to save it for my own sake and for the sake of my servant David."

Verses 33-35. Note the logical progression of thought thus far. In answer to Hezekiah's prayer, first of all he is reassured that he may take a triumphant attitude, over against his attackers; the attacker shall have to beat a retreat (vv. 21-29). Then it is indicated over what space of time these developments will extend, approximately three years (vv. 30-32). Then to be a bit more explicit, it is now plainly said that the king will not even be able to force an entrance into the city, even though other cities in Judah have surrendered by the dozens (vv. 33-35). Whether these three major thoughts were uttered in one breath, or whether they represent various stages by which, at intervals, the Prophet Isaiah enlightened and comforted the people of Jerusalem makes comparatively little difference. The chief point is now: "He will not come into the city." This is said twice over. All this is in keeping with other statements we have met with in the course of the book, like 10:33f.; and 31:9. In some mysterious way a tragic disaster will overtake him and defeat the purposes of the expedition. And all this the Lord will do (v. 35) for his own sake and for the sake of his servant David. Both reasons given dovetail into one another. For his own sake, indicates that human merit has no part in this result. On the other hand, since a great promise of grace had been given to David in II Sam. 7, God would have regard for the sanctity of his promise.

9. The Startling End of the Assyrian Campaign (vv. 36-37)

37:36-37 36. And the angel of the Lord went forth and slew in the camp of the Assyrians one hundred and eighty-five thousand; and when men arose early in the morning, lo, there were all dead bodies. 37. And Sennacherib, king of Assyria, departed and went home and dwelt in Nineveh. And it came to pass as he was worshipping in the temple of Nisroch, his god, that Adrammelech and Sharezer, his sons, slew him with the sword and escaped into the land of Ararat. And Esarhaddon, his son, reigned in his stead.

At this point it almost has become an established tradition to make the claim that this part of the account clashes with v. 7, where the cause of Sennacherib's retreat is said to be a rumor that comes to his attention. Dare there be only a single cause for a retreat in war? A combination of circumstances may easily occur. The rumor does not rule out the destructive work of the angel. When both concur, then a disastrous retreat becomes inevitable. Then also there are many who claim that the number of those slain by the angel of the Lord is far too high — some reduce it to one tenth of the Biblical figure. But it also has been pointed out that in the First Crusade the loss of life amounted to 300,000; and that of the Grand Army of 250,000 men which invaded Russia under Napoleon only 12,000 came back.

Verse 36. But how about the angel of the Lord? Analogous is the event recorded in the Exodus story (Exod. 12:23). There it usually has been assumed that a swift-striking pestilence was the deadly instrument that God's messenger employed. Note the similarity with II Sam. 24:13ff. A tale of Herodotus is usually compared at this point. He tells of an army made up of Assyrians and Arabians who found their camp invaded one night by an army of field mice, who gnawed through the bow strings and shield handles and so compelled the soldiers to beat a retreat. It is frequently suggested that these rodents may have been carriers of the bubonic plague, which is both swift and deadly in its working. The essence of what Herodotus tells may agree with the Biblical account. All this could have happened in part to a detachment of Assyrian forces left beneath the walls of Jerusalem, all of which would agree with Scriptures such as Isa. 33; Ps. 48 and 76.

Verse 37. In any case, Sennacherib found it necessary to retreat and go home, taking up his residence in Nineveh. The fact of the matter is that his assassination occurred some twenty years later, an item that is not told in our abbreviated account. But his two sons, Adrammelech and Sharezer, were the ones who perpetrated the deed, and apparently in this dreadful end of the life of the king, the writer would have us see a further instance of the judgment of God against a haughtly and insolent monarch.

Notes

Verse 3. The first verb cannot be translated, "They said to him" (*RSV*) because the beginning of v. 6 states that fact. Here the "and" represents a subordinate conjunction and so the translation is called for: "that they should say to him." Cf. *KS* 369 l.

Verse 9. The tension between the two *wayyishma's* of this verse is relieved by II Kings 19:9, which reads instead of the second one *wayyashobh*, i.e., "He again sent."

Verse 11. In the form "by destroying them utterly" the suffix is masculine, though it refers to "lands" which is feminine. Such irregularities are common. See *KS* 249 a. The question "and should you be delivered?" has no interrogative particle — another common occurrence. Cf. *GK* 150 a.

Verse 14. The word for "letter" is plural, involving, no doubt, the several folded sheets that made up the letter.

Verse 19. For "and have cast" the Hebrew makes a transition from the finite verb construction to the use of the absolute infinitive (*KS* 218 a; 413 q; *GK* 118 z).

Verse 22. "Daughter" in the expression "virgin daughter" is an appositional genitive. *KS* 337 n.

Verse 24. "Tallest of cedars" in Hebrew reads: "height of cedars" and is a device for using a noun to express a superlative. *GK* 128 r.

Verse 26. "Heaps of ruins" is a factitive object. *KS* 327 v; *GK* 117 ii.

Verse 30. For "this year" the Hebrew says "*the* year" — indicating the originally demonstrative use of the article. *GK* 126 b. The verb "eat" is an infinitive in apposition with the noun "sign." *KS* 400 d.

Chapter XXXVIII

C.   AN IMPORTANT INCIDENT IN THE MINISTRY OF ISAIAH (Chap. 38)

We have given this somewhat vague heading to this chapter chiefly to indicate that in this connection it had to do with *Isaiah's* activity rather than the *king's* experience. The event involved is also reported in I Kings 20, but there as a part of the life of the nation, where that which befalls the king is important to the people. But here Isaiah's ministry is involved and the reported incident is in this special setting.

The chapter may be outlined as follows:

1. Hezekiah's Sickness, Promised Recovery, and Confirmatory Sign (vv. 1-7)
2. Hezekiah's Psalm (vv. 9-20)
3. A Few Circumstances Attendant upon the Incident (vv. 21-22)

It is a matter of some concern whether this psalm (vv. 9-20) may rightly be ascribed to Hezekiah. Verse 9 says it is. As far as we can see, no valid ground for questioning the reliability of this statement can be adduced. Nothing in the psalm must necessarily be of late origin; the Aramaisms to be found are always an uncertain factor as to date. It hardly can be argued with any validity that since nothing in the psalm specifically points to Hezekiah, therefore he cannot have written it. Writers of psalms are known to have generalized their experiences so that others too might with profit employ what they themselves wrote.

It must be freely admitted that rather unusual difficulties surround the interpretation of the psalm as such, and that textual difficulties are numerous. But the drastic text revision resorted to by some is hardly warranted. It is an overstatement when it is claimed that the text is a "mass of

577

ruins" (*Truemmercharakter*) as *Begrich* claims in his famous treatise on the psalm.

But getting nearer to the overall character of the chapter is the helpful title of G. A. Smith, "An Old Testament Believer's Deathbed; or, the Difference Christ Makes." For it is true that the chapter tells with amazing clearness that concerning the victory over death there still was much to be achieved as far as the saints of those early days were concerned.

We may yet draw attention to the fact that quite a bit of effort has been expended on trying to determine the exact historical sequence of Chaps. 36–39. However, it must be admitted that historical sequence was not always sought by the Biblical writers. It is quite possible that in time order the chapters would be placed as follows: 38, 39, 36, 37. But even as the writers of the four Gospels often took liberties with the order in which they arranged materials, so other writers also sometimes thought in terms of subject-matter sequence. One cannot rightly quarrel with a writer for following a sequence other than the chronological one that we might have felt inclined to use.

1. Hezekiah's Sickness, Promised Recovery, and Confirmatory Sign (vv. 1-8)

38:1-8 1. In those days Hezekiah became sick unto death. And Isaiah the prophet, the son of Amoz, came to him and said to him: "Thus says the Lord: 'Set your affairs in order, for you shall die and not recover.'" 2. Then Hezekiah turned his face to the wall and prayed to the Lord, 3. and said: "Remember now, O Lord, I beseech thee, how I have walked before thee in faithfulness and with a sincere heart, and have done what is good in thy sight." And Hezekiah wept bitterly. 4. Then the word of the Lord came to Isaiah: 5. "Go and say to Hezekiah: 'Thus says the Lord, the God of David, your father: I have heard your prayer, I have seen your tears. Lo, I will add fifteen years to your life. 6. And from the hand of the king of Assyria, I will deliver you and this city, and I will shield this city. 7. And this shall be a sign to you that the Lord will do the thing that he has spoken: 8. Lo, I will turn back the shadow of the steps which has gone down on the steps from the sun, ten steps, and the sun will go back ten steps on the steps down which it went.'"

Verse 1. It could well be that the event narrated here took place about 704-703 B.C. and so, in point of time, should stand before Chaps. 36–37. Whoever the writer of vv. 1-7 was, he had no special interest in the strict time-sequence and so begins with the rather vague time-designation "in those days," much like 39:1. It seems a somewhat sudden sickness befell Hezekiah and a very serious one at that. It could have ended in death, in fact, it was moving exactly in that direction. It somehow seemed good in the eyes of the Lord to indicate the fatal character of the disease to the king, and to use Isaiah, the prophet, as his agent. The fact that this prediction is afterward retracted, indicates that God's intention with regard to the course of a man's life is not irrevocably fixed: the outcome may be contingent upon the attitude that the individual takes. There is room in God's plans for the prayers of man. At first it appears to have been the Lord's intention to let this sickness prove fatal. To this end Isaiah's message is very blunt: "Set your affairs in order, for you shall die and not recover." The Hebrew really says "Give your last orders," and seems to think in terms of an incident like I Kings 2:1-9, where David set his affairs in order before his death. The apparent bluntness of the message may have been required by the circumstances. God is not intentionally cruel. Or it could be that this is merely the substance of God's word to the king, which word the prophet may have communicated to the king with all due consideration, and may have softened the impact of the message as much as possible.

Verse 2. The king is a pious man. His first thought in the emergency is prayer. To be the less disturbed in his prayer he turns his face to the wall. He knew that the Lord has all possible regard for the prayers of his servants.

Verse 3. The substance of Hezekiah's prayer is to call attention to the fact that his conduct had been blameless in the sight of the Lord, in so far as man is capable of blameless conduct. "With a perfect heart" as *KJ* has it goes farther than the words involved actually state. But with good conscience the king can say that he had walked before the Lord. God was in his thoughts: his life was lived in the consciousness of his responsibility to God. The historical record underscores this; for II Kings 18:1-7 indicates that blameless conduct was the goal of his reign. We need not suspect that a spirit of meritoriousness breathes through this prayer. The assumption is that God delights in rewarding and hearing those who seek to do his will. That assumption in this case is upheld by the final outcome. To his prayers the godly monarch added his bitter tears, showing how deeply this sudden confrontation with death had disturbed him.

Verse 4. Apparently no one communicated to Isaiah what transpired between the king and his God, except God himself. For it pleased God in his sovereign wisdom to grant the request that had been addressed to him, and grant it rather promptly. For, as II Kings 20:4 states, before Isaiah had gotten as far as the "middle city" (or, according to some manuscripts, the "middle court") a second word of the Lord came to him countermanding the first.

Verse 5. The substance of this new word is, "I have heard your prayer and seen your tears. Lo, I will add fifteen years to your life." There are few instances on record where prayer was heard so promptly and the relief provided so decisively. II Kings 20:6 adds that on the third day the king would go up to the Lord's house. But in the initial part of this word the added apposition that this word came from "the God of David" his father, indicates a point so often made by the Scriptures that the blessings that descend from godly fathers to godly children are far richer than man is inclined to suppose. At this point v. 21 and v. 22 might be inserted to secure something like a strict time-sequence. For the account of the Book of Kings indicates that Isaiah gave the counsel to use the fig-poultice at this point. But the time-sequence is of no particular importance.

Verse 6. As Kings also indicates at this point, the prophet added the promise that city and king would be delivered "from the hand of the king of Assyria," and that God would "shield" the city. This promise is not so much out of place at this point in the text as many would claim. The Assyrian crisis already may have been in the making at this time, some two years prior to the events of Chaps. 36 and 37. God here merely may be granting what, prior to this sudden sickness, Hezekiah had been praying for long and earnestly. So the promise to help is expanded beyond the immediate request of the prayers made on the sickbed.

Verses 7, 8. It pleased God in the richness of his grace, on this occasion to make assurance doubly sure by granting the king a "sign." The account of II Chron. 32:24 merely indicates that a sign was provided without even mentioning wherein the sign consisted. But the sign provided strong confirmation that God can do exceeding abundantly above all that man can ask or think. Because the terms in which the sign is described seem to be technical in character, we cannot be entirely sure that an actual "dial," or merely something that could serve as a measure of the extent to which the shadow of the sun had moved is under consideration. For the word involved by itself alone seems to mean only "steps." The term "sundial" (*KJ*), for that matter, even may be correct. But all the needs of the case would be met if nothing more were thought of than that a certain pillar in the temple-court, or for that matter merely visible from the royal palace, was wont to cast a shadow which fell on certain palace or temple steps. According to the account of the book of Kings, Hezekiah was given the option of having the shadow retreat or advance. Our chapter merely gives the actual result, which in itself must have been a striking sign. For the shadow retreated, as the king had asked that it might, retreated for that matter, even ten steps. The account seems a bit verbose as here given, but that may be due to the fact that we fail to see how precisely the account was worded. Nor does it matter any that one version has it that the sun went back, and the other version that the shadow went back.

How far may we go in trying to determine exactly what transpired? We must guard against laying into the words used elaborate revelations that they were never intended to convey. Surely the text does not say that God stopped the earth in its movement. It makes no attempt to describe the mode of procedure involved. Had it been a case of "the whole world being thrown back on its axis" such an approach certainly poses a tremendous problem from the point of view of the physical consequences involved, though we would in no sense limit the omnipotence of God. But God usually seems to operate in harmony with the laws of this world which he himself has put into operation. Less difficulty seems to be involved if we think in terms of some fresh aspect of refraction of light, even as the mirage represents a strange phenomenon in this area. So vv. 6-7 have assembled certain important factors that grew out of Hezekiah's sickness and prayer: a promise of fifteen years added to his life; rescue from the power of the Assyrians; and a sign of confirmation. The writer apparently aims to do no more than bring these factors into the picture. Their sequence and deeper logical connection was of no particular concern to him. He is not to be criticized for having been pleased to arrange his material in this manner.

2. Hezekiah's Psalm (vv. 9-20)

a. *Complaint (vv. 9-14)*

38:9-14 9. A Psalm of Hezekiah king of Judah, composed after he had been ill and recovered from his illness.
10. My thoughts were that in the noontide of my days
   I must go hence;
I am consigned to the gates of Sheol
   for the rest of my years.
11. I thought: I shall not see the Lord — the Lord in the land of the living;
I shall not look upon man any more
   among the inhabitants of the world.
12. My dwelling is removed and taken away from me
   like a shepherd's tent;
I have already rolled up my life like a weaver;
   he cuts me off from the loom.
   From day to night thou dost bring me to an end.
13. I composed myself until morning;
   like a lion he broke all my bones.
From day to night thou dost bring me to an end.
14. Like a swallow, or a crane, so I moaned;
   I mourned like a dove.
My eyes looked languishingly upward —
   "O Lord, I am depressed; take my part."

Before we look at the individual statements of this psalm a few issues must be explored a bit more fully. We have above already indicated our position that we believe that Hezekiah may have written this paslm; and also have conceded that a number of unusual difficulties of interpretation will be encountered. We are well aware of the fact that the majority of commentators regard the psalm as merely being "traditionally ascribed to Hezekiah." That it is a "liturgical thanksgiving of a man rescued from grave illness," is another way of stating the opinion commonly held concerning this poem. Over against this approach we concede first of all that if another man had freely interpreted in this psalm the sentiments that Hezekiah expressed on this occasion, that would not necessarily be a dangerous assumption. But the evidence seems to point beyond this. Hezekiah's interest in sacred literature is indicated by the heading found in Prov. 25:1. His concern about helping to embellish the temple services is described in II Chron. 29: 25-30. The absence of specific references to his particular situation does not argue against our approach, as already indicated at the beginning of the chapter.

We would also add that it is not an extravagant statement to claim that this psalm is "the finest of the hymns of thanksgiving that has come down to us in Israel's tradition" (*Begrich*). The fact that it does not appear in the hymnal i.e., the Psalter; of the congregation indicates that it does not use the "collective I" speaking in the name of the congregation. It was the hymn of an individual. To this might be added the suggestion that we may attempt to visualize the use of the psalms, as some do, somewhat after this fashion: The king has recovered; a day of thanksgiving in the Temple has been appointed; the sacrifice is ready to be offered; the king steps forth and speaks the words of this hymn of thanksgiving; the assembled friends rejoice with him.

As to structure, it may be pointed out that the general pattern followed is five accented syllables per line, usually in a 3/2 pattern, the somewhat solemn measure of the Qinah verse. However, we also hold, on good grounds, that the meter-pattern was not so strictly followed by the Hebrew poets as some assume. Quite a bit of freedom in the matter of meter prevailed. Therefore to attempt a reconstruction of the psalm largely controlled by this meter-pattern is unwarranted; and that is the major defect that marks *Begrich's* otherwise very good treatment of the psalm.

Verse 9. The Hebrew really says that this is "a writing." Perhaps the reason for this colorless description is that for the present the text merely desires to ascribe the writing of this piece of poetry directly to the king, as the words used without a doubt do. This part of the testimony to authorship by Hezekiah is often too lightly brushed aside. The reason for inserting the psalm here between vv. 7 and 21 may be that the writer of the book, or of the section, Chaps. 36–39 — The Historical Interlude — is more intent on revealing the godly sentiments of the king on this occasion than on arriving at the exact historical sequence of things.

Verse 10. The first word of the verse carries more than usual emphasis; the word order amounts to this: "*My* thoughts were. . . ." Whatever God may have had in mind, *I* thought. . . . Just as his life has reached its zenith, or "noontide" when indeed a gradual decline might have taken its beginning, he suddenly found, at the prophet's announcement, that he "must go hence." To be deprived of the full measure of one's days, is almost always felt to be a sharp disappointment. The word rendered "noontide" is by many rendered as "quiet course." Either translation fits. We cannot be too certain about either of the two. The second half of the verse means: I have been given orders into the netherworld for the rest of my years. The "gates of Sheol" is an expression used by synecdoche, part for the whole, and it poetically recalls the very acts of passing through those dread gates. Sheol is mentioned quite frequently by Isaiah (cf. 5:14; 7:11; 14:9, 11; 28:15, 18; 38:18, etc.). The "gates of Sheol" appear in Ps. 9:13; 107:18. Sheol itself is that dismal, dreary place where the departed lead a dull and listless existence; that insatiable monster that swallows down all of the children of men in due course of time. For the hope of immortality glowed but dimly for most of the saints of the Old Testament. The king, at Isaiah's announcement, saw himself also going into that realm. The expression "for the rest of my years" means nothing more than: the years that I might normally have expected. These were his first thoughts at the sad news.

Verse 11. He next expresses the thought that he shall be deprived of all the things that had become dear to him in this life. First among these is the "seeing of the Lord," an expression, which according to Ps. 11:7; 17:15, and so forth, may be construed to mean, appearing before him in public worship. For if one worships aright, true and living contact with the Unseen One is established. It gives a man rare insight into the values that the king prized most highly to note that the privilege of worship is, as it were, his most cherished possession. Then he will also be deprived of fellowship with his fellow men. For to tell the truth of the matter, such contact with men greatly enriches life and is one of its most prized assets. Not every one would have thought just these thoughts at the prospect of death; but Hezekiah did.

Verse 12. He next pictures the termination of his life by the use of a number of expressive figures. In the first of these, life is likened to the tent of a Bedouin, which, as the circumstances of pasturage might demand, would be taken down and moved to another place. In the second, life is likened to a piece of cloth or carpet, which is finished on the loom and is cut off — a thought kindred to that of the Greeks who spoke of the Parcae (fates), one of whom spun life's thread, the second measured it, the third cut it off. But it is not primarily the thought of a colorful description of what life is like. The last line brings the major thought involved: "From day to night thou dost bring me to an end." The interpretation of these words (especially the phrase "from day to night") that appeals most to us is the one that thinks in terms of how swiftly the Oriental day passes from day into night. Just so swiftly was the king's life to be snuffed out. He literally was standing at the very threshold of death. The repetition of this sentiment at the end of the next verse indicates how prominent this thought was in his experience at that time.

Verse 13. This verse bristles with difficulties. We shall attempt to indicate what it says, according to our translation. After his initial alarm, the king composed himself and managed to achieve relative composure until morning. Then, by some turn of events, perhaps the arrival and message from the lips of the prophet Isaiah, disaster crashed down upon him like a lion pouncing upon him and breaking all his bones. Such an interpretation would fit aptly into the picture, although rather than speak of disaster as overtaking him, the king speaks of the Lord as crashing down upon him. Others note the fact that the first verb may also mean "be like," or "act like," and arrive at the meaning: I roared in my distress like a lion, loudly and fiercely. Other possibilities need not be considered now.

Verse 14. By a new set of comparisons the godly king now describes how he gave expression to the anguish of his soul. He gave vent to his distress by moaning, even as certain birds make low moaning sounds. He even mourned, "like a dove." It must be the mourning-dove that is under consideration, a bird whose mournful tones are well known. Abandoning all figures perhaps the royal poet pictures himself as actually "looking languishingly upward." Again the term used is a difficult one in this connection. But the translation suggested is not without good warrant. One final statement by way of direct petition sums up all that agitated his mind. "O Lord, I am depressed, take my part." The term "depressed," however, in this instance is too mild to catch the idea of the noun involved, which really covers oppression and extortion. Perhaps we should have said: I am crushed to the earth. At this point the complaint-section of the psalm suddenly comes to an end.

One word as to the structure of the psalm up to this verse. *Begrich*, in the monograph repeatedly referred to, following form-criticism approach rather closely, arrives at the conclusion that this psalm is primarily a psalm of thanksgiving. It should, therefore, begin with a strong word of thanks. Instead it opens with a bitter wail of pain. He feels this must have greatly startled the worshippers present with him at the sanctuary, and been very effective. We feel that such a claim uses the form-criticism method too rigorously, almost as if the Old Testament psalm-writers themselves had been scholarly students of the form in which psalms commonly appeared, whereas some of these approaches are psychologically easily understood and most natural quite apart from what the present-day form-critic expects.

b. *Thanksgiving (vv. 15-20)*

38:15-20 ¹⁵. What shall I say? seeing he hath both spoken to me and has also done it.
I will go meekly all my years
  in view of the bitterness of my soul.
16. O Lord, by these things men live,
and in all these things is the life of my spirit.
  Thou wilt restore me and revive me.
  17. Lo, it was for my own good
  that I had great bitterness.
For it was thou who didst hold me back
  from the pit of destruction.
For thou hast cast all my sins
  behind thy back.
  18. For Sheol cannot thank thee,
  death cannot praise thee.
They that go down into the pit cannot hope
  in thy faithfulness.
  19. The living, the living, he it is that will thank thee,
  even as I do this day.
The father makes known to the children thy faithfulness.
  20. The Lord is minded to save me;
  therefore we will sing to stringed instruments,
all the days of my life at the house of the Lord.

Verse 15. The tone of the psalm changes completely at this point, though this verse is still in the nature of a transition. The rhetorical question with which it begins bears witness to the astonishment that the king still feels at being so marvelously delivered, where hope seemed almost out of the question. One might compare II Sam. 7:20, where David received a remarkable promise of future greatness. The reply to the question put, sums up the whole experience: "seeing he hath both spoken to me and has also done it." Both the promise and the fulfilment lie before him. He himself is the living witness to both. This experience as a historical fact stands out. His own reaction to this experience is also concisely stated: "I will go meekly all my years in view of the bitterness of my soul." Such a rare favor received from God, if taken rightly, produces a feeling of

meekness; it is deeply humbling to be singled out for such
great mercy from God. When he mentions "the bitterness
of his soul" he is referring to the distress caused by the sudden confrontation with death, when the prophet's message
first came to him. That kind of experience leaves its in-
delible mark on a man. In spite of all gratitude, he will
carry the mark of it upon his being as long as he lives.

Verse 16. From here on the note of thanksgiving predom-
inates. Though the verse has its difficulties, largely because of its conciseness, and the somewhat different use
of pronouns than what we are accustomed to, it still calls
for no radical revision or extensive changes. The King
James translators made an almost classical translation of it,
and so did *Luther*, in practically the same form. These
translations are grammatically defensible and are readily
understood. The expression "these things" refers to experiences such as the king had just passed through. They become vital factors in our lives on which we base our entire
existence. Going a bit deeper, the writer then claims that
in experiences such as these lies "the very life of [his]
spirit." They are the wellspring of all existence. All this is
said in an effort to indicate how deep these things go and
how long they last. When he adds: "Thou wilt restore me
and revive me," it almost appears as if, in spite of his recovery, convalescence is still going on, and the writer is
sure that God will bring that also to a satisfactory conclusion.

Verse 17. Some further major insights that grew out of
this recovery are now indicated. The "great bitterness" that
came upon him at the prospect of an untimely death,
nevertheless had its beneficial effect: "Lo, it was for my own
good." In retrospect he sees how it benefited him. He
was granted new understanding of the loving heart of God.
Or another way of putting it: "It was thou who didst hold
me back from the pit of destruction." That God is in control even over death and destruction itself came home to him
now as a living truth. And another insight gained — all this
could be done by God for he had "cast all [the king's] sins
behind his back," that is to say, had put them completely
out of the picture. That some deeper connection between
sin, guilt, and suffering exists is clear to him, also that the

root cause of it all is sin. But now as never before he becomes reassured that God pardons sin, removing it completely. Cf. also Micah 7:19; Ps. 103:12. The psalmist does not, however, seem to indicate that corrective purposes, or chastisement, were involved in this whole experience.

Verse 18. Here the limitations of the faith of men of the Old Testament becomes very obvious. Hope burned but dimly, as far as the afterlife was concerned. As things appeared to the men of that time, praise of God came to an end when life ended. The shades (i.e., the departed ones) were no longer capable of such glorious activity as singing the praise of God. "Sheol cannot thank thee" apparently means: They that dwell in Sheol cannot thank. Quite parallel runs the thought: "Death cannot praise thee." For it means: They whom death has claimed come to a form of existence where praise cannot be engaged in. For both these statements the presupposition is that praise and thanks of men is valuable in the sight of God.

Lastly, analogous is the last claim: "They that go down into the pit cannot hope in thy faithfulness." On this subject, for reasons unknown to us, men's eyes were holden that they could not see the full measure of hope that is ours. In other words, as praise and thanks were out of the question so was hope. Strange as we find all this, there are similar passages that run quite parallel to the sentiments here expressed (see Ps. 6:5; 30:9; 88:11; 115:17).

Verse 19. Now the other side of the matter. The man still living, yes, the living, "he it is that will thank thee, even as I do this day." Men of days of old may have been less enlightened with regard to the future and what it held in store but they were not ignorant of the rich joy to be found in thanksgiving or of the value it had in the godly life. One catches the somewhat exuberant ring of the last clause, "even as I do this day." To be deprived of such a joyful occupation meant to lose much of what made life worth living. To this is then added one example of such thanksgiving, namely when the "father makes known to the children thy faithfulness." Such activity cannot be engaged in without becoming eloquent in the praise of God. Of this Exod. 12:25ff. furnishes a good illustration. Perhaps there is a somewhat plaintive note here: at this time Hezekiah did not yet have a son.

Verse 20. Bringing this psalm to a well-rounded conclusion, the author sums up God's entire attitude openly displayed in his own life: "The Lord is minded to save me." I may need help in many a situation in life. The Lord is always ready to give it according to his great wisdom. With such a God watching over me, who can question the validity of the resolution now expressed: "Therefore we will sing to stringed instruments all the days of my life at the house of the Lord." No regal plural here in the "we." The circle of his believing friends who feel as keenly as he does the mercy of the Lord, will blend their praise with his, and that as long as life lasts, and besides in public worship at the house of the Lord.

This last statement in no sense makes the impression of being some later liturgical addition from some editor's pen. *Begrich* very properly calls it, "a genuine conclusion and confession."

3. A Few Circumstances Attendant upon the Incident (vv. 21-22)

38:21-22 21. And Isaiah said: "Let them take a poultice of figs and let them apply it to the boil that he may recover." 22. And Hezekiah said: "What is the sign that I shall go up to the house of the Lord?"

Verse 21. It may well be that we are justified in evaluating the sequence of material in this chapter as follows: After the promise to Hezekiah that he will recover, the psalm of Hezekiah ranked first in importance. It was a true portrayal of the deep experience through which the king had lived. This having been recorded, there remained a detail or two that still needed to be added. The first of these dtails was that a remedy had been employed by the prophet to effect the cure involved. This remedy was "a poultice of figs" which had been applied at the prophet's own suggestion. The use of a remedy does not stand in conflict with the miraculous nature of the cure.

Verse 22. Then also (v. 22) an interesting detail was involved. The sign, referred to above (v. 7), had come in answer to the inquiry by Hezekiah himself; the king virtually asked that some token of assurance be given him. The writer had failed to indicate this above. He adds it now as a kind of afterthought. And this writer could have been Isaiah himself.

Notes

Verse 3. The sign of the accusative (*'eth*) in this case introduces as object the entire clause that follows. See *GK* 157 c and *KS* 384 e.

Verse 5. It is II Kings 20:4 which mentions that Isaiah had not yet gotten any farther than the "middle city," using for city the word *ha'ir*. The *Keri* and some manuscripts suggest that *chatser* should be read — in Hebrew these two words are much more nearly alike. The latter word means "court." It is also quite likely that for the imperfect *yosiph*, the participle *yoseph* should be read. *GK* 50 e; *KS* 344 o.

Verse 9. For the more vague *mikhtabh*, *mikhtam* could be read, the latter appearing in the heading of a number of psalms. But as *BDB* suggests this word is also of uncertain meaning, although *KW* suggests the meaning of *Sinngedicht*, or a "mystery poem," that is, a poem dealing with a problematic issue. The change, however, practically results only in substituting one problem for another. In the last three words of the verse the construction begins with an absolute infinitive and veers over into a finite verb construction, a common procedure. See *KS* 413 d.

Verse 11. The verse closes with the words "inhabitants of *chadhel*." This last word could mean "cessation" or even refer to Sheol. Eight manuscripts and the *Targum* read, by transferring two consonants, *chaledh*, which does mean "world." The latter reading would appear to deserve the preference.

Verse 12. The Hebrew reads "is removed, is taken" omitting the "and" between synonyms. *KS* 370 f. On the form *ro'i*, according to the versions, an *m* should be added, "shepherds" for "my shepherd," which latter form hardly makes sense.

Verse 14. The Hebrew has "crane" practically in apposition to "swallow," omitting the "or" of our translation. It could be that the word was inserted because of the uncertainty about the meaning of *sus* ("swallow"). The second ("crane") could be a gloss.

Verse 16. The word *yichyu* ("they live") is a clear case of the use of the third person plural for the indefinite "men." *KS* 324 g.

Verse 18. The negative *lo'* reaches over with its negative force into the following clause. *KS* 352 u; *GK* 152 z.

Verse 20. The *le* before *hoshi'eni* expresses an interest in something (*KS* 399 y). Therefore we translated "The Lord is minded to save me."

Chapter XXXIX

D. THE INCIDENT OF THE MESSENGERS FROM BABYLON (Chap. 39)

The time-issue in these last four chapters is not of great moment, for though Chap. 36 has an exact dating, obviously both Chaps. 38 and 39 are vague in their timesetting. Some indications as to how these items are to be arranged chronologically have been given. Here we merely add that the incident involved in this chapter takes us back prior to the time of 701 B.C., because according to Chap. 36, which played in the fourteenth year of King Hezekiah and tells of the heavy tribute that Judah's king had to pay to Sennacherib at least according to II Kings 18:14-16, it must be observed that our chapter plays in a time when the resources of the kingdom have not yet been dimished, for the king is able to display some measure of wealth to the emissaries from Babylon. So Chap. 39 perhaps might be dated at about 703.

In the interest of historical completeness we may yet draw attention to the fact that, as in II Chron. 32:31, one purpose of the coming of the ambassadors to Jerusalem was to make inquiry about the sun-dial incident (38:8), for being close students of astronomy, the Babylonians will have been attracted by the reports that had reached their ears concerning it.

But a certain difficulty must first be removed in approaching this chapter. According to 21:1-10 Babylon is to fall. In our chapter *Judah* is to fall and Babylon is to stand. However, both points of view may be considered as feasible. In our chapter Jerusalem will fall first and there is a Babylonian Captivity to be faced. Chapter 21 looks a bit farther and indicates that after Babylon has accomplished its mission of overthrowing Jerusalem, she herself will ultimately be overthrown. This sequence as such is not expressly indicated but may be very reasonably assumed.

Furthermore it is not expressly stated but implied that the

592

purpose of the coming of the Babylonian envoys was to prepare the way for some sort of Babylonian-Judean alliance.
On the surface it was a courtesy from one king to another.
A bid for closer cooperation against the common foe, Assyria,
is certainly involved, as practically all writers on the subject
agree. That ambassadors were going back and forth between
nations is made clear from the fact that at least two other
instances appear in the chapters studied thus far — 14:28ff. —
which involves the thought that emissaries had come to Jerusalem from Philistaea, and Chap. 18, which goes on the assumption that Ethiopian messengers were to be seen in the
Holy City in the prophet's days.

Then it should be noted that the general character of the
chapter before us is that it brings to a sort of conclusion
words of doom on a given subject. Micah brings his words
on the relation of Judah and Babylon to a head in 3:12 and
4:9ff., speaking also in terms of a Babylonian Captivity. It
should be remembered that Micah and Isaiah were contemporaries.

One word of caution is in order at this point. The one
thing that Hezekiah did according to this chapter by no
means should be regarded as the one and only cause of the
great disaster that befell king and people. Nor should we
suppose that the chapter is trying to say that the nation must
suffer for the sin of the king. Many are the sins of which
Judah and her kings were guilty. This last one made the
cup of her iniquity full; and though the sin is clearly that of
the king, it, no doubt, reflected an attitude that was shared
by the nation as a whole. At the same time it illustrates
how the good resolutions that came into the king's heart
upon his recovery from illness were all too readily annulled at the appearance of almost the first temptation that
crossed his path. *Luther* aptly remarks that the chapter is
directed against "that horrible beast called presumption."

The chapter may be outlined as follows:

1. Arrival of a Delegation of Babylonians and Hezekiah's
   Reprehensible Display of Resources (vv. 1-2)
2. Isaiah's Cross-examination of Hezekiah (vv. 3-4)

3. Isaiah's Announcement of Doom upon the King's House (vv. 5-8)

1. Arrival of a Delegation of Babylonians and Hezekiah's Reprehensible Display of Resources (vv. 1-2)

39:1-2 1. At that time Merodach-baladan, the son of Baladan, king of Babylon, sent a letter and a present to Hezekiah; for he had heard that he had been sick and had recovered. 2. And Hezekiah was glad over this and showed them his treasure house, the silver and the gold, and the spice and the fine oil; his whole armory, and all that was to be found in his storehouses. There was not a thing that Hezekiah did not show them in his house and in all his kingdom.

Verse 1. In this case "at that time" merely means a reasonable time after Hezekiah's recovery. The Babylonian king mentioned is Merodach-baladan, the son of Baladan. Baladan himself has not been identified from any other available source any further than that he was the father of the son mentioned. But Merodach-baladan himself is known to have reigned over Babylon twice, from 721-709 B.C. and for a short term of six to nine months in 705. This allows for the possibility that the event here recorded took place in 705. But to send letters of congratulations and presents to monarchs who had recovered is a custom of which we have ample evidence in history already in times of old. It seems quite obvious from the sequel of events that there was a further diplomatic objective behind these congratulatory tokens of good will, as already indicated. The silence with regard to this factor may indeed agree with the actual course of events. Nothing may have been said by the envoys about alliances and treaties. These purposes Hezekiah could detect only too readily. That a world-power so prominent as Babylon should show such kindly interest in so small a nation as Judah, must, on the very face of it, have proved quite flattering. Hezekiah caught the point, and acts accordingly.

Verse 2. The king of Judah may also have observed a discreet silence about the veiled purposes involved. But his actions spoke louder than words. They said in effect: If you seek military alliance with us against the Assyrians, we are not a weak and insignificant ally; we have resources; we can lend substantial aid. So first of all Hezekiah "was glad" to be treated as a potential ally, "and showed him his treasure house." We are told (II Chron. 32:27-29) that a good bit of the wealth of the kingdom was gained from trade with the Arabians. As a rule the Scriptures regard such items as of secondary importance and barely mention them. At least "the spices and the fine oil" may have come from this source. The "armory" was the repository of weapons. The "treasure house" contained such things as usually accumulated in such a storage. From the last remark that "there was not a thing that Hezekiah did not show them in his house and in all his kingdom," we get the feeling that this display was made in a somewhat boastful spirit. At the same time we cannot but have some misgivings about revealing how great the resources of the kingdom were. All nations are potential enemies or they are desirous of acquiring the wealth of other nations.

2. Isaiah's Cross-examination of Hezekiah (vv. 3-4)

39:3-4 3. And Isaiah the prophet came to king Hezekiah and said to him: "What did these men say and from whence did they come to you?" And Hezekiah said: "They came to me from a distant land, from Babylon." 4. Then he said: "What did they see in your house?" And Hezekiah said: "All that is in my house have they seen; there was nothing in my treasures that I did not show them."

Verse 3. When Isaiah is here designated as "the prophet" it implies that he spoke, not merely as a friend interested in what had transpired but in his official capacity as a called prophet of the Lord. He would seem to have appeared on the scene very shortly after the envoys had departed. He asked three questions of the king. It is significant that the first question was not answered — "What did these men say?" Hezekiah does display a certain naive pride in the fact that ambassadors had come from afar, from Babylon. It was not merely a delegation from some petty neighboring tribe.

Verse 4. The next question seems to carry an implied rebuke over the king's indiscretion: "What did they see in
your house?" The thought implied is: Is it wise to lay bare
the complete measure of your resources to a potential enemy? Still elated over the flattery connected with the visit,
the king fails to hear the indirect rebuke and blurts out that
there was nothing of his resources that he did not show these
envoys.

3. Isaiah's Announcement of Doom upon the King's House (vv. 5-8)

39:5-8 5. Then Isaiah said to Hezekiah: "Hear the word of the
Lord of hosts: 6. 'Behold, days are coming, when all that is
in your house, and that your fathers stored up till this day, shall be
carried away to Babylon. Nothing shall be left,' says the Lord.
7. 'And some of your sons who shall be born to you, whom
you shall beget, men will take, and they shall become eunuchs in
the palace of the king of Babylon.'" 8. And Hezekiah said to
Isaiah: "Good is the word of the Lord which you have spoken."
He thought namely: "There will be peace and stability in my
days."

Verse 5. In the background of Isaiah's pronouncement
stands the ghost of alliances, an involvement against which
the prophet had inveighed time and again, as appears from
30:1ff. and 31:1ff., where, however, alliance with Egypt was
denounced. The issue is the same. Doom is therefore pronounced upon Hezekiah as it formerly had been spoken
against Ahaz (8:5-8). The word before us is a typical word
of prophecy and of doom in particular, concise, brief, and
easily remembered. We have more than keen political insight
on the part of the prophet. He speaks with authority: "Hear
the word of the Lord of hosts."

Verse 6. The punishment fits the crime. The king had
made a boastful display of all the treasure of his house.
This same treasure that Hezekiah and his fathers had accumulated "shall be carried away to Babylon — this last word
is emphatic by its position in the sentence. To show how
total the judgment will be, he adds: "Nothing shall be left."
It will be noted that the sin that had been committed was
not defined. The king and the prophet both knew what it
was. The king's conscience clearly told him.

Verse 7. It will be noted from this point on that as further details are given, nothing is said about a possible deportation of the nation, the people of Judah. For the present: the sin was the king's; the punishment befalls the king and his house. Only one item is specified: sons of his, whom he himself had begotten, would be carried away to this famed Babylon to be "eunuchs in the palace of the king of Babylon." Daniel 1:3 gives a bit of sidelight on the fulfilment of this threat. We should be careful to note that, though Assyria was the world-power that threatened Judah at the time, Assyria is by-passed in this oracle. For the prophet already clearly foresees that Assyria's doom is also sealed and that she will be replaced by Babylon as dominant empire.

Verse 8. It almost seems as though when the king calls this word of the Lord "good," he means that it is far less severe than he now felt he deserved. In a chastened spirit he felt that the punishment to be inflicted could serve a good purpose. He certainly accepts the divine verdict with humility. He also drew the conclusion that since it was said that these things should befall his sons, the doom would not yet be ripe in his own day. This latter thought he expresses in the words, "There will be peace and stability in my days." To criticize the king sharply for this word, as though it carried the connotation, *Après nous le déluge*, is neither right nor kind. Hezekiah bows under the mighty hand of God. It even seems right to interpret the word spoken as giving evidence of repentance. Some have rightly spoken of "childlike humility" as manifested by this utterance. It certainly does not express "the acme of selfishness," to be glad that a calamity is at least deferred, and will strike the next generation and not the present one. Analogies are found in two other cases — I Kings 21:20f. (Ahab) and II Kings 22:18ff. (Josiah).

Notes

Verse 1. If in II Kings 20:12 Merodach's name is written Berodach, that is obviously a copyist's error.

Verse 2. The last word of the verse ("kingdom" perhaps should be translated something like "administration" (*Verwaltung*), as is the case in 22:21. For it is not too likely that Hezekiah took the Babylonian envoys on a tour throughout the kingdom.

Verse 3. The verb *yabho'u* ("they have come") is a case where the verb is separated from the *waw* conversive, but therefore still is to be translated as belonging to the past.

Verse 6. The clause "when all that is in your house" is a clear case of coordination of clauses in Hebrew, where the English demands a subordinate clause (*KS* 361 c).

Verse 8. The *ki* before *yihyeh* is an instance of the *ki recitativum* (see *BDB* p. 471, 1 b).

Exposition of

I S A I A H
Volume II
Chapters 40—66

Exposition of

ISAIAH
Volume II
Chapters 40 – 66

INTRODUCTION

Introduction

No one questions that the second half of this book commonly designated "Isaiah" begins at this point. Questions of authorship and composition have been sufficiently discussed in the Introduction in the first volume, so that we may address ourselves to the exposition of the chapters as such. We merely recall in passing that we still consider the possibility of unit-authorship of the entire book by the prophet Isaiah himself to be a reasonable and therefore tenable position.

Many are the outlines that have been proposed for these chapters. Almost each one of those proposed has its merits. We have found those of the character of *von Orelli's* as helpful as any. This writer suggests that Chaps. 40-48 deal with the Lord's measures for the Deliverance of his people; Chaps. 49-57 center attention of the Lord's Agent for the achieving of this work; and Chaps. 58-66 treat of the Consummation of the Lord's salvation.

We are not claiming that a close-knit sequence of thought is to be traced through each chapter. The logical sequence is not always expressed, but there is so obvious a measure of coherence that, though the case may be worded differently at times, the basic progression of thought is not hard to discover.

The material of the second part of Isaiah obviously implies that the Exile of the children of Judah has taken place: it has run on for decades. In fact its termination is about to take place. This fact is most clearly to be observed in Chap. 1.

Just about every author presents his own outline for the contents of these chapters. We offer ours as just one more attempt to confine the rich material of the chapters within the confines of a more or less logical outline.

DETAILED OUTLINE

I. THE SECOND PART OF ISAIAH (chaps. 40–55)

A. Judah's Impending Deliverance from Captivity and the Great God Who Brings It About (chap. 40)

1. Judah's Impending Deliverance from Captivity (vv. 1-11)
    a. The Theme: Comfort for God's Afflicted People — the Restoration from Babylonian Captivity (vv. 1-2)
    b. A Call to Make Ready the Way for the Lord (vv. 3-5)
    c. The Frailty of Man and the Enduring Character of God's Word (vv. 6-8)
    d. Zion's Proclamation: God Has Come to Her (vv. 9-11)
2. The Great God Who Brings This About (the incomparable greatness of the Lord) (vv. 12-31)
    a. Over Against the World He Has Created (vv. 12-14)
    b. Over Against the Nations of the Earth (vv. 15-17)
    c. In Contrast to the Vain Idols (vv. 18-20)
    d. In Contrast to the Mighty of the Earth (vv. 21-24)
    e. God's Masterful Control of the Stars (vv. 25-27)
    f. The Lord, the Source of All Power (vv. 28-31)

B. A Court-trial of the Nations and Their Gods (chap. 41)

1. A Summons to the Coastlands to Test the Power of Their Gods: Can Their Gods Bring up a Cyrus on the Scene as Yahweh Did? (vv. 1-4)
2. The Consternation of the Coastlands at the Rise of Cyrus, Manifested by the Manufacture of New Idols (vv. 5-7)
3. God's Reassurance to Israel That She Has Not Been Cast Off (vv. 8-10)

THE SECOND PART
OF ISAIAH

Chapter XL

A. JUDAH'S IMPENDING DELIVERANCE FROM CAPTIVITY AND THE GREAT GOD WHO BRINGS IT ABOUT (Chap. 40)

Many very suggestive titles for this chapter have been offered. Delitzsch gives the caption: "The Word of Comfort and the God of Comfort." von Orelli sets forth in the form of a statement: "Let Zion take comfort for her Mighty Lord draws near." We have chosen to capture what we deem the essence of the chapter in the heading: Judah's Impending Deliverance from Captivity and the Great God Who Brings It About.

As to form, this section is commonly rated as a modified "herald's-message" (*Botenspruch*). Before this type of terminology was in vogue, *G. A. Smith* had already labelled the piece as "The Four Herald Voices." There is a certain vagueness and indefiniteness about these beautiful words as far as the possible speaker of them and as far as the recipient of them is concerned. Four significant voices of messages sound sweetly and meaningfully on the ear. Present-day exegesis has tried to relieve this vagueness first by discovering a location from which the speaker proclaims his message. It is now quite commonly accepted that the setting for these words must be that heavenly council from which messages or courses of action are known to have emanated in times past, namely, the heavenly council of none less than Yahweh himself. Instances where this council may be referred to are Isa. 6:1 f.; Jer. 23:22; and I Kings 22:19. Some would add passages like Gen. 1:26 ff. We regard these passages for the most part as figures of speech by which, in a colorful way, the thought is brought home that certain decisions are the result of the careful planning of the Almighty. But already in Gen 1:26 ff. it may very reasonably be doubted whether the Scriptural statement aims to convey the impression that any one may serve as counsellor for the Great Lord in any of the works that he does. In Chap. 40 of Isaiah in particular, vv. 13 and 14 clash very directly with the very possibility of the Lord's ever seeking any counsel for the great tasks that he undertakes. It must be admitted that the material for construing a complete heavenly council as a session is hardly available in this chapter.

Another attempt to make what is intentionally left indefinite more precise and concrete: it is in our day commonly being suggested that the opening verses of Chap. 40 are a record of the call and commissioning of II Isaiah. This approach seems to grow out of the uneasiness felt over the fact that the so-called Deutero-Isaiah is an entirely anonymous figure and this anonymity is disturbing. But no one person stands out as recipient of the message to be spoken and so the whole of this approach rests on very fragile foundations.

A far more suggestive and unimpeachable approach in our day merits very serious consideration, and that is the observation that the whole chapter directs its glance to the Lord himself as the only one who can restore Israel and give her help. The material of this chapter is God-centered, not man-centered or problem-centered, as v. 9 puts it: "Behold your God."

It should also be noted that the tone of this chapter is rather at variance with the note so commonly sounded by the prophets of old. Very often these prophets were heralds of doom. If they did offer a brighter outlook for the future that outlook was directed to the good things that lay far in the future, in the final consummation of all things, in the perfection that God would bring as the climax of the Messianic Age. But this prophet offers the sweetest words of comfort for the time immediately impending.

1. Judah's Impending Deliverance from Captivity (vv. 1-11)

a. The Theme: Comfort for God's Afflicted Peo-

ple — the Restoration from Babylonian Cap-
tivity (vv. 1-2)

40:1-2 1. Comfort, O comfort my people, says your God.
2. Speak kindly to Jerusalem and proclaim to her
that her term of service is finished,
that her guilt is pardoned,
that she has received from the Lord's hand ample punishment for
all her sins.

Verse 1. This verse presents the theme of the book from
Chaps. 40-66; at the same time it presents the theme of this
particular chapter. Its abruptness is startling, and in a sense
annoying by its vagueness. Who is to be thus addressed appears clearly from v. 2. But there is no explicit indication as
to who is to administer this comfort. Apparently this vagueness is intentional. Prophets were not usually commissioned
in such vague terms. If priests were to be the speakers, nothing in the text points in this direction. Being so general a
statement it is best left in as general a form as possible. Anyone who catches the message that God would have comfort
spoken to his people should spread the good news. The time
has come to pass on the good word that comfort is at hand.
That something very specific is after all involved develops as
the reader moves on from step to step. It becomes increasingly apparent that the comfort to be offered is the good
news that restoration from Babylonian Captivity is about to
take place. This is exactly what the next verse conveys. For
the present let only this be added: The verb-form at this
point indicates that the Lord would have this comfort reiterated over and over again till finally the unbelieving and
doubting heart begins to accept it as fully determined in the
counsels of God. The repetition of the verb here, as often,
spells urgency. The help stands ready at the door.
Verse 2. The comfort involved is so rich that it takes a
number of statements to unfold the fullness of what is implied. It may be paraphrased: "Speak kindly to Jerusalem."
The expression involved is almost untranslatable. It means to
lay something tenderly close to the heart of another (cf.

Hos. 2:14). From this point on, more and more, terms like "Zion" and "Jerusalem" stand as synonymns for the holy people of God, the true believers in Israel. Like a gentle balm this message cools and soothes the troubled heart.

Or the message to be spoken may be paraphrased: "Proclaim to her that her service is finished." Literally the statement really runs as *KJ* has it, "that her warfare is accomplished." That means, however, that the harsh rigors of service on the field of battle are at an end. Nothing other than the hardships of the Captivity is meant by these words. The term of conscription is over; let her relax.

Or the message may be paraphrased: "her guilt is pardoned." Not every affliction is immediately to be traced back to sin as its source but, more commonly by far than not, this is the case. When Captivity struck Jerusalem it was for the obvious sins of the nation as the prophets had abundantly told. In sin lies the deepest and most virulent root of the evils that befall men. An obvious prerequisite is implied in all this. God does not pardon the impenitent. Therefore a preceding repentance must have been shaping up. In fact this matter of forgiveness is of such moment that another statement deals with it at greater length from another point of view: "she has received from the Lord's hands ample punishment for all her sins." "Punishment" from God is in the forefront of this statement. It had to be bestowed in full measure for the sin had gone deep and had been of long standing. But in so far as a correspondence exists between guilt and punishment, in this instance at least all the needs of the case had been fully met; "ample" punishment has been visited upon the heads of the guilty. Who other than the Almighty can determine whether all the needs of a given case have been adequately met? As one commentator puts it: her guilt has been "sufficiently expiated." — "Ample" is better than "double" (*KJ* and *RSV*).

b. A Call to Make Ready the Way for the Lord (vv. 3-5)

40:3-5 3. A voice is heard making a proclamation:
"Make ready a way for the Lord in the wilderness;
make a straight highway in the desert for our God;
4. Every valley should be filled in,
and every mountain and hill should be levelled off;
and the steep ground should be made level country,
and rugged heights a plain.
5. Then shall the glory of the Lord be revealed,
and all flesh shall see it together.
For the mouth of the Lord has so said."

Verse 3. Who is making the proclamation here referred
to? Answer: It does not matter, and therefore the speaker
is not identified. To say, it is to be done by hermits, introduces an utterly extraneous thought, which is not suggested
by anything in the text. To claim it is angels, is an equally
unsupported guess. The message as such claims attention,
not the one who speaks it. Preparations are to be made; a
way is to be gotten ready. Everything depends on the basic
approach here used. Who is to use the way that is to be prepared? Answer: the Lord himself. In that sense it is "the
way of the Lord." At this point nothing is more helpful than
to recall some thoughts that Ezekiel presented rather strongly
in his day. Comparing the following passages from this
prophet — 10:18, 19; 11:23; and 43:1-3 — it becomes apparent that where once the Holy City and the Temple had
been the dwelling place of the Lord, finally there came a
time, before the Captivity of the city, when the Lord withdrew from the holy place; he abandoned the city that he had
so highly honored. Ezekiel sees the glory of the Lord depart
and vanish out into the desert lands of the east. That state of
affairs prevailed during the entire period of the Captivity
(587-538 B.C.). Now says the prophet, a new day is dawning; God will again take up his habitation among his people.
If that be so, his people should give tokens of their appreciation and put things in readiness. In typical Oriental
fashion they are even to smooth the way for their king. Since
he went into the wilderness, from the wilderness he will
again come. Therefore even a highway should be made

ready for him. We must therefore abandon suggestions such as: This highway is for the children of Israel to travel on as they emerge from Captivity. But we must hold fast, as has now been abundantly shown by many writers, that the terminology of the Exodus pervades these chapters, especially the thought that the Lord is on the march through the wilderness, guiding the destinies of his people.

Verse 4. Of course, the language is a bit exuberant. With road-building in the state that it was among Oriental nations of those days, even the picture involved does not really think in terms of having all these preparations done according to letter of this pronouncement. But surely this much is meant: Make preparations for this monarch that are in keeping with the honor that he confers upon you by coming as he does: fill in valleys; level off mountains; make steep ground level; make rugged spots smooth. This is what you "should" do. In this sense the "shall" of our versions is meant (e.g., "shall be lifted up," etc.). This is an obligation that grows out of the dignity that God would bestow upon his people by coming to dwell among them again. In a general way all this is to be interpreted spiritually. The nation is to remove every spiritual barrier that might hinder the coming of their God. But that does not mean that each term ("valley," "mountain" etc.) is to be explicitly related to some form of spiritual block that lies in the way. The picture as a whole describes a situation as a whole.

Verse 5. If Israel properly prepares to receive its Lord, he will come. But this coming is here again spoken of in the terminology of the Exodus days. Then, when God appeared among his people it was often said: "And the glory of the Lord was revealed," as Exod. 16:7, 10; 24:15, etc. indicates. So here: "Then shall the glory of the Lord be displayed," means: The Lord will appear to you as in days of old. This need not mean an appearing which is physically visible. God's glory may be seen by the eyes of faith as well as by the physical eye. But the fact that the Lord has again taken an active part in the affairs of his people will be obvious to all who give any thought to what is happening to Israel. In other words, "all flesh together shall see it." Even the eyes of the unenlightened could not help but see that what happened to Israel in her Return from Captivity had to be a divine accomplishment. The heathen were made to marvel over the unique power of the Lord of Israel. With solemn assurance this fact is underscored by the concluding remark, "for the mouth of the Lord has so said." God is predicting Israel's deliverance. This deliverance must surely come to pass.

c. The Frailty of Man and the Enduring Character of God's Word (vv. 6-8)

40:6-8 6. A voice is heard saying: "Call out!"
Then some one said: "What shall I call out?"
"All flesh is grass,
and all its beauty like the flower of the field.
7. The grass withers, the flower fades,
when the breath of the Lord blows upon it.
Surely the people is grass.
8. The grass withers, the flower fades;
but the Word of our God shall stand forever."

Verse 6. Another voice! No connection between this one and the one preceding is indicated. But a deep underlying logic is nevertheless easily discernible. With the emphasis on how frail man really is and how enduring the Word of God, by contrast, must we not conclude that some connection like the following is being indicated? God's great work of Restoration of Israel has just been revealed. It is now being indicated that much as Israel might want to rebuild herself in her own strength — and who would not want a share in the achievement of great things? — human strength is too utterly inadequate a thing to achieve results like these. Only the powerful, creative Word of the Lord can suffice for such an achievement. This double truth is what this verse wants to have "called out." This verb is one that is frequently used for strong, emphatic prophetic proclamation. The brief dialogue indicates also how man may be at a loss as to what proclamation to stress particularly in these stirring times. "All flesh" after the analogy of Gen. 6:13, must refer to all forms of existence, to all creatures that live. But they are insufficient for an emergency like the present, for the word "flesh" already by itself connotes weakness in the Old Testament. This thought is further underscored by the assertion that "all flesh is grass." Grass came out beautifully in spring in the Holy Land and after a few weeks withered and shrivelled. So is man with his human strength. It demands greater resources than these to build in a lasting way in the kingdom of God. Passages like 37:27; Ps. 90:5; 103:15; and I Peter 1:24 f. convey the same thought of the inadequacy of man.

Verse 7. It takes nothing more than "the breath of the Lord" — we might say "any passing wind" — to bring about the quick withering of the grass and the fading of the flower. Now we have the measure of "the people," i.e., of mankind as a whole (cf. "people" used in the same sense in 42:5).

Verse 8. In solemn reiteration this thought is repeated. It falls on the ear with a certain mournful cadence. But the writer does not end on this note of weakness. He knows a power by the use of which eternal results can be achieved. That power is the Word of the Lord. Heaven and earth may pass away; not that Word. Trusting in that Word and using that Word, God's people can confidently face the future, which will bring for Israel results that are otherwise humanly impossible. We may aptly compare 55:8-11 at this point.

Summing up the three emphases that have thus far been set forth by this chapter, we learn first that comfort, hope of the nation's restoration, lies ready for Israel. But secondly she must remove all obstacles that sin has put into God's way, that is to say: She must repent. Then, thirdly, she must build not in, or on, her own strength but on the clear prophetic Word of the Lord. All of these are abiding truths that, for that matter, apply to every age and generation in the life of the church of God.

d. Zion's Proclamation: God Has Come to Her (vv. 9-11)

40:9-11 9. Get up on a high mountain, O Zion, heraldess;
raise your voice mightily, O Jerusalem, heraldess;
raise it, be not afraid;
say to the cities of Judah: "See, there is your God!"
10. Lo, the Lord comes as a mighty one,
and his arm rules for him.
Lo, his reward is with him,
and his recompense before him.
11. Like a shepherd he tends his flock,
and gathers the lambs in his arms,
and carries them in his bosom,
and gently leads those that are with young.

Verse 9. This is a sort of climax of the initial voices that have been heard. Put more abstractly, here is the last major emphasis for the day of Restoration.

The true believers among the people of God ("Zion") are to make known what their faith has grasped, the fact namely that God is graciously returning to his people, in fact, has returned. They are to publish these glad tidings throughout the whole land, i.e., "to the cities of Judah." If perhaps in the preceding verses, the setting was still the land of Captivity, now the scene is the Holy Land itself. That is a more satisfactory way of putting it than to say that it has shifted from heaven to earth. The message to be published is so momentous that Zion is bidden to go up into a high mountain in order that her voice may carry far and wide (cf. Judg. 9:7). The same behest is given to Jerusalem, which here apparently is used as substitute for Judah, since the term Jerusalem is used more than thirty times in these chapters for Judah. In fact, all the members of the nation are mutually to reassure one another of the good news that is breaking. All timidity about the future is to be banished — "be not afraid." This again is one of the key-notes of the message for a dispirited people, for it keeps recurring (cf. 41:10, 13, 14; 43:5; 44:2; 51:7; 54:4). When the title "heraldess" is used with Zion and Jerusalem, it is a term that could well be translated "bearer of good tidings," and is used in the feminine, for women were commonly regarded as the ones that did most to spread abroad the message of victory (cf. I Sam. 18:7). Or it could be said that the feminine is induced by the fact that personifications of cities usually regard them as female figures. But the message, the message that is to be proclaimed is: "See, there is your God." The proclaimers are, as it were, to point directly to the one who has just appeared on the scene, and to exclaim: He is in your midst.

Verse 10. Two figures are used at this point to convey somewhat of an impression of what manner of God the Lord is under the circumstances here involved. First of all, he is a conquering hero, or a "mighty one." The same thought is expressed by the statement "his arm rules for him." That is to say: His strength prevails and gains the victory. But the statement now following adds a very significant thought. The "reward" or "recompense" that this conquering hero brings with him is nothing other than his people, whom he has regained as his own and delivered from the power of the enemy. Though it may seem that at this point we are after all conceding that the road to be prepared was for the use of the returning captives, that is not the case. The figure of the road to be prepared (vv. 3-4) has by this time been abandoned. The victor and those whom he has redeemed are on the scene.

Verse 11. As so often, the figure swiftly changes. Now it is the Shepherd who is approaching, a figure often used in the Old Testament to describe God's relation to his people (cf. Mic. 2:12; Jer. 31:10; Ezek. 34:11 ff.; Ps. 78:52; 80:1). His most tender care is reflected in the various activities that the Shepherd engages in for his flock: "he leads them" not drives them. He gathers the newly-born lambs in his arms and carries them in his bosom. And where mother-sheep are almost at the point of giving birth to their young, he takes especial care of them. These are the things that Zion is to publish throughout the cities of Judah. But she cannot pub-

lish them effectively unless she first appropriates them in
faith. On this positive note the initial Four Voices of this
book begin.

2. The Great God Who Brings These Things About (the Incomparable Greatness of the Lord) (vv. 12-31)

Israel's initial reaction to the great promises God had just
given may well be: These things can never come to pass; no
nation has ever returned from a captivity and survived; how
could we? More significantly now than even before, the
message directs attention to the Lord himself. If he be kept
in mind and truly believed, this all can come to pass. It is with
this in mind that the incomparable greatness of God is now
very emphatically set forth by the prophet.

a. Over Against the World He Has Created (vv. 12-14)

40:12-14 12. Who has measured the waters in the hollow of
his hand,
and determined the measure of heaven with a span,
and gathered the dust of the earth in a measure,
and weighed the mountains in scales and the hills in balances?
13. Who has determined the measure of the spirit of the Lord
or given him instruction as his counsellor?
14. With whom did he take counsel and let himself be instructed,
and who gave him instruction in the way of justice
and taught him knowledge and imparted to him deep insight?

Westermann very properly draws attention to a peculiarity
of the style of the prophet, the fact namely that at times the
prophet resorts to the use of a series of double questions (cf.
40:12, 18, 25, 27) or a series of double imperatives (51:9, 17;
52:1) to introduce new subjects and so ties them together
into a unity. *Westermann* rightly regards this as indicative
of the fact that the material in this part of the book was intentionally arranged as a major composition and does not
consist of a series of detached fragments, which have been
casually placed side by side.

Here the remark is in order that the meter is a bit difficult to determine for this section and for the rest of the chapter. The meter keeps changing. As to form, it may be admitted that we have here a sort of "hymnic monologue" (*Muilenburg*). That the language is highly impassioned must also be granted at the outset. Nature is explored repeatedly from different points of view, especially as being under the sovereign control of God. Where this occurs it must be observed that such an approach can be very effective. *Westermann* reminds us that vv. 12-31 constitute a *Disputationsrede*.

A number of questions are asked. Though there is some merit in the suggestion that they could be answered: "God only," the fact of the matter still is that the speaker is looking about on earth, so that the more appropriate answer would be: "No one among the children of men can do these things." But all the activities mentioned could be achieved with comparative ease by the Almighty.

Verse 12. Especially in this verse the idea of God's doing of mighty works with great ease is achieved by employing a number of vessels and containers for measuring, that are of comparatively trivial size: the hollow of the hand, the span, the measure (a few pecks), scales and balances. Yet the things referred to are vast: the waters, the heavens, the dust of the earth, the mountains and the hills.

Verse 13. Perhaps the "spirit of the Lord" is here being thought of as the powerful agent through which he does his creative work. So the question asked amounts to this: Is there anyone who can determine the extent of the creative power of God? Again the answer is: There is no one. Or for that matter, in the use of his divine power, who could have given him instruction or been his advisor? Answer: the same (cf. Rom. 11:34; I Cor. 2:16). God is quite self-sufficient and far above the capacities of mere mortal man.

Verse 14. The questions are still further piled up to show man's utter incapacity and God's illimitable ability. In a word, could God be conceived of as sitting down at any time with one of the children of men to solicit advice! The "way of

justice" which he alone administers is the just apportionment
of all things that fall under his administration. He always
deals with men as they fully deserve. "Knowledge" and "insight" are lastly mentioned as qualities which he also possesses
and so never stands in need of having anybody provide him
with needed facts. He alone sees through things and is able
to judge impartially on the basis of the full knowledge of all
facts. So looking abroad at the world that came from the
Creator's hands, there is no question about it that he is able
to regulate the affairs in it, affairs like the destiny of Israel.

b. *Over Against the Nations of the Earth (vv. 15-17)*

40:15-17 15. Lo, nations are like a drop of water dripping
from a bucket;
they are reckoned like fine dust on scales.
Lo, he lifts up the coastlands like a bit of dust.
16. Lebanon is not sufficient to provide the fuel,
nor the creatures found on it sufficient for a burnt-offering.
17. All the nations are as nothing before him;
they are reckoned as ciphers and a vacuum.

Verse 15. The area of investigation to determine the
power of the Almighty shifts from nature to history, the
history of the nations. This verse could be misunderstood.
But it surely does not mean that God cares nothing for the
nations. Rather, if their importance over against him is to
be measured, they are of very trivial account. In the forefront of consideration, though not specifically mentioned, is
Babylon, the power that could attempt to resist the Lord's
efforts to free his people from Captivity. But the figures
setting forth the comparative unimportance of the nations
over against God are very striking. Nations factually
amount to no more in his sight than does a mere drop running down the side of a bucket as a man draws water from a
well. Or they could be likened to the light dust that has
accumulated on the apothecary's scales, which dust he lightly
blows away before he starts weighing. In fact he could, if he

were so minded, even lift up "the coastlands" as a man picks
up a bit of earth. The coastlands include all the far-distant
areas around the Mediterranean Sea, however remote they
may be. For there is no geographical limit to the Lord's
power.

Verse 16. Thinking in vast terms geographically, the
writer brings in an illustration of a different sort to make his
point. Suppose one were to think in terms of cultus, especially in terms of a sacrifice actually worthy of a God as
great as Yahweh is. Taking all the vast timber values of the
famous Lebanon range for fuel, and laying upon it all the
creatures that inhabit these forests, one still would not have
constructed a sacrifice worthy of him. In an effort to speak
in terms of vastness, momentarily the writer passes by the
obvious fact that the wild beasts of the forest are not fit for
sacrifice in the worship of Yahweh. In its character, this
comparison is much in place and need not at all be regarded
as intruding into what is purely an issue of history (contra
Volz).

Verse 17. Coming back to the point already made — how
the nations rank in the sight of the majestic Lord of all —
the author offers a few more hyperboles. The nations are
"as nothing," "as ciphers and a vacuum." Not the value of
the human beings that make up the nations is under consideration; but the potential strength and importance of the nations when contrasted with the God of Israel.

c. *In Contrast to the Vain Idols (vv. 18-20)*

40:18-20 18. To whom then would you liken God,
    or what likeness is there that you could array over
against him?
19. An idol! The craftsman casts it;
the goldsmith overlays it with gold;
and a metal-worker decorates it with silver chains.
20. A man too poor for such a contribution chooses wood that
will not rot;
he selects for himself a skilful craftsman
to prepare an idol that will not totter.

Looking about him for further comparisons of powers that are ranked as great, the author comes to a field where the whole world of that time thought that the greatest powers of all were to be found — the field of idols. As has been suggested, this section is not primarily a polemic against idols; it is a positive setting forth of the omnipotence of God by way of contrast. Similar passages are to be found: 41:6 f.; 44:9-17; 45:16; 46:5-7. We have here a practical exposition of the commandment: "Thou shalt not make unto thee any graven image" (Exod. 2:4). It is as though the author said: There simply is no being that can in any wise even remotely compete with God, or that could be "likened" to him. Since in those days idolatry among the nations was very real and a major factor in their life, Isaiah can very aptly bring the famous images of well-known heathen gods into the picture. Note, he does not admire the beauty, and the skill of the sculptor who produced the image, as art-lovers might be wont to do in viewing such idol-images of old as have been recovered through the years. Biting sarcasm falls from his lips, that is, implied, not expressed, sarcasm. In reality the author merely gives a precise account of the process of manufacture of an idol.

Verse 19. Take any idol — it is the work of the craftsman who cast it. Here is not a case of God making man, but one of man making a god. A product of solid gold would be both too heavy and too expensive. So the quality of the product lies practically entirely in the option of the manufacturer. He constructs a basic structure which then the goldsmith overlays with gold-plating. The silver chains mentioned are very likely only ornamentations. They could be thought of being used to hold the image in place lest it fall. The product in any case is a manufactured god. If it be protested that the heathen well knew the distinction between gods and idols that represented these gods, it has been noted time and again that in practice this distinction fell away and the common worshipper regarded the image as though it were the god.

Verse 20. But then there is the case of a devotee of a god, who desires to make an image of his god but lacks the means for a more expensive production, he chooses a suitable piece of a type of wood that will not rot. He must engage a craftsman to do the job, a "skillful craftsman," lest the image appear unworthy of him whom it represents. Besides, it took some skill to prepare an image that would not totter. The point that is being made has gotten enough attention for the moment; the writer will come back to it later.

In striking contrast to Isaiah's description of the process of the manufacture of idol images stands an Accadian directive which instructs a workman how to prepare certain smaller idol images for a great impending idol festival of the New Year. Materials and procedures are indicated. The workmen took their task very seriously. The document in no wise senses that there might be something trivial and ridiculous about the whole procedure (cf. ANET, pp. 331 f.).

d. In Contrast to the Mighty of This Earth (vv. 21-24)

40:21-24 21. Don't you know? Can't you hear?
Has it not been told you from days of old?
Haven't you understood since the world was founded?
22. It is he that sits enthroned above the circle of the earth
so that its inhabitants are like grasshoppers.
It is he that spreads out the heavens like a veil
and stretches them out like a tent to dwell in.
23. It is he who makes dignitaries of no account
and renders the judges of the earth as nothing.
24. Hardly are they planted; hardly are they sown;
hardly has their stock taken root in the earth;
then he blows upon them and they wither,
and the storm carries them away as stubble.

Though at first it would appear in this section that the Lord as the great Creator is under consideration, this his creative work is only brought into the picture for the purpose of providing the background against which the *mighty of this earth* function. These mighty ones are being evaluated over against the Almighty.

Verse 21. A certain tone of impatience, and even of exasperation, appears to be struck here at first. The prophet is speaking of certain elementary truths concerning which there should really be no need that he instruct the people of God. The facts at stake are too basic, and have really been set forth in one form or another "from days of old." "Since the world was founded" they were common knowledge among the people of God. He means, of course, the frailty of the ones who are esteemed great among men on a purely earthly level. In passing, a few typical works of the Lord are mentioned to remind men of his greatness. He, for example, being as high as he is, "sits enthroned above the circle of the earth" so highly exalted, as it were, that when he looks down upon the children of men they "are like grasshoppers." This "circle of the earth" means the dome of the heavens. Or to use another approach, as a man might with infinite ease spread out a light veil, so it in days of old cost the Lord no more effort when he for the first time created and "spread out the heavens." Or still a third approach, as a man pitches a tent, with ease and in quick order, this being a common occupation among men, with the same ease the Lord spread out the heavens like a tent to dwell in.

Verse 23. This Lord, now, is able to deal with "dignitaries" and has dealt with them in times past in such a way that he makes them of "no account." They just vanish off the scene when he decides that their work is done. Or, for that matter, "the judges of the earth" become as nothing when they have accomplished what he has assigned for them. How often have the mighty fallen in the course of history!

Verse 24. In another powerful figure their vanishing is described. They are likened to plants, which have just scarcely been planted, or sown, or have just begun to take root, when, because he is done with them, the Almighty One blows upon them and before the hot blast of his mouth they first wither and then are carried away by the storm; and, to use another Biblical phrase, "the place thereof shall know them no more." How great must he be who disposes of earth's mightiest men with such consummate ease!

One further bit of groundwork has to be built in before the prophet can bring things to the desired conclusion.

e. *God's Masterful Control of the Stars (vv. 25-27)*

40:25-27 25. To whom then would you liken me
that I should really resemble him, says the Holy One?
26. Lift up your eyes on high and see:
Who created these?
He who brings forth the host of heaven by number,
and calls them all by name.
As a result of the greatness of his might
and the abundance of his strength
not a one of them is ever missing.
27. Why do you say, O Jacob, and speak, O Israel:
"My lot is hidden from the Lord
and my rights are disregarded by my God"?

Verse 25. The incomparable greatness of the Lord is still under consideration and now in the light of a realm which he alone controls. But this is introduced by a reminder that nothing has in the present investigation been found to be in any sense worthy of comparison with him or is in any sense actually like him.

Verse 26. One of the realms that is under his control is "the host of heaven." What makes this comparison all the more meaningful is the fact that especially in the land of the Babylonians, where the children of Israel had been in bondage, the heavenly bodies were regarded astrologically, as controlling the affairs of men, that transpired down here on earth. Their control of these affairs was absolute, far beyond that of the gods themselves. Not so in the religion of Israel. There they appeared first of all merely as part of the creation of God. "Who created these?" allows for only one answer: the God whom Israel worshipped. And as they once originated with him, so they forever remain under *his* control, his "who brings forth their host by number." The spectacle of the starry skies, night for night, is, figuratively speaking, nothing other than a case where the Almighty Maker of the universe brings them out as a shepherd brings forth his flock. Besides, the count is made, as it were, night for night, and the sum-total remains the same invariably. The figure may be regarded as blending into another one at this point: the Lord of this heavenly host is a shepherd, who calls forth these sheep of his, night for night, as the shepherd calls forth his sheep one by one out of the fold. As it were, in his astronomy he has them all named from the time when they were created and he may be thought of as remembering their name. It is not due to the laws of nature and their normal operation that the stars all appear nightly. It is rather the "result of the greatness of his might and the abundance of his strength" that "not a one of them is ever missing." The utmost simplicity of argument is blended with the greatest of insight in this illustration.

Verse 27. Now comes the point toward which this whole discussion has been moving since v. 12. With such a God as its Lord, how could Israel ever have ventured to *have misgivings* about God, whether he be able to control the destinies of his people. For that was practically what they did when they made complaints such as, "My lot is hidden from the Lord." When they said that they meant: God is not even aware of what is befalling me from day to day. The same was true when they uttered the complaint: "My rights are disregarded by my God." By that they meant: I have certain rights as nation, particularly in view of his election of Israel as his people; but my God disregards them. But with a certain impatience again the prophet challenges these statements, when he exclaims: "Why do you say, O Jacob and speak [thus], O Israel?" Littleness of faith, failure to think things through is the reason for your attitude, charges the prophet.

Much of what is written in the second part of Isaiah is deeply colored by the terminology of the Psalms, as *Westermann* abundantly indicates. "Hidden" (v. 27) is an indication

of this fact (see Ps. 13:1; 22:24; 27:9; 30:7; 44:24; 69:17;
88:14; 102:2; 104:29; 143:7). "Rights" — i.e., "vindication"
or "justice" — is another such a word (cf. Ps. 26:1; 35:23;
37:6; 140:12; 146:7). In its distress during the Captivity days
Israel was finding expression for its distress of soul in the vocabulary of the well-known Psalms.

f. The Lord, the Source of All Power (vv. 28-31)

40:28-31 28. Have you not known, have you not heard?
The eternal God, the Lord, the Creator even of the
ends of the earth, does not faint or grow weary;
his insight is unfathomable.
29. He gives power to the faint;
for them that lack might he increases strength.
30. Even youths may faint and grow weary;
young men may utterly totter.
31. But they that wait for the Lord shall renew their strength;
they shall mount up with wings like eagles;
they shall run and not be weary;
they shall walk and not grow faint.

Verse 28. Again a few questions marked by a justifiable,
impatience; "Have you not known, have you not heard?"
These truths, such as, the Lord is the source of all strength,
have been proclaimed as long as Israel has been God's people.
The prophet makes his starting point, as he presses home his
argument, the concept of God as *Creator*. Should not he
that made the world and what is in it, be able to control his
creation? Besides, he is "eternal." Besides, he has created the
"ends of the earth." There is a vastness about the reach of
his power that is downright overwhelming. It is simply unthinkable with reference to him that he should "faint or
grow weary," especially in regard to the project that he has
in hand. Nor, for that matter, is there lack of insight with
regard to the issues that confront him; for "his insight is unfathomable."

Verse 29. The truth of the matter is really the very opposite. He not only does not lack strength. He supplies it,
supplies every bit of strength that man may ever need or has
needed.

Verse 30. A good comparison is the youth of the nation, these beings that seem so full of energy and so tireless at times. For contrasted with the Lord, they too will "faint and grow weary" from time to time. They may even "utterly totter."

Verse 31. Now comes the practical thought: How may men come to have a share in this boundless power of the Lord? They shall have it if they will learn to "wait for the Lord." This expression is merely a synonym for *faith*, and is one of the "cardinal expressions in the Old Testament" for this highly to be desired attribute (see 49:23; Ps. 25:8; 33: 20). It means to lean heavily on the Lord for strength and to bide his time till it comes. Such persons will have the experience that "they shall mount up with wings like eagles" above the difficulties they encounter. For that matter they shall even be able to go on miraculously, if need be, running and not wearying, walking and not growing faint. Here Israel's course and source of strength is clearly portrayed in an utterance of surpassing faith and insight.

Notes

Verse 1.   The verb *yo'mar* is perhaps best taken as the imperfect of continuing action. See *GK* 107 f.

Verse 2.   The three *ki* that appear in this verse, standing, as they do in a sort of series, should be translated alike, as "that," introducing the indirect discourse.

The noun *kipbláyim* does mean "double," but in this case it is not to be construed in the sense of careful computation, exactly twice as much as should be, for that would involve a criticism of God and his dealings. It should therefore be taken in a loose sense, perhaps as "ample."

Verse 3.   The opening word *qol* has been very properly translated as "hark." See *GK*. 146 b.

The phrase "in the wilderness" can be joined with what precedes or with what follows. Either makes good sense. It may be intentionally ambiguous and be construed both ways.

Verse 6.   The verb *we'amar* is usually corrected into *wa'omer* ("and I said" for "and some one — impersonal use — said"). Such a correction is not necessary. The message counts, not the person.

Verse 9.   We have not translated the phrase *lakh*, for it is one of those untranslatable ethical datives (*KS* 35).

Verse 10. The *be* before *chazaq* is the so-called "beth of essence" (*GK* 119), telling not only what one is like but what he actually is.

Verse 13. The *yodi'énnu* is one of the many imperfects that is in the imperfect because it is separated from the *waw* consecutive that really controls it. *KS* 368 h.

Verse 15. The phrase *middeli* is an instance of the use of a preposition instead of the construct state. *KS* 278 c.

Verse 18. We have here one of those peculiar constructions where a positive rhetorical question really has the force of a negative claim. *KS* 352 a.

The *mah* before *demuth* does not mean "what" but "what kind of." *KS* 69.

Between vv. 19 and 20 many commentators are persuaded that they should insert 41:6-7. This is a purely subjective opinion. The text makes perfectly good sense as it stands. The correction poses the question: How did the two verses of Chapter 41 slip from their anchorage into another chapter?

Verse 21. The noun *ro'sh* stands without article. This here makes it to be a sort of proper noun, "the absolute beginning." *KS* 294 f.

Verse 22. Gunkel has pointed out that the participles that appear here belong to the hymnic style of prophetic writings. They express that which is essential and abiding.

Verse 25. The "then" that we have inserted appears already in the *Septuagint*, and is at least logically quite in place.

Verse 29. The verb *yarbeh* is an instance of the construction where first the participle is used, then the finite verb. The same construction occurred in v. 26b.

Chapter XLI

B. A COURT-TRIAL OF THE NATIONS AND THEIR GODS (Chap. 41)

In the previous chapter Israel was addressed. In Chap. 41 the prophet addresses himself to the "coastlands," that is to the areas lying around the Mediterranean. In the previous chapter the incomparable greatness of God was strongly outlined; here the emphasis lies on the impotence of the idols. Besides this chapter is marked by a striking note of assurance on the part of a minority group, the children of Israel, who were thought of but lightly by the nations surrounding them, especially since the chapter thinks of this people in terms of a Captivity. A rather polemical note is sounded: the incapacity of the gods of the surrounding nations — they cannot begin to compare with the God of Israel.

The point of time to which the writer has transported himself is that period of history where Cyrus the Great was beginning to make great conquests and many nations were beginning to be alarmed at his success.

The whole chapter assumed more or less the form of a court-trial, as our heading indicates. It could be termed a kind of lawsuit. The Germans call it a *Rechtsstreit*, a literary form which appears rather commonly in the Old Testament. To state it a bit more accurately, it is, as G. A. Smith said, "loosely cast in the form of a Trial-at-Law," as Chap. 1 also is to an extent. The trial begins vv. 1-7. Then comes something in the nature of a digression, vv. 8-20. The trial is then resumed and summed up, vv. 21-29.

Some writers have pointed out that this situation takes us into the midst of the time when the Semitic era was coming to an end and the Persian era was taking its beginning.

1. A Summons to the Coastlands to Test the Power of Their Gods (vv. 1-4)

41:1-4 1. Listen to me in silence, O coastlands;
let the peoples pick up fresh strength.
Let them approach; then let them speak;
together let them draw near for a court-trial.
2. Who has stirred up from the east
one whom victory attends at every step?
He gives up nations before him,
so that he tramples kings under foot;
With his sword he makes them like dust;
like scattered chaff with his bow.
3. He pursues them [i.e., the kings], passes on safely,
by paths his feet have not trodden.
4. Who has wrought and done this?
He that calls the generations from the beginning,
I, Yahweh, the first and with the last, I am he.

Verse 1. This piece may be classed as a herald's call (*Heroldsruf*), except that in the first line, the sender of the herald himself speaks. It certainly is a divine pronouncement. It is addressed to the "coastlands." Since this special term refers to the irregular shores of the Mediterranean and beyond, it covers the West as over against the East of that day. But at this particular juncture in history the two outstanding leaders were Croesus of Lydia and Cyrus of Persia. The western nations had cast in their lot with Croesus. Yet in the divine purpose, Cyrus was the figure to which importance was to be attached. His importance is to be demonstrated to the western groups by this challenge. They particularly are being apprised of the fact that Cyrus is Yahweh's man of destiny. So they are being bidden to draw near in reverent silence into Yahweh's presence and listen to his instruction about the course history is taking. They are also encouraged to "pick up fresh strength," that is, as they recover from the shock of having stepped into the presence of the Most High God. Then they are to step still closer — "Let them approach." Already they are being spoken about, not spoken to, as they were in the opening address. The Lord is letting them feel a bit of the tremendous distance existing between them and him. They are then invited to speak, if they should have anything to say in the trial that is about to take place. They will be given a fair hearing. They are allowed to come as one huge group for this court-trial. All this is merely a figurative way of bringing home to them that some great issues have to be settled; a few basic facts have to be cleared up.

Verse 2. Now comes the issue that is at stake. Some one has appeared on the stage of history. For the present his approach is cloaked in a measure of secrecy. He is somewhat vague. The identification is far from clear. He is a person of mystery. All that is indicated for the present is that he has come from the East. As things develop, it becomes apparent that the East refers to Persia. The remarkable thing about him however is that he is one "whom victory attends at every step." Apparently there was but one person of whom this claim could be made at that time. This was Cyrus, the Persian. One after another of the nations fell before him. Yet such a claim is inaccurate since *Yahweh* was giving them up before him (cf. Josh. 10:12). This conqueror was virtually "trampling kings under foot." So little could men stand up against him that it is claimed that "his sword made them like dust;" his bow made them "like scattered chaff."

Verse 3. His career to date is further described as "pursuing" them, i.e., the kings of v. 2. The assumption is that he overtakes these kings whom he pursues, vanquishes them and then "passes on safely." He emerges from each battle unscathed. And as he passes on, it is "by paths his feet have not trodden." This statement is meant in the sense that he is always striking out into new territory; no opposition can stand before him. He does not have to retrace his steps.

These conquests of Cyrus are so important, especially for the children of Israel, that Isaiah comes back to this subject repeatedly. Cf. 44:28 and 45:1, where the conqueror is even mentioned by name; but cf. also 45:13; 46:11; 48:14-16. When it is claimed that Yahweh brought this king on the scene that is a claim analogous to the one of 10:5 and 15, where the Assyrian is described as a tool in Yahweh's hand.

Strangely at first glance it appears that in II Chron. 36:22 and Ezra 1:1, this word about Yahweh's bringing Cyrus on the stage of world-history seems to be attributed to Jeremiah. In fact what is ascribed to Jeremiah in these two passages is the fact of the restoration of Israel from captivity (see Jer. 25:11 ff.). The issue is not Cyrus' conquests.

Verse 4. But the main point at issue is not the coming of Cyrus as such, but the question who it was that brought Cyrus on the scene: "Who has wrought and done this?" i.e., who started this enterprise and finished it? That is, finished it as far as it has been finished to this day. The Lord himself gives the answer in terms of other things that may be attributed to him. First he describes himself as One who is wont to do even greater works than raising up one conqueror. For he is the one that "calls the generations from the beginning." It was he who brought generation after generation out upon the face of the earth, ever since generations have been appearing. Here "from the beginning" means from the very time of creation itself. So he further identifies himself and answers his own question by saying: "I, Yahweh, the first and with the last, I am he." Here he adds the claim that he not only brought the first and all other generations out upon the earth, but that he will also still be on the scene when the last generation that ever will appear puts in its appearance. It must be admitted that this last statement has a solemn dignity and serves admirably to close an effective answer. It is at the same time reminiscent of a similar divine utterance spoken with unusual emphasis, namely Exod. 3:13 ff.

2. The Consternation of the Coastlands at the Rise of Cyrus, Manifested by the Manufacture of New Idols (vv. 5-7)

41:5-7 5. The coastlands saw it and were afraid; the ends of the earth trembled; they drew near and came.
6. One helped the other

and said to his brother: "Have courage!"
7. The craftsman encouraged the goldsmith;
he that smooths with the hammer, him that pounded the anvil,
saying of the soldering: "It is good!"
and they fastened it with nails so that it should not sway.

Verse 5. The writer envisions what reaction the initial
successes of Cyrus produced way out in the western world.
He describes it all as having already taken place, so sure is it
to come to pass. When they noted the phenomenal success
of the opponent of King Croesus of Lydia, whom they
favored, they "were afraid; the ends of the earth trembled."
Panic seized the western world, even its remotest corners.
They begin first of all to congregate in order to map out
some course of action: "they drew near and came."

Verse 6. They are about to engage in concerted action in
one particular field of endeavor. The writer delays as long
as he can to identify what this field of activity will be, that
when it is named it may appear as the anticlimax that it actually is. Men are shown first of all as encouraging one another before the protective measure is undertaken. One says
to the other: "Have courage!" Some have rendered this
verb: "Cheer up!"

Verse 7. A momentary perplexity comes upon the reader
as he notes that a very particular class of men are being depicted as engaged in defensive projects. There is the "craftsman" — the word could also be translated "the ordinary
smith." He is speaking to the "goldsmith"; and besides, the
man who "smooths with the hammer" speaks to him "who
(pounds) the anvil"; and they are talking about soldering and
saying, in effect, You have made a good job of it. They have
fastened down something with nails "so that it should not
sway." Yet the objects made are not identified precisely.
What is this mysterious something on which these craftsmen
are working? Isaiah 40:19-20 gives us the needed clue. New
and better *idols* are being manufactured; perhaps even larger
ones. By such means the conquests of Cyrus are to be
stopped. Of course, here as so often, the image and the thing

it represents are practically being identified. So we could have said: the manufacture of new and better gods is their surest means of defense, it would seem. There is again a biting sarcasm behind what is here written. Very likely this was the best opposition that the coastlands had to offer at the prospect of the impending conquests of Cyrus.

3. God's Reassurance to Israel That She Has Not Been Cast Off (vv. 8-10)

Vv. 8-13 are a *Heilsorkal,* an oracle of salvation.

41:8-10 8. But you, Israel, my servant, Jacob whom I have chosen,
the descendants of Abraham, my friend,
9. whom I fetched from the ends of the earth,
and called from the remotest corners,
and said to you: "You are my servant,
I have chosen you and not cast you off;
10. fear not I am with you;
be not apprehensive, for I am your God;
I will strengthen you, yea, I will help you;
I will uphold you with my victorious right hand."

Verse 8. It has been rightly claimed that the style of speaking in this passage is marked by special solemnity. The main point at issue is indicated by the honorable title that is used in regard to Israel — "servant." Note the frequency of its use by the prophet: cf. 42:19; 44:1, 2, 21; 45:4; 48:20; as also Jer. 30:10; Ezek. 28:25; 37:25. When it is used, even though the basic meaning of the term is "slave," yet here its connotations are entirely honorable. This servant is the one who enjoys a relation of close intimacy with his master and has major assignments laid upon him. In fact, the title runs a close parallel with words: "Jacob, whom I have chosen." The election of Israel to be the Lord's own people is being discussed. What gives rise to the subject is that another "servant" of the Lord has just been brought into the picture, Cyrus. The fact that servant-functions can be ascribed to Cyrus, does not cancel out Israel's election by God. In a very special sense Israel too remains God's servant. Note here how frequently Isaiah makes reference to the election of Israel: cf. 43:1 f; 44:1 f, 21, 24; 45:11; 48:12; 49:7, 13; 55:5. Many are the passages in Scripture that associate Israel's election with the time of the Exodus — when in reality the already existing election was confirmed. Isaiah prefers to trace it back to the earlier event, the promise made to Abraham (Gen. 12 and 15, etc.). Note the words, "the descendants of Abraham, my friend" (Cf. II Chron. 20:7; James 2: 23). What far-reaching activity was involved in this call and election is indicated by the clauses of v. 9: "whom I fetched from the ends of the earth, and called from the remotest corners."

Verse 9. Though no passage can be cited where the words occur: "You are my servant; I have chosen you and not cast you off," this statement is nevertheless an effective summary of God's sentiments toward Abraham and to his whole people. Of course, the particular thought associated with "I have not cast you off" is: by now choosing Cyrus as my servant, *your* initial call is not revoked. When the claim is advanced that Abraham was called "from the ends of the earth" and "from the remotest corners," that certainly agrees better with the approach that these words were written in Palestine than in Babylon, and so may with some justification be ascribed to Isaiah, the son of Amoz.

4. God's Further Reassurance That Israel's Opponents Will Not Prevail against Her (vv. 11-13)

41:11-13 11. Lo, all who are incensed at you will be ashamed and confounded;
those who strive against you, will be as nothing and shall perish.
12. As for those who quarrel with you, if you look for them, you will not find them.
They will be as ciphers and nothing, the men that make war against you.
13. For I, Yahweh, your God, am making your right hand strong; I, who say to you: "Be not afraid, I myself will help you."

Verses 11-12. Where the preceding three verses laid down general principles defining God's attitude toward his people, these three verses now give the practical application of these principles. Reassurance is the essence of both sections. Though the opposition involved seems to be very generally all forces that might be arrayed against Israel, it is in reality *Babylon* that is under consideration. A new pattern of sentence-structure prevails: the subjects all stand at the end of each line. Besides the strophes mostly follow the 2:2 pattern instead of the 3:2 that had preceded. Furthermore, a climax is marked by the verbs describing the activity of those hostile to Israel. First they are described as being "incensed," i.e., filled with some kind of anger against this little Israel. Then they begin to "strive" with her; then an actual "quarrel" breaks out, which in turn develops into actual "making war." But in each case the form of hostility displayed is said to prove ineffective and futile. Some statements go so far as actually to describe the foe as vanishing off the scene, or as becoming "ciphers and nothing." Words more disparaging could hardly have been used.

Verse 13. The reason for the ineffectiveness of all this opposition is now disclosed: Yahweh, their own true God, is "making (their) right hand strong." He himself is breathing courage into them, saying: "Be not afraid, I myself will help you." So Israel faced catastrophe after catastrophe and came through it all victorious, although these words were in the first instance designed for the heavy days of the Captivity.

5. Rather, Israel Will Be Victorious over Her Foes (vv. 14-16)

41:14-16 14. Fear not, you worm Jacob,
    you men of Israel.
I myself will help you, says the Lord,
    and your redeemer is the Holy One of Israel.
15. Lo, I will make you a threshing sled,
    a new one with many teeth.
You shall thresh mountains and crush them;
and you shall make hills like chaff.
16. You shall winnow them and the wind shall sweep them away,
    and the storm shall scatter them.

But as for you, you shall rejoice in the Lord,
  in the Holy One of Israel you shall glory.

Verse 14. The opposite of a defeatist attitude is here suggested to small and seemingly unimportant Israel. The words,
which as to form are a *Heilsorakel*, i.e., a salvation oracle, aim
to inculcate a sense of victory over foes that seem practically
insuperable. Israel's own lack of strength, as she stands alone
by herself, is conceded. She is so small that she may be classified as being only a "worm." This is however not to be
construed in a derogatory sense, even as in the German the
diminutive *Luther* uses (*Wuermlein*) serves to indicate.
Rather it is even a term of endearment. Parallel runs the
expression "men of Israel," implying that there are not too
many of them. But the Lord places himself at their side and
promises to lend his aid. He describes himself as their "redeemer" and "the Holy One of Israel." A redeemer in the
original is one who stands in a relation of obligation to help,
over against him whose redeemer he is. God stands obligated,
for he has taken Israel to be his own. Strangely, this combination of the term "redeemer" (*go'el*) with the "Holy One of
Israel" appears seven times in these chapters, and in the use
of the word "redeemer" as such lie the roots of the whole
New Testament doctrine of redemption.

Verse 15. Now the prophet lists the achievements that
God's people will be capable of, as they proceed to move
forward in alliance with him. A bold figure is employed.
Israel is likened to a "threshing sled," or board, an instrument
drawn by oxen, which is used as a sled by the driver and
with its sharp attachments fixed in the under side of the board,
manages to break the ears of grain spread on the threshing-
floor and set loose the kernels. The nations, strong and
mighty as they seem, are the grain; Israel is the sled. This instrument is particularly effective. It is new and its teeth are
many. Though the amount to be threshed seems high as a
mountain, it still shall be controlled. For when it is said:
"You shall thresh mountains" that can only mean: huge

masses of the enemy, especially in the light of passages like
Matt. 17:20; Zech. 4:7; Mic. 1:4; cf. also Mic. 4:13. But assuredly the thought of the writer is not that Israel shall
achieve physical conquests of enemies in war, but rather
that she shall achieve moral victories of the highest sort, especially in the face of the present difficulties that confront her.

Verse 16. Staying within the limits of the figure that is
being used, the effectiveness with which Israel disposes of her
stronger enemy is described as a winnowing, in the process
of which the enemy, like the chaff and dust of threshing, is
swept away by the wind and scattered. But Israel on her
part, when she sees the outcome of her conflict with her
strong opponents, shall "rejoice" and "glory," in the Lord.
The sense of this last statement is that Israel, in her intimate
connection with the Lord, shall be filled with great happiness over the outcome of her struggle.

6. Israel, Suffering in Captivity, Will Dwell in a Paradise Rather Than in a Wilderness (vv. 17-20)

41:17-20 17. when the meek and the poor seek water, and
there is none,
  and their tongue is parched with thirst,
I, I the Lord, will answer them;
  I, the God of Israel, will not forsake them.
18. I will open streams on the bare hills,
  and fountains in the midst of the valleys.
I will make the wilderness a pool of water,
  and the dry land springs of water.
19. I will provide in the wilderness the cedar,
  the acacia, the myrtle and the wild olive tree.
I will set in the desert the cypress,
  the plane tree and the larch together;
20. that men may see and know
  and may note and understand together
that the hand of the Lord has done this,
  and the Holy One of Israel has created this.

Verse 17. Everything is highly figurative in this passage.
The chief question is: Is this, like 35:8-10, a passage that again

describes how the Lord will transform the *route* along which Israel travels as she returns to her native land? Or is this merely a poetic way of describing a beautiful metamorphosis that will take place in Israel's *condition*? We prefer to stress the second possibility. For there is no reference, even a remote one, to a nation on the march. So v. 17 then is to be regarded as first a description of the pitiful state of Israel as a captive nation: she is like a people that are dying of thirst in the wilderness. When the terms "the meek and the poor" are used to describe those who are suffering, these words would seem to carry the connotation of awareness of spiritual poverty, even as in Matt. 5:3, 5. Here are souls longing for the Lord's deliverance. First of all the strong reassurance is given them by the Lord that he will respond to their need and will not forsake them to their desolate lot. Yet behind the terms used there appears to be a reference to the wilderness experience, where Moses smote the rock.

Verse 18. The prophet now stays within the limits of the figure just introduced: water in abundance will be provided. That signifies all manner of spiritual blessings of which they stand in such sore need. These are then, words spoken to penitent souls, by implication. "Bare hills," which are never the source of water, are here spoken of as opening up with "streams" of water. In addition, down in the valleys where fountains would naturally arise, they do spring forth. Dry areas, which never produced water will stand in "pools of water." So also the "dry land." In the Near East the blessing of water is always appreciated to the utmost. This prerequisite to growth and productiveness now having been met, luxuriant growth can begin. It does in the next verse.

Verse 19. But this productiveness is painted in colors of trees and forests rather than in terms of crops and fields of grain. The emphasis just happens to be on the beautiful rather than on the utilitarian. That certainly will mean the transformation of the "wilderness" and the "desert." Although there may be a small measure of doubt on the exact identification of some of the first of these trees, the translation given is sufficiently close for all practical purposes. On the "plane tree" and the "larch" the identification is very dubious.

Verse 20. In any case, though a picture of verdant beauty was unfolded, the emphasis, as usual, is less on the beauty of the scene than on the hand of God who wrought these things. This picture eloquently describes how the Lord loves to deal with his children when, in their need, they feel moved to call upon him.

7. The Gods of the Nations Are Challenged to Give Proof of Their Divine Powers by Divulging the Future (vv. 21-24)

41:21-24 21. Present your case, says the Lord;
produce your strong arguments, says the King of Jacob.
22. Let them produce them and tell us what will transpire.
As for the former things, make known to us what they are,
and we will take note that we may know the outcome.
23. Make known to us what will come hereafter,
and we shall know that you are gods.
Yea, do something good or something bad,
and we will both be properly amazed and will see it.
24. Lo, you are less than nothing,
and your work is less than nought,
an abomination is he that chooses you.

It must be said at the outset that there is more involved here than just ability to foretell the future. The Lord can indeed do that. But at the same time he also has control of all the issues that the future may bring.

Verse 21. From v. 23 we gather that all these remarks are addressed to the *gods* of the heathen. The trial, from which the line of thought departed with v. 5, for the purpose of reassuring God's chosen people, this court-trial is here being resumed. Another point has to be made. True, God is indeed the attorney for the defense as well as the presiding Judge, but he is very fair and is giving the opposition every opportunity to present all available evidence. It is as though he said to them "tell . . . tell . . . tell," if you have anything to tell. If they have perhaps any "strong arguments" which have not yet been submitted as good evidence, now is the time to set them forth. That the judge is called "the *king* of Jacob" reflects both his great authority and his close relation to his own people. This title appears also in 6:5; 33:22; 41:21; 43:15; 44:6, etc. "Jacob" is merely a synonym for "Israel."

Verse 22. When he challenges them to "produce" what they may have in reserve he seems to intimate that till now they may have had misgivings about the validity of their own arguments and so were reticent about submitting them. But the challenge is "tell us what will transpire." There are two areas where evidence might be adduced. One is concerning the "former things," which in this connection seems to refer to predictions concerning Cyrus, made in the past and now obviously fulfilled. Such evidence will be duly noted if it can be adduced. The term "former things" is repeatedly used (cf. 42:9; 43:9, 18; 46:9; 48:3; 65:16 f.). Not in every case does it refer to things done by Cyrus. But there is still another possibility. Perhaps they could furnish advance information about things that Cyrus, a man of many achievements, may yet accomplish in the future. Therefore the challenge: "Declare to us things that are to come."

Verse 23. Much in the same vein is the challenge: "Make known to us what is to come hereafter." This is not a vague and general challenge but stays within the context of what *Cyrus* may yet do. Such knowledge will indicate that you have some measure of control, you idols, over the things that you predict, "and we shall know that you are gods." The challenge moves over into a third area, the most general of all: It says in effect, at least do *something*, for that is what the expression "do something good or something bad" means (cf. Gen. 24:50; 31:24, 29; II Sam. 13:22; Jer. 10:5).

We promise due amazement, virtually says the next remark. For it will be most remarkable if you can be proved to have accomplished something. There is a veiled sarcasm behind this statement. At this point in the discussion a long and embarrassing silence sets in. Not a sound, not a movement, nothing, on the part of those who have been summoned to this court-trial of the Almighty!

Verse 24. So the verdict has to be spoken. What is it that has been proved by the evidence, or lack of it, submitted? It is this: "Lo, you are less than nothing." This is the claim advanced with reference to the idols. They are a totally minus-quantity. So is their "work," and the futility of all that they stand for is reflected in those that worship them, for of such it must be said: "An abomination is he that chooses you." Not a mere blunderer; not a simpleton; but an abomination. As *North* aptly translates: "He that chooses you is as loathsome as you are." That concluding statement makes the clear outcome of the court-trial quite plain.

8. On This Score the Gods of the Nations Fail Utterly (vv. 25-29)

41:25-29 25. I have stirred up one from the north, and he has come;
from the rising of the sun one who proclaims my name.
And he shall come upon rulers as upon mortar,
as a potter tramples clay.
26. Who has declared it from the beginning that we might know,
and beforetime, that we might say: "Right!"?
Yea, there was not a one that declared it;
Yea, there was none that proclaimed it;
yea, there was not a one that heard words of yours.
27. I first have declared to Zion, Lo, lo, here they are;
and I give to Jerusalem a messenger of good tidings.
28. But when I look there is no man,
and from among them there is no counsellor,
that I might ask them and get an answer.
29. Lo, all of them are nought, their works are nothing;
their molten images are wind and confusion.

Verse 25. The issue involved is of sufficient importance to warrant an official summary of the outcome of this court-trial. This summary appears in this last section. God reiterates that he has "stirred up one from the north" that is from Media, which lies more to the north. Or the one called could be said to have been called from "the rising of the sun," i.e., the east. For if one regards the land of his birth i.e., Persia, this lies more toward the east. But what this one thus called actually does, is that he *proclaims* the name of Yahweh (cf. II Chron. 36:23). For so the expression which seems to say: "one who calls upon my name" is best rendered (cf. Exod. 33:19, 34:5). When this agent of Yahweh appears, opposition to him will be so ineffective that the leaders of it will be so completely at the mercy of the conqueror that they will be trampled under foot as mortar, or as the potter stamps on the clay.

Verse 26. Is there clear-cut evidence that anyone, god or man, foreknew, foreordained, and forecontrolled events to show that this situation was under his control? Did the words and the outcome so correspond that the conclusion had to be drawn: "Right," so it was? Not only was no declaration of a formal sort forthcoming; in fact, not a sound was heard.

Verse 27. Almost everyone admits that this verse poses difficulties. It appears to be extremely elliptical. But if it be viewed in its context some such obvious statement as "I have declared" must be supplied. So our above translation results. God had declared to Zion that the Conqueror would come, has pointed out: Here is the evidence. But for Jerusalem this news was like "good tidings" because it spelled the end of the Captivity. On the Lord's side, the facts are foreknown and the outcome is determined.

Verse 28. But to look at the opposition in this court-trial — No intimation, even the slightest, of awareness of what was to transpire may be detected. There simply is "no man," and "no counsellor." Only an embarassed silence. No answer was forthcoming. So the people on that side are "nought," "their works are nothing; their molten images are wind and confusion." Finis! The case and the trial are closed.

Notes

Verse 1. For "Listen unto me in silence" the Hebrew has a more compact form of statement, saying only: "Be silent unto me." This is properly classified as an instance of the *constructio praegnans*. Cf. *GK*, 119 gg; *KS*, 213 a. The words "Pick up fresh strength" also *Muilenburg* admits, are "not entirely out of place." As our interpretation shows, the peoples are thought of as frightened by the challenge from the Almighty. The verse begins with an address in the second person but almost immediately switches over into the third person.

Verse 2. *Tsédheq*, though it commonly means "righteousness," is best translated here as "victory." *KJ* makes of it an adjective, referring it to the one who is stirred up. In reality a relative pronoun could have been inserted immediately before this word. Then the translation used above results. The term connotes something that comes as a gift from God and is earnestly sought after by men.

Verse 3. *Shalom*, usually translated "peace," is best taken as an adverbial accusative and translated "safely." *GK*, 118 q.

Verse 4. In the expression "from the beginning" the Hebrew omits the article before the noun, thus, according to Hebrew usage making the noun practically a proper noun, and thus referring to the *absolute* beginning of things. See *KS*, 294 g.

Verse 5. When quite generally the words "they drew near and came" are treated as a gloss, they who do this seem to fail to see that men are being described as gathering together to perform a certain task. By these terms they are represented as coming together. That is the beginning of a colorful description. It is quite proper to have men assemble before they do their task.

Verse 6. These references to the futility of the manufacture of idols are by some called "idol interludes." *North* claims with regard to them that they read like "fugitive pieces," meaning apparently that they have been slipped in by editors but do not really fit where they stand. We believe it can be shown in each case that they fit well into given situations.

Verse 7. The "craftsman" is the smith who does heavier work in iron over against the one who does more delicate work and is termed the "goldsmith." Before the latter noun stands the sign of the definite object (*'eth*) usually used only when the noun has the article. Here this sign is used to avoid confusion as to which of the nouns is the object. See *KS*, 288 g.

Verse 10. *Tishta'*, according to a root found in the Ugaritic, should be derived from *shatha'* and is a Kal form. In the latter part of this verse all the perfects are perfects of confidence (*GK* 106 n). Or, according to *KS* 131, perfects of promise.

Verse 14. *Tola'ath* is in the construct state and therefore the next noun is a genitive of apposition. See *KS* 337 d. There is no need to change the next noun into "maggot" instead of "men." Least of all does the translation "louse" have good warrant (*contra Knight*).

Verses 14-16 are given an unusual interpretation by E. J. Hamlin (JNES, XIII, Jul. 1954, pp. 189 ff.) in that the "mountains" and "hills" of v. 15 are construed to signify figuratively the idolatrous religions of the nations. The evidence adduced from Accadian sources may establish the fact that such an interpretation was current in the religious literature of some nations of days of old. But it is none too likely that Israel's prophets were close students of all this literature or familiar with every bit of Accadian lore. Besides, looking at the context of our passage, especially v. 13, the enemies that threatened Israel's safety were the mighty empire like Babylon and Persia.

Verse 17. In the statement "their tongue is parched with thirst," five long *a*'s (*qametz*) appear, a king of *onomatopoea*, representing the stammering effects at speech made with a parched tongue (cf. *North*).

Verse 20. The *yachdaw* is a device often used by Isaiah to bind things together, something like a "once and for all" (*North*). Cf. also at the close of v. 23.

Verse 23. At the close of the verse, the word "and will see it," can be supplied with different vowels and then reads "and will be terrified." (*RSV*). We feel that "see" fits better in the present context.

Verse 24. In *me'ayin*, the *min* used is the *min* comparative. See *KS*, 352 z.

Verse 25. For *wayyabho'* ("and he shall come upon") many conjecture that it should be altered to *wayyabhas*, from *bhus* "to trample." But it can be shown that *bho'* ("to come") can also be used transitively (cf. *North*).

Excursus to 41:21-24

Above we gave the caption, "The gods of the nations are challenged to give proof of their divine powers by divulging the future."

If the question be raised: Is there any indication that in the religions of the nations round about Israel there was the possibility of foretelling events that were yet to come to pass? it must be admitted that a spirit of divination (foretelling the future) did manifest itself. It is true that preponderantly it was some form of doom (death, disaster, etc.) that was foretold. It is also true that in many an instance deception was practiced. False prophecies were submitted. It is equally true that oftentimes the oracular pronouncement was intentionally equivocal, allowing for an obvious double meaning, so that whatever the outcome, the word of the oracle still covered the case. But it must be admitted that sufficient evidence is available to demonstrate that mantic foretelling did occur. See Guillaume's *Prophecy and Divination among the Hebrews and other Semites,* Harper and Brothers, New York and London, 1938.

But does not this admission invalidate the prophet's challenge addressed to the gods of the surrounding nations to produce clear-cut instances of prediction? By way of answer it has been pointed out that there is every indication that the prophet knew of the existence of mantic powers among the heathen cults round about Israel. But it has also been shown (*Westermann*) that Isaiah is not interested in abstract prediction, that is, in bare foretelling. His challenge includes the predictive word and the actual subsequent fulfillment of the word, that is to say, realized prophecy.

In further substantiation of mantic phenomena among neighboring nations one may compare Claus Westermann, *Forschung am Alten Testament* (24) Theologische Buecherei, 1964, Chr. Kaiser Verlag, Muenchen, the essay, *"Die Mari-Briefe und die Prophetie in Israel."*

Chapter XLII

C. THE WORK OF THE SERVANT OF THE LORD (Chap. 42)

A break occurs between Chaps. 41 and 42: there is no transition made from the one to the other. This is the first of the so-called "Servant of the Lord" passages. Since these passages seem to fit a bit loosely in some cases into the context, some have assumed that they stem from some other writer and were merely inserted casually and without sufficient cause or motivation. The passages under consideration are 42:1-9; 49:1-7; 50:4-11; 52:13–53:12. But for the present let it suffice that good arguments can be adduced why these passages may be thought of as original parts of the book and not later insertions. *Muilenburg* indicates that without this strophe the poem would be incomplete.

As the chapter opens, the Lord is speaking as in 40:1 and in 41:1. But to whom is he speaking? Is it perhaps, as some suggest, to his heavenly council? We hardly believe so, for the heavenly council is largely a figurative representation employed for embellishment. As in Chap. 40, all who will take heed are being addressed.

But who is the "servant"? There has long been a division of opinion among commentators dating back to the Septuagint, which identified him with Israel, the nation. But as we proceed, we hope to offer sufficient arguments for maintaining that in the passages listed above, the person under consideration is none less than the one who in the New Testament goes under the name of Jesus the Christ. Other views, such as he is Deutero-Isaiah, or some ruler of Judah, etc., are quite unsatisfactory. And though it is true enough that in a certain sense Israel herself may be thought of as the servant of the Lord, as is the case in the second half of our chapter, nevertheless there are too many references of the New Testament that support our view of his identity with the Messiah. Yet we should note at the very outset that a certain "duality" runs through the Old Testament already, so that on the one hand the servant's work is done by a human agent, but on the other hand it is viewed as the work of God himself. The New Testament truth is therefore prepared for, which says with unmistakable clearness that this task is the task of the God-man, Jesus Christ. Let us note already that the Servant is thought of very clearly as distinct from the nation Israel, for in v. 6 he stands over against the nation as the mediator of the covenant and as its light.

By taking this position we do not rule out the fact that in a certain sense Israel, the nation, also shares in the work that the Lord would have his Servant do. But this is an achievement on a much lower scale, and this accounts for the fact that on the one hand the Servant can meet with God's fullest approval in his work, but yet (vv. 18-22) God may find his servant highly inadequate. Matthew sees the fulfillment of this passage in Christ's withdrawing himself from the multitude (Matt. 12:18-21).

1. The Servant of the Lord, Meek and Unassuming, Yet Successful (vv. 1-4)

42:1-4 1. Lo, my servant, whom I support,
      my chosen one, in whom my inmost soul delights.
I have put my spirit upon him
      that he may bring forth justice to the nations.
2. He will not cry out or raise his voice,
      nor make it to be heard in the street.
3. A crushed reed he will not [utterly] break,
      and a dimly burning wick he will not quench;
      he will faithfully bring forth justice.
4. He himself will not be dimmed or crushed,
      until he has established justice in the earth;
      and for his teaching the coastlands do wait.

Verse 1. Though the word "servant" in the original does mean a slave, it is in this connection an entirely honorable term. If he is the Lord's servant, his is an honored task. Many have been designated by this title: Abram (Gen. 26:24), the patriarchs (Deut. 9:27), Moses (Num. 12:7), David (II Sam. 3:18), prophets (Amos 3:7), even Nebuchadnezzar (Jer. 27:6), so the individual connotation of this title is far more common than the collective; in a few instances Israel is referred to by this title. So then we place this passage by the side of those passages which refer to the individual Messiah, passages like 7:14; 9:1-6; 11:1-9. Neither can we find that interpretation satisfactory which finds here the description of some prophet. Several assertions are made about this servant. First of all he is the Lord's own servant ("my"). Then he is a man whom the Lord upholds or "supports." He needs help in his task and he enjoys the very maximum of help in that the Lord upholds him in every difficulty. This is further indicated by the fact that the Lord calls him "my chosen one." In fact he does his assigned task so well that the Lord can say of him, He is the one "in whom my inmost soul delighted." In Matt. 3:17 and 17:5 the reference to this passage is so obvious that the evangelist must be viewed as indicating that this passage is a distinct prophecy concerning the Messiah. The past tense in this case ("delighted") is to be taken as stating that the Lord has taken delight in everything that his chosen one did. As a further description of what equipment the Lord gave him for his work there comes the claim, "I have put my spirit upon him." On the Old Testament level the reference to the "spirit" almost invariably connotes "power." So this statement means that the Servant is richly indued with power. But the particular task that is assigned to him is "that he may bring forth justice to the nations." It is almost impossible to find an adequate equivalent for the word that we, with many others, have translated as "truth," as "a norm of judgment," or even as "the true religion." None of these is quite satisfactory. The term implies all that the nations need for their salvation, the blotting out of their spiritual ignorance. But this much is clear, he is not to confine his activity to the children of Israel. In fact, this is the big part of his assignment, this bringing forth justice to the nations, for in these verses (1-4) the matter appears three times. For further instances where the equipment of men with the "spirit" is referred to, cf. 32:15; 44: 3; Ezek. 36:26; 39:29; Joel 2:28.

Verse 2. From assignment and equipment a transition is made to the manner in which this chosen Servant of the Lord will do his work. A contrast seems to be implied, particularly with that conqueror from the north, or east (41:2 ff.), who is ruthless and cruel, trampling the vanquished ones under his feet. This Servant is modest and meek. He is not loud and boisterous, he does "not cry out nor raise his voice, nor make it to be heard in the street." He is so sure of himself and of the cause he represents that he can well expect his message to carry itself successfully through every test. How often Jesus shunned publicity, even though his aim was to carry his gospel to all men! This description is hardly intended to be a contrast to the ecstatic prophets of days of old.

Verse 3. We move into the area of pastoral care, so to speak. Wherever he finds men wounded and bruised by the harshness of life's experience, or wherever he finds wounded and bruised consciences, whether among the Gentiles or in Israel, there he is most tender and delicate in the gentle handling of these souls. Such individuals are likened in the first place to a "bruised reed," bent but not quite broken. He takes care that such a one is not utterly broken. In the second place such persons are likened to a "dimly burning wick." The flame of faith and hope has begun to flutter but is not quite gone out. He cups his hand around the flame that it may not be "quenched" or, as one writer has put it, "snuffed out." This will be the manner in which he "will faithfully bring forth justice." What a contrast such dealings are with 41:15 f.! But how in harmony this is with Matt. 5:3! Never did a servant acquit himself better in the achievement of a difficult assignment.

Verse 4. This assigned task was by no means an easy one. The Servant might have been overwhelmed by its enormity. But no! "He himself will not be dimmed or crushed" — the same verbs being intentionally used here as in reference to the afflicted ones whom he himself helps — as he goes about his task. Here for the first time comes a faint indication in the Servant Songs that this will be a *Suffering* Servant. Again, with emphatic repetition, he will carry on his work "until he has established justice in the earth." But it will not be universal hostility and opposition that he encounters. Prevenient grace will have been doing some work on the hearts of men in the distant coastlands. So the encouraging word is added: "for his teaching the coastlands do wait." Sometimes their longing will be dimly and not consciously defined. But it will be there, even if at times it is little more than a negative preparation. The next portion, vv. 5-9, may be regarded as also belonging to this Servant Song. It certainly is closely connected with it.

2. The Lord's Relation to His Servant Defined (vv. 5-9)

42:5-9 5. Thus says the true God, the Lord,
    who created the heavens and stretched them out,
who spread out the earth and what it produces;
who gave breath to the people upon it
    and spirit to those that walk in it:
6. "I the Lord have called you in righteousness,
and grasp you by the hand and guard you,
    and give you as mediator of the covenant to the people,
    and as a light to the nations,
7. to open blind eyes,
    to bring prisoners from the dungeon,
    from the prison-house those that sit in darkness.
8. I Yahweh, that is my name;
    and my glory I will not give to another
    nor my praise to graven images.
9. The former prophecies, lo, they have come to pass,
    and now I declare new things;
    before they spring forth, I let you hear of them."

Verse 5. Here the Lord himself defines his relation to his Servant, addressing him in person. To try to relate all these pronouncements to Cyrus falls far short of the great things that are here set forth. Not just any god is the speaker (if the gods of the nations could speak!); the article used before the word "God" gives the sense of the "true and only God." He is about to speak of achievements so great that men might have doubts as to whether he is able to fulfill them. Therefore he reminds them of the fact that he is none less than the very Creator himself, who has power to make the earth of nothing. Here, as so often, the Creator-character of God is the guaranty of his power to achieve any and all of the things he proposes to undertake (see 40:12, 13, 26, 28; 41:20; 43:1, 8, 12, 13, etc.). Besides, he is the one who also stretched out the heavens, with the ease with which a man spreads out a cloth. He also spread out (literally "hammered out") the earth and made it to bring forth what it produces; for it is no sterile earth. He did greater things even than these. He put animating breath into bodies so that they became living animated beings, and even higher than that, put spirit, a capacity for higher things, into these beings. Four tremendous achievements of the Almighty are here called to mind. You might well expect of such a one that he could produce great things to this day as he did in days of old.

Verse 6. He now envisions his Servant as standing before him. First of all, the call of this Servant to the task that he has, emanated from God, and it was transmitted "in righteousness," that is, with saving purposes in mind. More, from the very outset, when the Servant appears on the scene, God is grasping his right hand to uphold and strengthen him for the seemingly impossible great task which is his. At the same time he is continually guarding him against the many dangers that would assail him and thwart his work. And now the ultimate purposes for which all this is set in motion are delineated: First of all he is to serve as a "mediator of the covenant." There once was a covenant made with Abraham. This covenant was significantly expanded to involve all Israel at Mount Sinai. A greater covenant is now under consideration, one that involves "the people," that is all the nations on the face of the earth. In some mysterious way the Servant himself is the essence of that covenant, not only the

one who transmits it. Some have tried to capture the force
of the statement by defining this title as "truth personified"
(*Volz*), which is helpful but not broad enough. This new
covenant is spoken of also in 54:10; Jer. 31:31 ff.; Ezek. 16:
60 ff. But even this significant epithet says too little. He and
his work may further be defined as being "the light of the
nations." There is no real truth by which men can walk
aside from him. He lightens the darkness of the natural
mind of man. Jesus claimed this role for himself (John 8:12;
cf. also Luke 2:32). Isaiah 49:6 again alludes to this outstanding work. But no less than "the nations," that is to say, all of
them, are the beneficiaries of his great work.

Verse 7. But having once gotten on the rich subject of the
work outlined for this Servant, the Lord himself cannot soon
drop it, for it involves infinitely more. A few bold strokes
fully round out the picture. He will come "to open blind
eyes." Obviously this refers to more than occasional instances
where he restored sight to eyes physically blind. Imparting
insight into saving divine truth is what is primarily under consideration (cf. 29:18; 35:5 ff.). Or, completely altering the
figure, his task is "to bring prisoners from the dungeon."
Again the spiritual interpretation of the task described alone
fits the needs of the case. For prisoners in dungeons often
must be kept in such confinement for the safety of mankind.
But when the parallel statement speaks of liberating those
that sit in darkness, again some sad spiritual plight is under
consideration.

It must freely be admitted that taken all together, these
are achievements which only Christ, the Savior, was able to
accomplish and still does on a grand scale. At this point attempts to interpret the passage in reference to a collective
object like Israel, completely breaks down.

Verse 8. The Lord is still speaking. By raising up and
sustaining this Servant of his the Lord achieves great honor,
honor of the highest sort, which he desires to achieve, as he
now asserts. He who bears the distinctive name of the God
of Israel, the name "Yahweh," is jealous of this honor of

his, and will not allow it to be snatched from him or awarded to any other, because this honor is so intimately tied up with the salvation of mankind. Least of all can "graven images" ever match what he does with comparable works done in their name.

Verse 9. But what does the prophet mean by the statement, "the former prophecies, lo, they have come to pass"? What are the "former prophecies"? Much perplexity has been caused by this expression. Perhaps it is best after all to follow the lead of those who refer to distinct passages in Isaiah and Jeremiah, which declared beforehand that Babylon would fall at the hands of the Medes, passages like Isa. 13 and 14 (esp. 13:17); 21:1-10; Jer. 50 and 51 (esp. 51:11, 28). No one could have foreseen that the Medes would be successful in this direction. But the prophets, by the spirit of the Lord, foretold that it would come to pass, and it came. And now the prophet is foretelling restoration from Captivity for Israel and salvation unto the ends of the earth through the Servant of the Lord. "Before they spring forth" the Lord tells of them. These are the "new things" here referred to. These future events will come to pass as certainly as did the predictions of days of old. This is one of the distinctive achievements of the God of Jacob and the great Lord of Israel. All this makes the work of the Servant of the Lord more glorious.

3. A Summons to Praise the Lord for the Work of His Servant (vv. 10-12)

42:10-12 10. Sing to Yahweh, a new song,
      his praise to the end of the earth,
   they that go down to the sea and that which fills it,
you coastlands and they who dwell in them.
11. Let the wilderness and its cities raise their voice,
the villages that Kedar inhabits.
Let the cliff-dwellers exult;
   let them call aloud from the mountain-tops.
12. Let them give glory to the Lord,
and make known his praise in the coastlands.

Here, as pointed out by *Westermann*, occurs for the first time in the second half of the book "an eschatological hymn of praise," further examples of which are to be found in 44:23; 45:8; 48:20-21; 49:13; 52:7-10.

Verse 10. *G. A. Smith* at this point very appropriately remarks: "God's commission to his Servant is hailed by a hymn." So this summons to praise the Lord looks back at the commission as such and regards it as being of such supreme benefit to all mankind that they should all break forth into singing at what is here being done for the good of all. As so often in the Scriptures, a new work that God does for the children of men is to be greeted with a new song (cf. Ps. 33:3; 40:4; 96:1; 98:1; 144:9; 149:1). But in this case the blessing under consideration is so vast that it affects all of mankind, and only praise from all can begin to do justice to its magnitude. So praise is to come forth and ring out "to the ends of the earth." They who are to participate include certain ones, here enumerated as being persons whom we are likely to overlook in so general a summons — persons that sail the seas, or to use the idiom of a people who lived in the hills and whenever they betook themselves to the sea had to "come down" from the hill country. Add to the sailors all the various kinds of creature-life that exists in endless variety in the waters of the sea, all forms of aquatic life, strange as it may strike us that they should contribute their share of the praise due to the Lord. Then there is, of course, the vast expance of "the coastlands," i.e., the very irregular Mediterranean shoreline, where people of many races live. What this Servant of the Lord will do, bears very great meaning for them also. They should join in offering praises for these benefits. But a still larger chorus and symphony orchestra are to be enlisted to make the praises worthy of him to whom they are directed.

Verse 11. So even "the wilderness" where people are comparatively few, yet even, by way of exception, "cities" (like Tadmor, I Kings 9:18) are to be found, are summoned to bear their share. So too "the villages (or 'tentdwellings')"

that Kedar (perhaps Arabia) inhabits" and which represent
the eastern fringe of the nations with whom Israel had contact, even as the "coastlands" represented the western borders. Add to this the very isolated groups like "the cliff-
dwellers" (or "denizens of the rocks" as *North* calls them).
They are to be exuberantly glad ("exult") for the Servant's
work is for their good, too. They are to ascend high mountains and from there "call aloud" that they may be heard far
and wide. All these are called upon to praise, for a work of
most tremendous proportions, affecting the wellbeing of all
of them, is being achieved.

Verse 12. All this praise is to be tendered to the true God
of Israel, Yahweh, who alone can do such wonderful things
that affect the destiny of all.

4. How the Lord Himself Will Participate in the Achievement of His Servant's Tasks (vv. 13-17)

42:13-17   13. The Lord will go forth as a mighty man,
      like a man of war he will stir up his fury.
He will raise the war-cry, he will roar;
   he will prove himself victorious over his enemies.
14. For a long time I have kept silent,
I have been still and restrained myself.
   As a woman in childbirth I will groan,
I will gasp and pant together.
15. I will lay waste mountains and hills,
   and dry up all their vegetation;
I will turn rivers into islands,
   and dry up the pools.
16. And I will lead blind people in a way they have not known,
and in paths unknown to them I will let them go;
   I will turn darkness before them into light,
and rough places into level country.
   These things I will do and not leave undone.
17. They that trust in graven images shall be turned back,
and utterly put to shame;
   they that say to molten images,
      "You are our gods!"

Verse 13. Another way of looking at what is now portrayed is to regard this as a description of the Lord's activity

about achieving his objectives. Or looking back at v. 9, our verse now begins to picture the eagerness with which the Lord takes his projects, the "new things," in hand. The Lord really appears now in a new role. He is no longer so much the deliverer as the successful conqueror. Those familiar with Akkadian and Ugaritic literature find many parallels here as to the role in which God pictures himself as a mighty warrior. In fact biblical parallels are not wanting (see Judg. 5; Ps. 18; Hab. 3; Zech. 14:3). *North* ventures the rather bold observation that the Lord is represented as stirring himself up to a kind of "berserker" rage, and offers as further biblical parallel Isa. 63:1-6. Note the "holy war" language.

From the very first word on, military language is being employed; for the verb "to go forth" is the technical term for venturing forth to battle (cf. II Sam. 11:1); and "mighty man" is merely another title for "warrior." Language here goes as far as it possibly could without impropriety in picturing one who will be terrible to encounter as he goes against his foes. He is said to work himself up into a veritable passion (*Kampfeslust*) (cf. I Sam. 17:20). When sufficiently aroused, "he will raise the war cry," challenging his foe to the conflict. He will even "roar" in his anger. Then he ventures to assert before the conflict has even started that "he will prove himself victorious over his enemies." In this whole section it has been noted that there are no less than fifteen verbs used in reference to the various forms of activity in which the Lord engages. The whole scene is packed with action.

Verse 14. This is still a description of the change in policy from former inaction to present, intense activity. The Lord is like a man who for good reasons of his own has refrained from action. This has been difficult with a situation that seemed to clamor for intervention. Still "for a long time, he kept silent," he has "been still," and "restrained" himself. Now he can hold back no longer. *Volz* goes so far as to claim (and to us the claim seems justifiable) that this inaction sums up the whole space of time up till this moment. Now comes the birth-hour of a new aeon. In the colorful portrayal of the strenuous activity now getting under way, the words beat a kind of staccato tempo indicative of intense action. But the figure of the warrior is abruptly abandoned for one which well covers the other aspect of this new activity. The new figure is that of a woman in travail. So God travails to bring forth the new: he groans, gasps, and pants. Certainly the least one can claim is that these verbs reflect the intense concern that God has for the achievement of his goals. The final "together" of the verse seems to lump all activities together into one and to impart to the various verbs used a kind of superlative intensity.

Verse 15. This verse seems to fit badly into the picture, whether we look at the warrior aspect of God, or the woman-in-childbirth aspect, or also when we think of the deliverance-of-Israel approach. Perhaps the solution lies in the thought that this is all eschatological language, the final-judgment aspect of history, all blending together into one vast scene of divine activity without regard for the time sequence. Mountains and hills are being devastated, as it were, by the hot blast that goes forth from his mouth. Vegetation withers. Where rivers ran, now islands appear; the waters having been driven away by the hot blast of the Lord's anger. Pools also disappear. But at this point things seem to blend into another kind of perspective.

Verse 16. The destructive work of v. 15 was preparatory to making a road that the captive people might travel as they go back to their old homeland. As so often, the Exodus tradition of Israel's past comes to the forefront: a new Exodus is in the making. God appears as leading his once captive people through a wilderness again, as he led Israel from Egypt to Canaan. He calls them "blind people" because they are not yet able to see God's great purposes that he has in mind for their good. Some measure of the blindness of unbelief is still upon them. They cannot for themselves detect the way they are to take, nor do they know the road to restoration. But he promises to give them light as the cloud of God's presence guided them in the way through the dread wilderness of old. So to speak, he will even make the rough places plain. And if these promises seem grand and unbelievable, he gives the nation the assurance, like as by an oath, "These things will I do and not leave undone."

Verse 17. What is deliverance for Israel at the same time becomes a defeat for her idolatrous enemies. They will not prevail against Israel any longer. The magnificent display of power on God's part will mark an hour of disgrace and impotence of her enemies, who, like true idolaters say to the molten image, "You are our gods."

5. The Blind and Deaf Servant Who Failed God and Suffered the Consequences (vv. 18-22)

42:18-22   18. Hear, you deaf,
and look, you blind, that you may see!
19. Who is blind but my servant,
and deaf as my messenger whom I send?
  Who is blind as my trusted one,
and blind as the servant of the Lord?
20. You have seen many things, but you took no note of them,
I opened (his) ears, but he did not listen.
21. The Lord was pleased for his righteousness' sake
to make his instruction great and glorious.
22. But this is a people robbed and plundered;
men have ensnared them all in pits,
  and they were hid away in prisons.
They have been given over to plundering, with none to deliver,
  for spoil, and no one says, "Restore!"

Verse 18. The "servant" now encountered is an entirely different person than the one met with heretofore in the chapter. He stands in sharpest contrast to the Lord and his zeal for Israel. This servant is blind and deaf. He is a collective personality. The note of comfort that is so outstanding since 40:1 ff., recedes into the background, and the Comforter becomes the Rebuker and Educator. For him this servant now is Israel, an Israel marked by one most serious shortcoming, blindness. It is not an excusable blindness but a reprehensible one which merits sharp rebuke. Perhaps no one questions that the servant here spoken of is unbelieving Israel. The nation is here sharply challenged for its lack of receptivity. It is blind, not by accident but through fault of its own. Cf. the situation of Isa. 6.

Verse 19. Though in a sense the whole nation appears to be indicted, no doubt the unbelieving exiles in Captivity are primarily under consideration, and that in spite of the fact that the Lord can refer to the nation as "*my* servant," and also as "*my* messenger whom I send." For this latter claim does apply to Israel: she was always a nation with a distinct mission from God. Other honorable titles may be used in reference to the nation. She is God's "trusted one," a one to whom important tasks were entrusted. She is still, summing it all up, "the servant of the Lord." She has never been dismissed from this post of honor. The blindness she is charged with appears to be chiefly her failure to recognize her commission as servant. To this must be added the resultant blindness that grows out of misunderstanding her assignment. Lack of all deeper spiritual perception grows out of this root-oversight.

Verse 20. This failure of the nation dare not be attributed to any failure on God's part to do for her what needed to be done. The Lord displayed mighty acts, especially acts of deliverance in great number before the eyes of his chosen people. But Israel saw what was done but failed actually to take note of what it meant. God could even go so far as to claim that he "had opened [his] ears, but he did not listen." The change in person within the compass of this one verse is very significant. At first Israel is addressed directly. Then the Lord, in a somewhat cool manner, appears to turn away from the more intimate second person to the impersonal third. This we have sought to indicate by inserting a parenthetical "his" before "ears."

Verse 21. At this point the Lord makes reference to the greatest of the gifts that he bestowed upon Israel to fit the nation for its task. "He was pleased . . . to make his instruc-

tion [Hebrew: *torah* in the broadest sense of the word]
great and glorious." The reference is to all the instruction
that was in God's providence bestowed upon the nation. And
this favor was granted "for his righteousness' sake," that is to
say, with saving purposes in mind. No nation was ever so
richly and so graciously endowed. Many have claimed that
this verse does not belong here but is a later addition. The
connection indicated above shows that it fits admirably into
the picture.

Verse 22. So, from having been a nation with a high potential for blessed activity, she became disobedient and unresponsive, with the result, she had to be given over to God's
judgment. So she became a "people robbed and plundered;
men have ensnared them all in pits, and they were hidden
away in prisons." All the needs of the figure used seem to be
met if we think in terms of a caravan that was attacked by
marauders out in the desert and cruelly deprived of all their
goods and of their very liberty, being allowed to languish
in places of captivity. This figure is still being followed in
the remainder of the verse: "They have been given over to
plundering with none to deliver; for spoil, and no one says:
'Restore!'" For the present at least no indication of a deliverance from this sorry lot is discernible.

6. An Indictment of the Deaf Servant for His Failure (vv. 23-25)

42:23-25 23. Who among you gives ear to this,
hearkens and listens from now on?
24. Who gave Jacob up to be plundered
and Israel to robbers?
Was it not the Lord against whom we have sinned,
and in whose ways men were not willing to walk,
and whose instruction they did not obey?
25. So he poured out upon him the heat of his anger
and the fierceness of war;
and it set him on fire round about,
but he did not note it;
and it burned him,
but he did not take it to heart.

Verse 23. It is as though this section (vv. 23-25) were saying, O that Israel might recognize that the present disaster, the state of exile prevailing, is a just judgment of God! Looking forward to 43:1-7, we might say that the present portion is a preparation for the mercy about to be proclaimed. Or thinking in terms of the form in which these words are cast, it would be quite in order to describe vv. 23-25 as an invective, but 43:1-7 as an oracle of redemption (*Muilenburg*). In any case, when the prophet wrote there was as yet no evidence of a spirit of repentance on the part of the nation Israel for its infidelity to the Lord. Surely here it cannot be claimed that the restoration came as a result of Israel's repentance. Much as in the preceding section, v. 23 charges the nation with dullness and lack of perception. The Lord was saying something to the nation by the way in which he was treating them, but no man listened. No one was paying close attention ("hearkens and listens") to the Lord's words, at least "from now on," careless as they may have been previously.

Verse 24. The Captivity of Israel was not something that just happened. By the form of question used the prophet indicates that a divine act of giving up the people was the cause of it all. That was how Israel got into the hands of "robbers," an allusion to the figure used in v. 22. Sin was the major cause, and this sin was against the Lord (cf. Ps. 90:11 ff.). When the prophet uses the first person plural ("against whom *we* have sinned") and includes himself, he is leading the nation to admit that here lies the root of their misfortune and seeks to induce them to make a frank and free confession. The sin involved could also be described as stubbornness ("in whose ways men were not willing to walk"), the right way was not unknown but the nation was not minded to go according to the course prescribed. The last statement adds a significant thought ("whose instructions they did not obey"): God had virtually spelled out for them what course his people should follow. This put them under obligation to obey; but they were at heart a stubborn and disobedient people.

Verse 25. What else was there left for God to do than to chastise them? And it was chastisement of the most severe sort: "he poured out upon him the heat of his anger and the fierceness of war." The figure is a telling one, emphasizing the painfulness of the experience. Wars are not primarily the result of economic, industrial and nationalistic causes, or of misdirected diplomacy. They are judgments upon the guilty. The heavier the crime, the greater the judgment of God. But Israel, in the midst of it all, could be described as a person actually set on fire and not noting what had happened; or as a person who was being burned but did not take it to heart. Physically such an attitude would be unthinkable, spiritually it was a fact.

Notes

Verse 1. The *Septuagint* already indicates what interpretation was much in vogue in the Jewish circles B.C. when it inserts the word "Jacob" before "my servant" and "Israel" before "my chosen one." The verb "I support" is construed with a preposition in Hebrew (cf. *KS*, 215 h). Both "my servant" and "my chosen one" are absolute nominatives in the original.

Verse 4. The construction "until he has established" — *'adh* with an imperfect — practically equals a future perfect (cf. *KS*, 387 g).

Verse 5. The participle *noteyhem* ("stretching them out") may be viewed as only seemingly a plural (*GK* 93 ss) or as a plural of potency (*KS*, 263 b and d; also *GK* 124 k). The expression "the true God, the Lord" occurs only here in the second half of Isaiah.

Verse 6. On the verbs from *we'achzeq*, where *we* is regularly used as connective (not *waw* conversive) the major versions, *Septuagint*, *Vulgate*, *Syriac* and *Targum*, do read the text as though it were the connective *wa*. It is better to let the masoretic text stand. These are all acts of the Almighty that are still going on and do not only lie in the past.

Verse 7. For *'asir* read *'asirim*, *m* having fallen out through haplography. The sense demands the plural. The subject of the infinitives may be Yahweh or the Servant.

Verse 10. *Miqtseh* should not be rendered "*from*" but "*to*" "the end of the earth," according to the common point of view reflected in the Hebrew approach in such instances. At first glance the emendation *yir-am* ("let roar") for *yoredey* ("they that go down") according to Ps. 96:11 seems attractive. But some of the color of the verse is lost by this emendation.

Verse 13. The context would suggest that *yetse'* is better rendered as a future than a present (*Koenig*). The comparison "as a mighty man" uses an article before the noun, as is pointed out and explained *GK* 126 or *KS* 299 m.

Verse 14. After the perfect, follows a series of unconnected imperfects. They constitute what is called "a synchronistic asyndeton," *GK* 120 c.

Verse 18. The vocative may use the article. *GK* 126, e, f.

Verse 19. The *Septuagint* not inappropriately read the plural "my servants" for the singular, as the Hebrew text allows.

Verse 20. For "*he* did not listen," some 60 manuscripts render "you." But the more difficult reading deserves the preference and shows the Lord, as it were, turning away from more intimate address to objective impartiality.

Verse 22. Before "plundering" the *le*, appearing before *baz*, is still in force (*GK* 119 hh).

Verse 24. The *zu* used here is really a demonstrative pronoun, which is here used as a relative. See *KS* 51, 385 b; *GK* 138 g. The *athnach*, marking the middle of the verse (under *Yahweh*) is usually regarded as being out of place in this verse; it should stand two words earlier. For some reason *bethoratho* is by some regarded as a "pious gloss." This is purely subjective opinion. Obedience is clearly related to the keeping of the law. Disobedience is the lack of it. As the verse swerves from the address of the second person to the objective style of the third person ("men were not willing") it marks a kind of estranged aloofness on the part of the Lord.

Verse 25. At the close of the verse the expression, "heat of his anger" does not offer the usual relation of the first noun being in the construct state ("heat of"). This is explained either as a kind of apposition: the heat, which was his anger (*GK* 131 k); or it is thought of as an instance where the north-Hebrew construct state on long *a* is used (*KS* 285 f).

Chapter XLIII

D. RESTORATION BY DIVINE GRACE (Chap. 43)

This caption only roughly gathers together what is covered by this chapter. For there are diverse elements pieced together here, diverse but not unrelated, as the outline demonstrates.

The tone of the chapter, as indicated by the opening words, is not at all what would be expected after the somewhat sharp close of the preceding chapter. For, to use some of the terminology employed by form criticism, the preceding chapter has closed on the note of a rebuke (*Scheltwort*). But rebukes are, as a general rule, followed by threats of disaster (*Drohwort*). But to our surprise we find a gracious promise (*Verheissung*). But this is only a seeming irregularity. For the prophet is a man with a message primarily of comfort. He delights in transmitting messages of grace. He can be, and is, a man of sharp rebukes on occasion. But his book (chaps. 40-66) is primarily a comfort book, as is commonly conceded. The antithesis between the close of the one chapter and the opening of the next is indicated by the opening particle, "but now." Besides, though addressing the nation, these words have a singularly personal tone (cf. *Westermann*).

1. Restoration of Israel Impending (vv. 1-7)

43:1-7 1. But now, thus says the Lord,
who created you, O Jacob, and formed you, O Israel:
"Fear not, for I have redeemed you;
I have called you by your name; you are mine.
2. When you pass through the waters, I am with you,
and through the rivers, they will not sweep you away;
when you walk through fire; you will not be burned,
and the flame shall not scorch you.

3. For I, the Lord, am your God,
the Holy One of Israel, your Savior.
I give Egypt as your ransom, Cush and Seba in place of you.
4. Because you are precious in my eyes,
    honored, and I love you;
therefore I will give men in your stead,
    peoples for your life.
5. Fear not, for I am with you;
from the east will I bring your descendants,
    and from the west I will gather you.
6. I will say to the north, Give up!
and to the south, Keep not back!
Bring my sons from afar, and my daughters from the end of the
    earth;
7. every one who is called by my name,
and whom I created for my glory,
    whom I have formed and made."

Verse 1. That a new oracle is about to be presented is indicated by the formula "thus says the Lord," as well as by
the adversative "but now." To give a solid basis for the claim
that the Lord is about to make to the effect that he will not
fail Israel in the present emergency, the word of the Lord
points to two major activities that may also be ascribed to
him in connection with his people — he "created" them and
"formed" them. They owe their origin as a nation to him as
well as any substantial thing that they have become (for in
spite of the disaster of the Exile, Israel was still a nation with
perhaps more than ordinary potential, at least as far as the
divine purpose was concerned). The essence of the particular word to be imparted at this time is "fear not." Israel may
have been very dubious as to her future as nation. Many may
have seen nothing less than national extinction staring them in
the face. Any people would view such a prospect with fear.
In Israel's case such fear is groundless. It is for this reason
that the divine "fear not," runs like a continuous thread,
through these oracles (see 40:9; 41:10, 13 f.; 44:2; 54:4).
To the two outstanding favors already mentioned, two
others are added: (1) "I have redeemed you," one of those
perfects that the Hebrew uses to indicate that an event is as
good as already done. The verb here implies that Israel has

been freed from a threatening danger by one upon whom she has some well-established claim for help. (2) "I have called you by your name," an idiom which means about as much as: I have appointed you for a very special purpose in a very direct way. The expression occurs in Exod. 31:2; 35:30; Isa. 45:4. In other words, summing up: Innumerable ties bind the Lord and his people to one another. To this must be added the statement in which the prophet himself sums it all up: "You are mine" (Exod. 19:5). That is to say: I have special claim on you, and you on me.

Verse 2. This is now spelled out by way of practical application. This verse is a kind of generalization. It applies not only to the prevailing crisis but to the entire history of the nation. No matter what kind of dangers are encountered, Israel can survive. Two types of danger are mentioned for the whole catalogue of them that might be enumerated — passing through water and through fire, as in Ps. 66:12. The nation is thought of as on a journey. She may have to ford streams — there were no bridges in those days. Should the waters prove dangerous, her comfort is: The Lord will be with her. His mere presence is the epitome of safety. The waters will not be able to sweep her away. Should a fire in the wilderness be encountered, like our prairie fires, she will not be burned or scorched. This last statement seems to be a kind of reverse of what was said in 42:25. When God's displeasure had to be vented on his people, they were burned. In the season of compassion that is about to begin, such suffering shall not overtake them.

Verse 3. That such assurance is well founded is here undergirded by several of the choice names by which the Lord designates himself: "your God, the Holy One of Israel, your Savior." As God he stands related to them as their proper head; as the Holy One he is devoted to their welfare; as Savior he can be depended on to deliver from every extremity. This last title is a favorite one of the prophet (see 45:15, 21; 49:24; 60:16; 63:8).

Perhaps it is best to construe the rest of v. 3 as implying

what God would be ready to do, should emergency demand it. That Israel might go free he would give up other nations as substitutes. Or, so to speak, the Lord is ready to pay a high ransom for his people. In this verse even three nations are mentioned: Egypt, Cush (sometimes translated Ethiopia, or even Nubia) and Seba. These three constituted all that was known of Africa in those days. So God is practically ready to sacrifice a continent to rescue his people. *Muilenburg* does well to point out that a "literalistic interpretation" would do violence to the meaning of the passage. But still it should be noted that if the passage should imply that the Lord would reimburse Persia, or Cyrus, for liberating the Jews and restoring them to their independence, then it did at least happen that Cambyses, the successor of Cyrus, conquered Egypt. But it may also be noted that physical dominion is not promised to Israel in reference to the nations of the earth. Strange to say, Ezekiel (29:17-20) has a similar passage in which Egypt again is promised to Nebuchadnezzar for Tyre.

Verse 4. These totally unmerited favors that God is willing to bestow upon his people are now traced down to their deepest root — the love of God. For reasons that man will never be able fully to fathom, the Lord loved Israel: she was "precious in [his] eyes," she was also "honored" and he "loved" her. Our prophet is not the only one who knows of this remarkable love that God bears to his people (cf. Hos. 11:1; Jer. 31:20). It is this love that prompts the Lord's redeeming activity. Expanding the thought of v. 3, the prophet claims that God will "give men in [her] stead, peoples for [her] life." There is, as *Wright* says, something "highly metaphorical" about this statement, which forbids putting a "precise historical interpretation" on these words. But there is at the same time something of a divine mystery here involved. It lay entirely in the free choice of the Lord whether he would select one people to be his own in a distinct sense, preferring them to others, even, as here claimed, sacrificing others in their behalf. But Israel was given preferential treatment, even though she certainly did not merit it. This passage is one of the strongest statements on the mysterious subject of the election of Israel. But the dominant tone of it all is not speculation but solid divine comfort. As *Westermann* rightly remarks, in v. 2 the Creator, the Lord of the elements, speaks; in v. 3b-4b, the Lord of history.

Verse 5. Therefore the prophet goes on with strong words of reassurance. However, little Israel may have merited it, God's attitude is still: "Fear not for I am with you." His presence is enough to allay all fear. But translating the election into terms of restoration, it implies that he will gather her scattered remnants from all quarters of the globe. For here "descendants" does not refer to future offspring but to her present membership. Each of the cardinal points of the compass is expressly given orders to give back what has been scattered there in any form of captivity due to historical circumstances. Apparently many cases of deportation of captives of war from Israel had taken place of which we have no record even in the sacred Scriptures, as would appear from 11:11, and from the findings of archaeology (cf. the discovery of the one-time existence of a great colony of Jews in Elephantine on the Nile). The diaspora was quite widely spread already in Isaiah's day. This is now quite generally conceded.

Verse 6. In highly poetic terms these various areas are commanded to restore these captives to their native land. As special motivation mention is made of the fact that the persons involved are really God's "sons," or children, a point of view that found expression also in passages like Exod. 4:22, 23; Hos. 11:1; Isa. 1:2, etc. By specifying "sons" and "daughters" separately, the Hebrew language would cover the *totality* of the nation. However, it could hardly be asserted that the prophet actually expected these nations personally to escort Israelites back home.

Verse 7. Still the prophet cannot refrain from indicating to his own people how deeply concerned the Lord is about this restoration and how profound his love for them is, stat-

ing the case in rich and expressive terms that are calculated to
make Israel aware of her rare prerogatives. So, for example,
the chosen people may be described as being "called by
[his] name." He is uniquely associated with them as with no
other nation. Besides, they are "created for [his] glory."
No ground here for nationalistic, chauvinistic pride. All this
was undertaken by the Lord to display his glory in reference
to Israel. Note the progression of the verbs used: created,
formed, made. From his first contact with them to the last
act that he does for making them to be what he has destined
them to be, his divine activity centers about them historically.
Here *Delitzsch* suggests that the three verbs involve the
ideas of "produce, shape, finish." But the Lord's ultimate
goal is his own glory, not Israel's, as has been correctly observed.

2. A Court Trial of the Idols (vv. 8-13)

43:8-13 8. Bring forth the people who are blind and yet have
eyes,
    who are deaf and yet have ears.
9. And all the nations have already gathered together,
    and the peoples have assembled.
"Who among them can declare this,
    and is able to show us former things?
Let them bring their witnesses to justify them,
    and let them hear and say: "That's true!"
10. You are my witnesses, says the Lord,
and my servant whom I have chosen.
that you may know and believe me,
    and that you may perceive that I am he.
Before me no god was formed,
    neither shall there be any after me.
11. I, I am the Lord,
    and apart from me there is no savior.
12. I declared and I saved and I let it be known,
    and there was no strange god among you;
and [so] you are my witnesses, says the Lord,
    and I [only] am God.
13. Also from henceforth I am he;
    and there is none that can deliver out of my hands.
    When I act, who can reverse it?"

The prophet has a special liking for presenting his material in the form of a "court trial." One whole chapter (41) used this approach. Here it appears again. But it should be noted that the tone of the passage is not that of calm, legal investigation, but rather one of passionate speech. The whole transaction may be conceived of as taking place in a court-room.

Verse 8. The author's particular concern is his own people. They are the ones who are to be brought into the courtroom. They are a group who have long languished in a dungeon, where the light was exceedingly dim. Still the thought is that as such the Babylonian Captivity was not a season productive of repentance and deeper insights. As in 42:18 ff. there is reference here to a reprehensible blindness. The capacities that the nation has for grasping the truth offered, have not been utilized. Such persons will always be found everywhere. They were the object of deep concern on the part of our Lord, who, basing his call on words like those here used by the prophet, often exhorted men: "He that hath ears to hear, let him hear." But the summons, "Bring forth" in the present context involves the idea of bringing the nation into the court-trial which is about to take place. Verse 8 refers to the summoning of Israel; v. 9 to that of "the nations."

Verse 9. Where v. 8 set the scene, v. 9 now quickly advances to the second stage: All persons concerned are thought of as having been notified and as having given heed, and as being now "already gathered" and "assembled" for the impending transactions. At once the Lord launches into the case in hand. What he said is not formally introduced by some familiar statement such as, "The Lord said." The verse suddenly veers over into direct discourse with the words, "Who among them can declare this?" The investigation which is getting under way is reflecting on two areas, first "this" and then "former things." The first seems to refer to the present situation where a restoration is getting under way. The second has in mind past instances of foreknowing the future and controlling it. The pronoun "them" in the question "Who among them . . . ?" may refer to such persons as were found in practically all nations of antiquity, namely soothsayers, men who claimed ability in some way to foretell the future. In the two areas just named not a one of the heathen soothsayers ever produced anything at all. They are challenged if they have any witnesses anywhere who can produce proof that the future was forecast; they are given free rein to produce their proof now. Then they might be justified in claiming that they have occult power of some sort. Now is the time and the place. Those standing by will themselves be able to render the verdict in such an event and say: "That's true!" — Utter silence greets this challenge.

Verse 10. All rivals to the honor of being God having been eliminated, Yahweh now moves the trial on to its proper conclusion. "Witnesses" for the opposition could not be found. Yahweh has such available — his own people. In fact that is in a sense their very destiny. Israel is not to be a mighty worldly power dominating other nations and exercising world-empire. She is to be witness to what God has done for her, witness by her very existence and witness by the testimony that she can bear orally. By thus witnessing she fulfils her calling of being God's "servant," whom he has chosen. First of all she must come to the overpowering conviction that Yahweh is the one that alone deserves to be called God. Monotheism is Israel's most precious insight. Whatever indications along this line had begun to glimmer here and there in divine revelation, all this now comes to clear expression and is finalized by our prophet. When he claims — letting the Lord speak the words — that no god was formed before him, he is not conceding that gods can be "formed." He is using about the only verb that can be used in a context like this. Before him no other god ever existed. None will ever spring into being in times to come.

Verse 11. Or, formulated very precisely, "I, I am the Lord." But this is not a barren monotheism, predicating sole existence of Yahweh. This is all extremely practical, one might say existential. For the rest of the statement is: "apart from me there is no savior." He is a God who acts. The consistent purpose of his mighty acts bears testimony to his essential unity.

Verse 12. Now the prophet is back on a favorite subject of his — the foretelling and execution of the restoration of his chosen people. He (God) saw it coming; he made it come to pass. "I declared and I saved and I let it be known" refers just to this issue alone. This constitutes overwhelming proof of his being. None could share in this honor: "There was no strange God among you." The approach is the same as in 45:5 f., 18, 22. There is not and there cannot be a god who shares even the least bit of the honor of the work done in behalf of Israel. And Israel knows this. So the author brings the matter to a conclusion: "And [so] you are my witnesses, and I [only] am your God. The words we have inserted in brackets are not expressed in the text but they represent the manner in which the case would be formulated in our day and language. Strangely the prophet does not quite say, "There is but one God." But he implies it. In a sense he says more than such a claim. He says: "I am he." In these verses (11-13) as *Muilenburg* has observed, there are twenty-nine words, twelve of which are in the first person.

Verse 13. Thus far the eyes were directed primarily to the past, to things accomplished. There comes a brief glance into the future: "Also from henceforth I am he." Gods cannot spring into being. *He* always was. But this again is not pure theory but the substance of Israel's experience. For "there is none that can deliver out of [his] hands." As he has sole existence so he has sole power. Therefore "When I act who can reverse it" (cf. also Amos 1:3, 6, 9, 11, 13, etc.). How strongly all this stands contrasted with what the heathen believed, appears from the fact that rank and power among the gods of the heathen was continually in flux. As has been remarked, in Egypt Amon replaced Re; in Babylon, Marduk replaced Bel, etc.

3. The Captivity of the Chaldeans (vv. 14-15)

43:14-15 14. Thus says the Lord, your Redeemer, the Holy
One of Israel;
"For your sake I will send to Babylon,
   and I will bring low as captives all of them,
   namely the Chaldeans, in the ships of which they were so proud;
15. I, the Lord, your Holy One,
   the Creator of Israel, your King."

In the court-trial of the idols (vv. 8-13) a note that had
stood out prominently was the summary and description of
the great things God had done in behalf of, and in control of,
his people. By way of contrast a brief section now follows,
in which the Lord indicates how he can, and does, control the
fortunes of other nations, even mighty Babylon.

Verse 14. This brief oracle is full of difficulties. We shall
briefly set forth how it may be construed, and briefly substantiate our interpretation. One writer has labelled it "Babylon in Panic" (*North*). This approach summarizes our understanding of the passage. Solemn introduction is made to
the passage by familiar formulas and names: "Thus says the
Lord, your Redeemer, the Holy One of Israel." This last
title does not stress the metaphysical attribute of holiness,
but marks God's "ethical activity."

But when the oracle that follows is introduced by the
phrase "for your sake," it should be noted that in the view of
the prophets the big movements of history center around
God's people and take place, under divine control with the
purpose of furthering God's designs in reference to his own.
The somewhat vague statement, "I will send to Babylon,"
involves perhaps the sending of Cyrus, who became the conqueror of Babylon. Not the instrument but the control of
history is stressed by this form of statement. That all the
Babylonians will be involved in what God does is indicated
by the statement, "I will bring low as captives all of them."
The verb used is usually translated "I will bring down."
"Bring low" seems to cover the issue more adequately.
These Babylonians are in the parallel statement described ac-

cording to the older geographical designation "Chaldeans." The point seems to be that when the city falls, sooner or later, Babylonian captives will be transported away on ships, on the very ships "of which they were so extremely proud." Literally this last statement reads "on the ships of their exultation." Babylon, on the Euphrates, controlled a tremendous world-trade. For this many ships were used. Any nation would be proud of its merchant marine. But there is a strange irony about having the objects of their pride become the means of their grief.

Verse 15. In concluding this brief oracle, the Lord uses a very solemn identification of himself, as the one who does all these things for the good of his people. He created them; he still is their "King." Though now in Captivity, Israel is still not without a king, and her King will assert his effective rule of his people.

Practically all interpretations of this passage portray, in one form or another, the defeat of the Chaldeans, the great super-power that had dominated a good part of history so successfully in the days of Isaiah and thereafter. *RSV* arrives at a feasible interpretation, largely by extensive textual emendations (always a somewhat dubious procedure) on the basis of too much confidence in the versions.

4. The Remarkable Exodus (vv. 16-21)

43:16-21 16. Thus says the Lord, he that made a way in the sea,
and a path in the mighty waters,
17. he that brought forth chariots and horses,
an army and warriors together, —
there they lie and can't get up,
they are extinguished, they are put out like a wick:
18. "Remember not former things;
do not consider things long past.
19. Lo, I am about to do a new thing;
now it is already springing up; haven't you noticed it?
I am also making a way in the wilderness,
and streams in the desert.
20. The wild beasts shall honor me, the jackals and the ostriches;

> for I give water in the wilderness,
>> and streams in the desert,
>> to give drink to my people, my chosen ones;
> 21. a people whom I have formed for myself shall declare my
>> praise."

Verse 16. It may be that *North's* caption is even better
than ours for this section — "Wonders of the New Exodus."
The old national traditions of his people live strong in the
remembrance of this prophet. "He that made a way in the
sea" reminds at once of the happenings that took place in the
days of Moses at the Red Sea. The parallel statement indicates what a remarkable work this was, for it actually involved the parting of "mighty waters" even though an area
was involved where the waters were comparatively shallow,
yet with a sudden change of the wind they may become the
equivalent of a mad tide. "Mighty waters" is no "exaggeration."

Verse 17. More of the ancient story is recalled. A turn is,
however, given to the thought which goes deeper than the
familiar historical account. The bringing forth of chariots
and horses, armies and warriors is attributed to *Yahweh*,
even as in Ezek. 38:4 it is *he* who leads the armies of God.
All this is merely a drastic way of saying that even the most
hostile forces that rage "against the Lord and against his
anointed" are still only doing the behest of the One True
God. That does not mean that Pharaoh, in sending forth his
chariots, was not a free agent. But it does mean that the incomprehensible God, who controls all things, was manifesting his mysterious control even when the Egyptians went
out with hostile intention. Yahweh was leading them to their
doom. For "army and warriors together" *North* suggests
"armies in mass formation." By a sudden change of the
Hebrew tense (?) we are introduced into the very midst of
the developing situation: without any agent apparently having been at work, the hosts lie low: "There they lie and can't
get up." Then by another sudden change of the Hebrew to
the perfect, marking the abruptness of the action, the whole

episode is over, done, finished: "They are extinguished, they are put out like a wick," even as Exod. 14 so dramatically pictures the incident.

Verse 18. The next step in the prophet's thinking is almost the very opposite of what we might have expected. He says not: "Remember," He says: "Remember *not* former things." Extreme forms of statement must always be regarded with due caution. In 46:9 Israel is bidden to "remember the former things." So the present statement must be meant in the sense of letting the memory linger on the events of the past, of dwelling nostalgically on what happened in the good old days. So the thought is this: Let the grand past be over-topped by the more glorious future. Cultivate hope, not re-membrance. The "new thing" that is to be eagerly antici-pated is the impending exodus from Babylon.

Verse 19. It is on the verge of happening. Alert minds can already discern traces of its coming: "It is already spring-ing up." Indications of its coming must already have been discernible. Israel could be challenged: "Haven't you noticed it?" Now comes the statement of what the prophet had in mind: "I am also making a way in the wilderness, and streams in the desert," for those returning from Captivity. Once it was a way through the waters; now it is a way through seemingly impassable dry, desert land. Then he re-moved the water; now he will furnish it.

Verse 20. But for this prophet, the area of grace and the area of what we call nature is a unit. Even the wild beasts have an interest and a share in what happens to God's people. It will make them glad to behold what God does for them, so glad that they, in their own way "will honor" him, even "jackals and ostriches" — creatures notoriously shy and un-friendly. The language is rhetorically rich and colorful: "I give water in the wilderness and streams in the desert, to give drink to my people, my chosen ones." Streams may never, in the course of this exodus have sprung up miraculously; but Israel never lacked for what was necessary for her subsis-tence during the return from Exile. In reality these statements cover the entire sweep of God's gracious dealings with his own for all times. They are truly eschatological in their scope.

Verse 21. God's people shall acknowledge the greatness of his works in their behalf. The future has mighty things in store according to the rich plans of the Lord.

5. Israel's Guilt — Yahweh's Grace (vv. 22-28)

43:22-28 22. "Yet you, O Jacob, did not call upon me;
but you have been weary of me, O Israel.
23. You have not brought me a sheep for a burnt offering,
nor have you honored me with your sacrifices.
I have not burdened you with offerings,
nor wearied you with [the demand of] frankincense.
24. You have not bought me sweet cane with money,
nor sated me with the fat of your sacrifices;
but you have burdened me with your sins,
and wearied me with your iniquities.
25. I, I am he who blots out your transgressions for my sake,
and will not remember your sins any more.
26. Remind me, and let us argue it out together;
you declare your case that you may be proved right.
27. Your first father [already] sinned,
and your mediators transgressed against me.
28. Therefore I profaned the princes of the sanctuary,
and gave up Jacob to utter destruction, and Israel to scorn."

How does this section (vv. 22-28) stand related to the one that preceded (vv. 16-21)? The connection is traced in so many words, but apparently the pattern: effect — cause, is in evidence. The effect, the new exodus, has just been emphasized. Now that which is *not* the cause is being reflected upon. There are times when the people of God are exceedingly prone to attribute favorable developments within the kingdom to some measure of worthiness or desert on their part. The prophet may have sensed something of that spirit among those to whom his message was being transmitted. Since such an attitude tends to the corruption of faith and is full of spiritual dangers of all sorts, he promptly launches into an invective (*Gerichtsrede*, like 50:1-3 — *Westermann*) which is strangely followed by a sweet declaration of divine grace (v. 25). We say "strangely" because grace is not the logical answer to a sharp denunciation. But God's grace so far transcends human logic that we shall never be able to grasp its full magnitude.

Verse 22. What follows is not a rejection of formal worship or a repudiation of the sacrifices of Israel, any more than is the case in Jer. 7:21-23; or Amos 5:21-25; or Isa. 29:13. But it is certainly a repudiation of the type of soulless worship that prevailed in those days. Priest and prophet were not pitted against one another in sharp antithesis, as they are so frequently represented to have been.

The first count on which Israel is indicted is worthless prayer; for prayer may rightly be regarded as the soul of all true worship. Prayers were no doubt made publicly and privately; but they did not amount to a calling upon the Lord. They must have had something of the spirit of the Pharisee who went up into the temple to pray, according to Luke 18. That such was the case is indicated clearly enough by the parallel statement of this verse: "But you have been weary of me." The performance of the rite of prayer proved a boring thing. If that be the case, then nothing that follows as part of the rites of worship can have any validity.

Verse 23. They may have offered sheep, but they did not sincerely bring them to the Lord. So the words appear to be construed: "You have not brought *me* a sheep." Or the matter might be regarded from this angle: The true spirit that should have motivated "a burnt offering," was noticeably lacking. So also the next statement is to be construed: "You have not honored me with your sacrifices." Of course, it must also be remembered that Israel in captivity could not meet the requirements of the cultus because the temple was destroyed and the priests were scattered. But that is not a major consideration of the prophet here. Apparently an attitude is being described which prevailed abundantly already while the temple still stood and has not been remedied since. God's side of the matter is covered by the second half of the verse. This appears at first reading as a repudiation of all that the law of Moses ascribed to divine appointment in the days after the Exodus from Egypt. But since such a flagrant contradiction within the sacred Scriptures is hardly reasonable, apparently the statements are meant in the sense that the Lord did not require these ceremonial acts as mere outward performances devoid of soul and sincerity. God certainly had not made what would be burdensome demands of "offerings." What God had appointed, the true worshipper would present, not as a heavy duty but as a meaningful outlet of deep emotion and inner need. So the offering of frankincense could be either a dead chore or a spiritual experience, depending on the attitude of the heart of the worshipper.

Verse 24. The "sweet cane" referred to was a part of the sacred anointing oil that is described in Exod. 30:23. How it was assigned to some form of use in the cultus otherwise, we do not know. In any case it was a rare article that was used by some in cultic practices. It may have constituted a special part of an act of devotion resorted to by some of the Israelites and may have been part of a very special observance. It could be meaningful. Here the prophet rebukes his people for not having ventured to do anything special of this sort for their Lord. And since the "fat of sacrifices" was regarded as a choice gift specially devoted to the Lord, Israel is here charged with not having ventured to do any such special act in a spirit of deeper devotion.

Summing up at this point for the moment, we must emphasize that we reject as totally unwarranted the contention of *Volz* that the prophet did not regard the prevailing laws regarding sacrifice as divinely appointed. God had, in other words, given no appointments about sacrificial rites. But we do regard the remarks of *Fischer* as entirely proper — "This is by no means a total rejection of sacrifices." Even more to the point is *Skinner's* statement: "This hardly amounts to a repudiation of sacrifice *in principle* on the part of Jehovah." This approach would be further well expressed by *North*, when he suggests as translation for v. 22 the following: "Do not imagine that it was me you invited to your feasting."

The second half of v. 24 shows what their sacrifice in those days actually amounted to. Taking the words from v. 23, the writer suggests that "burdening" was done, but it was Israel who did it to the Lord with their sins. So also some "wearying" was done, but again it was Israel wearying the Lord "with their iniquities." What could have been a delight and a helpful sacramental experience, instead became something offensive to God as well as harmful to man.

Verse 25. At this point the turn of thought comes very abruptly. Here, if ever, the invective could have been followed by a word of threat. Instead there follows one of the most gracious promises of the whole book. With heavy emphasis on the "I" as the author of this grace, the word says in effect: I, the very one whom you offended; I who have just cause to vent my anger on you to the full; I am the one who blots out the very transgressions that have so wearied and offended me. God, as *Delitzsch* rightly asserts, is the one who here proclaims the *sola gratia* (by grace alone) and the *sola fide* (through faith alone). That the motivation and the whole approach rests solely with him and not on any merit or worthiness on the nation's part is contained in the "for my sake." Another of the standard expressions for forgiving is set forth in the parallel statement: "I will not remember your sins any more." Under the circumstances it is true that the statement totally passes by for the moment the need of expiation or the method of it. It is not the prophet's intention to offer the total theology of redemption. But he is the strongest exponent of justification by faith found in the Old Testament, and here fully vindicates his right to that title.

Verse 26. Having for the moment relieved the tension by the assurance of divine grace, the prophet drives home still more fully the point of Israel's grave guilt. He does it by the use of the means of a court-trial again. For that is what the words, "let us argue it out together" clearly imply. Half ironic comes the introductory summons, "Remind me."

That apparently means nothing more here than: You shall have a fair hearing; no evidence shall be suppressed. In that spirit the words are added, "You declare your case that you may be proved right." From the sequel it appears that in the face of this challenge Israel never even ventured a word of excuse. Total silence testified to total guiltiness.

Verse 27. Here Yahweh charges that their "first father" already was a guilty man, stained by major sins. We do best to regard this as a reference to Jacob (not to Adam — who lies too far in the past; not to Abraham — who was also the father of Arabs and Edomites; not to David — to whom a title like "first father" scarcely applies). But Jacob who secured the birth-right by subterfuge and did other deeds of questionable character, is truly the father of this people who have been guilty of double dealing with God throughout their history. When we come to the second statement, "Your mediators transgressed against me," a number of reasonable possibilities confront us. The "mediators" could be priests or prophets (cf. 28:7); or "kings and prophets (*North*); or Moses and Aaron (cf. Num. 20:12). Israel often stood in need of mediation. Her "mediators" were almost as fallible as the nation they represented. They almost may be said to have led the way for the nation in disobedience. In the face of such indictments, the people could hardly have an easy conscience about the way they had treated their God. They could hardly take forgiveness lightly just because God was so gracious. As has often been remarked: here too "free grace is not cheap grace."

Verse 28. That God did not take their sin lightly is driven home more effectively by a reference to the recent experience of the capture of Jerusalem, the destruction of the temple, and the dragging of the nation into Captivity. For the "profaning of the princes of the sanctuary" may refer to acts like II Kings 25:18-21, where the execution of priests is expressly mentioned. That "Jacob was given to utter destruction" most likely is a reference to the Captivity as such.

So too, "the giving of Israel to scorn," or "to reviling" (*RSV*).

Notes

Verse 1. Both "I have redeemed" and "I have called" are to be regarded as prophetic perfects.

Verse 4. The singular "man" and the plural "peoples" both together constitute one of those pairs that aim to cover the entire scope of a certain concept. Cf. *KS* 94. This approach makes it unnecessary to attempt any textual changes (like *'adhamoth* for *'adham*).

Verse 6. "Sons" and "daughters" again is a means for expressing totality of a given concept. Cf. *GK* 122 v.

Verse 8. *Volz* decrees, we believe rather arbitrarily, that v. 8 must be dropped. But if viewed, as set forth above, as referring to Israel and v. 9 as referring to the nations, the two approaches make very good sense together. The initial word *hotsi'* is most commonly regarded as an imperative, which is made possible by a vowel change — *hotse'*. Cf. *GK* 53 m.

Verse 9. The verb *niqbetsu* need not be changed into an imperative form. It may be regarded as a future perfect "will have already assembled themselves," as *KS* 172 a, points out. This approach ties up well with the further suggestion that before *kol* a *waw* may have fallen out through haplography. That could serve as further indication how the two verses belong together.

Verse 10. Before *tha'aminu* the customary *waw* conversive with perfects is not used because the two verbs are synonymns.

Verse 14. When *Muilenburg* takes the material from this verse on to 44:5 and arranges it as belonging into seven strophies, "of approximately the same length," this strikes us as too highly artificial. Certain broader thought patterns are lost by such an arrangement.

On this difficult verse *North* suggests the emendation "drive the Chaldeans downstream" — at least a possible translation for *horadhti*. *Volz* relates *rinnatham* to the "noisy bustle" at the wharves (*Weltgetuemmel*).

Verse 16. *Nothen*, the participle, stands in a past context, and so must be translated "made," as *KS* 237a shows.

Verse 17. The perfects *da'achu* and *kabhu* are used to indicate the abruptness of the event they describe (*KS* 119).

Verse 20. For "jackals and ostriches" — at best a questionable translation — *North* suggests "wolves and owls."

Verse 21. V. 21 does not appeal to the taste of some commentators and so they eliminate it. Such purely subjective criteria of judgment are inadequate.

Verse 24. The *be* before *keseph* is the *be* or price (*GK* 119 p).

The verb *he'bhadhtanni* literally means, "you have made me your servant."

Verse 25. The "any more" at the end of the verse appears in the Isaiah (I) scroll of Qumran as *'odh* and seems to be very much in place. For some the entire verse does not appear sharp enough in a context of rebuke. But in Isaiah this often is the case. Therefore the verse need not be regarded as a later addition.

Verse 28. The word for "scorn" (*gidduphim*) appears in the plural — an intensive plural — like "to much scorn." Cf. *GK* 124 e.

Chapter XLIV:1-23

E. THE GOD OF GRACE VS. THE IMPOTENT IDOLS (Chap. 44:1-23)

The preceding chapter had closed with a strong word of rebuke (*Scheltrede*). But in this rebuke was imbedded one verse that indicated that this rebuke was not God's last word to his people, namely v. 25. The note struck in that verse is now taken up in our chapter and developed more at length in sharp contrast to the preceding rebuke. This creates the impression that rebuke and promise are inextricably intertwined, if not dovetailed together in a rather surprising turn of thought.

But this approach does not yet indicate the character of the chapter as a whole, which is a sharp contrast between two widely divergent concepts of God, or gods. For the true concept of who and what God is, as Israel held the faith concerning him, and the view held by the typical non-Israelite of that day, the idolater, are presented in the sharpest contrast that could possibly be depicted, as our above caption sets forth: The God of (effective) grace vs. the impotent idols.

We may pause for a moment at this point to indicate the pattern of this chapter as form-criticism sees it. In this type of approach vv. 1-5 constitute a salvation oracle; vv. 6-8 constitute an oracle of judgment; vv. 9-20 is excised and treated separately, as a passage that does not have its setting in this chapter originally; vv. 21-22 constitute an oracle of admonition (*Mahnrede*); v. 23 is a hymn. Leaving aside the problem of vv. 9-20, the rest of this approach gives the reader a feel of the nature of the chapter as a whole.

Centering again on vv. 9-20 for the moment it may be noted how G. A. Smith evaluates this section in particular.

He uses terminology that at least effectively catches the unique character of this passage, when he says: "A burst of laughter comes very weirdly out of exile." Though it may be sharp satire rather than "laughter," still one is made to feel the uniqueness of the passage. While engaged in evaluating this large sector of the chapter we may also now already take note of the fact that, as the same writer says, the style is not as smooth as the *KJ* version makes it. It does indeed have some irregularities about it. Many find it difficult to determine whether this piece is to be classified as prose or as poetry. *RSV* prints it as prose. Some measure of parallelism is no doubt to be detected throughout. Nevertheless we cannot help but feel that the grounds for denying this section to the author of the rest of the chapter are none too solid.

1. The Blessing of the Spirit to Be Poured on the Unworthy

44:1-5 1. But now hear, O Jacob my servant,
   and Israel whom I have chosen!
2. Thus says Yahweh, who made you,
   who formed you from the womb, who will help you:
"Fear not, my servant Jacob,
   Jeshurun, whom I have chosen;
3. For as I pour out water on the thirsty land
   and copious rains on the dry land,
so I will pour out my spirit on your descendants
   and my blessing on your offspring.
4. And they shall spring up in the midst of grass,
   as willows by the streams of water.
5. This one will say, 'I belong to the Lord,'
   and another will call himself by the name of Jacob;
and still another will write on his hand, 'I am the Lord's'
   and shall surname himself by the name of Israel."

Verse 1. The "but now" sets this new section off sharply from what preceded. "Jacob" and "Israel," being used together, in parallel lines seem to signify, as elsewhere, the entire nation. The lamentable division of the days of Jeroboam I, will be a thing of the past. Israel's role as God's "servant" is again stressed. The fact as such is held parallel to the fact that God has freely chosen this people as his own. Again and again God's choice of the nation as his people is the foundation of his further kindly dealings with them.

Verse 2. Other favors included in the original choice are brought to the fore. For one thing God "made" them to be what they are, the only nation enjoying this unique distinction. Or to stress still further God's favors, he may be said to have "formed [them] from the womb," which here means from the very beginning of their national existence. Therefore it follows freely that he will "help" them whenever help is needed. It may well have been that in the days of the captivity many a "fear" assailed the hearts of the godly in Israel whether they still had any future whatever to look forward to. Therefore the kindly assurance: "Fear not, my servant Jacob." In the parallel statement Israel is now addressed as "Jeshurun," a name which already appears in Deut. 32:15; 33:5, 26. It appears to be related to the name Israel, but no one seems to know just how. The idea that it is a tender diminutive has now generally been abandoned. It could be traced back to the root meaning "righteous," and then might be designed to describe the nation as righteous in God's sight rather than the "conniver" which is the root meaning of the name Jacob. But all this is dubious. At least it must be classed as a term of endearment. To it is added a second reference to God's free choice of the people.

Verse 3. Now comes the issue toward which this elaborate introduction has been leading. We follow the approach of those interpreters who see the first half of the verse as correlated to the second (as — so). One thing God is known to do the world over: he provides water and rain for the thirsty land and more often than not, does this work of his in a very generous fashion; he "pours out water." So in days to come (here indicated by the terms "descendeants" and "offspring") he will "pour out [his] Spirit." The divine power that created physical life will also be the source of spiritual life. For Spirit here, as so frequently, connotes the acme of divine power. This gift is also described as being a "blessing" which term again signifies an effective form of divine enrichment. The prophet had previously expressed a similar thought in 32:15 (cf. also Ps. 104:30). Ezekiel 37 also stands related to this approach. Again we recall in this connection that in the background some emphasis lies on the fact that a gift such as this to be bestowed upon the unworthy nation was a gift of free grace.

Verse 4. Rounding out the figure employed, the prophet now indicates that as a result of God's abundant outpouring of water a tree is to spring up, and the tree is Israel. More is meant than the mere fact that the growth involved merely germinates. It is implied that it will continue to grow and prosper. The fact that it is to spring up "in the midst of grass," would seem to imply that it stands in an area rich in other vegetation, which also thrives because of abundant water. In all this approach, though we recognize the figure of a tree, it may still be said appropriately "they [plural] shall spring up," because the tree idea covers the multitude of the members of the nation. Thus far the idea seems to limit itself to the nation Israel. *It* shall again grow and thrive and flourish and be a mighty tree.

Verse 5. Now the emphasis changes and the thought is stressed that outsiders shall take pride in becoming affiliated with this ancient and marvelous people on whom God's blessing rests in such abundant measure. The term "Israel" takes on new dimensions. It is no longer limited to the purely national; it takes on possibilities of an expanded concept of, shall we say, the congregational. It blossoms out into the super-racial. Several examples are given. One man will say: "I belong to the Lord," that is to say, to Yahweh, who was once regarded as the national God of *Israel* and no more. Now he will take pride in being under the authority of this God, whom he no doubt recognizes as being beyond such limitations. Another person will feel honored to be identified with the ancestor of the nation, Jacob. Still another will even "write on his hand, 'I am the Lord's.'" This could mean that he tatoos Yahweh's name on his hand that he may carry it before his eyes and see it continually as a reminder of his allegiance to the God of Israel. The fact that tatooing was forbidden in the Mosaic law (see Lev. 19:28; 21:5) was connected with the fact that this practice was associated with idolatry. But here it is regarded as the very antithesis to such a connotation. Even a fourth possibility is suggested: a man may "surname himself by the name of Israel." In addition to his native name, a man shall give himself the surname "Israel" as indicative of the highest honor that any name can bestow.

2. Redemption Guaranteed by Yahweh, the Only God Who Can Foretell (vv. 6-8)

44:6-8 6. Thus says the Lord, the King of Israel
and his Redeemer, the Lord of hosts:
"I am the first and I am the last
and apart from me there is no god.
7. And who is like me? Let him proclaim it;
let him tell it, and set forth before me what has happened
from the time when I set up nations in days of old.
Let them tell us what is yet to be.
8. Be not afraid nor perplexed.
Have I not told you from of old and declared it?
And you are my witnesses! Is there a god apart from me?
There is no Rock; I know none."

The emphasis now lies on the fact that the God of Israel in anything but one of the impotent idols. He works by grace but it is effective grace. And so the redemption that is held forth in prospect for God's people is a thing that will be definitely achieved. So a word is given from the mouth of the Almighty that sets forth this thought effectively.

Verse 6. The formula introducing this word from the mouth of the Lord first centers attention on three titles that fitly apply to him. He is first of all "King," one who administers affairs efficiently. But above all — here comes a favorite title — he is the "Lord of hosts," the one who has the entire host of created things always under total control. When such a one speaks he merits attention. What he says will as-

suredly come to pass. All this adds up again to the claim that
he is the only one deserving of the name God — monotheism.
The same approach was used in 41:21-29 and 43:9-13. When
he claims that he is "the first and . . . the last" he represents
himself as functioning throughout the entire course of history. He was on the scene when things began to be made.
He will still be on the scene when the stage of history is
cleared for the last time. The same statement appears also in
Rev. 1:8, 17 and 22:13. All of which amounts to the claim
that "apart from [him] there is no god."

Verse 7. This involves not only his exclusiveness but also
his being totally other than the rest of those who are called
gods. This verse would seem to be a challenge addressed to
the so-called gods. They are invited to a court-trial again.
If any one of their number is in any sense like him, let such
a one stand forth and say so, and tell it. The one area in
which this test can prove decisive is the ability of these who
are challenged "to set forth . . . what has happened," that is
to say, give instances where a coming event was predicted
and then came the fulfillment of the prediction. Perhaps
God, the challenger, has in mind cases like the foretelling of
the Flood in the days of Noah, an event which indubitably
came to pass just as it was foretold. We go back as far as
this because rather remote time seems to be under consideration, as the somewhat difficult statement indicates: "from the
time when I set up nations in days of old." But here again
Yahweh is in a class by himself, just as he is distinct from all
others in that he can tell "what is yet to be" in reference to
the things that lie in the future. The Lord keeps making this
point because the proof employed is distinctive and powerful.

Verse 8. Now comes the practical application of all this.
If these claims of the Holy One be true then there is no
ground for fear or perplexity. For even though the heathen
gods look very impressive in the light of their massive temples, their splendid processions, their costly images, their rich
ceremonial worship, the apparent success of the arms of their
worshippers, all this is nothing more than a fleeting shadow

when subjected to the test of time. God keeps reiterating that *he* told and declared things from of old and of that Israel in its long and impressive history is witness, a history that allows for only one conclusion: There is no god "apart from [him]." Or to phrase it all in terms hallowed from days of old: "There is no rock." He knows of none, and his knowledge is more comprehensive than theirs. (On "rock" cf. 26: 4; Deut. 32:31; it is a term used 33 times in reference to God in the Old Testament).

3. Idolatry, Empty Folly (vv. 9-11)

44:9-11 9. The makers of idols are all of them numskulls,
and their darlings [the idols] are useless;
and their witnesses neither see nor understand.
So they must be ashamed.
10. Whoever has formed a god,
well, he has cast an image to no avail.
11. And behold, all who are attached to them, will be ashamed,
and the workmen, they are but human beings.
Let them all assemble, let them step forth;
they shall be terrified and put to shame together.

In addition to what was said before on this section a few remarks are in order. Very much to the point is *North's* description: "the stupidity of idolatry." Furthermore the fact that vv. 9-20 may be omitted and then v. 21 will follow readily after v. 8 and make good sequence, that claim, we say, proves nothing. For any writer may interrupt a line of argument for a momentary digression, then continue with his former line of thought. What the critical claim says in effect is: Writers dare not make digressions. The sequence going from v. 8 to v. 9 is also readily seen to be a good and coherent one. If the subject under consideration had been "Redemption guaranteed," obviously v. 9 brings in a contrast: The useless idols could not work any redemption.

In approaching this section it should be noted, as again *North* has well said: "The Old Testament knows nothing of the distinction between an idol in which the god is supposed to reside . . . and the symbol." In other words, the Old Testament writers identify the image with the idol. For in practice that is the way the matter works out. The philosopher's reflections together with those of the historian on the subject were not to be found among the people at large. So the same approach prevails in each of the passages that satirize idolatry (cf. 40:19, 20; 41:6, 7, 29; 45:16; 46:5-7).

Verse 9. It must be borne in mind that it took courage in the face of strongly intrenched idolatry to make remarks such as are about to be examined. Idolatry seemed the very embodiment of success. Now comes the prophet and says the idol-makers are "numskulls." He goes farther: "Their darlings," i.e., the very idols themselves, are "useless." All who are addicted to idolatry (for they are the ones meant by the name "their witnesses,") "neither see nor understand." "So they must be ashamed" as is now historically the case virtually with all idolaters the world over. Idolatry stands discredited as utter folly.

Verse 10. Aside from the senselessness of the practice of it all there is the complete futility of it. This the prophet sums up in the claim that all who have made images have done something that was done "to no avail." No idol ever did anything.

Verse 11. He sees the day coming when all devotees of the idols will be ashamed. So will the workmen and all who commission them to produce an idol. For the workmen are "but human beings." But water cannot rise above its level. So the human cannot produce the divine. If a test case were to be made of it and all who had ever made idols were to assemble as one unit group and were to try to step forth in support of what they had produced, they could furnish nothing by way of upholding their bold claims about what they manufacture; they would all "be terrified and put to shame together." The whole crew of them would have been engaged in a totally futile project.

4. A Satirical Description of the Manufacture of Idols (vv. 12-17)

44:12-17 12. The ironsmith [makes] an axe and works it over
the coals;
with the hammer he shapes it,
and works it over with his strong right arm.
Then he grows hungry and has no strength left;
he drinks no water and is faint.
13. The carpenter stretches the measuring-line over it,
then shapes it up with a pencil.
He works with a scraping-tool and shapes it up with a compass.
He makes it to be like the figure of a man,
with all the beauty of a man—
to take its place in a dwelling.
14. He went out and cut down cedars for himself,
or he took a holm-tree or an oak,
and lets it become sturdy among the trees of the forest.
Or he even planted a fir and the rain nourished it.
15. Then it serves as fuel for a man.
Namely he takes some of it and warms himself;
he kindles a fire and bakes bread;
also he makes a god and worships it;
he makes an image for himself and falls down before it.
16. A part of it he burns in the fire
and over another part of it he eats flesh.
He prepares a roast and satisfies his hunger.
He also warms himself and says:
"Aha! I am warm; I feel the warm glow."
17. And the rest of it he makes into a god, his idol.
He falls down before it and worships it,
and he says: "Deliver me, for you are my god!"

In expounding this passage we are beset by two major difficulties. One, the names of the tools and implements used
by craftsmen in days of old are not very familiar to us. Two,
the writer does not follow through on the process of manufacture of the idol in strict sequence, but reaches back, it
seems, to a certain point; then reaches back even farther;
then even farther still. He reverses the procedure that we
would have been inclined to pursue. We may indicate at this
point that at least in the Apocrypha (Wisdom 13:11 ff.) a
fairly close parallel to this account is to be found.

Verse 12. Two types of craftsmen are depicted in their
respective activities — "the ironsmith" and (v. 13) "the carpenter." This is due to the fact that images, as has been long

understood by now, in days of old were so constructed as to consist of a metal plating over a wood framework. So a kind of cooperation between the two types of craftsmen is taken for granted in this description. We are not even sure of the meaning of the term we have translated as "axe." The point of the writer seems to be that even the necessary tools used in the process have to be manufactured before the task can be taken in hand. But even that part of the assignment makes the smith to grow weary with hunger and faint with thirst. So the basis of it all is clumsy tools and weak workmen. They are the source from which an idol springs.

Verse 13. Now it is as though the prophet says: Let us examine how the carpenter goes about his task. The measuring-line is stretched. Whether the idol has an inch or two more of height depends on that measuring line. His general shape depends on the "pencil" used. Lack of skill in this direction could result in a disfigured god. Then the carpenter works with a "scraping-tool" — perhaps a plane; and uses the "compass" to round out perhaps the shape of the head. Always in the back of the craftman's mind is the "image of a man," and not just any man, but one who has some measure of "beauty" or attractiveness. And in the process of all this work from time to time the workman already envisions the finished product occupying its place "in a dwelling," or a shrine. We failed to take note of the possibility that the carpenter may have had as basis for the entire model a solid tree trunk, rather than a light frame of wood.

Verse 14. Now the investigation into the procedure involved is pushed back a little farther, into the time when the idol to be was still in the tree-state, and the tree had not yet been cut down. Then the woodsman may have started out with several trees, "cedars" perhaps, intending after they were cut down to decide which would be best suited for his purpose. It might have been "a holm-tree or an oak," that was cut down, but even there some deliberation was involved. These last two mentioned may have been good prospects but were not quite tall enough. So they had to be nursed along for a while till they became "sturdy among the trees of the forest." So much were these idols creatures of chance; they could have turned out quite a bit different from what actually resulted in the end. To such an extent are the idols victims of circumstance. They do not control circumstance. Circumstance controls them. Or for that matter, the craftsman may even have supervised the process of selection back from the point where he even "planted a fir and the rain nourished it." The whole destiny of the idol was at each of these junctures hanging in the balance.

Verse 15. Now a number of possible uses to which the wood that made the body of the idol *might* have been put, and always it might have been the idol that was put to such uses. It could have been, as parts of it certainly were, used "as fuel for a man." The craftsman did actually use some of this same wood for kindling "a fire and [baking] bread," Such purely utilitarian uses! But the sentence goes on in one breath: "also he makes a god and worships it." It's all in a day's work, this manufacture of idols. Just to repeat: "he makes an image for himself and falls down before it." It's such a senseless thing to fall down before that which is the work of his hands, achieved with so much toil and trouble.

Verse 16. The particular point to be made is spelled out so that it may by no means be overlooked. Note the various uses to which "a part" of the wood has been put. It need not always be the same pattern. Not all men would necessarily do according to the letter of what is here outlined. But the uses involved could include: burning some in the fire; eating flesh over some of it; preparing roast over another portion; satisfying his hunger; warming himself, and expressing his satisfaction at having taken the chill out of his bones.

Verse 17. Now comes what to him was the climax: "the rest of it he makes into a god, his idol." Really that is a ludicrous anticlimax. The writer repeats, as much as to say: "He *actually* falls down before it and worships it." His prayer and confession follow: "Deliver me, for you are my god!"

5. The Idle Folly of Idolatry (vv. 18-20)

44:18-20 18. They still have not known and have not understood;

for their eyes have been smeared shut so that they cannot see,
and their minds so that they cannot understand.
19. No one gives the matter any thought,
nor has any one knowledge or insight enough to say:
"Half of it I burned in the fire,
    and I also baked bread on its coals;
    I am now roasting flesh and eating it;
and shall I now make the rest of it an abominable idol,
and shall I fall down before a block of wood?"
20. If a man feeds on ashes,
    a mind that has been deceived has led him astray,
and he cannot deliver himself,
    or say: "Am I not holding fast to a delusion?"

The heading we have set down for this section is practically the same as for the section 3. above. Repetition for the sake of driving a point home to the utmost! A bigger piece of folly can hardly be conceived of. Perhaps now a little more emphasis is put on the aspect of the *delusion* involved.

Verse 19. In this verse the use of the term "abominable idol" may seem a bit out of place. In fact, this is not a term that the idol-worshipper would actually have used. The writer has merely substituted a word out of his own vocabulary. Or else he feels so strongly that if the man were but honest he would himself feel impelled to use a term like this.

Verse 20. The opening of the verse sounds like a kind of proverbial saying. One feels instinctively that some form of self-deception is under consideration. Some have thought that the figure is derived from the idea of trying to graze sheep on a barren ash-heap. So the mind of the idolater is dealing with empty, fruitless concepts and is not doing any solid reasoning. Or it may be thought of as involving an attempt at self-help. But who could "deliver himself" by manufacturing an idol, who cannot even deliver himself when dangers draw near? The conclusion of the verse actually runs thus: "Is there not a lie in my right hand?" We have chosen one of the several translations which have been offered for this line in the words: "Am I not holding fast to a delusion?" It might be to the point to indicate that the "right hand" referred to in the text often involves the idea of a position of honor, and the word for "delusion" is literally "a lie." The whole attitude of the idol-worshipper then boils down to this: In his life and thinking the position of honor is occupied by a lie.

6. The Effective Pardon Bestowed by the Lord (vv. 21-23)

44:21-23 21. Remember these things, O Jacob,
     and Israel, for you are my servant.
I formed you, you are my servant;
   O Israel, you will not be forgotten by me.
22. I have blotted out your transgressions like a cloud,
   your sins like a mist.
O return to me, for I have redeemed you.
23. Rejoice, O heavens, for the Lord has done it;
shout aloud, O depths of the earth.
Break forth into singing, O mountains,
   your forest and every tree in it!
For the Lord has redeemed Jacob
   and will be glorified in Israel.

Verse 21. Now comes the practical application of the above. The issue of idolatry is so important, for the sin is so devastating and foolish. Demonstrations like the one just presented should not be forgotten. It is as though the words "these things" demanded some such unique presentation as the one just covered. This shows how well the entire section (vv. 9-20) fits into this context and is by no means extraneous material. Israel in her role as "servant" of the Lord has a high honor and should heed all things that contribute to her successful fulfillment of this role. The Lord is beginning again to set forth how different a God he is. His people "will not be forgotten" by him. He remembers them even when they have forgotten him. The idols, when appealed to, cannot remember, cannot, in fact, do anything at any time. There is a wealth of comforting assurance in words like these. They reveal God's heart.

Verse 22. But more than vague generalities are involved in Yahweh's attitude toward his people. It involves effective dealing with the most crucial issue of the lives of men — sin. And what does he do about sin? He "blots it out," even as the morning mists are dissipated by the heat of rising sun, and are dispersed so effectively as to be no more. They vanish. Clouds, higher up in the atmosphere and mists, clinging close to the earth, are both disposed of. That is the kind of God that mankind needs above all other needs. That more is involved than some kind of juggling of balances, in fact that a corresponding attitude, or reaction, to this forgiving grace is necessary, is suggested by the last line: "Return to me, for I have redeemed you." Unless there be a decisive personal turning to God, there is no receiving of pardon. Not that man's attitude gained the slightest merit in the transaction. In the whole context of Isaiah only grace without a particle of human achievement can be involved. Again Isaiah has proven himself to be the outstanding evangelist of the Old Covenant.

Verse 23. Again and again men have pointed out that the hymnic conclusion of this section is characteristic of the prophet. God does so many things for which he is to be praised resoundingly. To such praise the prophet not only admonishes but provides the very terms to be used convenient at hand for immediate use. Again the feeling that the mercy bestowed is so great that it calls for more praise than man is normally capable of offering, and so all of nature is summoned to contribute its share: heavens above and the depths of the earth beneath; mountains and forests and trees. This praise is due to him for on the one hand "He has done it." In this context that seems to refer to the fact that he has effectively acted. He has actually bestowed pardon. Or it can also be stated in terms like this: "He has redeemed Jacob and will be glorified in Israel." More than national restoration is under consideration here, though that too is reflected upon. And so once again a section has been concluded on the "theocentric" note. It may even be, as *North* suggests that the Lord "points to Israel as his crowning achievement."

Notes

Verse 3. Though it is not fully expressed in the Hebrew, the nature of the two successive clauses is clearly correlative, and may well be translated in this way: "as . . . so" (Cf. *KS* 371 l).

Verse 7. After "Who is like me?" the *Septuagint* inserts the verb, "let him step forth" which fits very appropriately. The clause beginning *missumi* is admittedly very difficult, but may be construed as an infinitive clause of time (*KS* 401 d).

Verse 9. The pronoun *hemah* has a row of points over it in the Masoretic text, apparently to indicate that the very presence of the word in the text is questionable. It may safely be omitted. At the close of the verse the clause introduced by *lema'an*, would seem to express purpose, but is one of the many instances where purpose should rather be construed as *result*.

Verse 10. The word *chabheraw* ("who are attached to them") in its root meaning appears with about the same connotation in Hos. 4:17.

Verse 11. We have translated *me'adham* as "but human beings"; the expression may also be rendered "despised of men" or "less than human." Cf. *KS* 402 e.

Verse 12. The verb is missing at the beginning of the verse and so the *Septuagint* already inserted one ("*sharpened*"). We preferred to use "makes."

Verse 13. In this verse too there are the names of tools and instruments which do not appear elsewhere in the Scriptures: "Pencil," and "scraping tool." The last word of the verse is construed without a preposition, something like "to occupy a shrine." *KS* 211 e.

Verse 14. In this verse the initial word apparently has to be supplied, "he went out."

Verse 16. What we translated "a part of it" actually says in Hebrew "half of it." Then the second half is referred to, then that which is left over. Apparently terms are not being used with mathematical exactitude. Therefore our translation.

Verse 18. "Smeared shut" does not agree with its subject in gender and number, a common observation in Hebrew when the verb stands first and the gender and number of the subject have not yet been determined. See *GK* 145.

Verse 21. In the last word *tinnascheni* the pronominal suffix is dative in character (*KS* 21; *GK* 117 x).

Chapter XLIV:24—XLV:25

F. THE COMMISSIONING OF CYRUS, THE AGENT OF THE RESTORATION (Chaps. 44:24—45:25

There have been two references to Cyrus in the second half of Isaiah's book thus far (41:2-4, 25). In neither case was his name mentioned. The references were vague in character. He was the man of mystery. Now his name is prophetically disclosed; he appears as the one whose success was so miraculous. We still hold to the view of the fathers that it was Isaiah, the son of Amoz, who made these prophecies more than 150 years prior to the time they came to pass. In God's sovereign control of history this is merely the agent who carries into effect plans and purposes long prepared for by the Lord. Cyrus makes the liberation of Israel from Babylonian Captivity a reality.

But it is a strange thing how Isaiah envisions these things that shall come to pass. Like so many other Biblical writers he sees the Cyrus-epoch and the End-time flow together into one. The time-sequence is unimportant, in fact, it is very likely not even discerned by the prophet. He merely knows that these things will come to pass. He seems to have no knowledge in what order or after how much time has elapsed these things will come to pass. Their coming is certain; their sequence is not yet clearly seen.

In fact, Isaiah seems to think in terms of a conversion of Cyrus to the true God, Yahweh, and as subsequent result to this conversion, the acknowledgement of Yahweh by all the world. Neither of these two hopes was realized, nor are they to this day. Was the Prophet in error? We shall attempt a solution of the difficulty as we come to the specific verses that are involved.

But another matter may be disposed of now, the similarity

of the statements of this chapter with the statement made about Cyrus and the relation of the gods, Marduk, Bel, and Nebo, to him. There are three statements in particular that call for examination. We cite as parallels to the Biblical text from *Ancient Near Eastern Texts* by Pritchard (Princeton, 1950). 45:1-2 give the words "whose right hand I have grasped" and "I will go before you." The Cyrus cylinder says "going at his side like a friend." 45:4 says: "I call you by your name" and "I surname you." The cylinder reads: "He pronounced the name of Cyrus." Again 44:28 says: "He is my shepherd" and the cylinder: "Whose rule Bel and Nebo love." Is the Isaiah material after all perhaps dependent upon the Cyrus cylinder? In the first place, it is commonly acknowledged that the Cyrus cylinder is later in point of time than the Biblical passage. And in the second place it will have to be conceded that the statements involved are of a general character that might have been used quite commonly in all languages when the relation of a victorious ruler to some god is being described. For aside from these three parallels the material in the two documents involved has precious little in common.

1. The Commissioning, a Work of the All-powerful Lord (44:24-28)

44:24-28 24. Thus says the Lord, who has redeemed you,
                 he who formed you from the womb,
"I am the Lord who made all things,
    who stretched out the heavens, I alone,
    who spread out the earth (who was with me?);
25. who nullifies the omens of the charlatan prognosticators,
    who makes the diviners appear as fools,
    who refutes the wise,
and shows up their knowledge to be folly;
26. [but] establishes the word of his servant,
    and fulfils the purpose announced through his messengers;
who says to Jerusalem, 'She shall be inhabited,'
    and to the cities of Judah, 'They shall be built,'
    and their ruins I will raise up again.
27. who says to the ocean-deep, 'Be dry,'
    I will dry up your rivers;

28. who says to Cyrus, 'He is my shepherd,
    he will execute my whole plan
        by ordering Jerusalem to be rebuilt
    and the temple-foundations to be relaid.' "

Verse 24. This section is one sentence, one of the longest in the Old Testament, each clause practically beginning with a participle (there are nine participles involved). Some classify the piece as a *Selbsthymnus*, a hymn in which God sings his own praise. The connotation is unfortunate; a better designation will have to be found. God does proclaim his own honor, an entirely proper procedure, for he is in reality all that he predicates concerning himself. He proclaims with authority things he has done, is doing at the present, and will yet fulfill in the future. The emphasis is strong on history, which is entirely under God's control without being predestined. The first reference is to Israel's redemption from Egyptian bondage, the one great act that welded Israel into a unity and gave her her national existence. Parallel runs the statement "he who formed you from the womb." The reference is to all the things done in the grand and glorious days of Moses. At this point the pronouncements veer over into the first person. When he claims that he is the Lord "who made all things" two areas are apparently under consideration — creation and history. For he created all things that are and still majestically controls them by determining the outcome of history. Other works of creation that fit very properly into the picture here are: (he) "stretched out the heavens alone" (cf. 40:22). And he similarly "spread out the earth" and there was no one who was needed to be of assistance. Creation is the sole work of God. Here we have a brief assortment of the most marvelous achievements attributable to God alone.

Verse 25. Now a second area in which Yahweh's all-powerful character is discernible is subjected to scrutiny. It is the area of magic, divining, astrology and kindred pursuits. For activity in these fields all the nations of antiquity were known. Babylon perhaps excelled them all. "Omens" were

carefully observed. Prognostications were continually resorted to. "Diviners" were even officially appointed by the
state. Since all these activities lay outside the field of the
exact sciences, many a "charlatan" would be found studiously
framing double-talk. All of them could take refuge behind
their ambiguous prognostications. Perhaps the prophet is
here thinking of efforts along these lines spoken at the approach of Cyrus to Babylon. Success for the Babylonians
was abundantly foretold. Even if that had not been the case,
God had still made all the efforts of the fortunetellers of
none effect. He "nullified" the omens to which they attached
so much importance, made their authors appear as fools,
refuted the wise and made all their "knowledge appear to be
folly." So lengthy a refutation of the hollowness of their
endeavors was quite in keeping with the importance men
attached to this subject.

Verse 26. What now follows further establishes how all-
powerful the Lord is. His effective work is contrasted with
the futile efforts of their pseudo-science. Therefore we inserted an adversative "but" in our translation. The Lord also
has men who deal with the possibilities that the future holds.
There is first of all his "servant," the prophet himself,
through whom he had repeatedly made his purposes and the
future outcome of things known. All his messages are
summed up as being a "word." But this prophet is not the
only one whom he has in reserve; there are also his "messengers," the men of whom Israel's tradition and Israel's
sacred writings had many a clear-cut word on record.
Through these he had announced his "purpose" and what
had been announced had invariably come to pass. Now
comes the comfort that the prophet was strongly setting
forth for Israel. He is on record as having promised to his
people that Jerusalem would again be inhabited and that the
cities of Judah would again be built, and the ruins would
again be raised up. This is the first clear prediction of the
restoration of Jerusalem, the name of the city being plainly
indicated (*Westermann*).

Verse 27. The negative (v. 25) having thus been met by a positive (v. 26), the prophetic word moves on, building up to a skillful climax. Men are not quite sure how they should construe the meaning of the "ocean-deep," perhaps all needs of the case are best met if it be thought of as a historic reference to the crossing of the waters of the Red Sea in the days of the Exodus, and if the drying up of the rivers be thought of in connection with the crossing of the Jordan, all in highly poetic terminology. The reference then appears to be to the validated acts of a historic past. They abundantly testify how all-powerful the Lord is, whose acts are now under review.

Verse 28. Now the climax! The mysterious personage, whose coming has repeatedly been alluded to, is now mentioned by name. It is a man called Cyrus. According to our position (whose merits we shall not argue here) it was granted to the prophet by the omniscient God to foretell the coming and the name of the deliverer from Babylonian Captivity more than 150 years before these things transpired, an approach that the heathen idols through their priests and prognosticators could not make, as the prophet had contended again and again. This Cyrus now functions as the Lord's "shepherd." This is a name frequently used in the Scriptures for rulers (see Gen. 48:15; II Sam. 5:2; 7:7; Jer. 3:15; Ezek. 34:23; 37:24, etc.). The care and guidance of a nation are conferred upon its shepherd. Whatever the relation of Cyrus to his own nation may be said to be, for Israel he distinctly functions as shepherd. He, whether he is aware of it or not (both possibilities may be urged) "will execute (God's) whole plan." In essence this will involve that the capital city of Israel be rebuilt and that the temple-foundations be relaid. These are the tasks that are assigned to Cyrus by the Lord at the time when he commissioned him, an act which he himself ascribes to himself in this verse. It may yet be added that the emphasis in the matter of the restoration of the temple at Jerusalem is not on providing a place for authentic cultic worship — though this too is by no means unimportant — but chiefly to provide a place where Israel can have assurance that the Lord's presence is in the midst of his people.

It must yet be added that when it is said of Cyrus that he will "execute the Lord's whole plan" that form of statement need not be taken in the sense that whatever plans God has even down to the end of time for his people and for the whole world will, in the thinking of the prophet, come to total fulfillment in the days of Cyrus. Eschatological statements are sometimes cast into a somewhat loose form and dare not be pressed with undue emphasis on the very letter.

2. The Resultant Success of Cyrus Attributable to Yahweh's Dominion (vv. 1-7)

45:1-7 1. Thus says the Lord in reference to his anointed one, to Cyrus — "whose right hand I have grasped,
in order to trample down nations before him,
    and to strip kings of their weapons;
to open doors before him,
    that gates shall not be shut.
2. I myself will go before you,
    and level off the hindrances that would block your path;
I will shatter doors of bronze,
    and hew in pieces iron gate-bars.
3. And I will give you treasures stored up in dark chambers
    and such as are buried in secret hiding-places;
that you may know that I am the Lord,
    the one who has called you by your name, the God of Israel,
4. For the sake of my servant Jacob,
    and of Israel, my chosen one,
I call you by your name,
    indeed I give you a title of honor,
although you did not know me;
5. I am the Lord and there is no other;
    apart from me there is no God;
I arm you though you did not know me;
6. in order that men may know from the rising of the sun
    and from the west that there is none besides me.
I am the Lord and there is no other God.
7. I form the light and create the darkness,
    I make weal and create woe.
    I am the Lord who does all these things."

Here Yahweh presents Cyrus to his people as the "agent of
her salvation." Because he is addressed in terms of intimacy
some read into the text that Cyrus is to be thought of as going
over to the faith of the children of Israel and accepting the
worship of their God. Then they add that the prophet expected this step to sweep all the nations along with him.
Such an approach claims more than the evidence of the case
here warrants. But this much is clear that the success that
Cyrus had is attributed to Yahweh's dominion. So much the
prophet clearly claims. Throughout the passage terms are
used that are proverbial for the ceremony of the crowning
of kings both in, and outside of, Israel (cf. *Westermann*).

Verse 1. Here Cyrus is mentioned by name a second time.
He is even given a most distinctive title, the "anointed one."
The word used happens to be the word that coincides with
the name Messiah, although it should be remarked at once
that this title is never used in the Scriptures of the Old Testament for the Christ that is to come. That usage developed
in the time between the Testaments. It is however used for
kings like Saul (I Sam. 12:3, etc.); for the people of God
(Hab. 3:13); and even for the patriarchs (Ps. 105:15). It
does not necessarily imply that an actual anointing of the
person in question took place. It is a designation of honor.
Here now it is used of a heathen ruler whom God is employing for a very special purpose. To say then that Cyrus was
God's Messiah is technically correct but very misleading.
God has a proclamation to make with reference to this
Cyrus, a proclamation which is lengthy and weighty. It
discloses things that neither Cyrus nor Israel nor the Gentiles
could have sensed. The first claim is that in the work of conquest which Cyrus is engaged in, God is upholding him
("whose right hand I have grasped"). By thus being upheld by God, Cyrus is enabled to have success wherever he
goes. But it is the Lord who "tramples down nations before
him," a colorful way of describing the success that Cyrus
had. The same Lord "strips kings of their weapons" before
him. The verb for "strips" really is "ungirds," that is to say

either: "loosens the girdle" and so lets flowing garments hamper his activity; or it means "loosen the belt to which the sword is attached" and so disarm the man. We prefer the latter interpretation. (cf. I Kings 20:11). A third form of activity that Yahweh engages in for Cyrus' benefit is "to open doors [of cities] before him that gates [of cities] shall not be shut."

Verse 2. It is as though the Lord himself personally took a hand in the issues involved, came down from heaven, led the way for Cyrus and cleared away the obstacles that towered in his path. To make it all more personal and intimate, at this point the Lord addresses himself to Cyrus directly. In other words the Lord's proclamation moves over into the second person. In highly effective figures, the Lord represents himself as actually battering down strong bronze gates that seemed to guaranty the safety of the cities, and actually hewing in pieces iron gate-bars, and all this in the interest of Cyrus, "his anointed one."

Verse 3. A further item of God's guiding of the destinies of this servant of his is that he allows the conqueror to amass rich treasures, such as are wont to be kept for safe-keeping in dark, sometimes subterranean, chambers, or may be buried in secret hiding-places — so to speak, the Fort Knox-installations of days of old. The treasures amassed by Babylon must have been fabulous, for they are also referred to in Hab. 2:6-8; Jer. 50:37; 51:13. The purpose expressed in reference to Cyrus' acquisition of treasures is quite unexpected and a bit unusual. It is that Cyrus may know that Yahweh is the Lord, the one who has called him by his name, the God of Israel. The difficulty here involved is unduly increased if these expressed results are associated only with the acquisition of treasure. It is rather the sum total of all the things that the Lord did for Cyrus, from vv. 1-3, that bring home a more intimate knowledge of the Lord God of Israel to the Persian conqueror. This almost seems to demand something that the Hebrew tradition, as reported by Josephus, brings to our attention, that namely these prophecies concerning his success were shown to Cyrus by the Jews and were known to have deeply impressed the monarch. In any case, at least in some way, not disclosed to us, Cyrus became aware of the fact that the God of the Jews had willed and contributed to his success. The verse before us does not directly say that Cyrus confessed the monotheistic faith, or his acceptance of it, but he came close to taking this step as the two passages II Chron. 36:22 f. and the parallel Ezra 1: 2 ff. indicate. But perhaps this particular decree is to be rated no higher than an analogous one, which Nebuchadnezzar in his day set forth, as recorded in Dan. 4:1-3. For from the Cyrus cylinder, referred to above as given in Pritchard's *Ancient New Eastern Texts*, we learn that Cyrus attributed his success in his enterprises and in the capture of Babylon to the Babylonian god, Marduk. It is entirely possible that both the Biblical and cylinder accounts come from Cyrus, and that from his polytheistic point of view he was able to make these, to us, conflicting statements.

Verse 4. The previous verse indicated what purpose the Lord had in mind with regard to Cyrus when he gave him Babylon and all the rest of his phenomenal success. Now the Lord adds what it was that he had in mind with regard to his own people Israel. It may be said to have all been done "for the sake of my servant Jacob." This honorific title ("servant") for Israel occurs often enough in the course of the book (see 41:8; 42:1; 43:10; 44:1-2; 49:3-6). To it is added the further title "my chosen one." Both together show how high Israel stands in the Lord's esteem. True this is traceable to the covenant relationship. But it still makes it apparent why he will use so select an instrument for the liberation and restoration of his people as Cyrus. He has much at stake as Lord of his people. In addition he honors Cyrus by calling him by his name, even as he did Israel (43:1), and also asserts that he has given to this instrument that he uses "a title of honor." That the personal merits of Cyrus were not the determining factor in God's choice of the man, good though he otherwise was, appears from the further assertion here made: "you did not know me." God's dealings with man can never be motivated by the merit and achievements of man. That thought bridges over to the next verse.

Verse 5. This type of dealing with man on the basis of pure grace is then the distinctive mark of his dealing with all mankind. In a sense that is the mark of the monotheistic Lord. In all relations between men and gods, so called, merit is the distinguishing factor, at least to some extent, passing by for the moment the occasional strange whims of these same gods. But grace is the determining issue between the *Lord* and men. We might then well say that sole grace and sole deity are factors that mutually determine one another. On this basis one more of the favors bestowed on Cyrus comes to the forefront: "I arm you though you did not know me." The total sovereignty of God must be maintained at any cost. Therefore this additional reminder.

Verse 6. One further factor that entered into the choice and equipment of Cyrus is added here: the impression that all this is calculated to make on men the world over, from "the rising of the sun and from the west." Somehow God's choice and guidance of Cyrus will bring his sole claim to deity to the attention of men, wherever they may dwell. Though we have no corroborative material available from historical sources, it is still possible that results and effects were produced at that time that are far in excess of what we might have thought likely. That men will then follow through logically on this basis and will, the world over, renounce their inferior gods and turn to Yahweh, that is not claimed by the prophet, although some men feel that this is actually his position. This subject may be explored a little more fully. Two claims at least may be made in this connection. One is that Cyrus does appear in this passage as a kind of pioneer in advancing the claim of monotheism. Yet as noted above from the historical records it appears that his own insight was a bit confused: Cyrus ascribed his success to Marduk also. It would then appear that in his better moments he championed to an extent the monotheism of Israel. The other claim that may be made on the basis of this passage is that Cyrus is represented hopefully as a possible convert to the Lord of Israel. This is in reality merely another form of the first of these two claims.

Verse 7. This verse attempts to further clarify the big issues that are at stake. Monotheism involves that Yahweh must be regarded as sole ruler and controller of the universe. Of course, he is never the source of evil. But both good and evil, no matter with whom they originate, are never out of God's control. Basic are the two elements, light and darkness, and all that they represent in common parlance. Equally basic almost are the two possible types of deeds of men, the good and the bad, or as here stated: "weal" and "woe." All heathen systems of religion were basically dualistic, having two separate sources for all that is done, one good and one evil, and one as powerful and efficient as the other. This dualism is disavowed strongly by this text. We have here then not a disavowing of the position of the dualistic Persian religion only, but of all systems that were known to antiquity outside the revelation and faith of Israel. The form in which this claim was cast in the old King James version could well prove disturbing, when it said: "I make peace and create evil," although the Hebrew would allow for such a translation. But it is not the morally good and the morally evil that are being attributed to Yahweh, but things good and bad are said to lie totally in his power, as far as their physical aspects and consequences are concerned. The *RSV* version does full justice to the issues involved when it says: "I make weal and create woe." Note similar statements in Amos 3:6b; and Isa. 14:24-27. "I am the Lord who does all these things" aptly sums it all up, and obviously ties back to 44:24 — obvious evidence of careful composition.

3. A Prayer for the Realization of This Work (v. 8)

45:8   8. Distil moisture, you skies above,
and let the skies rain down success!

Let the earth open, that salvation may grow forth,
  and let it cause success to spring up also!
I the Lord have created it.

Who is speaking? We seem to have one of those situations
where the prophet so completely identifies himself with the
objectives of the Lord that the words of the Lord and his
servant merge into one. The opening line of the verse may
well be classified as "the yearning cry of the prophet," and
so may be regarded as a prayer. The last line represents the
Lord as speaking. In any case, poetically both heaven and
earth are appealed to to bring to pass the good blessings that
the Lord has in store for his people. The world is a unit.
Heaven and earth are sympathetically thought of as both interested in the achievement of the Lord objectives. These
objectives are "success" and "salvation." Both are regarded as
being furthered by the coming of a fructifying rain and by
the springing forth of a growth of God's blessings. The in-
jection of this touching prayer indicates how deeply the
prophet was concerned about having the good things of
which he prophesied come to pass. A kindred approach is
to be seen in Ps. 85:12 and Hos. 2:21 ff.

4. Rebuke of Those Who Are Critical of Yahweh in His Use of Cyrus (vv. 9-13)

45:9-13 9. Woe to the man who would find fault with his Maker,
a piece of mere pottery among pieces of earthen pottery.
Dare the clay say to the potter, "What are you making?"
  or your work say: "He has no hands?"
10. Woe to him who says to his father: "What are you begetting?"
  or to his mother: "To what are you giving birth?"
11. Thus says the Lord, the Holy One of Israel,
  and he who formed it:
"Inquire of me concerning things to come?
  give orders concerning my children
  and about the work of my hands?
12. It is I who made the earth
  and created man upon it;
it is I whose hands stretched out the heavens
  and appointed all their host.

13. It is I who raised him up for a saving purpose,
    and will make straight all his ways.
It is I who will build my city
    and liberate my exiles;
    not for a price and reward," says the Lord of hosts.

Verse 9. So it has just been indicated that the Lord is going to use as his instrument for restoring Israel the conqueror Cyrus. That purpose may indeed meet with some measure of disapproval on the part of some of the children of Israel. Their attitude would be: A heathen like that is not worthy for the achievement of God's high purposes. This objection would not be raised, as has been indicated, by faint-hearted unbelief, but the very verb "find fault" may also be translated "strive." That would imply stubborn opposition, an attitude of knowing things better than the very Lord himself. The prophet cannot but denounce such an attitude. He points out several analogies, each of which would be equally reprehensible. Such a man would be like a "piece of pottery among pieces of earthen pottery" — that means: a mere potsherd — finding fault with the potter. Not a complete finished article, but the mere remains of a broken dish. The "potter" in this instance, of course, is God. This approach is found in 29:16; Jer. 18:1 ff.; Rom. 9:20.; cf. Isa. 10:15. Carrying this approach farther — would there not be a strong impropriety about having a lump of clay remonstrate with the potter, if it could speak words, and say by way of criticism: "What are you making?" Or to make the insolence of it still more apparent — what if some cup or saucer ("your work") were to take the potter to task for making it, charging him with incompetence ("He has no hands!") or lack of skill, implying that for hands he has mere clumsy stumps (or, as we might say of a man: "He is all thumbs").

Verse 10. The prophet is so indignant with the impudence of the critics of the Almighty that he must carry this line of reasoning a few steps farther. He continues in a strong vein of indignation, as the second "woe" indicates. It is as though a child were questioning the propriety of having a father

beget it and bring it into the world, an uninformed, inexperienced child. It is as though at any point in childhood any
youngster were to remonstrate with his mother: "To what
are you giving birth?" As unheard of as that is and as unthinkable as it should be, so is Israel's criticism of the means
God employs for the achievement of his sovereign designs.

Verse 11. In a tone of solemn majesty the prophet continues: "Thus says the Lord, the Holy One of Israel and he
who formed it," as much as to say, it is this Lord whom you
are in fact belittling. What follows is difficult of interpretation. We take the two verbs as they stand, as imperatives,
spoken, however, with strong indignation as a question in the
sense: ("Will you) inquire of me concerning things to come?"
i.e., will you remonstrate with me about things that have
not yet come to pass? i.e., sitting in judgment upon them before they have even happened? Or the second question is in
the nature of the protest of an astonished parent whose dealings with his children are being questioned by an outsider:
("Will you) give me orders concerning my children and
about the work of my hands?" For an outsider to interfere
with a parent dealing with his children in a case of discipline
is usually rightly resented. So here.

Verse 12. The Lord now proceeds to indicate what manner of works he is in the habit of engaging in, in order to
make the conclusion obvious that if he resorts to the use of
certain minor plans in readjustments among the things that
need readjustment in his creation, he surely must be entirely
capable of making the proper choice of means and agents.
Here are the things that he lists as being in the ordinary
range of the projects he engages in: Making the earth; creating man upon it; stretching out the heavens with his hands;
appointing all the host to their proper place and sphere. Who
would even dream of advising one who is capable of handling
issues of such dimensions?

Verse 13. Once again the Lord patiently defines his purposes and the place of Cyrus within these purposes of his.
Though the term is not used it is made very plain that Cyrus

merely functions as agent of the Almighty. What things he accomplishes the Lord does through him. The project on which the Lord is working is described by a number of terms: "a saving purpose," "his [Cyrus'] ways," "build my city," "liberate my exiles" — all of which have been previously set forth and are now being re-enumerated that one may see that they are projects vitally related to the future of Israel and well worthy of the best thoughts of the God of Israel. The closing remark of the verse presents a difficulty. All this is being done in Israel's behalf "not for price nor reward." If this be construed to mean that neither Israel nor any man or group of men are producing something that could be valued as a due and proper payment for so great a favor, and so God is not in any way being repaid for what he does, this is a proper statement which no man could call into question. Construed thus, as referring to a ransom that might be paid by man to God, this passage presents no problem over against 43:3 f., as *North* has claimed it does. This previous passage speaks of the reward that the *Lord* either would be ready to pay, if it were necessary, or that he would be ready to provide to offset what Cyrus loses by giving up his claim on Israel.

5. The Submission of Nations Validates God's Work (vv. 14-17)

45:14-17 14. Thus says the Lord:
"The wealth of Egypt and the merchandise of Ethiopia
and of the tall Sabeans shall come over to you and be yours.
   They shall follow you [Zion], they shall come fettered;
   They shall prostrate themselves before you
      and make supplication to you:
   'God is only with you, and there is no other;
      no God besides you!' "
15. Surely thou art a God who conceals himself,
   thou God of Israel, the Savior.
16. All of them are put to shame and confusion,
   the manufacturers of idols shall be totally confounded.

17. But Israel shall be saved by the Lord
   with an everlasting salvation;
you shall not be ashamed or confounded
   forever and ever.

Verse 14. Men cannot agree how they are to label this section. *Haller* says it is one of the songs of Zion. *Volz* calls at least vv. 15-17 a word of prayer and a prophetic word of doom. *Begrich* sees here only an oracle of salvation. The piece evidently does not fit into the usual categories. *Skinner* regards v. 14 in particular as addressed to Cyrus, which sounds very strange for the end of the verse. Zion is being addressed. When different national groups with their treasures are pictured as coming to Israel in a spirit of submission, this is analogous with what is stated in 2:2-4; 18:7; 23:18; 60:5 ff. First the bringing of treasures is stressed — treasure from Egypt, from Ethiopia and from the Sabeans, from southwest Arabia (cf. 43:3). Also the "merchandise" that is the exportable articles from these nations. Israel is then regarded as heading a march of the nations; the others follow. Besides "they shall come fettered." This is either a hyperbole used to express total submission, or better still, this indicates "a deference approaching worship." They have manacled themselves voluntarily. Political domination by Israel is not even remotely thought of. Their cheerful prostration before Israel shows a spirit of submission like that described in 2:2-4. When these nations are said to "make supplication" to Israel this statement seems to regard them as imploring Israel to be allowed to share her spiritual treasures and to accept the treasures they bring in gratitude. The words, "God is only with you, and there is no other, no God besides you," are the confession of a faith and an insight which stands behind their present approach. Insight has come to them that there is only one nation whose God has true existence; all other gods so-called are fiction. This then describes the marvelous day, even now but partially realized, when the knowledge of the living God shall have spread to all nations and shall have been accepted as the treasure that it is. This statement of the case does not necessarily mean that *all* men will at some time actually accept what is told them of this saving truth. That possibility is not reflected upon.

Verse 15. Now the prophet breaks forth into a prayer of adoration, moved by the mysterious character of God's dealing with Israel. Above (vv. 9 ff.), an unwholesome attitude toward God's dealings with Israel was repudiated. Here a right attitude is pictured: falling down, as it were, before him and singing his praises. The word could perhaps be construed as reflecting the attitude of the nations mentioned in v. 14. But it seems better to think of it as a prayer in which the prophet leads his people in veneration of the Lord. Yahweh is a "God who conceals himself," a concept for which *Luther* employed the classical title *deus absconditus* ("the hidden God"). He conceals himself, as it were, behind the fact that he lets Jerusalem be destroyed; or by the mysterious manner in which he lets history develop. Several Scriptures have the thought of his self-concealing, as Ps. 97:2; Exod. 33:17-23; cf. also, for the more positive side, Rom. 11:33. But this concealing of himself does not cancel out the constructive side of this attitude; for he still is for Israel "the God of Israel, the Savior."

Verses 16, 17. But even as v. 14 showed that God's dealings would bring about the submission even of the distant Gentiles, so the negative may properly be brought into the picture. They who are in their native benightedness, or refuse to come out of it to the light, that is to say, "the manufacturers of idols," they shall be totally confounded, they "shall be put to shame and confusion." But still reflecting upon the fact that God's ways with Israel have been productive of good, the prophet sums up the good that will be achieved (v. 17). She shall "be saved by the Lord with an everlasting salvation." She shall not be "ashamed or confounded forever and ever." The outcome will prove how well the plans of the Almighty were laid. So God's work is fully validated.

6. Appeal to the Survivors of the Nations to Acknowledge the Only God (vv. 18-21)

45:18-21 18. For thus says Yahweh, who created the heavens
— he is God —
who formed the earth and made it — he established it —
   he did not create it to no purpose;
   he formed it for men to dwell in,
"I am the Lord and there is no other.
19. I did not speak in secret,
   in some place in a land of darkness;
   nor did I say in vain to the offspring of Jacob, 'Seek me.'
   I am the Lord, I speak the truth;
     I declare what is right.
20. Assemble yourselves and come;
draw near together, you survivors of the nations!
   They who carry their wooden idols are utterly without knowledge,
   as are they who pray to a god who cannot help.
21. State your case and present your arguments —
yea, let us have a conference together —
Who has made this to be heard long ago
   and declared it long since?
Was it not I, the Lord?
and there is no God besides me;
a righteous God and a Savior;
   there is none except me."

Verse 18. Two points are stressed in this and the following verse, creation and revelation. Both are clear and orderly. The Creator did not form this world of his "to no purpose," or as some translate, as "a chaos." "He formed it for men to dwell in," and it gives overwhelming evidence of being adapted to that purpose. It also bears testimony to the oneness of God, a truth, which the prophet presses home at every possible point. Both these great truths find their oneness in God himself. They reinforce the faith of Israel in monotheism.

Verse 19. Whenever God has spoken it was done with such clear light that his meaning was immediately apparent to all who would lend an attentive ear. No veiled disclosures! No need of groping around in "a land of darkness" where the disclosures of heathen prognosticators so often left men. In other words, God did not deal in esoteric knowledge which was available only for a select few. When God said "Seek me!" that involved that he could be found, "seeking" here being taken in the sense of seeking his face in worship, as "seek" so often signifies. One major trait of God's deity was that what he spoke was "truth" and "right."

Verse 20. This much was needed to provide a solid foundation for the appeal to the "survivors of the nations" which was about to be made. A sort of court-trial comes into the picture. A test is to be made openly and publicly. The survivors of the nations are those who have lived through the recent major world-wide upheavals, contingent upon the conquests made by the Persians under Cyrus. In the midst of the readjustments that come after such an up-heaval the minds of many may be ready for new things, open for new truths. The idols and faith in them are inade-quate for trying times such as those that had befallen men. So it is quickly pointed out that they who "carry their wooden idols," cannot seriously expect these helpless blocks of wood that have to be carried about, help those who have to carry them. So the idol-worshippers "are utterly without knowledge." They are as badly off as any who keep on praying "to a god who cannot help."

Verse 21. But these persons are not merely to submit unconditionally. They are to present their arguments and state their case in a public examination of the issues involved. In the prophet's mind there is no doubt as to how such a test, honestly conducted, must turn out. He cheerfully in-vites the opposition to "a conference." But immediately he produces the strong argument with which he has operated successfully so many times in the past: "Who has made this to be heard long ago and declared it long since" (cf. 41:22). The answer is, of course, Yahweh, the God of Israel. He has declared things beforehand, also the coming and the success of Cyrus, as Chaps. 41-44 have so conclusively demonstrated, especially 13:2-4, 17-25; 21:1-10. This the survivors of the nations are asked to take under advisement. If they do and examine Yahweh's claim, "Was it not I . . . ?" they should be moved to the acceptance of him, as v. 14 already indicated that this outcome would be the result.

The broad outlook and the high hope for the nations outside of Israel, as reflected in this chapter, make this section to be one of the high points of the message of the prophet.

7. God's Objectives Reach to All the Ends of the Earth (vv. 22-25)

45:22-25   22. Turn to me and be saved, all the ends of the earth;
for I am God and there is no other.
23. By myself have I sworn;
truth has gone forth from my mouth,
a word that shall not be nullified:
   "To me every knee shall bow
   and every tongue shall swear allegiance!"
24. Only in the Lord [men shall say]
do I have full righteousness and strength;
to him shall come, utterly ashamed,
   all that were incensed against him.
25. In the Lord all the offspring of Israel
shall be justified and shall glory.

Verse 22. If a large segment of mankind was under consideration in the preceding section, now the prospect widens still farther. All the ends of the earth are taken into the picture. This verse might have been tied up with what preceded by the use of a "therefore." For if God's concern is so warm for the "survivors" then it is but logical to assume that it is without limit. In fact, as *Haller* rightly remarks, the "door of salvation is thrown wide open" at this point. Or as *Volz* suggests, "universalism follows from monotheism," but, mark well, universalism in the Biblical sense. All nations, ignorant of the living God and his ways, are thought of as all faced in the wrong direction and going in this direction. They are invited "to turn," which definitely here involves a reversal of their direction. If they turn and throw themselves upon the mercy of the Lord, in one word "be saved," God will receive them. The verb involved could more accurately be rendered "let yourselves be saved." For in conversion as such, man is completely passive. He contributes nothing to his salvation. When the "ends of the earth" are referred to, that approach does not eliminate those areas that lie in between. So the appeal is truly universal. God would have all men to be saved. No narrow nationalism blurred the vision of men like our prophet. The supporting argument should be noted: "for I am the Lord and there is no other." Since he is God alone, his interest in mankind is a unit interest that involves all mankind.

Verse 23. This is an issue of such tremendous moment that the Lord supports his invitation by a solemn oath. Since there is no one greater by whom he could swear (see Heb. 6:13) he swears by himself. The parallel statement ("truth has gone forth from my mouth") clinches the point being made. A third parallel ("a word that shall not be nullified") makes assurance doubly sure. The truth that is being uttered is still that of v. 22, that God's mercies are all-inclusive. But the emphasis now rests not on the fact that God can rescue those whom he invites, but on the other side of the matter, that these people shall be brought to the point where in adoration they acknowledge his sole lordship and saviorhood. "Every knee shall bow" for there is no other posture permissible for man nor worthy of him when he steps into the presence of the All-holy (cf. also Rom. 14:11 and Phil. 2:10 f.). This might all be misread as supporting an unbiblical universalism. The two New Testament passages cited indicate that in this connection men must still think in terms of a final judgment. So that we might interpretively paraphrase: "To me every knee — of those who are ready to acknowledge the Lordship of the Christ — shall bow; but even they that do not acknowledge him as Christ, must admit his sole sovereignty, though perhaps grudgingly." For, to be exact, the verb "swear" that follows does not of itself mean "swear allegiance," but merely swear in the sense of acknowledging the highest authority and appealing to it.

Verse 24. Still on the same high level of confessing the

breadth of the purposes of God is the claim, "Only in the Lord (men shall say) do I have full righteousness and strength." The one Lord is set forth as the only source of help and deliverance. At this point the prophet is speaking. The aspect of the word "righteousness" that is here under consideration is the righteousness that justifies, even as this appears in Holy Writ from Gen. 15:6 on. And where faith grasps this righteousness a new hidden source of "strength" opens up that man can appropriate in no other way. From this point onward the pronouncement of the prophet drops to lower levels of enthusiastic insight. This drop is unduly magnified when it is claimed that the rest now "limps along lamely" and this rest is even discarded as a poor afterthought of an uninspired glossator. For the things referred to are still great and glorious. Is it not indicative of a great victory when those "that were incensed against him" now approach "utterly ashamed," convinced of the utter folly of their former ways? This new attitude grows out of the clear insight how wrong they once were, how far removed from the true center of life.

Verse 25. The prophet also deems it worthy of mention that Israel herself shall occupy the same position as the rest of the saved and "shall be justified and shall glory" in what they again possess. When this attitude of Israel is ascribed to "all the offspring of Israel" it is difficult to determine whether this refers to the entirety of the nation of Israel, which is to be thought of as involved in an almost national conversion, or whether the *spiritual* Israel is under consideration.

Notes

Verse 24. We prefer to follow the marginal reading on the last word of the verse, as suggested by the Jewish scribes, namely *two* words, *mi 'itti*, "who (was) with me."

Verse 25. The word *baddim*, "empty talk," or "empty talkers," is in our day frequently taken in the sense of a known type of Babylonian priests, namely *barim* priests, an interpretation requiring the change of *d* to *r*. These *barim* priests were regarded as great prognosticators. But something vital is lost in making this change, the fact that they are really "charlatans."

Verse 26. Should we read the consonants as involving a singular or a plural in the case of the word we have rendered "his servant"? Parallelism would suggest the plural. The singular, supported by the Hebrew tradition, makes the word refer to the prophet himself. The decision is difficult. We prefer the latter sense.

Verse 27. Does the reference to the "ocean deep" here inject the "chaos-dragon" motif? Many hold that to be the case. We believe that the mythological approach is being sadly overworked and that such an approach contributes nothing helpful to the interpretation.

Verse 28. For the opening word of the second half of this verse where the word *le'mor* (infinitive) occurs, the *Septuagint* and the *Vulgate* have the participle, in line with the type of construction which appears from v. 24b onward. Much may be said in favor of such an emendation. The last two lines of the verse are regarded with suspicion as being repetitious. We believe they should be retained, for they re-emphasize an important point. It has been noted that this is the only occurrence of the word "temple" in the second half of the book.

45:2 In the case of the verb "level off" we feel that the *Keri* should be followed *'ayyasher* (*Piel* imperfect).

Verse 4. It is believed by many that vv. 4-6 are more or less in a state of confusion. We believe that our interpretation shows that a good measure of coherence marks the passage.

Verse 8. In approaching the verb "open," some hold that it should be thought of as assuming as its object the words "her womb." Then this would be a kind of carry-over, having "erotic associations" with Baal religion, which however are here rather "sublimated." Such assumptions are neither helpful nor can they be demonstrated to be valid.

Verse 9. The *RSV* seems to have an attractive solution of the difficulty at the end of the verse when it renders, "Your work has no handles." But as has been pointed out that translation would require the *masculine* plural form rather than the *feminine*.

Verse 10. On the somewhat unusual ending for the verb "begetting" see *GK* 47 o.

Verse 16. In this verse the *athnach* should stand with *yachdaw*.

Verse 19. For "right" the Hebrew has "right things" — an amplificative plural (*GK* 124 s).

Verse 22. "Let yourselves be saved" is a *Nifal tolerativum*, see *GK* 51 c. The imperative conveys a note of assurance, see *GK* 110 f.

Verse 24. Where we have rendered "men shall say" the Hebrew has the plain perfect, 3. singular *'amar*, here used impersonally, "one says" or "men shall say."

Verse 25. It will remain an open question whether the first verb should be translated "triumph" (*RSV*) or "justified" (*McKenzie et al.*). Usage allows for either.

Chapter XLVI

G. YAHWEH AND IDOLS CONTRASTED (Chap. 46)

We now move a step forward after considering how Cyrus was to be commissioned as the agent of the restoration of Israel. The other side of the coin is looked at: after Israel's restoration comes the story of Babylon's downfall — to be more exact, first the downfall of her gods, then her own collapse in Chaps. 46 and 47 respectively. But just as Yahweh was a vital factor in the restoration of Israel, so Babylon's idols are a factor — purely negative of course — in the overthrow of the greatest city of the then-time world. We say "negative" because they are totally impotent to avert the impending downfall.

It is for this reason that some of the following captions have been devised for this chapter: "Bel cowers, Yahweh sustains to eternity" (*Volz*); "Gods impotent and the Lord God omnipotent" (*North*); "Bearing or borne" (*G. A. Smith*). Though there is a high strain of victorious faith in evidence in this chapter and though the heathen idols are spoken of in a somewhat derogatory manner, this is hardly "a mocking-song" as *Muilenburg* has rightly pointed out.

As *North* again has maintained, the chapter is easily discerned to be a unity. There is no need to attempt to eliminate certain verses, as many writers are only too prone to do. The coherence that pervades the chapter is made obvious in part already by the outline.

1. Babylon's Gods Will Be Borne into Captivity (vv. 1-2)

46:1-2 1. Bel will bow down, Nebo will stoop;
their images will be consigned to beasts and cattle;
your items of baggage will be loaded up

135

as burdens for weary beasts.
2. They [the gods] will both stoop and bow down;
   they will be unable to save their load;
   they themselves will go into exile.

It has been rightly pointed out that this chapter begins like a proclamation of victory, the defeated ones being Babylon's gods.

Verse 1. Bel was the principal god of the Babylonians. He is usually identified with the Greek god Mercury, who was the spokesman for the gods. Nabu (or Nebo) was his son. When in the course of time Marduk became the chief divinity of Babylon he was also called Bel, by that convenient identification of old gods with new that was achieved so easily among the ancients. Bel, of course, is only a variant from of the Canaanite Baal. When however Marduk became so prominent the rank of his son Nebo became more outstanding, as is indicated by the frequency with which names were compounded with Nabu (Nebuchadnezzar, Nabopolassar, Nabonidus). Bel's major temple was in Borsippa, which lay twelve miles to the south of Babylon. According to Herodotus the image of Bel found in this temple was gold and twelve cubits (*ca.* eighteen feet) tall.

Now of these two outstanding Babylonian gods it is said that they "will bow down and stoop." This is meant in the sense of being carried away *by their worshippers* into safety at the time of the approach of the enemy to capture the city and its idols. The words could be interpreted as referring to the fact that the images would be carried away by the victorious enemy as booty of war. In either case the great Babylonian gods will suffer a shameful humiliation. Not only are they to be a burden to weary beasts and cattle, but they will be loaded up unceremoniously on these baggage animals and suffer all the indignities of such treatment. These two are mentioned as examples of how all Babylonian deities will be treated. (*Pritchard's* ANEP, No. 538 gives an apt illustration from the monuments.)

Verse 2. The impotence of these two gods in this time of

extremity is now further indicated. When the two verbs "stoop" and "bow down" are used a second time it is to stress the utter humiliation that they will experience. They (the idols) can contribute nothing to their own salvation. They are just so much dead weight. Being unable to deliver their worshippers from exile they must themselves experience that very fate.

But at this point attention is commonly drawn to the fact that Cyrus in his capture of the city of Babylon did nothing by way of humiliating the city's gods, nor did the inhabitants transport them away at the advent of Cyrus. In fact the capture of Babylon was not marked by the customary plundering and destruction and loss of life. As far as the Babylonian gods were concerned, Cyrus not only let them remain in their temples, but besought that prayers be made in these temples for his own success and that of his son Cambyses. So Isaiah erred in his prediction? That is a hasty conclusion. Fact of the matter is that the prophet had not specifically said that the downfall of the Babylonian deities would take place when Cyrus captured the city. He merely asserted that it could take place. Of their overthrow he was entirely certain. We do not even know whether he perhaps personally expected that the two events would coincide. This chapter may rightly be said to be marked by supreme confidence in the downfall of these impotent idols, and fall they did.

2. Yahweh Has Borne His People Faithfully (vv. 3-4)

46:3-4   "Hearken to me, O house of Jacob,
        all of you of the house of Israel who are left;
you who have been borne from birth,
    carried ever since you came forth from the womb.
4. Even to your old age I remain the same,
    and till your hairs are grey I will support you.
I have done so and I myself will carry you,
    yea, I myself will support and save you.

Verse 3. At this point without formal introduction direct discourse begins, God addressing his people. Two names are used for this people — Jacob and Israel. Both, of course, in this context refer to the same group, being used in parallelism for variety's sake. The clause "who are left" really is made up of the noun "remnant" (found only here in chaps. 40-66) which here is not used in the customary sense of "the remnant of Israel," but merely to indicate that the persons involved constituted a pitifully small group. When it is said that from birth they have been "borne" and "carried," this is merely a repetition of the two verbs that appeared in the first two verses in reference to the idols: *they* were borne; *God* bears his own. "From birth" and "from the womb" merely signifies: from the time when Israel became a nation, she has been the object of God's solicitous care and protection (cf. 44:2, 24; 49:5; also passages such as 63:9; Deut. 1:31; 33:27; Isa. 40:11).

Westermann very aptly draws attention to the fact that it is a stylistic peculiarity of the prophet to begin larger sections of his material with imperatives ("hearken", cf. v. 12, etc.).

Verse 4. When it is asserted that God will remain the same in his attitude toward his people "even to your old age" that surely does not imply that when they come to the point of old age his care for them is terminated. So the faithfulness of God is not set forth in terms of abstractions but in a practical and most comforting manner, as is often the case in this second half of Isaiah's book. When the word "carry" is used, the root meaning involved means to bear a heavy burden. There is a half-reproachful note in this, for God had often found Israel very burdensome in her self-will and stubborn pride. But the major emphasis lies on the fact that it is Yahweh himself who has taken these obligations upon himself for his people; for five times the emphatic personal pronoun "I" appears in this verse.

3. The Idols Are Utterly Impotent (vv. 5-7)

46:5-7   5. "To whom then will you liken me, or equate me, or compare me that I will really be like?

6. Those who pour forth gold from a purse
   and weigh out silver in balances
   and hire a goldsmith to make a god of it,
and then prostrate themselves before it, yea, worship it;
7. they lift it up upon their shoulders and laboriously transport it;
   they set it down in its place and it stays there.
      He cannot move from his spot.
   Even if one cries out to him he cannot answer;
      he will not deliver him from his distress."

Is this section perhaps an intrusion or a later addition?
Some claim this to be the case because the polemic against
idols has now been repeated a number of times since 40:18-
20. But it must be obvious that this section forms a strong
contrast to the faithfulness that Yahweh displays over against
them that truly serve him. Besides should not a vital point
be driven home again and again? This is a fresh statement of
a point that has indeed been previously made. A number of
commentators strongly defend the authenticity of these verses.

Verse 5. Yahweh is in a class entirely by himself. That
Israel understood well and the prophets taught it with emphasis. There is no being that can even remotely be compared with him. A class word for Yahweh and other beings
cannot be found.

Verse 6. So the way is prepared for a realistic estimate of
the heathen idols. They are of man's manufacture. The
process may be thought of as beginning at the moment when
a person, having a sufficiency of precious metal, pours it
forth from the money-bag that it may be weighed in the
balances. Coined money was not yet in common circulation
in the days of the prophet: metal had to be weighed out in
balances. An additional amount has to be weighed out to
hire the goldsmith "to make a god of it." Till now it was
merely a mass of metal. The rest of the process is in this case
passed by, having been described sufficiently already in 44:
12 ff. We move up at once to the use to which the finished
object is put. That use is this: they "prostrate themselves before it, yea, worship it." Combining the two ideas, *North*
comes up with the rather apt translation: they "prostrate

themselves full length." They adore and implore the work of their hands, of which they can rest assured, they may expect nothing by way of help. Not after such an origin of the object involved! Perhaps there never was a greater folly than idolatry. But before he drops the subject, the Lord, here still speaking, expands one feature that clearly reveals the ridiculousness of it all, viz. v. 7.

Verse 7. The whole approach centers around the fact that the idols can become so heavy a burden for a man. He "lifts it up upon his shoulders and laboriously transports it" to the place destined for it. The sweat streams from the face of those who do the work. Finally they get to their distination. There "they set it down in its place and — what else could be the result? — it stays there." The god is rigidly held in place by the law of gravity; "he cannot move from his spot," in fact cannot budge so much as an inch by his own power. Let the worshipper now step before him; let him present his petition modestly. Or, if he pleases let him "cry out." Still "he cannot answer" or give any token of having even heard the voice that cried. Summing it up: "he will not deliver him from his distress." Idolatry is the height of futility. — This portion is immediately followed by one of those striking contrasts so characteristic of the prophet (vv. 8-11).

4. Yahweh's Total Control of All Things Made Apparent by the Fact That He Can Foretell the Future (vv. 8-11)

46:8-11   8. "Remember this and show yourselves firm;
          lay it to heart, you rebels.
9. Remember the former things of long ago;
     for I am God and there is no other,
          very God and there is none like me,
10. declaring the end [outcome] from the beginning,
     and long beforehand things not yet done;
saying, 'My purpose stands,
     and I will execute all my good pleasure;
11. calling a falcon from the east,

from a far country the man who shall carry out my purpose.'
  I have both spoken and will also bring it to pass;
I have formulated my plan and will also carry it out."

Another approach may be used in taking this passage in
hand. *Volz* captions it, "A warning addressed to rebels." It
is that too, for v. 8 calls those who are being addressed
"rebels." So this passage to an extent runs parallel with 45:
9-13, where those addressed also find fault with what the
Almighty is doing. But as to content the passage does set
forth Yahweh's total control of all things; and so our title
may be retained. In that the passage used the proof from
prophecy as indicative of the fact that he has all things
under his control, it presents a parallel to 41:22-24; 42:9;
43:9-13; 48:3-5.

Verse 8. Yahweh is still speaking. He is still addressing
Israel as was the case since v. 3. However it is only a portion
of the people whom he challenges. He calls them "rebels."
They seem to be an impenitent element in the nation that
in spite of all that God has done for his people still take a
critical attitude. The prophet falls into a tone of a somewhat
unusual severity not otherwise characteristic of him at all.
The same somewhat harsh tone appears again in v. 12. Apparently they wavered in their whole attitude and were far
from taking that trustful position that they should have.
Therefore the challenge: "Remember this and show yourselves firm; lay it to heart," spoken somewhat in the tone of
I Cor. 16:13. Continual vacillation, trusting the Lord one
day and being dubious about him the next, is most unwholesome and dangerous.

Verse 9. To reinforce this challenge, the prophet once
more resorts to the proof from prophecy that he seemingly
loves to operate with. He invites the rebels to turn their
thoughts back far into the past, recalling "former things" like
perhaps the Exodus, or other such mighty works of God
done for Israel. These works of his demonstrate, as nothing
else can, his consistent attitude toward his people, that he has

proved himself to be their God, and there is no other. He is "very God and none like [him]."

Verse 10. Now follows the rest of the proof built up on this fact. What he purposed to do for his covenant-people he also declared from the beginning, demonstrating his control by specifying what the end would be from the very beginning of time. The Lord's deeds are thought of as a series; the predictions that these deeds would come to pass are also a series. These two series correspond with one another: they match up. The foretelling always came "long beforehand." Only the Lord can do or has done things like that. The very magnitude of the conception of God that is displayed by all this guarantees for Israel what a reliable and able God she has. Another way of stating the case is: "My purpose stands and I will execute my good pleasure." Previous passages where this approach was used are 41:22 and 42:9.

Verse 11. Now the argument is brought down to the present instance: The Lord has called "a falcon from the east, from a far country the man who shall carry out [his] purpose." The reference is obviously to Cyrus, who previously was described as the man from the *north* (41:25). A specific bird is not really mentioned, for the original means a swooping bird; could be an eagle or any bird of prey. A similar figure is used in Jer. 49:22 in reference to a bird of prey coming against Edom. In the present instance a swift and deadly thrust against Babylon is under consideration. But the point is: this is not merely another conqueror. This is a divinely commissioned conqueror whose coming the Lord has foreseen and determined, guarantying his success at the same time. The full certainty of God's control of the situation is reflected in the concluding statement: "I have both spoken and will also bring it to pass; I have formulated my plan and will also carry it out."

This whole declaration (vv. 8-11) has aptly been described as a "superb expression of the prophet's theology," in other words, of his concept of God. The future lies in God's mind, but does not lie there "dormant." God foresees, predetermines, and brings his purposes to completion. More complete control of the issues of history could not even be visualized.

In conclusion it may yet be remarked that in the use of the figure of the eagle there is hardly an allusion to the fact that on the imperial standards of Persia the symbol of the eagle appeared, as it also did at a later date on the battle flags of Rome.

5. Yahweh's Deliverance Will Soon Take Place (vv. 12-13)

46:12-13   12. "Hearken to me you stubborn-hearted,
        you who are far from righteousness.
13. I have brought near my righteousness,
    it is not far off,
        and my salvation will not lag.
    I shall give my gift of salvation in Zion,
        for Israel my glorification."

Verse 12. The class who are now being addressed as the "stubborn-hearted" will most likely be the very "rebels" of v. 8. The two failings are akin, and they are still in the same general category. First this group is described as not submitting to the divine word but rebelling against it. Then they are thought of as having made their hearts obdurate against divine truth. Such an attitude puts them far away from "righteousness." Though the tendency is strong in our day to use the perfectly permissible translation "deliverance" for this word, still that aspect of the case seems to be covered by the word found at the end of v. 13 — "salvation." We find good ground therefore for taking the word in what many are pleased to call the "forensic sense," i.e., practically synonymous with "justification." For as long as men harden their hearts against God's promises and refuse to appropriate them they certainly are not in a situation in which God can pronounce them to be what they ought to be in his sight. They are "far from righteousness." Speaking more nearly in terms applicable to the Old Testament we could say, these persons are not obedient to the demands of the covenant of their God and to faith in its promises, as it has been aptly claimed.

Verse 13. But God's graciousness far exceeds what man might expect. So he still promises to grant unto them this righteousness, which he alone can impart or impute. It has, as it were, been brought so close by him that all they on their part need to do is to stretch forth their hand and take it. But he also has another gift at hand, the "salvation" they as a nation so badly need; for they are far from fully restored from the Captivity. This salvation is described as a gift by the use of the word "give." To make this apparent we have translated: "I shall give my gift of salvation in Zion," a promise which is further amplified by the parallel statement, "for Israel (I shall give) my glorification." Thus noun "glorification" has nothing to do with the glory of God, which in different instances he allowed to appear and to dwell among his people. This refers to the singular honors that he bestowed upon his people, giving them a glorious name. On this note the contrast between the mighty God and the impotent idols comes to a close. Yahweh is not only mighty but mighty to give whatever his people need or desire.

Notes

Verse 2. The two perfects *qaresu* and *kareʻu* are used without conjunction (the customary *waw* consecutive) as is frequently the case with synonymns. See *KS* 370 h. "They themselves" in Hebrew reads "their souls," souls being used for persons.

Verse 4. In *'esbol* we have an instance of the growing usage in later Hebrew to avoid the *waw* consecutive construction. See *KS* 40. In *'asithi* (perfect) and *'essa'* (imperfect) we should note the distinction. The perfect expresses the nature of an act; the imperfect, the display of that nature.

Verse 5. The last verb *wenidhmeh* seems to coordinate this verb with the preceding by a *waw* consecutive, but this is really a consecutive clause "*that* I will really be like." *KS* 364 n.

Verse 7. When the construction switches to the singular with *yitsʻaq* it is the distributive singular ("any one") that is actually being resorted to. See *KS* 348 w.

Verse 8. There is no need to try to emend the text at this point when *hith'oshashu* is used just because this is the only instance of the use of this verb *'ashash*. The *Targum* already renders it "take courage." An Arabic parallel root would seem to confirm this approach.

Verse 10. *Re'shith* is used without an article; that virtually stamps it as a proper noun, the absolute beginning (*KS* 294 g).

Verse 11. We follow the *keri 'atsathi*, rather than "*his* purpose" which yields no usable sense. The threefold use of the *'aph* in the second half of the verse gives a kind of staccato effect.

Chapter XLVII

H. THE OVERTHROW OF BABYLON TRIUMPHANTLY PREDICTED (Chap. 47)

This overthrow is not just the overthrow of one more city during the course of history; it is the overthrow of the proud world-capital of the time.

We have before us a poem in the form of a "taunt song," or "mocking song." In mood and content it is like the preceding chapter, which told of the overthrow of Babylon's gods. Where however this type of poem might degenerate into something cheap and trivial and thus quite unworthy of being the utterance of a man of God, that is not the case here. The taunt is the taunt of faith; the mockery is based on the certainity of God's judgments. God has determined to overthrow a city marked by overweening pride; the author of this poem concurs fully in what is determined and sees both the justice and the wisdom of what God has determined. So, as *North* has said, this is a "magnificent taunt song." Nor should we think of it as offering a certain type of philosophy of history, namely an illustration of the validity of the ancient rule that things move in cycles, empires too. The kingdoms of this world keep rising and falling in a ceaseless round. True as that is to an extent, for the present writer, the prophet, Babylon's fall is an instance of the absolute control of history by Yahweh, the Lord God Almighty. A defeated God of a defeated people boldly asserts that he will take a victorious nation in hand and execute vengeance upon her, as *Westermann* points out. A striking thought!

When some claim for this song that it is not as vengeful as Nahum's song about Nineveh's overthrow, we fear that such a comparison is inept. As stated above, the writer concurs in the judgments of the Almighty and is glad over them

146

because they are right. The one to be punished has fully
merited the judgment contemplated. When justice therefore
is done, that is something to rejoice over. Such rejoicing can
be true and wholesome without the note of an unholy
gloating.

It is a bit difficult to determine who it is that is speaking.
Some think that it is God addressing Babylon. Others feel
it is the prophet. Still others, that it is the nation of Israel
itself. There is a propriety about each approach. It could
have been any one of these three. It really does not matter
in this instance which interpretation one prefers. It still
clearly is a prediction of what must befall Babylon.

Breaking the poem up into component parts is not easy, at
least not achieving an outline that is fully convincing. There
are advocates of a three part division, of a four, five, or six
part division. Again it does not matter too much which pattern is followed. The six-part division has the most enthusiastic adherents, calling it, in terms of pattern, "a poem of
outstanding artistry." That it is in any case. But where certain arrangements are arrived at by deletions and corrections,
we admit that such procedures may be classed as being questionable. All writers in our day practically agree that the
qinah (lament) meter is employed to a very large extent.
The artistry claimed for the poem involves such elements
as imperatives freely used, repetition, onomatopoeia, a striking introduction, a similar conclusion, and the like.

The thing at which this song strikes out sharply is the
overweening pride and heartlessness of the Babylonian empire, in controlling the destinies of the nations comprising her
empire. Some surmise that it was this factor that made Babylon the type of the Antichrist, as it is in the New Testament, rather than Assyria, an equally renowned empire (cf.
Rev. 17 and 18).

Comparing the taunt songs that stand out, we find in Isaiah
14 dealing with Babylon's wicked king, Chap. 46, with her
impotent idols, and Chap. 47 with the dethroned queen.

Let us underscore one point a bit more strongly. The fact

just alluded to is what we have in mind. In the Scriptures, Babylon is sometimes a historical entity, sometimes it is practically only a symbol of concentrated wickedness, ripe for judgment. She is a pattern how world empires grow, become exceedingly proud, and are drastically overthrown.

1. It Is Impending and Inevitable (vv. 1-5)

47:1-5
1. Down with you and sit in the dust,
    O virgin daughter of Babylon;
sit on the bare earth dethroned,
    O daughter of the Chaldeans.
For no longer shall you be in a situation that men
    shall call you tender and delicate.
2. Take a mill and grind meal;
remove your veil; strip off the train;
    lay bare the leg; wade through the streams.
3. Your nakedness shall be uncovered,
    and your shame shall be seen.
I will take vegeance; I will yield to no man.
4. Our Redeemer — the Lord of hosts is his name —
    is the Holy One of Israel.
5. Sit down in silence and go into darkness,
    O daughter of the Chaldeans;
        for you shall no more be called
    the queen of kingdoms.

Verse 1. It is a common practice to let a nation be personified as a woman. In this case the designation of "virgin" is added, signifying that she is to be thought of as sexually unconquered (cf. 23:12 — Sidon — and 37:22 — Zion). Whether this woman in question is to be thought of as a queen or as a prominent member of the royal harem, is not immediately clear; we feel the former possibility has greater likelihood. It is, however, quite clear that a severe humiliation is in prospect ("virgin daughter" regularly introduces doom oracles). So, being also the object of divine displeasure, she is somewhat rudely addressed: "Down with you"! and: "Sit on the bare earth"! and "Sit in the dust"! Sitting on the bare earth is sometimes to be construed as a gesture of mourning; here it involves humiliation, even as does the designation "dethroned." From being as high as women can rise, she is to be as low as they can descend. Perhaps *North* goes a little too far when he takes the second imperative to mean: "sit among the rubble." For the picture has not yet been developed enough to allow for the thought of ruins in the picture. "Tender and delicate" is virtually a quotation from Deut. 28:56, describing a pampered person, who has enjoyed every luxury. Some explain the terms as involving sensuous and sensual living in the extreme, which could certainly be asserted concerning Babylon of old.

Verse 2. Having been demoted, as it were, from queen to slave, she is next bidden to engage in the most menial of tasks — to "take a mill and grind meal." All pleasant and luxurious living is at an end: the garments of luxury must go, "veil and train." At this point the figure of the slave is abandoned and the woman is conceived of as being led away into captivity. In the course of being led away she must ford streams and in doing so must lay bare the leg and wade.

Verse 3. The figure continues in terms of wading across a stream. The water is thought of as deeper than was expected. So the garment had to be raised higher. Result: exposure, unavoidable, of "nakedness," and also (her) "shame" — genitalia — shall be seen. No need here to go to extremes of interpretation, as though rape, for example, were being described; or even, that the woman is being thought of as stripped like an adulteress, or that she shall be put on public display on the slave market, naked. Similar expressions are found in 20:4; Nah. 3:5; Jer 13:22, 26. All this that is thus figuratively described is now approached from another point of view: God is "taking vengeance." Here this noun is apparently being used in the constructive sense of righting wrongs long due for correction. What befalls Babylon is her just punishment and well deserved. The last statement of the verse — "I will yield to no man" — is merely another way of saying: Her doom is irrevocable; intercessions in her behalf will be of no avail. She has gone too far.

Verse 4. This verse looks like an uncalled for interruption of the train of thought, however, it is anything but that. It asserts that a higher point of view is to be noted in regard to what is happening to Babylon. The "Redeemer" of Israel, who, as "Lord of hosts" has all things under his control, and stands in a unique relation to his people, having set himself apart for their care and protection ("the Holy One of Israel") is the one under whose aegis all these things are happening to the once proud capital of the empire of Babylon. All history is God-related and remains totally under his control. Here there are no cheap and trivial retaliations. Here is controlled history. Nor should this verse be regarded as an afterthought. It reflects the very heart and soul of what happened when Babylon fell.

Verse 5. As this section began so it ends with a summons to step down and begin to lead a different type of existence. Babylon is to be removed from high station and is to "sit down." She is to move out of the spotlight of prominence and popularity and is to sit "in darkness," that is to say, in comparative obscurity. "Chaldeans" is here merely used as a synonymn for Babylonians. In one word, she is no longer to be a "queen" — a parallel to this would be the designation of Venice as "the queen of the Adriatic."

2. It Is Largely Due to Her Misunderstanding Israel's Overthrow (vv. 6-7)

47:6-7 6. I was indeed angry with my people,
I profaned my heritage,
and gave them over into your hand.
But you showed them no mercy;
even upon the old men you made
the yoke press very heavily.
7. You thought, "I shall be queen forever,"
you did not lay these things to heart;
you did not consider how all this would end.

Verse 6. It is quite clear that Yahweh is now speaking. He is outlining for Babylon what it is that has actually happened. But what he claims happened is hardly what a nation like Babylon would have deemed possible. The little nation of God's people suddenly moves into the picture as a matter of even greater concern than mighty Babylon. History has as its very center God's people and not the mighty empires which seem to dominate the world. So what actually happened was this: Israel had led a life unworthy of her destiny as God's people. This called forth God's just anger. The nation persisted in its wilfulness, and so God had to act. He did act, and so doing "profaned his heritage." This somewhat weighty statement involved that he allowed his people to be profaned, which here means "polluted," or "defiled." He gave them over to the spoiler or plunderer. "Heritage" could here mean Israel itself. The term is sometimes also used for the Temple, or for the Holy Land. Which ever is thought of, the net result is about the same. But the Lord gives over his prized possession into the hands of the enemy. The ultimate control of what befalls nations in their conflict with one another rests with the Almighty. So Babylon conquered Judah. But in the process of working out the results of such a victory there were certain normal limitations that reason dictated for the conqueror in the treatment of the vanquished. These obvious humane limitations Babylon did not observe. She ignored what the natural law taught all nations. The victor cannot let his vilest passions rage against the nation overcome in war. But Babylon behaved very arbitrarily; she "showed them no mercy." One instance of such unpardonable behavior is cited: "even upon the old men you made the yoke press very heavily." Harsh cruelty was the order of the day as though Babylon could let its basest and most cruel passion have free range. Her success in war called forth the worst in her. There are indications also in the Scriptures that even heathen nations felt that they were instruments in the hand of God when they gained victories over other nations.

Verse 7. But Babylon thought that perpetual success was bound to be her destiny. In other words: "I shall be queen forever." Whatever lessons of history and suggestions of conscience there were, Babylon disregarded them proudly. She made her calculations without thinking "how all this

would end." She should have known that if she played her
role badly she would have to answer to the Deity himself.
These aspects of history are obvious but they have been misread over and over again by the nations. The prophet has in
these words allowed us a glimpse behind the scenes of history. Now we know why Babylon had to fall. She defied
God's purposes with his people.

3. But It Is Also Due to Her Own Unseemly Pride (vv. 8-11)

47:8-11   8. But now hear this, you voluptuous one,
            who dwell securely,
who say in your heart:
   "I am, and there is none besides me;
   I shall not sit as a widow
     or know the loss of children."
9. And yet both these things shall befall you,
   suddenly, on one and the same day:
   the loss of children and widowhood shall come upon you
     in their full measure,
   in spite of your many sorceries,
     and in spite of the great power of your spells.
10. But you felt secure in your wickedness.
   You said: "No one sees me."
   Your very wisdom and your knowledge led you astray;
     and you said in your heart:
   "I am, and there is none besides me."
11. But there will come upon you evil,
   which you shall not know how to control.
Catastrophe, such as you have not known,
   shall suddenly befall you.

Verse 8. The key to this section lies in the fact that the
proud claim of Babylon is presented twice, in v. 8 and v. 10.
Twice she is represented as saying: "I am and there is none
besides me." Still it is true that, as to form, this passage is introduced as a "prophetic oracle" in the form "of a threat,"
following "the invective" (*Muilenburg*). Babylon is addressed as "you voluptuous one." She may be harsh in her
dealings with others; she pampers herself, as happens so often.
At the same time she lives under the illusion that no evil can

befall her, or "she dwells securely." (cf. Zeph. 2:15, where Nineveh is represented as taking the same attitude). When however Babylon makes her proud boast, "I am and there is none besides me," it should be noted first that elsewhere in the book this is the language used by none less than Yahweh himself (cf. 45:5, 21; 46:9). This therefore amounts to self-deification, as is also indicated by Ezek. 28:1-10, in the case of Tyre. This therefore is no ordinary boast but a most arrogant and presumptuous one. For sheer daring this boast cannot be matched. It defiantly challenges God himself. By way of further comparison, 14:13 f. may appropriately be examined. In her presumption the nation therefore likens herself to a woman who is happily married and has a goodly number of children and now regards her position as impregnable. The folly of such a boastful attitude is only too apparent. No position offers the promise of total security. The suddenness of the overthrow of proud Babylon is historically well attested.

Verse 9. So the prophet punctures the bubble of false security, proclaiming that the very thing the nation deems impossible will come to pass, yes, both things, "loss of children and widowhood," and that very suddenly. Babylon sat on top of the world one day and the next she was in the hands of the Persians. And all this in "full measure." Total collapse! Certain resources on which Babylon particularly prided itself would avail nothing when her time came upon her, resources such as "sorceries" and "spells." In these areas Babylon was known to be very much at home. These practices were assiduously cultivated by all nations of antiquity, and by none more than by the men of Babylon. *Haller* aptly described Babylon as "the promised land of astrology and magic." These pseudo-sciences were cultivated in a manner "incredibly elaborate" (*North*). In spite of all this, the *mass* of sorceries and the *great power* of the spells would prove utterly futile.

Verse 10. But such an attitude which assumed that one can get along well without God is more than a grandiose delusion. It is "wickedness." It sadly misleads him who harbors it. Yet there is something of an awareness of guilt involved in such an attitude. For when the remark is added: "You said: 'No one sees me,' " that very statement indicates that the speaker was aware that something reprehensible was involved. Superb pride also is one of those things that shuns the light because it is wicked, and seeks to remain hid. What had happened was that that very type of abstruse knowledge and wisdom that was being cultivated by these occult sciences was the thing that was utterly misleading the nation. Confidence was placed in the stars and their courses and not in the power of the Living God. Here is where the proud attitude of self-glorification is referred to again. For trust in the knowledge that a man can concoct leads man astray.

Verse 11. Now comes the threat of the inevitable disaster. It will be of such a sort that Babylon will not be able to control it. The futility of the devices she has been employing will become very evident on the day of judgment. Incantations and magic formulas, and the endless repetition of them is futile procedure. In fact it will all lead up to a catastrophe so overwhelming that the like will never even have occurred to Babylon. All this may be summed up in the one word: "God resisteth the proud."

4. Sorcery Is of No Avail in This Calamity (vv. 12-15)

47:12-15 12. Step forth now with your spells
and your many sorceries,
with which you have toiled from your youth;
perhaps you will terrify [me].
13. You have wearied yourself with your many consultations;
let them step forth and save you,
those that divide the heavens,
that gaze on the stars,
that at the new moon make known
something of what will come upon you.
14. They are nothing but so much chaff
which fire consumes.
They cannot deliver even themselves
from the power of the flame.

It is not a coal for warming oneself,
no firelight to sit by.
15. Such have they become with whom you have labored,
the men who have done business with you from your youth
up.
Each one strays about in his own random way;
there is no one to save you.

Verse 12. There was a passing allusion already to sorcery in the previous section. Now the prophet goes at this subject at some length, because he had to demolish completely the confidence that men might put in such deceptions. The nations esteemed sorcery as very important. Israel may sometimes have envied the nations the possession of such mysterious powers. But they were no powers; they were grand delusions. The prophet strikes a devastating blow at the whole structure of sorcery. He hurls a challenge at the Babylonians. They are to step forth on the scene for a show-down, equipped with all the wealth of resources that sorcery has devised in the course of the centuries. She had not trifled with these factors. She had "toiled" with them from her youth. Astronomy and occult arts had been drawn on heavily. It took years of intense study to become a competent exponent of magic, spells, and sorcery. When the prophet adds, "perhaps you may yet succeed," he does not vaguely anticipate that something will be achieved after all. This is sarcasm, as is the following statement, "perhaps you will terrify" says the Lord. At this point we have added a "me" in parenthesis, because it seems to be implied. Nor is sarcasm unexpected in a taunt song.

Verse 13. The many hours of study devoted to these arts are represented as having already wearied the nation, who through her men of learning, particularly the Chaldeans, has engaged in "many consultations." Again and again it would be attempted to unravel the skein of the future. The ones with whom learned consultations were held are challenged to "step forth and save." They will be given a fair chance to do something helpful, if they can. The ones who are particularly in the mind of the prophet are the "ones that divide the heavens." The reference would appear to be to the astrologers and classification of spheres of influence, as the signs of the zodiac. For they are also described as those "that gaze on the stars," or as those "that at the new moon make known something of what will come upon you." All this is not too precisely defined and may be a reference to things astrological that we are not in a position to describe. But interesting is the careful phrasing, "*something* of what will come upon you." These prognosticators will sometimes hit the right thing, but all they offer will be fragmentary, and unsatisfactory.

Verse 14. Now the verdict upon this pseudo-science, pretentious but hollow! The whole lot of the college of fortunetellers, maintained at great expense and devoting much effort to the project, in the last analysis is "nothing but so much chaff," stuff worthy only of being consumed by fire. The writer charges them with not even being able to deliver themselves, let alone others, "from the power of the flame." Here flame stands for the divine judgment, which is often likened to a flame. The flame-figure is at this point given another turn and developed more fully. A flame could serve the good purpose of warming a man when cold. Not so this fire. Or it might be thought of as a cheery fire, or "firelight to sit by." Not even that may be claimed for this fire. Astrology is in fact the epitome of futility.

Verse 15. When it is stated that these men had worked hand in hand with the Babylonians, this may be a reference to the well-known fact that these groups of purveyors of secret arts had been furnished private quarters at national expense and had enjoyed special privileges, like priests. Of course, they are men who have been so long in the picture that they seem to belong there. These men have done business with the nation from her youth up. They are something distinctively Babylonian. But when the great reckoning comes, which the prophet describes as being in the offing, these persons will stray about aimlessly and helplessly, unable to save themselves or any other man. On this note of the utter futility of astrology ends this "magnificent taunt song."

Notes

Luther begins the new section with 46:12. We fail to see good grounds for so doing.

Verse 1. On the idea of a nation personified as a woman see *KS* 248 f. On the unique way of expressing the idea of "no longer to do a thing," see *GK* 120 c and *KS* 361 h.

Verse 3. Some would claim that this verse is an inept expansion of the idea involved, at least 3a. That approach is purely a matter of subjective impression. The first half of the verse rounds out the thought quite effectively.

"Will yield to no man" is a defensible translation of *'ephga'*, which *BDB* translates as "entreat" and *KB*, as "yield to asking." No matter how it is translated the net result is about the same.

Verse 4. Following the lead of the Septuagint some feel that this verse should be introduced by *'amar* ("he says") and then have v. 5 as that which the Holy One says, a harmless emendation but unnecessary.

Verse 7. The initial verb *'amar* is generally admitted also to have the meaning not of "say" but of "suppose." See *BDB*, p. 56.

Verse 8. In *'aphsi* the final syllable may be the remnant of an old case ending (*GK* 90 m).

Verse 9. The verb *ba'u* is a prophetic perfect.

Verse 10. For "in your wickedness" the Dead Sea Scrolls substituted "in your knowledge" substituting an initial *r* for *d*. Though that would make good sense, so does the text as it stands.

Verse 11. For "which you shall not know how to control" *KJ* has: "thou shalt not know from whence it ariseth." The word involved is *shachar*, "dawn." The rendering involved in *KJ* is, as *BDB* indicates "improbable." The word is now usually traced back to a kindred Arabic root meaning "to charm" or "to bribe away."

The initial verb of this verse appears in the masculine with a feminine subject, as is often done in Hebrew. See *KS* 345 b.

Verse 12. Elaborate emendations on this verse are attempted, but when all is said and done it still seems best, with *North*, to keep the text as it stands.

For "that divide the heavens" the *Septuagint* actually uses the word "astrologers."

Chapter XLVIII

I. A SHARP REBUKE AND A GRACIOUS CHALLENGE (Chap. 48)

As our caption indicates we see two elements set forth in this chapter, the first element, rebuke, is preponderant; the second, grace, here plays a secondary role. So we are in sympathy with those who term the subject of the chapter to be a summary word of admonition to the unconverted, or, as some put it: "Once again an attempt had to be made to stir up a people who had their doubts about good prospects for the future" (*Koenig*).

Our chapter presents a number of unique problems. We shall not attempt to describe and evaluate the various solutions that have been offered. But we do draw attention to one of the latest, one that has been worked out with great care. We refer to *Westermann's* treatment of the case. He takes issue with the obvious fact that two kinds of material appear in the chapter: some words speak graciously to the nation Israel, some words prefer sharp indictments of the same group. *Westermann* believes to have gotten around the difficulty involved by attributing the second group of words to the class of secondary additions, leaving the question open whether these additions stem from the author or from some other writer. Secondary materials are: vv. 1e, 4, 5cd, 7c, 8cd, 9, 10, 11c. This would certainly result in a chapter that had been abundantly reworked. But the critic is positive that we have anything but a unit chapter. The writer is always wavering between two types of material.

It must be admitted that a sharp, clear-cut, logical progression of thought is not in evidence in the chapter. But the truth of the matter appears to be that there are two sides to the author's message. We have sought to cover this as-

158

pect of the case by the chapter-caption: "A sharp rebuke and a gracious challenge." Both aspects of the message clamor for a hearing. Hardly has the one side of the matter been presented when the prophet feels the need of emphasizing the other aspect of the case. This is a situation like so many in the prophetic writings of the Old Testament: they present a blend of law and gospel. Somewhat harshly *Westermann* refuses to allow the question of what is genuine and what is not even to be raised in this context.

We choose at this point to present a condensation of the contents of this chapter in a somewhat more detailed outline.

a. vv. 1-2. A solemn introduction of a sharp rebuke. God is about to make a pronouncement and describes the spiritual state of those to whom this rebuke is addressed.

b. vv. 3-5. The beginning of the pronouncement. God's *fore-knowledge of past history* is an index of his full control of history. Thereby he anticipates and cuts short Israel's willful misinterpretation.

c. vv. 6-8. The same control of history is displayed by God's *foretelling of a new set of events.* No one knew of these things save God alone. God had to operate thus to shame rebellious Israel.

d. vv. 9-11. God's sparing of the sinners is due solely to his grace.

e. vv. 12-13. All things take their beginning from the Lord, and he survives them all.

f. vv. 14-16. The sending of Cyrus and the foretelling of his success is further proof of God's absolute control.

g. vv. 17-19. If Israel had hearkened to God in the past, she would now be most abundantly blessed.

h. vv. 20-22. Israel is invited to go forth from Babylon rejoicing.

Though outlines of the chapter like *North's* (*Prophecy and History*) have some value, they are too brief to be of much help.

One thing that almost every writer comments on is the extreme sharpness of the rebuke administered by our prophet.

We feel that too much is being made of this type of approach. Sharpness? Yes. Extreme sharpness? That is a matter of opinion. Passages marked by some measure of sharp rebuke would be the following: 42:18-25; 43:22 ff.; 46:8 ff.; 50:1-3. It becomes very difficult to determine which of these is to be labelled as the sharpest of all.

Another somewhat striking thing is the fact that idolatry is ascribed to the nations, whereas the opposite observation has frequently been made that idolatry becomes a dead issue for Israel after the Captivity. This is no longer a dominant sin after the Return from Babylon. The relative truth of this chapter on the subject appears to be this, that, though by and large idolatry lost its hold on the nation, it still survived as a private sin on the part of some and still constituted at least some measure of a threat to her healthy spiritual life as a nation.

1. Solemn Introduction of a Sharp Rebuke (vv. 1-2)

48:1-2 1. Hearken, O house of Jacob,
who are called by the name of Israel,
and have come forth out of the waters of Judah,
who swear by the name of Yahweh,
who call to remembrance the God of Israel
but not in good faith and sincerity.
2. For they call themselves after the Holy City
and lean upon the God of Israel:
the Lord of hosts is his name.

Verse 1. The prophet is speaking. This solemn introduction savors more of the spirit of the prophet Ezekiel than of the comfort of Isaiah. In fact this harsh note prevails till v. 11. The "this" of "hear this" (*RSV*) refers to what is about to follow. The ones addressed as "house of Jacob" are simply the ancient people of God, here designated after their historical ancestor. They have in addition the more honorable title of "Israel" — the covenant nation. A third term is used to heighten the solemnity of the address — they have come forth "from the waters of Judah" (the tribal ancestor of the southern kingdom). This somewhat difficult expression, which has invited a number of textual emendations, perhaps has nothing more in mind than a tributary derived from the main stream. So the majority of the people, being Jews, stem at this post-exilic date which is envisioned, from the main-stream Judah. In the somewhat eloquent description that follows, certain spiritual prerogatives are set forth, prerogatives that are distinctly her own. The nation may use the name of Yahweh wherever solemn oaths are required. She calls upon him to witness what they say, and he hears. Furthermore, she may call to remembrance whatever God has done for her in the past, praising his holy name. Such adoration is a further privilege. But alas, these sacred usages have degenerated to the point where they are no longer done "in good faith and sincerity." The whole verse then speaks of rare privileges bestowed but abused and regarded lightly. The fact that the two verbs last used ("swear" and "all to remembrance" (frequently have liturgical connotation, by no means puts the stamp of a liturgical gathering upon the people mentioned in the text in question. For to use verbs that have liturgical connotation does not say that such usage immediately conjures up a liturgical act as such.

Verse 2. Further bad habits that have been developed by this favored nation indicate in what area the bad faith and lack of sincerity just referred to are to be found. These people are wont to associate themselves with "the Holy City," unholy though they themselves are (on "Holy City" compare 52:1 and Dan. 9:24). They also are in the habit of "leaning upon the God of Israel, Yahweh of hosts is his name." But here too the implication is that they put their trust in him on occasions where such confidence is unwarranted. For "Yahweh of hosts" is the God of all worlds and is not lightly to be used as a refuge in connection with unhallowed purposes. So ends the solemn, ominous-sounding introduction.

2. The Beginning of the Pronouncement (vv. 3-5)

48:3-5 3. "The earlier prophecies I have declared from of old;
from my mouth they went forth and I made them known.
Suddenly I acted and they happened.
4. Since I knew how stubborn you are,
and that your neck is like a sinew of iron
and your forehead is of bronze;
5. therefore did I declare things from of old.
Before they happened I published them,
lest you say: 'My idol did them,
my carved image and my metal image have ordered it.'"

Now the Lord begins to speak.

Verse 3. The prophet represents the Lord as also operating with an argument that he has been using effectively, the argument about God's foreknowledge of things that happened in the past. Here the emphasis lies mainly on the effect that this fact should have had on Israel and how it should have influenced the nation's thinking. In times past — here the line of demarcation in point of time is drawn where the Babylonian Captivity comes to pass. The significant events of Israel's history were again and again declared before they happened: Abraham's destiny, Israel's Bondage in Egypt, Israel's Liberation from this Bondage, the Conquest of Canaan, the coming of the Babylonian Captivity. The references to these events are the "earlier prophecies" here mentioned. They reach far back ("from of old"). Either speaking directly to individuals when he appeared to them, or through the mouth of his holy prophets, "which have been since the world began," God made the coming of these events known. People often knew a long time in advance of the coming of these events. Then "suddenly [he] acted and they happened."

Verse 4. A unique motivation for the prediction and for bringing the predicted event to pass is now given. Among other reasons that may be advanced for God's doing this, God advances this new one: "I knew how stubborn you are . . . therefore did I declare things from of old . . . lest you say:

'My idol did them.' " God's course of action was calculated
to forestall some unwholesome attitude on Israel's part. She,
as nation, was so stubbornly addicted to idolatry that she
would be inclined to attribute such unusual acts of God to
her idols, whereas the glory belonged to God. This stubbornness is often referred to in the Scriptures (see Exod. 32:
9; Deut. 9:6, 27; Jer. 3:3; Ezek. 3:7). Here there is attributed to Israel a "neck like a sinew of iron," and a "forehead of bronze" ("your effrontery is brazen" translates
North). Yahweh would nip in the bud this inclination to
give the idols credit for what Yahweh did.

Verse 5. One is taken aback a bit by this reference to
idolatry on the part of the Israel of the Exile. It is usually
claimed that the Babylonian Exile cured Israel of her pro-
clivity to idolatry, which had to be scored so frequently by
the prophets, especially Jeremiah. The explanation for this
seeming discrepancy may lie in this that the public and open
practice of idolatry did fall away with the heavy yoke of the
Captivity coming as a punishment for Israel's unfaithfulness.
But even so, evils like idolatry have deep root, and the secret
worship of idols may have still gone on behind the scenes.
Witness the stubbornness with which withcraft is held fast
and practiced in many areas, always in secret and in the
dark of the night. It could well be that when two types of
idol-figures are mentioned ("carved image" and "metal image") the intention is to show that various forms of this old
sin were still in evidence. Although it is also possible that the
figure of speech called "hendiadys" is involved, two terms
used for a composite single term, both together amounting
to "metal image."

3. The Same Control of History Displayed by God's Fortelling of a New Set of Events (vv. 6-8)

48:6-8 6. "You have heard all this; now regard it,
and will not you yourself declare it?
From now on I make you to hear new things
and hidden things which you have not known.
7. They are being created now, not long ago;

and until now you had never heard of them;
lest you say: 'Of course I knew them.'
8. On the contrary, you neither heard nor knew;
and besides your ear has long been completely closed.
For I know how very treacherous you are,
and you have been rightly called: 'a rebel from birth.'"

Verse 6. It has just been indicated that God had in times past revealed things which were to come, things here referred to as "earlier prophecies" (v. 3). Now another manifestation of divine foreknowledge is put forth — "new things," a term which refers to events that still lie in the future. But before turning to these "new things" the Lord once more encourages his people to cast one more glance back at these "earlier prophecies," to "study them" or as we translated above "now regard them," i.e., scrutinize them with care and take note of the fact that they were in a very significant way foretold with a purpose. In fact so striking is their prediction that Israel, as a result of her scrutiny of them, is challenged. For she must feel impelled, she herself, the stubborn one, to "declare it," that God so often foretold and so regularly brought to pass what was foretold. The thought is cast in the form of a challenging question. But all this lies in the past. "From now on" God is going to declare some "new things" to his people with a similar purpose in mind as when in times past he told them of impending events. Until now, not a one of the things he will declare has been disclosed; they are "hidden things," undisclosed for the present. Though not mentioned here, events like the overthrow of Babylon might be thought of. Though Isaiah had prophesied this (13:19) the fact as such was as good as unknown, for Israel had as yet not taken it to heart. Or perhaps it would be better to leave it undetermined what events the prophet had in mind, and so let the claim stand there in all its breadth. Or else, as *Delitzsch* expounds, the reference is to the New Testament era as such, the facts of which are abundantly set forth by God's prophets.

Verse 7. Working with this last assumption, as perhaps

the most reasonable one of them all, we can understand what the prophet now means when he says: "They are being created now, not long ago." Two thoughts blend into one: God creates these events; and, now first they are in the making. God's sovereign control of history for one thing is asserted. It may rightly be said that he "creates" the events that come to pass. But then the second thought, the details of what the Messianic age would bring in the days to come had never yet been revealed, "until now you had never heard of them." So the Lord delights to work in his control of history, that his overruling providence might prevail and that Israel might not say, "Of course, I knew them." For Israel was always sidestepping God's work in her behalf. She would not acknowledge freely what God had done and that the control of his acts was solely in his hands.

Verse 8. At this point the Lord resumes his sharp indictment of Israel. He charges the nation in its spiritual intractability, practically with never having learned her lessons in the past ("you neither knew nor heard"). She had degenerated in the course of time to the point where her ear has "long been completely closed." More than a measure of dullness or weakness is attributed to Israel. She has long been "very treacherous," a charge that God makes in a tone marked by some impatience. He seems to imply that the nation kept misconstruing what was told her. Sharpening the charge still more, the Lord advances to the point of asserting that if in times past it was claimed that Israel was "a rebel from birth" the accusation was correct. "Rebel" is the strongest term for sin and the sinner. One may well construe the whole charge as mounting to an ever higher pitch, until "rebel" is reached, as an almost thunderous close.

4. Sparing of Sinners Due to God's Grace (vv. 9-11)

48:9-11 9. "For my name's sake I will defer my anger,
for the sake of my renown I will lay restraint upon myself,

that I may not cut you off.
10. I have assayed you — and not found you to be silver.
I tested you in the furnace of affliction.
11. For my sake, yea, for my sake I act thus —
for why should (my name) be profaned?
And my honor I will not give to another."

Verse 9. The tone changes abruptly. The sermon-call to repentance turns about and becomes a consolatory address (*Fischer*). In a truly evangelical spirit these words flatly reject any human merit or achievement as the possible basis for this radical change of attitude. God has a "name" or, we could say, a reputation for deferring anger. This attribute of his is called "mercy." That it is that motivates his dealing kindly with the sinner. The "renown" that he gets for dealing thus with the unworthy could also be designated as the "praise" that is given to him. The word involved could be translated either way. The description is rather colorful. The restraint that he lays upon himself, according to the root-meaning of the verb used, could be said to be a muzzle, preventing him from speaking the word of condemnation that is so richly deserved. For if he acted otherwise, the evidence of the case demands that he "cut off" his people.

Verse 10. This verse may be thought of as having been spoken with a sigh, a deep sigh. It underlines the lack of worth on the part of God's people still more strongly. To determine if there be not some good in them, he played the part of the assayer, he tested them in the "furnace of affliction," which is known to bring out hidden qualities in men. But the results were disappointing: (I have) "not found you to be silver." On the verse as a whole it is interesting to observe that the two verbs employed (assayed and tested) appear together many times (see Zech. 13:9; Jer. 9:7; Ps. 17:3, 26; 66:10; Prov. 17:3, etc.).

Verse 11. God's sole initiative and sovereignty could hardly be emphasized more than they are here — twice over "for my sake." The thought of v. 9 is being recapitulated. When a causal clause is added, "for why should my name be profaned?" the thought is that if God were minded to deal with his people as sternly as they deserve, then the affliction brought on his people might lead their heathen neighbors to make statements to the effect that God had left his own in the lurch, and so the honor of which he was deserving might wrongfully be attributed to other gods. Ezekiel 36:19-23 might serve as a sort of commentary on these verses.

5. All Things Take Their Beginning from the Lord (vv. 12-13)

In this half of the book, Isaiah is preoccupied with God and not with man, as has been often remarked. The passage about to follow is a good illustration of this.

48:12-13 12. "Listen to me, O Jacob, and Israel whom I called. I, I am the first, also I am the last.
13. Yea, my hand laid the foundation of the earth, and my right hand spread out the skies.
When I call them [into being] there they stand!"

Verses 12, 13. First Israel is reminded of how she stands related to the Lord: she became his people as a result of his call addressed to her. He is "the absolute Originator" (*von Orelli*). He is on the scene before all things else. He calls all being into existence. But also when all things temporal shall have had their day and pass off the scene, he will still be there. To state the case a bit more concretely, His "hand laid the foundation of the earth," not only the earth as such but also the "foundation" (whatever that may be) on which the earth rests. This does not necessarily demand that there be concrete foundations as such for the earth to rest on. Whatever holds her in place, he put it there. Even more impressive is the next work mentioned, his "right hand spread out the skies." When he called earth and skies and all other created things into being at once, there they stood (cf. Ps. 33:9; Gen. 1:1 ff.; Rom. 4:17). That is the kind of God that called Israel to be his own people. That is the one with whom they are now dealing. He is the one who is now as-

serting his right to maintain them and not cast them off. The
tone of the passage is one of consolation. The ground has
been prepared for the great works of his that are yet to follow and that Israel might think him incapable of doing. For
the prophet is about to come back again to the subject of
Cyrus and his successful overthrow of Babylon.

6. The Sending of Cyrus Further Proof of God's Control (vv. 14-16)

48:14-16 14. "Assemble all of you and hear:
            who among them foretold these things?
He whom Yahweh loves will achieve his purpose against Babylon,
and his arm will be against the Chaldeans.
15. It is I, and I only who have spoken and have called him;
I have brought him on the scene and his purpose will prosper.
16. Draw near to me; hear this:
        'Indeed I did not speak from the beginning in secrecy;
Ever since things came to pass, there am I.'
    And now the Lord has sent me endowed with his Spirit."

Verse 14. If God's sovereignty and absolute control in
general were under consideration in vv. 12-13, now comes a
specific instance of such control, to which the Lord pointedly
draws attention. Here everything centers around the work
and mission of Cyrus again (cf. 44:28).

Apparently these words address themselves to the people
of Israel, who are invited to assemble; for important disclosures are about to be transmitted to them. They are invited to listen closely to what is said. It is really an old argument that is again being submitted: the impotence of the
idols to disclose the future (see 41:21-24; 45:21 f.). In
"Who among them . . ." the "them" refers to the idols. They
knew nothing and could disclose nothing about what and
who were about to appear on the scene and do significant
work. At once the Lord assures his people that there is a
man whom he is about to send, and for him he has particular
affection because he will successfully achieve a work committed to him by the Lord; and this work is directed "against
Babylon" involving her overthrow in fact. "His arm will be

against the Chaldeans" signifies that his power will be in evidence against this mighty nation with headquarters in Babylon. It is now quite obvious that the thing implied is the total conquest of Babylon by Cyrus and his armies.

Verse 15. The Lord insists on it that he brought Cyrus on the scene, having himself spoken and called him. Others may not be aware of this. Cyrus himself may have sensed it but dimly. But the Lord actually brought this his instrument on the scene and prospered his efforts.

Verse 16. This verse is in the same vein as the preceding. Israel is still the one being addressed. The nation is invited to draw near and give heed both to the claim that the Lord is the revealer of things and is the one who exists prior to all things. The former claim appears to the effect that when God did reveal things that were about to happen, he spoke plainly and openly so that men had a clear prediction of what was to come to pass. Everything was done openly and above board. The proof for God's ability to predict is strong and irrefutable.

But now comes the last line, a crux for interpreters if ever there was one. *Muilenburg* despairs of a solution. Most commentators resort either to the claim of corruption of the text or the other claim of editorial addition. We freely admit that the difficulty is great, great already in this that suddenly the speech changes from the word of the Lord to the comment of the prophet. We offer an interpretation with some diffidence. The prophet speaks of his own mission as being one of the acts of that God who ordains and controls all things; and he adds that he comes "endowed with his Spirit," the Spirit whose coming to the nations would come like a copious outpouring of power on his own (see 44:3). This, we admit, is an unexpected turn of the thought but not an impossible or an unreasonable one. The prophet comes, sent as a herald of the victorious mission of Cyrus.

7. If Israel Had Hearkened in the Past (vv. 17-19)

48:17-19 17. Thus says the Lord, your Redeemer,
                 the Holy One of Israel:
"I am the Lord your God, who teaches you for your own good.
  and directs you in the path you should go.
18. O that you had listened to my commandments!
Then your peace would have been like a river,
and your righteousness [prosperity] like the waves of the Sea.
19. Then your descendants would have been as numerous as the
      sand,
and your offspring like its grains;
their name would never be cut off,
  nor destroyed from before me."

Verse 17. All this (vv. 17-19) seems to be spoken to offset
the possible criticism: If God is as kindly disposed toward his
people as he is now asserting since v. 9, why his harshness in
dealing with them in even allowing a captivity? He replies
to this implied criticism by reassuring them that in all this he
is still their "Redeemer, the Holy One of Israel." He is still
"the Lord [their] God." In times past he had made it possible for them to fare well. He had taught them for their
own good, and had even gone so far as to map out their path
for them, the path in which they should go.

Verse 18. Had Israel listened to his commandments, which
were the substance of his guiding directions, a number of
very substantial blessings would have fallen to their lot.
These commandments seem to be thought of as sufficiently
well known by the children of Israel, for they were, with
more or less regularity, read in assemblies of public worship.
The resultant blessings that God would have been pleased
to bestow would, first of all, be "peace," a general state of
well being, extending over the whole of their existence.
This peace would have been abundant and rich like a strongly
flowing stream (a figure appearing also in Amos 5:24; Isa.
11:9; 44:4). This stream is in contrast to the shallow, flash-
flood streamlets, or wadis, which are so much more common
in the land of Palestine than are perennial streams. The Lord
would bestow his gift copiously. Similar is the figure of
abundance with regard to the "righteousness" bestowed,

which here too implies the idea of abundance. For "waves of the sea" are certainly not to be numbered over the surface of the vast ocean. The whole verse bears a striking similarity to the passage in Ps. 81:13-16.

Verse 19. In addition numerous offspring would be granted to the nation by the Lord. The ancient promise of Gen. 15:5 would then have been realized to the full, descendants like the sand by the seashore. Such a nation would never be cut off or destroyed.

8. Israel Invited to Go Forth from Babylon (vv. 20-22)

48:20-22 20. Go forth from Babylon,
haste away from Chaldea.
Declare it with a shout of jubilation;
let this be heard.
Tell it out to the end of the earth;
say: "The Lord has redeemed his servant Jacob!"
21. And not did they thirst in the deserts
through which he led them;
he made water to flow forth from the rock for them;
he cleft the rock and the water ran out.
22. "There is no peace," says the Lord, "for the wicked."

Verse 20. The meter had been mostly 3:3 up to this point in the chapter. It now changes mostly to 2:2. *Muilenburg* calls the form "staccato imperatives."

Instead of announcing formally that the method of achieving his gracious purpose will be a glorious deliverance from the prison of Babylon, the prophet dramatically challenges his people to go forth, as it were, on their own initiative (cf. Gen. 19:15-22). As the people then answer the challenge and go forth they are to proclaim with jubilation that this deliverance is the Lord's work. So vociferously are they to make their proclamation that it will resound to the end of the earth. When the one redeemed is described as "his servant Jacob," this implies that after his deliverance Jacob will have work to do in the service of his God. Tasks yet to be done lie before him.

Verse 21. As the prophet visualizes what is to happen in this deliverance, it may be best to regard this verse as a kind of reflection upon the past of Israel's glorious history. Particularly, since a vast desert lay in the space intervening between Babylon and Palestine, an area where they who pass through might perish from thirst, the prophet lets Israel reflect upon the past as though it were a guaranty for the future. When God even gave water from the rock to his people Israel on two occasions (see Exod. 17:6; Num. 20:11), faith may well draw the conclusion that he will not fail his people in the present emergency. It is not said that a repetition of that miracle will again take place, but faith is allowed to draw inspiring hope from the events of the past.

Verse 22. This brings us to what is usually esteemed a later editorial addition that stands utterly unrelated to what has been presented in this chapter. Besides this same statement, word for word, appears in 57:21, closing off the second major section in the second half of the book of Isaiah. Is this then merely to be regarded as a somewhat artificial device for marking off sections one from the other? We believe there is more to it than that. The unique "peace" that they enjoy who listened to the Lord's commandments (v. 18) stands in sharp contrast to the lack of peace on the part of the wicked. Is that sharp reminder out of place in a chapter which on the whole bears the stamp of a sharp rebuke? Even though the tone in the second half of the chapter had turned to one of consolation, is it entirely inappropriate to let an undertone of rebuke sound forth once more before the close? The approach then would be the very opposite of that used by Paul in Gal. 6:16.

Notes

Verse 1. The construction goes from the finite verb (hear) to the participle ("the ones called"). Cf. *KS* 413 k. Then it goes over into the third person ("have come forth"). For "waters" some conjecture "from the loins" (*RSV*) by a slight vowel change; others go to an entirely different word with the Septuagint "from the seed". The Hebrew is plausible as construed above.

Verse 4. The infinitive is used to express the equivalent of a causal clause (*KS* 403 d).

Verse 6. "Will not you yourself declare it" is a statement labelled by *Volz* as not making any sense whatever. We believe we have shown above that it does make sense, especially if it be noted that the insertion of the personal pronoun makes it emphatic that *they themselves* declare what is so very obvious. By the use of the personal pronoun a transition is made from the singular to the plural.

Verse 8. Instead of *pittechah* (a *Piel* form) we read the passive, *puttechah* (a *Pual* form), making the statement a case of litotes (denying the negative to obtain a stronger positive).

Verse 9. The compound preposition (*lema'an*) extends over into the second stich, and so takes a second object (*GK* 119 hh).

Verse 10. The expression "but not found you to be silver" is very much condensed in Hebrew — "but not as silver." It must surely be meant in a sense somewhat like our version.

Verse 14. "Who among *them*" involves a somewhat harsh change of person from the second to the third. Transitions like this are not uncommon. Some forty manuscripts retain the second person form (*bakhem* for *bahem*). Let the reader take his choice. "Against the Chaldeans" is another case where the preposition is not repeated (see *KS* 319 m and l).

Verse 16. Where the Hebrew merely says (he) "has sent me and his Spirit" it seems to catch the intended force of the statement if the word "endowed" be inserted, thus: "endowed me with his Spirit," as some commentators do.

Verse 21. The Hebrew form *holikham* represents a relative clause with the relative pronoun, so-called — omitted. Cf. *KS* 380 c.

Chapter XLIX

J. THE SERVANT'S ASSIGNMENT REDEFINED AND ISRAEL REASSURED OF RECOVERY (Chap. 49)

It has been observed by some that the subject under consideration now for the next seven chapters is the redemption of Israel. Again there are those who hold that the major theme of these chapters is The Servant of the Lord. The difference between these two approaches is not as striking as it might seem. Our above caption indicates that we incline more toward the second approach, all the more so since in Chap. 53 the Servant towers above every other consideration.

That we have actually come to a new section of the second half of the book is made obvious by the fact that a new series of subjects stand in the foreground, or, better, certain subjects that stood out in Chaps. 40-48 have retreated into the background. Among these themes that are absent is Babylon; also Cyrus; then, polemics against idols; court trials are lacking — a favorite theme for some time; and lastly Jacob and Israel have receded backstage to be replaced by Zion-Jerusalem.

We do well to take issue with a major problem which must be settled sooner or later: Who is the Servant of the Lord who appears speaking in the first seven verses of the chapter and is prominent through the rest of the chapter? The literature on the subject is voluminous. The problem is perennial. The difficulties involved in the problem are not simple or easy of solution. Even if some one solution is accepted, a relative validity of other approaches has to be conceded. The name "the servant of the Lord" is rich in connotation.

In addition to what has been said on the subject in Chap.

42, we should like to submit the following considerations. Though in this chapter in v. 3 the person under consideration is plainly called "Israel" that does not settle the question, because Israel may be taken in the nationalistic sense or as descriptive of the idea that God held up before his people in a spiritual sense. We reject the term as referring to the corporate Israel — the nation — for the following reasons: There is something a bit unnatural to have the *nation* have as object of its efforts the restoration of the *nation*. A nation cannot well restore itself. We speak soberly on the subject: this seems too much like exhorting a nation to draw itself up out of trouble by its own bootstraps. *North* contends that this is no more inappropriate than to say "that the first mission of the church is to the church." But this observation does not eliminate the fact that such a task could hardly be called a "mission," for mission means "sending": a group cannot be sent to itself.

Furthermore, it would be quite unnatural for a nation to say of itself that it was named (v. 1) "from the body of (its) mother." Such imagery may well apply to an individual, not to a nation.

For the present we add only one more consideration. Throughout the chapter the mission and the achievements of the Servant are described in such glowing terms as to be entirely beside the point as far as Israel's achievement of its mission could be concerned. Israel's achievements always fell so far short of the ideal, were so incomplete and inadequate that to describe them as is done in this chapter savors of a certain idle rhetoric, or a failure to face facts squarely.

Aside from this, there is the problem of the state of the text. Too many writers allow themselves too much freedom in the treatment of the text as though it were in a very sad state of confusion. Problems are involved, but it can hardly be claimed that there are many additions, many inversions, many omissions, much need of correction. By way of offering a sampling at the very beginning of the chapter, one writer would rearrange the verses as follows: 3, 5b, 4, 5a,

6, 7. Just because the prophet did not let his thought appear in the sequence we might have chosen hardly warrants a re-arrangement according to our preference.

1. The Servant Disappointed but Recommissioned (vv. 1-6)

49:1-6 1. Listen to me, O coastlands;
give attention, O peoples from afar.
The Lord has called me from birth,
while I was yet in the womb
he gave me a name to be remembered.
2. He made my mouth like a sharp sword,
in the shadow of his hand he hid me.
He made me a polished arrow,
he hid me away in his quiver.
3. And he said to me: "You are my servant, Israel,
in whom I will be glorified."
4. But I said: "In vain have I toiled;
I have spent my strength in vain and to no purpose.
But yet my right is with the Lord,
and my reward is with my God."
5. And now the Lord says,
he that formed me from birth to be his servant,
to bring back Jacob to him,
and that Israel might be gathered to him.
(So I was honored in the eyes of the Lord,
and my God became my strength).
6. He says: "It is too light a thing that you should be a servant
of mine,
to raise up the tribes of Jacob,
and to restore the preserved of Jacob.
I will also give you as a light to the Gentiles,
and to be my salvation to the end of the earth."

Verse 1. Some have suggested that the Servant, whoever he may be, is in reality telling the story of his life (*Volz*). Our approach to the problem of the identity of the Servant is that he is in the last analysis none less than the Messiah. By the Spirit of prophecy, the prophet is given the privilege of seeing the Messiah and is initiated into the problems of his (the Messiah's) ministry. It is more clearly apparent than in Chap. 42 that in some mysterious way it is to be the lot of the Messiah to achieve his purpose by suffering. He is the

Suffering Servant of the Lord. The full measure of his suffering will be indicated presently. For a short time his ministry is marked by the suffering that disappointment brings. But the experience is of world-wide significance.

And so he begins by inviting the distant shores of the West ("the coastlands"), representative of all remote areas of the then-known world, to give close attention ("listen"). Note the same approach in 46:3, 12; 51:1, 7; 55:3. The parallel statement invites "peoples from afar" to give attention also. The big issues of the history of mankind are to be weighed. What men should become aware of first is that the unique person who is under consideration has been destined by the Lord himself, even before birth, to a task of incomparable magnitude and importance. God's plans are not improvised as he goes along. They are distinctly made long in advance. The speaker is a man of destiny in the highest sense of the word. This fact is in line with the magnitude of his mission. One might say that in this respect he is a counterpart, even of higher standing than Cyrus, whom God also prepared beforehand for his unusual task. Besides, one thinks almost at once of the similarity of this case with that of Jeremiah, called before his birth (Jer. 1:5). The speaker has a sense of divine mission analogous to that of the great prophets of Israel, who were deeply imbued with a sense of divine commission.

But not only was this person divinely appointed before his birth to perform an unusually high task, he was also equipped with the requisite gifts to achieve his destined purpose.

Verse 2. The instrument with which he works is the word, spoken by his "mouth," which spoke words that were to be startlingly effective ("sword"), which is kept in such a way that its sharp edge will not be blunted, but be ready for effective use. "Shadow of his hand" signifies protection, or careful preservation. A number of parallel Scriptures come to mind in this connection: Heb. 4:12; Rev. 1:16; cf. also Jer. 23:29; and Eph. 6:17. A second telling figure clinches the point: the speaker is to be like "a polished arrow," kept in reserve in its proper quiver, to be fully effective when circumstances require it. The ministry of the man in question apparently is calculated to wound men for their own good. His ministry to men may involve pain and suffering on their part; it will have deep-going effects.

Verse 3. But the ministry of the man in question is summed up more comprehensively in the definition of it that the Lord himself gives: he is to be the Lord's "servant," a person totally committed to execute the commission that the Lord has laid upon him. This assignment is more fully covered by the fact that he is to be a new "Israel," the man who in a strange way carried on the Lord's work and fulfilled the destiny that was assigned to the nation Israel at large, to be the bearer of the message of divine truth to the nations, a task which the Israel after the flesh executed but poorly, but which awaits accomplishment. He is to be the true spiritual Israel, doing God's work, achieving the Lord's objectives in such a manner that it will redound to the great glory of God.

Verse 4. But this aspect of positive achievement of the Lord's work is for the moment pushed into the background. In spite of marvelous equipment for the task, the Servant's work will be marked by disappointing results. None will feel that more keenly than the Lord's Servant himself. He is represented as voicing his inner pain over his apparent lack of success. He says: "In vain have I toiled; I have spent my strength in vain and to no purpose." More clearly even than the New Testament Gospels the disappointing aspect of Christ's earthly ministry is here indicated at least for his three years ministry on earth. The fruits of this ministry were startlingly meager. The servant would put his best efforts into his labors, toiling and spending his strength. Visible results would not be in evidence. But still he knows that his efforts will not be totally fruitless, to state the case mildly. He has the "right" to expect some fruitage from the Lord, and he can safely leave the outcome in God's hands. The same ground is covered by the parallel statement: "My reward is with my God," i.e., the reward of my faithful work, for God will give success.

Verse 5. The Lord has an answer to the complaint of his servant. As the servant reports what God said, he brings into the picture a fuller statement of the Lord's plans for his servant. He recalls first the fact already emphasized, that he has been destined for his office before birth. Then he sets forth more fully that Israel's restoration was his assignment, and indicates that this assignment involved the spiritual revival, that is to say, nothing less than bringing the nation back into fellowship with the Lord. He adds to this parenthetically that he was aware of the fact that such a commission reflected an unusual honor upon him and that for the fulfillment of his task God "became his strength." So richly did God equip his servant and honor him. It is as though the servant were recalling the tremendous issues involved in his task.

Verse 6. Now the new form of his commission stands out the more distinctly. But once again in giving the fresh statement, the Lord recalls how comprehensive the original assignment was — for the issues involved were of a most tremendous scope — but the Lord does not withdraw from the obligations assigned, nor does he lighten the burden of responsibility laid upon the shoulders of his servant. Rather God adds much weightier burden to the one already being carried. Two terms indicate the new area of assignment. The first is that the servant is to be a light to the Gentiles. His person is to be such a light, or as it is often rephrased: the servant is to be the bearer of light or the instrument of light to them. No human agent's assignment ever involved such responsibility. For this reason in part, as indicated above, we consider this to be a definition of the work laid upon the Messiah himself. Of practically equal force is the definition of duty, that he is to be (God's) "salvation to the end of the earth." He is not only to be the bearer of salvation, but in his own person is to be the Savior. This is the second statement of the servant's new commission. The word of Jesus

(John 8:12) "I am the light of the world" agrees well with the first half of this commission. How true it is that men walk in darkness till Christ has come into their life! How true it is that he is "salvation" wherever men are to be found!

2. The Servant's Reassignment in Terms of a Glorious Restoration of Israel (vv. 7-13)

49:7-13
7. Thus has the Lord spoken;
the Redeemer of Israel, his Holy One,
to a one deeply despised, to one abhorred by the nations,
to a servant of tyrant-rulers:
"Kings will see [what is happening] and respectfully rise;
princes will prostrate themselves;
because of the Lord who is faithful,
and because of the Holy One of Israel, who has chosen you."
8. Thus has the Lord spoken:
"At a favorable time I have answered you,
in a day of salvation I have helped you;
and I will protect you
and give you to be a covenant to the people,
in order to establish the land,
and in order to reallot the desolate heritages;
9. saying to the prisoners: 'Step forth!'
and to those in darkness: 'Show yourselves!'
They shall feed along the roads,
and even on all sand-dunes shall be their pasture.
10. They shall not suffer hunger nor thirst,
neither parching heat nor the sun shall smite them.
For he that has compassion on them shall lead them,
by the springs of water he shall let them rest.
11. And I will make all my mountains to be pathways,
and my highways shall be set in order.
12. See! Some come from afar,
and see! Some from the north and some from the west,
and some from the land of Syene."
13. Rejoice, O heavens and exult, O earth;
break out, O mountains, in jubilant shouts!
For the Lord has comforted his people;
he will have compassion on his afflicted.

Verse 7. According to our above caption for this section, now first of all what the Servant's reassignment means in terms of Israel's experience is given in detail. Various phases of what the Servant can and will do for Israel are explored.

This means that the Restoration from Captivity in particular will be brought about by the Messiah. Strangely, *before* his Incarnation he brings blessings to his people. People of the Old Covenant may sometimes have dimly sensed this fact. He is represented as addressing his people by a prophetic word of reassurance (*Heilsorakel*), which he transmitted to the prophet, who asserts that this word comes from him who is both the "Redeemer of Israel" and the "Holy One." The first of these titles lays emphasis on the work of salvation which he achieves; the second on the work of judgment which he performs. His own are rescued; the oppressors will be severely dealt with. But now comes the startling aspect of the case: the Redeemer is anything but an impressive figure, for he is the one "deeply despised" and even "abhorred by the [outside] nations." As to rank and station among persons of authority, it must further be admitted that he ranks no higher than "a servant of tyrant rulers." They who judge by what the eye sees find no glamor in this deliverer at all. But though that may be the first unfavorable impression on the outsider, that shall all be changed. At this point the word of the Lord begins. Upon *his* authority we have it that men of highest ranks — "kings" and "princes" — will rise from their throne, surprised and impressed, and will go the limit, as far as showing honor is concerned and prostrate themselves before him. Something will have happened to elicit this act of adoration; he had said that he would restore his people and he proved himself "faithful" to his word. All honor is due to this Servant. It was not that the nation Israel possessed so much toughness and resiliency to stage a political comeback. It was a case of God's faithfulness. He who had once chosen Israel would not invalidate his choice (cf. Hos. 11:9; Isa. 5:16). He was "the Holy One of Israel."

Verse 8. We are taken behind the scenes and are allowed to hear another word, directly addressed to the Servant. The word is a promissory declaration of impending salvation. The Servant had cried out in despair. God heard him. The "favorable time" for answering had come. It was a "time of

salvation," so God gave his help for Israel's deliverance. For
the work that still remains to be done the Lord promises
protection and fulfills the high destiny that he has in mind
for this elect Servant. For his Servant is to be by divine appointment "a covenant of the people" that is: the mediator
through whom he will bring his salvation of Israel to pass, as
he had promised. In the course of realizing this objective
the achievements of God through his Servant will include the
rehabilitation of the land, and, so to speak, the ancient heritages which had lain waste during the Captivity would be
reallotted to the families to which they traditionally belonged.

Verse 9. Still more is included among the achievements of
this Servant: Of course, all this is cast in terms of an ideal
and it is not to be expected that literal fulfillment will necessarily come to pass. But among the blessings listed are also
these: they that were, so to speak, in the prison-house of the
Captivity will receive the command to step out and show
themselves. Prison walls can no longer hold them. Shackles
fall from their limbs. At this point the figure undergoes a
great change.

Verse 10. Israel is likened to a flock with its shepherd, the
Servant. The figure is familiar since 40:11. Israel is being
led from Babylon. New aspects of the case are that ample
pasturage will be, as it were, provided along the sides of the
road. Even, for that matter, the utterly unproductive sand-
dunes shall produce sufficient pasturage as the flock passes
by. Physical hardships (v. 10a) will be alleviated. Hunger
and thirst, a seemingly unavoidable difficulty under such circumstances, will offer no obstacle. The parching heat of the
sun shall be no problem. All these blessings are traceable to
the deep compassion of the shepherd for his sheep. He shall,
as it were, know how to find springs of water and suitable
places for rest.

Verse 11. Now the prophet comes back, in the word of
the Lord to the familiar concept of nature transformed for
the convenience of the returnees. The rough and difficult

mountains shall present no obstacle. For he who can call them "*my* mountains" because he made them, can also transform them to be mere pathways. Even, for that matter, "highways" will be readied for convenient passage.

Verse 12. The word of the Lord invites readers and hearers of his promise to look with the eyes of faith and they will see the flock coming in great numbers from all points of the compass, even from so far distant a land as Syene, which most likely was the modern Aswan, to the extreme south of the land of Egypt.

Verse 13. Such gracious deeds of the Almighty, done for his covenant people, demand a response. They are deeds done on so grand a scale that the whole of God's creation is pictured as taking note and they are here invited, by a bold personification to make their praises vocal. The heavens, the earth and the mountains are bidden to bear their part in the joyful task. For, to sum it all up: "the Lord has comforted (effectively comforted) his people." By changing the tense at this point, so to speak, the prophet seems to indicate that there are several stages in which the Lord's task will be performed: He *has* comforted; "he *will have* compassion" on his afflicted ones. This summons to praise rounds off this section masterfully.

3. Misgivings of Zion Alleviated (vv. 14-26)

a. The Lord Has Abandoned Us (vv. 14-18)

49:14-18 14. But Zion said: "The Lord has abandoned me;
my Lord has forgotten me."
15. Can a mother forget the child she suckled,
so as not to have compassion on the son she bore?
Even these may forget,
but I for my part will never forget you.
16. See, I have engraved you on the palms of my hands;
your [new] walls are before my eyes continually.
17. Your children are already making haste;
those who destroyed and desolated you are going out from you.
18. Lift up your eyes, look all around,
all of them have gathered and are coming to you.

As I live, says the Lord,
  you shall put them on as ornaments,
    You will fasten them as a bride does.

Verse 14, 15. Though the prophet speaks very confidently of a glorious future, it is by no means easy under the circumstances to accept the message as true. Zion has several misgivings. Experience had proved in the past that nations led into captivity failed to return. Could Israel really return? Her Captivity had gone on for decades. So voices were being heard here and there to the effect: the Lord has written us off — "abandoned," "forgotten" (cf. Lam. 5:22). By way of reassurance comes one of the loveliest words of the entire Old Testament. The Lord's concern for Zion is likened to what may be the most selfless love that mankind knows, mother's love. As impossible as it is for a normal mother to forget a child that she nursed at her breast, in rare cases an exception will be found, but the Lord's love for Zion is indestructible.

Verse 16. To change the figure, it is as though the Lord had deeply engraved the name, or picture, of Israel on the palms of his hands, that his eyes might lovingly dwell on her features and be continually reminded of the one whom he so deeply loved. Before his mind's eye he sees the city as she shall be, strong and well protected by walls that the enemy shall never demolish.

Verse 17. To this the Lord adds a vision of the future as he sees it from the divine perspective. Zion's children, the captives in Babylon, are already making haste to come back home. While they draw nearer and nearer, others are leaving the site to which her children are coming. Those leaving are "those who destroyed and desolated" the Israelites. Since the land and the city are therefore to be thought of as ready to be occupied, the whole body of the captive nation is thought of as responding to the invitation. In reality these words sketch what could have happened had Israel had a responsive and believing heart. The reality did not quite conform to the ideal visualized. In another charming figure the prophet describes what will happen. As a bride puts on her ornaments on her wedding-day and so enhances her beauty, so shall those who return enhance the nation's attractiveness. From the nature of the figures used it appears how dear to the Lord's heart and the prophet's heart the whole matter is.

b. The Land Is Waste and Its Inhabitants Few (vv. 19-23)

49:19-23 19. But as for your wastes and desolations
and your devastated areas,
you will be cramped for space to live in
and those who swallowed you up will be far away.
20. The children of you, the bereaved one, shall yet say within
your hearing:
"The place is too narrow for me,
make room for me to live in."
21. And you will say to yourself;
"Who has borne me these?
I was childless and barren, exiled and turned away;
and who has brought up these?
I was quite alone;
where have these come from?"
22. Thus has the Lord God spoken:
"See, I will lift up my hand to the nations
and raise my signal to the peoples.
And they shall bring your sons in their bosom,
and your daughters shall be carried on their shoulders.
23. Kings shall be your foster fathers
and their queens your nursing mothers.
With their faces to the ground shall they do reverence to you;
and they shall lick the dust on your feet.
And you will know that I am the Lord;
they who wait for me will not be disappointed."

Verse 19. There is another strong misgiving that many in Israel felt in those days: The land lay waste and its inhabitants were few in number. This factor is not couched in so many words, labelled as a misgiving, but from the manner in which the Lord makes mention of it, it clearly appears that he was putting into words what they felt and had no doubt often said. At once the reassurance is given that the evil will be completely remedied. The people will be so many that they "will be cramped for space to live in" (cf. Zech. 2:5). At the same time those that afflicted Israel will be off the scene. They can no longer engage in their oppressive acts, nor can they afflict Israel. The very opposite situation will prevail (v. 21). Mother Israel watching over her children shall overhear them saying in effect that the land is over-crowded with inhabitants. The words that will now be used are: "The place is too narrow for me; make room for me to live in."

Verse 21. Mother Israel is further pictured as saying: "Who has born [*KJ*: "begotten"] me these?" Something must be added to the mother-children figure. Those that she brought forth herself and those that others bore for her count as her family. During the Exile, Mother Israel was not having children: Israel's numbers were not increasing. She was "childless and barren." She views her offspring at this point (purposely left vague) with great astonishment. They are numerous, or, they will be at some still undefined future. So Israel keeps saying over and over again with amazement: "What happened? How did all this come to pass?"

Verse 22. In this verse the Lord himself answers Israel's question. He represents himself as having given the signal to nations the world over that harbored captives from Israel to gather and bring these unfortunate ones home. The captives are thought of as young children that are to be carried in the bosom or on the shoulder. In fact so radically will the situation have changed (v. 23) that they whom Israel served (kings and queens) will serve *Israel*, and will count it an honor, as it were, to tend her children. In token of rever-ence, not for Israel but for the God that dwells in the midst of Israel, these dignitaries will fall with their faces to the ground, and in a somewhat exaggerated figure, when they have their faces bent so low, they will practically lick the dust on the feet of those to whom they pay homage. At this point it would seem that the figure before whom they do reverence shifts to Zion. When these things come to pass, discouraged Zion shall take fresh courage, for they will again have been offered a proof that the Lord is God, keeping the promises which he has made to his ancient people. Or as it is often stated in the Old Testament: "They who wait for the Lord will not be disappointed." "Waiting" in such situation implies that the soul has been fixed on the Lord and on his gracious promises.

c. Captives Cannot Be Liberated (vv. 24-26)

49:24-26 24. Can the prey be taken from the mighty man, or the captives of a tyrant be rescued?
25. Surely this is the word of the Lord:
"Even the captives of a mighty man may be taken, and the prey of the tyrant may be rescued.
Whoever contends with you, I myself will contend with him, and I myself will rescue your children.
26. And I will make those that maltreat you devour their own flesh,
And they shall be drunk with their own blood as with new wine.
And all mankind shall know that I am the Lord, your Savior, and your Redeemer, the Mighty One of Jacob."

Verse 24. Now comes the third misgiving that would plague the nation Israel in Captivity: Captives, especially captives of a weak nation like Israel in the hands of a mighty nation like Babylon, are irretrievably lost. Note here how Babylon is actually called "the mighty man" and "a tyrant."

Verse 25. Over against such misgivings the prophet pits a clear and promissory word of God, "Surely this is the word of the Lord." At first this word of the Lord merely sets the Lord's word over against doubts and misgivings. In this word that the Lord pronounces in Hebrew a very emphatic "I" stands as subject: "Whoever contends with you, *I* myself will contend with him" and "*I* myself will rescue your children." Who can contend with the Almighty? Therefore Israel will be rescued as surely as God is God.

Verse 26. A somewhat revolting picture is presented of the fate of the Babylonian conquerors: As they maltreated Israel so shall they be given over to internecine strife, civil war. For the expression "to devour their own flesh" involves a meaning of "own flesh" as in 58:7, namely their next of kin. The same thought is contained in the following line, being in strict parallelism with the one preceding. With this half of the verse Ezek. 38:21 and Zech. 14:13 may be compared. It should however be noted, that though the resurrection, the political resurrection of Israel, is indicated and promised, there is no thought here of Israel dominating the world and gaining world-wide victories; nor of Israel taking revenge on her conqueror. But it is indicated that what the Lord does by way of restoring Israel will attract the attention of nations over the wide world. They will recognize that Israel has a Lord and Savior. To this are added a few more glorious titles in the exuberance of joy that the passage breathes. It should be noted that all these are titles that the Lord gives himself.

Notes

Verses 1-7. Some would rearrange the verses of this section as follows: 3, 5b, 4, 5a, 6, 7. We believe the regular sequence which the text presents makes as good a sequence, if not a better, than the rearrangement propounded. Perhaps "named my name" (v. 1) may be rendered "gave me a name to be remembered" which gives a more colorful translation.

Verse 5. "To bring back Jacob to him." In Hebrew the "to him" reads "not," both forms being pronounced the same. It has been conjectured that a pessimistic view of history led the scribes to read the negative, though the other reading is given in the margin. The marginal reading is quite commonly accepted.

Verse 7. For "tyrant rulers" the Hebrew has a mere "rulers." However the word seems to be meant in the sense of tyrants as is also the case in 14:5.

Verse 15. In *merachchem* the initial *min* is a *min* separative (*KS* 406 n). The *gam* following shortly thereafter is used in a concessive sense (*KS* 394 d).

Verse 18. The article in *kakkalah* is used generically.

Verse 20. *Geshah* — is imperative feminine from *nagash*, "to draw near." Very strangely from meaning "to move closer" it comes to mean "move farther away," or "to make room."

Verse 24. If v. 24 is read in the light of the answer given in v. 25, then *tsaddiq* must be replaced by *'arits* ("tyrant") as the *Septuagint*, the *Syriac* and the *Vulgate* do.

Chapter L

K. ISRAEL SELF-REJECTED, THE SERVANT STEADFAST (Chap. 50)

As for a general approach, we are still going on the assumption that Chaps. 49-55 center around the Servant of the Lord. Opinions are rather widely divided as to the exact nature of the material in this chapter. Is it a lament? Is it a psalm? a prayer of complaint? a royal psalm of confidence? Or is it perhaps a prophetic confession? The wide variety of form of the material of this chapter shows that form criticism does not always stand on firm ground. A person who seems to fill a prophetic office seems to be making a confession of the difficulties he experienced in the performance of the duties of his office. Though this applies to vv. 4-11, how does the section vv. 1-3 fit into the picture? We expect to demonstrate as we move into the chapter that its thoughts are coherently developed. The chapter is unified.

Delitzsch has a simple outline on which ours is based; but by labeling vv. 1-3 as another "misgiving," we have also indicated how our chapter reaches back into the one that precedes.

Perhaps, as far as the metrical structure of the lines of the chapter is concerned, *Skinner's* approach may still hold true: "The scheme is obscure."

1. Another Misgiving Alleviated: Is the Covenant Abrogated? (vv. 1-3)

50:1-3 1. Thus has the Lord spoken:
"Where is the certificate of your mother's divorce
with which I put her away?
Or which of my creditors is it
to whom I sold you?
Nay, it was for your iniquities that you were sold,

and it was for your transgressions that your mother was
  put away.
2. Why, then, when I came, was no one there to meet me?
  why when I called, no one to answer?
Is my hand really inadequate to redeem?
  Or have I no strength to deliver?
Nay, by my rebuke I dry up the sea,
  I turn its ocean currents into a desert;
their fish would stink for lack of water and die for thirst.
3. I clothe heavens with blackness,
  and make sackcloth their covering."

Verse 1. A court hearing is being conducted by the Lord, similar to 42:18-25 and 43:22-28. Israel is guilty of misconduct but is not ready to admit it. She is behaving as though the Lord had put her aside and cancelled the covenant that he had made with the nation at Sinai. The Lord follows through on this situation treating Israel as though she were the wife and he her husband. The analogy leads to a striking refutation of the claim that he might have cast off his people. For according to basic Mosaic law (cf. Deut. 24:1) if a man did divorce his wife he was legally bound to give her a certificate to make the transaction legal. There is no such certificate in existence. Therefore no divorce has taken place. A separation? Yes, a temporary separation. But not a divorce.

Then in this hearing a second analogy is drawn upon: Did the Lord sell his own into slavery? Here again, as Exod. 21:7; II Kings 4:1; Neh. 5:5, indicate, a man might sell his own children into slavery to pay off a debt that he might owe to a creditor. Is it thinkable that some one has a financial claim upon the Lord because of which he must sell his own people into slavery? Preposterous! Israel is in slavery and she is separated from God, but that is not the Lord's fault. Israel is guilty. She has brought this calamity upon herself, by her iniquities and her transgressions. At this point we may well suppose that a stunned silence pervades the court room. Being charged with guilt she had to admit her guilt.

Now to sum up this somewhat difficult first verse —

looking at Israel's present plight in her Captivity, is it thinkable that this all came about because the Lord, as a hot-
tempered husband, cast off his wife and finalized the transaction by a writ of divorcement? Of course not. Or is it
possible the the Lord was in debt to some one and unable to
pay and had to resort to the sale of the very members of his
family to meet his obligations? Such an assumption is equally
out of place. Israel brought all its misery upon itself. She has
not been overtaken by some heavy doom. She misconstrued
the Lord's share in what had transpired.

Verses 2, 3. Why then should the nation behave as though
the Lord had been the cause of their doom? She was obviously taking such an attitude. When the Lord came, speaking by the mouth of his prophets, nobody responded. Any
gracious overtures that he made were ignored. When he
called by the prophets that Israel should come back, why
this dead silence on the nation's part? Or to consider another
possibility — had the Lord grown weak so that he was no
longer capable of redeeming his people as he was wont to do
in times past? To prove the contrary, the Lord cites a few
instances of works of power that he can perform. It is true
that the works cited are of a *destructive* nature to clinch the
point that he can work *constructively*. But the point at issue
is that the Lord has power unlimited. A sharp word of command from his lips, and the sea dries up, as happened at the
Red Sea passage in the days of Moses. Similar rebukes are
noted in 17:13; Job 38:11; Ps. 104:7; 106:9. With equal ease
he can control the currents, or tides, of the ocean, reducing
the area to the dry land of the desert. Adding a bit of color,
as striking evidence of what his power can do would be the
mass of fish, wriggling about, squirming and dying and stinking. To add a third example of works of power of which he
is capable (v. 3), he is even able to work mighty signs on the
face of the heavens covering them with blackness. Has this
word anything in particular in mind? Is there here an allusion to the darkness that engulfed Egypt in the Exodus days?
Or perhaps to some heathen creation epic? Or may this

word be pointing to the future, when the great judgment of God shall overtake the earth? The last mentioned possibility has as much likelihood as any. There is a certain grandeur and sweep to the style which magnifies the great Creator God. Sackcloth as covering for the heavens is merely another colorful way of saying that the very heavens must suffer when the Lord displays his power as the final Judge of all things.

2. The Servant, an Example of Trust in Adversity (vv. 4-6)

50:4-6 4. The Lord God has given me an expert tongue,
to know how to sustain the weary with a word.
Morning for morning he wakens, he wakens my ear,
to hear as those who are taught.
5. The Lord God has opened my ear
and I was not rebellious, I did not turn backward.
6. I gave my back to the smiters
and my cheeks to those who tore at my beard.
My face I hid not from shame and spitting.

Verse 4. The Servant, whom we already met with in Chaps. 42 and 49 appears, one might say, unexpectedly, speaking a monologue. He tells what he suffered for his people's sake, and without saying so, sets an example for God's people, showing them how they should steadfastly trust in the Lord. As to form, his words are *kinah*-like, i.e., in the customary lament patterns, for there is something of a tragic tone in this recital. It is really the so-called "lament of an individual" that appears here, something like the laments of Moses, Elijah, and Jeremiah, telling the burden of the prophetic office which these men bore heroically. These words also have rightly been said to describe the Servant's "Gethsemane." Four times from vv. 4-11, a double name of God is used, introducing vv. 4, 5, 7, 9. Literally translated the title is "the Lord Yahweh." We have been translating Yahweh as "Lord." So to avoid the troublesome "Lord, Lord," we resorted as did *RSV*, to the somewhat inaccurate "Lord, God."

This, being one of the Servant-passages, so-called, is often regarded as a later insertion into the text by some later writer. But if the four Servant-passages are set side by side it becomes apparent that, as *Skinner* remarks, this passage is an "indispensable link" in the chain, letting the measure of suffering that the Servant must endure come increasingly obvious.

The Servant begins by pointing out what unusual gift had been given him for the fulfillment of the duties of his office, primarily the gift of an "expert tongue." The Hebrew describes it as the "tongue of learners," i.e., a tongue adapted to deliver effectively the message that is given him to communicate. This is one of the distinguishing marks of the Servant. This gift enables him in particular "to sustain the weary with a word." Who are these weary ones? Since, according to Chap. 49, the Servant's mission has to do both with Israel and the Gentiles, the "weary" apparently are to be sought in both groups, Israelites laboring under the burden of the law and finding no peace, and Gentiles laboring under the oppressive burden of idol-religions that afforded no peace to the burdened conscience of the sinner. We regard the "word" employed by the Servant in the fulfillment of his tasks as being nothing less than the gracious gospel (cf. Matt. 11:27). In addition to the expert tongue, the Servant has the gift of a listening ear. That gift enabled him always to be able to give because he was always receiving from God what he needed to give. God is described as supplying every day, as a necessary gift, an alert ear, keeping it sensitive to the divine teaching. As true man he had to receive continually the message of life. As a result he remained a "learner" all his days. For the Hebrew has it: "to hear as learners," the same word used in the beginning of the verse. So the servant had the "tongue of learners" and the "ear of learners."

Verses 5, 6. Once again the Servant alludes to the fine care with which he was taught to listen indicating that the Lord had virtually opened his ear. But if a man has this double equipment — ability to hear well and to speak well, the message being what it is, often in the spirit of sharp reproof where the nation's sin was involved, it was bound to happen that dangerous opposition would be encountered. The Servant knows this. He could have refused the obligation that these gifts imposed, claiming that too much was at stake. But as the Servant emphatically claims, he on his part was not rebellious. He did not turn away from this assignment. Here the propriety of the use of the adjective comes obviously into the picture, the adjective "suffering" — the Suffering Servant of the Lord. That Israel would be rebellious, even to the point of cruel treatment of the Lord's Servant, was intimated already in Jer. 7:13, 25. It is true, no further details that were to be involved in this situation are given. But the nature of the types of painful suffering that would be encountered is foreseen very accurately. For one thing he would be smitten painfully upon the back; scourged, in fact. Men would tear at the beard that covered his cheeks. They would spit upon his face. But he, consistent in his behavior would so readily accept it all, that he even offers himself to his tormentors. That these were traditional forms of treatment of criminals in the Orient in days of old appears from passages such as Neh. 13:25; Num. 12:14; Deut. 25:9; Matt. 26:67; 27:30.

Special mention should be made in this connection that the case in hand was the first instance, as *Westermann* rightly remarks, where the suffering involved in a prophetic mission was willingly incurred, because the person in question recognized that the suffering involved was God's will. These thoughts come to a climax in Chap. 53. Such suffering undertaken with complete willingness marks the highest and most fruitful type of suffering.

3. The Servant Also an Example of Steadfastness (vv. 7-9)

50:7-9 7. But the Lord God helps me;
therefore I have not been disappointed;
therefore I have set my face like flint;
and I know I will not be put to shame.

8. My Vindicator is near:
   who will start a lawsuit with me?
Who is my adversary?
   Let him come near to me.
9. Behold, the Lord God helps me;
   who will pronounce a verdict against me?
Nay, they will all wear out as a garment,
   and the moth will eat them up,

Verse 7. There is something triumphant about the tone of this part of the chapter. The suffering involved may be very heavy. The victory will be all the more glorious. The passage soars on the same level as Rom. 8:33, which passage grounds on this one. The certainty of divine help makes all the difference; "The Lord God helps me." If the preceding section laid emphasis on the "trust in adversity" that the Servant manifested, the present section seems to make a point of the "steadfastness" that he displays. The key-note is sounded first — "The Lord will help me." In the past he has not been disappointed when he fell back upon the Lord. That certainty of help has made such an impression on him that he has "set [his] face as a flint." He will not give his adversaries the satisfaction of seeing him flinch when maltreated. He is certain that in the future he "will not be put to shame." There are at least two parallels in prophetic literature: Jer. 1:18, Ezek. 3:8-9. But in no instance was this word fulfilled more marvelously than in the case of Christ.

Verse 8. But this steadfastness is based on nothing other than the nearness of his Vindicator, not on any capacity of his own to absorb punishment. Therefore with this Helper always accessible he challenges any and every opponent to "start a lawsuit" with him or be his opponent in a public trial. In the steadfastness begotten in rich experience he knows he can meet any challengers and come through victorious.

Verse 9. The same certainty of ultimate success, in whatever task he was engaged by divine assignment, that was expressed in v. 7, is reiterated in v. 9. On the ground of the Lord's help the Servant stands as upon a firm rock. Charges may be hurled at him. They fall to the ground, repelled by the shield of divine protection. In fact, in the end not he but they will wear out and come to ruin, as the expressive figure now used indicates: "they will all wear out as a garment" eaten by moths. A rare measure of confidence and steadfastness are displayed here, a steadfastness not based on inflated opinions of self but upon a divinely wrought certainty necessary for the fulfillment of the task assigned by the Servant's Lord. It must be admitted that the Servant depicted is a very striking figure, whose potential is met fully only in Jesus Christ.

4. There Is Light for the Faithful, Judgment for the Adversaries (vv. 10-11)

50:10-11 10. Is there any one among you that fears the Lord,
obeying the voice of his Servant, who walks in deep darkness,
    not even a glimmer of light guides him?
Let him trust in the name of the Lord
    and firmly rely upon his God.
11. Lo, all of you who strike fire
    and surround yourselves with a girdle of sparks;
by all means walk in the flames of your fire,
    and among the sparks you have kindled!
This is destined for you from my hands;
    you shall lie down to suffer torments.

Verse 10. The Lord is obviously speaking in these two verses, indicating that two possible outcomes are involved as an outgrowth of the attitude that men take to the Servant of the Lord, for he is a personage of such tremendous importance. In the first three lines he describes the attitude of a God-fearing man, who finds difficulty arising for him from the fact that he takes the right attitude toward the Lord's Servant and obeys his voice. They who follow the Lord without reservations, may frequently find themselves in situations of "deep darkness," even to the point where "not even a glimmer of light guides [them]." Such persons are counselled by the Lord to "trust in the name of the Lord and firmly rely upon God." This counsel carries with its echoes from the preceding verses. They in reality describe the attitude of the Servant of the Lord. He should serve as example for such. That is the connection of v. 10 with what precedes. The Servant may be a man of mystery. But the time will come when his example will serve as a welcome guide.

Verse 11. Now the other side of the matter, the judgment of the adversaries. One expanded figure is set forth. The wicked machinations that they are guilty of over against the godly are like sparks with which the wicked try to hurt and harm those who fear God. The wicked are like a man who is striking a flint that the sparks may be used to kindle the fire. These sparks fly in every direction. They encircle or engirdle the man. Those who kindle the fire are half-sarcastically bidden to go right on in their course. For in the destiny that God controls for all such, they shall find the sparks falling on themselves, kindling their own garments, kindling a fire that they cannot extinguish. They shall lie down in torment and perish miserably. On this ominous note the passage closes. It is a part of the work of the Servant to make the wrath of man praise him.

Notes

Verse 2. In *mippedhuth* the initial *min* serves to introduce a negative clause of result. Cf. *KS* 406 h. Again in *me'ayin* the *min* involved is the *min* causal.

Verse 4 To understand the structure of this verse we do well to note that *nathan* is a perfect, speaking of what God had already given, whereas *ya'ir* is an imperfect, indicating what he continues to do.

Verse 9. The *hu'* after *mi*, though it is the personal pronoun only serves to add a certain livelier tone to the question (see *KS* 353 r).

Verse 10. We have kept the pointing of *shome'a* as the *MT* has it, a *kal* participle. This makes good sense, though the *kal*, imperfect, according to the *Septuagint*, could have been used. *Chashekhim*, being also a plural, marking a kind of superlative, is construed adverbially as a *beth* of sphere.

Verse 11. It would seem that *North* has done more than any commentator to clear up this somewhat difficult verse.

Chapter LI

L. COMFORT ABUNDANTLY ADMINISTERED
(Chaps. 51:1-52:12)

Chapter 48 had addressed itself to the unfaithful in Israel. Chapter 49 had introduced something of the same sort. A different approach now lets the word of the Lord address itself to the faithful, as v. 1 shows. However the thought-sequence of the chapters would seem to call for the first part of 52 as still continuing the preceding chapter. Besides in a rather natural progression of thought ten units present themselves, apparently planned by the writer and all falling naturally into place under a title like "Comfort abundantly administered." All of which shows that the initial message, whose keynote was sounded in 40:1 is merely being developed more thoroughly. Various captions might be used to advantage, for the material here as usual in the second half of Isaiah is extremely rich. Some would use a caption like "Salvation" and find added to this note certain eschatological overtones. Besides one can easily detect a high level of sanctified emotion very especially in this section. The meter again is mostly 3+ 3 with occasional 3 + 2.

1. The Lord Can and Will Establish His People (vv. 1-3)

51:1-3 1. O listen, you who eagerly pursue righteousness,
you who seek the Lord.
Look to the rock from which you were hewn,
and to the quarry from which you were digged.
2. Look to Abraham, your father,
and to Sarah who bore you.
For he was but one when I called him,
and I blessed him and made him many.
3. For [even so] the Lord will comfort Zion,
he will comfort all her waste places.

He will make her wilderness like Eden
and her desert like the garden of the Lord.
Joy and gladness will be found in her,
thanksgiving and sounds of praise.

Verse 1. Men find it hard to agree on the translation of the word that is most commonly rendered "righteousness." "Deliverance" (*RSV*) has a measure of propriety. So has "integrity" and the German *Heil*. But here it seems proper to think in terms of several concepts. The word may mean imputed righteousness in the sense of being put right with God. But one need not stop short with that concept. For such imputed righteousness, if sincere, always brings with it the desire to produce ethical conduct worthy of a justified man. So we take the entire phrase "pursue righteousness" as a description of sincere godliness, and the mark of a faithful member of God's chosen people. An apt parallel expression is to "seek the Lord," that is to say to reach out eagerly and sincerely for true fellowship with God. Such true Israelites are invited to "look to the rock from which [they] were hewn, and to the quarry from which [they] were digged." We are not left to vague guesses as to what the call has in mind, for v. 2 gives the official interpretation.

Verse 2. The rock is Abraham; the quarry is Sarah. The propriety of the figure in regard to Abraham is rather obvious: from the one column of rock the individual rocks were hewn. What was first a unit rock is the one from whom many came. Exactly how Sarah is to be construed in the figure "quarry" seems a bit puzzling, since this is the only instance of the use of this particular word in the Old Testament. Perhaps the figure means about the same in both cases. Besides, the fact that Abraham may rightly be regarded as the father of the nation is clear enough. In the second instance to say that Sarah "bore" the nation must not be pressed too strongly. But the point in both instances is distinctly made when the text goes on to point out that Abraham was called when he was "but one," and the prospects of developing into a nation were most unlikely. But it pleased God to "bless him and make him many." As he once did in days of old he can surely do again. The *Jerusalem Bible* uses an apt translation in this connection when it says: he "was all alone." We should remind ourselves here that increase in population was regarded as one of the prime blessings for the Lord to bestow (cf. Hos. 1:10; Jer. 3:16; Ezek. 36:10, 11; Zech. 8:5) and a prominent feature in eschatology.

Verse 3. Other modes of establishing Israel are indicated. First the whole process is comprehended in the one term "comfort," which includes feeling sorry for the one in need and also administering help, as *Westermann* especially loves to point out. Echoes of 40:1 ring out rather clearly at this point. A colorful figure is resorted to. Israel in Captivity is thought of as a waste land, whose desolation is to be brought to an end, so that what was like a waste now will be like the famous paradise of days of old before he calamitous fall into sin. This one far-reaching change in the land is indicative of many similar ones that shall stand out. Four more items are listed as being in evidence throughout the nation. "Joy and gladness" will again be found because of the transformation that is to take place. And the response on Israel's part will be "thanksgiving and sounds of praise." This last part could be reminiscent of Jer. 30:19.

2. The Lord's Salvation Will Endure (vv. 4-6)

51:4-6   4. Hearken to me, you my people,
          and give ear to me, my nation.
For instruction will go forth from me,
    and my norm of judgment will I appoint
        as a light for people.
5. My victory is near, my salvation has gone forth,
    the coastlands wait for me
    and for my arm they hope.
6. Lift up your eyes to the heavens,
    and look to the earth beneath.
For the heavens will disintegrate like smoke,
    the earth will wear out like a garment;
        and they that dwell in it will die like swarms of gnats.
But my salvation will be forever,
    and my victory will never be annulled.

Verse 4. The Lord is about to make a solemn pronouncement to which he wants his people to give strict attention.
What is about to take place in Israel is not a mere passing
phase of history. For God builds solidly; he promises an enduring future for them. Heaven and earth may pass away
but the Lord's kingdom will endure forever. God is deeply
concerned for the future of his own. Israel is the basis of all
development, but what is developed there is for the people
generally. All this growth and development is to begin with
"instruction" that Israel gets as to the big issues involved. Besides he will appoint a lasting "norm of judgment" for Israel's
use in estimating values. But the light kindled in Israel will
throw its kindly beams "for people" the world over.

Verse 5. The same prominent word occurs here as in v. 1,
but it is now to be translated as "victory," a possibility that
cannot be reproduced in English. In fact all the keywords
used here are practically synonymous: instruction (law),
judgment, righteousness, victory. All point to the achievement of the Lord's glorious objectives. This has led some to
translate "victory" as the "fulfillment of my promise." All
this is spoken of in the perfect tense, for it all refers to things
that have as good as happened. God's successful overall rule
could hardly be described more simply and clearly than in the
words, "my arm will rule the people." All the issues of history lie in the hollow of God's hand. Ultimately these benefits will accrue to all nations. The nations themselves in the
secrets of their heart wait for the time when they will have a
share in these blessings. And so it may rightly be said by the
Lord: "The coastlands [the shorelands of the Mediterranean]
wait for me, and for my arm [i.e., the proper display of
divine power] they do hope."

Verse 6. By way of contrast, the Lord invites his people
to consider things that seem unalterably fixed and sure —
the heavens above and the earth beneath. Nothing appears
to be more stable than these works of the Lord's hands. But
they are not among the things that endure to all eternity.
And when they go off the scene, the "heavens will disin-

tegrate like smoke," vanishing as though they had no substance. But the old earth will gradually wear out and be cast
off like an old garment. The dwellers upon the earth will
share in the same lot in the great judgment, perishing like
swarms of gnats, in a merciless and total judgment, many
though they may be at the time the judgment takes place.
Those seemingly durable things shall all vanish away. All
that last will be God's "salvation," the deliverance from all
evil, for which we have been taught to pray. Or to state the
case differently, "my victory shall never be annulled."

It may yet be remarked that this section (vv. 4-6) contains a number of expressions that are clearly echoes of the
Servant passages, a matter which we cannot now pause to
trace down.

3. Slanderous Attacks by Enemies Cannot Harm Israel (vv. 7-8)

51:7-8 7. Listen to me, you who know righteousness,
 you people in whose heart is my instruction.
Fear not the reproach of men;
 do not be alarmed at their revilings.
8. For the moth will eat them up as a garment,
 and the clothes-moth will eat them as wool.
 But my victory shall last forever,
 and my deliverance to the last generations.

Verse 7. The voice of authority that speaks is that of the
Lord himself. He deals with what may have been a painful
issue in those days. Men, especially the Babylonians who
were Israel's captors, had heard what claims this little nation
had made about its relations to the Lord and about the glorious future that lay in store for her. Since everything
seemed to be going amiss with Israel, they readily became
the objects of scorn of their powerful captors. Reproach,
scoffing, and reviling, Israel had to endure aplenty. No
doubt, this all became a painful experience for Israel. For
insults may be very difficult to bear, especially when they are
unwarranted. So the Lord now proceeds to speak a reassur-

ing word to his true people, those who in v. 1 were described as "eagerly pursuing righteousness." Here they are said to "know righteousness," where "know" implies a deeper and earnest acquaintance with (cf. Josh. 23:14; Jer. 31:33 f.). That the ones addressed have more than an externalistic knowledge of the Lord appears from the fact that they are said to have God's instruction in their hearts. The Lord here exhorts his faithful ones not to let themselves be intimidated by reproach and revilings.

Verse 8. This summons to go on bravely is supported by an argument like that found in v. 6. For the Lord points out that they who revile his chosen ones will vanish as even the heavens and the earth shall. The familiar figure again appears, the garment devoured by moths. But among the things that endure are God's victory and deliverance, which he shall work for his people. So the emphasis up to this point has been on the enduring things that the Lord is building.

4. Display Your Power, Arm of the Lord (vv. 9-11)

51:9-11
9. Awake, awake, display your strength,
    O arm of the Lord;
awake as in days of old,
    in generations long past.
Were you not the arm that hewed Rahab in pieces,
    that pierced the sea-monster?
10. Was it not you that dried up the sea,
    the waters of the great deep?
you that converted the depths of the sea into a way
    for the redeemed to pass over?
11. And the ransomed of the Lord shall return
    and shall come to Zion with shouts of joy;
everlasting joy shall be their crown,
    and sorrow and sighing shall flee away.

Verse 9. Verses 9-11 are an answer in the form of a prayer to all the assurance that the chapter has offered till now. For till now the chapter has been a challenge to have confidence in the cause of Israel that the Lord espouses. Emboldened by his word the prophet, in the name of the people, prays that

God may bring all these things to pass. At the same time these three verses apostrophize the arm of the Lord (cf. 52: 10; Luke 1:51), challenging it as though it were a responsible agent ready to go into action. The arm of the Lord *is* powerful. Now let it furnish proof of it. God's arm has been known historically to achieve great things "in days of old." One outstanding victory that it achieved was the mighty act wrought in the crossing of the Red Sea. This event is referred to when "Rahab" is mentioned. For the name Rahab means the one that "acts stormily or boisterously." It is a name used several times for Egypt (see 30:7; Ps. 87:4). At the same time Egypt (or her ruler) is referred to as the "sea monster" (see 27:1; Ezek. 29:3; 32:2). When the proud and boisterous Egypt acted defiantly over against God's demand to let his people go, then the arm of the Lord went into action and "hewed into pieces" the wild beast, or to use a parallel expression, it "pierced the sea monster," or overcame Egypt. The slaughter of the wild beast is proof of the power of God. The arm of the Lord did such a mighty work once. He can do it again. Whether there is a reference here to a mythical sea-monster of the Babylonian Creation Epic, will be examined in an Excursus at the end of this chapter.

Verse 10. The prophet brings in a direct historical allusion to the Exodus when in bold terms he describes what happened as a drying of the sea and the waters of the great deep. What was depth of water was converted into a path for the children of Israel to pass over. Mighty works like this should be pondered. They furnish excellent groundwork for faith to build upon.

Verse 11. Now comes the well-grounded conclusion relating to the situation involved. The big question that kept troubling Israel was, Can the Lord actually bring back his people from Captivity? He both can, and is able to do it with a unique display of power and glory. Those whom God will free, "the redeemed of the Lord" — they will not break their own shackles — they will return, not merely making a feeble attempt to do so, and "shall come to Zion with shouts of joy." The description of the experience is one of the most gladsome scenes of all that the Scriptures present. A joy that cannot be quenched will take possession of the returnees: "everlasting joy shall be their crown." They are virtually likened to kings and royalty. A joy, not self-induced, but overpowering, shall irresistibly take possession of them ("overtake them") "and sorrow and sighing shall flee away."

This verse is identical with 35:10. The prophet appears to be quoting himself. Why not? The sentiment well bears repeating.

5. A Reassuring Answer from God (vv. 12-16)

51:12-16 12. I, I am he that comforts you.
　　　　　　 Why should you be afraid of man who dies,
of the children of men who fade away like grass?
13. and forget the Lord, your Maker,
　　who stretched out the heavens
and laid the foundation of the earth —
　　and be continually afraid all the day —
of the oppressor, when he sets himself to destroy?
　　And where is now the wrath of the oppressor?
14. The crouching captive already makes haste to throw off his shackles, and he shall not die in the deep dungeon nor shall he lack bread. 15. For I am the Lord your God, who stirs up the sea so that its waves roar. 16. And I have laid my words in your mouth; with the shadow of my hand I covered you, planting the heavens and founding the earth, and saying to Zion: "You are my people."

Verse 12, 13. Man prays; God answers (v. 12-16). We are not dealing with a superficial optimism, nor with unfounded promises, but with divine assurances deeply grounded. Therefore with a doubly emphatic "I" the Lord points out that he is condescending to speak "comfortably" (!) to Jerusalem. To get the right measure of this divine comfort we must estimate who it is that might inspire fear. It is "man who dies," vs. the living God. It is "the children of men who fade away like grass." To be intimidated by these opponents amounts to "forgetting the Lord [their] Maker."

The prophet never tires of stressing that the Lord is the omnipotent Creator. With never-ceasing wonder he recalls that the mighty heavens were stretched out by him, and the foundations of the earth were laid by him. Whatever may have given solidity and firmness to the earth, there can be no question about it that on God's part it was solid building. Can he who engages in such mighty and enduring works find the control of the children of men to be a problem? Only by overlooking tremendous works of God such as these can men lapse into fear of men when they oppose God. In fact at this point it appears how silly man's misgivings in reality are, when the work of the Lord is considered.

Here the sentence structure grows a bit complicated — not unclear just complex — for the writer is packing away big thoughts within a narrow compass of lines. But we are reminded that there is an "oppressor" — no doubt the strong Babylonian world-power. This oppressor, we are reminded, "sets himself to destroy." The ancient animosity of the world over against the kingdom of God is involved. But already the enemy is as good as defeated, for that is what the question implies, "Where is now the wrath of the oppressor?" As antagonist God must view the strength of the destroyer as ridiculously small.

Verse 14. The next three verses may be prose (not according to the *RSV*). But that has no further bearing on the interpretation, in fact it may be purely accidental.

Verse 14 as such is fraught with much difficulty, which we shall not endeavor to explore, giving, if possible, merely a feasible exposition. "The crouching captive" is the nation Israel. He crouches because the prison envisioned is small, low, and cramped. Since God wills it so, the freedom he is about to enjoy lies within his grasp, if in faith he will lay hold of it. All he needs to do is to throw off his shackles. For the next clause we take our cue from the Jerusalem Bible translation. This clause merely restates from another point of view what, by the grace of God, is actually happening: "He shall not die in the deep dungeon." He seemed destined

to death. His case seemed hopeless. It is far from that.
Rounding out the picture, one minor but colorful item is
added, the force of which we may catch by the insertion of
the adverb "ever," viz., "nor shall he [ever] lack bread."
After his captivity is ended, all his wants will be so adequately supplied that he shall never suffer hunger again.
This interpretation of the verse is not forced or unreasonable,
and vindicates the verse against those who magnify the difficulties, claiming among other things that everything in the
verse is "clumsily patched together" (*zusammengestoppelt*).

Verse 15. Another reference by the good Lord himself to
his successful control of the forces of nature ("stir up the
sea so that the waves roar") shows how well founded all his
claims of control are.

Verse 16. In this verse the Lord concludes his comforting
reassurance. Having just described what enormous resources
are at his disposal, he now indicates how he purposes to use
them. In a word, he works through men, enabling them to
achieve results. But again he works through men first of all
by laying his words in their mouth. Resorting for a moment
to New Testament terminology: the Lord enables his faithful servants to speak his powerful gospel message, that
"power of God unto salvation." They speak and God remakes men through the word spoken. And where this work
involves dangers, it pleases the Lord to cover them with the
shadow (protection) of his hand. The three participles —
infinitives in Hebrew (*KS* 402 z) — that follow are a bit difficult to construe: "planting . . . founding . . . saying. . . ."
All three describe divine forms of activity. It seems best to
regard them as describing those works that God will do as the
grand climax of his saving work, when he establishes the
new heavens and the new earth, where all things are right.

6. No Ground for Israel's Despair and Inaction (vv. 17-20)

51:17-20 17. Bestir yourself, bestir yourself,
                   up on your feet, O Jerusalem!

You who have drunk at the hand of the Lord
   the cup of his wrath.
Yea, the beaker of reeling
   you have completely drained.
18. Of all the children which she brought forth
   there was not a one that acted as her guide,
not a one that took her by the hand
   of all the children she had raised.
19. These two things have befallen you —
   — and who shall be sorry for you?
devastation and destruction, famine and the sword;
   who will comfort you?
20. Your sons have fainted;
   they lie at the head of every street
     like an antelope caught in the net.
   they have experienced the wrath of the Lord to the full,
     the rebuke of your God.

Verse 17. Apparently the calamity of the Captivity was so heavy that the nation practically lay there utterly prostrate, unable to even think of any constructive enterprise. In this section the pitiful state of the nation is pictured. The prophet seems to be addressing the nation. But in spite of all that has befallen, the nation does not need to take a defeatist attitude. In view of all that has been said, despair and inaction are not called for. Rather she is to be active about her assigned task. Still the prophet does not press the point of action; in deep sympathy he pictures her misery in all its depth. The figure that dominates this description is that of the cup of divine wrath that the nation has been obliged to drain. The Lord thrust this cup at her. The contents was God's righteous wrath at the people's sin. The nation had no choice. She had to drain it completely. She then fell to the ground. None could help her. The hour of God's judgment was upon her. There she lay prostrate till the divine anger had spent itself. How common this figure in its various aspects is, appears from the following passages: Jer. 25:15-31; Hab. 2:16; Ezek. 23:13-15; Lam. 4:21; Zech. 12:2; Ps. 60:3; 75:8; Mark 10:38 f.; John 18:11.

Verse 18. A pathetic touch is added when it is noted that none of her children, figuratively speaking, could lend her any assistance. The Lord appoints and no man can say him nay. He appoints the times of judgment.

Verses 19, 20. In a word, clearly patterned after 47:9, the misery of the unhappy nation is summed up, first in terms of what befell the city — "devastation and destruction" — and then in terms of what befell her inhabitants — "famine and sword." One aspect of a siege-scene is developed a little more at length (v. 20). The siege of the city is in progress. Men are falling in the streets, perishing with hunger, or cut down by the weapons of the enemy. They are hopelessly entangled in death, "like an antelope caught in the net," as the apt comparison has it. The force at work behind it all was the "wrath of the Lord" which dare never be trifled with.

7. The Cup of God's Wrath Is Being Transferred from Israel's Hands to Those of Her Enemies (vv. 21-23)

51:21-23 21. Therefore hear this, you afflicted one,
  drunk but not with wine.
22. Thus says the Lord, Yahweh;
  and your God, who defends the cause of his people:
"Lo, I have removed from your hand the beaker of reeling,
  the cup of my wrath you shall not have to drink any more.
23. And I will put it into the hand of your tormentors,
  who say to you, 'Lie down flat
    that we may trample over you,'
  and you have made your back like the ground,
    like the street for men to pass over."

Verse 21. The cup-of-wrath-idea is to be developed a bit more fully. A second term has appeared, parallel to the "cup of wrath," an expression that we have translated "the beaker of reeling," which second name suggests one possibility that is also connected with drinking of this cup, namely staggering blindly and helplessly under the impact of the drink. The nation is being invited by the Lord to give particular heed to the announcement about to be made. These are not two separate cups, but two names for the one cup, the term "beaker" being used only here. This verse may be patterned after 47:8, the taunt song on Babylon.

Verses 22, 23. It now appears that he who had dealt with Israel in wrath, still, strange to say, will deal with them in mercy and champion their cause publicly, a course that has repeatedly been taken (cf. 41:1; 42:4; 43:8-13; 50:8-9). A beautiful name is coined by the prophet for the Lord, faithful in all his dealings with his people, the name "the Defender of the cause of his people." He it is who alone can determine how long the cup of wrath shall be in a nation's hands. He has decreed in the present instance that the day of affliction is over. This cup will still be in the picture, but now it will be given into the hand of the tormentors (v. 23). From this it appears, from the fact that they are called tormentors, that the victors (the Babylonians) had practiced the usual cruelties on the vanquished. Not only had they used a gesture of conquest (like Josh. 10:24; cf. also Ps. 110:1) but had trampled over the backs of the captives, yea, had made a street of them for "men to pass over." They who practiced cruelty will suffer cruelty in return.

Notes

Verse 1. "From which you were hewn" — in this clause the "from" and the "which" have been omitted. See *KS* 380 c and *GK* 155 k.

Verse 4. The possessive "*my* people" . . . and "*my* nation" should be retained as *RSV* has it. The chapter is concerned with the nation Israel, not with the nations. The last word of this verse may be retained and rendered "I will appoint." No need of emending the text to obtain the adverb "suddenly." The words that appear in this area — *torah, mishpat, tsedheq, yesha*ʿ are practically synonymns for the Lord's help which he will reveal in due time.

Verse 6. We have followed the prevailing trend to translate *ken* as "gnats," even though no case occurs where the singular is thus used. To translate it "so" makes it difficult to extract a plausible sense.

Verse 11. It would appear that a conjunction (*waw* conversive) has fallen out before *nasu*. In 35:10 the *waw* stands.

Verse 12. In "comforts you" we prefer to read the singular suffix with the *Septuagint* and *Symmachus*.

Verse 13. "Sets himself" (*konen*) involves a verb which is used in the figure of setting the bow on the string.

Verse 15. "Stirs" (*roga'*) is a participial form. See *GK* 65 d.

Verse 17. In "beaker of reeling" a genetive construction is involved where the genetive expresses the result: a beaker that causes reeling (*GK* 128 q).

Verse 19. In the last word, *y* should be substituted for *aleph*, which latter expresses the first person, which is intolerably harsh.

Verse 22. "I have removed" is a perfect of certainty, often translated as a positive future.

EXCURSUS ON "Rahab."

Verse 9. At this point it is customary to refer to a Babylonian myth, which is supposed to be in the background of the prophet's mind, the battle of Marduk with Tiamat, the monster of the great deep. Six (or seven?) passages are referred to in this connection. They are: Isa. 30:7; 51:9 f.; Ps. 89:10 f.; 87:4; Job 26:2 f.; 9:13; Ps. 40:5 (?). The name Rahab appears in all these passages and is supposed to be this monster. A careful examination of the passages, one by one (as made by Eduard Hertlein, ZATW, 1919/20) does not support this approach. For in every case "Rahab" which means the "boisterous one" is a standing designation of Egypt, without any mythological undertones. For Egypt as world power in her day was "noisy, proud, boisterous." No passage of those commonly referred to in this connection contains a reference to some mythological creature. Our passage, in particular, interprets itself. For v. 10 describes, without figure, what is being thought of, namely the overcoming of the waters of the arm of the Red Sea, which was the obstacle in Israel's way in the Exodus days. Verse 9 describes the allusion in terms of a figure. God overcame Egypt that stood in the way of the Exodus. Verse 10 abandons the figure and makes an obvious reference to the dissipating of the waters of the Red Sea. So it is consistently: Egypt is always the entity thought of when the word Rahab is used in these passages.

We concede that there may be mythological language used in Scripture, because there just is a mythological flavor in certain current expressions in familiar usage. Nothing indicates that "Rahab" has such a flavor.

Chapter LII:1-12

L. COMFORT ABUNDANTLY ADMINISTERED (cont.) (Chap. 52:1-12)

We consider Chap. 52 as being the continuation of Chap. 51, as our outline at the beginning of the book indicates.

In approaching this chapter a number of major difficulties stare us in the face. They may be summed up about as follows: vv. 1-2 is said to begin a certain thought which is not brought to a conclusion; after v. 2 some lines dropped out; then a glossator added vv. 3-6 in prose; but no one quite seems to be able to make a consistent thought out of these verses. We hope to be able to indicate in a measure that logic and coherence mark the opening of this chapter.

The thoughts move on a high level of joy and exultation; these are some of the grandest passages of the great prophet. In vv. 1-2 the prophet addresses first the city, then its inhabitants to take an aggressive, hopeful attitude. Verses 3-6 the Lord is speaking showing what justification he has to set his people free and help them.

8. Zion Awake! (vv. 1-6)

52:1-6 1. Wake up! Wake up!
 Put on your strength, O Zion;
put on your glorious garments,
 O Jerusalem, the holy city.
For no more shall there come into you
 the uncircumcised and the unclean.
2. Shake yourself from the dust,
 rise and sit on your throne, O Jerusalem.
Loose the bonds off your neck,
 you captives, you people of Zion,
3. For thus says the Lord:
 You were sold for nothing, and you shall be redeemed without money.
4. For thus says the Lord, Yahweh: "My people at the first went down to Egypt to sojourn there. Also Assyria oppressed them for

no reason at all. 5. Now therefore what do I find here?" — this
is the word of the Lord — for my people have been taken away
for nothing. They that rule over them shriek out [harsh orders]
— this is the word of the Lord: "continually all the day long my
name is blasphemed. 6. Therefore my people shall know my
name; yea, therefore shall they know on that day that it is I that
am saying, Here I am."

Verse 1. This summons to Zion obviously constitutes a
contrast to the taunt-song on the daughter of Babylon (47:
1 ff.), who is bidden to go down into the dust and take on the
role of a slave. Zion is to come up from the slave-status and
become a queen. She is to awake from the stupor of captivity, bestir herself and take on her regal functions, for the
day of her deliverance has come. She *was* clothed in the
habiliments of a slave. She had put aside, among other things,
even her strength. All she felt was weakness. Now she is to
resume her former strength and engage in her tasks assigned
to her by her God. Rich, glorious, sumptuous garments be-
fit the state in which she now finds herself. For she will
again be the "holy city." This includes, among other things,
that the "uncircumcised and the unclean" shall no more appear as attackers within the city. Obviously the prophet is
not speaking of the political entity called Jerusalem, but of
the ideal city of God as she shall appear in the consummation
of all things.

Verse 2. The figure just used (the queen putting on
strength) is developed a bit more in detail. She is pictured as
rising up from the dust in which she had lain, shaking off
the dust, standing up and walking with queenly dignity to her
throne; as she goes she looses the bonds from her neck, as
captives are often represented in monumental inscriptions as
bound together to one another by ropes around their necks.

Verse 3. The basis on which this deliverance rests is now
set forth by an unusual argument. The Lord is represented
as advancing the justification for his deliverance of Zion —
"for thus says the Lord." In one simple statement this justification is set forth; "You were sold for nothing." Ap-

parently this is a figurative way of describing the Babylonian Captivity. This can be likened to a sale, a one-sided sale. Babylon acquired Judah but paid nothing for it. Therefore the people of God can be freed for nothing, without the payment of a special price, simply on the strength of a divine order. Judah can be redeemed without money. Apparently the issue is not redemption from sin, nor a question of whether Jerusalem was guilty and deserving of punishment. The Lord appears as champion of his people. Babylon, from one point of view, was guilty in her treatment of Judah. Judah, from one point of view, was innocent over against Babylon. The Lord, without setting any further forces into play, could call for the freedom of his people. Without further ado, the nations would have to liberate them at his call.

Verse 4. In fact a kind of historic pattern is disclosed by the prophet as prevailing during the entire period of Israel's existence. In Egypt Israel appeared as guest. Egypt had no claim upon her, when Moses demanded that she be released. But her rights were violated by Pharaoh. Then centuries later Assyria appeared on the scene of history. Though from one point of view, the prophet viewed Assyria as a tool in God's hands (10:5 ff.) to punish Israel's apostasy, still from the point of view of Assyria as a nation, she had no rightful claims on Israel. This is implied in the brief statement in reference to Assyria. Assyria oppressed Israel "for no reason at all." This approach shows what broad insight the prophets in their day displayed in their evaluation of current events. They could appreciate both sides of an issue.

Verse 5. The seemingly vague statement, "Now therefore what do I find here?" in context clearly refers to the Lord looking at the Babylonian situation, particularly in so far as the Captivity of Judah was concerned. The answer to the question that the Lord poses to himself must run somewhat as follows: In the case of Babylon we have a matter like that of Egypt and Assyria. Here, too, Israel was taken in without her conqueror's having paid an adequate price, without Babylon's having due right and title to what she held.

Too much of selfish imperialistic designs were mixed up in Babylon's claims. God was entitled to the privilege of demanding that his people be set free. Babylon's rulers in the meantime were "shrieking out harsh orders" in typical tyrant-style. Some oppression of captive Israel had definitely been practiced. God's verdict in the matter is contained in the claim that by thus riding rough-shod over Israel Babylon was dishonoring the Lord. For no doubt many a time the conqueror said to the conquered: "Where is now your God?" (cf. Ps. 42:10; 115:2; Joel 2:17). So the holy name of the Lord was being blasphemed all the day long.

Verse 6. All that has just been said amply justifies the deliverance from Captivity. When the Lord thus vindicates himself and what he is doing, Israel will have a truer and deeper knowledge of the Lord ("My people shall know my name"). In this deliverance it will be as though they would see their God standing in their midst, identifying himself and saying: "Here am I." It is in this spirit that Zion is to awake and put on her strength and become a true queenly personage.

9. How Beautiful upon the Mountains Are the Messenger's Feet (vv. 7-10)

A different meter prevails in this section; it is in a tripping 2:2 pattern. Besides the imagery is drawn from the battle field. The battle is over, the victory won.

52:7-10   7. How attractive upon the mountains are the feet of
           the messenger,
  announcing, "All is well!"
bringing good news, proclaiming deliverance;
      saying to Zion: "Your God has proved himself king."
8. Hark, your watchmen, they have raised their voice!
    together they shout for joy.
For eye to eye they see
    the return of the Lord to Zion.
9. Break forth into joy, sing together,
    you waste places of Jerusalem;
for the Lord has comforted his people,
    he has freed Jerusalem.

10. The Lord has made bare his holy arm,
    before the eyes of all the Gentiles.
All the ends of the earth
    shall see the salvation of our God.

Verse 7. Practically each line is a jubilant note of victory. As indicated above the scene is cast in military terms — just after the battle. People and officials are gathered anxiously waiting for a report on the outcome of the battle. Strictly speaking this however was not a battle. The question pending is, How is it with the captives in Babylon? Is their liberation achieved? Suddenly they spy a runner. He must be the messenger with a report on the outcome. All can tell even at a distance from the eager attitude of his running that good news is speeding his course. Oh, how "attractive" those feet appear! The whole scene is laid in Palestine; the mountains are those of the Holy Land. The Babylonian country is a flat plain. As the messenger comes near, his first cry is "All is well!" The announcements tumble over his lips: "good news," "deliverance." He finally manages to sum it all up effectively: "Your God has proved himself king." Of course, Yahweh has been king right along. But now, by liberating his people he has demonstrated conclusively that the reins of world-government are firmly in his hands. He can achieve whatever he pleases. This special meaning of the verb "rule" appears elsewhere (cf. Exod. 15:18; Ps. 93:1; 97: 1; 99:1; Isa. 24:25).

Verse 8. Now the whole group of those who had been anxiously awaiting the messenger's report break out simultaneously into a loud shout of joy. Shouts of joy fall pell-mell from their lips. For one thing is now perfectly clear to them: The Lord has again turned to his people with favor, he has come back and deigns to dwell in their midst as in days of old. Where his glory had departed from his holy city with the coming of the Captivity, this glory again enters in to take up its dwelling there. Or, as some have stated it: Israel has again become the center of the Lord's manifestation (cf. 40:9).

Verse 9. Verses 9 and 10 are a typical feature of Isaiah, a jubilant hymn bringing to a triumphant conclusion a line of thought that depicts what the Lord has done. Other hymnic conclusions of a similar sort are to be found: 42:10-13; 44: 23; 48:20 f.; 49:13. It is as though the prophet offers for the use of the congregation a hymn suitable for the occasion. At the same time he exhorts the people to be sure to offer sacrifices of thanksgiving. But very strangely and quite poetically he addresses himself to the "waste places of Jerusalem" in what some have called "an exuberant paradox" to "sing together" in harmonious chorus. It is as though all along even the ruins had felt the unhappy state of the nation. There could be no greater comfort for the holy city than to have her freedom restored.

Verse 10. The Lord's munificent blessing for his people is further described as a case of his "making bare his holy arm before the eyes of all Gentiles." During the Captivity the Lord's arm had, as it were, been swathed in the folds of his garments, preventing him from using it freely. In 51:9 the nation had appealed to the arm of the Almighty to manifest its saving strength. This prayer has been answered. Even the dimmed eye of the Gentiles cannot help but see that the Lord has gone into action. In fact, "All the ends of the earth have seen the salvation of our God." Israel's return from Captivity was an event that challenged world-wide attention.

10. Leave Babylon (vv. 11-12)

52:11-12 11. Depart, depart. Go out from there
    Touch nothing unclean.
Go out from the midst of her.
  Purify yourselves, you who bear the vessels of the Lord.
12. For you shall not go forth in haste;
  you shall not leave as men who flee.
For the one who leads the way is the Lord;
  the God of Israel is your rearguard.

Verse 11. In a sense Babylon is the epitome of wickedness as well as the prisonhouse of Israel's captivity. From both points of view she is to be left behind by the people of God. For the expression "Go out from there" the Jerusalem Bible has translated rather aptly: "Leave that place"; and for "Go out from the midst of her" it offers the translation: "Get out of her." Both translations help us understand more clearly by their very abruptness that we have a call for immediate action. Babylon is not mentioned by name in this verse but no one can doubt that she is the place that is to be left behind. The added summons, "touch nothing unclean" indicate the whole attitude that the prophet aims to cultivate. The stain of sin, worldly pride and idolatry is upon the city and upon everything in it in spite of the splendor and glory of the empire. She is the very spirit of worldliness. Therefore she and all that she stands for must be disavowed. Here the prophet somehow realizes that in the Return the holy vessels, once taken from Jerusalem's temple, will be given back to Israel, and though it may appear a very external thing, so completely shall the people regard their Return not as a nationalistic achievement but as a Holy enterprise. Ritual cleanness is a proper counterpart to true sanctification. One cannot be indifferent to ceremonial uncleanness with impunity. They who are entrusted with the vessels of the Lord (perhaps the priests and Levites) are to be mindful of this injunction.

Verse 12. The Return of Israel is now described in terms of a great deliverance of days of old, the Exodus from Egypt, only there will be certain notable differences. For one thing, in days of old Israel had to flee posthaste. Now it shall be a leisurely and dignified procedure (cf. Deut. 16:3; Exod. 12:39). But the last point made is one of similarity. As the Lord went before and followed after Israel so shall he on this occasion "lead the way" and also "be the rearguard" (Exod. 13:21 f.).

So Israel is exhorted to take part in a glorious experience. So the prophet administered comfort.

Notes

Verse 2. Because the Hebrew text, as it reads, seems to say: "Rise up, sit down" many feel impelled to make a slight emendation, which results in the rendering: "Arise, O *captive* Jerusalem"; but even that minor emendation is not necessary. For the word *shebhi*, "sit down," may be taken in the rather common sense of that verb: "sit on your throne," a translation offered already by the *Septuagint*.

Verse 3. The statement, "You were sold for nothing" seems to clash with other statements of the prophet, such as 50:1; 42:24; 43:22-24, where the thought is expressed that Israel's Captivity-experience was the result of her many and great sins, a fact which cannot be denied. But at this point the prophet is not attempting to give an all-sided treatment of the causes of the Captivity. It simply is true that if the Captivity is viewed as a financial transaction God gained nothing by selling his people into captivity. But if it be claimed that he did not sell them for a price, for no cause of guilt at all, then the statement applies to the godly remnant in Israel. For that remnant was not being punished, as *Koenig* in his commentary, rightly points out. But the simpler rendering still is: The Lord gained nothing by the transaction when he sold his people to Babylon.

Verse 5. We are, of course, reading the last word of the verse as *meno'ats*, not *minno'ats*.

Verse 6. When it is pointed out that the expression "in that day" appears only here in the second half of the book, it should be pointed out that they that accept the unit-authorship of the book can also point to 7:18, 20, 21, 23. And it should be remarked that an author's earlier style must not always correspond to the style employed later in life.

Verse 8. The phrase "eye to eye" has an utterly different meaning in English than in Hebrew. In English it means something like agreeing completely in one's approach and outlook with another. In Hebrew the meaning is "close at hand," something like being so near that you can see the whites of the eye of the person approaching. See *KS* 402 i.

M. THE SUFFERING SERVANT SUCCESSFUL IN HIS REDEMPTIVE WORK (Chaps. 52: 13—53:12)

We come to the fourth and greatest of the songs of the Suffering Servant. Unfortunately it is often overlooked that the Song begins with the last three verses of Chap. 52. This complete section quite obviously divides itself into five strophes, each significantly marked by one (or two) initial keyword. As this poem progresses, or gathers momentum, the verses grow in weight and length. But it should be indicated from the outset that we have here a kind of song of triumph, as the opening line already suggests.

This Servant Song presupposes the previous three (cf. chaps. 42, 49, and 50). It can hardly be understood without those that precede it. It prepares for Chap. 54:1 ff.

Yet there is a plaintive and even sorrowful note in the poem. As *G. A. Smith* has indicated, the style is "broken, sobbing and recurrent." The light in the poem is very bright, and the shadows are exceedingly dark. We may safely brush aside the suggestion that some one other than the prophet wrote this chapter. To catch the full flavor of this Song we must not overlook the fact that nowhere in the course of it does the Servant himself speak, nor does he appear. He is the object of discussion. He "haunts" the poem.

Textual problems stare us in the face. There are some difficult lines in the poem. *Volz* speaks of the text as sadly corrupted, *schwerverderbt*. Each commentator almost attempts generous corrections. A few, like *Muilenburg*, dare to make the assertion that there are good grounds for maintaining the text as it traditionally appears in the form accepted by the Hebrews. The *RSV* showed admirable restraint when they accepted only two variants in the chapter. When numerous changes are made, conjectures for the most part, the distinctive features of the chapter are largely lost. It is also true that, as some have counted, twenty-six words appear that are found in this chapter only (*hapax legomena*). Some seem to be trying desperately to rob the chapter of both its uniqueness and its originality, when, for example, they stress what they believe to be kinship with Babylonian Tammuz legend, his dying and recurrent rising. But the differences between the two are far more striking than the points of similarity. All that needs to be conceded in this area is that the Hebrew prophet may have had some knowledge of the Babylonian material, but hardly used it in this poem.

And who was its author? Two major schools of thought stand out. One school says it was Deutero-Isaiah, the Great Unknown, the writer of the rest of the material of this second half of the book. The second school says it was a totally unknown stranger. There is still a third group, larger than is usually supposed, who attribute this, as well as the rest of the book, on good evidence, to Isaiah, the son of Amoz (1:1).

As to the title to be set at the head of this section we have chosen "The Suffering Servant Successful in His Redemptive Work." It is almost impossible to find a title comprehensive enough to do justice to the chapter. "The Fourth Servant Song" is a bit prosy as title. Our own title lacks a reference to the big theme that underlies the whole, vicarious atonement.

As to the form in which this material appears, some have noted the similarity with laments. But that is a merely superficial similarity. Some, with better justification, label its character as a praise psalm, (*Lobpsalm*). But to stop short with that approach, proper as it is in part, overlooks the somber minor key in which it is written. But it still comes closer to the triumph-note that marks the psalm as a whole.

One unique feature that stands out most prominently is

the fact that the author delights to devise certain basic themes which he stresses when he first presents them. But as the poem progresses, he keeps recurring to these major themes (the vicarious suffering, total obedience, utter willingness to suffer, the guilt of the people of God, divine approval). These keep reappearing as themes or sub-themes in this grand symphonic poem.

A marked feature that is quite significant is that it is being recognized more and more that the poem bears no traces of the environment from which it sprang. It is virtually impossible to assign any period of Israel's history as the age in which it originated. Intimately connected with this feature is the question, How did the unique insight (vicarious atonement) originate and find expression? The only tenable answer we seem to be able to find is, it was a divinely imparted spiritual insight that did not spring from the prophet's mind, or result from meditation over great theological issues, nor did the native genius of the writer arrive at these conclusions. But still for all that it develops with unique emphasis the deep possibilities of vicarious sufferings, develops it in a measure not outdone even by the New Testament writers.

Before we examine the text as such, it may prove helpful to point to a problem the full answer to which we are not able to offer. We refer to the *time* factor in the poem. At times the point of approach seems to be that a certain feature of the prophet's message lies in the present; it is discussed as happening. Then the issues seem to lie in the past; they are an accomplished fact. Then again all the good things envisioned seem to lie somewhere in the future, even the remote future. We offer a very partial solution to the problem. There appears to be a certain timelessness about the issues discussed. In the counsels of God they are as good as realized. They are in one sense also in process of realization. Certain factors are still to be accomplished. A disregard of the time-factor enshrouds the whole picture.

Yet for all the difficulties that the chapter offers it is and

will forever remain one of the grandest and most dearly beloved passages of Sacred Writ. Faith grasps these verities,
gratitude feeds on them; hope is nourished by them.

What this chapter meant in the early life of the Christian
church has been shown in a striking booklet by Hans Walter
Wolff, *Jesaia 53 im Urchristentum*. He shows that from the
earliest days it was regarded as a prophecy of eschatological-
messianic character. He, however, also defends the approach
that Deutero-Isaiah, the supposed author of Chaps. 40-66,
experienced in a measure the things foretold in this chapter
and so Deutero-Isaiah becomes a type of the Messiah. But
the main point of his treatment of the subject is that the
church always construed the passage in a Messianic sense.
Wolff shows that the New Testament stands on this ground,
as well as early fathers like Clement, Barnabas, so too the
Didache, and other New Testament Apocrypha. Special
importance is attached to Justin the Martyr. Wolff greets
with delight the fact that the exponents of the theory that
the Servant in Israel is losing ground.

1. Greatly Exalted after Being Deeply Humiliated (52:13-15)

52:13-15 13. Lo, my Servant shall be successful;
he shall be high and lifted up and greatly exalted.
14. Just as many were awestruck at you —
his appearance was so distorted from that of a man,
and his form scarcely seemed human —
15. so again shall he startle many nations.
At the sight of him kings shall hold their mouth shut;
because they have seen what had never been told them;
they have taken note of something the like of which they had
never heard.

These three verses contain in capsule-form what is unfolded at greater length in Chap. 53, only the thought is in
reverse order: In these three verses success is stressed first,
then the lack of it. In Chap. 53 humiliation comes first, exaltation second.

Verse 13. The Lord is speaking. He is asserting that, ap-

pearances to the contrary, his Servant will achieve what he
sets out to do. The verb could be translated "he will deal
prudently" (*KJ*) but the stress lies rather on the results of
prudent dealing-success, (or *RSV*): "he shall prosper." The
same verb is used in the Lord's promise to Joshua (Josh. 1:
7, 8) and with reference to David (I Sam. 18:14). It is
also used specifically with reference to the Messiah (Jer. 23:
5). In the latter connection it fits most admirably. For
who ever achieved greater success than the Lord's Christ?
That a superlative degree of success is being thought of appears from the three verbs heaped up in the rest of the
verse ("be high and lifted up and greatly exalted"). So
God grades the work of his Son. Success of every sort and
description shall be rightly attributed to the Servant. He
did his work very well.

Verse 14. At this point the sentence structure, though
clear, becomes somewhat involved. The first line of v. 14 is
to be followed up by the first line of v. 15, the two intervening lines constitute a kind of parenthesis. As men were awestruck at his extreme disfigurement, so will nations be
startled at the totally unexpected development that things
will ultimately take in the further turn from humiliation to
exaltation. The parenthesis indicates that when the Servant
was brought low this was something also physical. It actually
involved bodily disfigurement. He was to be thought of as
badly mutilated, more than man could bear; it was suffering
that borders on the unthinkable. This being poetry, it does
not require that every item specified was of necessity carried out to the letter. But still the striking correspondence
between the thing prophesied and the fulfillment again and
again fills us with wonder. Little wonder that many of the
fathers of the church of days of old claim that the account
reads as though Isaiah had sat at the foot of the cross.

Verse 15. So the amazement of the nations will be over
the happy turn for the better that the lot of the Servant will
take. He who had been brought so low will be so greatly
exalted that, for example, kings, who are entitled and are

wont to speak up on all manner of important occasions, will feel themselves to be so inadequate to even construe rightly what is happening that in embarrassment will hold their mouth shut. For what is happening will be quite beyond them. The like of what they here see and hear was never encountered by them before. Never was man brought so low; never was anyone raised so high. This situation is, as it were, a divine conundrum which calls for further elucidation, which is now about to follow.

The Suffering Servant is

2. Totally Misunderstood because of His Seeming Insignificance (53:1-3)

53:1-3 1. Who believed what we heard?
and to whom was the arm of the Lord revealed?
2. And so he grew up before him as a shoot,
as a root coming up from arid soil.
He had neither form nor dignity
that we should regard him;
and no beauty that we should delight in him.
3. He was despised and shunned by men;
a man weighted down by sorrow and acquainted with grief.
He was like a thing from which a man turns away his face;
so we despised him and deemed him insignificant.

Verse 1. A different speaker is heard from this point on. Some would say he is the prophet and those who are spreading the message of comfort of 40:1. Others claim it is the nation Israel. We suggest a different approach. In these verses we seem to overhear the believing portion of the nation as they discuss the tragic death that occurred in their midst, the death of the Servant of the Lord. Luke's account (24:13 ff.) where the two disciples on the way to Emmaus discuss recent events would be a good parallel to what our chapter offers. So to speak, here we seem to hear two disciples standing on a street-corner in Jerusalem reviewing the things that happened on Good Friday in the light of the better insight that came after Pentecost. They express especially their amazement at the complete misunderstanding they were guilty of in regard to the remarkable figure that appeared as the great Sufferer in their midst. Who believed what reliable witnesses told about him, especially his claims to divine sonship? The nation's first reaction was total unbelief. The believing, penitent Jews after their baptism still marvel that they could have been so obtuse. What they here say is almost a penitent confession, at least it grows out of a penitent spirit. The second question drives home the point more strongly. That the Lord was at work and employing his divine strength of arm in what was happening on Golgotha never entered any one's mind. They still marvel as they reflect on this blindness.

Verse 2. It has been rightly remarked about the following verses that they tell the life's story of the Servant from the cradle to the grave. The humble beginnings of his life seemed so inauspicious. When he grew up as a lad in the streets of Nazareth, who took any particular note of him? He could be likened to an insignificant "shoot," a bit of vegetation that is scarcely noticed. Yet this term points to the Messiah (cf. 11:1, 10). So no one attaches particular importance to "a root coming up from arid soil." It seems doomed to wither away early. From this point onward it almost seems that the person described is Jesus of Nazareth hanging on the cross, or standing in the judgment hall of Pilate. At that particular juncture of life there was nothing attractive about this person. He may even be said to have been the epitome of repulsiveness. What beauty of form he may have had, had been virtually beaten out of him by his tormentors. Since with significant assignment there usually goes corresponding "dignity" it is rather striking that in this case such dignity of bearing seemed to be totally absent. Not only among the Greeks in days of old but practically among all people, beauty was regarded as a kind of prerequisite of greatness. At this juncture of his life the Servant did not meet this requirement. When the Servant was on trial no one considered him worthy of defense. No one would have thought of choosing him as a deliverer. The language at this point is like that of the psalms of lament, because the lot of the person in question was a lamentable one.

Verse 3. The impression made by the Servant at one point in his career was not only a case of being unimpressed by him but even a matter of being repelled by him: "he was despised and shunned by men." This reaction was not that of a special few but it was universal. The nation rejected him. This impression is now cast in terms that have become proverbial: he was "a man weighted down by sorrow and acquainted with grief." The first expression is usually rendered "a man of sorrows." This again translated literally would run "a man of pains." An abject and pitiful figure comes to mind. Not that he was such in reality. This expression seeks to cover the most extreme form of misunderstanding that prevailed. He was in reality everything but that. Add one further factor to all this and the impression of wretchedness is complete: "He was like a thing from which a man turns away his face" (cf. 49:7). By this time the lowest point is reached in what becomes almost a dreary repetition : "So we despised him and deemed him insignificant."

In reality the Suffering Servant was

3. A Willing Substitute for the Guilty Ones (vv. 4-6)

53:4-6 4. Surely, ours were the ailments that he bore;
ours were the sorrows that he loaded upon himself.
But we on our part esteemed him a marked man,
smitten by God and afflicted [by God].
5. Yet he was pierced through by our transgressions,
crushed because of our guilt.
The punishment producing our welfare was upon him;
and by his wounds healing came to us.
6. We had all gone astray like sheep;
each of us had turned his own way.
But it was the Lord who made the guilt of all of us
fall upon him.

Verse 4. Verses 1-3 were a record of a pitiful misunderstanding. Verses 4-6 reveal the real facts of the case. There-

fore the initial "surely" marks a strong adversative to what
went before. It could also have been translated: "but in fact"
(*BDB*). By a kind of rhyme — an unusual feature in Hebrew
— a feature that we attempt to capture by moving "ours"
forward, the adversative character of the verse is made all
the more evident. Nothing was wrong with him; all was
wrong with us. He on his part became the substitute for us.
The more familiar translation has it: "Surely he hath born
our griefs." The word really means "sicknesses," but is used
for a wide variety of ailments. The verb following allows
for taking the burden and carrying it for us as well as for
bearing the evil consequences that should have fallen to our
lot. While he was doing all this, we on our part were still
laboring (say these converted Jews) under the misapprehen-
sion that, because so heavy burdens lay on the Servant's
shoulders, he must be "a marked man," whom God had
singled out for unusual punishment because of unusual guilt
on his part. Yes, God had both "smitten" and "afflicted"
him.

Verse 5. Nothing could be farther from the truth. It was
our transgressions that had pierced this Servant of God
through. They had "crushed" him. Strong verbs are used
because the effects falling on this man were so extremely painful. It will be noted that at this point the figure changed
from that of a sick man to that of a wounded one. It would,
however, be undue pressing of the letter to insist on it that
the Servant actually was also afflicted by sickness. The next
line probes still deeper into these divine, saving mysteries.
The very familiar *KJ* version says little to the average
reader: "The chastisement of our peace was upon him."
This is an entirely un-English mode of speaking. *RSV* has
clarified the issue a lot by rendering: "Upon him was the
chastisement that made us whole." None have rendered this
line better than *Luther*: "The punishment was laid on him
that we might have peace." Though the word used in almost
every case bears the thought of *corrective* suffering, i.e.,
"chastisement," we hold with those who take the word in

the sense of "punishment" (*Strafe*), because otherwise the sin-bearer himself would stand in need of correction. And, oh, the marvel of it all: "by his wounds healing came to us!" "Wounds" is actually "stripes," the welt left by the lash on the back of the man scourged. On "punishment" cf. also von Rad, *Theologie des A.T. des Alten Testaments, II, p.* 267.

Verse 6. It yet remains to point out the fact that there was no hope for rescue anywhere in the human race. They who speak are still the Jews, but the reader cannot help but feel that if even none of *God's people* could achieve deliverance, there would be none in the wide, wide world able to help. But here it is pointed out that all had "gone astray." How could they show others the way? Self-willed, men were going the way of their own sinful choosing. So the Lord had to take the man of his own choosing and lay the burden of the task on him. In this area — and it all again and again adds up to vicarious atonement, stated and restated, defined and redefined — in this area, we say, lies the explanation of the unparalleled suffering that the Servant had to undergo.

4. Utterly Innocent, Totally Submissive (vv. 7-9)

53:7-9 7. He was harrassed, though he humbled himself,
    and did not open his mouth.
As a sheep that is led to the slaughter
    and as a ewe before its shearers is dumb,
    so he did not open his mouth.
8. By oppression and an unjust sentence he was taken away;
    and as to his fate, who gave it any thought?
        For he was cut off from the land of the living,
    because of the transgression of my people was he stricken.
9. Men gave him a grave with wicked persons,
    and with a rich man in his death;
        although he had done no violence;
        and there was no deceit in his mouth.

Verse 7. It is no longer the Lord who is speaking. Perhaps it is the prophet. The unique degree of suffering that the Servant endured is a matter of constant wonderment for the prophet. Equally striking is the fact that all suffering was borne without a word of protest or complaint. This latter fact is an indication that the Servant endured willingly whatever was laid upon him. Had he suffered under protest and reluctantly, his suffering would have been impaired as to its effectiveness. In this respect the Servant stands in sharp contrast to men of the Old Testament who had a large measure of suffering to endure, like Job and Jeremiah. They were very vocal in their cry of anguish and in their protestations of innocence. So the comparison with a sheep, or a sheep-mother (a "ewe") is very much in place. The last line of the verse is not an idle repetition, or a clumsy copyist's mistake. It stresses an important point that should stand out. Here also lies the basis for the very choice name that John the Baptist used for Jesus, "the Lamb of God" (John 1:29, 36).

Verse 8. This has been rightly labelled "a notoriously difficult verse." What we offer as interpretation is merely what appears to us as feasible and in agreement with the context. The first line could well be a summary description of how judgment was passed on the Servant as a result of his trial. The verdict rendered was a glaring instance of oppression and at the same time a flagrant example of an unjust sentence. "Fate" in the line that follows is not what the Greeks and Romans meant by that term (an inscrutable power working ruthlessly) but merely *what befell him* in the course of the trial just mentioned. Men witnessed a grave miscarriage of justice and did nothing about it: they gave it no further thought. The next line implies a cruel and unjust termination of a human life: "he was cut off from the land of the living." The speaker, overwhelmed by the importance of the substitutionary atonement involved, falls back once more upon it as the only explanation of an outcome so strange. A momentary personal note enters the picture when the prophet observes the fact that it was his own people ("*my* people") that were the beneficiaries of this strange transaction.

Verse 9. As the Servant's suffering was strange and perplexing so there was a significant series of happenings associated with his *burial*. For one thing, the totally innocent one was given a kind of treatment that would have been more in agreement with the career of a "wicked person." "He was reckoned with the transgressors." To be very exact about it all, the classification with wicked persons applies to the company in which he suffered and died. Not to his burial. But who would quibble about such trifles. In the line that follows usually the difficulty is removed by a textual change which eliminates the term "rich man." We prefer to let the text stand as it is and to see one of the strange marvels of predictive prophecy which however was well worthy of record. For by an unusual and entirely unexpected turn of events, Jesus (i.e., the "Servant") was given a decent and honorable burial (Matt. 27:57 ff.). The concessive clause "although he had done . . ." reaches back to the second line preceding: he was given unseemly treatment though he had been guilty of no major crime deserving dishonorable treatment. In fact, not only of no heinous misdeed, but not even of an improper *word* was this Servant guilty: "no deceit was in his mouth."

5. Amazingly Successful in His Life's Work (vv. 10-12)

53:10-12 10. Yet it was the Lord's will to crush him. He put him to grief.
When he shall make a trespass-offering,
   he shall see offspring — he shall prolong his days;
And that which pleases the Lord [his plan of salvation]
   will prosper in his hands.
11. And so after the toil of his soul he shall see satisfaction.
   By his experience he, my righteous Servant,
      shall make many to be accounted righteous.
   He, namely, will take their guilt upon himself.
12. Therefore I will allot to him the spoils of victory among the great,
   and he will divide the booty with the mighty.
   For that he poured out his soul unto death,

and was counted with the transgressors;
when in reality he bore the sins of many,
   and intervened for the evildoers.

Verse 10. This Song began (52:13) on a victory-note. It comes to a conclusion on the same note. Though it dwelled extensively on suffering, for the Lord's Servant's sufferings were many, yet pain in God's service leads to glory, as G. A. *Smith* remarks. This suffering was not accidental. It was a part of a great divine plan. "It was the Lord's will to crush him," though "crush" in this case surely implies no hostile purpose. Even so *KJ* may be misunderstood when it says: "Yet it pleased the Lord to bruise him," if one insists on introducing sadistic thoughts at this point. In these words the emphasis lies on divine causality, also in the statement "he put him to grief." Suddenly the tense of the verbs changes; all is now viewed as future, perhaps with the intent of showing that what is viewed as accomplished still remains to be done: "When he *shall* make a trespass offering." The language of the Old Testament sacrificial system is at this point employed, not with the intent of indicating detailed specifications but perhaps only because in the trespass offering "all the blood was scattered over the altar" (Lev. 5:14 ff.). Intricacies of types of sacrifices might be explored here in the spirit of the Letter to the Hebrews. But perhaps no more is intended than stress on the fact that the Servant's anguish was in every way the fulfilment of a great divine plan. It had been foreshadowed by sacrifices. Nothing about it was accidental. But the main point seems to be indicated in the line that follows: "he shall see offspring — he shall prolong his days." This certainly involves a strange paradox — he has died, yet he prolongs his days. We cannot avoid the conviction that this points forward to the death and resurrection of Christ. The "offspring" mentioned, it would appear, are spiritual, although in view of the fact that the Old Testament deems it a great blessing to live long and have many descendants, one might rightly think of this aspect of the case. In any event he that died lives on and carries on the work that God has entrusted to his care — the work of salvation. Translated into New Testament language, the work of governing and guiding the church in its task of saving souls "will prosper in his hands."

Verse 11. The pronouncements of this verse are weighty. The success the Servant achieved is being spelled out at greater length, for his achievements are many and without a parallel in the annals of mankind. So that in the second line the Lord himself again begins to speak. For only he himself can do full justice to an adequate description of this phenomenal success. But echoes of the great suffering keep recurring — "the toil of his soul." When that is ended "he shall see satisfaction," that is, he shall look back upon a task well and brilliantly done. For the salvation of many a soul is involved. It might well be expected that when the Lord himself sums up the work of his Servant that he would begin with a statement of the work that is the most momentous of all. He does just that when he ascribes to him the work of "making many to be accounted righteous." In other words what he achieves is justification by faith. This then is briefly and simply redefined: "He, namely, will take their guilt upon himself," again an echo of vicarious atonement.

Verse 12. It has been rightly claimed that no passage of the Old Testament presents more problems than this. Yet it is quite obvious that a note of triumph prevails throughout and echoes of the great issues that have been dealt with in this chapter keep ringing throughout. In post-battle language the scene is first of all one of distribution of spoils after a decisive victory has been won. "The great" and "the mighty" are on the scene and the Servant among them receiving his well-deserved share, in fact, receiving the lion's share, to use a slightly incongruous figure. The Lord indicates why he, the Servant, is so strikingly deserving of the major share of booty; "He poured out his soul unto death," a more expressive way of saying that he gave his all in the great conflict in which he was engaged. This calls to mind that he even went the limit of being "counted with the transgressors," as set forth at great length in v. 9. Fact of the matter is, as the Lord keeps reiterating, in reality "he bore the sins of many," as vv. 4-6 had so clearly set forth. All these encomiums come to an end in a most effective summary in the words: "He intervened for the evil-doers." The verb here used really says more than "made intercession." It means to go all out in acting in behalf of another person. For this reason we claim that the statement is so apt a conclusion.

Notes

It is utterly impossible within the narrow compass of this exposition to give exhaustive treatment of all the issues that clamor for attention — word studies, grammatical niceties, textual problems, etc. We are able only to furnish an elementary approach and give in summary fashion the findings that grew for us out of a somewhat detailed study of the issues involved. We contend that a careful cursory reading of the fourth Servant Song impresses the reader with the rare merits of this singular Scripture. This impression keeps growing, the deeper one probes.

In our *Notes* we shall attempt to touch at least upon the major critical problems involved.

52:14. The third word of the verse (*'alekhah*) ("at thee") is usually changed to "at him" (so *RSV*), a reasonable emendation, following the lead of the Targum and the Syriac. But the text may be allowed to stand as the Masoretes have transmitted it. Then it will be interpreted as a sudden address of the Servant, whom the Lord regards as standing in his presence. Then the discourse turns to the third person from the first. In Hebrew such a change of person is far less disturbing than in English.

52:15. "Startle." This verb has long been a bone of contention. *Luther* and *KJ* represents the tradition that the verb means "sprinkle." In more recent times an Arabic root has been found which allows for the meaning "startle," an approach followed already by the *Septuagint* translation (*thaumasontai*). Men like *Hengstenberg, Edward J. Young* (*Westminster Theol. Journal*, May, 1941) and *von Rad* have ably defended the traditional meaning "sprinkle" in the sense of ceremonial purification. Perhaps the majority of scholars prefer "startle." The latter approach has as its major support the fact that an obvious contrast is demanded by the verse between "were awestruck" and our verb *nazah* ("to sprinkle"). But *to be awestruck* and to *sprinkle* do not constitute a contrast. Therefore we incline slightly in the direction of the majority in this instance, although even *BDB* admits that the second meaning is a bit "dubious." *North* suggests a rather far-fetched translation: "So shall many nations guard against contagion by him."

53:1. For "who believed," *Westermann* suggests the translation, "Who could have believed?" — a translaton which suggests that the contemporary unbelief was but natural and lifts the responsibility for unbelief off the shoulders of the nation.

On the use of a question to obtain a negative conclusion see *GK* 151 a.

Verse 2. Striking instances where national deliverers were also men of striking attractiveness would be Joseph (Gen. 39:6) and David (I Sam. 16:18).

Verse 3. For "weighted down by sorrow" many still use the *KJ* translation "man of sorrows." It should be noted, however, that "sorrows" is an intensive plural, constituting a kind of superlative, a fact which our translation seeks to capture.

Verse 5. Rather striking instances where the idea of substitution appears are the following: Gen. 18:23 ff.; 19:29; I Kings 11:13, 32, 34; II Kings 19:34; 20:6; Ps. 89:4.

Verse 7. The repetition in this verse of the words, he "did not open his mouth," is not relieved by glibly describing this as a gloss.

The difficult word in this verse is *dor*, the simplest meaning of which is "generation" i.e., "men living at a particular time" (*BDB*). *RSV* apparently takes the word in this sense. *Volz* suggests "descendants." "Fate" seems to fit most readily into the picture. See *KB*, p. 206.

Verse 9. Strangly for "in his death" the Hebrew has a plural "deaths." The simplest explanation may lie in the fact that the word for "life" (*chayyim*) also is a plural noun, which in the plural form indicates life in its many-sidedness; in its complexity. So "death" in the plural indicates the many things involved in dying.

Verse 10. We have translated the third line: "when he shall make a trespass offering." For this *KJ*, for example, offers: "when thou shalt make his soul an offering for sin." Fact of the matter is that the Hebrew word "his soul" may be an emphatic subject for "he." In this instance this is the simplest rendering of all, and relieves us of the need of textual emendations.

Verse 11. The *min* in *me'amal* is a *min* temporal (*KS* 401 f.). The second line of the verse is described by *North* as "grammatically execrable." It is true that it does not flow too smoothly. But it still is a glorious and comforting word.

Verse 12. The last word of the verse is an imperfect, *waw* consecutive separated from its *waw* by a phrase, a fairly common construction in Hebrew. Cf. *KS* 368, h, i, k.

Chapter LIV

N. AN EXAMPLE OF THE SERVANT'S SUCCESS (Chap. 54)

The preceding chapter, though not usually regarded from this point of view, had a deep undertone of success running through it. It began with the statement, "Behold, my Servant shall prosper" (52:13) and ended with a comprehensive description of the Servant's manifold success (53:10-12). We may therefore well regard Chap. 54 as being set forth in the same vein. It presents a significant example of this success, and so the close connection of thought between Chaps. 53 and 54 is clearly indicated. We make a special point of this, because the tendency is still somewhat strong to regard the "fourth Servant Song" as a later insertion between 52:12 and 54:1. Aside from other points which indicate that Chap. 53 rightfully holds and held its present position apparently from the time of the first writing of the book, this is a significant point.

Still the title that we have given this chapter is far from exhausting all the rich possibilities that the wealth of material of this chapter offers. So, for example, *von Orelli* uses a title like "Zion's Blessed State of Grace." *Muilenburg* gives as heading "The Consolation of Israel."

As to form men are inclined to regard this as a salvation oracle. The summons with which the piece opens are reminiscent of hymns of praise (cf. 44:23; 49:13; 52:9). We may also take note of the fact that an obvious strain of deep pathos marks Chap. 53, whereas Chap. 54 is marked by a deep note of joy. *Calvin*, quoted by *G. A. Smith* makes a rather pertinent remark: "After having spoken of the death of Christ, the prophet passes on with good reason to the church that we may feel more deeply in ourselves the value and efficacy of his death." This statement is surprisingly like *Luther's* opening remarks on this same chapter: "Even as in the preceding chapter the prophet had described Christ as the head of the kingdom, so here his body, that is the church, is described, as being oppressed, unfruitful, and forsaken. But he comforts her and promises her great offspring."

Some writers find six strophes, clearly outlined, within this chapter. Others find two. We incline to a tripartite division.

1. A Promise to Zion of Numerous Offspring (vv. 1-3)

54:1-3 1. Shout for joy, you barren woman, who have not born a child;
burst forth into shrill and joyous shouts,
you who have not been in labor.
For more numerous are the children of the forsaken one
than the children of the married woman.
2. Enlarge the area of your tent,
and spread out the curtains of your habitation;
make plenty of room;
lengthen your tent ropes and plant your stakes firmly.
3. For you will burst forth in every direction,
and your descendants will take possession of the Gentiles;
and they shall cause desolate cities to be populated.

Verse 1. The passage before us is one marked by strong emotion. Shouts and shrill cries are called for; there is great occasion for joy and jubilation. The one in whose life this great joy appeared is not mentioned by name, but no one doubts that it is Zion, the Old Testament church. During the Exile she had been greatly reduced in numbers. So to speak, the curse of sterility had descended upon her, a curse felt more keenly in Oriental countries than among us. This curse was to be taken from her. Her children were again to become numerous. From having been a Rachel she was to become a Leah. Rounding out the picture a bit more fully: Her husband, none less than the Lord himself, had forsaken her. She could have no children. But the promise here runs

to the effect that her children will ultimately be more in
numbers than those of a woman not forsaken. This is a familiar subject in the Scriptures (see 49:18 ff.; 51:1 ff.; Zech.
2:1-5; Hos. 1:10-12). To be a little more specific, the destruction of Jerusalem could be likened to the divorce from
the husband; the period of the Exile was the season of bar-
renness. This was not however a promise that saw immediate fulfilment. There was indeed an appreciable increase
in numbers on the part of the Jews after the Exile, but nothing that could come in any wise near to the situation here
described. Here is a divine promise which is in process of being fulfilled but awaits total fulfilment in the ages to come.
Lest man gain the impression that the Lord's promises are
taken lightly by him, the closing reassurance, "thus says the
Lord," is appended.

2. If the Lord spoke the preceding word, this verse may
now be regarded as an amplification of the thoughts of v. 1
spelled out by the prophet himself. In anticipation of the increase of the number of the members of this family, the
mother is bidden to take steps to accommodate the new additions to the family by marking out a larger space as tent-
area, by spreading out larger tent-curtains, and by using
longer ropes and firmer stakes. In fact she should make
"plenty of room." Nothing is gained in the overall picture
by using the term that Israel is likened to a "beduin-prin-
cess." An ordinary enlarged household is under consideration. The terminology is reminiscent of the sacred days of
the wilderness wanderings of Israel, when the nation dwelt
in tents, a harmless anachronism.

Verse 3. Now three figures are used to describe the experience. First from every side children burst forth from
the tent — a "population explosion." So it becomes apparent
why the enlargement of the tent just spoken of is necessary.
One wonders that one tent could have held so many. Next
follows a total change of the picture in terms of occupation
of territory: the numerous nation, Israel, shall overflow into
the territory of the Gentiles. This figure is followed by a

third one: deserted and abandoned cities are taken in hand by Israel's overflow population. So a nation which had been thinking in terms of possible extinction and of gradually dying off is reassured that such is not the case.

2. This Promise Reinforced (vv. 4-10)

54:4-10 4. "Don't be afraid, for you will not be made ashamed;
be not confounded, for you will not be embarrassed.
For you will forget the shame of your youth;
and will not remember the disgrace of your widowhood.
5. For your husband is your Maker,
'Lord of hosts' is his name.
and your Redeemer, the Holy One of Israel.
6. For you were a woman forsaken and deeply grieved,
when the Lord called you.
Would the wife of one's youth indeed be disowned?
says the Lord.
7. For a brief moment I left you,
but with great compassion I will gather you again.
8. In a flash of anger
I hid my face from you for a moment;
but with everlasting kindness,
I have had pity upon you,"
says your Redeemer, the Lord.
9. "This situation is to me like the days of Noah,
when I swore that the waters of Noah's days
should not again sweep over the earth.
so now I swear that never again
will I be angry with you or rebuke you.
10. For mountains may depart
and hills fall away;
but my loving kindness shall not depart from you
and my peace-pact shall not fall away,"
says the Lord who has compassion on you.

Verse 4. All the visible evidence pointed to the contrary conclusion, namely that Israel would continue to lose ground; and Israel may well have been most reluctant to believe the promise just given. So a special word of the Lord is given, bidding the nation to cast its fear and confusion aside. She will not be in a position where she set her hopes high and then found them all evaporating into thin air and so she would be laughed at for having indulged in idle dreams. A strong double assurance is given that this shall in no event happen. In the second (i.e., parallel) statement two verbs are used which are usually distinguished in the following way: "confounded" involves being actually in a state of utter confusion; "embarrassed" refers to personal embarrassment, being painfully aware that things have turned out disastrously. When the prophet adds, "for you will forget the shame of your youth" that might be a reference to the humiliating experience of the ancient bondage in the land of Egypt and might at the same time be thought of as including all disasters of old. For the humiliation of the Egyptian bondage burned deep into Israel's consciousness. Then the prophet adds: "and [you] will not remember the disgrace of your widowhood." Here the reference must manifestly be to the Babylonian Captivity. The blessing that the Lord is about to give will completely eradicate all remembrance of these painful experiences. So v. 4 summed up from a fresh point of view, the first three verses of the chapter. Now follow the words that reinforce all this.

Verse 5. Impossible as all that is promised may seem, it will yet come to pass. Now the statement comes back to the figure used above: God, the husband; the nation, the wife. And this husband is none other than the nation's "Maker." He could, and did create a nation. He can remake the same nation for he is also "the Lord of hosts," i.e., he has the whole host of created things always at his beck and call. He further rightly bears the title "Redeemer," a name which connotes responsibility for the well-being of another. At the same time he bears the name, "the Holy One of Israel," which title involves the fact that he is flawless in the performance of his obligations to his chosen people. To cap the climax, he "is rightly called the God of all the earth." All these descriptive names of the Lord reinforce his present promises to Israel. The Lord knows it will be a long while till these promises are fully realized. Therefore he strongly grounds them in eternal verities.

Verse 6. Using once again the figure of a woman abandoned by her husband, the prophet helps the nation recall how bitter her lot once was when he called her back into a state of divine approval. But that *unhappy* state now lies entirely in the past. For there is another angle to this case: This forsaken one once enjoyed the distinction of being, as it were, the "wife of [the] youth," when lovers love ardently, living through experiences which can never be completely forgotten (cf. Prov. 5:18; Mal. 2:14 f.). In the spirit of the Hebrew language the use of a pointed question ("Would the wife of one's youth indeed be disowned?") is the equivalent of a very positive assertion. God says in effect: I cannot give you up.

Verse 7. The Lord is still making "assurance doubly sure." He does this now by two clear and meaningful figures. The words "for a brief moment I left you" employ the figure used above, the figure of a wife abandoned by her husband. Though sometimes the Babylonian Captivity is regarded as having lasted quite a while, here, in retrospect, it is said to have been only "for a brief moment." The thought continues by blending into another figure, that of children that have been scattered by some disaster and are now being sought out again and gathered into one congenial group. This gathering is said to have been done "with great compassion."

Verse 8. The thought of v. 7 is restated in v. 8 under still another figure, that of a man in just anger flaring up for the moment. But pity gets the upper hand over anger. This turn of attitude is traced back to the Lord's "everlasting kindness." It may here be noted that the statement attributing all these mercies to the Lord grow in extent at the conclusion of v. 6 and v. 8 and v. 10. Here (v. 8) it takes the form "says your Redeemer, the Lord." The vv. 7-10 have rightly been labelled as the high point in the poem, v. 10 in particular, as a "corepassage" (*Kernstelle*) of the Old Testament (*Haller*). Certainly words of strong consolation could hardly be expressed more aptly.

Verse 9. More is to follow by way of reinforcing God's

gracious promises. A historical incident is referred to by way of fitting illustration. The writer knows the history prior to God's particular dealings with Israel; specifically the event of the great Deluge in the days of Noah. When the Flood had done its work, God gave solemn assurance to the human race in the person of Noah (Gen. 8:20-22) that flood waters should not again sweep over the earth, though strictly speaking no formal oath was pronounced. But we may well claim that a solemn promise under the sign of the rainbow is as much of a guaranty as any oath. As God promised then, he swears now that there will be no repetition of the disaster of the Captivity — "I will not be angry with you or rebuke you." If at this point a man recalls that there came a similar disaster nevertheless in the destruction of Jerusalem in A.D. 70 it should be remembered that in our statement the emphasis lies on the faithfulness of the Lord in keeping his promise, not on unconditional blessing. For all of God's promises are in a sense conditional.

Verse 10. Comforting reassurance could not be spoken more tenderly than in this verse, a favorite passage of the people of God through the centuries. The point is that God-wrought salvation endures. A favorite method of Biblical writers to express this thought is to use "cosmic comparisons" (*Muilenburg*); (cf. 51:6; Jer. 31:35; 33:20, 21). The hills and the mountains in particular are here referred to as symbols of that which endures (Ps. 36:6; 46:2 f.; Hab. 3:6). It might be conceded that these "eternal hills" could totter and collapse; but it cannot be conceded that the Lord's "loving kindness" (this seems the richer translation in this context) shall not depart. More precisely stated, "my peace-pact shall not fall away." This reference to the "covenant" (we used the word "pact" in our translation) seems to involve a subtle allusion to the work of the Servant of the Lord in passages such as 42:6 and 49:8. At this point the citation formula grows broadest of all: "Says the Lord who has compassion on you." This was certainly one of the grandest of Old Testament passages.

3. The Future Glory of Zion (vv. 11-17)

54:11-17 11. O you afflicted one, storm-tossed, disconsolate,
lo, I will lay your stones in mascara,
and set your foundations with sapphires.
12. And I will make your pinnacles of rubies,
your gates of carbuncles,
and all your boundary walls of precious stones.
13. And all your sons shall be taught by God,
and great shall be the prosperity of your sons.
14. You shall be established on a foundation of righteousness,
and you shall be so far from oppression
that you shall not fear.
And from terror, that it will not come near you.
15. If indeed you should be attacked
that will not be my doing;
whoever attacks you shall fall to ruin upon you.
16. I am the one who has created the smith
who blows upon the fire of charcoal,
and produces implements to work with;
and I have created the ravager to destroy.
17. Every weapon that is forged against you must fail;
every tongue that rises up against you in court
you shall prove guilty.
This is the inheritance of the servants of the Lord,
and their vindication coming from me,
says the Lord.

The future glory of Zion involves

a. Costly Building Materials (vv. 11-12)

Verse 11. As the address begins, the Lord has before him one who is "afflicted, storm-tossed, disconsolate." She is bidden to envision for herself a glorious future where everything will be enhanced "down to the very stones" used in construction. It is true that this describes a kind of architectural approach to the glories of the future. Yes, even that. In the somewhat detailed description now following we find ourselves to be a bit perplexed because the terms used appear to be technical building terminology. This is partly because we cannot quite tell whether the precious stones referred to constitute building material or describe their use as lending beauty to the stones that they encircle.

It is even possible that some mosaic-like pattern is involved. To add to our difficulty, no one quite knows exactly what stones are referred to. But perhaps strangest of all, these stones, common and precious, are not being used in the construction of a place of worship but seem to appear on buildings and city walls. This is a far cry from Ezekiel who, in Chaps. 40 ff., practically limits himself in his description of the temple buildings. But still the impression created by our passage is one of rare beauty and high glory. Passages like 26:1 ff.; Rev. 21:9 ff., 18-29 may be compared.

A few details: "antimony" seems to have been a kind of "mascara," though it strikes us a bit strange that the tuck-pointing of common stones with a sort of black border should lend beauty to the ordinary stone. Yet the effect could have been striking.

Verse 12. A hint as to what may be involved in this verse — The "pinnacle's" could refer to the upper fringe of the battlements, where the red, glowing rubies give a rare setting to the whole picture. It next appears that the gates themselves were made of one precious stone each. The "boundary walls" may be a reference to the encircling walls of the city. Sumptuous as it may seem, precious stones are used for plain city walls, for in this picture there is nothing plain.

b. Fear Vanquished (vv. 13-14)

Verse 13. Now some of the spiritual values of the new Jerusalem! The two verses, 13 and 14, constitute what may be called *Segenszusage* (a promise of a blessing). Such promises are usually given to an individual. Here they reach out over a glorified city. Passages in the same vein would be Ps. 91; 121; Job 5:17-26. The substance of our passage is "all your sons shall be taught by God." Superior, divinely-inspired knowledge shall be freely given to the children of God, knowledge which it shall be life eternal to have (cf. John 6:45). As a result of such knowledge or perhaps, in addition to it, shall be the great "prosperity" that these true children of God shall enjoy. In the Hebrew the word here rendered as "prosperity" is that rich, comprehensive term "peace," which in addition connotes victory and in general a state of total well-being.

Verse 14. By recasting the order of the words of this verse we seem to get closer to its import. The emphasis appears to lie on the stability of the new state of affairs ("you shall be established"). Then upon the good foundation which is requisite for such stability — "righteousness." At this point the question suggests itself: Is this the righteousness of good conduct or the righteousness imputed to faith? We incline to the opinion that both may be thought of, primarily the latter, which is the basis of all life acceptable to God. Here one result, growing out of this situation is especially pointed to — the absence of fear and terror. God's people will not be living in a state of continual apprehensiveness; this in contrast to their life during the Exile, where fears haunted them by day and by night.

But there was still the thought of being open to attack by the powerful enemy; for the enemy was strong and Israel was weak. The word here given offers separate treatment of the subject.

c. *The Futility of Enemy Attack (vv. 15-17)*

Verse 15. The first part of the verse could be paraphrased: Should it after all really happen that some one should venture to attack you . . . the estimate to be put upon such an attack is that it has no divine sanction: "it is not from me." (*RSV*) Or, as the *Jerusalem Bible* puts it "that will not be my doing." In fact, such unholy efforts will strike back on them that plot them: "Whoever attacks you shall fall to ruin upon you." The thought here leads us to recall Luke 20: 18. This last statement is difficult and may be translated in different ways. The situation is hardly so bad as to call for the verdict that the text is "badly corrupted." It fits well as it stands in the context in which it appears.

Verse 16. This situation calls for a further development

of the thought that all issues are continually under complete divine control. Rather unusual is the expression given to this thought. The point really is that even the smith who makes weapons and the weapons that he makes are possible only because God has also both of these under total control. That makes for the result that the smith who blows upon the coals at the smithy is enabled by God to function. The instruments he works with remain in the Lord's possession. They may sometimes be used by him as agents for destruction, for, as he says: "I have created the ravager to destroy." This "ravager" would seem to be a world-conqueror, like Sennacherib. God lets weapons be made, he creates him that wields them. He may let them loose as he once did against Israel, his people. But that is not the case now, as v. 17 indicates.

Verse 17. The illustration of the smith and the weapon is still under consideration. God's present attitude toward his people is: "Every weapon that is forged against you must fail." For that matter, any other attack that the tongue of man might direct against God's chosen ones shall also come to nought. In other words, Israel shall be publicly vindicated as enjoying the Lord's favor. The attackers shall be indicted. To this vindication of God's people as enjoying God's favor a few more pertinent thoughts are added. For one thing, Israel has not merited such favors from the Lord; they are a divinely bestowed "inheritance," freely granted upon his "servants." They, the nation, cannot merit such favor; but it surely will not fall to the lot of the unresponsive, who are not concerned about the doing of his will. God is the sole author and originator of his mercies. Isaiah always strikes the evangelical note — free grace, unmerited pardon.

Notes

Verse 1. In the first line of this verse there is a change from the second person to the third, a procedure followed rather frequently in Hebrew. Cf. *GK* 144 p.

Verse 5. The word for "Maker" is the plural form of the participle being a kind of plural of excellence. Cf. *GK* 124 k. The noun for "husband" is drawn into a similar plural.

Verse 6. The words "deeply grieved" in Hebrew are "grieved of spirit" — the last word being the well-known Hebrew *ru(a)ch*, which is sometimes used for an equivalent of a mood.

Verse 9. Two schools of thought prevail on the translation of the first word of this verse — *kimey*, which may involve either the plural of the word "days" in the construct, or it may involve the plural of "waters" in the construct. We have cast our vote in favor of the former. Strangely the meaning is hardly affected either way.

Verse 10. Grammatically the first clause of this verse may be translated as we have it, or it may be rendered by a concessive clause. See *KS* 394 b.

Verse 11. The second word "storm-tossed" is a *pual* participle with the initial *m* omitted. The situation is the same with the fourth word.

The verse is shorter than the rest. Has half a verse been lost? Who can tell?

Verse 14. What we translated as "shall be far," is really an imperative (*rachaqi*), but in Hebrew an imperative may be used as an imperfect to express assurance. Cf. *GK* 110 c.

Verse 15. The initial *hen* is distinctly an Aramaism and is to be treated as an "if," not as "lo."

The word *me'othi* is merely a variant form of *me'itti*, which is only a stronger form of "from" and means literally, "from with me."

Chapter LV

O. ZION CALLED TO APPROPRIATION OF SALVATION (Chap. 55)

Chapters 40-55 of Isaiah constitute a distinct phase with characteristic marks all its own. Our present chapter spells an appropriate close of the section. Or with a slightly different approach, Chap. 55 is the Epilogue of this piece even as Chap. 40 was a prologue.

As is usually the case with this prophet, such a wealth of material is offered that every commentator finds difficulty in trying to find an adequate caption for the chapter. *Muilenburg* suggests: "Grace Abounding." *Skinner* offers: "A Call to Individuals to Embrace Salvation." *The Oxford Annotated Bible* feels this is "A Hymn of Joy and Triumph." *North* follows an entirely different approach, suggesting: "Come for All Things Are Now Ready." The diversity of approach could hardly be more diversified.

But looking at the issue from a broader point of view, we may at least take note in passing that in the second half of this book, the first major subject was: The salvation God has prepared (chaps. 40-48). Then there was heavy emphasis on the agent who prepares this salvation — the Suffering Servant of the Lord (chaps. 49-55). This outline of the whole material makes it plausible to think at this point of the salvation prepared and the need of appropriation. This at least shows that there is some propriety about the caption we have suggested above.

First comes a gracious invitation, which has analogies elsewhere in the Scriptures, especially where wisdom is represented as calling men to the good things she has prepared (see Prov. 3:18; 9:5, 6; Matt. 11:28 f.). We said in the above heading that "Zion" is called upon to appropriate. Still this

248

is less a corporate invitation. It addresses itself to individuals, to anyone who may be ready to take what is offered. It might be spoken of as an appeal made to a group of earnest-minded men assembled in a synagogue or in whatever meeting may have been customary in the prophet's day. In any case the prophet seems to be the speaker in the first seven verses. He addresses an appeal to his hearers which seems to be an Old Testament counterpart of the Parable of the Great Supper.

1. An Invitation to Accept God's Free Blessings (vv. 1-3)

55:1-3 1. Attention, every one that is thirsty, come for water;
even if you have no money come!
Buy grain that you may eat, but come and buy grain;
without money and without price, wine and milk.
2. Why should you pay out money for what is not bread,
and your earning for what does not satisfy?
Just listen to me and eat choice food,
and have inmost delight in nourishing food.
3. Give close attention and come to me;
listen, that you may really live;
and I will make an enduring covenant with you,
namely the utterly reliable manifestations of mercy granted
to David.

Verse 1. Some writers have a feeling that things are somewhat in a state of confusion in this verse. It may be more to the point to think of some spots as being a bit rough grammatically because of the urgency of the appeal addressed to the prophet's hearers. Others find this verse a bit "unmetrical." But Hebrew poets were far less bound by the rigid rules of a metrical system than we are inclined to be. Being a call to action this verse is almost all imperatives. The speaker has gifts ready to distribute, primarily food — rich and tasty food — and drink — water and wine. These terms stand as symbols of impending salvation. This salvation is primarily thought of in terms of restoration from the prevailing Exile. The hunger and thirst plaguing the people are the weariness and discontent of the Exile (*Skinner*). Now the big point of this verse is that the food and drink offered to relieve the people's need is *free*. God has provided it. It is now ready. All that is required is an open hand, or an opened mouth, to take freely what is abundantly ready. Provision has apparently been made for every form of nourishment for every form of want of body and soul. We do well to think of the invitation as couched in terms of a ringing call proclaimed in stentorian tones. It may at the same time be said that the spiritual gifts hinted at by the terminology of food and drink are all incorporated in the one concept — the Word of God. The verse is a most urgent plea to accept freely all the good gifts that God has now in readiness for his own.

Verse 2. The plea grows more urgent. A contrast is pointed out. The nation with its many-talented people is devoting much effort to the acquisition of the lesser values. As has been suggested in this context, the Jews in Captivity in Babylon have put much effort into the pursuit of the lesser human values and had made themselves quite comfortable in the possession of material comforts. Why do that? cries the prophet, spending money for that which cannot satisfy, and is not the real bread of life. Here we hear echoes of the age-old truth: "Man shall not live by bread alone" (cf. Deut. 8:3; Isa. 44:3; Prov. 19:7 Matt. 4:4; John 4:10). If only this present plea be heeded there is available for all who will give heed, satisfying, nourishing, rich-tasting, soul-satisfying food.

Verse 3. When offers like this are made and God is ready to pour out of his super-abounding riches, then men should "give close attention." For men are then at the vital crises of life. It is an issue as simple as it can be. He is saying: "Come to me." All man needs to do is "come." Or stated differently: "listen." Then, from that point on, they may be said to "really live." At this point the prophet seems to feel that the offers of a present salvation can best be described in terms of the rich spiritual history of Israel's past, in the era of

the stirring days of King David. In particular the truth now
offered can be stated in terms of the covenant which God in
his day freely gave to this great king. God promised to this
man, once only an ordinary shepherd lad, great things, a
dynasty and a kingdom. He had, to date, kept his promise in
a striking manner. History was full of "reliable manifestations of mercy granted to David." As the Lord fulfilled the
promises given to David, so he would now fulfill them for
his ancient people, in the way in which the fourth verse more
specifically indicates.

2. If Israel Accepts, Zion Will Become a Blessing to the Nations (vv. 4-5)

55:4-5 4. As I once made him a witness to the nations,
          a leader and commander for nations,
5. so shall you call heathen whom you had not known,
   and nations you were not acquainted with shall come running
        to you,
because of the Lord your God
   and because of the Holy One of Israel;
      for he will have glorified you.

Verse 4. The reference to David is expanded at some
length. The spiritual side of his call is spelled out. For in addition to making David's throne an everlasting throne, David
was singled out to make the Lord known in a measure to the
nations. For the many and unusual victories that David
gained as king of Israel, he was making his Lord known to all
the surrounding nations. David in this sense was a "witness."
At the same time he was "a leader and commander for nations." The nations will not necessarily have arrived at a full
and comprehensive knowledge of the Holy One of Israel.
But that there was something unique about Israel's God will
have begun to dawn on some. One may compare I Kings
5:7 in this connection. It is also a well-known fact that all
the nations from the River of Egypt to the Euphrates acknowledged the sovereignty of David. Here, however, the
"spiritual primacy" (*Fischer*) of David is under considera-

tion (cf. also Ps. 18:43; and I Sam. 13:14). But the main
point now being made in vv. 4-5 is: What the Lord once did
for *David* that will he now do again for *Israel*, if she will
but come and freely "buy" what he so freely offers.

Verse 5. The promises once made to David will now be
laid with equal validity on David's people, a marvelous expansion of the scope of these promises. The first statement to
this effect involves that Israel shall have power and authority
to summon nations she had not known to help her carry out
her mission. In fact nations are even represented as so filled
with eagerness to share in the task that they "shall come running." What shall impel them to such eagerness of participation is covered by the phrase "because of the Lord your God
and because of the Holy One of Israel." On this note this
strophe comes to a "theocentric" conclusion, as Isaiah loves
to do. This section then describes in a far-reaching prediction all that men did to witness for the Lord God in days of
old and particularly what was done in New Testament times
by way of sanctified proclamation. Every victory gained by
the gospel is a fulfilment of this passage, and constitutes a
part of the true glorification of Israel ("he will have glorified you.") For the Israel of old becomes "the Israel of
God" with the coming of the days of the New Testament
(cf. Gal. 6:16).

Is there then nothing Messianic about this passage? Not
in the sense that we have here a direct reference to the Messiah. But he who is familiar with II Sam. 7:8-16, will not be
content to leave the matter rest with such a remark. For in
addition to promising to David an "everlasting throne" in
the passage just referred to, the Lord promised to David
one who would sit upon that throne. That factor is the
greatest glory of this passage. So we shall have to say that
though the prophet in this chapter does not dwell on the
messianic content of the passage before us, the figure of the
Messiah from David's line stands in the shadows and may not
be ignored. Our passage is indirectly Messianic. Behind the

David referred to in these verses stands "great David's Greater Son."

3. But These Blessings Must Be Eagerly Sought with a Penitent Heart (vv. 6-7)

55:6-7 6. Seek the Lord while he may yet be found;
           call upon him while he is near.
7. Let the wicked man give up his way of life;
   and the worthless fellow his thoughts;
let him turn back to the Lord that he may have mercy upon him,
   and unto our God, for he will abundantly pardon.

Verse 6. The Lord had been speaking in the fore part of this chapter. Now it appears that the prophet takes up the line of thought (vv. 6-7). What he says appears to be of a general character, applicable to men everywhere and at all times. But this word has a special relevance to the issue in hand and the situation just described (vv. 1-5). His words tie up with the initial summons to "come" and "buy." When gracious invitations are addressed to any body of men, the hour of grace has struck. It is a time for action. God is reaching out his hand; that hand must be grasped. God is seeking man; man must seek the Lord. Similar words spoken by the prophets are to be found in Amos 5:4; Jer. 29:12-14. Frequently the expression "Seek the Lord" is meant in the sense of offering a sacrifice. Here it would rather mean to seek him by prayer. But God is not always equally accessible. Sometimes he must withdraw his presence. Seasons of opportunity must be made the most of while they last. Sometimes he is "near," sometimes he removes himself. When he is near then he must be "called upon," that is, summoned to give his help.

Verse 7. But the other side of the coin is that sin must simultaneously with one's calling be laid aside, sloughed off and abandoned. Aside from this double action which holds good at all times, there seems to have been a special need at the time this appeal was made to break with sin. There seems to have been those who in Babylonian Captivity im-

mersed themselves so deeply in the stream of life of that
worldly capital that they became the prey of the corrupt
mercantile procedures and were perhaps growing rich by devious devices. They were the "wicked man" and the "worthless fellow" who are being specifically summoned to break
with their sinful way of life. That is the negative side of
the summons. But the necessary positive aspect is contained in
the words that follow: "Let him turn back to the Lord."
That involves a complete right-about-face. As man backs
away from sin he must draw consciously closer to God.
Though the word penitence is not used in this context it is
definitely implied. And he who penitently draws near to
God will experience that he will by no means be cast out.
God "will have mercy upon him" and "abundantly pardon." Pardon has to be abundant because apparently there
was such an abundance of sin. One can hardly speak more
comfortingly to the soul troubled by sin than is done in
these words.

4. God Is Magnificent in Forgiveness (vv. 8-9)

55:8-9 8. For my thoughts are not your thoughts,
          neither are my ways your ways, says the Lord.
9. For as the heavens are high above the earth,
   so are my ways higher than your ways,
     and my thoughts than your thoughts.

Verses 8, 9. Again we have what looks like a general
truth, applicable to all manner of situations. But in this
special context the statement describes God's method of dealing with sin. For when the word of the law strikes home
with a man and the enormity of his guilt disturbs him, then
it seems impossible that God's grace might cope with sin.
The present text says that such misgivings are unfounded.
There is something magnificent about the greatness of God's
mercy. Far-reaching comparisons must be made to catch
the full measure of God's pardon, comparisons like: "As the
heavens are high above the earth. . . ." There is a beauty and

a measure of reassurance about such utterance that is overwhelming. The evangelist of the Old Testament is speaking. Here *Luther* remarks: "Thus far goes the admonition;
now he begins to raise up the weak." The prophet has offered proof for his previous claim about the magnificence of
God's forgiveness.

5. This Forgiveness Comes by Way of the Word of God (vv. 10-11)

55:10-11 10. For us the rain comes down and the snow from heaven,
  and does not return there but waters the earth,
and makes it bring forth and sprout,
  and gives new seed to him that sows
    and bread to him that eats;
11. so shall my word be that goes forth from my mouth.
  It shall not return to me empty.
But it shall achieve what I please,
  and be successful in the thing for which I commissioned it.

Verse 10. There is a tangible point of contact between
God, the merciful one and the sinner, the penitent one. That
point of contact is the word of God. Here God deigns to
explain how his word is as though it had a built-in quality of
"self-fulfilling energy." That divine word is dynamic. It is
sent forth by the Lord as a sort of messenger, who has a
specific commission. In a strikingly simple and telling comparison the Lord shows how he operates. His word is like
the rain and the snow that come down and stay in the earth
on which they fell; and they moisten and fructify the earth,
making things to stir with a hidden energy and to sprout,
so that the eternal cycle of seed-time and harvest fulfills itself, and new seed is provided for the man that sows and for
the man who needs bread to eat.

Verse 11. For God, who has again been speaking since
v. 8, now spells out in detail exactly how the word that
comes forth from his own mouth, and also after that from
the mouth of his prophet — how this word, we say, operates.
It comes forth like God's mighty creation word, omnipotent

and irresistible. Then it does its assigned task. At this point the figure of a messenger enters upon the scene: the word of God is such a messenger. He does not return with a mission unaccomplished. When he reappears he has finished what it pleased God to send him for. The task laid upon it has been successfully accomplished. Though this description always applies to the saving word of the gospel wherever it is sent forth, in this particular case the return from Babylonian Captivity seems to be specifically thought of. But the efficacy of the word of forgiveness, as outlined in vv. 8-10, is also not to be lost sight of.

6. The Great Joy Resulting from the Deliverance from Captivity (vv. 12-13)

55:12-13 12. For with joy shall you go forth,
and in peace shall you be led forth.
The mountains and the hills before you
shall break forth in jubilant shouts;
and all the trees of the forest shall clap their hands.
13. Instead of the thornbush shall come up the cypress;
instead of the nettle shall come up the myrtle.
And it shall be to the Lord for a memorial,
for an everlasting sign which shall not be effaced.

Verse 12. This section (chaps. 40-55) and Chap. 55 very appropriately come to a close on a note of joy, joy over the impending Return from Babylonian Captivity, a point of view that has been continually appearing and reappearing. The language discriptive of this great event is borrowed from the account of the Exodus from Egyptian bondage. As there was joy then, there shall be joy again. So also this Exodus shall be "in peace," not in panic or in haste but in the full assurance of faith in the God who has often redeemed his people. That figure of a band of men released and coming back free is replaced by the language of a festal procession, where men keep a feast and mark the occasion by jubilant shouts. To catch the exuberance of the festival spirit, we must note that the expressions of joy are so overwhelming that even "the trees of the field" are swept along into it and clap their hands for joy as a king of rhythmic accompaniment to the swelling chorus of joy. "The trees of the field" are the wild trees that grow promiscuously here and there; even they feel that they must join this happy chorus.

Verse 13. This new Exodus has been variously described and, as remarked above, is a favorite theme of the prophet (cf. 40:3-5; 41:17-20; 42:16; 43:1 f., 19-24; 48:20 f.). In highly figurative language that prophet now describes a marvelous transformation even of the vegetation along the road of the Return. Common, worthless desert plants, like the thornbush and nettle, will along the road of the Return be changed into trees of distinction and beauty, like the cypress and the myrtle. But all this shall serve not for the glorification of Israel, but for the enhancement of the glory of Israel's God. He shall thereby, as it were, erect a memorial (Hebrew: "name") for himself, and establish an everlasting sign for himself, which can never be effaced. The language seems reminiscent of the procedure of kings of the Orient, who were wont to record their achievements, especially those of a military sort, in the rocks, that they might be read by generations to come. But new conquerors often appeared on the scene and mutilated or destroyed inscriptions left by their predecessors. The memory of God's salvation-acts can never be destroyed.

Notes

Verse 2. "For that which does not satisfy" is an expression that uses the *be* of price and a compound negative noun, "not satisfaction." See *GK* 152 a.

Verse 5. "Because of" is twice used toward the end of the verse. The first time it reads *le ma'an*, the second time just plain *le*, which is merely an abbreviated form of the preposition. See *KS* 319 o.

Verse 6. The verb "may be found" is a good example of the so-called *Niphal tolerativum*.

Verse 7. "Abundantly" is a good case of the use of the *Hiphil* in place of an adverb. (*KS* 399 m). *North* has a simplified rendering of "he will abundantly forgive" in the words: "He is always ready to forgive."

Verse 10. We have translated the second half of the second line with an adversative "but" ("but waters the earth"). Some translate it "except." It all depends on what the writer's conception of things meteorological was. Did he know of evaporation, condensation, and super-saturation? If he did then it would be good to translate the *ki 'im* as "except."

Verse 11. If "the word" refers to the word by which the Lord appointed the Return from Captivity then it might be well to point *yetse'* as *yatsa'*, referring to a word already pronounced.

THE THIRD PART
OF ISAIAH

Chapter LVI

II. THE THIRD PART OF ISAIAH (Chaps. 56—66)

A. A SUPPLEMENT TO CHAPTER 55 (Chap. 56)

Since 1892 (*Duhm*) the rest of Isaiah's book (chaps. 56-66) has by the majority of Old Testament scholars been considered as belonging to a third author, who for want of a better name has been labelled as Trito-Isaiah, that is: Third Isaiah.

The reasons for giving him a separate entity are in brief the following. A vocabulary appears from this point onward, not entirely new, but one that brings in quite a few new features. Besides the theological position brings with it new emphases which had not appeared in Second Isaiah. With a new vocabulary and a new theological position goes, of course, new subject matter, which neither Isaiah himself, nor Second Isaiah dealt with. As to the general tone of the material offered in these chapters it is commonly asserted that Trito-Isaiah does not display quite as high a level of inspired fervor: he is not so often swept off his feet into truly inspired and inspiring utterance. Then, among other things, the words of this writer are said to stand out against a different historical background than that of all the material preceding.

We do not find these arguments very impressive. New vocabulary brings in new material. But one merely needs a simple additional assumption: As the years passed the prophet attained to new insights: he kept growing all his years. The more mature prophet presented his new insight gained by continuing inspiration. Similar is the matter of a different theological position. Old truths acquired new depths under the guidance of the Spirit. Must a man remain static in his theological position? Add to all this the fact that the prophet enjoyed a rather long ministry during which the historical situation may well have changed quite a bit. Add further the fact that it is quite reasonable to believe that as Isaiah prepared his people for the Captivity, so he also prepared them by material calculated to fit the nation for the era after the Return.

These are but a few of the considerations which induce us to discount the theory of a Trito-Isaiah.

We are not hostile to the idea that Chaps. 56-66 contain a core of material traceable to Isaiah, to which core relevant material may have been added by faithful disciples of Isaiah, writing at a later time in the spirit of the matter. But the idea should not be too repulsive and too unbelievable that the Lord let inspired men produce prophetic messages that in exceptional cases were calculated to serve for the guidance of God's people, being produced at some time prior to the development of this new situation. Compare also 41:12-14, where God challenges the gods of the heathen to match him in the power of being able to disclose the future. So we are quite content to hold to the view that the original prophet Isaiah is the author also of Chaps. 56-66.

At first glance 56:1-2 seems unrelated to what went before. Chapter 55 was concerned about having the nation appropriate to itself the free grace of God. But even then already free grace was not cheap grace. It meant not only to accept God's mercy, but also put men under obligation to live a life worthy of the calling wherewith they had been called. To such a position Isaiah calls his people. He says: Live lives that are in harmony with being saved by grace. Incidentally one of many indications that the author of the present chapter is familiar with what is commonly called Second Isaiah, we may note that 56:1 voices the same thought as 46:13.

Here may be the place to indicate that our chapter does not become guilty of an unhealthy emphasis on external things when it stresses the keeping of the Sabbath and the Law. Only by divorcing Chap. 55 from 56 can such a position be arrived at. Exposition must consider the context.

The state of the Hebrew text is on the whole good, in spite of *Duhm's* charge to the contrary.

1. The Importance of the Observance of the Law (vv. 1-2)

56:1-2 1. Thus says the Lord:
"Keep the Law and do what is right.
For my salvation is about to come;
And my righteousness is about to be revealed.
2. Oh how very happy is he who does this
and the son of man who holds fast to this;
keeping the Sabbath so as not to profane it;
and restraining his hand from doing any evil."

Verse 1. The first two verses constitute a *Heilsorakel* (salvation oracle). They are introduced with a solemn, "Thus says the Lord." As indicated above, the word aims to inculcate faithful observance of the Law. It is therefore Torah-instruction. Our translation is a slight oversimplification. But "Keep justice" (*RSV*) ignores that which constitutes "justice," has been spelled out by Israel's codes. And "Do righteousness" is an un-English mode of speech. It has therefore been aptly rendered: "Do what is right." The *Jerusalem Bible* says, very much to the point: "Have a care for justice and act with integrity." The reason why the nation should be meticulous about the faithful observance of the Law is that the intervention of the Lord in the affairs of Israel is about to come. We could say that the case is like that of the New Testament writers, who reinforced the call to godly living by a reference to the impending coming of the Lord to the Final Judgment. And that is practically what the last line means: "My righteousness is about to be revealed." For "righteousness" may be construed (*Fischer*) to signify "righteous intervention." God is about to take a hand in the affairs of his people; let them live accordingly.

A sense of immediacy marks the word, even as did John the Baptist's preaching (Mark 1:15).

Verse 2. What was recommended in v. 1 is pleasant and brings blessings with it, as this beatitude ("Oh how very happy, . . .") indicates. The "this" of v. 2 refers to the attitude stressed in v. 1, viz., the blessedness of godly living. Only at this point the attitude of the *individual* is indicated. Personal religion as well as corporate piety gets its due emphasis, with a bit more of stress on the corporate aspect of the matter in the earlier days. An unexpected aspect of godly living seems to appear at this point, the observance of the Sabbath. This observance had apparently grown in importance during Israel's Captivity experience. For the keeping of the Sabbath was one area in which faithful adherence to the Lord could effectively demonstrate itself as an act of confession. In Mosaic times (Exod. 20:8 ff.) the Sabbath enjoyed distinction. This distinction was greatly enhanced in Exilic and post-Exilic times, as the following passages indicate: 58:13; 66:23; Ezek. 20:12 ff.; 22:18, 26. To this one item of importance, a reminder of general character, is added as an obvious expression of the good life: "restraining [one's] hand from doing evil." Some consider this a reference to social wrongs. But the word is broader. It covers all sins against one's neighbor. Both verses taken together show close affinity of spirit with Ps. 1.

2. Admission of Strangers and Eunuchs to the Congregation of Israel (vv. 3-8)

56:3-8 3. Let not the stranger [i.e., proselyte] who has joined himself to the Lord say:
"The Lord will utterly separate me from his people."
And let not the eunuch say:
"Lo, I am a withered tree."
4. For thus says the Lord:
"To the eunuchs who keep my Sabbaths,
and choose the things that I delight in,
and hold fast my covenant;
5. to them will I give in my house and on my walls
a monument and a name

better than sons or daughters.
   I will give to such an everlasting name
which shall not be cut off.
6. And the strangers [proselytes] who join themselves to the Lord
   to minister to him and to love the name of the Lord,
even to be his servant,
   every one of them keeping the Sabbath so as not to profane it,
and holding fast to my covenant;
7. these I will bring to my holy mountain,
   and make them glad in my house of prayer.
Their burnt offerings and their sacrifices
   shall be accepted on my altar.
For my house shall be called a house of prayer for all people."
8. An oracle of the Lord God,
   who gathers the scattered of Israel:
"I will gather others to him
   besides those already gathered."

Verse 3. How this section (vv. 3-8) attaches itself to vv.
1-2 is difficult to ascertain. It could be that the importance of
observing the Law in those days was in danger of being over-
done in some respects. Important as it was to prevent persons not cleaving to the God of Israel from being allowed to
hold membership with the true people of God, there were a
few areas where this caution could have been unduly rigor-
ous. These areas had to do with proselytes and eunuchs.
The proselytes are described as "strangers who have joined
themselves to the Lord." That is saying merely this: These
persons have been attracted to the One and True God and to
his pure and spiritual worship. That there were some worthy
Gentiles of whom this was true appears already from a word
in Solomon's dedicatory prayer (I Kings 8:41-43). Now
it is true that Deut. 23:3-6 forbade the admission of Moabites
and Ammonites into the congregation of Israel. It appears
now in these later days these prohibitions were about to be
expanded so as to cover the case of other innocent Gentiles,
especially since it almost appears that proselytes were becoming somewhat numerous. Some may have been overheard saying: "The Lord will utterly separate me from his
people." A note of sadness seems to have crept into such a
pronouncement, for Israel's religion had strongly attracted

them. In like manner a class of unfortunates, eunuchs, were in danger when considered as material for membership in Israel, of being shut out from the inner circle of true worshippers. This could even have included such outstanding personages as Nehemiah. And such too might have been overheard saying, with a note of sadness, "Lo, I am a withered tree." For Deut. 23:1 could have been made to apply to their case. Both classes of personages are advised not to take such a glum view of things. The Lord, in this verse virtually grants true-hearted men of this type the privilege of full membership among his people.

Verse 4. Taking the case of the eunuchs first — the Lord advises them that if their life gives evidence that they are sincere in their desire for membership, they will in no wise be barred from entrance with God's people. A few typical examples are cited of practices that they will follow in such a case. They will, for one thing, keep the Lord's Sabbaths by proper observance of the day. They will also manifest delight in the things that the Lord delights in, like the keeping of his commandments. They will hold fast God's covenant. This would include the rite of circumcision. But it would involve more than that: it would base the entire relationship with God on his covenant-word and promise, even as would any true-hearted son of Abraham.

Verse 5. The word of the Lord to the eunuchs continues. If they have done their part, he, on his part, will grant them certain rewards and emoluments to give evidence of his approval of their sincere quest of him. The first of these need not be taken literally. It guarantees to the eunuchs what we might call a memorial plaque, hung up on the walls of the Lord's house. In addition the Lord promises to such persons a "name," that is a reputation, among the people of Israel, which will indicate what these people are reputed to be, a reputation more outstanding than that of having left behind numerous offspring, a blessing which the Orientals even then already prized very highly. In fact the "name" will be such that it "shall not be cut off."

Verse 6. And now the proselytes — here called "strangers" or "foreigners" — of them it is also expected that they will give some positive evidence that it is a deep-seated concern for them to knock at Israel's door that they may be admitted. A few samples of such evidence are submitted. First, their quest is given a favorable appraisal in that they are said to be consciously joining themselves to the Lord, as was already said of them in v. 3. Their objectives and motives are set forth: they want to engage in "ministering" to the Lord, that is to say, participate in the meaningful worship at Jerusalem with God's people. They also want to give visible expressions to that impelling motive that urges them on in this quest, namely they "love the name of the Lord," to which must be added that fine objective that they want "to be his servants." That is, they want to be used up in doing the will of the Lord. Again (as in v. 2) the keeping of the Sabbath plays an important role. For he that walks carelessly can in short order "profane" this holy day. But they have learned how to sanctify it. Here we may inject that there are some indications in the Scriptures that proselytes were more numerous than we might have imagined. We are thinking of the passages where these possibilities are more fully spelled out, passages like Isa. 2:2-4; 60:1-14; 66:18 f.

Verse 7. Now a listing of the mercies that God has in store for earnest seekers after the truth. The "mountain" to which the Lord will bring them is the temple-mountain. They know that the truth of God is centered and preserved there. And when they are admitted to this sanctuary and what it stands for, the Lord will "make them glad in [his] house of prayer." The joy of worship, of which the Scriptures so frequently speak, will then be realized, and somehow it will involve "prayer." There prayer will be made and answered. Speaking in the language of those days, and especially of the Old Testament, there "their burnt offerings and their sacrifices shall be accepted on [his] altar." A man of those days, also in Israel, thought of worship primarily in terms of sacrifice. And that proselytes might have a strong desire to share in sacrifices to the true and living God is apparent from Lev. 15:14 ff.; 22:18 ff.; 17:8 ff. That a type of *universal* religion was contemplated for the future appears from the assertion here made: "My house shall be called a house of prayer for all people." The distinct emphasis of this promise lies on the last words, "for all people" (cf. also Mark 11:17).

Verse 8. This line of thought is rounded out by this verse, which for emphasis' sake is labelled as "an oracle of the Lord God." It states that not only will such unusual persons as proselytes and eunuchs be granted admission to the fellowship of Israel, but "others" — apparently a sizeable contingent — will be gathered to him "besides those already gathered." This promise is uttered in the spirit of the well-known passage (John 10:16) concerning the other sheep that the Lord has.

3. Israel's Degenerate Leaders (vv. 9-12)

56:9-12 9. All you beasts of the field, come to devour;
yea, all the beasts of the forest.
10. Her watchmen are blind;
the whole lot of them know nothing.
They are all dumb dogs that cannot bark.
They lie about dreaming,
they love to slumber.
11. And these dogs are voracious;
they can never get enough.
Such are shepherds who have no intelligence.
Each one has turned to his own way;
every man entirely to his own profit.
12. "Come, let me fetch wine,
let us guzzle strong drink;
and tomorrow shall be like today,
only much more so."

Verse 9. This section actually runs on to about 57:13, dealing with the degenerate leadership of Israel. But because of the chapter division, we are letting Chap. 57 appear almost like a separate entity. Verse 9 has been described as resisting every effort at interpretation. The situation is hardly as des-

perate as that. The verse does initiate a proclamation of
judgment (*Westermann*). As the thought is further developed it becomes apparent that the unworthy leaders of the
nation are under sharp scrutiny. They are utterly remiss in
performing their official duties. It is assumed that the judgment of God has already befallen them. Beasts have overrun
the land and slain many. These beasts are now invited to
come and finish their bloody business by devouring the bodies of the slain. Perhaps the "beasts of the forest" are considered more ferocious than "the beasts of the field." Both
together are serving the purpose of being agents of God's
just judgment. Ezek. 34:1-10 has some analogy to this passage.

Verse 10. The leaders of the nation are called "watchmen"
for the obvious reason that they are to keep on the alert to
warn the nation of approaching dangers. The only question
is then whether these watchmen are prophets or priests.
Prophets seem to be assigned more commonly to this function as may appear from Jer. 6:17; Ezek. 3:17; 33:7. Occasionally priests seem to be appointed to this task (see Jer.
14:18). A sweeping indictment is pronounced: These watchmen are "blind." They fail to see that dangers, grave dangers, threaten the welfare of the nation. Not seeing what is
obvious enough, they have grown entirely ignorant as to
what the nation really lacks: "The whole lot of them know
nothing." With almost insulting plainness of speech the
prophet indicts the leadership by the charge: "They are all
dumb dogs that cannot bark." Any cur might raise the
alarm when a thief or a robber enters. These men have sunk
beneath this level. They all have taken their responsibility
so lightly that they spend their time dreaming and slumber-
ing.

Verse 11. As suggested by the figure of the previous
verse, these watchmen are for the moment classified as watch-
dogs. But about all they seem to do is to feed themselves
greedily. They are voracious, of ravenous appetites. That
is what the "shepherds" are like — another sudden turn of the

figure. They have so little appreciation of the responsibility of their assignment that they may be said to have no intelligence at all. The only concern they seem to have is to go the way of their own choosing, each man looking out for his own profit.

Verse 12. Without introduction — the reader can readily discern who is talking and to what purpose — a word is suddenly flashed on the screen presenting a typical utterance of one of these degenerate leaders, setting forth another prevailing vice, drunkenness. They crave variety in their drinking-bouts, wine one day, strong drink the next. One leader volunteers to go out and get the drinks. "Guzzle" implies copious indulgence. The height of their ambition seems to be to have the morrow outdo today in the quantity consumed.

The indictment of these irresponsible leaders continues into the next chapter.

Notes

Verse 3. The word for "stranger" in Hebrew is "son of the foreigner" with no emphasis on the word "son." *Ben* is merely a relation word.

Verse 4. The verb "hold fast" is participial as to form, the progression being from finite verb to the participle — not an unusual construction in Hebrew. See *KS* 413 r.

Verse 5. The Hebrew word for "monument" is *yadh*, i.e., "hand." The same word appears in I Sam. 15:12.

Verse 6. "To profane it" — in Hebrew the construction is the infinitive with a *min* separative. Both together make a negative result clause. (See *KS*, 406 n.)

Verse 10. We prefer to follow the *keri* (Hebrew marginal reading) of the participle *tsophaw*, reading a *yod* before the *waw*, so making the suffix plural. The word for "dreaming" comes from a Hebrew root which may read in its initial letter either as a smooth *h* or as a rough *ch*. The former means "seeing a vision" the latter "dreaming." We prefer the latter.

Verse 12. The text reads, as we have rendered: "let *me* fetch," one man volunteering to go for the group. That fits the situation so well as to make textual emendation, based mostly on the versions, unnecessary.

Chapter LVII

B. THE TRIUMPH OF DIVINE GRACE OVER ISRAEL'S INFIDELITY (Chap. 57)

As we look back on Chap. 56 we recall that it ended on a note of lament over faithless shepherds, or rulers. This lament continues, now with the faithless *people* in mind. In other words the emphasis shifts from the shepherd to the flock. For the most part, commentators are of the opinion that this material was composed before the people left Palestine for the Babylonian Exile. There appears to be evidences of a background that is distinctively Palestinian — terebinths (possibly), wadis, clefts of the rock, etc. The lament which runs through both chapters turns into an indictment by the prophetic word. But where in our chapter a blistering denouncement opens the chapter, a kindly portrayal of divine grace comes strongly on the scene and so we arrive at the caption used above.

1. The Perishing of the Righteous — an Unheeded Warning (vv. 1-2)

57:1-2   1. Even the righteous have been wiped out,
     and there is no man that lays it to heart;
and loyal men have been taken away
   and no one took note of it.
For the righteous are [always] taken away from the evil to come.
2. He enters into peace,
   each one who has walked straightforward shall rest upon his
   bed.

Verse 1. To get some kind of setting for this chapter we may suppose, as some do, that this material may have been presented by some prophet (perhaps Isaiah himself) at a kind of synagogue meeting in the holy city. First of all an event that should have caused some alarm is drawn to the attention of the hearers: Good men have been dying off in surprising numbers (cf. Ps. 12:1; Mic. 7:2). By this fact God is trying to say something to his people, but they have failed to take notice. So the prophet is telling them what it all means. Good people, the "salt of the earth," have been taken away, very likely by an unexpected death. Why does God allow that? That is the way things usually go before great calamities break in: "The righteous are alway taken away from the evil to come." This phenomenon has been observed so often that it may be laid down as a general rule. Thus the righteous man is spared, being off the scene before the calamity breaks. This does not seem to imply that their death is to be attributed to the violence which prevails on every hand, making life unsafe. But generally speaking, men are so dull-witted that they usually fail to see what God has in mind, and how he is sparing his saints much grief. Two passages from the apocryphal book of Wisdom may be compared (3:1-3; 4:7-17).

Verse 2. To present this truth in proper balance, two more thoughts need to be added. First of all, such a righteous man's death means for him that "he enters into peace." For him, "life's fitful fever" is over. To this thought the second one is a corollary, that they were truly righteous is evidenced by the fact that "they walked straightforward" and so their godly life testified to a right relation to God in faith. The "bed" upon which such are said to rest is their grave (cf. Job 17:13). It can rightly be asserted that this verse contains a certain measure of the hope of everlasting life, which was not much in evidence in the days of the Old Testament.

But the point toward which this thought moves forward is the fact that the numerous deaths of "loyal men" portended the breaking in of a major calamity, of which no man seemed even remotely concerned. This calamity could again be the Babylonian Captivity, which the prophet foretold abundantly but to which warning no man gave heed.

2. Rebuke of Sorcery and Idolatry (vv. 3-10)

57:3-10   3. But you there, come over here,
 you sons of the sorceress,
  you offspring of the adulterer and the harlot.
4. Whom are you ridiculing?
  against whom are you opening your mouth wide?
   and stretching your tongue far out?
Aren't you a brood of transgressors, a pack of liars?
5. You who burn with lust over the idols
  under every green tree;
and slaughter your children in the stream-beds
  among the clefts of the rocks.
6. And among the smooth stones of the streams in your portion,
  and to them you have poured out your drinkofferings,
7. Upon every high and lofty hill
  you have set up your bed,
   and you have gone to offer sacrifice even up there.
6. And among the smooth stones of the streams is your portion,
  you have set up your plaques;
and having turned away from me, you have uncovered,
  and gone up to, and made spacious your bed;
and you have made a bargain for yourself with them.
  You have loved their bed and gazed upon nakedness.
9. You have journeyed to Molech with oil;
  you have provided an abundance of perfumes.
You have also sent your envoys far off,
  and made obeisance even to Sheol.
10. You wear yourself out with your many journeys,
  but you never admitted, "It's all in vain!"
You found new life for your vitality;
  therefore you did not weaken.

Verse 3. This section (vv. 3-10) is a pronouncement of judgment (*Gerichtsrede*). It would fit into the days of Manasseh, under whose patronage every form of idolatry flourished. After the first two verses, which hinted at calamity that stood before the very door but was believed to be still far off, it is very proper to give an indication what the deep-seated cause of this calamity was: sorcery and idolatry, both in a highly developed degree. The passage carries echoes of Jer. 2:20 ff. and Ezek. 16:23ff. In Isa. 56:10 the tone of rebuke was comparatively mild. In this chapter it is sharp and brusque. The opening address is a harsh imperative. A person authorized to rebuke bids the sinners before the divine judgment. They are called "sons of the sorceress," implying that they are strongly addicted to sorcery — magic arts, black magic, and all forms of witchcraft. The mother, so to speak, innoculated the children to practice such rites. The second choice title by which the sinners are addressed is "offspring of the adulterer." Apparently spiritual adultery, that is, idolatry, is meant. Though the difference between the two was often not clearly marked. Spiritual infidelity led to carnal adultery. So adultery here means defection, as in Hos. 7:4; Jer. 3:8 f.; Ezek. 23:37, etc. The first of the indicting titles, referring to the mother, would be keenly felt by those rebuked, because the Oriental felt deeply any slander against his mother. But the prophet is unsparing.

Verse 4. These persons now, the ones addicted to sorcery and adultery, adopted a superior attitude and looked down on those who faithfully held to the worship of the true God of Israel, and gave expression to their conceit by ridiculing the exponents of the ancestral faith. They gave coarse and insulting expression to their feeling of superiority by "opening their mouth wide" in a gesture of derision, and even far more so by "stretching [their] tongue far out." As a result, though the objects of their ridicule were in the first place fellow countrymen, in the last analysis, what they did was directed at the Lord Most High. For such who are so brazen in their rejection of the Lord, the prophet has two more very appropriate titles: "brood of transgressors" (i.e., rebels), and "a pack of liars." These are not merely harsh invectives but entirely fitting descriptions of what these unfaithful in Israel really were.

Verse 5. A multifarious variety and types of idolatrous cults was cultivated by the nation, whose God had done so many good things for them. These further classes of infidelity are treecults, child-sacrifice, and cult of stones. The description becomes a bit lurid. The idolaters are described as inflamed by unholy lust in pursuing this nature-cult and practicing it "under every green tree," an obvious hyperbole and a quite proper one to characterize the zeal with which these abominable practices were followed. This cult alone must have had adherents aplenty (cf. Deut. 12:2; Ezek. 6:13; II Kings 17:10; etc.). From the frequency with which child-sacrifices are alluded to, this specially horrible cult must have taken deeper root in Israel than we usually believe. See by way of illustration: Jer. 7:31; 19:5; Ezek. 20:31; 23:39; II Kings 23:10. Besides, apparently, a favorite place for performing such child-sacrifices was "in the stream-beds," or among "the clefts of the rocks," i.e., small caves in the wadi-beds which furnished a weird background for such practices.

Verse 6. Exactly what is meant by the "smooth stones of the streams" and what spiritual aberration is involved seems almost impossible to determine. But according to the context an idol-cult of some sort must be involved. Perhaps stones fantastically shaped by wind and sand (*Fischer*) were treated as particularly potent fetishes. In any case, the idols involved were regarded as Israel's "portion," that is, her prized inheritance, her most valuable possession (cf. Ps. 16: 5; 142:6; 119:57; Josh. 22:25). To objects such as these, drink-offerings and cereal offerings were dutifully brought. God has all this time been charging the nation with gross rebellion and transgression. He interrupts his indictment with the question: "Shall I be calm over these things?" For all such worship was also shot through with fertility-cult sexual extravagances.

Verse 7. A second description in even more vivid colors follows. We gather from the nature of the description that in this picture the Canaanite fertility-cult is largely being depicted, even as it is in Hosea and Ezekiel. Or it may be called the worship "in high places." Again with a measure of permissible hyperbole these things are said to take place upon "every high and lofty hill." Setting up the bed in these places implies preparations for the practice of the rites of the fertility-cult. Though all this involved some laborious hill-climbing, nevertheless "even up there" the sacrifices and what went with it were performed.

Verse 8. We cannot be entirely sure that we have rightly caught the details of the next act of infidelity that is described. We may have a fairly correct picture of what was practiced according to this description. Deuteronomy 6:9 and 11:20 had taught the people of Israel to write key-words of the Mosaic law on their doorposts and gates. These memory-verses (we called them "plaques") were, however, by this generation set back *"behind* the door" so as not to serve as uncomfortable reminders of the true God of Israel. Having thus turned away from him they are ready to practice the abominations which were characteristic of this cult. In fact the participants in these rites did not, as prostitutes were wont to do, make a bargain for money to be received, but instead made a bargain for themselves with them (i.e., the Canaanites), *paying them* to engage in such things. Nor was all this done with some measure of repugnance and reluctance. But those of Israel "had loved the bed" of lust and had even "gazed upon nakedness." In other words they delighted in indecent exposure, devoid by this time of all sense of shame.

Verse 9. The collection of prophetic oracles goes on, now in a kind of historic retrospect of things that are a matter of record of days gone by. The words are a bit difficult to interpret, but in these verses it seems to be a record of what troubles Israel went to, to engage in her nefarious conduct. Journeys were taken into other countries in order to take part in rites. So, for example, they sought participation in the rites which belonged to Molech, the chief divinity of the Ammonites (see I Kings 11:5, 7). To enhance the practice engaged in, even costly perfumes in abundance were procured. They sent "envoys far off" in order to make further contacts, even if sometimes humiliating obeisance had to be resorted to to get concessions. That is perhaps all that is involved in the phrase "made obeisance even to Sheol." We fail to see here an allusion to attempted contact with the deities of the nether regions, or to necromantic practices.

Verse 10. Yes, it might even be said of Israel that she "wore herself out" in the multiplicity of idolatrous practices. Especially in view of the journeys involved (see also II Kings 16:10 ff.; II Chron. 28:22 ff.). But she never tired of her pursuits. She was never ready to make the obvious admission, "It is all in vain," or as the *Jerusalem Bible* puts it, "I give up." The next sentence again is a bit puzzling. It may suffice to note a bit of the sexual connotation in the translation, "You found new life for your vitality." All these practices practically reinvigorated the idolaters. Therefore they "did not weaken." So ends the excursion into the area of the Canaanite fertility-cult.

Now comes, quite appropriately,

3. The Threat of Judgment (vv. 11-13)

57:11-13 11. Whom did you dread and fear
     so that you behaved treacherously?
And me you did not remember,
     nor take things to heart.
Did I not keep quiet at all this, even from way back?
     But me you did not fear.
12. I for my part will expose this righteousness of yours;
     these doings of yours, they shall avail you nothing.
13. When you cry out for help, let your loathsome idols save
     you, —
     yea, the wind will carry them away,
     and a breath will take them away.
But he that takes refuge in me shall possess the land,
     and inherit my holy mountain.

Verse 11. It would seem that some nameless fear impelled those idolaters on their course. Did the Canaanites themselves perhaps spread the rumor that, if their deities were not appeased, evil would befall those who were negligent? That may have been a major motive by which guilty Israel was driven. Of course, that involved that (they) "did not remember" the Lord, nor "take to heart" his gracious dealings with his people in times past. The Lord indicates that he had never made inordinate demands upon his people: he "kept quiet at all this," as far back as the memory of history reaches. He was patient and longsuffering. His self-restraint could have indicated to Israel what a gracious God the Lord was. But they were dull of perception. Him they "did not fear."

Verse 12. Now finally judgment is pronounced. God will now at last bring to light what it really is that has been going on and reveals how he himself will bring to light what has been happening. You feel secure in that you have kept the ordinances of idolatry. Such keeping was your "righteousness" — spoken ironically. If true righteousness was a worthy garb in which to appear before the throne on high, then Israel's righteousness, based on idolatrous practices surely was a garment of "filthy rags." God is going to make that very apparent. So he spells it out: "These doings of yours, they shall avail you nothing."

Verse 13. A threat of judgment is implied at this point, the nation will be driven into such extremities that they will "cry out for help." When the real test comes then it will become apparent how wretched deities the idols were. They are here called "loathsome idols" because their inability will, in such emergencies, be appalling. When the real test comes, they will be so helpless that any wind or breath will remove them off the scene. But grace triumphs over justice. The section comes to an end on a very positive note. All that the Lord requires, even of these guilty ones is that they "take refuge" in him. If they do this then the old covenant blessing made to Abraham will become a reality: they "shall possess the land" and enjoy all the blessings attendant upon such possession. When it is said that they will "inherit [his] holy mountain" this mountain is the mountainous territory of the land of Israel.

4. A Promise of Salvation (vv. 14-21)

57:14-21 14. And it shall be said:
          "Build a road, build a road, prepare a way.
Remove every obstacle from the way of my people."

15. For thus says the high and exalted One,
    who sits enthroned forever, whose name is Holy:
"I dwell in the high and holy place,
    and also with him who is crushed and low in spirit,
to revive the spirit of the lowly,
    and to revive the heart of those who are crushed.
16. For I will not contend forever,
    neither will I always be angry.
For [every] spirit would faint before me,
    and the souls which I have made.
17. I was indeed angry because of the sin of covetousness,
    and I smote him, hiding my face in anger.
But he went on backsliding in the way of his heart.
18. I have seen his ways, yet I will heal him;
    and I will lead him and I will give him full consolations,
        and also to his mourners,
19. producing as the utterance of their lips:
    'Peace, peace to those afar off
        and to those who are near'
says the Lord: 'and I will heal him.'
20. But the wicked are like the stirred-up sea,
    for it cannot calm down;
        and its waters toss up mud and slime.
21. 'There is no peace, says my God,
    'for the wicked.'"

Verse 14. Logic or strict justice would at this point have launched into despair about Israel's future, or would have dictated harsh punishments. Grace is that quality which rises beyond logic and justice. It tells what God will do in spite of all that points to the contrary. Who it is that speaks and when and where is unimportant. Therefore these words are introduced by a mere: "And it shall be said." Thus the message as such is underscored. This word is *Heilsverheissung*, a promise of salvation. It demands constructive enterprise: "Build a road." The terms are reminiscent of 40:3. Only in the former passage the road was to be built for the Lord to travel on, and to come to his people. Here it is the road that leads to the achievement of God's purposes and is prepared for the people to travel on and thus come to their goal. That involves the removal of all obstacles that lie in the way of achieving what has been promised the nation. Littleness of faith, doubt, discouragement are to be pushed out of the way, for God is with his people. He is very near. He is at hand to help. Salvation in all its fulness is to be aimed at.

Verse 15. To strengthen them still more, a second word of encouragement is added. He is not too high and mighty to let himself be concerned about what is happening to his own. Indeed he is "high and exalted." He has always sat enthroned. His name "Holy" means here total dedication to his purposes. But exalted as he deservedly is, he is also pleased to take up residence with "him who is crushed and low in spirit." These words might seem to describe men who are deeply contrite over their sins, but in the whole context it rather applies to those who are deeply discouraged, who have lost heart, who are held down by discouragement. They have not utterly lost faith, but they badly need revitalization; and that is what the Lord promises to give them.

Verse 16. The thought that God is not too high to take note of lowly man in his misery is being developed further. When man goes astray God does not merely let him drift: he takes him to task. In Biblical language he "contends" with him (cf. 54:7-9; Gen. 6:3; Jer. 3:5, 12; Ps. 103:9). Or another way of stating the case is: he "will not always be angry. For the manifestation of his anger, unrestrained, would have as result that "every spirit would faint before [him]" for his anger is a consuming fire. Then all the souls which he had made would perish.

Verse 17. The thought of God's anger is not to be dismissed; it is a very real and stern concept. God here dwells on the fact that he had just grounds for being angry. There was one sin in particular which had provoked him, the sin of "covetousness." Apparently this sin played a larger role than we usually admit. It is doubly heinous because it usually gives birth to social injustices. Even after the Israelites came back from Exile they still nurtured this sin in their bosom. So the Lord hid (his) face in anger. He let them painfully feel his displeasure. Did that treatment move them to abandon this sin? Far from it. "He went on backsliding in the

way of his heart." Now comes the surprising reaction of the
Lord to all this.

Verse 18. The opening statement looks back for a moment, as much as to say: The Lord is fully aware of Israel's
attitude. And "*yet* he will heal him." This form of presentation constitutes one of those surprising triumphs of grace over
justice. The healing spoken of is one of a spiritual nature,
being reminiscent of Exod. 15:26. This thought is quite appropriate here, for the sin spoken of in v. 17 was a serious
malady. The Lord's gracious attitude is covered by a few
more verbs showing his kindly attitude toward the undeserving: "I will lead him and I will give full consolations."
Perhaps the last phrase is best interpreted by translating a bit
differently than we have, namely: "and *especially* to his
mourners." The more deeply they grieve, the more do they
become the objects of the Lord's pity.

Verse 19. The structure of this rather long sentence becomes a bit difficult, though the thought is clear. When the
Lord takes pity on his children that will now produce grateful acknowledgment in the form of thanksgiving and praise,
which are here described as being the "utterance of their
lips." The same thought is found in Heb. 13:15 and Hos. 14:
2. How "Peace, peace" fits into the picture is perhaps best
covered by *Muilenburg's* explanation: "One is tempted to
view this as Yahweh's greeting (*shalom, shalom!*) to all who
enter the city of Zion." These blessings are available to
"those afar off and to those who are near," that is to the
Hebrews gathered in their own land as well as to those who
have not yet returned. Or, repeating the former thought of
v. 18: God's blessing on his own may be adequately covered
by the statement: "And I will heal him." Ephesians 2:14 may
also be compared on the second line of the verse.

Verses 20, 21. Over against the fortunate lot of those who
have let themselves be admonished by the Lord, stands as a
proper conclusion a description of the situation of the wicked
and impenitent. They have anything but peace. For they
are like "the stirred-up sea" which cannot calm down, and

who may be said "to toss up mud and slime." In a sense this statement is a warning; in another sense it is a stern conclusion. The earnest tone of the law comes into the picture over against the gospel tone, which had for a time come to the forefront. The same stern note is sounded in v. 21, which appeared already in 48:22 and marked the conclusion of a major section. When men advocate to excise this verse at this point they are overlooking how well the verse fits in after v. 20.

Notes

Verse 1. *Koenig* in his commentary classified the "taken away" (*ne'esaph*) as a gnomic aorist, which fact we sought to display by inserting "always" in the translation. For the translation of *mippeney* three possibilities are to be reckoned with: *min* separative, *min* temporal, and *min* causal. We believe that *min* separative agrees best with the context.

Verse 3. For *wattizneh* ("and she played the harlot") the *Septuagint*, the *Syriac*, and the *Vulgate* read *zonah* (*kal*, feminine participle) which makes for a smoother translation.

Verse 6. There is a play on words involved: *cheleq* from one root means "smooth" and from another means "portion." *von Orelli* has caught the point in his translation: Des Tales *Kiesel* hast du dir *erkiest*.

Verse 8. The word rendered "nakedness" in Hebrew is the word "hand." To render it "nakedness" seems at best a guess, but a fairly reasonable guess at that.

Verse 13. The word *qibbutzim* (with suffix) from the root *qabhatz* could mean "the collected ones" which has led to the translation "your collection of idols" (*RSV*), a translation which fits very well at this point. Our translation, "your loathsome idols," builds on the fact that *qibbutzim* seems to be patterned after the word for "loathsome ones," which in Hebrew read *shiqqutzim*.

Verse 15. For "who sits enthroned forever" *KJ* and *RSV* have the seemingly impressive "who inhabits eternity," which does not seem to yield a very clear thought.

Verse 16. The word "spirit" in the second half of the verse has no article. This fact makes the thought more general. We have sought to render this fact by inserting an "every" before the word. The last clause of the verse could be very properly translated: "And I myself have made life." We offer it as an alternate translation (a la *Volz*).

Verse 18. The second verb in the verse is best taken as introduced by an adversative conjunction. See *KS* 369 f.

Chapter LVIII

C. ABUSES THAT RETARDED THE RECOVERY OF POST-EXILIC ISRAEL (Chap. 58)

From this title we draw the conclusion that the chapter is predominantly a preaching of law; and so it is. It may be properly labelled an admonition (*Mahnrede*). Fitting things into a historical situation we may conclude that the fortunes of the children of Israel are at low ebb; recovery has been slow. But there are very special reasons why this is so. According to the main issues of this chapter two major abuses have been pointed out that have retarded recovery. These two are: a misdirected fasting and an inadequate Sabbath observance. Because of shortcomings in the area just indicated the people stand there as utterly undeserving of divine favors. It would then appear that the time into which this passage fits is neither the pre-exilic, nor the exilic, nor the time immediately after the Return from Exile, but perhaps the decade following the Return. Although we feel that the days of the prophet Isaiah need not be ruled out completely. The indications of a possible background are so utterly meager and consist mostly in facts like no mention of a temple — as though fasting and Sabbath observance could not be discussed without mention of the Temple — if it had already been rebuilt.

It is true that the author of this chapter speaks as a teacher and instructor, or even as a *Seelsorger* and not with the characteristic approach of a prophet. But that could happen even if the speaker had been Isaiah. For these prophets were not one-talent men; and they had many different situations to combat.

Restating the major thought of the chapter briefly, we might say: It is not externalistic piety that paves the way for Israel's restoration but true, active righteousness (*Fischer*).

1. The Wrong Kind of Fast (vv. 1-5)

58:1-5   1. Call mightily, do not let up;
 lift up your voice like a trumpet
and tell my people their transgressions
 and to the house of Jacob their sins.
2. Indeed, me they seek daily;
 they take pleasure in the knowledge of my ways,
as if they were a nation that did what is right
 and had not forsaken the law of its God.
They demand of me righteous judgments;
 they find pleasure in drawing near to God.
3. "Why have we fasted and you have not taken note?
 Why have we afflicted our bodies, but you are not aware of it?"
Lo, on the day when you fast, you find time for your business,
 and oppress all your workers.
4. Lo, when you fast, it is for strife and squabbling,
 and for hitting with a wicked fist.
When for the present you fast
 it is not to make your voice heard on high.
5. Or shall it be a fast such as I approve of,
 a day of mortification?
Is it to bow down one's head like a reed?
 or to bed one's self in sackcloth and ashes?
Will you call this a fast,
 a day acceptable to the Lord?

Verse 1. The *Jerusalem Bible* catches the spirit of this verse rather well when it renders: "Shout for all you are worth." The attitude conveyed by this word is: Speak clearly and loudly; spare no one; be sure they all hear you. Sin is to be labelled as sin. When they come with excuses, like v. 2, in answer to your charge, do not weakly capitulate. The sin is great. It is rooted strongly in the nation's life.

Verse 2. But the hearers are hurt, not wounded unto repentance. They have several excuses to offer. A certain religiousness marks their assemblies, whether they be in the synagogue, the temple, or the home. For they engage in religious subjects even so important a matter as the Lord's "ways," that is to say, the ways of proper conduct that the Lord would have them follow. On the surface they appear to be interested in godly living. But there is a fatal defect in their life and conversation: they have "forsaken the law of [their] God," and so they are not a nation that "did what is right." They have the form of godliness but they deny the power thereof. In fact, on the basis of their ungrounded assumption, they feel they have a right to "demand of [him] righteous judgments." This appears to mean they are demanding of the Lord rewards for their fidelity and punishment of their enemies, on the basis of their own religiosity. In addition to all this they behave as though they were on terms of familiarity with their God: "they find pleasure in drawing near to God." Godly exercises such as prayer, godly helps such as reading the Sacred Scriptures, seem to come easily and naturally to them. For they are sure that they are God's favored people.

Verse 3. Words such as the opening of this verse display in part where the trouble lies. They have fasted but God has not taken their fasting into account; God does not seem to notice that they have achieved a certain measure of merit by their godly exercises. When men blame God for what is befalling them there is something decidedly unwholesome about their attitude.

A brief evaluation of fasting is in order at this point. Fasting was suggested by the Mosaic law only in one instance and that was in the observance of the annual Day of Atonement (Lev. 16:29). In that connection the term used was the same as the one here used as second term: "afflict or humble the person" (*nephesh*). That meant to subdue and control the desire for food by abstaining from the use of it. Occasions where the nation Israel fasted are recorded I Sam. 7:6; Judg. 20:26; I Kings 21:12; Jer. 36:9. In all these instances the fasting seems to have been entirely wholesome and self-imposed. A special type of fast is mentioned as having been engaged in after the Fall of Jerusalem, where the outstanding days of divine judgment were commemorated by the nation, like the capture of the Temple by the Chaldeans. All instances of this sort are mentioned by Zechariah (7:3; 8:19). As Zech. 7:1-6 shows, the value of this observance had become doubtful for the people and so they inquired of the prophet whether these fasts could be abrogated. It appears, then, that fasts were chiefly regarded as "signs of sorrow." As already indicated the fasts under consideration were not wholesome for they had as their object the achievement of a measure of merit. But above all things certain flagrant abuses were tolerated and much in evidence on fast days, as the rest of v. 3 now begins to show.

The prophet follows them to their place of assembly on a fast day. There, off in a corner, two men are not evaluating their own conduct and that of their nation; they are not seeking the face of God in true repentance. They are carrying on a business transaction. Or again, while they are publicly engaged in holy exercises, at home the laborer who is working for them is slaving under heavy burdens and is being oppressed. Heavy social wrong-doings are being tolerated and practiced.

Verse 4. More than that, while they fast to obtain peace with God, as it were, their abstaining from food makes them so irritable that quarrels and squabbles are continually occurring, and that publicly; yes, even to the point of making a public spectacle of it all, by engaging in fisticuffs with their fellow men. There is something telling about the term used in this connection: they hit with "a wicked fist." No thought is given to the high and noble purpose for which the fasts were designed, the expression of sincere sorrow for manifest sins. In other words, it is not with the design of "making [their] voice heard on high."

Verse 5. Now the prophet uses a different approach (for the subject has several sides). The opening words of this verse could perhaps be given in a simpler form like this: "Or is this something you would label as a fast?" He begins to dwell particularly on the idiom of "afflicting one's body," or as some call it: "mortification." The form in which this aspect of the case also expressed itself was "to bow down one's head like a reed." This is what Jesus described in the Sermon on the Mount as making the face "look dismal." The colorful expression used here is "to bow down one's head like a reed." Is that an approach that appeases and gratifies the Almighty? Some made a special show of the physical discomfort to which they were ready to expose themselves by making a kind of "bed for themselves in sackcloth and ashes." *G. A. Smith* caught the spirit of this act when he rendered the term rather well: "they grovel in sackcloth and ashes." With intense sarcasm the prophet rightly calls out: "Will you call *this* a fast?" No one would hesitate to call all this "the Wrong Sort of Fast."

2. The Right Kind of Fast (vv. 6-7)

58:6-7 6. But rather is not this a fast such as I should choose?
Free the person unjustly bound;
loose the bonds of the yoke;
set the oppressed free,
and rend every yoke.
7. Or is it not this?
that you share your bread with the hungry,
that you take into your house the wretched refugees?
When you see a man inadequately clothed,
you provide garments.
And do not hide yourself from your own flesh?

Verse 6. The opening statement (Is not this a fast?) may be said to look both ways. What has just been described, deserves to be called a true fast. What is about to be described, likewise. In substance what now follows comes under the general classification: He who would obtain mercy from God must first show himself merciful, as *Duhm* already remarked. How very similar all this is to the words of Jesus (Matt. 25:35 ff.) is only too obvious. Jesus' words may rest on our passage. Social suffering, wherever it is found, is to be relieved as much as lies in our power. Steps are to be taken to free those unjustly imprisoned, if to do so is possible. The prophet's contemporaries, the men who were engaging in fasting, were often the ones guilty of their imprisonment. Different kinds of oppressive measures ("the yoke") were being employed. Under a pretense of justice men were being "oppressed." All these things lay in the area of judicial procedure.

Verse 7. Now comes a list of procedures that come under the head of relief of the poor and needy. The list of opportunities of helping the helpless is rather long because oppression by those in power has always been rather a common thing. Under this head comes, not only *giving* bread to the hungry, but "sharing" it. That could involve going half-hungry oneself. "Not what we give but what we share." — In the same spirit "wretched refugees" are not simply given an improvised hovel as shelter against the wind and the cold, but are, if need requires, to be taken into one's own house. Such is the nature of true mercy. Similar help is to be provided for those "inadequately clothed." In no case is a man to evade the issue involved (i.e., to "hide himself from his own flesh"). It would seem to us that this expression covers any human being who may be encountered as being in need, not only our own blood-kin. Not many in our day dare take the broad demand of this passage seriously, even as already in the prophet's day men avoided the broad scope of its demands.

3. Blessings That Will Result from a Proper Fast (vv. 8-9a)

58:8-9a 8. Then shall your light break forth like the dawn,
and your healing shall develop speedily;
and your integrity shall go before you;
the glory of the Lord shall be your rearguard.
9a. Then you shall call and the Lord will answer;
you shall cry out for help and he will say: "Here am I."

Verse 8. The Lord loves to reward them that do his will. Keeping a fast in the manner just described will induce him to bestow blessings. The first of these will be that the "light" of the nation shall break forth like a brilliant dawn. This "light" would seem to be true national prosperity. In addition where the people were suffering from grievous maladies "healing shall develop speedily." Where all progress and prosperity had ground to a halt, now the nation will again begin to march forward led by a trusty guide, "integrity," that is irreproachable conduct as people. Echoes of the march of Israel through the wilderness in the days of Moses seem to ring through this description. The nation will be protected by a rearguard none less than the Lord himself (cf. 52:12). Here some claim that, since the verbs appear in the singular, the prophet is addressing himself to the individual members of the nation. That is hardly likely. The nation is merely being regarded as a unit.

Verse 9a. One further blessing is recounted as enjoyed by the nation, the fine spiritual blessings of being heard when they pray: dialog with God. Where in v. 3 God was charged with being unresponsive when his people looked up to him, now the moment they cry, he will answer them, and remind them that he delights to hear their petitions.

4. The Abuses That Are to Be Put Aside (vv. 9b-10a)

58:9b-10a 9b. If you remove from your midst the yoke, the pointing with the finger and speaking wickedly
10a. and you offer to the hungry man the bread you crave, and satisfy the hunger of the afflicted.

Verse 9b. The speaker is back again on the subject of righting social wrongs, of which there were many. He is making a complete appraisal of the ills that are blocking the approach of the nation to God. Every bit of oppressive treatment is to be done away with. So are unkind modes of treatment of the one by the other, like pointing with the finger in a derisive gesture with not a word spoken. Gestures can hurt. And the tongue can hurt, "speaking wickedly" by way of slander. Slander rather than curses and wicked charms appear to be under consideration. Again (v. 10a) the subject of feeding the hungry poor is mentioned by the prophet. To expect God to hear our cries when we will not let the cries of the poor reach our heart is quite unreasonable.

5. A Further Group of Resultant Blessings (vv. 10b-12)

58:10b-12 10b. Then shall your light rise in the darkness,
and your gloom shall be as the noonday.
11. And the Lord will guide you continually,
and he will satisfy your hunger in the sun-parched desert;
and he will make your bones sturdy,
and you shall be like a well-watered garden,
like a spring whose waters fail not.
12. And your people shall build again your ancient ruins,
the foundations of many generations shall you raise up again;
and you shall be called "Mender of the Breaches"
"Restorer of Streets to Dwell in."

Verse 10b. The prophet is back again on the subject of blessings that will come to those who engage in a right fast. It is as though he had a kind of afterthought. He had already dealt with this subject in vv. 8-9a. This coming back and resuming a subject is called by some "palindrome" (i.e., "running over again"). Also for that matter, above (v. 8) he had used the figure of "light" breaking forth. Instead of the darkness of misery that enshrouds the nation the cheerful light of prosperity shall prevail, or, as the parallel statement puts it, there shall be a change from gloom to noonday.

Verse 11. A new series of blessings is listed. The first one is continual guidance by the Lord himself. One seems to catch echoes of Ps. 23 at this point. Besides, in an area where food is liable to fail one ("the sun-parched desert") enough food will be found to completely satisfy hunger. Besides, instead of old and brittle bones in the framework of the nation the Lord will give sturdy bones. Then too the nation shall present a flourishing appearance like a well-watered garden. Even the sources of water-supply will not fail. So by the use of a number of colorful figures the prophet shows how richly the Lord will bless those who engage in the loving service of their fellow men.

Verse 12. It is a foregone conclusion that a disaster will first strike the nation before things can get better. After the disaster, ruins will be left throughout the land. The blessings that will afterward come upon the land can be conceived of in terms of ruins rebuilt and cities and towns restored. True restoration shall finally come about. Once deserted streets shall be lined with houses for people to dwell in. Special honorable titles shall even be given the nation for this work, the first of which has been well rendered as "Breachmender" (*Jerusalem Bible*).

6. A Kindred Reform in the Matter of the Sabbath (vv. 13-14)

58:13-14 13. If you will restrain your foot from the Sabbath, from doing your pleasure on my holy day,
and will call the Sabbath a delight,
    and wilt call the holy one of the Lord honorable;
if you honor it so as not to go your own ways,
    so as not to find what pleases you, or to talk idly;
14. then you shall take delight in the Lord
and I will make you to ride in triumph over the
    high places of the earth,
and give you to enjoy the heritage of Jacob, your father;
    for the mouth of the Lord has spoken it.

Verse 13. Some have called the Sabbath the "grandest rite" (*grossartigste Einrichtung*) of the Old Testament religion. It had been established in Mosaic days. It served as a unique confession of the Jews during the Babylonian Captivity. Its importance was reasserted by the prophet, who in this case becomes a teacher of his people. Other prophets reasserted its importance: Jer. 12:19 ff.; Ezek. 20:12 ff.; 22:8, 26. For its proper observance could bring rich blessings upon the nation. A re-evaluation akin to that of fasting could be a very wholesome and helpful cultic rite. Above (56:7) a similar preaching of the importance of the proper observance of the Sabbath had already appeared. It is here not so much a rest-day (Exod. 20:8-11) but a day for sanctified observance. The things that are inculcated as belonging to proper observance are the avoidance of rash profanation of the day. For that is what it means to restrain one's foot from the Sabbath, an act like trampling on a pretty flower-bed. Another thing to be avoided is doing one's own pleasure, i.e., business, on that day, letting thoughts of business transaction claim attention — unholy thoughts on the holy day. This might give rise to the view that this day was one of rigid restraints, whereas quite the opposite ought to be the case — "call the Sabbath a delight." When referring to it, a man was to imply by his whole attitude that it was esteemed as an "honorable" day. In fact any kind of activity that catered to personal and selfish activity was to be shunned; not to "go one's own way," and "not to find what pleases you." In fact the tone of the activities of that day was to be kept at such a high level that all trivial and idle talk was to be avoided. The supreme honorific title applied to the Sabbath is "the holy one of the Lord."

Verse 14. Palindromically (see v. 10a) the prophet returns to the subject of blessings that the Lord will grant to those that seek to please him, whether it be in the area of fasting or Sabbath observance. The first blessing will be that they "shall take delight in the Lord." Their chief good will be to have their fellowship with the Lord a source of deepest pleasure. Practical values will result: men will surmount difficulties and obstacles, or, as is here said: they will "triumph over the high places of the earth." In addition his people shall "enjoy the heritage of Jacob." That is to say, be rewarded by God with enjoyment of peaceful possession of the Promised Land (Gen. 28:13 f.). All this concludes with a solemn promise, almost like an oath: "for the mouth of the Lord has spoken it."

Notes

Verse 2. The expression *qirebhath 'elohim* ("the drawing near of God") can in Hebrew be construed as a subjective or an objective genetive: God's drawing near to man or man's drawing near to God. In the light of the same expression in Ps. 73:28 it would appear that it means "drawing near to God."

Verse 5. The infinitive *lakhoph* ("to bow") is dependant on the verb that follows *tiqra'* ("will you call"). So the infinitive comes first and is in the absolute position (*KS* 341 k).

Verse 7. In the light of what was said above (v. 10b) on the use of the figure called "palindrome" it becomes quite unnecessary to rearrange the verses into the pattern: 9b, 10a, 8, 9a, 10b, 11, 12.

Verse 10a. A rather unusual use of the term *nephesh* appears here, the meaning "appetite." So "your appetite" comes to mean "the bread you crave."

Chapter LIX

D. THE HAND OF THE LORD IS NOT TOO SHORT TO SAVE (Chap. 59)

The material offered in this chapter is so multifarious as to make it difficult to discover a unified theme that could serve as title. However when we reflect upon the beginning of the previous chapter, recalling that the prophet was bidden to lift up his voice and to "spare not," we begin to note that in reality the prophet had not yet made a vehement proclamation in the course of Chap. 58. He first does that in Chap. 59. Then, besides, the prophets are frequently seen to observe the basic rules of good rhetoric, such as employing a meaningful topic sentence at the head of a new chapter. Then we see that the opening statement covers Chap. 59 rather adequately: "The hand of the Lord is not too short to save." Besides, the well-organized unity of the chapter is highlighted. We note at the same time that the chapter may be regarded as the continuation of the one that precedes (58). All of this need not shut our eyes to the fact that the difficulties involved are many and great. Yet on the whole a comparatively clear message emerges as we proceed.

Nor is it easy to find a convenient point in time into which this chapter may be fitted. Yet it seems safe to assume that it fits the needs of the nation as they developed a decade or two after the return from Babylonian Captivity. Does this eliminate the possibility of authorship by Isaiah? Not really. In the providence of God he may have been guided to prepare beforehand materials that stood the returned Israelites in good stead; and may even for that matter have served a purpose for Isaiah's contemporaries, where a situation may have developed much akin to that of post-exilic days. Thus the supposition that Isaiah wrote this chapter is not too farfetched.

As to the form in which the chapter appears, it must be admitted that there are elements of a "community lament" (*Westermann*). But it must be admitted that a rather ugly description of the moral state of the nation is also drawn. There is also a free and frank confession of sins done in the community. At the same time a hopeful note is sounded of what God, for all that, still proposes to do in behalf of his people.

We doubt very much whether it will yield any profit to regard this chapter as a liturgy. It does not fit well into that category. We are equally dubious about classifying it as a sermon. Elements of a lament and a goodly amount of prophetic instruction must be conceded to make up most of the chapter. Rehabilitation seems to have taken place to quite an extent after the Return. The elements of a settled community, or commonwealth, seem to have been established. The title given by the *RSV* — "Confession of National Wickedness" — elevates one incidental factor to the level of supreme importance. So does the caption of the *Oxford Annotated Bible* with its: "Call to National Repentance."

Quite a diversity of opinion exists also with regard to the issue of the unity of the chapter. Some seem to detect verses that are later additions. We are quite content to be in the company of *Westermann* and *McKenzie* who hold to the "obvious unity" of the material included in this chapter.

One unique factor in this connection is the fact that key terms like "justice" and "righteousness" appear with varying meanings, e.g., sometimes "righteousness," sometimes "salvation," as we shall indicate in the exposition that follows.

1. The Nation's Ungrounded Complaint (vv. 1-2)

59:1-2 1. Lo, the hand of the Lord is not too short to save; nor his ears too dull to hear;
2. but your iniquities have interposed a barrier between you and your God,
    so that he could not hear.

Verse 1. The prophets of the Lord had prophesied things in connection with the Restoration of Israel, things which they were wont to depict in such glowing colors. The Restoration took place as a result of the decree of Cyrus (II Chron. 36:22; Ezra 1:1-4). But the hoped-for glories failed to materialize. It was an age of bitter disappointment. Israel complained. The easiest way out of the dilemma was to blame the Almighty, charging him with inability to bring his promises to pass. We seem to hear echoes of 50:1-3. The first figure ("hand too short") is expressive. Israel has fallen into deep waters. His arm cannot catch hold on them. So impatient and short-sighted minds are inclined to conclude. The second figure is much the same as the first. Far from the haunts of men a traveler is in distress. He cries out aloud for help. He cries and keeps on crying. The Lord seems like one incapable of hearing. Fault is persistently found with the divine administration of things. With some measure of impatience the prophet rejects the charges made, crying out "lo" — translated "no" (*Jerusalem Bible*). The blame must be sought on the other side of the equation. Not with God! with the *people!*

Verse 2. Putting it as bluntly and unmistakably as possible, the prophet faults Israel. It is no light offense to charge God for things whose fault lies at our own doorstep. A "barrier" has been interposed between the nation and God. For "so that he could not hear" does not imply inability on God's part but thinks in terms of a moral impossibility. From being the accuser, the nation suddenly has the role of the defendant thrust upon her. Sin, not repented of, becomes the source of many evils.

2. The Unrighteousness Prevailing in Israel (vv. 3-8)

59:3-8   3. For your hands are stained with blood,
       and your fingers with iniquity;
your lips speak lies,
    and your tongues mutter injustice.

4. Nobody makes charges justly,
   no one goes to law honestly.
But each one trusts in nothingness;
   and speaks emptiness.
They conceive violence and bring forth iniquity.
5. Viper's eggs do they hatch out
   and spider's webs do they spin.
He who eats their eggs will die,
   Crush one, and out comes a viper.
6. Their webs cannot be used to make a garment;
   a man cannot wrap himself in what they make.
Their products are works of iniquity,
   and deeds of violence are in their hands.
7. Their feet run to do evil,
   they hurry their pace to shed blood.
Their thoughts are thoughts of wickedness;
   destruction and ruin are found in the roads they build.
8. The way of peace they do not know,
   and there is no justice in their paths.
Tortuous trails they make for themselves;
   he that walks in them will know no peace.

Verse 3. The prophet goes on to specify what grounds he has for the accusation he made in v. 2. His line of argument is easy to follow; he finds that hands, fingers, lips, and tongues are separately chargeable with malfeasance. He cannot be accused of implying that every member of the nation is guilty of each of the misdeeds mentioned. Still he would have us know that the nation shares in this corporate guilt.

Verse 4. At this point some believe that vv. 4-8 is a later addition; v. 3 is thought to be enough of an indictment. But one can easily see that the prophet with good reason brought the heavy hammer of the law down on the conscience of the evil-doers. Therefore vv. 4-8 are not a weak afterthought but a forceful elaboration. Verse 4 takes us into the law-courts, where justice and equity should prevail. But it soon becomes apparent that miscarriage of justice is the order of the day, a rather common subject for Biblical writers (see 1:17, 23; 3:14; 5:7, 23; 10:1, 2; — just to cite instances from the book of Isaiah). But to tell the truth, the verse begins in the courts of law and soon branches out into every walk of life. The rather general idea of "conceiving" and "bringing forth" is to be found also in Job 15:35; Ps. 7:14; Isa. 33:11.

Verse 5. From this point onward the thoughts of the writer do not move forward in a given line. Rather do we find an accumulation of separate, more or less, unrelated examples of the abundance of evil fruits that evil hearts produce. The sum total becomes appalling and overwhelming. The beginning of the verse may have been in the mind of John the Baptist (Matt. 3:7) when he uncovered the hypocrisy of the Pharisees. One item in this connection cannot be entirely cleared up — the "vipers." We seem to be unable to discover what kind of serpents are meant. There are two difficulties: Who *eats* vipers' eggs? and: Vipers *do not* lay eggs. Under the circumstances, we shall have to think in general terms of some type of poisonous serpents known well enough to the prophet's hearers. The general picture of all the mischief these evil-doers hatched out is clear enough.

Verse 6. In a sense this verse is the application of the principle: "By their fruits you shall know them." Nothing substantial comes from a life that has the marks just described. Their works have the quality of spider-webs. As little as you can weave a warm garment out of such material, so little does what these evil-doers produce have any worth or value. Worse than that: some things are produced but they are downright wickedness and deeds of violence.

Verse 7. More still must be made mention of if a complete picture is to be produced. Not only are wicked deeds the order of the day; these persons display *zeal* for the achievement of their fell plots. They approach each new wicked enterprise with zeal and alacrity. All their thoughts pivot about the center of wickedness. How could the net result be anything less than "destruction and ruin." By a clever alliteration the prophet makes this result stand out the more evidently (the Hebrew says: *shodh washebher*). If what life produces may be likened to roadbuilding, these people build elements of destruction and ruin into the very roadway.

From this point on throughout the next verse four separate terms for "road" are used, showing how much prominence the writer attaches to this figure. We all build for ourselves the roads on which we walk through life. Paul quotes this verse in Rom. 3:15-17.

Verse 8. It would seem that "peace" in this context means something like "well-being" and "prosperity." He that walks on the road with these evil-doers will be unable to find peace. For people minded, as these road-builders are, have no room for things like justice as they shape their lives. As their minds are ("tortuous") so are the roads they build for themselves — twisted. For a man living with such associates, the prophet repeats it again: they "will know no peace."

3. The Resultant Moral Confusion (vv. 9-11)

59:9-11 9. That is why justice is so far from us,
and righteousness does not overtake us.
We wait for light, and lo, there is darkness,
and for brightness, but we walk along in gloom.
10. We grope along the wall like blind men;
like persons without eyes do we grope.
We stumble at noonday as if it were twilight;
among men of lusty strength, we are like dead men.
11. All of us growl as bears,
and mourn sadly as doves.
We hope for justice, but there is none,
for salvation, but it is far from us.

Verse 9. Given a set of conditions as such depicted in vv. 3-8, moral confusion is bound to follow, even as it is here sketched — "Justice" is far off, that means: justice in the sense of deliverance. The "righteousness" here mentioned seems to refer to the same thing: the restoration of which the prophets spoke in such glowing terms. "Light," as is so often the case in contexts such as this, refers to a bright and happy state of affairs. "Gloom" and "darkness" by way of contrast serve to describe a wretched state.

Verse 10. A few lines may yet be added to the picture of the prevailing moral confusion. Spiritual blindness has taken hold of the nation. People are groping to find a way out of their dilemma. Even in the brightness of the noon-day sun they stumble along. At this point a difficult word occurs, which has led some to assert that the text makes no sense. The word involved may, according to good lexicons (see *Koenig*, Hebr. *Woerterbuch*) be translated as "men of lusty strength." It would then refer to the oppressors of Israel, who feed themselves fat while Israel languishes. The verse as a whole seems to refer back to Deut. 28:29.

Verse 11. This verse also has its difficulties. The growling like bears seems to imply discontent. Mourning like doves seems to point to sad longing (cf. 38:14). Again the terms "justice" and "salvation" appear, pointing to blessings that are being sadly missed. Both terms seem to refer to the restoration of his people that he so often promised them. By stating that these blessings are still "far from" them, the message of the prophet harks back to the beginning of v. 9, and so rings a note of hopelessness.

4. A Frank Confession (vv. 12-15a)

59:12-15a 12. For our transgressions before thee are many; and our sins testify against us.
For our transgressions are with us,
   our iniquities — we are conscious of them;
13. Transgressing, and denying the Lord,
   and turning away from following after our God;
speaking oppression and defection,
   conceiving and uttering from the heart lying words.
14. Justice is pushed into a corner;
   righteousness must stand at a distance.
Truth is made to stumble in the market-place,
   and honesty can find no entrance.
15a. Security is missing;
   and he who avoids evil makes himself a prey.

Verse 12. At this point the sense of sinfulness on the part of the people seems to have been awakened. The dark picture that the prophet had painted seemed to be only too true. He feels that the time is ripe for a frank confession. He is merely expressing what the community feels. The confession is sincere and wholesome. There is no trace of trying to make light of a single charge that the prophet had leveled against them. The various words for sin that may be used are practically all employed. It is admitted that these sins are "many," they "testify" against the nation. They are "with them" like leeches clinging stubbornly to them. Men are "conscious" of the evil they have done.

Verse 13. With deep insight into the real truth of the situation the prophet goes on with the confession, indicating that the sins confessed are not merely a loose accumulation of deeds and practices, but going into the deeper implications of the case traces the nation's guilt and moral confusion to the fact that the proper relation to God has been disturbed ("transgressing, and denying the Lord"). Or to word it differently: "turning away from following after our God." Even the next line presents an element of this sort when it speaks of "defection" which basically means "turning aside." Note that the writer lets the first commandment dominate all the rest. Here the prophet adds a few misdeeds that play into the area of the Second Table of the Law, sins not yet mentioned ("conceiving and uttering from the heart lying words") — a thought uttered by the Savior himself: "Out of the heart proceed wicked thoughts." To claim at this point that vv. 13-15 are a later insertion into the text, fitting very poorly into this context is an approach which fails to do justice to the prophet.

Verses 14, 15a. Though this verse is still a description of a deplorable state of affairs in the land and so rings somewhat the note of lament, it is still primarily a part of a contrite confession. It takes us into the field of jurisprudence and of procedures prevailing in law-courts. In this use of terms "justice and righteousness" are legal terms. These two attributes of upright lawyers and administrators, together with the last two mentioned, "truth and honesty," are all four of them being abused and maltreated, "pushed into a corner," "stand at a distance," "stumble in the market place" and "find no entrance." To this description of judicial malpractice v. 15a quite naturally attaches itself. For while "security" is built on the foundation of unimpeachable courts of law, under the conditions just described, insecurity must prevail on every hand. And should a man be conscientious about his behavior and conduct, such a one, instead of gaining the approval of all right-thinking persons, is instead singled out for persecution and oppression: in other words, such a one "makes himself a prey." With a sign the present-day reader lays this confession aside. It rings only too modern.

5. The Lord's Intervention (vv. 15b-21)

59:15b-21 15b. And the Lord saw it and it displeased him that there was no justice.
16. And he saw that there was no man,
and was astounded that there was no man to intervene;
and his own arm brought him victory,
and his righteousness supported him.
17. He put on righteousness as a breastplate,
and a helmet of salvation on his head;
and he put on garments of vengeance for clothing;
and wrapped himself in zeal as a garment.
18. According to men's deeds so will he repay;
wrath to his enemies, requital to his foes.
To the coastlands he will render requital.
19. And they from the west shall fear the name of the Lord;
and they from the rising of the sun, his glory.
And he shall come like a pent-up stream,
which the wind of the Lord drives.
20. And he will come to Zion as Redeemer,
and to those in Jacob who turn from transgression, says the Lord.
21. "And as for me, this is my covenant with them, says the Lord: My spirit, which is upon you, and my words which I have put in your mouth, they shall not depart out of your mouth, or out of the mouth of your children, or out of the mouth of your children's children, says the Lord, from this time forth and even forevermore."

Verses 15, 16. The two sections just examined — the resultant moral confusion and the frank confession — constituted an ugly enough picture in themselves for any one who viewed the state of affairs soberly. How much more so would that have been the case if the Lord scrutinized what is going on. The situation constituted an emergency that might seem to drive any right-minded man to step forth to do what could be done to set things right. God's reaction is now described. Humanly speaking many might have been expected to intervene. But on closer inspection there is found to be such a measure of downright indifference that it was enough to astound the Almighty (v. 16a). He feels he must himself enter the arena and use his own arm. At this point "righteousness" would seem to remind us that where men have done everything wrong, He, the impeccable and entirely faultless One, appears on the scene as an adequate deliverer.

Verses 17, 18 pictures how the well-armed warrior prepares himself for the conflict. His righteousness as a breastplate renders him, so to speak, invulnerable. His whole person radiates "salvation," which is likened to his helmet. Since all who oppose his plans and purposes are his enemies and deserve to have his vengeance strike them, he is pictured as clothed in vengeance. Nor can he be thought of as engaging in his task languidly. "Zeal" envelopes him. He works his deliverance wholeheartedly. Nor will he do his work in blind zeal but whatever is inflicted on enemies will have been fully merited. It is a bit difficult in v. 18 to define clearly who are the "enemies" and who the "foes." Perhaps the two terms cover all men who oppose themselves to his laudable purposes. As the term "coastlands" comes into the picture it brings in also the far-distant areas that lie to the west — the Mediterranean shorelands. The Lord appears as *warrior* also in 42:13; 49:24 f.; 52:9.

Verse 19. But enough of that negative side of the picture! Positive results will also be attained. Men who do not wilfully oppose him, when they behold his deeds will be taught a reverent fear of God. Others will see in what he does a display of divine glory. But the Lord himself shall carry on his work like "a pent-up stream, which the wind of the Lord drives." That is to say, with irresistible power.

Verse 20. But for Zion it will appear time and again that his is the attitude of a Redeemer. And *that*, all penitent souls shall experience, i.e., those who "turn from transgression." This is a promise that has met with fulfilment for the Old Testament church many a time and for the Zion of the New Testament times without number. This theophany is reminiscent of the many theophanies recorded in the Scriptures (40:5; 60:1, 2; 66:18, 19, etc.). In Rom. 11:27 Paul gives a Messianic interpretation of the passage.

Verse 21. So vv. 15b-20 offered a description how the Lord finds that he must deal with his enemies that afflict his people. He will be stern but just. But now once again he gives a brief account of how much differently he will deal with his own people and the generations following. All his dealings are covered by the term "covenant," which embodies the mercies that he has time and again promised to them. Here the substance of the covenant is set forth in two terms, "my spirit and . . . my words." The concept spirit is practically synonymous with power, strength in the inner man. This promise met with its richest fulfilment on Pentecost. "Words" here seems to connote cheerful testimony, for it is said, "my words . . . shall not depart out of your mouth." It must be admitted that on the Old Testament level, spirit and words are an unusual combination. But both belong together and amount to spirit-filled testimony. Not only in a momentary fulfilment will this be the case, but as the generations roll on, such testimony will be characteristic of God's people "from this time forth and even forevermore."

Viewed thus v. 21 is not a loose editorial addition or a more or less vague gloss. It closes a unified chapter in an effective way.

Notes

Verse 2. The word for face, *panim*, strangely appears without the article. The versions (*LXX, Syriac, Targum*) have added a suffix (*his* face), which is probably the correct reading.

Verse 3. The form *nego'alu* is pointed both as *niph'al* and as *pu'al*, take it either way; the sense is about the same.

Verse 4. The infinitives absolute in 4b, describe what is being universally done.

Verse 7. The alliteration in *shodh washebher* is reproduced by Fisher as *Verderben und Sherben*.

Verse 11. Some suggest that the text may be improved by the following sequence: v. 11, 12, 15b, 16-20. Nothing is gained by this approach.

Verse 12. The verb *'anethah* appears in the singular with a plural subject, "sins," as is sometimes the case with feminine nouns which are plurals of abstraction. See *GK* 145 h.

Verse 13. Again the infinitives absolute are used to describe things which are universally done, as above in v. 4. The words for "conceiving and uttering" should perhaps be pointed differently, again as two infinitives absolute (*haro* and *hago*). The verb for "pushed into a corner" *hussagh* is a *hophal* from *sugh*.

Verse 19. The first word "and they shall fear" should be left as it is, coming from *yare'* (to fear). To substitute a form from *ra'ah* (to see) results in a meaningless phrase: to see the name of the Lord.

Chapter LX

E. ZION'S FUTURE GLORY (Chap. 60)

There is a world of difference between this chapter and the preceding. The mood of Chap. 59 is dull and gloomy. The situation involved is depressing. Chapter 60 breathes high hopes. It moves on a high level of poetic beauty and ardor. Great expectations are expressed, involving earthly prosperity and blessings. Or, as some have put it, economic prosperity rather than political are held up in prospect. But there is not a single note of world domination on the part of Israel.

The attitude of the foreign nations to Israel is much improved from what sometimes is sketched by the prophets. Hostility toward Israel is vanished. The nations are bringing their best treasures and are freely laying them at Israel's door. Strange as it may seem, there is no special act of deliverance expected or promised. But it might be said that such an act is presupposed. It strikes us as unnecessarily derogatory when *Duhm*, attempting to catch the spirit of this chapter, suggests that the prophet starts out on a lofty flight, then tires somewhat, and continues limping along in a prosy, repetitious style. Obviously no writer is able to move on the same high level uninterruptedly. We are safe in claiming inspired utterance for the author. The chapter is a literary unit, and bears evidence of careful composition.

No two writers arrive at the same results when they outline the chapter; but it must also be admitted that in the spirit of diversity of approach many outlines come to strikingly similar conclusions.

1. A Summons to Zion to Greet the Light that Is Dawning upon Her (vv. 1-2).

60:1-2 1. Arise, shine forth, for your light has come,
and the glory of the Lord has risen upon you.
2. For, lo, darkness covers the earth,
and a heavy cloud, the people.
But upon you the Lord rises as the sun,
and his glory is being seen upon you.

Verses 1, 2. Imagine the whole earth wrapped in total darkness. Imagine Zion, the Old Testament church, also as being overcome by this darkness of hopelessness. Then of a sudden to her, and her only, the glory of the Lord flares up. It is as though the day had dawned with the abrupt rising characteristic of the Oriental sun. This sun is God's heavenly glory, this glory of which Isaiah speaks so frequently (cf. 6:3; 24:23; 40:5; 58:8), this glory which some have called the central theme of the chapter. The vision goes on to show that the rest of the world is still shrouded in darkness (v. 2): "darkness covers the earth, and a heavy cloud the people." Zion at least can see where she is going. She can arise and be about her tasks. She is the only one to whom the light has come; the "upon you" is in emphatic position in Hebrew. Zion has been singularly favored.

Historically, what has happened? The prophet dramatically pictures the moment when Israel's liberation from Babylonian Captivity takes place, as though it had been one great burst of glory. The "light" spoken of is Israel's salvation, as is also the case in 58:8; 59:9. A salvation which took years and centuries is pictured as a sudden and instantaneous event. Viewed in spiritual perspective, all its glory is concentrated in a flash of glory: "his glory is being seen upon you."

2. What Men Are Bringing to Zion from the West and from the East (vv. 3-9)

60:3-9 3. And nations are coming to your light,
and kings to the brightness that has risen upon you.
4. Look about you on every side and see:
all these have assembled together, they come to you.
Your sons are coming from afar,
and your daughters are being borne on the hip.

5. Then you shall look and be radiant,
　　and your heart shall be in awe and expand in joy;
for the wealth of the sea is being directed to you,
　　and the rich resources of the Gentiles shall come to you.
6. Camels in throngs shall cover your land;
　　young camels from Midian and Ephah;
all those from Sheba shall come;
　　and gold and frankincense shall they bring,
and gladly declare the praises of the Lord.
7. All the flocks of Kedar shall be gathered to you,
　　the rams of Nebaioth shall minister to you.
They shall come up for acceptance to your altar,
　　and I will glorify my glorious house.
8. Who are these that fly like a cloud,
　　as doves to their windows?
9. Indeed, the coastlands wait eagerly for me,
　　and the ships of Tarshish first in order,
to bring your sons from far,
　　together with their silver and gold
for the name of the Lord your God,
　　and for the Holy One of Israel;
because he has glorified you.

Verse 3. The picture, or the motion-picture, expands. Zion is, as it were, rubbing her eyes and beginning to take notice. The Lord, or perhaps his prophet, is standing by her side, calling her attention to notable things that appear. People are coming, streaming in from afar, bearing gifts. The light at Zion has attracted them, the only bright spot on the whole earth's horizon. Already it is becoming apparent not only that "nations" are on the march but also "kings."

Verse 4. In fact, they are streaming in "on every side." First they congregate in groups preparatory for setting out to Zion and its holy hill. Among those that come, some are already discernible that are especially dear to her — "your sons and your daughters." By some strange magic they can be distinguished though they are still at a great distance. The little ones among her daughters that cannot travel far are being "borne on the hip," a typical Oriental mode of carrying children. These are children whose parents had apparently been led away into some Western captivity.

Verse 5. Now the prophet, who is addressing Zion, points

out to her what happy emotions are being engendered by this experience. Looking, she becomes "radiant." Her "heart," here the center of the higher emotions, is filled with the awesomeness of the experience and "expands in joy." Lesser values, but still important, are being detected as constituting a notable part of what is being transported, "the wealth of the sea and . . . rich resources of the Gentiles." The first of these may well be wealth gained by commerce, which goes largely by way of the sea. The second includes all the things that the Gentiles call precious. They are bringing their best as tribute to Zion.

Verse 6. Zion's attention is drawn to the areas that lie to the east of her. That being mostly desert land, caravans have come from there, throngs of them. First of all from Midian, where camel-Bedouins are to be found, people who had originally lived mostly to the east of the Gulf of Aqaba. Together with them are people from Ephah, an allied tribe (cf. Gen. 25:4). Now another half-turn and Zion is looking to the south, to the land of Sheba in southern Arabia. This is a land famous for its gold, which in this instance the caravans have brought, together with frankincense. All these are at the same time proclaiming the praises of the Lord, as do, for that matter, all people who have gathered in this large company; for they have all come to know the God of Israel and the knowledge of him has made them glad.

Verse 7. All this economic wealth of one kind or another that has been brought, is further increased by "flocks of Kedar" — an area that lay between Arabia Petraea and Babylonia. So Kedar gave its best. So too Nebaioth, another Arabian tribe descended from Ishmael (Gen. 25:13). This nomadic tribe was famous for its rams. The expression "rams shall minister to you" means: They shall do so by ministering to your worship needs, as it is also explained: "They shall come up for acceptance to your altar." This figure is a bit overbold, for it ascribes to the rams willing self-surrender that they might be offered in sacrifice. A slight allowance may be made for poetic exaggeration. But this much is sure, ample provision shall be made for the cultus at Zion. All these factors will contribute to a glory in worship that shall be impressive.

Verse 8. At this point Zion, now wide awake, begins to review the situation, turning back again to the West. A moving cloud seems to be sweeping toward the Holy City. In reality these are ships with their white sails swiftly moving toward Zion. In the distance they are not at once clearly discernible. The Lord has been speaking and continues to speak putting the question that is uppermost in Zion's mind: "What are these . . .?" By a somewhat attractive figure the sails of the ships give the impression of doves flying to the windows of their cotes.

Verse 9. At first glance there appears to be a sort of break in the continuity of the thought, especially as far as the first line of this verse is concerned. Having turned first to the East and then to the West, then back again to the East, it is as though the speaker (the prophet speaking in God's name) remembered that he had not yet indicated what it was that was causing such a stir among people the world over. He supplies the answer: "Indeed, the coastlands wait earnestly for me." It is the natural hunger on the part of man for contact with the living God. The "coastlands" refers to all lands adjacent to the Mediterranean. Now, on with the marvelous story of people and things streaming in toward Zion! Leading the way across the Mediterranean come the "ships of Tarshish," the technical name for the largest sea-going vessels (Tarshish is the name for smelteries in Spain). These huge vessels bring a double cargo — precious metals and a human cargo, scattered "sons" from far countries, children once dragged into captivity by some now unknown foe. At this point the author feels impelled to ascribe the whole movement in all its parts to Yahweh, the God of Israel and the only God, giving a theocentric motivation. This great stir and commotion is in the last analysis being caused "for the name of the Lord," Israel's God. It tends to the glorification of the "Holy One of Israel." Incidentally it is also tended to glorify the holy people of God.

3. The Attitude of Those Who Are Coming to Zion (vv. 10-12)

60:10-12 10. Foreigners shall build your walls, and even kings shall minister to you.
For in my wrath I smote you,
but in my favor I have had mercy upon you.
11. And your gates shall stand open continually;
neither by day nor by night shall they be shut;
that men may bring in to you the wealth of the Gentiles,
with their kings led in procession.
12. For the nation and the kingdom that shall not serve you shall perish,
and those nations shall be utterly destroyed.

Verse 10. According to vv. 3-9 nations with gifts were flocking in from every side. Now in vv. 10-12 the Lord probes deeper to determine the motives behind their coming. Attention first centers upon the Holy City. Building projects are under way here. On closer inspection it appears that the builders are foreigners. Traditionally foreigners were hostile to Israel; they were the ones who had destroyed the walls and the city. Now they are seen to be builders of the walls themselves. Even more than that, kings are offering their services in any need that Israel may have. 49:23 has this thought in slightly different form. If it be asked what is the moving force behind this friendly attitude on the part of so many toward Israel? the answer is, the Lord's attitude has undergone a change in reference to his people. He had been angry, and justly so, over against his ancient people. They on their part have now changed. So he can again show mercy to them (cf. 54:7). Again the Lord is the sole author of all good that may come to Israel.

Verse 11. The highly poetic and picturesque description of the nation's state and condition is again resumed. It is true, the emphasis is rather strong on material blessings. But they too come from God and are tokens of his good will.

Here the stress is on such a stream of "wealth of the Gentiles" that the caretakers do not even get an opportunity to shut the gates through which they flow in: "neither by day nor by night shall they be shut." But note! there is a break in the sequence of what enters. There appears a lone figure, a king, yea, several kings, who apparently, have willingly joined the procession to bring themselves and their goods as token of fealty to the Great King. It appears that they both come willingly and are also led with marks of great respect by those who are in charge of the proceedings.

Verse 12. Repeatedly, like in v. 10b, an effort is being made to trace some of these surprising happenings back to their ultimate cause. One principle — and to tell the truth — it is one that strikes a momentary harsh and solemn note, may profitably be regarded at this point. It is this: when God begins his dealings with the nations, trying to induce them to appropriate Israel's blessings to themselves, issues are dead in earnest. The nations that refuse to serve the King of kings "shall be utterly destroyed." This verse is not a misfit. It is not uncalled for. It does not grow out of a misunderstanding of the tone of the passage. It is a warning side-light and a wholesome one. As *von Orelli* rightly says: "A nation's welfare depends on whether it submits to Israel," or to Israel's God.

4. The Attitude toward Worship Displayed by Those Who Are Coming to Zion (vv. 13-17)

60:13-17 13. The glory of Lebanon shall come to you,
the cypress, the ash, and the fir tree;
to make the place of my sanctuary beautiful,
to glorify the place where my feet stand.
14. And the sons of those who oppressed you, shall come, bowing reverently,
and all that despised you will do worship at the soles of your feet.
And men shall call you the city of the Lord,
the Zion of the Holy One of Israel.
15. Instead of being forsaken and hated, and no one passing through,

I shall make you an eternal excellency,
a joy for generation after generation.
16. You shall suck the milk of the nations,
even the breast of kings shall you suck.
And you shall know that I, the Lord, am your Savior,
and that your Redeemer is the Mighty One of Jacob.
17. Instead of bronze I shall bring gold,
and instead of iron I shall bring silver;
and instead of wood, bronze; and instead of stones, iron.
I shall make peace your government,
and righteousness your ruler.

Verse 13. Beginning with v. 13 the sanctuary at Zion becomes the center of interest. The very structure shall be glorious. The attitude of all men, natives and foreigners, shall be one of deep reverence when they think in terms of Israel's sanctuary. The most beautiful and costly building materials will not only be used for the structure, but shall even come of their own volition, to use a figure of hyperbole. "The glory of Lebanon" refers, of course, to the famous cedars. It must be conceded that when cedars are mentioned and also cypress, ash and fir trees, these could be thought of as planted in the temple area as objects of beauty. Perhaps it is best to allow for both possibilities, construction materials and ornamental trees. They all have conspired, as it were, to make a beautiful sanctuary, or "to glorify the place where [his] feet stand." For surely the Lord may be thought of as having taken his stand in his own sanctuary to be present among his people (cf. also Ezek. 43:7).

Verse 14. Now for a quick glance at an assembled worship-congregation. The strange sight presents itself that the very children of those who once were Israel's oppressors have come of their own volition, "bowing reverently," even, for that matter, the very ones that once despised lowly Israel "will do worship at the soles of [her] feet." The superior character of Israel's religion will be generally admitted. In reverent prostration in the sanctuary they will come to lie at the feet of Israelite worshippers and think it an honor to be allowed to worship there. The holy city itself shall be called by holy titles such as "the city of the Lord, the Zion of the Holy One of Israel."

Verse 15. There was a time when Zion was "forsaken and hated and no one passing through." No one sought contact with the forsaken city. That shall no longer be the case. Instead she shall be "an eternal excellency." That is to say, an object of pride, and joy for generation after generation.

Verse 16. This verse may be briefly summed up in a statement like this: In that glorious future that is to come only the best will be good enough for Israel. Zion is likened to a nursing child, who feeds on the choicest products of the nations. Only persons of highest station shall be deemed good enough for such services for Israel. Israel shall then be aware of the fact that it is the Lord who has wrought this changed attitude on the part of those who once were hostile to her. The names here given to the Lord as a result seem to stand in a sort of climax: Savior, Redeemer, Mighty One of Jacob (cf. 49:26b).

Verse 17. In the first three lines of the verse it may well be that two passages from past history are in the background of the thinking of the speaker. One, I Kings 10:14, 17, 22, 27, which reminds us of the abundance of precious metals which was available for Israel in Solomon's reign. So shall it be once again. The second, I Kings 14:26 f., telling of the humiliation that came on Rehoboam after the sack of Jerusalem by the Egyptians, how bronze shields were placed in the sanctuary as substitutes for the golden shields that had made the temple glorious in Solomon's day. Our passage indicates that the reverse of that humiliating experience shall come in the latter days. So the precious building materials shall take the place of the inferior. Of course, all this cannot take place before the glorious consummation of all things. Then in the last two lines of v. 17 the subject changes: The effective and perfect administration of government is stated in terms rich and glorious but which almost defy definition and paraphrase. "Peace" shall occupy the chief seat in government and so wars will become impossible; and in domestic rule all will be well for "righteousness" shall sit enthroned.

5. The Higher Level of Life in Evidence in the New Jerusalem (vv. 18-22)

60:18-22 18. Violence shall no more be heard of in your land,
nor destruction and ruin in your borders.
You shall call your walls Salvation,
and your gates Praise.
19. The sun shall be no more your light by day,
neither for brightness shall the moon give light to you.
But the Lord will be your everlasting light,
and your God your glory.
20. Your sun shall no more go down,
neither shall your moon wane;
for the Lord will be your everlasting light
and your days of mourning shall be ended.
21. Your people shall all be righteous;
forever shall they possess the land,
the shoot of my planting, the work of my hands.
that I might be glorified.
22. The least one shall become a clan,
and the smallest one a mighty nation
I, the Lord, will hasten it in due time.

Verse 18. The drawing of the highly idealized picture of Zion is coming to a close. Every city from days of old has had its criminal element. This Holy City shall be an exception. There would usually be those who wrought "ruin and destruction" in periodic outbreaks of "violence." Not so in the Jerusalem which shall come down from heaven. Two notable component parts shall be in evidence in this city, "Salvation" and "Praise." The first of these may be thought of as a protective wall, the second, as her sturdy protective gates. Here it may be pointed out that strangely the most important factor is still missing — the Messiah. He, it may be said now already, will come to the fore prominently in the next chapter.

Verse 19. Sun and moon shall no longer function as they once did, for a higher source of better light shall replace them, a point which is taken in hand by John in Revelation

21:23 and 22:5. This first part of the verse might have been rendered: You will no longer stand in need of a sun and a moon. For the Lord will condescend to be their light and shall be dwelling perpetually in their midst. Even so wonderful a thing as physical light shall be replaced by an unspeakably more marvelous light.

Verse 20. As the chapter draws to a close, the feature that stood out prominently at the opening of it again comes to the forefront — light. Perhaps more particularly what light stands for in the Old Testament. As *McKenzie* remarks, it symbolizes two things: first the presence of God and secondly salvation. We may well think of these two at this point. This verse emphasizes that there will be no fluctuation of this true light of God's presence, and the city shall glow, as it were, with salvation. To this may be added that light frequently symbolizes joy. Therefore "your days of mourning shall be ended."

Verse 21. But a city is unthinkable without inhabitants. A weighty declaration about the inhabitants is actually given: "Your people shall all be righteous." This thought is not foreign to Isaiah (cf. 53:11). This does not so much appear as a claim of irreproachable conduct, as a declaration that a righteousness above reproach is to be imputed to them through faith, as 53:11 also signifies. In addition, long-time possession of the Land of Promise is alluded to in the words: "Forever shall they possess the land," reminding ourselves that more precisely the Hebrew word "forever" does not necessarily mean "eternity," but time long drawn out (German: *unabsehbar*). This would be in fulfillment of the promise already given to Abraham (Gen. 17:8). The two phrases "the shoot of my planting" and "the work of my hands" modify the noun "people." The people will be like a tender fruitful shoot planted with loving care by the Lord, and giving promise of much fruit. Besides they will not be people strong in self-sufficiency, but strong because the Lord gave them strength: his hands made them sturdy.

Verse 22. Wholesome growth in numbers is also promised,

unimportant individuals growing into clans and mighty nations. All these are objectives which the Lord has set for himself and will achieve in due time. Great as this promise is, it may be questioned whether this is the climax of climaxes, as had been claimed. Quite appropriately Isa. 9:7 may be compared, as another significant pronouncement, attributing all success to the Lord.

Notes

Verse 1. We have translated the verb *zarach* as a perfect in English, well aware of the fact that some commentators regard this as a prophetic perfect, i.e., a future. The issue is as long as it is broad; the event is regarded as having practically occurred.

Verse 2. We regard the article before "darkness" as a clear case of dittography. Cf. *KS* 297 b.

Verse 14. "Bowing reverently" is really an infinitive construct used as an infinitive absolute; cf. *KS* 221.

Chapter LXI

F. GOOD NEWS FOR ZION (Chap. 61)

Note the progression of thought in the last few chapters. Chapter 58, "Abuses that retarded the recovery of post-exilic Israel"; the fault of slow recovery lay at Israel's door. Chapter 59, "The hand of the Lord is not shortened to save;" his power is omnipotent. Chapter 60, "Zion's future glory"; heavy emphasis on the glories of the Messianic age. There is an obvious forward movement of thought. But Chap. 60 left one thought completely out of the picture — the Great Messianic King. Chapter 61 brings Him on the scene. He introduces himself and his work in the monologue with which this chapter opens.

But it has long been a matter of controversy whether the speaker at the beginning of Chap. 61 is the *prophet* (Isaiah — some would have it to be a so-called Deutero-Isaiah, some even a so-called Trito-Isaiah) or whether he is the *Messiah* himself, in the light of Luke 4:18, 19. We take the position that the latter is the case, the Messiah is speaking; and that for the following reasons. In describing the work that he is commissioned to perform, the speaker assigns such significant achievements to himself that one might well question whether any human being could ever venture to deal with and accomplish issues so grand and wonderful. In the mouth of the Savior the tasks he claims as assigned to him are most fitting and proper. Here the word applies: "Man never spoke like this man." If the prophet had claimed such notable achievements for himself he might well have been charged with having a most highly exaggerated opinion of himself.

Add to this the obvious fact that in the second half of his book Isaiah keeps himself modestly in the background; then this sudden outburst of self-assertion strikes us as most inappropriate.

We grant that in the position we take we are identifying the speaker with the Suffering Servant of 42:1, etc. We must also freely admit that our chapter does not mention the term "Servant," but preconceived notions on our part of the terms to be used will hardly settle the issue. Though *G. A. Smith* boldly claims that it is a minor question to whom this passage was intended to first apply, we can hardly concur. We regard the passage as directly Messianic prophecy, and must believe all other attempts to meet with fulfillment to be inadequate. So after Zion's future glory has been dealt with, the chapter following presents him who brings this glory to pass. Or to word the case somewhat differently, as some do, Chap. 60 speaks more of the outward glory of Zion, Chap. 61, of her inner glory. With equal propriety it may be claimed that the chapter is a message of joy for the grieving community of Israel (*Fischer*). Therefore it is quite uncalled for to combine Chaps. 60 and 62, and to let 61 follow. It may also be noted in passing that in Chaps. 60-62 five passages are quoted verbatim from 40-55.

1. The Messenger Who Brings the Good News (vv. 1-3)

61:1-3 1. The spirit of the Lord God is upon me,
because the Lord has anointed me to bring good tidings to the meek,
he has sent me to bind up the brokenhearted,
  to proclaim liberty to the captives,
    and an opening to them that are bound;
2. to proclaim a year for the Lord to show favor,
  and a day of vengeance for our God;
to comfort all who mourn;
3. to appoint for them that mourn in Zion —
  to give them a headdress instead of ashes,
the oil of gladness instead of mourning,
  a mantle of praise for a spirit of despair;
and they shall be called oaks of righteousness,
  a planting of the Lord with which he may glorify himself.

Verse 1. At once one recalls that the Servant of the Lord was described (42:1) as having as characteristic mark equipment with the spirit of God for the doing of his work. For the Messiah from the line of David this also holds true (11:2). The importance of being equipped with the spirit for doing the work of the Lord is also attested by Zech. 7:12; I Sam. 16:14-23; II Sam. 23:1-7. How proper it is to be thus equipped appears also from the fact that the spirit of the Lord and power are synonymous. Even the preposition "upon" is significant; it conveys the thought that the spirit comes down from on high. This spirit then is the strong taproot of the life and being of the one who speaks. And when was there ever a one so uniquely endowed with the spirit as to warrant his bearing the name of the "Christ" — the truly anointed one. The significant word "anointed" at once appears in the text to indicate that there was a significant act of imparting the spirit, a procedure found quite commonly when men were inducted in office. Here, since most of the activities described have to do with the *word*, it is the *prophetic* office for which the spirit is given.

In an ecstatic gush of eloquent terms the multiplicity of tasks that fall to the Messiah's lot are recited, all of them flowing from, and growing out of, the fact that a generous anointing has been bestowed upon him. Six infinitives and numerous objects of these infinitives are employed. The first gracious activity that he engages in, is really the sum of them all and in a sense the source of all that follow. It is found in the words "to bring good tidings to the meek." This stands first in emphatic position here, even as it stands last in emphatic position in Christ's statement to John (Matt. 11:5). Of all the gracious work that the Savior did, none was more important and more all-inclusive than this. The expression at the same time defines who will be the recipients of this good news — "the meek," i.e., persons whose hearts have been rendered receptive by God's prevenient grace. Such will humbly accept rebuke and gladly embrace God's gracious pardon, and so will be saved. The many forms that this grace will take are now unfolded in detail, showing how many-sided God's grace is.

There follows a list of grievous disabilities that men may become afflicted with. They fall into the categories of the physical, the mental, and the spiritual ills that afflict the children of men and from which they cannot deliver themselves. The second kind of relief listed, for which this Deliverer is sent, is "to bind up the brokenhearted." This can include all that are deeply grieved over their sins as well as those that have been all but crushed by life's adversities. To this is to be added "to proclaim liberty to the captives." In this class may be found those who are socially bound by some unhappy lot. In the background of this statement there would seem to be a reference to Lev. 25:10, in which passage the fiftieth year of jubilee was to be proclaimed throughout the land. Some render the next achievement listed as being "the opening of the prison," in which case wholesale deliverance of criminals can hardly be thought of. Our rendering, omitting the word "prison," is somewhat broader and does imply deliverance of the innocent.

Verse 2. The next two lines may be approached in two different ways: first, the contrast between "year" and "day" may be stressed as of a ratio, as it were, between 365 and 1, asserting then that "favor" will be superabundant, but "vengeance" will be exacted only as much as must be. A similar ratio to stress God's loving kindness is employed in Exod. 20:5, 6. Secondly, there is the approach which construes the term "vengeance" positively as "restoration of wholeness." Aside from the fact that there clearly are cases where the Hebrew root carries the meaning of "punitive justice" and the further fact that God's vengeance is not tainted by a spirit of unwholesome retribution, we consider the familiar meaning of the term as too well established to allow for the precarious meaning of "vengeance." These two lines then, taken together, make a strong declaration of grace abounding.

The last line asserts as one of the expressed objectives of

the Messiah's mission "to comfort all who mourn." This is a common thought in Trito-Isaiah, so called, over against Deutero-Isaiah, so called, who never expresses this thought. Using New Testament terminology, this comfort consists chiefly in the forgiveness of sins, though this message bestows other forms of comfort as well.

Verse 3. Dwelling still on what this speaker can give to mourners, the speaker asserts that his mission includes relief for those who "mourn in Zion," most welcome relief. The wholesome mourning over sins is under consideration here. Another possibility is available: the words may be translated ". . . those who mourn *over* Zion." Then the consolation available deals with the persons who grieve over the sins and shortcomings of the people of God. But that there is much need of administering comfort to men is obvious. Not only is the cause for grief overcome, but a positive ground for joy is offered — here: "a headdress in place of ashes." In place of a disconsolate mourner seated on an ash-heap, strewing ashes on his head, there is the figure of a man arranging a gaily-colored turban as his headdress for a festive occasion. The contrast tells its own story. Wholesome joy is made available. An analogous figure — instead of a mourning-robe, perhaps sackcloth, a man is given a precious and fragrant perfume to cover himself with. The same thought virtually is expressed by a new figure to which the speaker quickly turns: there is to be given "a mantle of praise for a spirit of despair." This illustration grows out of the fact that a man may, so to speak, wrap himself in his moods, like the mood of "despair." Instead, grace is given to him to be enshrouded completely in "praise." The favors bestowed by the speaker make him so joyful that his mouth overflows with vocal praise.

Summing all up, those men, to whom God's grace has been administered, now stand, to borrow a figure from the vegetable kingdom, as sturdy trees abounding in healthy foliage. These persons are "sturdy living symbols of salvation" (cf. Ps. 1:1; 92:13 f.). Carrying the figure a bit farther, they may be thought of as trees planted by the care of the Lord's hands, trees which he has set out for the glory of his name. Whether the tree-name should be translated as "oaks" or as "terebinths" is not yet determined with finality.

2. A Nation Fulfilling Its Destiny by Accepting This Good News (vv. 4-7)

61:4-7 4. Men shall build places long lying waste,
 desolate spots where ancients lived of old.
They shall build anew waste cities,
 places that had been desolate for generations.
5. Strangers shall stand alert and pasture your flocks;
 aliens shall be your plowmen and vinedressers.
6. But you shall be called priests of the Lord,
 and men shall refer to you as ministers of our God.
You shall consume the wealth of the nations,
 and of their riches you shall boast.
7. Instead of your shame you shall be doubly rewarded,
 and instead of your ignominy you shall exult
 over what was their good fortune.
Therefore in their territory you shall possess a double lot.

Verse 4. The healing quality of the good news just described shall transform those who accept it. No individual, no nation can fulfill its destiny without accepting this news. That means among other things that in such a nation there will be no waste places, no desolate spots. Even areas that had once been inhabited but had long become proverbial ruins. In fact now everything flourishes. Even cities that had been so completely destroyed, so that it seemed useless to attempt to rebuild them are to be restored, no matter how long they have lain in ruins. The reference does not seem to be to the restoration from Babylonian-Captivity ruins; rather it tells how successful every national enterprise will be.

Verse 5. Going into another area of national life, the relation of the nation to those who were traditionally hostile, the acceptance of the good news will there too make all things new. Not that the former enemies will have been subdued or conquered but they shall have come in a spirit of cheerful cooperation so as to take the more menial tasks off Israel's hands that the people whom God had once chosen as his own might more effectively fulfill its spiritual destiny. The strangers shall pasture Israel's flocks, as it were, and aliens shall take care of the field work. All this is highly idealized description which the world will not see until there be a new heaven and a new earth, where all is right. But the gospel carries such vast potential, if room is only made for it.

Verse 6. The spiritual aspect of the glorious state which is here held in prospect is now detailed more fully. God had already said to Moses that Israel was destined to be "a kingdom of priests" (cf. Exod. 19:6). What the priesthood was for Israel, that Israel shall be to the nations. To what extent the "spiritual Israel" of the New Testament times may be involved is almost impossible to say, but in some very positive way Israelites will be "ministers of our God." Besides, in a way that we can hardly conceive of, God's people will live off the wealth of the nations, and Israel shall be able to boast of the riches of the Gentiles as though they were their own. The highly idealized level of thought must be maintained and nothing cheap or mercenary dare be imputed to this description, as *Volz* does when he claims that all that is said at this point is not exactly a "refreshing portrayal of Israel's faith in its specific election."

Verse 7. The somewhat exuberant tone of the description of the nation fulfilling its destiny continues. Whereas in times past Israel was often but lightly esteemed among the nations, her good name is to be fully restored. Israel shall reap where others have sowed.

3. God's Hand in Evidence (vv. 8-9)

61:8-9 8. For I the Lord love righteousness,
I hate robbery with transgression;
and I will faithfully give them their recompense,
and an everlasting covenant will I make with them.
9. Their descendants shall be known among the nations,
and their offspring in the midst of the peoples;
All who see them shall acknowledge them,
for they are descendants whom the Lord has blessed.

Verse 8. The Lord now speaks. The marvelous transformation of the nation is traced back to him and particularly to the fact that he loves and upholds fair play, here referred to as "righteousness." When Israel was led away into Captivity by the Babylonians there was many a deed of wanton cruelty laid upon them. They were deprived of their rights as normal human beings. This is here called "robbery with transgression." And this the Lord who watches over, and rules, all nations, hates and is now in the present restoration and in the coming future perfect restoration going to uphold righteousness and vindicate his people. In this sense he will "faithfully give them their recompense." So he will vindicate his "covenant" which he made with his people at Mt. Sinai (cf. 59:21).

Verse 9. Since one aspect of a thriving and successful people is numerous population the prophet develops this aspect of the case, tracing the development of this blessing to the Lord. The descendants of Israel instead of being ill-spoken of among the nations, shall "be known," i.e., "famous" (*Jerusalem Bible*). Men will "acknowledge," not slight them. Men will recognize that the blessing of the Lord is upon them. In the light of the rest of the Scriptures, this cannot be thought of apart from their acceptance of the Christ and his salvation.

4. The Nation's Joy at the Lord's Blessing (vv. 10-11)

61:10-11   10. I will greatly rejoice in the Lord,
        my soul shall be glad in my God;
for he has clad me with garments of salvation,
        he has covered me with the robe of righteousness,
as a bridegroom decks himself with the fine care of a priest,
        as a bride decks herself for her wedding.
11. For as the earth puts forth its sprouts,
        and as a garden makes the things sown in it to shoot forth,
so the Lord God will make salvation and praise
        to sprout before all the nations.

Verse 10. After describing a choice number of great blessings that the Lord will bestow upon his penitent people, the text breaks forth into an exclamation of joy over the rich grace of God — which is most appropriate and fits most aptly into the text at this point. The speaker is the nation, or Zion. Summing up all the great things promised and using a new figure, the nation describes itself as having been clad by God in spendid robes ("garments of salvation, robe of righteousness") using terms that are reserved in the New Testament for gifts like justification through faith. A very choice figure to cover the case is used by reference to how bridegroom and bride adorn themselves for their wedding day. This, on the part of the bridegroom, is likened to the meticulous care employed by the priest as he equips himself for the performance of his sacred duties (cf. Exod. 29:5-9; Zech. 3: 4 f.). For the high point of joy marked by the wedding day, see Ps. 19:5; Jer. 33:11; Rev. 21:2; Matt. 22:2.

Verse 11. Since the Lord often seems to accomplish work in a tardy fashion, the prophet indicates that a powerful drive and forward surge marks the Lord's carrying out of his purposes. It is like the thrust in the realm of nature when in spring vegetation bursts into bud and flower. Just as certainly as spring brings the impulse for growth and sprouting, just so surely will the Lord's plans for Israel eventuate. In other words "salvation" and "praise" for this salvation will burst into evidence in the sight of all the nations.

Notes

Verse 1. "Lord God" is slightly inaccurate as translation, since *Yahweh* is regularly translated as Lord and so is *'adhonay*. But "Lord Lord" is most objectionable. Therefore "Lord God."

Verse 2. To gain the thought "*a* year" the Hebrew inserts a *le* — sign of the dative. Cf. *KS* 280 n. The last three words of the verse could be prefixed to v. 3, chiefly for the sake of a better Hebrew verse, as the *Kittel* text has it.

Verse 3. Having said "appoint," after a pause the writer resumes with "to give" as a more appropriate verb. In the expressions "oil of gladness" and "mantle of praise" we have two genetives of apposition (oil which *is* gladness, etc.). Cf. *KS* 337 l.

Verse 8. The expression "robbery with transgression" constitutes a sort of superlative, and is more easily understood than "robbery for burnt offering" (KJ). The *Septuagint* also reads "with transgression" a reading for which the text allows.

Verse 10. The verb "decks himself with the fine care of a priest" is a rare and colorful one, and should be retained, although *yakhin* for *yekhahhen* would be permissible.

Chapter LXII

G. THE IMPENDING SALVATION (Chap. 62)

No two writers come up with the same theme and parts on these chapters. Still a measure of unity prevails. An undertone runs through these chapters — God has great things in store for his people; of that he assures and reassures Israel unwaveringly. We might say that in this chapter in particular God testifies to Israel that her salvation is near at hand, long as he may have waited and seemingly delayed.

It does not matter too much into whose mouth the words of this chapter are laid. In days of old they were ascribed to the Lord. Most more recent writers claim that the Prophet is speaking. Even so they attribute the message to the Lord. Ascribing this message directly to the Lord appeals to us most, especially from v. 6 onward. If then at times the Lord would be speaking of himself in the third person, that is a rather common feature in Old Testament prophecy.

If some writers fail to find the deeper things of the prophetic message, things like forgiveness; that is not a serious defect, if a defect at all. Discourse, also prophetic discourse, may with full propriety touch upon the Lord's gifts at their various levels. Pardon and forgiveness are implied even if not expressly treated. To make it obvious that rich prophetic words cannot soon be caught in their richness of meaning by way of outlines, we mention a few titles chosen for this chapter more or less at random. "The Prophet Cries Out for Zion's Salvation" (*Fischer*). "The Messianic People" (*Muilenburg*). "The Progressive Achievement of Jerusalem's Salvation (*Delitzsch*).

1. The Lord's Objectives for His People (vv. 1-5)

62:1-5   1. For Zion's sake I dare not remain inactive,
      and for Jerusalem's sake I dare not merely look on;

328

until her vindication comes forth as a light,
and her salvation as a torch that burns.
2. And nations shall see your vindication,
and all kings your glory;
and you shall be called by a new name,
which the mouth of the Lord shall designate.
3. And you shall be a glorious crown in the Lord's hand,
and a royal diadem on the palm of your God's hand.
4. You shall not any more be called Forsaken [Hebrew: *Azubah*]
and your land shall not any more be referred to as Desolate
[Hebrew: *Shemamah*]
But you shall be called My Delight is in her [Hebrew: *Hephzibah*]
and your land shall be termed Married [Hebrew: *Beulah*]
For the Lord delights in you,
and your land shall be [so to speak] married.
5. For as a young man marries [i.e., takes possession of] a virgin,
so shall your children take possession of you.
and as a bridegroom rejoices over a bride
so shall your God rejoice over you.

Verse 1. We seem to catch the spirit of the passage better
by translating the verb in the imperfect by the use of the
auxiliary "dare." The Lord, for reasons of his own, has apparently been doing nothing by way of furthering Israel's
interests. He dare not continue thus any longer without
creating the impression among the neighboring nations that
he has lost interest in his people. Zion and Jerusalem represent a major investment of his. It is true that God often is
deliberate in his actions. His "mills grind slowly" as the
proverb has it. In his own wise providence the time has come
for her vindication (Hebrew: "righteousness") to be made
manifest. The Lord must furnish visible proof that Israel's
interests are a matter of deep concern. As the Oriental dawn
flashes across the skies suddenly so must Israel's vindication.
Or it must shine forth "as a torch that burns." Isaiah foresaw
a time when Israel's situation would demand divine interfer-
ence. Such periods, demanding intervention come repeatedly, even down to the very end when the consummation of
all things comes to pass.

Verse 2. Such vindication, whether it pertains to Israel of
old, the Old Testament community, or whether it is done in

behalf of the spiritual Israel, will often be done in a most manifest fashion, demonstrating that the Lord has not forgotten his people. "Nations shall see it," "kings shall behold [Israel's] glory." The new situation that shall therefore develop will be so radically different that the old vocabulary will no longer be adequate. A new name must be employed to cover the new situation. That name is not given at this point. It is merely indicated that it will be a matter of divine choice. There are other passages in Scripture in which the new-name concept appears (1:26; Jer. 3:17; 33:16; Ezek. 48:35). These various new names do not rule out one another. They merely supplement each other. Each new name expresses some valid aspect of God's dealings with his people. Even the New Testament deals with this concept (cf. Rev. 2:17; 3:12).

Verse 3. How utterly glorious the people of God shall be when God remakes them is indicated by another attractive illustration: Israel shall be "a glorious crown." This illustration locates the crown in this case, not upon the King's *head*, but in his hand. The Lord is inspecting it, looking at it from different angles. The work of his hands contributes to his glory. The parallel statement says the same thing in other words, but it still has the "diadem" in the Lord's hands.

Verse 4. A few samplings are given of such new names of the Lord's choice. Two negatives are rejected as no longer appropriate. Two positives are added by way of showing how many possibilities are involved. The negatives are "Forsaken" and "Desolate." These two names could once have been aptly applied to her in the days of her Captivity. God abandoned his people and they became desolate. Here he asserts that this shall no more be the case. The word speaks in terms of the ultimate achievement, and is conditioned by Israel's attitude, whether she remains humble and penitent, and continues to hold her faith in the Lord. This verse thinks in terms of an ideal situation.

Two positive names follow. "My Delight is in her" and "Married." God's people shall adopt such an attitude that it provokes his strong delight. He cannot cast her off but will remain married to her. Her infidelity in that case shall not be in evidence: the Lord will not cast her off. That these names are not fantastic or unnatural appears from the fact that the mother of Jehoshaphat bore the name Azubah, i.e., Forsaken (I Kings 22:42), and Manasseh's mother bore the name Hephzibah, i.e., My Delight is in her (II Kings 21:1). All this is reminiscent of 54:1-8 and deals with the same general picture largely taken from married life. In the last line we have inserted the brackets "so to speak," because strictly speaking one cannot be married to a *land*. Still the figure conveys the thought of being strongly attached, and loyal to the people and their land.

Verse 5. To ward off the inferior approach that attributes the Lord's kindly dealings with Israel to a sense merely of obligation, this verse shows the deeper and kindly feelings that are involved. The analogy used as illustration is the warm love displayed by a young man to a virgin. A use of words comes into the picture at this point, because of the double meaning of the Hebrew *ba'al*, which means "marry" and also "take possession of" or "become master of." So the incongruous picture of sons marrying a mother does not appear in the original, but rather the children will fulfill their obligation in the family. To this the second half of the verse adds the note of joy and warm satisfaction that marks the new relation to the Lord, as deep and true as that of a faithful bridegroom. This is the brief sketch of the objectives which God has in store for his own.

2. God to Be Implored to Carry Out His Objectives (vv. 6-7)

62:6-7 6. Upon your walls, O Jerusalem,
I have appointed watchmen.
All the day and all the night
they shall never keep silence.
They are the ones that keep reminding the Lord:
Take no rest.

7. Do not grant him any rest,
   until he establishes Jerusalem
   and makes it famous in the earth.

Verse 6. A new theme is introduced, Watchmen on the walls continually at prayer. Ordinarily watchmen were a safety-device, appointed to guard a city from a surprise attack. Here that feature does not appear. The sole duty of these watchers is "to continue instant in prayer" that Jerusalem be established inwardly and outwardly. It is somewhat difficult to determine the identity of these watchers. Looking at Dan. 4:18 and I Kings 22:19 we might incline to the opinion that they are angels. Since intercessory prayer is not elsewhere noted as a particular function of angels we may prefer to think that the watchmen are faithful prophets of the Lord. Perhaps since nothing definite is asserted on the subject we may hold the opinion that they are merely a means for having faithful and earnest prayer to be made. For "day and night they shall never keep silence." There is something anthropomorphic about it all: if enough persistent prayer is offered God will yield and finally see to it that Jerusalem is re-established. 49:16 presents an analogous point of view from the divine angle. They go too far who deduce from this verse that at the time these words were spoken the walls of Jerusalem had already been rebuilt. Watchmen could stand and offer prayer on ruins of walls. One thing certainly is not intended by these words, that is to create the impression that man could be more concerned about the welfare of the people of God than he himself.

Verse 7. God honors believing prayer and heeds the intercession of his children. The objective of the prayer in this case is twofold: first to "establish Jerusalem," that is to give her inner strength and stability; secondly, "to make her famous in the earth." That means to give her rank and standing in the world, that is commensurate with her spiritual importance. The watchmen are not to rest till both are achieved.

3. Successful Achievement Guaranteed on God's Part (vv. 8-9)

62:8-9 8. The Lord has sworn by his right hand,
and by his powerful arm:
"I will not again give your grain
to be food for your enemies,
and foreigners shall not drink your wine
for which you have toiled.
9. For they who have gathered your grain shall eat it,
and shall praise the Lord.
and they who have gathered your vintage shall drink it,
in my holy courts."

Verse 8. And they that prayed faithfully will not have prayed in vain. The Lord assures them of this by an oath. The oath is not required to make the Lord's word valid, but it is added by the Lord because of the frailty of man's faith (cf. also 45:23; 54:9). The "right" and "powerful arm" are mentioned as the customary gesture accompanying the oath. Surprisingly that which is guaranteed by the oath is more economic in character than spiritual — grain guaranteed and wine. But this must be understood in the light of Deut. 28:30-33, where one of the most striking marks of divine displeasure is the disappointing experience of having one man sow the field and have the enemy come along and reap it. So this word does nothing more than to guaranty tokens of divine approval. These blessings are not exhaustively listed, but are mentioned by way of significant examples. The "foreigners" could be the Persian officials, or even the Samaritans and Edomites.

Verse 9. The success that the Lord will achieve is recounted in some measure of detail. In the second half of the verse the "gathering" of the vintage obviously includes the treading out of the same. One last touch reminds Israel of her high festivals where food and drink were partaken of in the "holy courts" of the Lord, a memorable and happy custom.

4. Israel Invited to Make God's Salvation Her Own (vv. 10-12)

62:10-12 10. Go out, go out through the gates;
prepare the way for the people.
Grade up, grade up the highway;
    clear it of stones;
lift high an ensign over the people.
11. Behold, the Lord has made a proclamation
    to the ends of the earth:
"Tell the inhabitants of Zion:
    'Lo, your salvation is coming
lo, his reward is with him
    and his recompence before him.' "
12. And men shall call them The Holy People,
    the Redeemed of the Lord.
And you shall be called "Sought Out" [Hebrew: *derushah*]
    a city not forsaken.

Verse 10. Repeated imperatives are common to our
prophet — "Go out, go out" (see 40:11; 51:9, 17; 52:1; 57:
14; 65:1). It would seem that this word addresses itself to
those who have stayed behind in some of the cities of the
Captivity. Here the theme of the wonderful road comes into
the picture again (cf. 35:8-10). Add the figure of the ensign, as a sign of invitation for people to congregate. Echoes
of Chap. 40 are beginning to be heard.

Verse 11. To make the invitation to join the assembly
and go up to the holy city more attractive this verse points
to a proclamation emanating from the Lord to the effect that
he himself is coming along this road accompanied by those
who have heeded his call. They are his "reward" and "his
recompense," whom he has won for himself in bitter conflict (cf. 40:10 again).

Verse 12. Another look is cast in the direction of these
people who are coming along this road. They are called by
an old name, the "holy people" or also "the redeemed of the
Lord." They would seem to indicate that more than *Zion's*
children are involved, or even the Jews of the Dispersion;
but all the children of God. All the saints of God down to
the day of the final judgment are envisioned in this scene.
Here comes one last backward glance: She who was for-

saken and abandoned (the ideal Holy City) will be an object of interest and concern. She shall no longer be forsaken.

Notes

Verse 1. An attractive suggestion has been offered inasmuch as this verse speaks of the "coming forth of the *light*," the suggestion that this chapter was spoken originally on the occasion of the festival of booths (cf. John 7:2 and 8:12), where Jesus referred to himself as "the light of the world." The only difficulty is that the abundant use of lights, which was actually associated with this festival at Christ's time hardly seems to have been in use at as early a date as this.

The difficulty of v. 5, where "children take possession" of their parents, which we have interpreted to mean that they fulfill their obligation to their parents, may be met in another way. Many take the consonants *bnykh* and by inserting a new set of vowels arrive at the meaning "thy builders" or singular "thy builder." Especially the singular would in this case refer to the Lord, who, as the builder of Israel takes charge of her.

Verse 6. *Hammazkirim* presents an interesting case of how a participle takes up the line of thought. Cf. *KS* 411 e.

Verse 7. *RSV* makes a rather genial move, quite in keeping with the thought, when it takes the object "Jerusalem" and moves it up into the preceding clause.

Verse 10. The *min* before *'ebhen* conveys the idea that not a single stone remains. *KS* 406 p.

Chapter LXIII

H. ESCHATOLOGICAL UNDERTONES (Chaps. 63—65)

Things are rather loosely woven together in these last chapters of Isaiah. Strict logic does not control the situation. It is difficult to find a unit title for our chapter. Therefore we have chosen the one we have, which could serve as title for the rest of the book. Then we can observe, too, how v. 1-6 may be worked into the picture: they offer a part and aspect of eschatological truth that belongs to a well-rounded treatment of the subject — judgment on God's unrelenting foes. This is an aspect of divine righteousness. For righteousness is a two-sided attribute of God. It deals with blessings and rewards for the faithful servants of the Lord, as well as with stern judgment of the ungodly. These verses (1-6) have been much misunderstood, as though they savored of a spirit of hatred and revenge. Fact of the matter is that the Edomites, wherever they appear on the scene in Scripture are cruelly spiteful and vindictive. Edom's hatred of Israel is proverbial (cf. 34:5-15; Obad. 20 ff.; Ezek. 35:1-15, to list but a few). Therefore we even hesitate to use captions like "The Terrible Treader of the Winepress" (*Volz*), for it could imply that the Almighty had lost control of his anger. These verses involve a stern truth but a wholesome one. Besides, too much stress should not be put on an incidental feature of the passage. It may be said that it speaks not in terms of punishment so much as in terms, seemingly, of destruction. What the passage wants to assert is that God has his foes totally under control, even when they are doing their worst. So *Muilenburg* has spoken well when he classifies the passage as "belonging to the literature of eschatological judgment." He also speaks well when he says that the characteristic style and terminology of the *lament* prevails, although it might be safer to say that some undertones of lament appear in vv. 1-6.

Duhm and those of his class speak in a derogatory fashion of the chapter, insisting that it begins on a high level, but gradually subsides and drops into a weak repetitiousness or even a repulsive overornamentation (*unangenehm wirkender Redeputz*).

Care also should be taken in regard to the Messianic interpretations of vv. 1-6. They look upon the passage as a description of the blood-stained Messiah in his great passion. But the blood is that of his enemies. Furthermore it is a punitive task that is here ascribed to the figure appearing on the scene. There is nothing redemptive about it.

This passage furthermore is very difficult to pin-point as to time and circumstances under which it was first spoken or written. 64:10-12 would seem to point to a date after the fall of Jerusalem and the destruction of the Temple. In that case, according to our conviction that one Isaiah wrote the whole book, Isaiah, the son of Amoz, these chapters would involve prophetic prediction, divinely inspired, revealing what would come to pass and preparing Israel for it.

1. God's Program Includes Vengeance on Edom and on All Like Her (vv. 1-6)

63:1-6   1. Who is this that comes from Edom
       in crimson garments from Bozrah,
he is glorious in his apparel,
    striding along erect in the abundance of his strength?
"It is I who dictate righteousness,
    who abound in ability to help."
2. Why this redness on your garments,
    why are your garments like those of one
       who treads in the wine-press?
3. "I have trodden the wine-press alone
    and no one of the nations was with me.
And I trod them down in my anger
    and stamped them down in my wrath;
and their life-blood spurted on my garments;
    and my whole garment became sullied.

4. For a day of vengeance is in my heart,
   and my year of redemption has come.
5. And I looked out,
   but there was no one who could assist;
   and I was amazed,
   but there was no one to stand by me.
   So my own arm gave me help,
   and my wrath supported me.
6. And I stamped on nations in my anger,
   and I made them drunk in my wrath,
   and let their lifeblood run down to the ground."

Verse 1. The prophet suddenly beholds a majestic figure striding toward him, coming from the direction of the people of Edom. He cannot identify the person approaching. It seems significant that he is definitely coming from the neighboring nation to the south, as though he had had dealings with them. The prophet seems to have suspicions that the one approaching did some punitive work on this southern brother-nation. Another notable feature about this figure, a feature that at first glance stands out, is his blood-bespattered appearance. The garments, though rich and costly, may almost be said to have been dipped in blood — a scene bound to startle any beholder. So the prophet utters a rhetorical question, which expresses his eagerness to identify the one coming on. A third striking thing about the on-coming one is that he strides along like one who has achieved a notable bit of success. His whole bearing emanates success and victory. We must fall back on the totality of Scripture to determine why Edom (also often called the land of Seir) and its one-time capital Bozrah, should be singled out as apparently deserving of exceptional punitive treatment. Then it appears that whenever Edom appears over against Israel, Edom's attitude is one of unyielding, never changing hostility. So Edom is guilty in itself and at the same time a symbol of unreasonable hostility on the part of surrounding nations.

Though the one who answers the question put in v. 1 is not formally introduced as speaking, it is immediately obvious that the one about whom the question was raised is the one who himself supplies the answer. As the chapter progresses it becomes increasingly clear that the one who gives the answer is the Lord. For the present one particular attribute of the Lord is to be stressed. He is the one who "dictates righteousness," that is, speaks with authority, that righteousness may be upheld and prevail throughout the world, an assignment that includes that they who have been wronged are assured of their rights. In this respect he "abounds in ability to help." So this particular function of his might be stated thus: I direct the affairs of history.

As to the *form* in which this section (vv. 1-6) appears, there is hardly enough evidence to arrive at the conclusion that these verses fall into the category of "the sentry's question." The following passages, though they employ the rhetorical question form, may hardly be used as evidence to the contrary (cf. Song of Sol. 3:6; 6:10; 8:5; also Ps. 24:8 and 10).

Verse 2. One item still intrigues the prophet, though he may have been able to form a shrewd guess as to source of the blood that so abundantly stains the garments of the victor, yet to make sure that he is construing rightly what he sees, he addresses him in a clear question: "Why this redness on your garments?" The only one to whom he can liken the man in stained garments is the man who treads the wine-press, an occupation which invariably caused spattering with the blood of the grape. So he puts a direct question: "Why this redness . . . ?" At least twice in the Old Testament, the same figure is employed (Joel 3:13; Lam. 1:15).

Verse 3. The One in the wine-press was the Lord — he accepts the figure as quite proper, but adds a second feature that should be noted: He was "alone." In times past when judgment-work was to be done, especially on Israel, the Lord used other nations (e.g., Egypt, I Kings 14:25 or Assyria, Isa. 10:5 f.). In this case none appear to have been available. So he stresses that works of judgment are, in the last analysis, *his own*. He is the only one qualified for such acts of supreme importance. God's "anger" is a wholesome indignation. It was the motivating force behind his actions. If the account given and the figures used are a bit on the gruesome side, they are no doubt meant to be, for judgment is gruesome business. In reference to Israel the same figure was employed in 59:16.

Verse 4. In the nature of the case, times for such action on God's part are so essential that one may very properly assert that the Lord has a "day of vengeance." These days are in his heart, that is to say, are part and parcel of his plans. But never are features like this stressed unduly. God's vengeance may be said to be held in balance by his "redemption," which also will have its day, and, in fact, in a ratio of 365 to 1 over against vengeance. For where sin abounds, grace does the more abound. This aspect of the case keeps everything wholesome.

Verse 5. This verse describes the Lord very anthropomorphically. He may be likened to a man who is confronted by a tremendous task. In such a situation one almost instinctively looks for men to stand by him. It would seem that his is so clearcut a case of being in the right that there would be many who would flock to his banner to help support a just cause. But there is no volunteer. The Lord must fall back on his own resources exclusively, and these resources are entirely adequate: "(his) arm gave him help and (his) wrath supported him."

Verse 6. In keeping with the approach of the beginning of the chapter a type of description is used that strikes the present-day reader of Scripture as unnecessarily gory and cruel: "nations" thrown into a vat, nations made drunk with the wine of God's wrath, blood running to the ground in streams from the veins of the guilty nations. Not that Hebrew writers, in a spirit of revenge, gloated over the disastrous fate of their adversaries. But judgment is grim business. "Be not deceived, God is not mocked." So ends the description of the Lord's Judgment on Edom. But the

words may not be limited to Edom. For all that display the
spirit of Edom will suffer the vengeance that befalls Edom.

2. A Comprehensive Prayer for Those Days in the Spirit of 62:6 (63:7-64:11)

It is impossible to tell whether this prayer stems from Jerusalem or Babylon. Consequently the dating of it is fraught
with difficulties. From our point of view it was divinely provided for evil days which are ominously beginning to
threaten on the horizon. As prayer it has a character all its
own. It has a heaven-storming aspect. It is impetuous. It
devises motive after motive why God should hear and come
to the redemption of his people. It also has a generous element of the lament in it.

a. Recalling a Glorious Past (vv. 7-9)

63:7-9   7. I will call to mind the deeds of loving kindness of
         the Lord;
    the praiseworthy acts of the Lord;
according to all that the Lord has done for us,
    and the great goodness to the house of Israel,
which he granted to them according to his mercy
    and according to the multitude of his lovingkindnesses.
8. For he said: "Surely they are my people;
    they are children who will not prove faithless,"
and he became their Deliverer.
9. In all their affliction he was afflicted,
    and the angel of his presence helped them.
In his love and in his pity he delivered them;
    he took them up and carried them
        all the days of old.

Verse 7. Looking at the contents of 63:7–64:11 *Delitzsch* says rather aptly that it is "a prayer of thanksgiving,
penitence, and petition." Looking more at the outward form,
Westermann calls it "a community lament." It has much
of the flavor of Pss. 77, 78, 105, 135, and 136. Some things
are reminiscent of Deut. 32. First the whole of the history of
the people of God is reviewed (vv. 7-10), then the history
of partriarchal times (vv. 11-14). Verses 7-10 carries echoes

of 1:2-3. The beginning of v. 7 is translated literally by
KJ: "I will mention the lovingkindnesses of the Lord."
Clearly we would say "deeds of lovingkindness" ("steadfast love" here fails to catch the intimacy of the expression).
In recalling God's deeds of mercy the writer's heart grows
warm and his tongue eloquent; thoughts gush forth. For certainly Israel's history was a catalogue of merciful dealings
on God's part. Seldom has the pen of man captured this
truth more fittingly. Especially the deep taproot of his dealings is detected: goodness, mercy and lovingkindnesses.

Verse 8. This verse seems to clash with reality. For Israel
was most stubborn and continually going counter to the revealed will of the Lord. None knew that better than the
Lord himself. Surely, the Lord was not blindly deceiving
himself. Again we have a striking instance of anthropomorphic speech. Love might induce a man to put the better construction on all that the nation does. Strict reasoning is not
going to fathom the depth of divine love. This verse surely
says with emphasis that the Lord's favors toward the nation
were utterly undeserved. The last statement of the verse
may be a reference to what God did in Egypt and the wilderness.

Verse 9. There is something touching about the manner
in which the Lord identified himself with his people's sufferings. This is divine empathy at its best. This empathy led
him to delegate a notable messenger of his to appear on the
scene again and again, "the angel of his presence," about
whom the generation of the Exodus seems to have had an
understanding which went farther than our speculations can
reach. God appears to have manifested his presence through
this uncreated angel in a kind of incarnation before the
Great Incarnation. He was the nation's best gift from God.
His mere presence was a deliverance (Exod. 33:15). Where
the prophet might have dwelled on the Lord's *obligation*
toward the people whom he has chosen for his own, he goes
deeper into the warm and affectionate heart of God and ascribes all "to his love and pity." He concludes this approach

by likening God to a compassionate father who "took them up" when they fell down and "carried them" till they forgot their hurt. Here we find ourselves almost at the point of the New Testament approach of "our Father." The prophet, and the nation speaking after him, ascribe this attitude not merely to a few exceptional cases but to "all the days of old." What a delightful way of recalling the past!

b. Why Divine Mercies Then and Not Now (vv. 10-14)

63:10-14 10. But they on their part rebelled,
   and grieved his holy Spirit.
So he turned to be their enemy;
   he even fought against them.
11. Then his people remembered the ancient days [Moses]
   Where is he that brought us from the sea
      the shepherd of his flock?
   Where is he that put in the midst of them
      his holy Spirit?
12. causing his glorious arm to go
      at the right hand of Moses;
   dividing the waters before them,
      to make for himself an eternal name;
13. leading them through the depths?
   As the horse in the plain, they did not stumble.
14. As the cattle go down into the broad valley
   so the Spirit of the Lord always gave them rest.
Thus didst thou lead thy people.

Verse 10. Now comes the stern reality: Israel did not measure up to specifications. Stubborn-hearted and stiff-necked, they manifestly and again and again rebelled. To this stubborn rebellion the divine reaction was that he "was grieved." Divine love was wounded. The Holy Spirit enters into the picture unexpectedly. He does not often appear in the Old Testament. He is more than a potency; more than an attribute. For he can be grieved, which is a purely personal reaction. His reaction was more than a mood of temporary displeasure. When Israel rebels something of extreme value and importance has been despised and rejected, causing a powerful and stern reaction: "he turned to be their enemy; he even fought against them." This is strong reaction. When he fought against them that was apparently done through the world powers: God gave Israel over into the hands of nations greater and mightier than themselves and let them be subjugated. It is an evil thing to have God go on record as hostile to a nation, Egypt and Assyria being their lords. All this is recorded against a background of sincere repentance.

Verse 11. The several textual problems involved in this verse will be discussed at the end of the chapter in the *Notes*. — Affliction set Israel thinking time and again. In the good sense of the word they remembered "the good old times." This was wholesome because it was done penitently. The Mosaic Age in particular seemed to be rich in comfort and instruction. Here is the essence of this section, Israel crying out: Why help *then* and not *now?* The figure used to exemplify this is that of a shepherd (Moses) leading his flock (Israel) into a situation of grave peril but coming out — (shepherd and flock) unscathed. The reference to God's "putting in the midst of them his holy Spirit" would seem to be an allusion to the incident in Num. 11:24-30. For though it was not the whole nation which at the time was indued with the gift, still it was a rare token of good will designed to help a nation get its bearings. A further overall description of the deliverance at the Red Sea follows in v. 12.

Verse 12. The figure employed is unusual but clear. As Moses, the shepherd, strode along, there was, visible to the eye of those who believed in the Lord, the "glorious arm [51:9; 52:10; 62:8] [going] at the right hand of Moses." God's arm is here personified. Without the use of a rhetorical figure, it might be said that God's omnipotent power at every point sustained and upheld Moses, enabling him to do the impossible, like dividing the waters (Exod. 14-16) before the nation and removing an insuperable barrier to their escape This act enhanced the "name," i.e., the renown and reputation of the Lord (cf. 55:13; 56:5; 64:2) with an undying lustre.

Verse 13. Moses led Israel; God's right arm led Moses; God directed his arm. Under this effective triple leadership the nation passed safely through "the depths." Though the waters of the Red Sea, as far as we know were comparatively shallow, in the situation immediately confronting Israel these waters constituted an insurmountable obstacle. Two rather effective illustrations help the reader to catch the point. The first — the "horse in the plain." A level plain, encumbered by no obstacle, makes the passage of the horse swift and safe. Such was the nature of the passage of the sea by the nation. To sum it up, the words are added: "they did not stumble." In other words, an insuperable obstacle becomes not even the least bit of an obstacle.

Verse 14. Abandoning the illustration of smooth passage, a pastoral figure is now employed. Cattle having grazed on a hillside drift down easily into the valley, where water may be found and thirst slaked. But the chief point at issue is that time and again, where there might have been distress and trouble, God's Spirit "gave them rest." Many are the instances where God thus helped his people in what might have been grievous trouble. "Thus didst thou lead thy people." A kind of nostalgia pervades the account. But the point as a whole still is: Why *then* and not now?

c. Bitter Lament over Present Misfortunes (vv. 15-19a)

63:15-19a 15. Look down from heaven and see,
from thy holy and glorious habitation.
Where is thy zeal and thy might?
The yearning of thy heart and thy compassion
toward me are withheld.
16. For thou art our father —
for Abraham does not know us
and Israel does not recognize us.
But thou, O Lord, art our father,
Our Redeemer from of old is thy name.
17. Why then didst thou make us stray from thy ways?

Why didst thou harden our heart,
    so that we no longer fear thee?
Return for the sake of thy servants, the tribes of thy inheritance.
18. Thy holy people possessed thy sanctuary
    but a little while.
Our enemies had trodden it under foot.
19. We have become like those over whom
    thou hadst never ruled,
  like those over whom thy name was not called.

Verse 15. The lament proper does not commence before v. 17. Verse 15 is a plea to be heard by the Almighty. Heaven apparently is far removed and the Lord seems to have withdrawn himself into his glorious habitation. He appears indeed to have become, in the language of *Luther*, a *"deus absconditus"* (a hidden God). He appears to take no note of what is going on against his children. This criticism is implied, not spoken. Another failing on God's part would seem to be that where once he manifested "zeal" in the interest of his people, this all seems to have vanished. "Zeal" coupled with "might" made an invincible combination. But both are not in evidence. The change might be said to have taken place deep in the heart of God. Compassion for Israel once dwelt there. Now all this seems to be cancelled out. The whole verse constitutes a restrained and reverent complaint.

Verse 16. The Jews felt that the patriarchs were interested in the welfare of their descendants, as Luke 16:22 would seem to indicate. Yet that interest would have its limitations and be inadequate for an emergency like that of the present. Now nothing less than the paternal concern of the Lord himself could cope with the present. That this was not a meaningless concept appears from the words, "thou art our father." But that again seems to avail little. Somehow the blessing of this truth has become momentarily submerged. For reasons not specifically known, the Lord has cancelled out the "yearning of [his] heart and [his] compassion" as the close of v. 15 states the case. But here is a truth that the prophet and the nation will not let go, "thou, O Lord, art

our father." And for emergencies this means "our Redeemer." There is no doubt about it; *that* prayer reached its
mark.

Verse 17. The commentator's last word on this verse has
not yet been spoken. It is doubly difficult if the first verb
is taken as a straight causative, which it actually is, and then
translated: "thou didst make us stray" rather than to soften it
a bit: "thou didst let us stray." The first of these two seems
to agree best with the Hebrew idiom. Then the blame for
present misfortunes is squarely laid at God's door, both the
straying from his ways and the hardening of the nation's
heart. If God is sole ruler of the lives of men then some
conclusion such as this could be reached. But that involves
God in the sin of man, in fact, makes God a sinner. Men no
longer fear God, but God made their hearts hard so that they
could no longer fear him. A nation in distress, trying to solve
the problem of sin and evil in this world has recourse to such
logic but sin is illogical. So we consider this as an example
of how man can get entangled in his thoughts, especially on
the question, How does, or did, sin and evil originate? As for
the rest of this verse, we believe that its difficulties are best
solved by a translation like this: "Be kind again for the sake
of thy servants, the tribes of thy inheritance." It is in this
way that God is to "return" or turn back, or, become as he
once was. As basis for this attitude the prophet in this lament
adduces the fact that there still are some within the "tribes of
[God's] inheritance" who are "servants" of the Lord. He is
urged to take these into consideration.

For a fuller treatment of this involved subject the reader
may consult our *Exposition of Isaiah, Vol. 1,* Excursus, p.
142 f.

Verse 18. Another motive is set forth why God should
hear and help his people. The destruction of the temple is
reckoned with as an inevitable consequence and is stated, as
in the whole of the second half of the book, as having practically happened. The specific point that is involved is that
the temple of Solomon functioned as national shrine but a

"little while." Then the enemy took and destroyed the city and "trod it under foot." This is a unique plea for being heard. It practically amounts to this: the Lord appears as unable to maintain himself for any length of time. The Lord's honor is at stake.

Verse 19a. From the point of view of looking into the future and seeing the great calamity that is inevitably to come, still another motive is provided, to press home upon the Lord. The space of time where the Lord effectively upheld his people was comparatively so short that is hardly seemed worth considering. It is as though he "had never ruled" over his people. It was so short a space of time that it was as though God's ownership of his people had never actually been realized. For to call one's name over a people is a way of pronouncing that he is their lord, and is strongly committed to see to their welfare. If God does not help, he will appear remiss in looking after the welfare of his people.

Note: we are taking v. 19b together with Chap. 64.

Notes

Verse 1. "In crimson garments" in Hebrew reads: "crimson of garments," the latter word being an accusative of specification — "crimson in respect to garments." *KS* 336 h.

Verse 3. We have translated *darakhti* as a perfect: "I have trodden." The possibility of translating it as a prophetic perfect, that is, as a future, must be allowed for. In that case the time of the whole section (vv. 1-6) would point to the future.

The difficult form *'egh'aleti* points to either a piel or a hiphil. One seems to fit as well as the other. See *GK* 53 p.

Verse 6. *'ashakkerim* ("I have made them drunk") appears to some to be overbold language to use in reference to the Lord. Quite a few manuscripts read *b* instead of *k*, arriving at the meaning: "I have broken them." The burden of evidence appears to be on the form: "I have made them drunk."

Verse 7. *RSV* has also at this point translated *chesedh* as "steadfast love." We believe "loving kindness" in this case deserves the preference.

Verse 9. We prefer to follow the ancient Hebrew tradition where the Masoretes read *lo* ("to him") rather than *lo'* ("not"), although both were pronounced the same. Much further evidence points in the same direction.

Verse 11. Everything falls into place in the first line of this verse if the last word (*'ammo*) is regarded as subject "his people remembered. . . ." The word "Moses" is inserted parenthetically indicating what area of history it was that the people remembered. That approach eliminates the need of changing the noun *'ammo* to *'abhdo* ("his servant"). The second line of this verse may be treated as follows: strike the final *m* of the second word (a clear case of dittography). Then the object of this participle is the word "shepherd" which is not plural construct ("shepherds of") but a singular construct to be written with a final *h*. This makes Moses the one whom the Lord brought up from the sea, and the one in whose midst he put his holy Spirit. This entire approach eliminates the need of many changes of the text.

Verse 14. The verb "he gave them rest" (*tenichennu*) is apparently a frequentative imperfect and therefore suggests the insertion of "always" in the translation (*KS* 157).

Verse 15. The word "might" in Hebrew appears as a plural of potency (*KS* 262 b) and amounts to a kind of superlative.

Verse 18. To try to make this verse interrogative, as *Koenig* does in his Kommentar, results in a very artificial construction.

Chapter LXIV

d. *Prayer for Divine Intervention (63:19b—64: 11)*

This prayer began at 63:15. It has rightly been termed one of the prayer-gems of the Old Testament. With Chap. 64 it begins to narrow down to a prayer for divine intervention, or that the Lord might display his might and power in behalf of his people to the world. *Fischer* has rather aptly called this chapter a cry to Yahweh that he might bestir himself.

It has long been a question whether 63:19 should be included with Chap. 64 as its beginning or as the conclusion (according to the Hebrew notation of verses) of Chap. 63. Following the lead of the *Septuagint* and the *Vulgate* it seems best to let the verse constitute the beginning of a new chapter (64).

They who see a third major author of the book in Chaps. 56-66, find some difficulty in dating the chapter, but advance the suggestion that it may be assigned to some date between 538-520 B.C.

(1) The Prayer in Brief (vv. 1-3)

64:1-3 1. O that thou wouldest rend the heavens and come down,
O that the mountains might sway at thy presence —
2. as fire ignites brushwood,
as fire makes water to seethe —
to make thy name known to thy adversaries,
and that the nations might tremble at thy presence;
3. when thou dost work awe-inspiring deeds,
which we had not anticipated;
O that thou mightest come down,
and that the mountains might sway at thy presence.

Verse 1. It appears in the time set for this prayer as though the Lord had withdrawn himself from men, had spread out an impenetrable garment across the heavens and hidden himself from his children. This prayer makes bold to beseech God to tear this covering wide open and appear in the rift of the clouds. The Sinai event (Exod. 19), as the first major appearance of this sort of which we have record, is thought of as basic for future interventions. One outstanding element in all passages where the same thought occurs is "fire" (cf. Ps. 144:5; Deut. 32:22; Judg. 5:4-5; Mic. 1:3-4; Hab. 1:4-6; 3:3-15; Ps. 18:8-16. So much so is this the case that the New Testament has summed it up effectively in the statement (Heb. 12:29): "Our God is a consuming fire." As remarked above, God is asked to appear in the clouds, then to go one step further, and "come down." A notable side-effect, visible to all eyes when the theophany occurs will be that the mountains would sway at his presence. A huge created object, like a mountain trembles, so to speak, with awe and reverence in the awesome presence of its Creator.

Verse 2. The first two lines of this verse are parenthetical. They indicate that something must happen to the earthly, material object when brought into the presence of the Holy God. Fire kindled near dry brushwood ignites and consumes quickly. Hot fire brought into touch with water makes it to seethe. As natural as these results are, so it is the normal thing for mountains to "quake" (*KJV*). But far more striking is the effect of the divine theophany on those who thought they might confront the Almighty without fear. Were they to be confronted by the Lord, they would come to know the "name" of the Lord, that is, become aware of his superlative majesty. But if such awareness did not result they still would be strongly affected, overcome by fear and trembling. That the prayer is not dealing with things purely imaginary and fantastic is made plain by the fact that at the close of each of these first three verses appears the phrase "at thy presence." God can and will intervene in a drastic, visible appearance.

Verse 3. This is the continuation of one long sentence of

prayer. The theophany of God is now thought of as part of a general plan, namely the doing of "awe-inspiring deeds," which the nation had not thought possible ("awe-inspiring" is better than "terrible.") For such an event as God appearing on the scene is too overwhelming for words. Since the essence of what is asked for in this prayer is that God might actually intervene in person, this item is repeated at this point. The last two lines are therefore not an idle repetition, or a copyist's mistake.

(2) God, the Sole Author of Effective Intervention (vv. 4-5a)

64:4-5a 4. From of old, men have not heard,
    nor has the ear perceived,
  nor has the eye seen a God besides thee,
  who does deeds for those who wait for him.
5a. O that thou wouldest come to meet him,
  who rejoices to work righteousness,
those who remember thee in thy ways.

Verse 4. The uniqueness of the God of Israel is under consideration. He alone has been known to appear unto the help of his people. Go back as far as the annals of history or the memory of man can carry you, there is nothing on record like deeds which the Lord has done. There are involved here not idle appearances to no effect or purpose. The Lord has "[done] deeds for those who wait for him." That is the uniqueness of Israel's tradition that their God has manifested himself in visible and audible fashion. His people did not call upon him in vain. Therefore they make bold to call upon him again.

Verse 5a. It fits better with the spirit of this word to take it to be a direct prayer and petition: the wish introduced, v. 1, by "O that" is still going on, only now God's appearance is thought of as encounter with man rather than as simple manifestation to the eye and the ear. However man must also meet certain conditions if the appearance of God is to become a reality. God's favors are not bestowed according to deserts but man must be receptive for what God has to give.

Such receptivity is measured by the attitude that a man "rejoices to work righteousness," that is to say, he remembers what God has taught his people to do and delights in doing it. But always God is in the background of such a man's thinking, or man remembers him in his ways. He cannot forget how God has helped and is sure that he will help again.

(3) Renewed Misgivings and Hopelessness (vv. 5b-7)

64:5b-7   5b. Lo, thou wast angry and we kept on sinning;
            in our sins we have been a long while,
and shall we be saved?
6. And we have all of us become like an unclean person,
   and all our righteous deeds like filthy rags.
We all fade like a leaf;
   and our iniquities bear us away like the wind.
7. And there is not a one that calls upon thy name,
   bestirring himself to take hold of thee.
For thou hast hid thy face from us,
   and thou hast delivered us into the power of our sins.

Verse 5b. Prayer has its moods. It may fluctuate. In the preceding words a fact was firmly established: God is well able at any time to take things in hand for his people. But this note of confidence is now lost for the moment. Misgivings assail the individual and the nation. A touch of hopelessness takes hold. Where the speaker had come to some measure of assurance about pardon for his sins, he now feels that there may be some doubt about forgiveness. He feels that he and the nation are still under God's anger (cf. Ps. 90: 9). In spite of the fact that the nation knew that God was displeased, they had to admit "we kept on sinning." Sin had become a strongly ingrained habit. They had been so long in this unhappy state that it had become second nature. They even felt for that matter, that they were perhaps beyond the point of recovery: "shall we be saved?" (cf. Ezek. 33:18). A series of comparisons, describing Israel's miserable state now follow. In a sense they have become untouchable like a leper (Lev. 13:45), ceremonially unclean, but still unclean. They are not in a state of worthiness to approach God and his sanctuary. Or they may be likened to a woman, ceremonially unclean because of her monthly period. This may be an unusual comparison, it may offend the fastidious taste of our day, but it does convey a feeling of deep sinfulness. The ethical and the ceremonial aspect of things blend here somewhat uniquely. No matter how you construe it, it speaks of a deep awareness of sin, and is a powerful word: "All our righteous deeds are as filthy rags." The next comparison illustrates the blighting effect of sin: "We all fade like a leaf," for sin separates man from the source of life, and so he withers away. The last comparison stresses the total instability of the life of sin: "Our iniquities bear us away like the wind." The disruptive effects of sin are under consideration.

Verse 7. The note of hopelessness becomes stronger. No encouraging signs may be detected. No one recalls that God is a God who forgives. So no one dares venture to approach the Lord to take him by the hand and claim mercy from the all-gracious Lord. Whatever of repentance there is, it has not dared to claim any of God's gracious promises as including him, the poor sinner. All they can sense is the negative side of God's attitude: "Thou hast hid thy face from us." That things then must go from bad to worse is all that seems to be left under the circumstances, as the concluding word of this section indicates: "Thou hast delivered us into the power of our sins." Similar is the case of the Gentiles (Rom. 1:28).

(4) Various Reasons for Divine Intervention (vv. 8-12)

64:8-12 8. And yet, O Lord, thou art our father;
      we are the clay and thou art our potter;
and we all of us are the work of thy hand.
9. Be not angry, O Lord, over us;
    do not remember iniquity forever.
Behold and see, we are all of us thy people.
10. Thy holy cities have become a wilderness;
    Zion has become a wilderness, Jerusalem a desolation.
11. Our holy and glorious house, where our fathers praised thee,
    has been burned by fire;
        all our treasure has become a desolation.

12. In the face of all these things,
    canst thou stand aloof?
    canst thou keep silence,
    and afflict us still more?

Verse 8. The mood changes in this prayer. Recalling God's deeds in the past, all of them a matter of record among God's people, the writer displays a certain inventiveness for finding motives why God should intervene in behalf of his people. The first of the motives mentioned is the fact that the nation is made up of children of his. They are "the work of [his] hands." This is merely a variation of the theme that they are children. The potter/clay figure indicates that they owe their very existence to him. The Lord will not abandon that upon which he has bestowed infinite pains and care. Here the potter-figure and the children-figure blend into one, also the potter-figure and the father-figure. It may be questioned whether in this passage the heavier emphasis lies on God's being the father and in 63:16 Israel's being the children (*Westermann*).

Verse 9. Another reason why the Lord should show consideration under the circumstances is brought forth — Israel are "[his] people." The election of Israel by God is being recalled. If being God's people means anything it implies that God will be ready to forgive after his justifiable anger has flared up. In fact he cannot "remember iniquity forever" (cf. Ps. 79:8).

Verse 10. The writer now goes on to reflect upon the desolate sight presented by all the cities, by Zion and by the city of Jerusalem. This does not necessarily mean that this part must have been written after the fall of Jerusalem (586 B.C.). Prophetically he may be foreseeing a situation that will ultimately arise if Israel persists in her sins. But such a scene of utter ruin should stir the Lord's compassions. The cities are called "holy" because they lie in the Holy Land.

Verse 11. In a sense the chain of thought that is being developed rises to higher values. Now comes the Temple, the Lord's "glorious house," which is thought of as lying in ruins, as it needs must ultimately be if the nation continues to go on in its present sinful ways. One major purpose that was served by the Temple was this that it furnished a place for the true fathers of Israel to praise the Lord. Those were deeply satisfying experiences. Many holy aspirations were associated with this national shrine; here they are called Israel's "treasure." This even may include such items as the altar of burnt offering, the sea of bronze, the beautifully ornamented buildings, and the like.

Verse 12. So now this verse appropriately sums up and presses home its point: "canst thou stand aloof? canst thou keep silence, and afflict us still more?" It takes boldness and the courage of faith to pray thus. The intense earnestness of this prayer is touching.

Notes

Verse 1. The *Jerusalem Bible* renders the first verb quite effectively in the idiom of our day: "tear the heavens open." The two effective comparisons how fire operates, may not be quite the same as some that *we* might have used, but that does not yet warrant the criticism that they are "lame" and "do not fit the situation" (*Duhm*). In the second of these two, the verb goes over from the infinitive construction to the finite verb.

Verse 3. "Terrible things" (*KJ, RSV*) could carry wrong connotations in our day. Therefore we have rendered "awe-inspiring deeds."

Verse 4. When Paul cites this verse (I Cor. 2:9) he seems to be quoting freely from memory. He sees new possibilities in this verse.

Verse 5. It seems better to take the verb "and we sinned" as a durative, "we kept on sinning." So the logical sequence of things is preserved; or perhaps with *Delitzsch*: "We stood there as sinners." *Bahem* (lit. "in them"), can well, according to the context, refer to sins. Therefore *RSV* did well to translate "in our sins," injecting the word "sins." To take the last verb of the verse as a plain indicative produces a strange effect (*KJ*). To construe it as interrogative seems much more to the point.

Verse 9. The *Jerusalem Bible* goes too far when it translates the opening words: "Do not let your anger go too far," as though God needed the supervision of man.

Chapter LXV

3. God's Answer to Israel's Prayer (Chap. 65)

The caption for this chapter looks back to Chap. 64, which we had labelled "Prayer for Divine Intervention." However two major approaches to the subject treated in the present chapter are to be noted. Some go so far as to claim that such a title fits the chapter so poorly as to make it impossible. On their part they who take this position maintain that the subject under consideration is "the Faithless and the Obedient" (*Westermann*). This conclusion is arrived at as a result of a slightly dubious observation, namely, that in this chapter for the first time in prophecy in the pronouncement of doom, this doom is not any longer regarded as befalling the entire mass of Israel but the nation is approached from the angle of being a divided group — some guilty and deserving of punishment, others faithful and to be spared when the punishment is meted out. We believe that the division of the nation into faithful and faithless was implied by the prophets who seemed to be pronouncing doom on the nation *en masse*. It would appear then that at this point that which was previously *implied* now is expressly *stated*. Chapter 65 is therefore closely bound to Chap. 64. Prayer and answer to prayer go hand in hand.

It should however be noted that an unusual omission seems to be characteristic of this chapter. The outstanding sins of the nation are spelled out. Nothing however is said of the forgiveness which God's grace grants to the sinner when he is penitent. On the other hand, when the salvation is depicted, which God has prepared for his people, the emphasis lies largely on the external things involved. This is unusual but is not to be regarded as a shortcoming of the state described. Oftentimes, especially in the Old Testament, the external, visible blessings bestowed by God's grace are rated as obvious manifestations of God's benevolent goodness.

Then it should be observed, as *Fischer* remarks: In the sequence of things as portrayed in this chapter, first comes a judgment which separates the godly from the ungodly; then salvation itself is to be bestowed.

As to details — this chapter may fit the needs of the returned exiles, of the date of about 538-521 B.C. From our point of view of the composition of the entire book by Isaiah, that would mean: God allowed the prophet to anticipate that a state of affairs would develop after the Return of the exiles, where they would need to be taught why God delayed answering their prayer, and furthermore a division of the people into the faithful and the renegades would take place.

The meter is somewhat difficult — sometimes 3 and 3; sometimes 3 and 2. *Westermann* prints the whole chapter as poetry. Most writers agree that vv. 8-16 may be more readily scanned.

a. His Answer Is Delayed because of the Unwholesome Attitude of Many of His People (vv. 1-7)

65:1-7 1. I made myself available to those who did not ask for me;
   I was ready to be found by those who do not seek me out.
I said, "Here am I; here am I"
   to a nation that was not called by my name.
2. I spread out my hands all the day
   to a stubborn nation,
that walked in a way that was not good
   after their own devices;
3. a people who continually provoke me brazenly,
   who sacrifice in gardens,
and burn incense on bricks;
4. who sit about in tombs,
   and spend the night in secret places;
who eat the flesh of swine,
   while the broth of repulsive meat is in their vessels;
5. who say, "Stay by yourself;
   do not come near me,
lest I make you taboo."
These persons are a smoke in my nostrils,

a fire which burns all day long.
6. Lo, it stands recorded before me;
   I shall not keep silence until I have repaid them,
and I will repay them in their bosom.
7. Your iniquities and those of your fathers
   (saith the Lord)
   which you sacrificed upon the mountains,
and by which you reviled me upon the hills;
   now I shall first measure out to them
their recompense in their bosom.

Verse 1. It should be borne in mind that this chapter shows how God is minded toward his people and their prayers. God was willing enough to be approached by his people; he had done enough to make himself available. The first approach did not begin with Israel. They were a people who did not seek *him* out. He was hoping that he might be found by them. But they were a people who did not make advances. His friendly attitude was manifest by his invitation: he represents himself as continually saying: "Here am I; here am I." The last line of this verse seems to invite a textual change: they were a people who were not calling upon his name. But the passive, a people "called" may well be retained. For that unique expression signifies to be regarded as the Lord's own special property. But they were not behaving as God has a right to expect that they would. So the point made by the verse is: Israel was calling upon the Lord; that action seemed good; but it was disappointing because there was no outreach on the nation's part to the Lord.

It is obvious according to our translation and interpretation that we regard v. 1 as describing *Israel's* attitude toward God, just as v. 2 clearly refers to Israel. Isaiah is making it clear why even Israel's prayers had to be rejected. Strangely Paul (Rom. 10:20 f.) quotes these first two verses, applying v. 1 to the *Gentiles* and v. 2 to Israel. According to the text and context Paul does not abide by the letter of the passage. It would appear that, according to the Greek translation, the words lent themselves to a fresh application of the words used. Paul is not employing strict scientific exegesis, but with great freedom is readapting the original as an effective statement of his case.

Verse 2. How eager this outreach on *God's* part was is indicated by the gesture accompanying his call — "[he] spread forth [his] hands all the day" — a pleading gesture of tender invitation. Whatever religious practices they, as nation, may have engaged in, they were still "a stubborn nation," and "[walking] in a way that was not good," as the prophet is about to explain. They were walking "after their own devices."

Verses 3, 4. The indictment grows sharper. In the Lord's sight, Israel, after its Return from Captivity, was far from being a dedicated people. There was an element among them that continually provoked God brazenly, an offensive form of conduct which is charged against the nation continually, especially in the historical books. Now follows a list of specifications — instances of offensive conduct that prevailed within the nation, although they are misdemeanors which hid their face and were often done in secret. The sins that had done particular damage to the nation and were the distinct vices prevalent among the renegades, were mostly in the area of cultic practices, as the next six lines clearly indicate. All manner of strange and even repulsive procedures are mentioned. Detailed explanations are not offered, but, no doubt, the nation understood the references made. First of all sacrificing in gardens seemed to have achieved popularity (cf. 1:29; 66:17). No doubt the cult involved planting delightful gardens in honor of certain deities that were reputed to love such homage. Then there was the burning of incense on bricks, which is usually explained as involving the use of incense jars. Incense figures in many religious practices. Then sitting about in tombs was involved in certain other rites. That would seem to have involved expecting messages from the dead. It could have involved contact with demons which were somehow associated with tombs (cf. Matt. 8:28; Mark 5:3-5). For messages from the dead cf. 8:19; 29:4. When it is charged that men spend the night in secret places that could have involved the same irregularities, though "secret places" means places difficult to access. Secrecy lends some kind of attraction to forbidden practices: "stolen waters are sweet" (Prov. 9:17). Besides they did eat the flesh of swine, a practice forbidden (Lev. 11:7). Swine were sacrificed among many nations; Israel frowned upon offering a creature of unclean habits. Exactly what is meant by "the broth of repulsive meat is in their vessels" is hard to determine, but it may be in line with the eating of pork. *JB* translates: "using unclean foods in their kitchens."

Verse 5. What now follows may well exemplify the "conceit of the cultist." Because of their exotic practices they believe that they have achieved a superior grade of holiness, which might be contaminated by contact with those who have not engaged in these unusual rites, or may even prove harmful to the unsanctified, if they but touched these high ranking religionists. "Stay by yourself" means: Do not touch me, as the next line suggests: Do not even come near me. Some of the "taboo" might rub off on the outsider. In a strongly anthropomorphic expression, the degree of vexation that these super-saints convey to the Almighty are said to be "smoke in [his] nostrils," or "a fire which burns all day long." So irritating to the Lord are those that employ rites that stem from idolatrous usages. Yet these persons esteem themselves to be persons of superior sanctity.

Verse 6. The remaining two verses of the section develop the thought that God will not remain passive in the face of prevailing irregularities that stain his people. He has recorded their misdeeds as something that calls for action. They are scheduled for attention. Punishment is announced with a certain solemnity. To declare that God will not remain inactive, the writer used a special expression: "I shall not keep silence" (cf. 62:1; 64:12). He further represents himself as coming to the renegades in person to mete out just punishment, we might say, "upon the head" of the guilty. The Hebrew idiom has it that evil will "repay them in their bosom," for which again we might say: "into their very lap" the entire unholy mess is to be deposited.

Verse 7. This verse indicates that there is such a thing as "mass guilt," where the sins of generation after generation are not completely broken with and the amount grows higher and higher. Ultimately, or time and again, it then happens that God visits the "sins of the fathers upon the children." The fathers had sacrificed upon the mountains; the children had continued the pernicious usage. God had warned; prophets had expostulated; the renegades had continued after as before. Israel prided itself upon such irregularities, which really amounted to a "reviling" of God upon the hills. The "first" issue noted down by God as the order of the day was to measure out to them their recompence in their bosom. All this must have made it abundantly clear to Israel why her cries for help were not meeting with a divine response.

b. The Wholesome Element to Be Spared, the Renegades to Be Punished (vv. 8-16)

65:8-16   8. Thus says the Lord:
       "Just as men find new juice in a cluster,
    and they say, 'Don't destroy it
      for there is a blessing in it,'
so shall I proceed for my servants' sake,
    so as not to destroy everything.
9. And I shall bring forth descendants from Jacob
    and from Judah inheritors of my mountain;
and my chosen ones shall inherit it,
    and my servants shall dwell there.
10. And Sharon shall become pasturage for flocks,
    and the valley of Achor shall be for cattle to lie down in.
for my people who have sought me.
11. But as for you who forsake the Lord,
    who forget my holy mountain,
      who prepare a table for Fortune [Gad],
    who fill up a drink offering for Destiny [Mani],
12. Lo, I will destine you to the sword,
    and all of you shall bow down to the slaughter;
because I called and you did not answer,
    I spoke and you would not listen;

but you did what was evil in my sight,
    and you preferred what I did not delight in."
13. Therefore, thus says the Lord, Yahweh:
    "Lo, my servants shall have food, but you shall be hungry;
        lo, my servants shall have drink, but you shall be thirsty;
    lo, my servants shall be happy, but you shall be put to shame;
14. lo, you shall be exultant for joy of heart,
    but you shall howl for pain of heart;
        and shall wail for anguish of spirit.
15. And you shall leave your name behind
    for a curse to my chosen ones;
        and the Lord Yahweh shall slay you
    and to his servants he shall give a different name.
16. So that he who blesses himself in the land
    will bless himself by the God of truth [Amen]
and he that swears in the land
    will swear by the God of truth.
Because the former troubles are forgotten,
    and are hid from my eyes.

Verse 8. At this point a distinction sets in: punishment is
not pronounced indiscriminately on good and wicked members of his people but what was often implied before is now
plainly stated: the wicked shall meet with just punishment.
An excerpt is quoted perhaps from an old vintage song. A
cluster of grapes is picked up with quite a few bad grapes in
it. Shall it be thrown aside, good and bad grapes together?
The verdict will be: "Don't destroy it." The reason? "There
is a blessing in it": the juice of the good grapes is worth the
saving. So shall the Lord proceed for "his servants' sake, and
not destroy everything." What happens to the evil-doer
need not be spelled out. It was already stated above in v. 7.
As "servants" the faithful have a claim upon their Lord. He
honors their claim. This is the doctrine of the remnant cast
in a new and different form.

Verse 9. In particular in this verse the achievement of one
blessing is stressed: the possession of the land by the generations to come. The land is described as "my mountain" because almost all of the Promised Land was mountainous territory.

Verse 10. Just a casual glance at the land already presents

a picture of idyllic peace and security throughout its entire breadth, from the plain of Sharon to the west to the valley of Achor to the east (cf. Josh. 7:24). For wherever one looks in the land there is an abundance of cattle with an abundance of pasturage. Against such a background of prosperity those loyal to the covenant spend their days.

Verse 11. In sharp contrast to the ones just referred to, stand the unfaithful. Their behavior betrays how they are minded toward him who should be their Lord. One overall descriptive phrase covers their case; they "forsake the Lord." Hand in hand with their infidelity goes neglect of the holy temple-mountain, i.e., true worship is not maintained as the seed-bed for faith. Rites honoring other foreign deities are resorted to, honoring, for example, the god of good luck (Hebrew: *Gad*); honoring him by preparing a counterpart to the table of shew-bread (cf. Exod. 25:23-30) that symbolically represented a fellowship meal with the Lord. Or they honored the less-known God of Destiny (Hebrew: *Mani*) who may have been resorted to to ward off all evil destinies that might befall. In any case, by honoring these Israel pushed the Lord aside.

Verse 12. God actually destines men as justice demands. Note the play on words (God destines [*manithi*] rather than destiny [*mani*]). His destinies are stern — "to the sword" and "to the slaughter." Personal infidelity brought this doom down on their heads: for he called but they did not even deign to answer. He spoke and they would not listen. They went farther than that. They added to do evil in his sight and preferred what he did not delight in.

Verses 13-14. Two lines of destiny run parallel to one another, according as men have chosen for themselves. For though in a sense they are parallel they are also opposites at the same time. Two great chapters of old furnish the material for these two verses, Lev. 26 and Deut. 28: having food versus going hungry; having to drink versus being thirsty; being happy versus being put to shame; being exultant versus howling for pain.

Verse 15. For a moment the prophet looks at the final outcome when the congregation of evil-doers will have perished from the land. Only one thing will they leave behind — their name to furnish a new curse for the chosen ones to refer to as a horrible example. In contrast to this he will give a new name to his servants that in its meaning will cover how richly God has blessed them.

Verse 16. The phrase "in the land" seems to indicate that the people may have been out of the land for a time. When they come back they will wish blessings on themselves and on others by the name of the Most Holy One, "the God of truth," which may be translated "the God of Amen." Oaths generally will be made in the name of this God whose utterly truthful word will have taken on a new meaning. The truth of the matter is that the new state of affairs that the Lord will create will be so completely blessed that it will blot out completely "the former troubles" (cf. 43:18 f.). A higher state of perfection cannot be conceived.

c. God's New Creation in All Its Splendor Is Portrayed (vv. 17-25)

65:17-25 17. For, lo, I shall create new heavens and a new earth,
    and the former state of affairs shall not be remembered,
nor shall they even come to mind.
18. But rejoice and be glad forever,
    over that which I shall create.
For, lo, I shall create Jerusalem a rejoicing,
    and her people a joy.
19. For I shall be glad over Jerusalem
    and rejoice over my people;
nor shall be heard in her anymore the sound of weeping
    nor the sound of an outcry.
20. Nor shall there spring up from there a child
    living but a limited number of days;
nor an old man
    who shall not get his full measure of days
For a lad of a hundred years may die,
    and he who falls short of a hundred years
        shall be reckoned accursed.
21. And men shall build houses and inhabit them,

and they shall plant vineyards and eat the fruit of them.
22. They shall not build and another inhabit;
    they shall not plow and another eat their fruit,
for like the days of a tree shall be the days of my people,
    and my chosen ones shall use to the full
        the work of their hands.
23. They shall not toil in vain,
    nor shall they bring forth children for terror
for they are a race of the Lord's blessed ones;
    and so are their offspring;
24. and it shall come to pass
    that before they call I will answer
        and while they are still speaking I will hear.
25. The wolf and the lamb shall be in the same pasture,
    and the lion shall eat straw like the ox,
and dust shall be the serpent's food.
They shall not hurt nor harm in all my holy mountain,
    says the Lord."

Verse 17. From this point to the end of the chapter the New Age is being depicted. Faith here rises to new levels; nowhere in the Old Testament is a more glorious picture of the future kingdom drawn. There will be a new heaven and a new earth. Both together spell a new universe. According to analogous Scriptures, transformation of the old is involved, not destruction of the old followed by a new creation. Yet the transformation will be so complete that the former state of affairs on this old sin-ridden earth shall not even be remembered or come to mind (cf. also 51:6).

Verse 18. The point now is that not only is there ample occasion for joy, but it is a joy that will last forever. Strangely at this point Jerusalem, the newly created Jerusalem, enters the picture as the center about which everything in the new creation rotates. To create "Jerusalem a rejoicing," of course, means an object of rejoicing. Note the emphasis that all this is work of God, the Creator. Even the people shall be transformed so as not to be a cause of vexation, but also an object of rejoicing.

Verse 19. The Lord reiterates the thought just expressed that he will have ample occasion for joy over his people. The negative aspect of the situation is now spelled in fresh colors: the sound of weeping and of an outcry shall no longer dull the picture (cf. 25:18; 35:10).

Verse 20 is concerned with another blessing that shall stand forth prominently — longevity on this new earth. This passage as such does not rise to the level of maintaining that there will be an eternal life, but merely a long continuation of life on this earth enabling man to taste to the full this pleasant existence. Therefore the level of 25:8 is not achieved here. The truth concerning the eternal blessedness of God's children was, in the providence of God but slowly revealed through the centuries. Approaching the issue from this angle it is asserted that the dying of children will be out of the question, in other words a child "living but a limited number of days." Then there is the additional claim that old men shall not die prematurely; each man will "get his full measure of days." With the light on this whole issue glowing but dimly, a new measure of long life is promised. At least this much is granted that, should a man die in youth at least he would not die at less than a hundred years, for less than that would mark a man as accursed.

Verse 21. One unique reward, so to speak, of the Old Testament saints was the fulfillment of the hope of not being subject to frustration, such as building a house and not getting to live in it, or, planting a vineyard and not getting to eat the fruit of it. Such disappointment would have been caused perhaps by war or other calamities.

Verse 22. Repeatedly in the Old Testament the long life of a man is compared with the long life of a tree (see Ps. 1:3; Jer. 17:8; Ezek. 19:10). No disappointing defeats will be encountered in this New Age. What a man achieves will be enjoyed by him who achieved it. Such is an effective way of saying: a man will get full satisfaction from life (cf. Ps. 92:12-14).

Verse 23. This verse continues on the note that the new earth shall not be marked by disappointments and frustrations. Common, everyday toil shall not be marked by futility, and be done "in vain." One striking example of major disappointments in life could be to have children, whose life would be shortened by accident and disaster, that is, not realizing the promise "that it may be well with thee and thou mayest live long on earth." The expression "to bring forth children for terrors," might be another way of saying "for death," for according to Job 18:14, death is "the king of terrors." This would then be the very opposite of the ghastly scene mentioned in Ps. 137:9. Instead, God's faithful, here called "the race of the Lord," shall be manifestly blessed, they and "their offspring." God's enduring blessings shall extend over generations.

Verse 24. A new aspect of God's blessing bestowed upon his children will be experienced in the field of prayer, where before they have uttered their prayer God will already be answering them; while they are still speaking, he will hear them.

Verse 25. Suddenly the thought veers over into the area of nature, characterized by peaceful coexistence of, and with, what were wild beasts. Instead of regarding this as a valuable supplement to what has already been described as a new creation, this verse is treated by some as suspect, as an unfortunate addition. This is an example of the type of criticism which we rightly deplore. For this addition beautifully illustrates how far-reaching the blessings of this new creation will be. True, the passage may be a take-off on 11:6-9, but even our Lord sometimes repeated himself in his discourses spoken here on earth. At least the critic would have us consider the line "and dust shall be the serpent's food" as a gloss. But even this is a colorful item. It indicates with a kind of half-sigh that the fallen state of man will not be entirely forgotten. As a reminder from Gen. 3:14, it indicates that the propensity of the serpent to attack man will be a thing of the past. It shall indeed "eat dust," i.e., taste defeat, but its presence in the picture shall not mar the perfection of God's new creation. In fact (and now quite naturally comes the crowning touch), nothing shall savor of imperfection and harm: "They shall not hurt nor harm in all my holy mountain" says the Lord. As in 10:9 we must allow for the possibility of the "holy mountain" being a reference to the entire land.

Notes

Verse 1. The first word of the verse could be translated as a passive — witness *KJ* and *Luther*. But to take the *Niphal* as a *Niphal tolerativum* — witness *RSV* — is much to be preferred. Cf. *GK* 51 c. To add a pronominal suffix object ("ask of *me, as Septuagint* and *Targum,* do) brings the construction in line with the other verbs of the verse.

Verse 2. "Not good" — a case of litotes. Cf. *KS* 385 d.

Verse 7. "Your iniquities" (Hebrew text) is changed to "their iniquities" (*RSV*). Yet the Hebrew makes good sense, and, being the more difficult, should be retained, though most versions make the change.

Verse 10. The words "and Sharon shall become pasturage," seeing that Sharon was rich grainland, could be construed as involving a demotion. But as we have construed it above, it shows the thought involved is rich pasturage for cattle.

Verse 14. The unusual form which we have translated "howl," is explained *GK* 70 d.

Verse 15. "Your name" (*RSV*) for "their name" is an obvious improvement.

Verse 20. *RSV* translates the latter part of the verse "the sinner a hundred years old," which makes a very difficult translation. The word rendered "sinner" (Hebrew "*chote*") comes from a basic root which means "come short" or "miss the mark." So we have translated: "he who falls short of a hundred years" — a translation which makes good sense.

Chapter LXVI

I. ISRAEL'S HOPE (Chap. 66)

The prophet's book has built up to a climax by way of a well-ordered progression. Though apparently written long in advance by a prophet living in the seventh century, yet it builds up to a logical conclusion. A good number of the people is to return from the Babylonian Captivity, and will be faced with the problem of setting up a state, and a temple for purposes of worship. The main altar for burnt offerings was functioning daily; the temple may have been restored, but unfortunately it was not the scene of a truly spiritual worship. Only the externals of worship were at hand. No concept of the greatness of the God of Israel was in evidence. At least the unspiritual worship could be corrected by ousting those who held only to routine procedures. Just who it was whom the Lord was to repel and remove is difficult to determine. But from the last two chapters of this book it appears that the prophets, and the men of deeper spiritual insight began to regard these as unworthy and as a blemish upon the fair name of the nation. Our chapter takes direct issue with such.

Time and place, where and when, these words were spoken, are difficult to determine. To think that the opening verses are directed at the Samaritans is a case of judgment on the basis of insufficient evidence. The same holds true in the case of classifying vv. 17-24 as a later addition by some unknown editor.

1. Corrupt Worship (vv. 1-4)

66:1-4 1. Thus says the Lord
The heavens are my throne
and the earth my footstool,
What manner of house is it that you would build for me?

370

And what sort of place would be the place of my rest.
2. All these things my hand has made,
 and so these things have come into being,
  says the Lord.
Yet to this man will I look, namely to the man
 that is humble and of a contrite spirit
and trembles with awe at my word.
3. He that slaughters an ox is as if he slew a man;
 He that sacrifices a lamb is as if he broke a dog's neck.
He that offers a cereal offering
 is as if he offered swine's blood.
He who makes a memorial offering of incense
 is as if he blessed an idol.
These have chosen their own way;
 It is their abomination that their soul delights in.
4. So I too will choose their calamity
 and bring their fears upon them;
because when I called no one answered
 I spoke and they would not hear.
But they did what was evil in my sight;
 they chose that in which I took no delight.

Verse 1. This first verse is much like Ps. 113:5 f. Besides, I Kings 8:26; Ps. 50:9-12; Amos 5:21-25 may be compared. This verse shows what great and mighty issues are involved when an individual or a group assembles for worship. He, before whom they come, has a throne that is indeed nothing less than the heavens. He has a footstool — the earth in all its vastness. It is, so to speak, almost presumptuous for earth-dwellers to erect a structure to serve as, and to be called, the Lord's habitation. Or what could serve as the place where he takes up residence. These things being so, there will always be a wholesome awe when men, as they worship, come to what is known to be a temple for the Almighty.

Verse 2. To expand the thought a bit more — all things that are within the compass of heaven and earth still in spite of their vast number are things that came into being as the work of his hands. They are his creatures. Some of mankind, in the nature of the case, are people in whom he takes pleasure; some he cannot delight in. Who are they that stand in the shade of his pleasure? The answer that comes from the lips of the Lord is one that man could hardly have thought possible. It is the man "that is humble and of a contrite spirit." This implies that the person in question has some awareness of the sins he has done and sincerely regrets that by his misdeeds he has incurred the displeasure of his Creator. None are good enough of themselves. Sinless persons cannot be found. The Lord can make something of those who sincerely repent of what they have done. And somehow, since they have heard of the mercy of the Lord, they have a deep respect for every word that falls from his lips: "they tremble with awe at [his] word."

Verses 3, 4. This difficult verse shows how the lack of penitence mars every act they may engage in, in the practice of worship. Suppose a man goes to some expense in connection with an act of devotion: he offers an ox. In the eyes of God, that which he performed counts as nothing better than if he had slain a man and had blood dripping from his hands as he stands before the Lord on trial. Or, another example — in the course of his worship he might bring a lamb as an offering to the Lord's temple. If such a one steps forth not actually penitent, he gains no more favor by his offering than if he had broken a dog's neck. A third example: suppose an impenitent person offers a comparatively unimpressive offering, through the agency of his sacrifice he has achieved no more than if he had offered swine's blood. Or suppose that which was presented was a memorial offering, the fact that it was not prompted by a contrite spirit would make what he did drop to the level of praise spoken in honor of a pagan god. Apparently some of these whom the prophet was rebuking were attempting to carry the Lord's worship on one shoulder, and idolatry on the other. They certainly were not choosing to walk in the ways of the Lord. As a result, all acts of piety and worship amounted to no more than "abomination" before the holy God.

2. The Lord Stands by His Faithful Ones (v. 5)

66:5 5. Hear the word of the Lord, you that tremble at his Word;

Your brethren, who hate you
 and thrust you out for my name's sake, say:
"Let the Lord step forth in his glory
 that we may see your joy."
But it is they who shall come to grief.

Verse 5. A deep line of cleavage runs through the congregation of Israel. There are unworthy ones who actually hate and despise the meek souls among God's people. They regard themselves as the elite and have already thrust out from the community these whom they despise. They are so sure of themselves that they are ready to take their case up to the court of heaven. In their presumption they venture to challenge the Lord and vindicate themselves before their very eyes. They speak sarcastically, as much as to say, You are claiming the Lord as standing on your side, or yourselves as having special relations with the Lord. Bold as they may be, they will find that their presumption is ill-founded. The opposite is the case: "It is *they* who shall come to grief."

3. Sending Recompense on the Ungodly (v. 6)

66:6   6. "Hark, an outcry from the city
  and uproar from the city,
 Hark, the Lord will render recompense
  to his enemies.

Verse 6. Suddenly and without warning the enemy strikes. All over in the city shouts of men engaged in conflict! They are even battering away at the temple gates. In its deeper aspects the Lord is at work in the conflict which is developing. But we seem to be totally at a loss as to the historical incident that the prophet has in mind.

4. Miraculously Rapid Birth of the New Nation (vv. 7-9)

66:7-9   7. Before she [the city] was in labor she gave birth,
  before her pains came upon her,
 she was delivered of a son.
8. Who has heard of such a thing,

who has seen things like these?
Shall a nation be born in one day?
Shall a nation be brought forth at once?
For as soon as Zion was in labor
she brought forth children.
9. Shall I bring to the birth and not cause to bring forth?
says the Lord.
Shall I who cause to bring forth, shut the womb?
says the Lord.

Verse 7-9. It may well have puzzled even the faithful in Israel when the new and prosperous ones in Israel pondered how things would go with God's people. For though God's promises were known it seemed too much as if even the strength of the Almighty was insufficient to accomplish the things promised. So the Lord speaks in terms of the birth of a nation. Who the mother is that is to bring forth, not children but an entire nation, we are not told. But speaking in eschatological language the prophet insists that the miracle will be accomplished. It is now as though the labor pains were about to begin, and already the birth has taken place. The hyperbole employed is bold and speaks in terms of the seemingly impossible. Dropping the figure used, we could regard those experiences like Pentecost where as a result of one sermon three thousand were added to the church.

The section just covered begins to take on eschatological coloring. Commentators list the following as items that are typical of the treatment of the "last things": many people, Zion's happy state; judgment on the Lord's enemies; revelation of God's glory in the sight of his enemies. Yet one could hardly expect a strict logical arrangement of the items listed.

5. An Exhortation to Rejoice over the New Nation (vv. 10-11)

66:10-11 10. Rejoice with Jerusalem and be jubilant over her
all of those who love her
Rejoice greatly with her
all you who mourn for her;
11. that you may suck and be satisfied

with her consolotary breasts,
in order that you may drink deeply and enjoy it,
   from her bountiful bosom.

Verse 10. Such good things are in store for Jerusalem,
that is, in the last analysis, inclusive of the church of the New
Testament, that when they who wish her well consider the
situation, they will be moved to rejoice and be jubilant. This
includes those who mourned over her when her lot was a
less happy one.

Verse 11. Here is the spot where true satisfaction is to be
found. To drive this thought home, the prophet uses an
analogy which is very meaningful, though it might draw an
indulgent smile to the lips of a modern reader. The true
satisfaction that a healthy and normal child enjoys at its
mother's breast may be somewhat naive for the sophisticate
of our times but it is still very meaningful and instructive.

6. The Lord Is with His People and against His Enemies (vv. 12-14)

66:12-14 12. For thus says the Lord:
   "Lo, I am offering prosperity like a river.
and the wealth of the Gentiles, like an overflowing stream;
   and you shall be nursed, and carried on the hip,
      and dandled on the knee.
13. As one whom his mother comforts, so shall I comfort you;
   even in Jerusalem shall you be comforted.
14. You shall see and your heart be glad;
   your bones shall flourish as the grass.
And it shall be known that the hand of the Lord
      is with his servants,
and his indignation is with his enemies,

Verses 12-13. God is speaking through his prophet. The
sum of all blessings is here contained in one word, "peace."
We translated this by "prosperity," of which an abundance
will be available, as is indicated by the words used: "river,"
"overflowing." Then comparisons are borrowed from the
intimacies of the care of young children. Another area of
life is drawn on to describe how precious God's resources

are. He comforts men (v. 13) as only a mother can. To make this comfort more precious, the prophet lets it be given against the rich prospects of the Holy City — even Jerusalem.

Verse 14. All these good things will not only be idle dreams: Israel shall see them with her own eyes. The happiness caused by the experience shall go deep, that is, down to the very marrow of her bones. It shall be obvious to all who share in the event that God has once again had a hand in the course that things took, that the hand of the Lord has been at work, in behalf of his servants. But for his enemies indignation lies in store.

7. The Lord Coming for Judgment on His Opponents (vv. 15-19)

66:15-19   15. For lo, the Lord will come in fire,
and his chariots like the storm wind
   to render his anger in fury
and his rebuke with flames of fire.
16. For the Lord will hold judgment by fire
and by his sword upon all flesh;
and the slain of the Lord shall be many.
17. They that sanctify and purify themselves to go into the gardens,
following one in their midst.
   eating swine's flesh and the abomination and mice
shall come to an end together, says the Lord.
18. But as for me, their deeds and their thoughts have come to my attention.
   to gather all Gentiles and tongues;
and they shall come and behold my glory.
19. And I will set up a sign of remembrance among them. And from them I will send survivors to the nations, to Tarshish, and Pul and Lod, who draw the bow; to Tubal and Javan, and to the far-off coastlands, who have not heard about me; and have not seen my glory, or made known my glory among the Gentiles.

Verse 15. Evidently, ever since especially Exod. 19:18, fire in one form or another was an index of the Lord's coming to judgment. Two things blend into one another. Either fire is the element which God uses for inflicting punishment upon the guilty, or else fire is the agency in which he envelopes himself for purposes of the theophany. The overtones of this chapter seem to emphasize the second aspect of the case. His purposes are indicated in this as being "to render his anger in fury." His anger is a very real and stern thing.

Verse 16. Aside from the fire-aspect of his theophany this verse shows the warrior-aspect of his nature. He has a sword, the use of which will make the slain of the Lord to be many.

Verse 17. Certain sins have in a special way roused his indignation. These cult-gardens are briefly described. They required a functionary who led the way in the performance of certain rites. Certain repulsive things were eaten, swine's flesh; then something called "the abomination," and lastly mice. Of all the rites and foods involved, none shall be left; they "shall come to an end together." They thought they had kept these repulsive things secret. But they have come to the Lord's attention. It seems that the prophet pictures the scene as involving "all Gentiles and tongues" so as to have them witness the scene where the Lord let his fury burn upon his people. For such a scene could involve a stern beauty and a certain beauty of holiness. — On the whole issue cf. also Ezek. 8.

Verse 18. The Lord has been aware of what his people are doing, though they thought that it had been kept from him. The Lord speaks anthropomorphically, as though he had just become aware of it all. But this verse actually thinks in terms of beholding God's glory in the sense that God's just judgment both on Israel and upon the Gentiles is also a glorious thing.

Verse 19. That is what v. 19 has in mind when it speaks of "a sign of remembrance." That which these spectators will behold is the judgment, dead bodies of those who opposed the Lord. A certain ironic tone falls on the beholding of the dead. This is also considered as beholding the Lord's glory in Joel 3:2; and Zeph. 3:8. At least they who did not appear to witness this display of glory are sent out as ambassadors of the Lord to the far corners of the earth, to Tarshish, far to the East in Spain; Put, in East Africa; Lud, also in Africa; Tubal, in the Caucasus, and Javan, in Greece; also the coastlands of the Mediterranean. All that did not perish in the first onslaught, are the survivors who are thought of as agents, to make known abroad the glory of his name. So there is one positive factor in the whole transaction.

8. New People for a New Earth (vv. 20-23)

66:20-23 20. And they shall bring all your brothers from all the Gentiles as an offering to the Lord on horses and wagons, and in litters, on mules and on dromedaries to my holy mountain at Jerusalem, says the Lord, as the children of Israel are wont to bring offerings in clean vessels to the house of the Lord. 21. And some of them I will also take for priests and Levites, says the Lord.
22. For just as the new heavens and the new earth
   shall continue before me, says the Lord,
so shall your descendants and your name continue.
23. And from new moon to new moon
   and from Sabbath to Sabbath
all flesh shall come to worship before me,
   says the Lord.

Verse 20. The turn of thought that comes as a glorious climax grows out of the thought with which the chapter opened — new heavens and a new earth. That calls for a new people deeply consecrated to the Lord. This group shall be made up of Israelites and of Gentiles. As an index of the wholesome feelings that shall prevail when the endpoint shall be reached, all the so-called "survivors" shall deem it an honor to bring their scattered brethren, especially from the Gentiles on all manner of vehicles and conveyances. As Israel brought offerings to the sanctuary so shall these new ministers bring people as an offerings to the Lord. Of these Gentiles in particular the Lord will select certain ones to serve as legitimate priests and Levites. All this is, of course, New Testament thought cast in Old Testament language.

Verse 22. All the things promised will not soon pass off the scene but shall be as stable and fixed as the heavens and the earth themselves, for, in the last analysis, God builds for eternity. When it is said that these, worshippers and ministering personnel, shall "continue," that does not imply merely long continued existence, but involves being deeply in the Lord's service and in the joy of that service.

Verse 23. Festivals in particular shall mark high days in this new people that resort to this sanctuary, as God's new people. The particularism of the Old Testament is brushed aside and "all flesh shall come to worship before the Lord in spirit and in truth."

9. The Sad Fate of the Impenitent (v. 24)

66:24 24. And they shall go forth and shall look upon the dead bodies of the men who have rebelled against me; for their worm shall not die and their fire shall not be quenched. But they shall be an abhorrence to all flesh.

Verse 24. The enduring nature of the lot of those on whom the sentence of eternal death shall be visited is here unequivacally set forth, so much so that in certain editions of the Old Testament a notation appears to the effect that v. 23, with its more ironic tone is a more apt conclusion.

Peace eternal and death eternal! On this note the book of Isaiah comes to a close.

Notes

Verse 15. The Hebrew preposition *b* may be translated "in" or "b" fire. See *G.K.* 119 l.